VERONESE

Renzo Villa   Giovanni C.F. Villa

VERONESE

SilvanaEditoriale

Cover
Supper at Emmaus, approx. 1560, detail. Paris, Musée du Louvre, inv. 1196

On pages 8-9
Consecration of David, 1552-1555 (?), detail. Vienna, Kunsthistorisches Museum, inv. 40

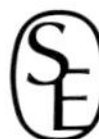

Silvana Editoriale

Chief Executive
Michele Pizzi

Editorial Director
Sergio Di Stefano

Art Director
Giacomo Merli

Editorial Coordinator
Natalia Grilli

Copy Editing
Cristina Pradella

Translations
Cristina Pradella

Layout
Evelina Laviano

Production Coordinator
Antonio Micelli

Editorial Assistant
Giulia Mercanti

Photo Editor
Silvia Sala, Barbara Miccolupi

Press Office
Alessandra Olivari, press@silvanaeditoriale.it

The deep geometric backgrounds,
the unrivalled Belfagorian teaching,
remembering Adele Plotkin
and Carlo Ferdinando Russo

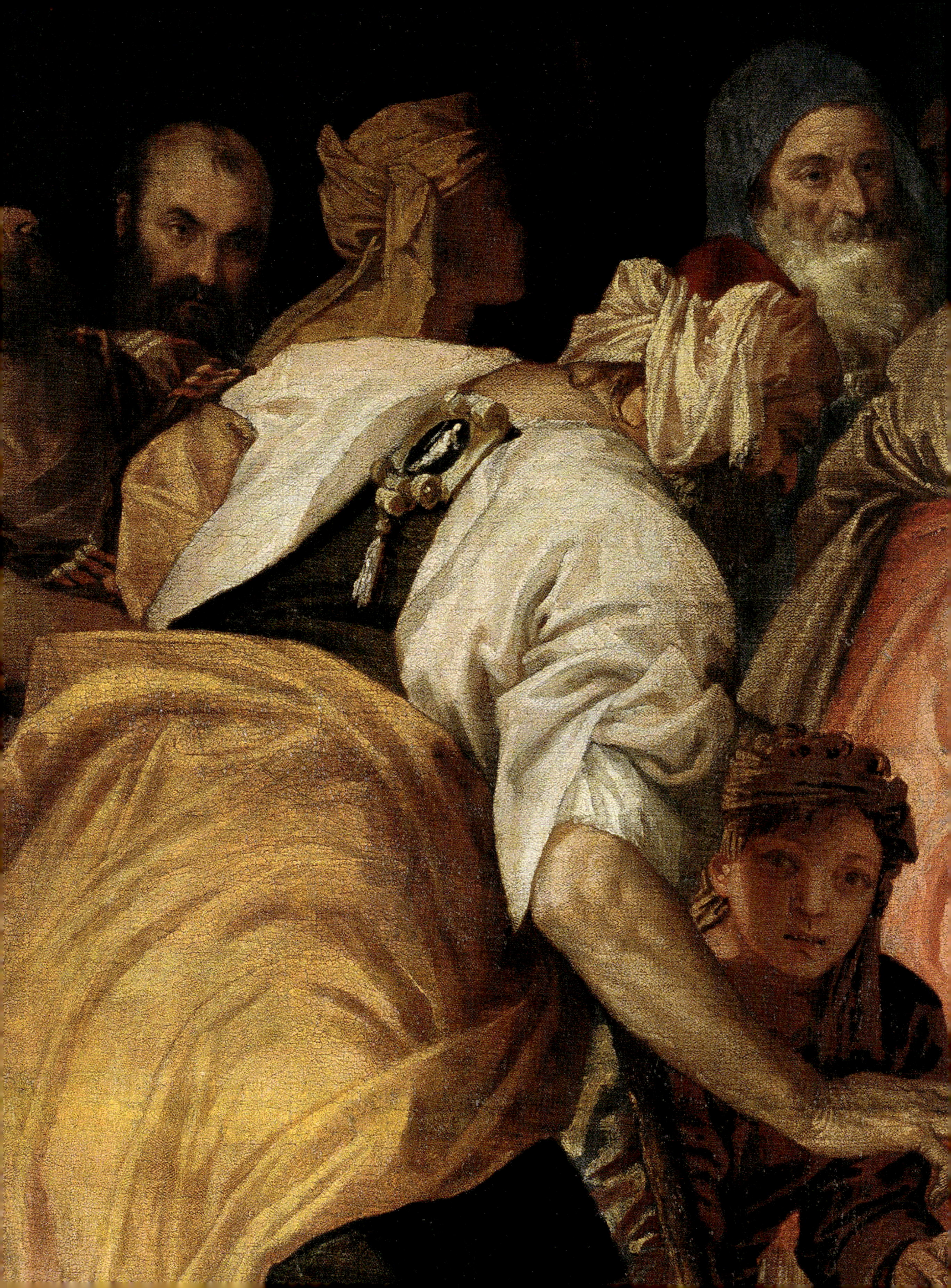

In recent decades, with new scholars and numerous new researches, and above all with radical restoration and scientific study operations – all occasions for important exhibitions – Veronese's image has changed. No longer is Paolo seen as either the skilled decorator, but cold, distant from the world, careful to celebrate the glories of the Serenissima with magnificence and obsequiousness, or the term of a homogeneous triad – Titian Tintoretto Veronese – or a "mannerist" who equips the great performances of the *Conviti*, nor the painter of scenes of sacred pietism already inspired by the Council of Trent and by the seventeenth century. Veronese is the interpreter of a great civil and cultural season of the Patrician Republic, he represents its tastes and presents them with new colours and inventions, grandiose and unexpected yet measured and balanced solutions; he also knows the folds of a lively religious life, quarrelsome and heated in doctrinal disputes, in the autonomous Venice and in constant conflict with the papal see.

Finally, he is always capable of inserting a very personal spark of irony, of allusive invention, of illusionistic play. He reveals himself so poetically ambiguous, open to interpretations and readings. He knows the artifices of rhetoric, the multiplicity of meaning of images. For this reason, scholars and exegetes are always proposing new interpretations, chasing multiple possibilities and explanations, still questioning his scenes, offered to multiple possibilities. Never truly dramatic, never terrible, balanced and decent, Paolo Caliari shows himself, in his almost endless production, the excellent interpreter of the very idea of painting as a pure relaxation of figures, a vision of a possible world, endowed with a life of its own, thought, conceived, imagined; not the historical truth, but an equally true possibility.

For a century, starting with a fundamental exhibition curated in 1939 by Rodolfo Pallucchini, knowledge and attention for Veronese have accelerated, with a sequence of exhibitions of his canvases, occasions for restorations and studies, rediscoveries and new attributions through techniques of modern analyses, in the commitment of museums and public and private institutions. In following the emerging aspects of a life and of a very rich production, we propose the most illuminating results to better understand and admire the masterpieces of the painter who for forty years worked with a colouristic invention that has few equivalents in the whole history of art.

The following chapters were drafted by Renzo Villa
The iconographic choices and the apparatuses are by Giovanni C.F. Villa

CHAPTER I

Vernissage in Venice

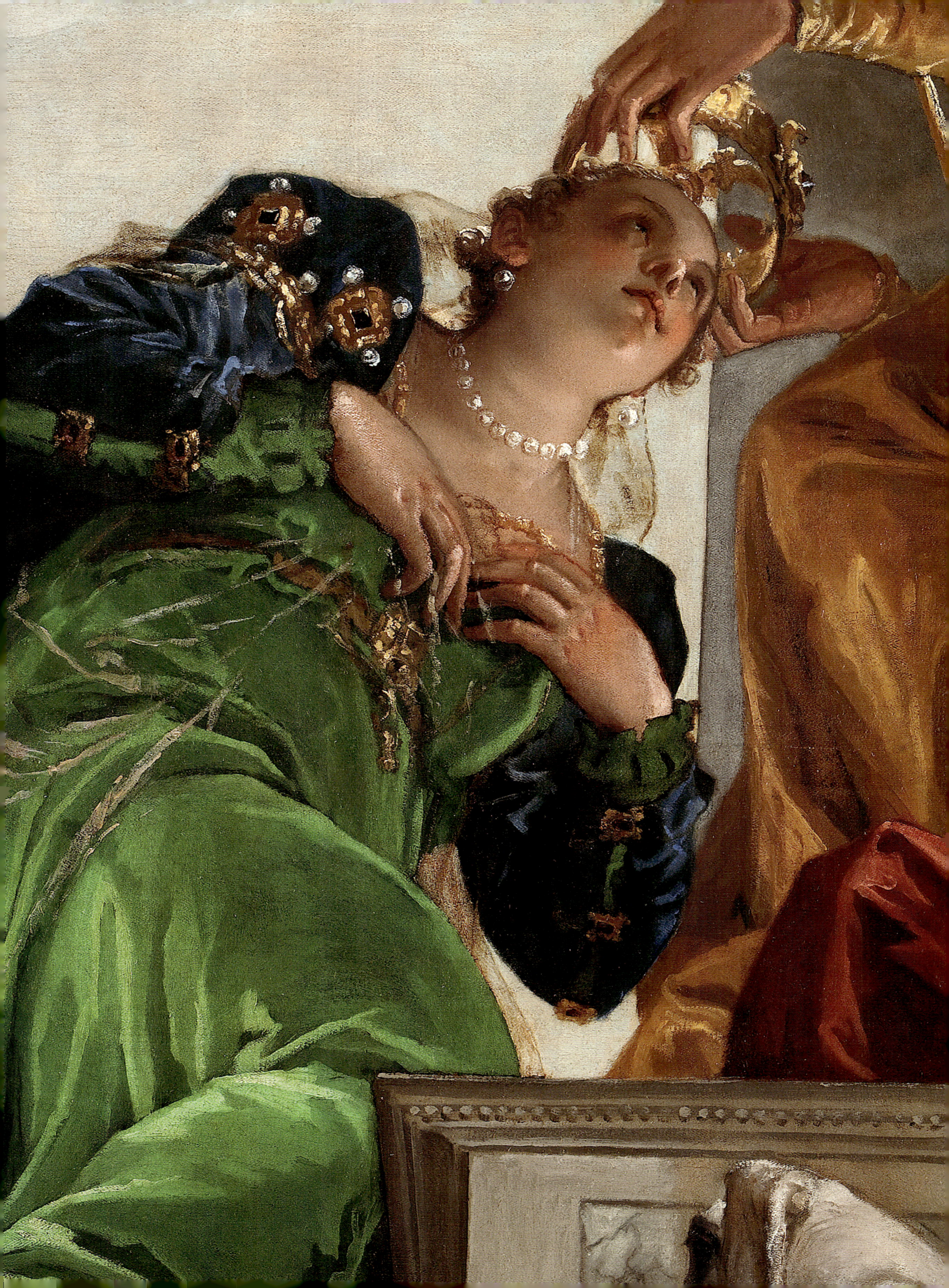

Going along *Calle dell'Avogaria* towards the Giudecca, in Venice, one sees an elegant backdrop made out of the façade of a church, fully visible at the top of the short bridge over *Rio di San Bastiàn*. Traced with an almost elementary geometry – a square surmounted by a triangle – it shows on the facing in light Istrian stone the dark voids of the four single-lancet windows, a single entrance portal, the oculus of the rose window. Such simplicity is barely adorned by architectural reliefs, tympanums and arched pediments, and is marked off by a balanced cornice, supported by slender semi-columns; the crowning of the tympanum is completed by the statues of three saints. The building can be measured by taking a few steps in the *campazzo*: the side is in masonry, with a simple side portal, and ends with a semicircular apse. The quadrangular bell tower is tall and proportionate, with mullioned windows; the octagonal bell crowning is covered by a small flattened dome.
This is how the church of San Sebastiano – the *San Bastiàn* protector from the plague –appears to us today, and so it appeared, just finished in 1548, to a painter in his early twenties, who had reached Venice for the first time. He will be destined to see it over and over again, and to work inside it, frequently, for decades. And San Sebastiano will welcome him one last time, now a well-known artist, the most celebrated not only in the city, bitterly mourned by his orphaned family members, escorted by the prayers of the friars in procession with the extinguished candles, and by a large crowd of Venetians who had learned to admire and esteem him above all. Paolo Caliari, called the Veronese, is still buried in the church, his bones lie under the floor, a bust and an epigraph remind him. He has rested there since the date of his demise, on 19 April 1588, when he was sixty years old. With him is buried Benedetto, the inseparable brother, his indispensable collaborator.
San Sebastiano is Veronese's church, the testimony of the art to which he dedicated himself with absolute passion, to make his unique and recognized ability to narrate and use colour visible to all. His taste for daring combinations, his oil and fresco technique, on canvas and on paper, his surprising inventions. And his very peculiar ability to insert allegories, allusions, details that require attention and study and are not always easy to interpret. As we will get to know in an extraordinary, truly unique and almost superhuman pictorial production.
Paolo had been called by the prior, the fellow citizen Bernardo Torlioni who, on behalf of the bishop of Verona Matteo Giberti, had come to give new rules to a somewhat problematic convent. The Hieronymites, or the Poor Hermits of Saint Jerome of the Congregation of the Blessed Peter of Pisa, founded in the period of the great Western Schism, between 1378 and 1417, on pauperistic ideals, or rather a return to the original poverty of the Church, had been agitated by reforming wills, by very questionable, disorderly behaviour, open to uncontrolled adventures, for which the Church of Rome, with Pope Paul III, in 1538 had acted for a corrective action on the *factiosi et discoli* friars with interdict and excommunication, until the arrival of Torlioni.
The prior had received Paolo in the sacristy, a relatively small space to the left of the nave, almost 13 feet high (about four meters).

The Coronation of Esther, 1556, canvas, 450 × 370 cm, detail. Venice, church of San Sebastiano, ceiling

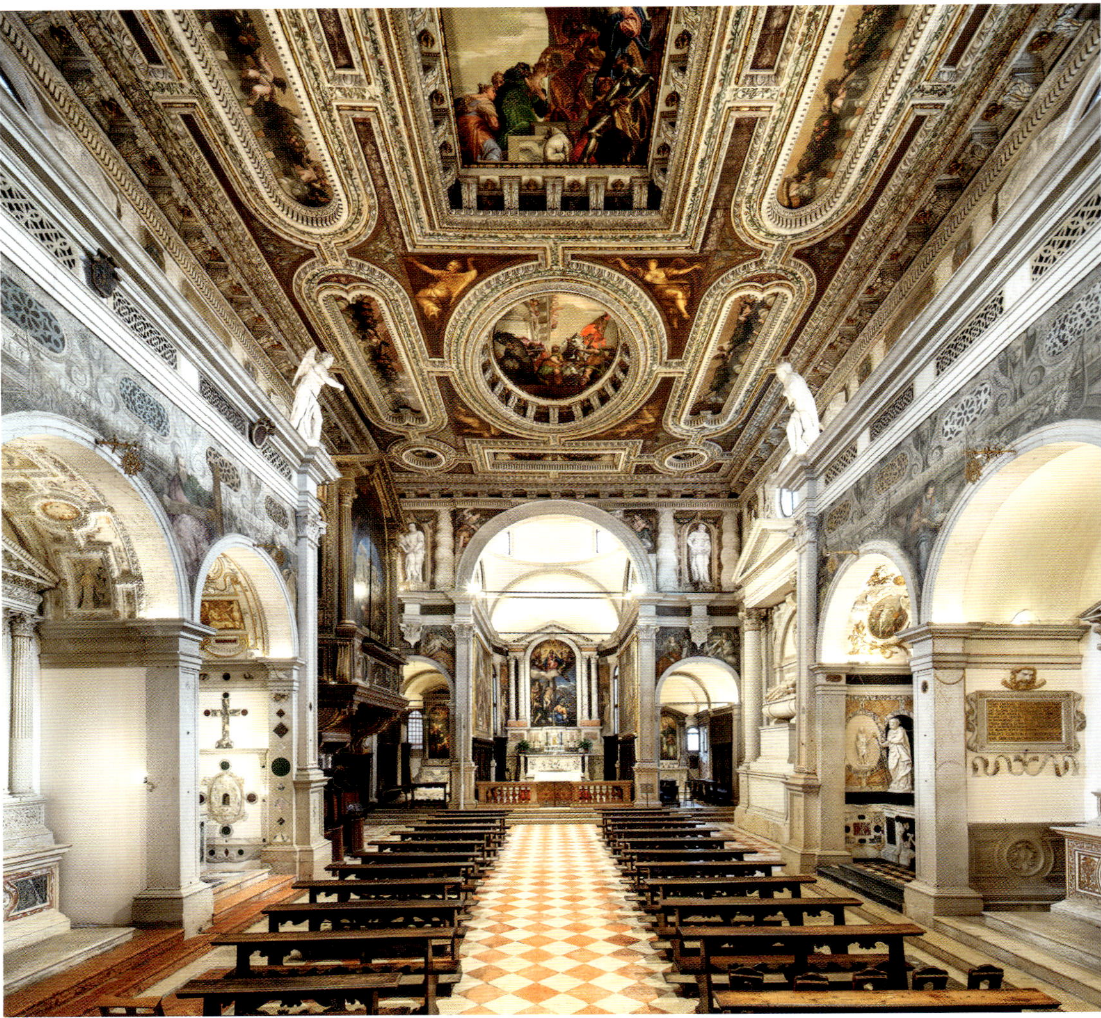

Venice, church of San Sebastiano: view from the entrance portal towards the presbytery and the high altar

The nave is limited by the side chapels, supporting the *barco*, or monks' choir. At the end of the chapels, on the left, the organ with the doors decorated by Veronese, and on the right Sansovino's funeral monument to the archbishop of Nicosia, Livio Podacataro. The whole decoration is the result of subsequent interventions by Veronese.

A Convent Church

A church among the many in Venice, certainly not the most grandiose or suggestive among those built and rebuilt in the golden age of the arts and architecture in Venice, the century opened by the supreme humanistic elegance of Mauro Codussi, traversed by the splendid ornate institutional and cultural buildings by Jacopo Sansovino, updated on the taste for a return to classicism, and finally concluded and equipped with the jewels of Andrea Palladio. This church was built by a craftsman, builder and entrepreneur who we could define as non-innovative and yet capable of constructing buildings that still mark the face of the city. It was designed and also materially supplied by Antonio Abbondi, known by all only as Scarpagnino, who unfortunately died when the façade was just completed. Originally from Valtellina, Abbondi had first been superintendent of the reconstruction of the Fondaco dei Tedeschi and then, appointed proto or chief architect of the *Officio del Sal*, he had had the decisive task of planning the reconstruction of the entire Rialto area, devastated by the furious fire of 10 January 1514. A feat criticized by artists such as Vasari, but in reality extremely functional and with an economical value, having reused everything possible, then decorating it with minimal but elegant decorations. Like the brick church dedicated to the miracle-working saint, created with the lightest possible masonry according to the construction rules necessary for the city, built on floors supported by a centuries-old forest of poles forcefully inserted into the mud of the lagoon, and now turned into stone, also forming the bottom of Dorsoduro. A construction completed in bits and pieces, every time the friars had a little money: almost forty years to finish the building.

In 1542, at the start of the last building campaign, the prior of the convent, Bernardo Torlioni from Verona, had asked Scarpagnino to build six chapels, three on each side. In this way, the single nave would have been animated by a *barco*, the friars' choir, extended on the side chapels, reproposing Codussi's solution in San Michele in Isola. The chapels would have made it possible to collect the ducats

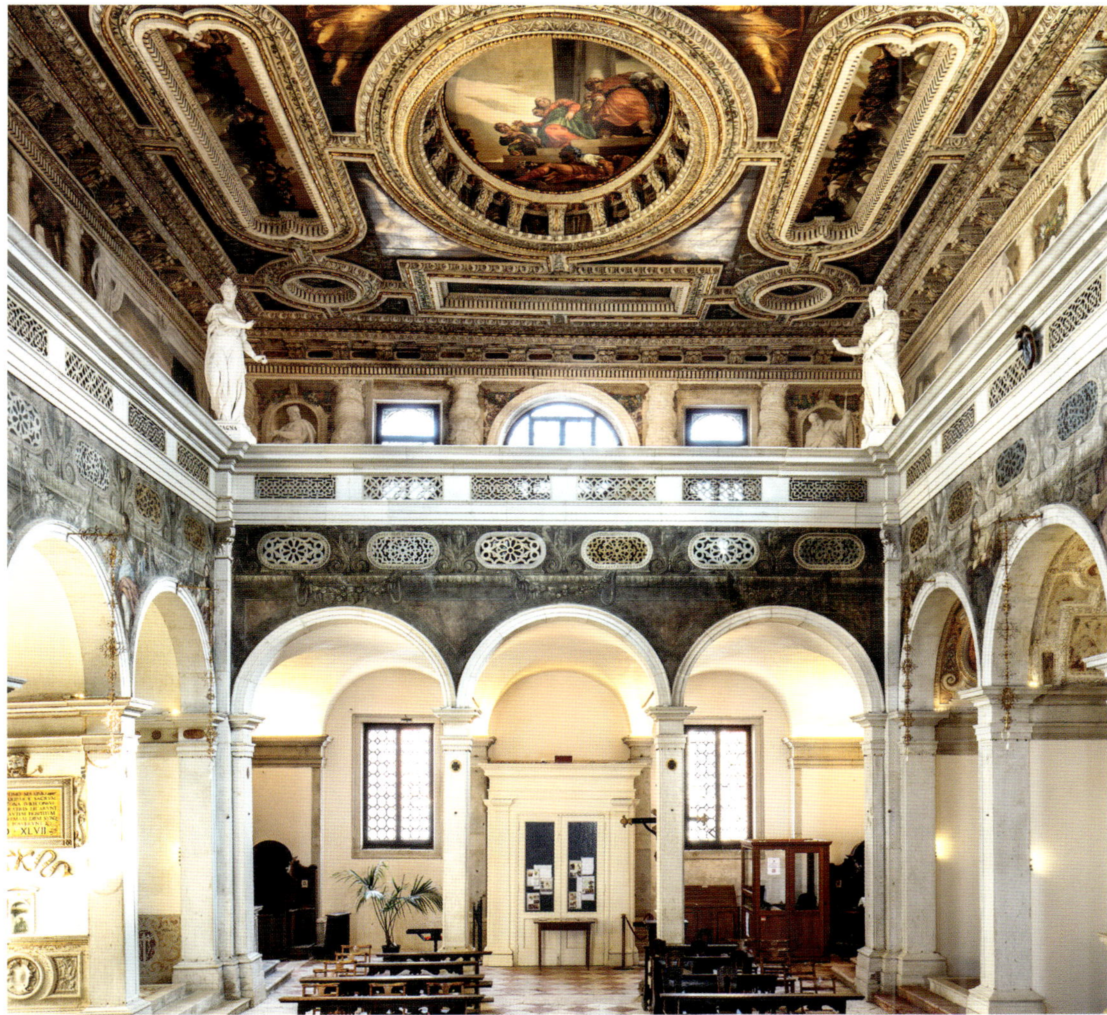

Venice, church of San Sebastiano: view towards the atrium and the entrance portal

The walls of the *barco* were the first to be frescoed by Veronese, visible and appreciated only by the monks. To be noted is the choice of placing the scene with the *Repudiation of Vasti*, or the separation from the bridegroom, towards the exit from the church, following the allegorical, Catholic reading of the biblical text.

necessary for the decorative enterprise planned by the friars, which should have been very expensive, so the donations collected in the neighbourhood, such as bequests and prebends, would have been insufficient. The chapels offered for the burials of rich patrician families, guaranteeing the celebration of masses "forever", made it possible to collect the hundreds, indeed thousands, of ducats necessary for the decoration and completion of the coffered wood ceiling, necessary to avoid spilling onto the lateral walls the weight of a masonry vault, which would have hidden the beam covered with tiles. The nave was ended by a square presbytery surmounted by a dome, completed by the semicircular apse and flanked by two chapels. From the atrium the *barco* of the choir continued with two wings above the chapels, three on each side, opened by arches on pillars. Openwork plutei were the parapet of the choir loft, which could only be accessed by the friars of the convent, the hermits of Saint Jerome. Slender mouldings and pillars marked the architectural design.

Here a *Crucifixion* was exhibited. The canvas had been delivered five years earlier by Raffaello, Bernardo's nephew, that took up a model created by Domenico Riccio "il Brusasorci", a painter who was a close friend of Paolo. The ceiling and the wooden furnishings of the sacristy, wardrobes and counters had instead been made a decade earlier: in March 1546 the *marangone* Luca had recorded the delivery of the wooden structure made up of rooms of different shapes and sizes, with frames suitable for welcoming canvases to be executed at the right time. And the right moment had now arrived thanks to the generous help of Marcantonio Grimani, financier of a chapel.

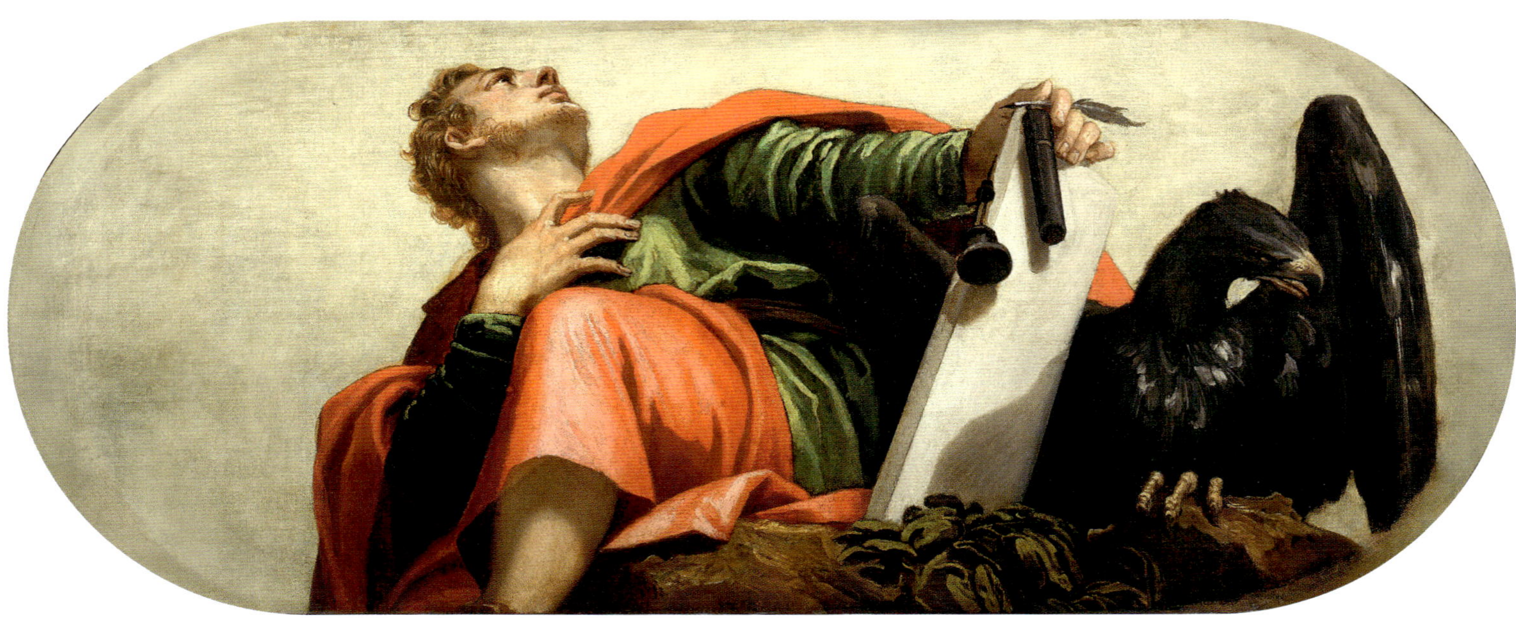

Torlioni had known Paolo since at least 1548, when the young painter had painted a *Deposition* for the church of the Hieronymite friars, in Santa Maria della Vittoria Nuova in Verona. The work was already appreciable for the articulation of the mourners, in a tight group on the left, caught in gestures and expressions of dignified desperation, and the opening to the right towards a distant space, with Golgotha against the clouded sky, the fainting of a wan Mother, and the kiss of a kneeling Magdalene, whose hairstyle was blatantly Venetian.

Paolo, twenty-seven, was by now known and appreciated also in Venice, the capital of the arts, having created canvases for ceilings even in the Doge's Palace, in the Hall destined for the work of the Council of Ten, the most important and formidable judiciary of the Republic. Bernardo and Paolo can therefore plan on a grand scale, imagine a decoration of the entire church: a public masterpiece, the demonstration of the painter's skills, abilities and inventions, and of the foresight, taste and prestige of the prior, in the greater glory of his convent. Before more demanding constructions, it was necessary to intervene in the sacristy. Afterwards, once the results have been approved, other works would follow: the large canvases painted for the ceiling of the nave, then the wall frescoes, other paintings in the presbytery, the altarpiece on the high altar, the organ doors. It will be the monument of Paolo Caliari, the Veronese, the exceptional anthology of his pictorial production over the course of twenty years of activity. A unique un-

Saint John the Evangelist, 1555,
canvas, 85 × 240 cm.
Venice, church of San Sebastiano, sacristy

Saint Luke, 1555,
canvas, 85 × 200 cm.
Venice, church of San Sebastiano, sacristy

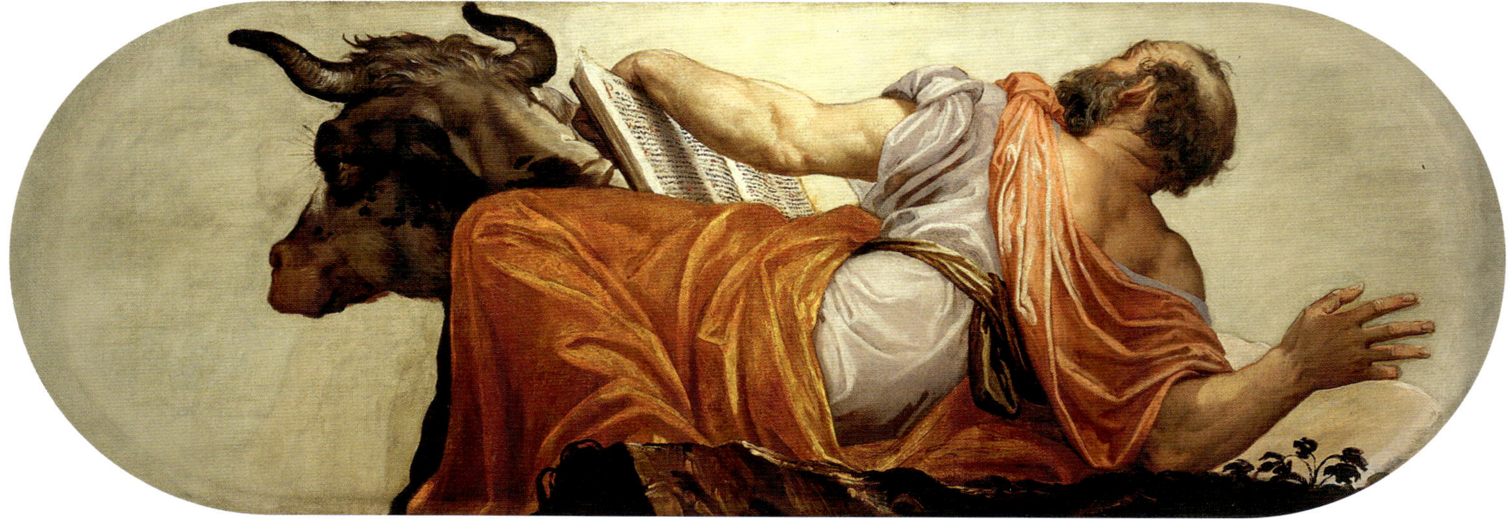

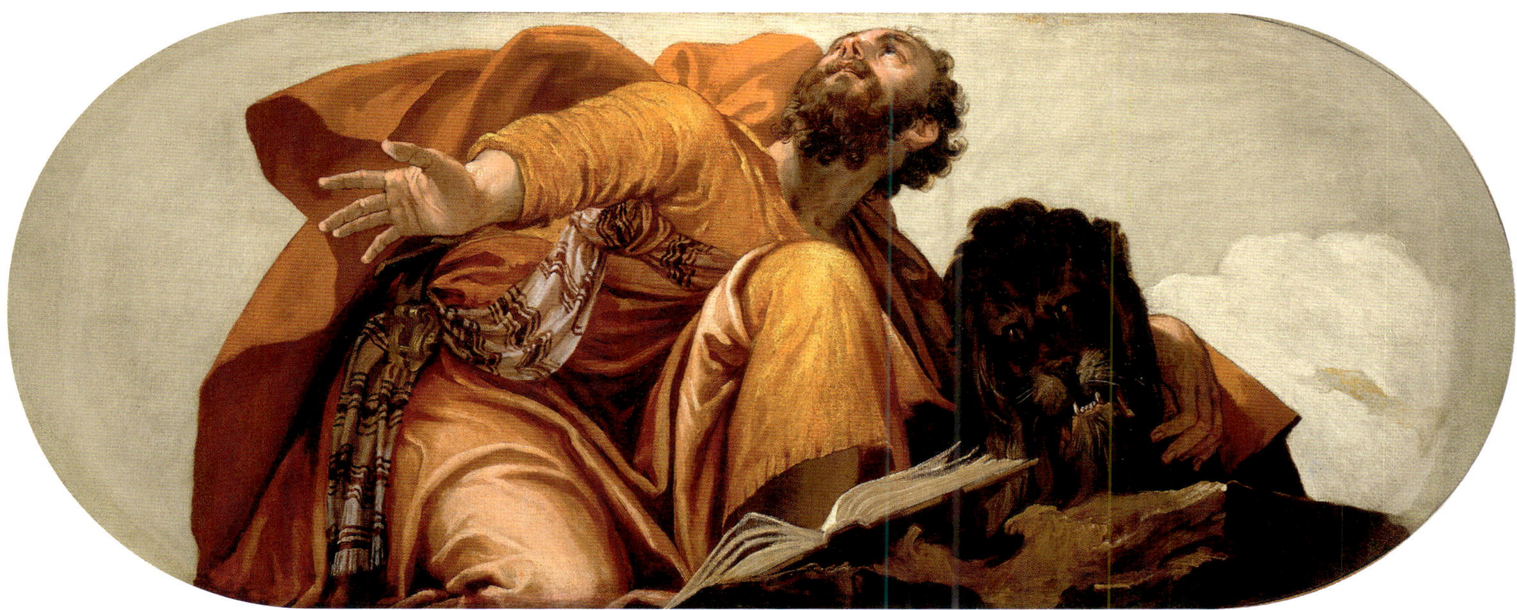

dertaking that would inspire only one other painter: Jacopo Robusti, the Tintoretto, when he managed to be entrusted with the entire decoration of the Scuola Grande di San Rocco.

But now Paolo subscribes to the commitment for the sacristy. The contract calls for a central panel, other canvases for the elongated spaces on the sides, further medallions at the corners. The central theme is the coronation of the Virgin, alongside the four Evangelists; in the roundels angels, or cherubs. Paolo would then have decorated the entire wooden structure, creating an ornamental continuum composed of festoons, scrolls, false bronzes and stone effects.
The crowned Mary represents the Glory of the Mother. But it is also something more, in Venice: it is the glory of the patroness, the central figure of the popular faith. Venice is the city dedicated to it, since the legendary date of its foundation, remembered and commemorated: the mythical 25 March, the day of the Annunciation, in the distant 421, a Friday, the day of Venus. Under the protection of Mary, Venice had remained "virgin" over the centuries, i.e. untouched by enemy armies: intact and defended not by walls, but by salty waters. Virgin and beautiful, Venice is Venus, the celestial Venus. The image of Mary, in the glory of the Coronation, was therefore central, the last figure to whom the priest looks in reverence as he prepares for the sacred rites.

Saint Mark, 1555,
canvas, 85 × 200 cm.
Venice, church of San Sebastiano, sacristy

Saint Matthew, 1555,
canvas, 85 × 240 cm.
Venice, church of San Sebastiano, sacristy

In the colour choices, like the red and green areas of John's robes, and in the daring foreshortenings in Mark and Luke, or in the angel of a Matthew hinting at Michelangelo's style, Veronese publicly shows the results of the complete maturation from the first tests in Verona and Mantua up to those at Palazzo Ducale, always in 1555.

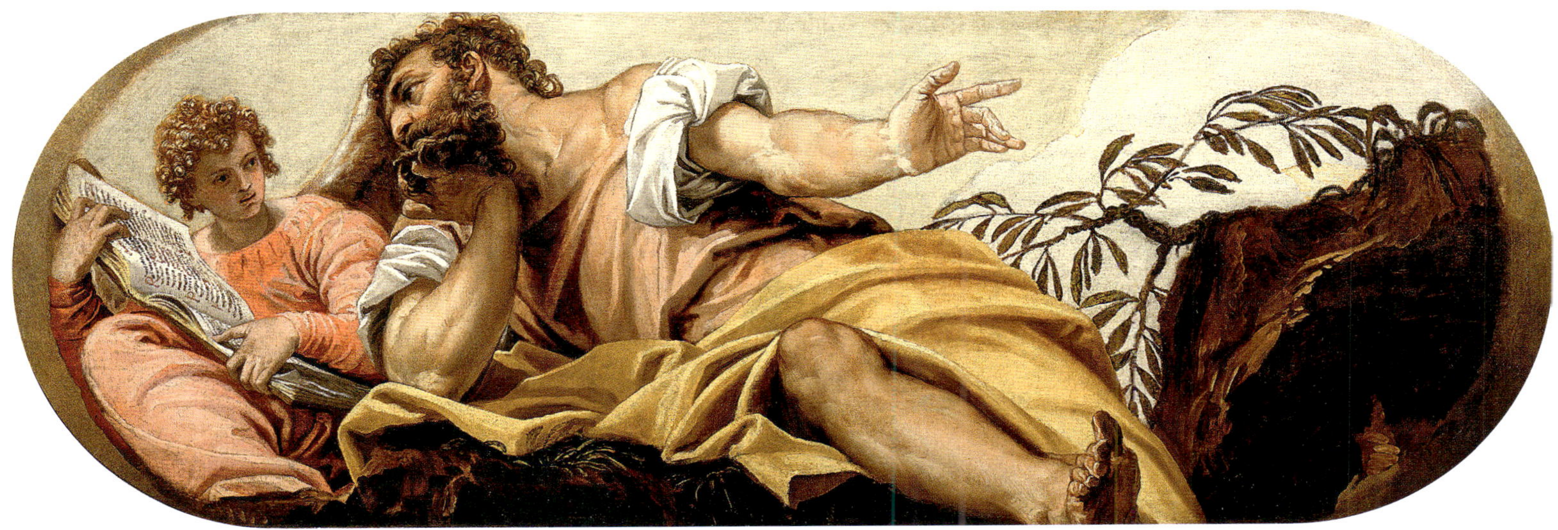

After four and a half centuries we still admire the ceiling of the sacristy: in the central compartment there is *The Coronation of the Virgin*, surrounded by four ovals with the figures of the Evangelists. The *Coronation* corresponds iconographically to the traditional manifestation of the Trinity: the Father – the face of a bearded elderly man – the Son portrayed in the fullness of an established maturity, the face of classical beauty, wavy and curly hair like the rich beard. The Mother is young, her face is idealized in the canons of oval perfection. Two little angels escort the great light in which the Spirit appears, the ritual dove with large wings. It is a "private" coronation compared to many scenes painted with a flood of saints: here we perceive the essential, the divine. The triumph of light, the most evident element of Veronese's colourism, determines the great movement of the drapery, where the shadows are coloured, with particularly evident effects on the reds and blues of the garments. The brightness of the sky, captured in the backlight effect, is the most evident pictorial datum, with an explosive effect.

The Coronation of the Virgin, 1555, canvas, 200 × 170 cm.
Venice, church of San Sebastiano, sacristy

Where the painter's art shows itself to be extraordinarily virtuous is in the invention of the four Evangelists. He had to deal with decidedly anomalous measures: two spaces of 200 centimetres, another two of 240 centimetres for only 85 centimetres wide; in these oblongs he must insert the bodies, faces and attributes that help identify the four: Mark's lion, Luke's ox, John's eagle, an angel holding Matthew's table. The postures, all varied, present extremely artificial but not forced figures, characterizing the expressive faces in the different ages of life, from the youngest Giovanni to the elder Luca. The bodies of the evangelists stand out against a clear sky, and this light avoids forcing bold glimpses: each character seems to be able to "see" the divine spectacle, beyond the edge of the canvas. Something similar had been admired in Venice a decade earlier, in the aerial figures painted by Vasari for the ceiling of Palazzo Corner Spinelli, but now these evangelists appear more natural, more full-bodied and at the same time moved and light. Natural and authentic in the sky of unreality.

The ceiling is completed by some minor monochrome scenes: eight present the *Creation of Man*, while four polychrome roundels are illustrated by *Cherubs*. At the corners there are still the *Cardinal Virtues* created with rapid brushstrokes in red earthenware. If it is legitimate to hypothesize that Paolo conceived these scenes, it is equally legitimate to consider the assignment of the drafting to the two assistants mentioned in the contractual agreement – his brother Benedetto, already defined as *depentor*, and an "Antonio", perhaps that Giovanni Antonio Fasolo who had already worked with Paolo – as well as a few assistants in his workshop for the preparation of canvases and colours.

While the rich and elaborate frames suggest an invitation to memory and prayer, the colour choices immediately appear very effective. Paolo used light, luminous and brilliant colours, full-bodied shades with iridescent effects using complementary hues, colouring the shadows, obtaining a significant effect of opening in a relatively low ceiling, further accentuating the angle of the frames. The work also reveals his visual training: while Parmigianino and Correggio inspire the refined figuration of the divinities, Giulio Romano oriented the massive figures, even in the confined spaces, which make the Evangelists grandiose.

In October the finishing touches and ornaments were given by the *indorador* Bartolomeo da Bologna. On 23 November 1555 the pictorial work was completed. The date is written on the Old Testament book shown by one of the cherubim on a lateral roundel; the other presents the New Testament. Another pair of cherubs carries tombstones with inscriptions for the glorified Virgin, and other scenes have been painted in chiaroscuro on the ceiling: Adam and Eve, the first parents, hint at Mary as the new Eve, the one who will make mankind reborn; and the four cardinal Virtues accompany stories from the Old Testament. Temperance seems to illustrate the episodes of David versus Goliath and the Judgment of Solomon; Prudence accompanies Moses' prayer before the battle against the Amalekites, but also, strangely, Cain and Abel; the Fortitude is shown with Abraham and Melchizedek, and with Judith and Holofernes; Moses

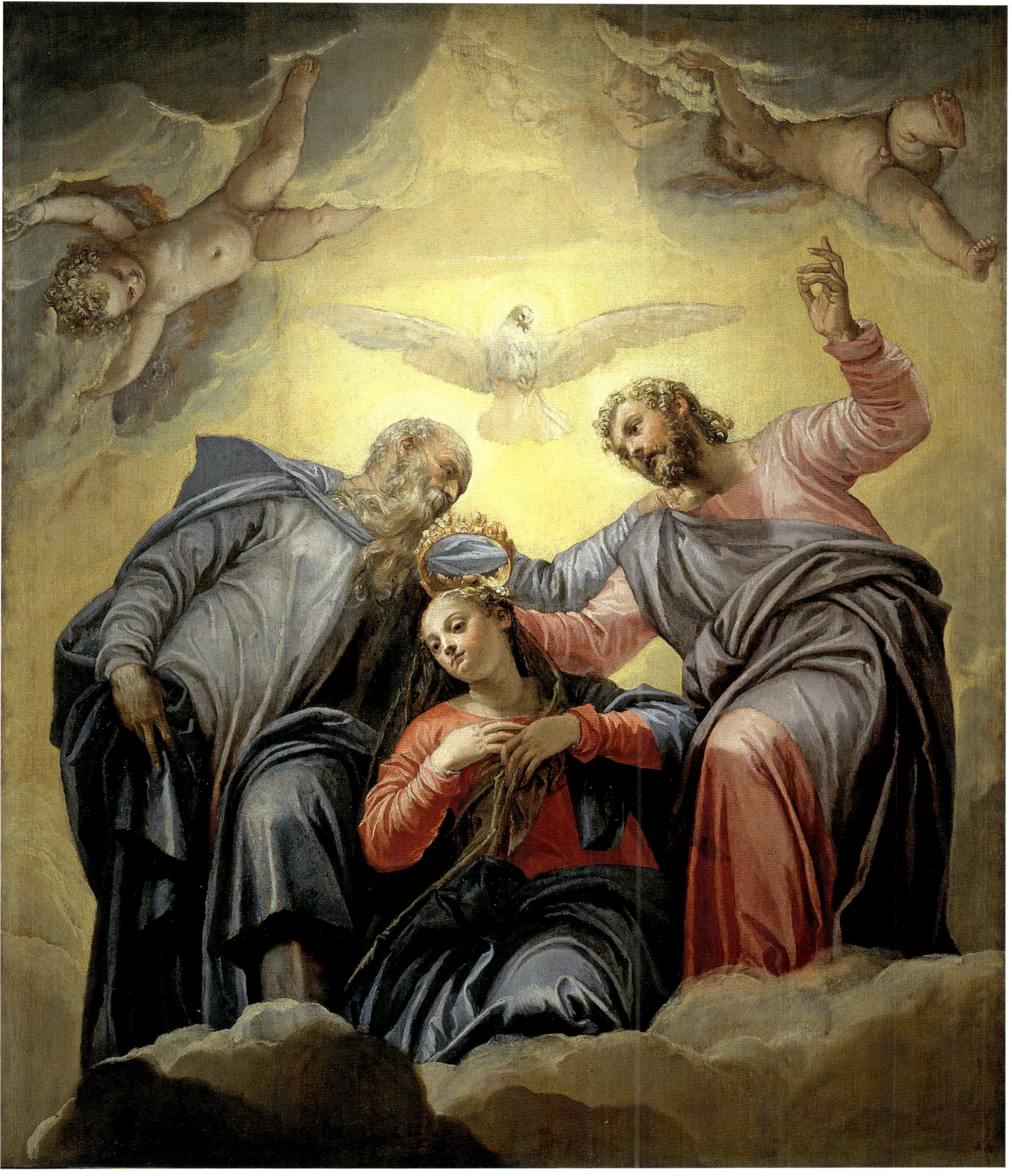

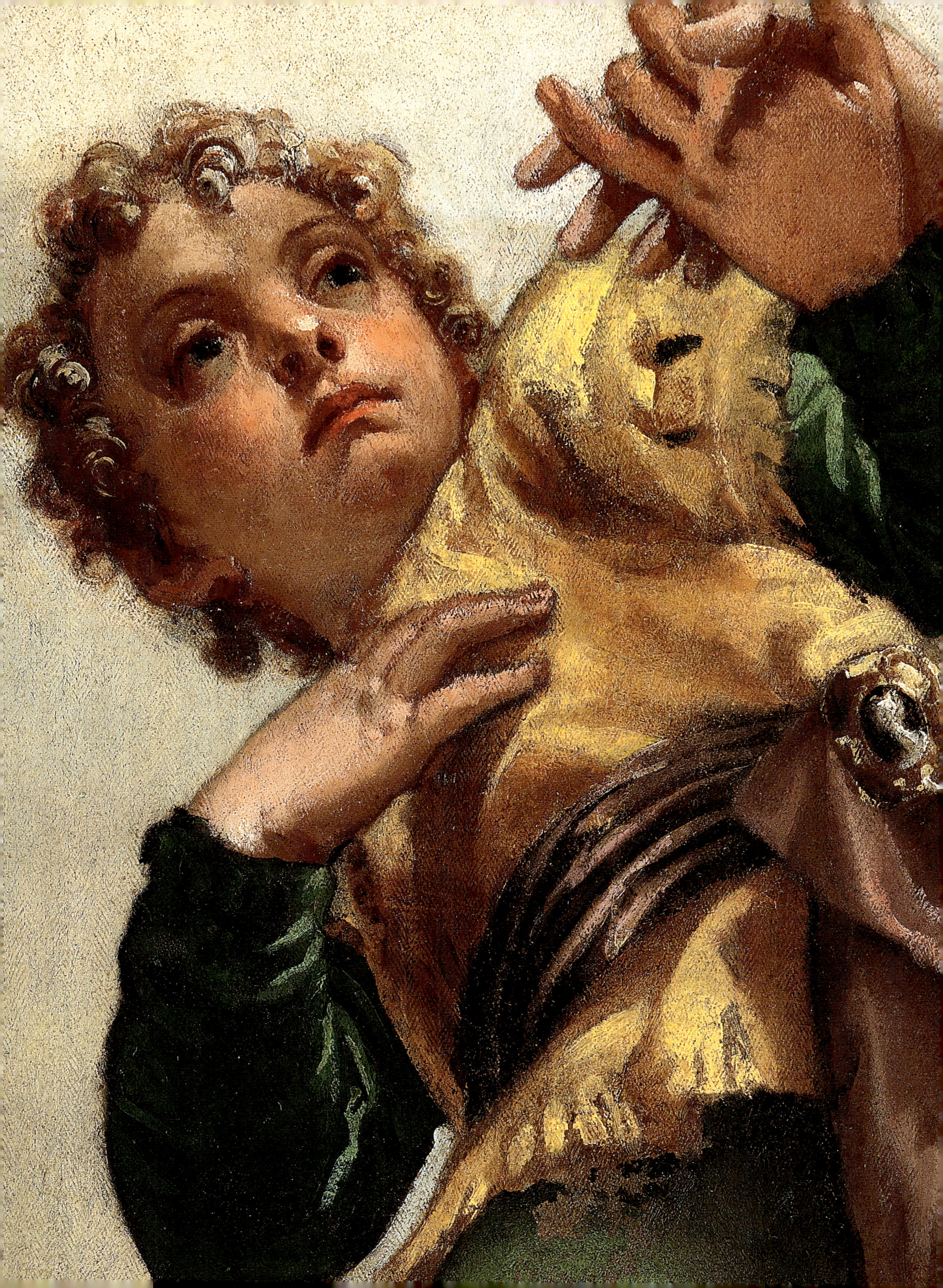

with the Tables and Esther and Ahasuerus are near Justice, the figures that will soon be potrayed on the ceiling of the hall. The admirable sacristy will be completed years later with other Old Testament stories on the walls, attributed by art historians to various painters. The names of Antonio Palma il Giovane, Bonifacio de' Pittati, Maarten de Vos have been mentioned. And then Brusasorci, Raffaello Torlioni before his death while still very young, Andrea Schiavone and Natalino da Murano. Almost all painters active in Venice between the eighth and ninth decades of the sixteenth century.

The Repudiation of Vasti, approx. 1556, canvas, 500 × 370 cm, detail. Venice, church of San Sebastiano, ceiling

The approval of Paolo's work, obviously not only from the prior, is unanimous. A few years later it will be confirmed by the high assessment of Giorgio Vasari. Now, immediately, on 1 December 1555, Paolo signs the contract for the execution of the canvases intended for the ceiling of the nave. The painter "pledges himself to paint the three main paintings which are in the middle of the ceiling of the church of San Sebastiano, with figures, and beyond the eight areas which go from the bands and the four rounds and all the snails that will be made there. He will get the colours of all sorts at his expenses, according to his convenience, as well as the finishes and everything in oil. We will give him the canvases and *telari*, and as a price for the mentioned work we will give him n. one hundred and fifty". So the prior wrote in his own hand, sure that "we will be satisfied and happy": the document is in the State Archives of Venice, Mani morte, Convento di S. Sebastiano, b. 93, processo 7, cc. 94-95. All the paintings were delivered on 31 October 1556, the date of payment for a work done with striking speed and absolute perfection. And in the meantime the indefatigable Paolo signed another contract: on 3 January 1556 he received a down payment from the cellarer of the convent of Saints Nazaro and Celso in Verona as evidenced by the State Archives of Verona, SS. Nazaro and Celso, reg. 11, cc. 78r-81r., for a *Supper in the House of Simon*. A fundamental work, as we will see, for the stylistic and narrative expression of Paolo Veronese.

ON THE RISKY LADDERS

The new enterprise really lives up to the qualities of a master already fully mastering perspective and colouristic techniques; an even literal height, since the ceiling that covers the entire nave is twelve meters above the floor, and therefore needs to be seen from below, at an adequate size and perspective. For the spaces left empty by the *marangoni*, Paolo has prepared three large canvases, one square and two ovals, to which are added minor decorations and scrolls. The fee of 150 ducats, excluding the canvases, is fair, the equivalent of five years' rent of Paolo's Venetian home with a patrician of the Zen family. In relatively few years and with a further donation from Marcantonio Grimani, Torlioni succeeded in collecting the "treasure" necessary for the enterprise – in reality the wooden work is much more expensive than the painted canvases – and above all in obtaining ecclesiastical and institutional support, the recognition and support from important patrician families for the religious building of a convent with a hard, tiring and discussed life.

The ceiling canvases must show the biblical *Book of Esther*; contour figures of Angels, the Cardinal Virtues – Faith, Charity, Hope and Justice on the corners – various decorative festoons and cherubs. These works, considered minor, were usually destined to his brother Benedetto and to Antonio Fasolo, and always according to Paolo's idea. But after the excellent restorations of 2009-2011, the *Allegories of the Virtues* – round works of 100 centimetres in diameter in monochrome – have proved to be just as masterpieces in terms of care, iconographic invention, quality of drapery and expressions. Four female figures of complete perfection, which only the height and grandeur of the main canvases have been able to obscure over the centuries, with the aggravation of a poor state of conservation and damage due to water infiltrations.

The scene organization, the grandiose architectures, the spatial ability and the brightness characterize the entire ceiling which has as its absolute protagonist a little-known Old Testament story: the story of Esther, from the book bearing the same name.
We summarize schematically: a Persian king, Ahasuerus (who could be the one we know as Xerxes, but the book has no actual historical substance), repudiates his wife Vasti, who refused to show herself to the king's guests in all her beauty, we could suppose wearing only the crown. Ahasuerus then chooses a very beautiful young woman, Esther, as his wife. She is of Jewish descent, but her uncle and adoptive father, Mordechai (popularly Mordecai), the guardian of the Royal Palace, suggests that she should hide her birth. A minister of Ahasuerus, Amman, hates Mordechai who has not paid his respects appropriately, and wants his death. In addition, he decides that all Jews in Persia will be killed. But Mordechai discovers a conspiracy against the king, and Esther warns the king. After days of anxiety and fear, Mordechai is praised, and Amman is sentenced to death. The Jews celebrate by killing in turn all the Persians who wanted the end of Mordechai. The memory will last forever and ever: it is the feast of Purim.
Paolo chooses three moments from this story: *The Repudiation of Vasti*, representing the repudiated bride as she descends a ladder and leaves the palace; in the central scene we see *The Coronation of Esther*: dressed in Venetian style she ascends the steps to the throne with contrition, kneeling; Amman witnesses the scene, clad in an imposing armour; *The Triumph of Mordechai* sees the glorious march of the guardian, dressed as a sovereign, on a white horse; he is still escorted by evil Amman on black steed. But the scenes are seen in the opposite order: whoever enters going towards the presbytery will first see the triumph, then the coronation, and when he turns his back on the altar he will witness the repudiation.
The choice of narrative moments is personal: Vasti descends from a ladder, returns to the harem with an accompaniment of which there is no trace in the book; the coronation of Esther in the presence of Amman is not narrated, and also the particular form of the triumph with the two enemies side by side, and the abyss in front of them, is pure pictorial invention. The three choices were made for exclusively expressive reasons: to be able to show a descent and an ascent by accentuating the perspective and the upside down, marking the spatial effect, thus favouring the rendering of movement over narrative fidelity and also tradition. Michelangelo had preferred the punishment of Amman in the Sistine Chapel. Lotto had chosen the fainting of Esther in front of Ahasuerus in the design of the marquetry for Santa Maria Maggiore in Bergamo; the emotionally involving episode, a consequence of the sovereign's reproach for having presented without being called, will be preferred by Tintoretto in a canvas for the Escorial, and Veronese himself will take it up again many years later, in one of the canvases of the so-called *Duke of Buckingham Series*.
The sequence in San Sebastiano is therefore completely original and adapted to the need to be seen from below towards the ceiling, therefore in a strong foreshortening, obtaining effective movement and balance of the scenes, all three being exactly aligned on a common median line.
Various figures flank the named characters, the actors on stage. A little boy holds Vasti's hand as she descends turning her head in silent reproach and disappointment; a beggar with his dog is at the foot of the ladder representing hopeless ruin; two are the maidservants accompanying Esther crowned by Ahasuerus, while two dignitaries observe the scene; another dog is at the foot of Amman addressed, not without concern, by a buffoon dwarf; a prudent soldier grabs the bridle of Mordechai's horse, saving him from a probable fall. All presences for whom a possible allegorical reading has been proposed. The child was attributed ignorance or rather that naive inexperience that motivated the dangerous pride of Vasti; the beggar, however powerful and in full maturity, was given the function of remembering the humility that would have saved the beautiful favourite from repudiation. Instead, it will be the buffoon, the fool, who will intuit and predict the dangers that will arise from the role of Esther for the too ambitious Amman. Interpretations, however, not required by the scenes painted by Paolo, scenes that must create a

The Repudiation of Vasti, approx. 1556, canvas, 500 × 370 cm. Venice, church of San Sebastiano, ceiling

In his first public work in Venice, Veronese presents himself with his novelties and perfectly accomplished skills: narrativity and allegorical taste; the innovative and daring sets; the richness of colours in unprecedented, clear and brilliant associations; here the greens and the sensational variations around yellow-orange. He proposes fantasy portraits of great and expressive realism, painting of animals of rare effectiveness, energy and volumes in the male musculature. It is a pictorial repertoire that immediately impresses and fascinates the city public.

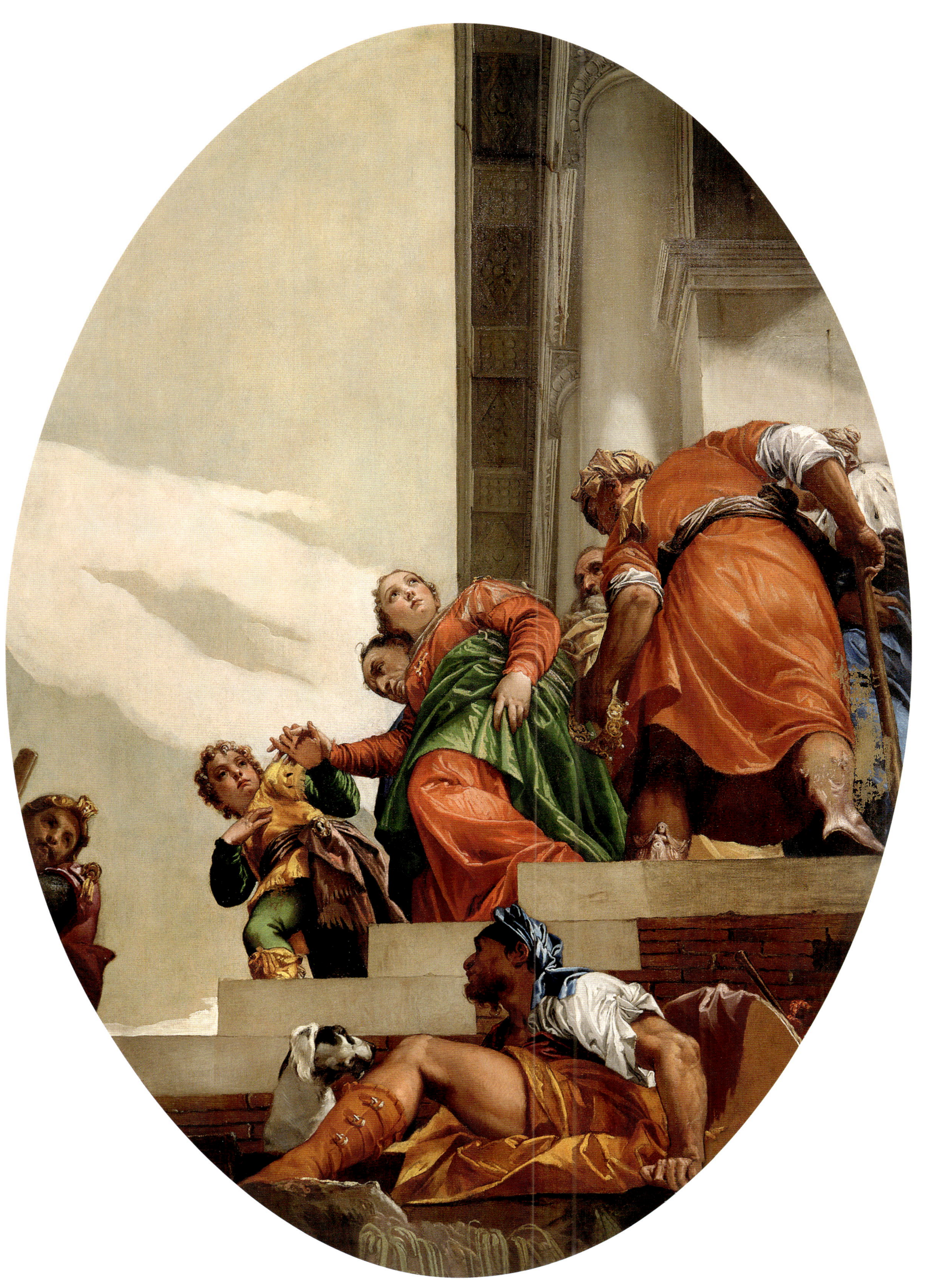

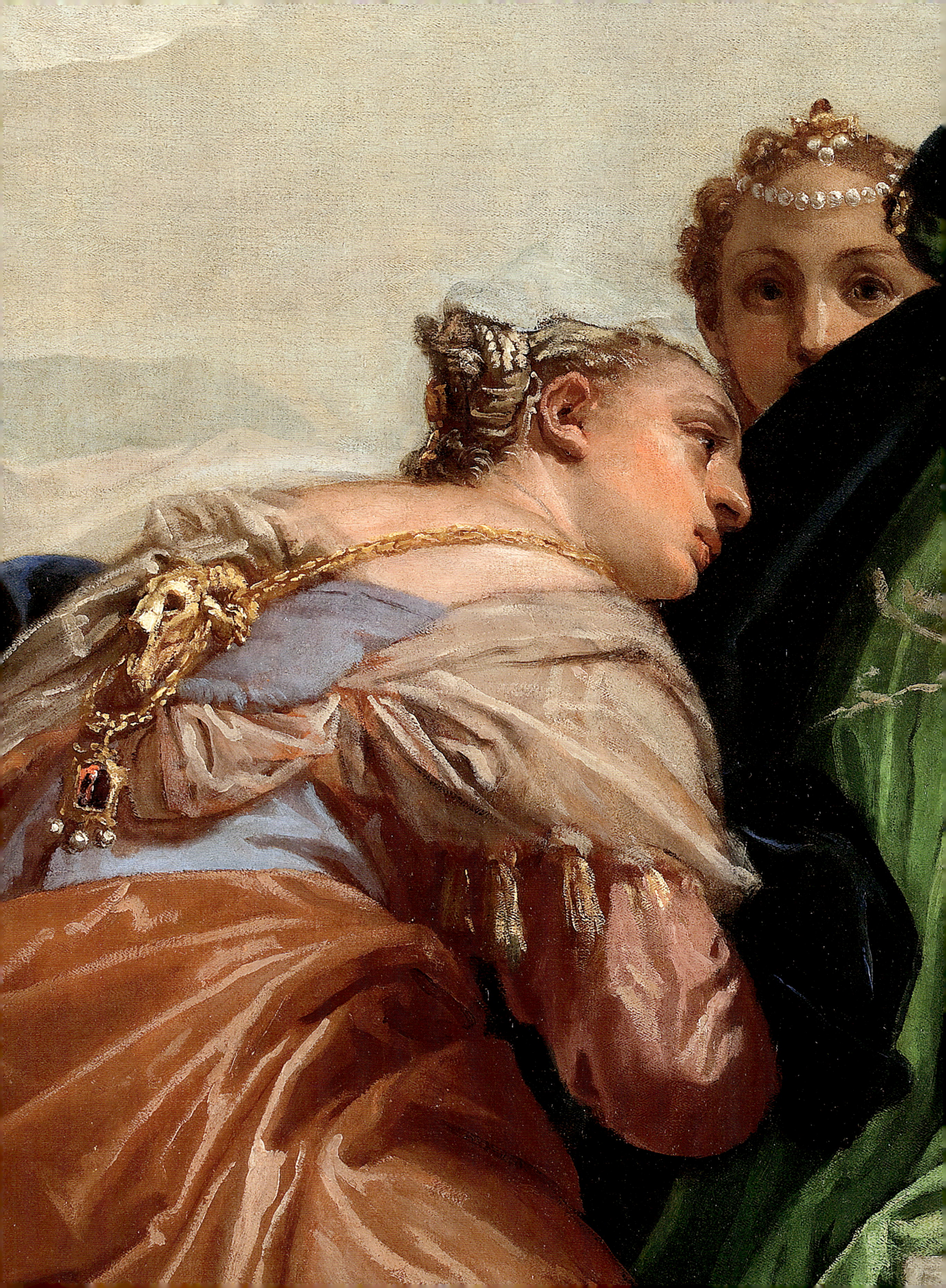

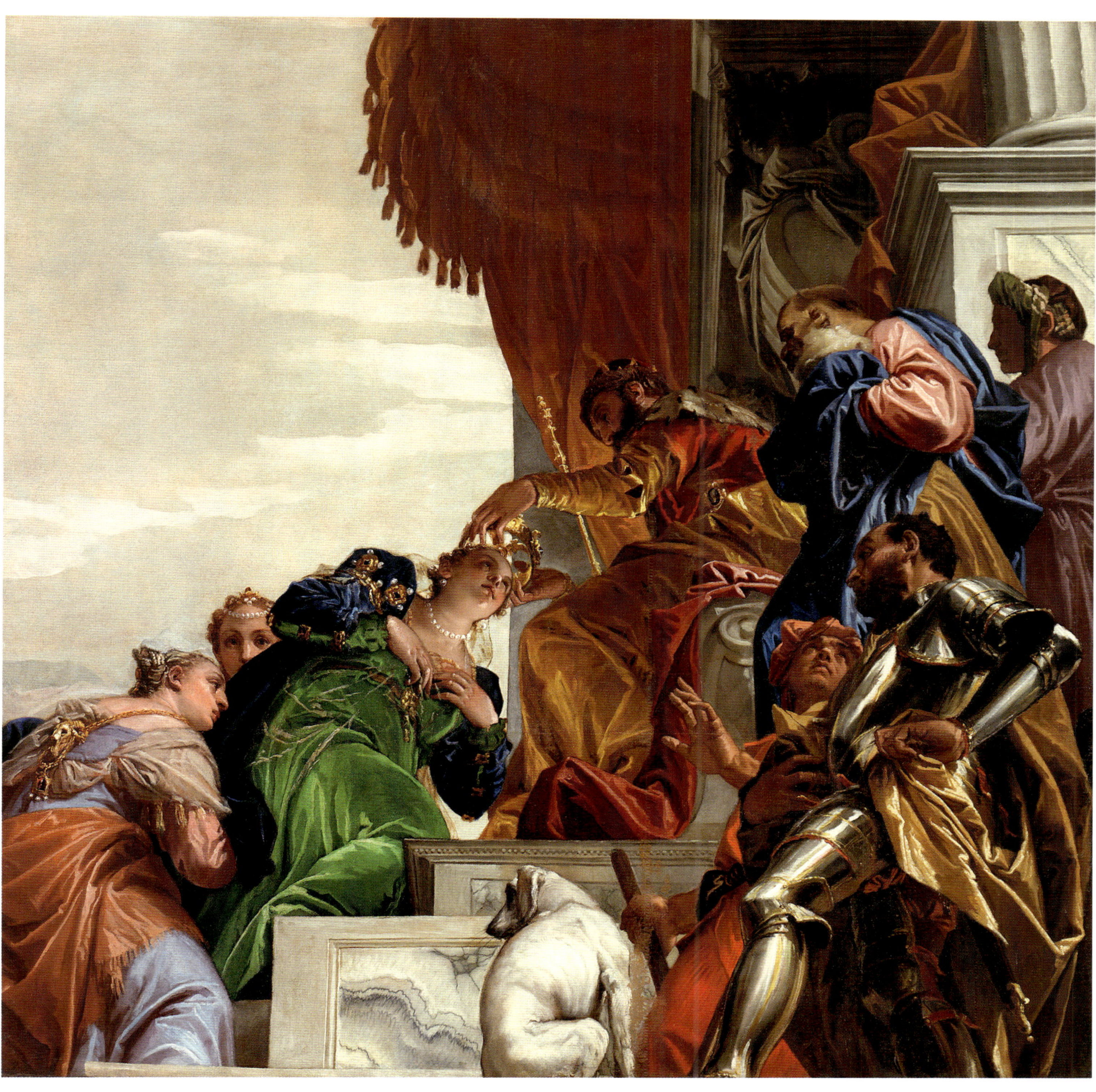

The Coronation of Esther, 1556, canvas, 450 × 370 cm.
Venice, church of San Sebastiano, ceiling

Veronese immediately proposes some solutions which he will then resume throughout his production: the taste and fashion of the time in hairstyles; balance and mirroring in the group of female faces; the mirrors and the flashes of light in armour; the presence of the jester and the classical herms in monochrome; the colouring of the shadows and the same use of the shaded faces.

The Coronation of Esther, 1556, canvas, 450 × 370 cm, detail. Venice, church of San Sebastiano, ceiling

balance of presences and colour backgrounds, and are above all evidence of his surprising structural and perspective capacity in joining space and figures in admirable unity. The space is built through architectural fragments, stairways and, in the *Triumph*, the base of a grandiose twisted column and an entablature that acts as a frame from which the crowd that follows the progress of the horses on the busy road overlooks. Those two big horses are impressive for the spectator who sees them from below, they give the impression of being about to fall on him. Those who raise their eyes to the ceiling for the first time cannot help but feel this illusionistic effect, created with perspective perfection and extreme narrative effectiveness. And then they will appreciate the details, the expressive faces and the admirable horse heads, marked by fluttering manes, a memory for many other painters, starting with Rubens. The first and intended effect is an amazing theatrical, imaginative and surprising result in the brightly coloured scenography.

If the staging is spectacular, it also has an allegorical and typological meaning, it shows the relationships between the Old and New Testaments, between History before and after the Grace. These are the motifs of the Ladder and the Fall. The ascending ladder is the ascent to Paradise, Jacob's ladder; the descending ladder represents the exile of the Jewish people in the interpretation of the Midrash. The rebel angels fall, one falls into sin, into the mortal risk of temptation: Mordechai will not fall, Amman will fall. Typologies explained in the *Speculum humanae salvationis*, the Mirror of human salvation, an imposing text, certainly known to the prior, written in the first half of the thirteenth century and attributed to Vincent de Beauvais, showing the deep links between human history, episodes of the Ancient Testament, meaning of the New.

The choice of the horse seen from below, which falls on the spectator, was present in the painting of the ceilings made by Giulio Romano in Palazzo Te and will be taken up again a few years later by Domenico Brusasorci in Phaeton's chariot in Palazzo Chiericati, Vicenza; but it had already been studied by Paolo Veronese, probably only a few years earlier, in a ceiling canvas whose destination and possible context we ignore: it is the *Marcus Curtius* where the same large crowd of the Triumph also appears, this time on balustrades just mentioned, in a forest of spears. The legend, referred to in the *Stories* of Titus Livius, tells of a great chasm that suddenly opened in the Roman Forum, a bottomless abyss. The augurs decreed that it would expand to engulf the city: the only way to avoid that precipice in the underworld was to throw into it what was most precious. The young warrior Marcus Curtius threw himself with his horse into the void, offering his greatest good, life, to the Manes gods. The abyss never widened and the Romans recognized in Marcus Curtius the supreme expression of *devotio*. The sacrifice of the soldier immolated for his country, the gesture of offering himself to the gods with arms wide open, underlined by the devout expression, the crowd around, even the incisiveness of the horse's muzzle, contribute to the grandiose effect of a canvas certainly destined for a spectacular ceiling. Replicated and indeed duplicated in the *Triumph*.

If there was a need for confirmation of the painter's illusionistic abilities, decidedly the most modern in Venice, the canvases with the story of Esther were proof of it. What further aroused admiration, however, was the colour, the striking use of greens, the hairstyles, the fabrics, the jewels rendered with luminous touches, that brilliance of the armour, those rendered by the fabrics. As Francesco Valcanover wrote: "With the contrast of cold tones with other warm ones, he gives an extraordinary detachment to the images. Having done away with black, he colours the surfaces in light and shadow with the reflections of neighbouring colours. He doses the amount of light in each coloured area in an ever-new scale of ratios and passages of richness" (Valcanover, 1988).

A test of technique and solid theoretical training on perspective and illusionistic solutions, also theorized by Sebastiano Serlio, of which Veronese would confirm himself as a master, and a test of drafting speed. On the canvas made rigid and smooth by a mixture of plaster and glue, a light pictorial support, or priming, Veronese sketches a few strokes in charcoal, with the function of memory; he then traces the lines of an essential drawing with a thin brush, still visible up close

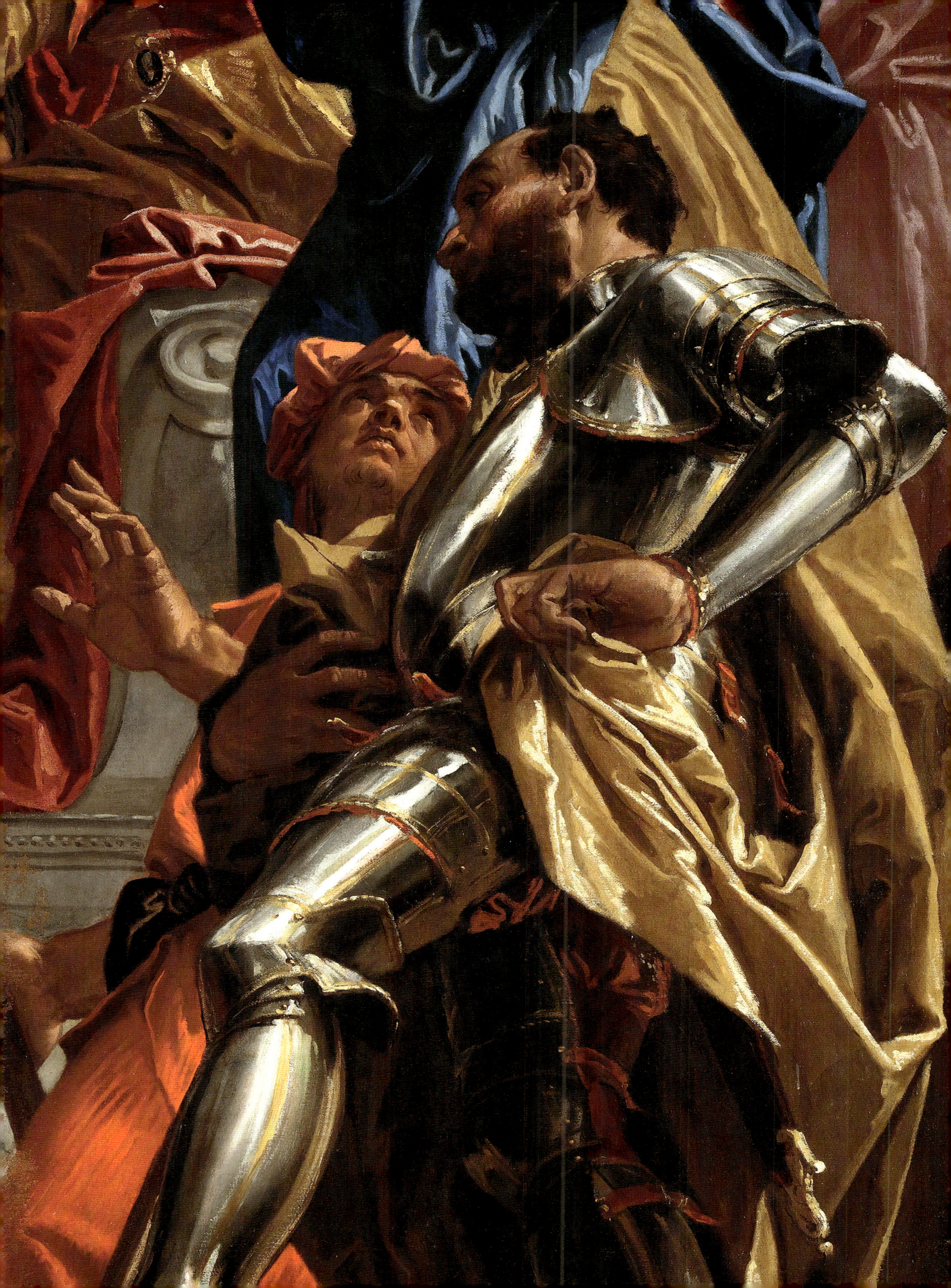

under the more transparent backgrounds. A graphic trace of simple suggestion, because the painting will define and create the volumes, since the coloured brushstroke completely outlines the shape. Paolo begins the work with the half-tone, applied in a thin layer, even very light, with broad blended brushstrokes; subsequently the lights and shadows build the volumes; finally, with quick touches of a denser colour, he defines the details, providing them with that particular light, diffused and clear, which is his distinctive trait. The details of Amman's armour show very well the succession of gestures, boasting an exemplary skill.

The Triumph of Mordechai, 1556, canvas, 500 × 370 cm.
Venice, church of San Sebastiano, ceiling

The majestic twisted column, the impressive musculature of the soldiers, the clamorous waving of the Albanian flag; the human expressiveness of the horses: even in this spectacular oval the Veronese varies his invention, presenting original motifs and solutions with effects of strong prospective illusionism.

ESTHER BETWEEN JEWS AND ALBANIANS

Prior Torlioni had proposed to the painter a biblical book, only relatively known; the only one in which the name of God is not mentioned. Paolo already knew it, if we owe him a small canvas with *Ahasuerus Orders the Triumph of Mordechai*, and another with *Esther before Ahasuerus*, in pendant with *The Punishment of the Eunuchs*, now in Museo di Castelvecchio. The Council of Trent will place the book among the canons, while for the reformers, and in particular for Martin Luther, it does not represent the divine word, but a narration of archaic aspects of Jewish culture; a judgment however communicated privately, in what will be the so-called "conversations at the table", or an opinion still unknown in mid-century Venice. For the Jews who live and pray in the Venice Ghetto, it is a book that recalls the bitterness and shame of the exile, and illustrates the courage to remain oneself, the pleasure of deception and revenge. It is the book that explains Purim, the feast where children dress up and drink until good and evil can no longer be distinguished, and Amman and Mordechai swap roles. The celebration of the reversal of fate, of the upside-down world, recalling how much the Jewish people have known how to survive, often in daring ways. A story of Fortune, of foresight, dissimulation and tenacity, even fidelity to oneself, later translated by Catholic pedants and liturgical scholars into the history of Providence which rescues the brave.

We do not know how many of the possible meanings the prior of San Sebastiano wanted to communicate to the faithful. However, we know that he read the text translated by Saint Jerome, the saint to whom the confraternity referred, with the additions in Greek, later than the Hebrew text, where we read a prayer of Esther addressed to God, which the Catholic liturgy proposes for meditation on Thursday in the first week of Lent. For Saint Jerome, Esther's role was to prefigure Mary's function in the salvation of all humanity. The prior will also have known another fundamental commentary on the Book, made in the 9th century by Hrabanus Maurus, the *Expositio in Librum Hester* of which a manuscript is kept in the Capitular Library in Verona. Hrabanus Maurus was very clear: "Tunc enim mystica Hester, id est ecclesia, de nationibus apostolica praedicatione ad regem Christum per sanae fidei credulitatem et baptismatis sacramentum introducebatur". The Carolingian scholar, abbot of Fulda, therefore states that "the mystic Hester, that is the Church, was introduced into the nations through apostolic preaching to the King Christ, through the clarity of sound faith and the sacrament of baptism". Esther is therefore the Church, which receives the task of bearing witness, and Mordechai is the one who protects and defends her, he is a witness, as her triumph demonstrates. Mordechai is a guide of prudence and shrewdness in which any shepherd of souls can recognize himself, even the Prior Torlioni.

Let's look again at the scene of the triumph: what is the reason for that waving red flag? Observing it, the stylized eagle can be seen in the centre, recognizable by its wing and paw. But it is not the eagle of the Habsburg Holy Roman Empire, which stands out on another colour, never red. It is the Albanian flag, the heraldic coat of arms of the Castrioti, the insignia of Giorgio Castriota Scanderbeg. The national hero, who died in 1468, had been an ally of the Venetians, interweaving a large part of his history with them, and was well present in the city's memory,

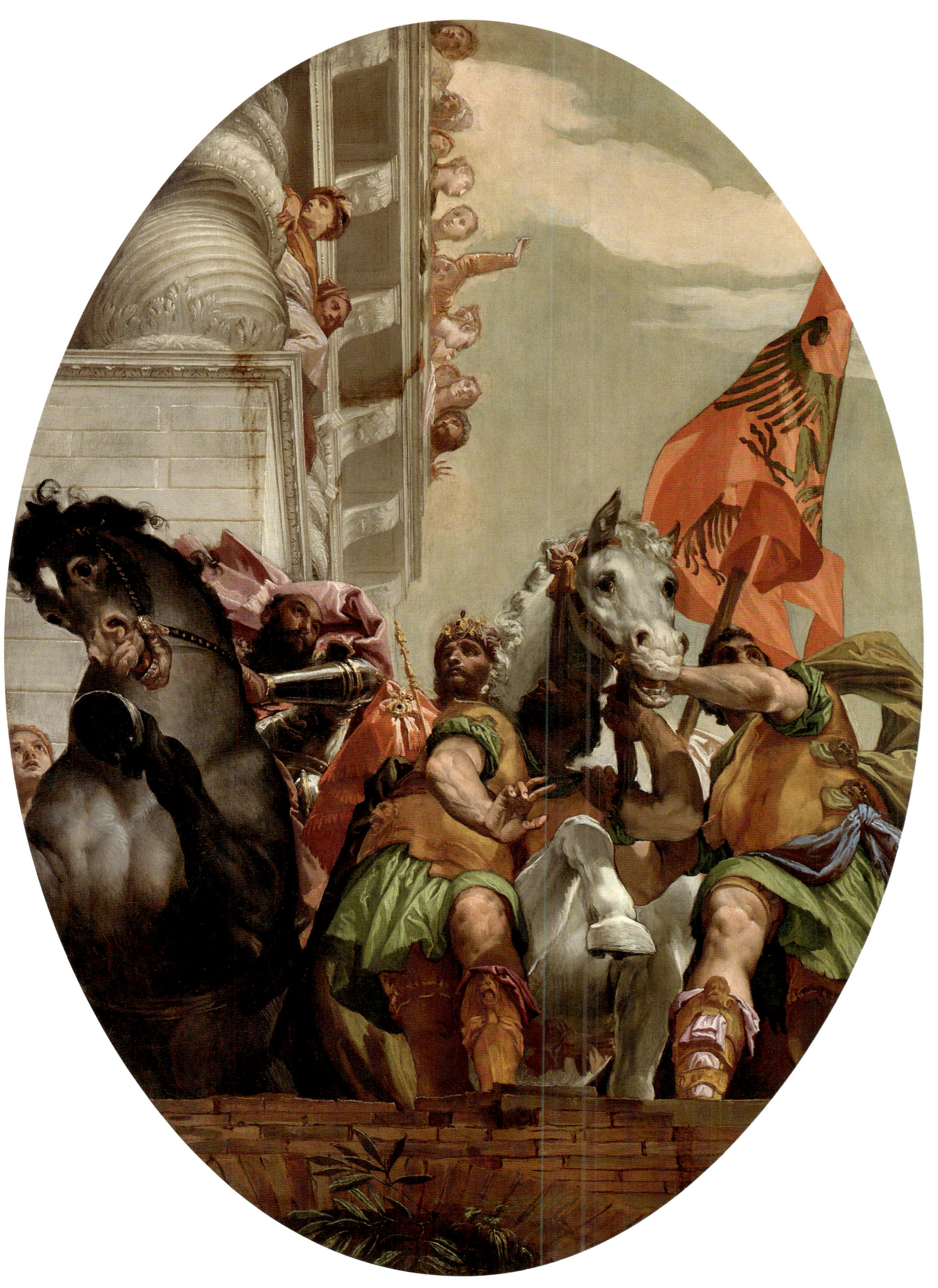

The Triumph of Mordechai, 1556, canvas, 500 × 370 cm, detail. Venice, church of San Sebastiano, ceiling

and obviously in the community of Albanians who fled after the tragic loss of Scutari. The memory and exaltation of the resistance of Venetians and Albanians, men and women, in 1479, remained a founding myth of the diaspora, well present, active and integrated into Venetian society. The façade of the Scola degli Albanesi recalled the event, and even today in Campo San Maurizio we see the beautiful bas-relief with Mohammed II, saber drawn, threatening the fortified castle subjected to bombardment by Ottoman artillery for months and attacked five times. Their loyalty to Venice and the benefits of the Senate are remembered in the marble wanted by the exiles, and in the epigraph. Walled up in 1532, the sign identified a frequented Scola, adorned with the cycle with the *Life of the Virgin* by Vittore Carpaccio. In Venice, the story of the siege narrated firsthand by Marino Barlezio, *De obsidione Scodrensi* published in 1504 and then re-published was well known. A Catholic priest, Barlezio was also the author of a life of Scanderbeg translated into various languages, disseminated and considered the main source for the life and deeds of the Albanian hero. Paolo Veronese will return to the story in 1582 with a large canvas in the Doge's Palace. It was the Venetian scholar Lucia Nadin who rediscovered with passionate attention many other traces of flags and figurative references to the Albanians in the pictorial system in San Sebastiano: it would therefore seem that the prior and the painter wanted to remind the faithful and the Christian people of the dangers from the *Signor Turco*, also illustrating, in addition to the moral sense, the prophetic value of the Old Testament, its perennial lesson, proposing both literal image and allegorical meanings.

The Text thus becomes fully explicit, as the painter who shares common tastes, sensitivities and readings will be able to do on many other occasions. But what relationship is possible between Sebastian, to whom the church is dedicated, and Esther, between a Roman soldier of the late empire who would have been killed for his faith, and a Jewish girl at the time of Xerxes, with a patriotic uncle? Between a Book perhaps written two, three centuries before the coming of the one whom others, non-Jews, will consider the Messiah, and the story handed down for centuries, and then well reproposed by a Ligurian friar, Bishop Jacopo born in Varazze in the 13th century? Or what is the relationship between Maria, the *Ecclesia* and the *Miles*? The link can only be explained through Catholic theology, relating the salvific value of sacrifice and that of intercession for the salvation of the faithful. It is the allegorical interpretation of the Hebrew text: Esther intercedes for his people with the king, as Mary and the Church intercede with the Son for the salvation of humanity; Sebastian accepts martyrdom as Christ accepted it for the salvation of human beings. Furthermore, Sebastian's model is that of the fighter, ready to sacrifice himself for the defence of faith against its enemies. A model for monks and Venetians. Over time, the scenes taken from the *Book of Esther* have also suggested different readings, including the triumph of Faith over Heresy, a theme that is always present in Christian iconography, but here without precise doctrinal or iconographic references. The Hieronymite fathers will have explained the most obvious meaning to the scarcely literate people: Sebastian accepted death to show his faith, Esther saved her people from the evil will of their enemies. Sacrifice, defense: the Venetians understood this well, since for years they had to defend themselves from the Turkish enemy, and at the same time from the attacks of many pretenders to the lands of the Serenissima Republic. And then the figure of Mordechai also evoked what everyone believed was the true shield of the Republic, the very reason for its existence and survival: Justice. Also Dante, now well-known and printed in Venice, had written about it: in the Comedy, in Purgatorio XVII, Dante recalls "One crucified, disdainful and ferocious [Amman]"; whose death is witnessed by "the great Ahasuerus, Esther his wife, and the just Mordechai, Who was in word and action so entire."

The pilgrim has a vision of it in the midst of a dream, in that sort of swoon that catches him as he ascends the mountain. And it is a vision of punitive justice, what the Jews will then do, atrociously taking revenge on the threatened genocide.

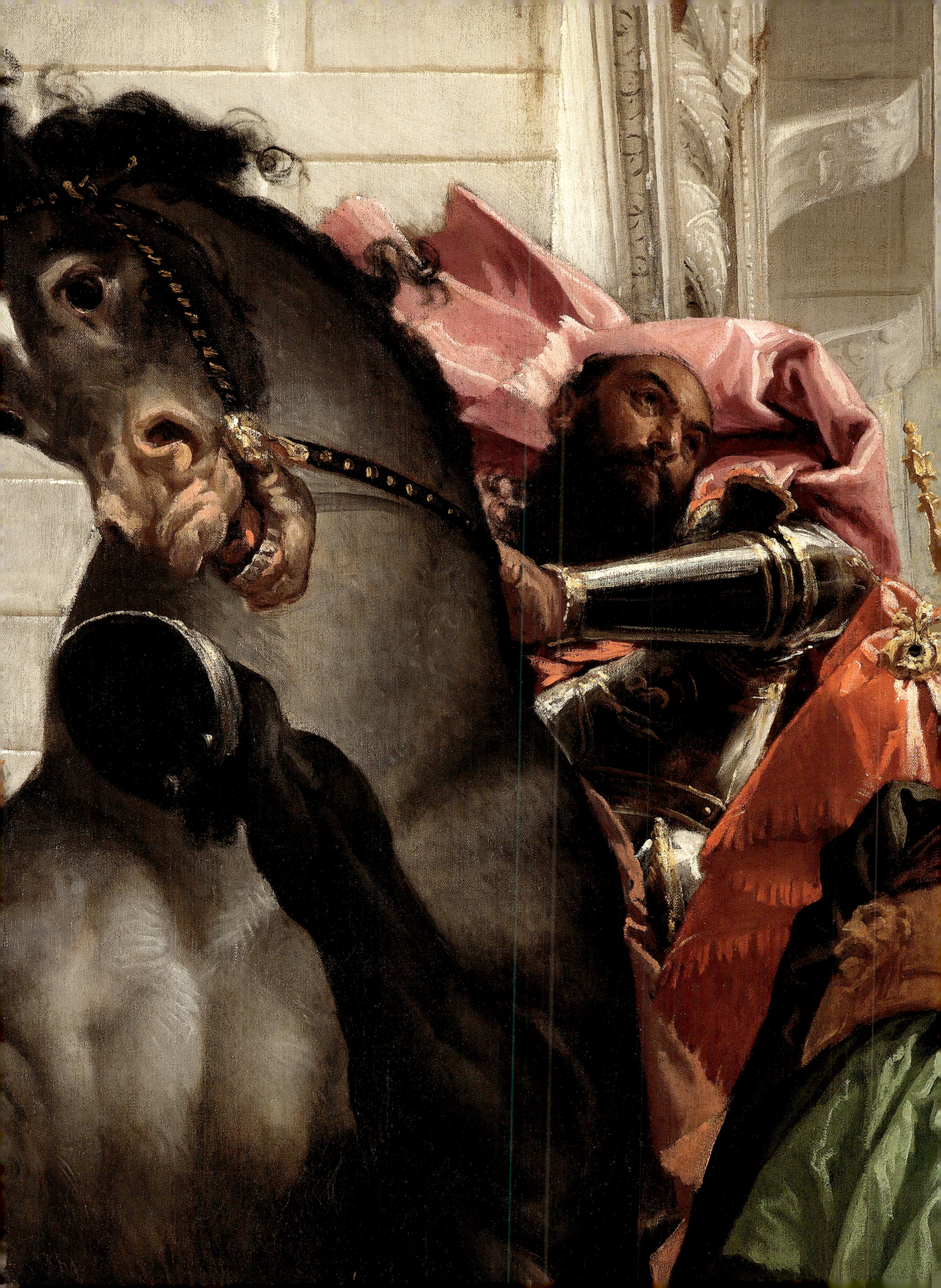

In those mid-century years, in the interval between deadly clashes, when the Turks had by now conquered all the Aegean islands, fugitives and refugees continued to arrive in Venice, even if not to the extent of the exiles who fled after the fall of Scutari fifty years before. Venice was still and always crossed and interwoven with stories and memories of persecutors and persecuted, of great conspiracies, of betrayals and bloody vendettas, of threatened genocides and carried out massacres; of stories of exile and domination, yokes, vexations and martyrs. Very human and very lagoon stories, in the city that had tried to defend a large part of its *Stato da Mar* to the point of exhaustion, welcoming fugitives, moved by the heroic feats in the defence of fortresses and cities, and which had had to sacrifice and faint to reconquer the friendly cities of the *Stato da Tera*. All stories from which to draw lessons and teachings, proposed to an audience enthralled by the categories practiced by preachers: the allegorical readings, the moral keys, the stock of the anagogical, or prophetic sense. Therefore the *Book of Esther* could speak and be understood by every Venetian.

An evidence of that feeling is the most grandiose tomb in the church of San Sebastiano: the cenotaph of the last archbishop of Nicosia on Cyprus, moreover *in commendam*, since the prelate never reached the most distant island. The splendid tomb, opposite the organ, on the right side of the building, was designed by Jacopo Sansovino for a nobleman of Greek ancestry, the humanist bishop Livio Podocataro, who died on 19 January 1556 just when Paolo was beginning the decorations. The tomb of the prelate would be completed by 1559, a further occasion for exchanges between Paolo and Sansovino, the architect with whom, after Sanmicheli and Palladio, Veronese collaborated and talked constantly. In relation to the design of the tomb, whose imposing size is immediately evident in the church, Veronese will design and decorate the organ case. And subsequently he will adapt the windows illuminating the high altar on the model of those illuminating the tomb: episodes of dialogue "on par" between the architecture and the decoration that adorns, colours and uses the spaces and lights of the architectural structure.

In the meantime, with his work in San Sebastiano he publicly showed the Venetians – the Doge's Palace in fact could be visited by exceptionally few guests of the Republic – his skills in architectural perspective and drawing, and brand new colours – clean and clear, bright and ringing compared to the choices and tonal traditions of Titian and Tintoretto, as well as a rapid mastery of work and an effective direction of a group of painters. Whereby Ridolfi will end: "The paintings having been discovered not only for the novelty of the structure, but for the singular works of Paolo (since similar beauties have not been seen before in the heavens of times), numerous people came to admire them, giving immortal praise to the author".

The Sacrifice of Marcus Curtius, 1550-1552, canvas, Ø 239 cm. Vienna, Kunsthistorisches Museum, inv. 6744

The sacrifice of the Roman soldier to save his city is an early work, certainly for a ceiling, expressed in melodramatic tones: here the impression of both the great lesson of Giulio Romano, and the contiguity with Brusasorci and all the coeval group of the Veronese painters with whom Paolo had studied, is more evident than in the oval of the *Triumph of Mordechai*.

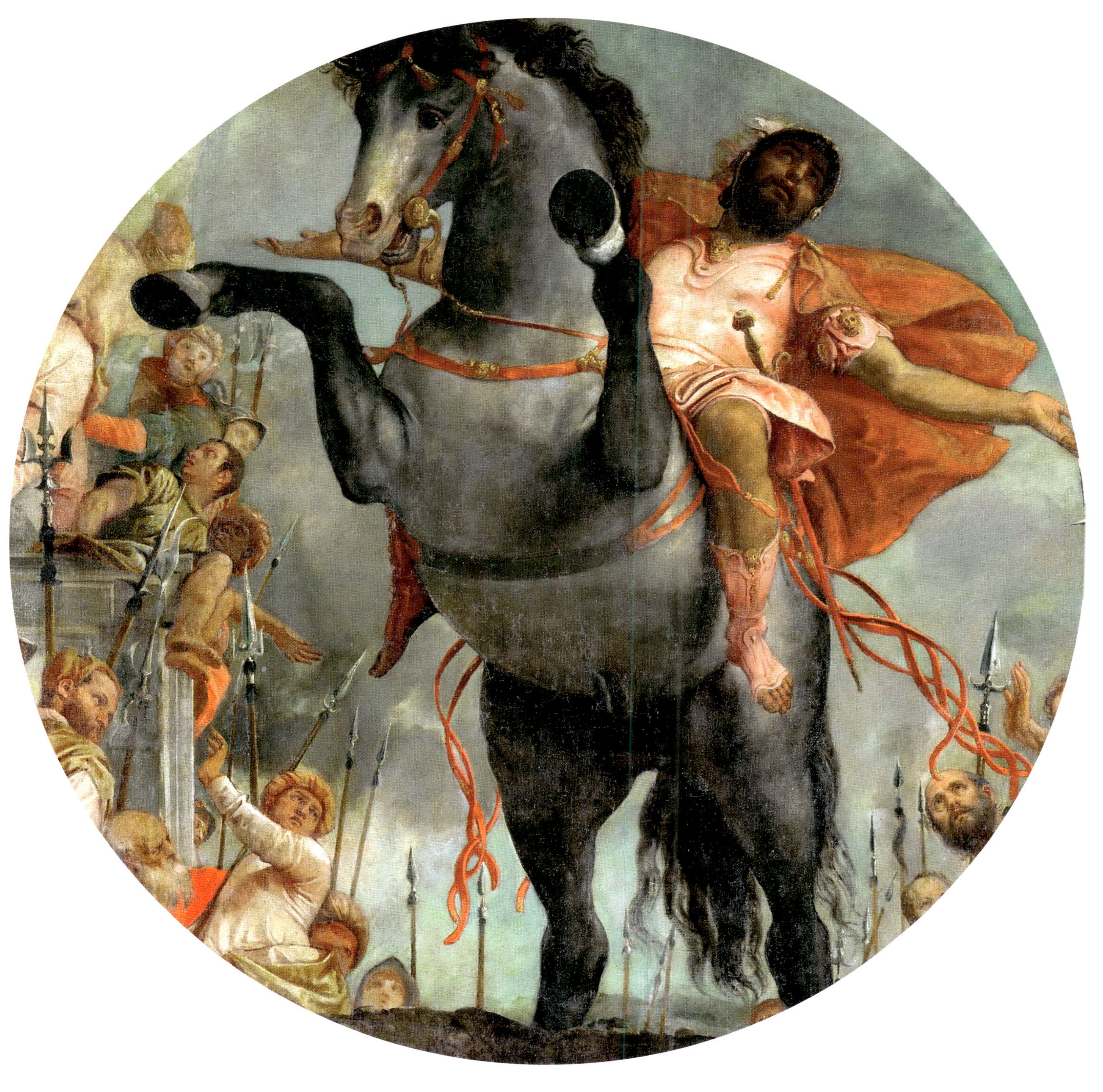

CHAPTER II

Debut in Verona

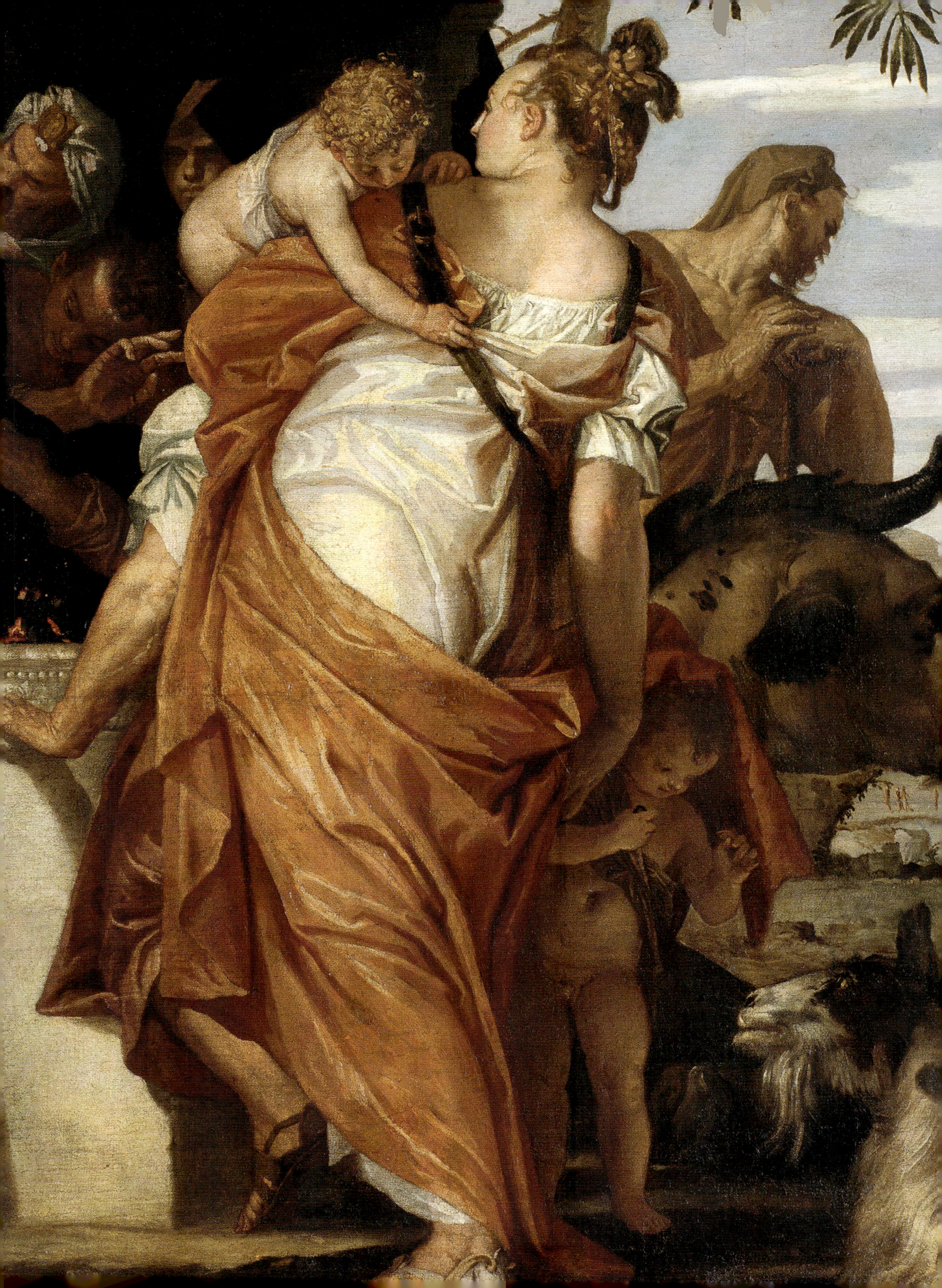

The large family of a stone-cutter craftsman, known by all as Gabriele *spezapreda*, lived in San Paolo district of Campo Marzio, near the river Adige, within the solid defensive walls designed and built under the guidance of Michele Sanmicheli. He was called so not by surname, unusual for artisans and people, but for his work: the dialect word indicated someone who knew how to work stone, not only the coarse stonecutter or the simple stonemason: also sculptors and marble workers, and masters capable of drawing and create altars, balustrades, polychrome and varied floors called *salezade*. A family trade: the father Pietro *spezapreda* had come from Bissone on Lake Lugano, registered in the Veronese cadastre since 1502, where he was registered with his son and his wife Lucia. Gabriele, born in 1497, married Caterina when he was very young. She was the natural daughter of the noble Antonio Caliari and of Maddalena Dragina. They had numerous children: the first, Margherita, followed by Francesco, Antonio and Laura. Then in 1528 Paolo was born, followed by Cassandra, Benedetto and finally Giovanni Battista. The very first document available to us is a personal data, rather rare given the times but also, like everyone else, somewhat insecure in the transcription of the age of the members of the family nucleus. In the Anagraphs of Contrada San Paolo, preserved in the State Archives of Verona, reg. 889, dated 1529, the following are listed: "Piero spezapreda 50 years, Lussia his wife 47, Gabriel his son 25 (instead of the more probable 33); Catharina his wife 30; Sons: Malgarita 11; Zuanfrancesco 9; Antonio 7; Laura 6; Paulo 1". In the registry office of 1541 Gabriele and Caterina will be recorded as being of the same age as 45, while Paolo is given ten years, already reporting him as "Depentor"; then in the registry of 1553 Gabriele is attributed 60 years, Caterina 50, Paolo 20. As can be seen, the age data, the spelling of the names, the absence of surnames make the sixteenth-century registry offices unsure, to be considered with great caution.
A large family in any case, a certainly solid and continuous activity: it is obvious that the children followed their father's work from infancy, imitating him and showing different talents, trying their hand at first mixtures of earth, roughing out workable stones, drawing; in this way it was possible to recognize, encourage and support any potential abilities. Those who showed talent were initiated as a trainee, apprentice with some master, a master builder, preferably a colleague friend. While the second son, Francesco, will be trained following his father's trade, Antonio will become an embroiderer, at the time a popular craft activity. Paolo first and then Benedetto, perhaps with his brother, will follow the training as painters. Gabriele knew several decorator craftsmen with workshops, because most of them lived right in that district, managing workshops that were operating for several generations.
The registry office of the Santa Cecilia district in the State Archives of Verona, Register 149, documents on 2 May 1541: "Antonius Badillus pictor q. Hieronymi 20 (years); Paulus ejus discipulus seu garzonus 14 "while in a previous one dated 16 April Paolo was registered in his family, qualified as "depentor". "Paulus ejus discipulus" will still be fourteen in a registration from 1542. The inscription on the back of the altarpiece in the church of Santissimi Nazaro e Celso in Verona, dated 1543, declares Antonio to be twenty-five.

Consecration of David,
1552-1555 (?), canvas,
173 × 365 cm, detail.
Vienna, Kunsthistorisches
Museum, inv. 40

The apprentice painter

Normally apprentices had to be at least twelve years old, and were qualified as *garzone*, apprentice; at the end of the apprenticeship they received their wages as workers; having passed an exemplary test, they could be recognized as masters by the corporation, having the right to exercise it. The professional association guaranteed protection and solidarity by following practices and rules indicated in the ancient statutes, the Venetian *mariegole* or master rules. The apprenticeship lasted from five to seven years; the condition of worker from two to three years; the masters could work independently or in association with each other, in single construction sites or in workshops for particular orders. Some masters specialized as fresco painters, landscape painters, portrait painters, genre scene painters, furniture decorators; at the top were the *figuranti*, i.e. painters of figures. In Venice, the Scuola di San Luca dell'arte dei dipintori, at Santa Sofia, also included *miniadori* and *cuoridori*, i.e. decorators of painted and punched leather; *cartieri* and *maschereri*, i.e. makers of papier-mâché masks, draftsmen; *casselleri* and *coffaneri*: coffins and chests were reserved for wedding trousseaus and for the preservation of clothes and tablecloths. So the term "painters" concerned a series of highly specialized craft activities.

Raising of Jairus' Daughter, approx. 1546, oil on paper mounted on canvas, 42 × 37 cm. Paris, Musée du Louvre, inv. 1419

It should be the preparatory sketch, or the copy by heart, of an early work, a lost painting. The majority of Veronese art historians place it as an autographed work, among the very first proofs. For its structural elements – the group of figures in close dialogue, the architectural backdrop in the background – and for the use of clothes and colours, it can be considered exemplary of the early achievements of the young painter.

Those few and uncertain personal documents, confirmed by the traditional seventeenth-century historiography, were recovered by a distant descendant of the painter, Pietro Caliari (1841-1920), a teacher and priest, also a poet and storyteller, author of a fundamental biography of his ancestor. A reference book, adorned with some lyrical and romantic momentum, which confirms the first period of learning under Antonio – third of his name within the Badile dynasty – who grew up with his uncle Francesco in a very active workshop. A formation first indicated by Raffaello Borghini in that curious essay in dialogic form, divided into four books, two theoretical and two historical, which is entitled: *Il Riposo di R. B. in cui della pittura e della scultura si favella, de' più illustri pittori e scultori e delle più famose opere loro si fa mentione, e le cose principali appartenenti a dette arti s'insegnano*. Treatise originally published in Florence in 1584, dedicated to Giovanni de' Medici, the work of the Florentine playwright with an agitated life – from an important but economically decayed family, who stayed for a long time in France – an exponent of a courtly and academic environment that was now dying out. The news collected by Borghini would be only relatively reliable, but will also be confirmed by his nephew Giuseppe Caliari, son of Paolo Veronese's eldest son Gabriele. Giuseppe communicates the biographical traits of his grandfather, however unknown, to Claudio Ridolfi, born in Verona and a painter himself, as well as the author, in his early fifties, of the *Vita di Paolo Caliari*, printed in 1646 for the types of Matteo Leni, an anticipation of his most recent book known and widely used by art historians, published in 1648 under the title of *Le maraviglie dell'arte*. Two ponderous tomes which, on the model of Giorgio Vasari's *Lives*, reconstruct the history of Venetian painting through more than one hundred and fifty biographies of artists: the style is of the time, bombastic and moralizing but the information, even very anecdotal, is an irreplaceable source.

Teachers and prompters

There are many rich visual sources, represented in Verona by churches, public and civil buildings, open to the possibilities of study and to novelties from large centres such as Mantua, Brescia, Venice. Two painters in particular kept up to date and were, for Paolo, son of Gabriele *spezapreda*, the probable first training opportunity in terms of technique and taste. Tradition has it that Antonio Badile (about 1518-1560) was the first teacher even if he was just ten years older than the pupil; among the proofs of Antonio Badile we find in 1540 a *St. Nicholas of Tolentino*, followed by an altarpiece for the church of Maria Consolatrice, the *Madonna Enthroned between Saint Dionysius and the Magdalene*, now visible in the Museo Civico di Verona (inv. 380), where the teachings of the Carotos and the visual memories of the painting

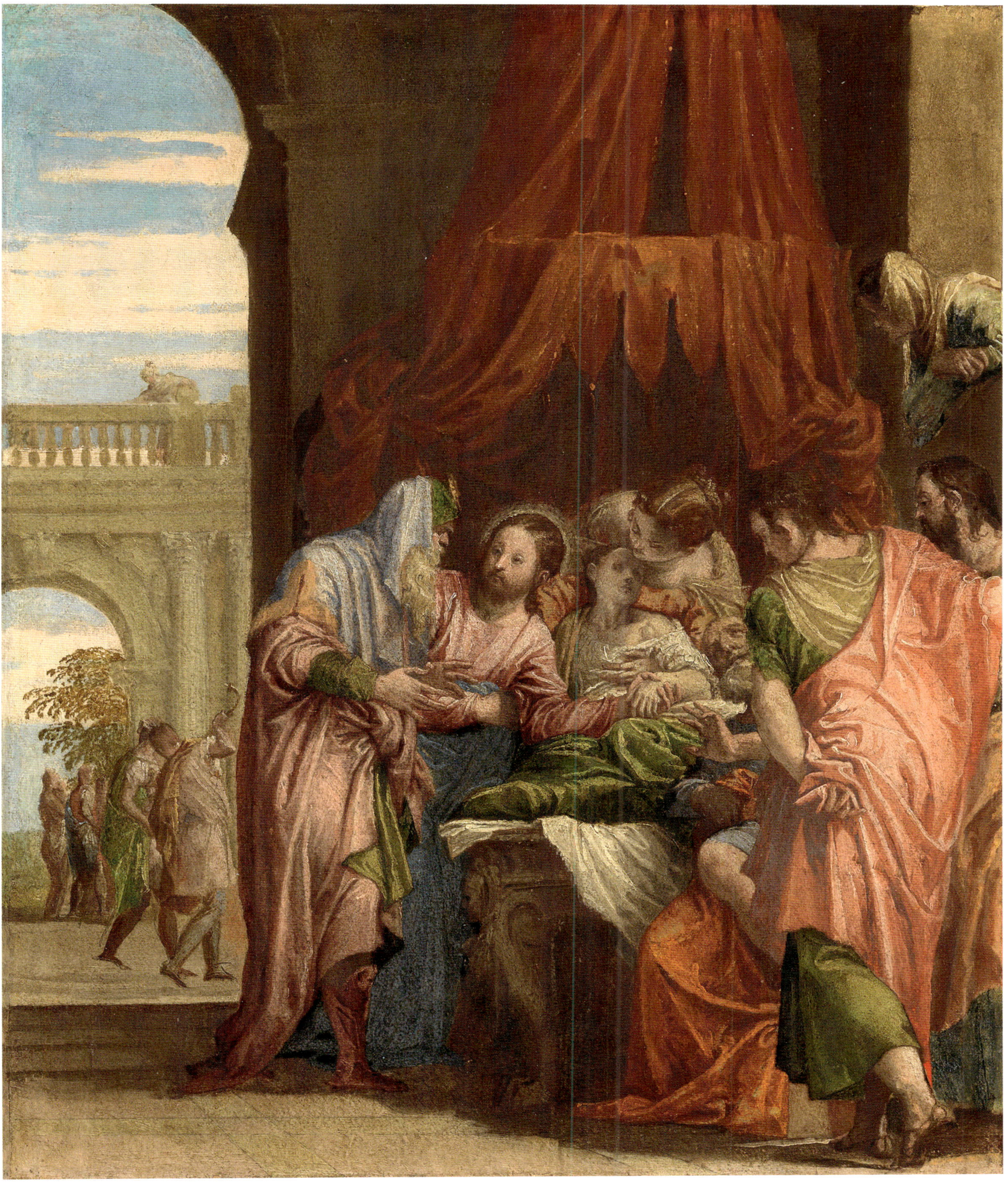

from Brescia and Veneto area, Moretto and Lotto can be recognized. Then the important altarpiece in the church of Santissimi Nazaro e Celso, delivered and signed in 1543 according to the testamentary will of the Veronese merchant Giovanni da Gandino. In the altarpiece someone wanted to recognize the portrait of Paolo in the little page that accompanies that sacred conversation, and again the *Virgin in Glory with the Saints Anthony Abbot, John the Baptist and Blaise*. A contemporary of Badile, Domenico Riccio "Il Brusasorci" (1516-1567), also a son of an artist, must have been a further reference to Paolo, and then also a friend and collaborator. After Badile, Paolo was perhaps a pupil, even if only for a short period, of the much more experienced Giovanni Caroto (1488-1566), a well-known and esteemed artist, attentive to Venetian painting, in particular to Carpaccio and Bellini, and a masterful painter of architecture as shown in the *De origine et amplitude civitatis Veronae* by Torello Saraina from 1540, an example of study of the monuments of the Roman age, a source and reference for the architects of the time.
The Carotos and Badile were the reference painters with whom other peers of Paolo also trained, a "Veronese brigade" who would share experiences of decoration and friendship: Bernardino India (1528-1590) a pupil of Brusasorci; Paolo Farinati (1524-1606), also present in Paolo's private life several times; Giovan Battista Zelotti (1526-1578), who also collaborated with him in Venice; Giovanni Ermanno Ligozzi (1525-1605). Belonging to families of painters, who went to the workshop with colleagues and friends, they will form a real group with exchanges of relationships, reciprocal stimuli coming from the different clientele. Always oriented, presented and followed by the Caroto brothers and by Sanmicheli, active in many construction sites. The most important families of the city turn to them for decorations and portraits, and the ecclesiastics for the decoration of the churches, requested and solicited by Bishop Giberti. In the words of Pallucchini, their common horizon is a pictorial culture updated on the novelties of Tuscan-Emilian Mannerism, on "a chromatic language defining the plastic form almost harshly, with timbral breaks, always set in spaces full of luminosity". To all this we must add the Mantuan novelties of Giulio Romano and architectural classicism.

Paolo *spezapreda*'s training is therefore defined by family, knowledge and relationships in an environment of open and up-to-date art craftsmanship, participating in the antiquarian tradition of the city, aware of recent developments in colour, decoration and perspective, in close dialogue with the architecture renewed by Sanmicheli, which takes up and updates the classical lesson with an unprecedented functional taste towards urban and spatial modules of eurythmic geometry.
All the early lessons are found in the *Raising of Jairus' Daughter* that, according to Ridolfi, was placed opposite Badile's *Resurrection of Lazarus*, signed and dated 1546 on the verso. Located in the chapel of the Avanzi family in San Bernardino di Verona, it would constitute Paolo's first public test: the eighteen-year-old master would have represented an episode from the Gospels of Mark (5, 21-43), Luke (8, 40-56) and Matthew (9, 18-26), an unusual iconographic choice.
The Gospels narrate the request to Jesus of the head of the synagogue of Capernaum in Galilee, Jairus, desperate for his daughter's condition. Arriving at the priest's house, accompanied by Peter, John and James, Jesus finds the girl now dead, and miraculously brings her back to life. Paolo creates a dynamic composition on two different levels: the first is characterized by the crowding of the various characters in front of the girl's bed, while in the distant second level he paints the perspective glimpse of a garden bordered by an architectural backdrop, a classic loggia crowned by a balustrade, with distant, almost evanescent people. All the figures, on both levels, appear slender and elegant, dressed in loose and colourful clothes, portrayed in expressive gesticulations. While the touches of light on the clothes give airiness to the scene, particular attention is paid to the female hair. All these will be typical elements of Veronese's creations of the following years. But the original canvas disappeared in 1696, sold or exchanged or stolen, in any case replaced by a mediocre copy. What we can consider today is only a small paper pasted on canvas, now in the Louvre, whose origins we do not know but which presents characters of immediacy and spontaneity of touch for which it is attributed to him, as a sketch, or a sort of copy – a later reminder.

Precocious and talented, the young man quickly learned by dealing with important texts, clearly visible in the Veronese churches. Sanmicheli, the most prestigious operating architect in Verona at that time, immediately appreciated Paolo's talent and introduced him to his patrons, families of the patriciate and the rich bourgeoisie. Antonio Badile fostered relations with ecclesiastical circles, fundamental for public visibility and very active in the modernization of religious buildings. The most important families, through the patronage of the altars, financed the ornament: this is the case of the altarpiece, unanimously considered fully autographed, attributed to the twenty-year-old painter, the *Madonna Enthroned with Saints John the Baptist and Louis of Toulouse, and Two Donors* from the Bevilacqua chapel in San Fermo Maggiore, today in Museo Castelvecchio in Verona and dated around 1548. The Galleria degli Uffizi also houses a small painting considered a sketch, or copy, of that canvas. Compared to the original, which unfortunately underwent heavy restorations in the 19th century, the Uffizi canvas seems more intense and involved, and shows greater adherence to Chatsworth's preparatory drawing. The couple of donors "en abyme", hypothetically Giovanni Bevilacqua Lazise and his wife Lucrezia Malaspina, is portrayed with a rather archaic formula, in the low angles, in humility, in profile and three-quarter view; the dynamics is given by the sudden movement of Saint Louis of Toulouse who turns disturbed at the vision of the Virgin, raising his head from the reading of the sacred texts in which he was absorbed. His silky coat receives the strokes of light that illuminate the page. The placement of the Marian seat on the side, a Titian innovation also present in Badile, would later become a compositional choice of the young painter. The architectural datum is also important, decidedly in the spirit and taste of Sanmicheli, with the column that recalls the Marian litanies: *Alma mater: Virgo potens,/ Tu columna nostra fortis,/ Nos conforta in hora morti*, listened who knows how many times by Paolo. If the altarpiece was created in the year of completion of the chapel, 1548, the work shows the already mature personality of a twenty-year-old painter.

From this work derives a group of canvases that confirm an achieved mastery, some original solutions, and also the different visual contributions that Paolo introjects and makes his own. In fact, between 1548 and 1553, the first certain and documented date, therefore when he was between twenty and twenty-five, several canvases were distributed, including the *Presentation in the Temple* in Dresden, unknown in its original location, mentioned by Boschini and also attributed to several painters, until the current attribution to the young Paolo. In the *Presentation* there is already what will become one of his typical motifs, the child who embraces a dog, here a bloodhound, in addition to the architectural elements in the Doric style. The narrative concatenation of the different figures is exemplary, for which several scholars would prefer to date it to a slightly later and more mature years, close to 1555. The *Consecration of David* should be dated later: it was purchased in 1595 in Venice by the diplomat Charles de Croy, Duke of Archot, a wealthy Flemish collector in the service of Philip II of Spain. A canvas made for a private patron, with the crowded group of characters around Samuel in the act of anointing the young man. The landscape foreshortenings on the sides of the scene are splendid, one wild, with ruins now abandoned to nature, the other with a building very close to the Palladian Basilica in Vicenza and a stone bridge adorned with classical statues. Once again, the reference to the world before and after the Grace. Distant and already misty landscapes, while the large group around the elderly Samuel presents some men with precise physiognomic features, so one would be tempted to see them as portraits. In the foreground, a woman from behind is holding a child, a typical Venetian study subject. In this canvas, Emilian suggestions are combined with a composition indebted to the friezes of Roman sarcophagi, thus motivating the order and characterization of the mature characters. If the subject is indeed quite rare, and the result of educated suggestions, the colour treatment is extremely effective: the refined mixtures so typical of Paolo are present, from dove gray to coral pink, from tobacco to gold, from yellows to the most acrid greens.

Following pages

Madonna Enthroned with Saints and Donors, preparatory drawing, pen and brown ink with lead white highlighting, 243 × 32 cm. Chatsworth, Devonshire Collection, on. 287

Madonna Enthroned with Saints John the Baptist and Louis of Toulouse, and Two Donors (Bevilacqua Lazise altarpiece), approx. 1548, canvas, 233 × 172 cm. Verona, Museo di Castelvecchio, inv. 4284-1B243

Although this is the work of a twenty-year-old painter, it already shows substantial personality in the transformation of a "sacred conversation" into a vision also emotionally engaging. The result of study and tests in the gestures and the definition of donors, it reveals the homage to Sanmicheli's classical architectural solutions and the presence of careful reflections on Parmigianino, particularly in the figure of the young Madonna.

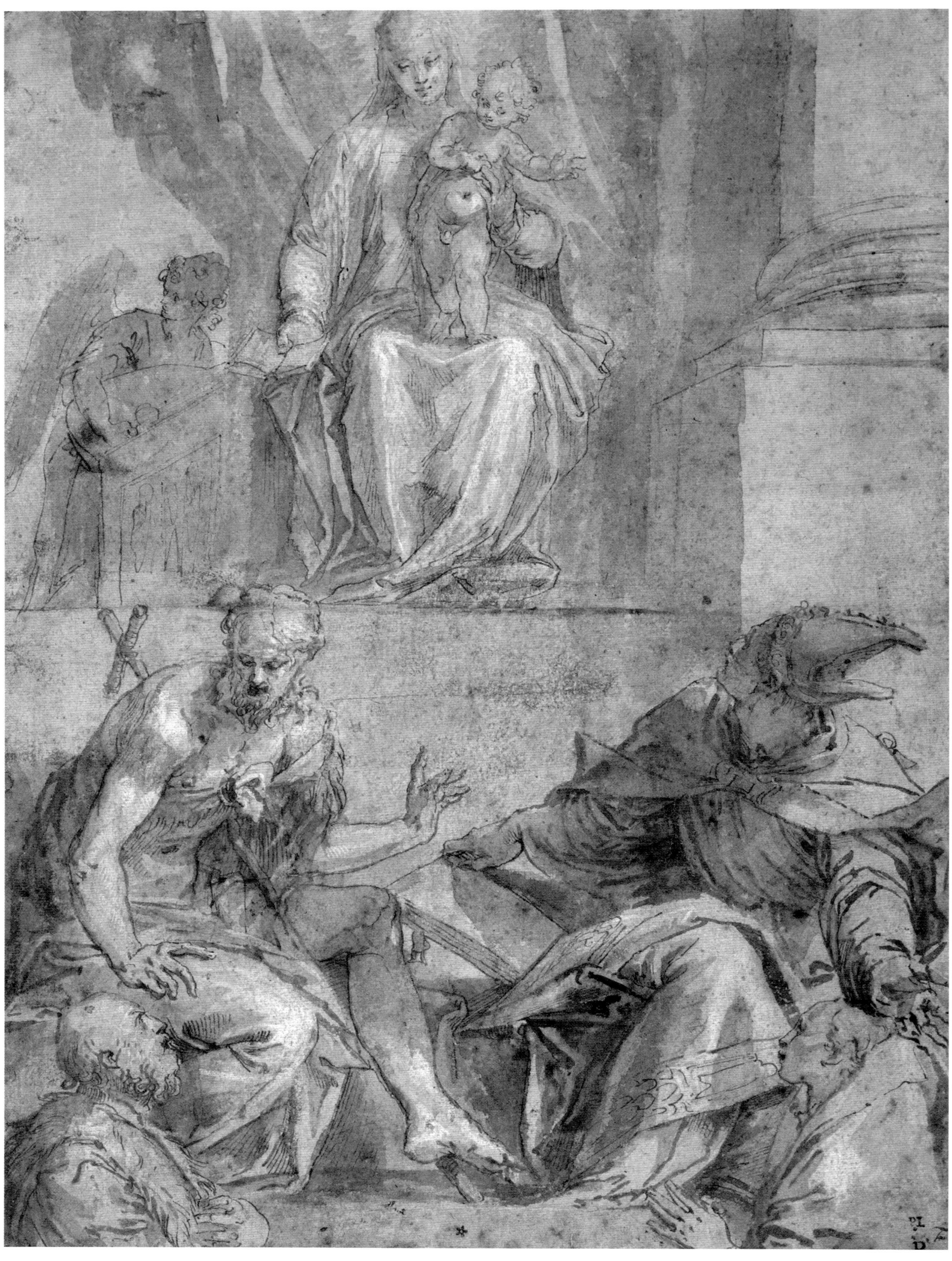

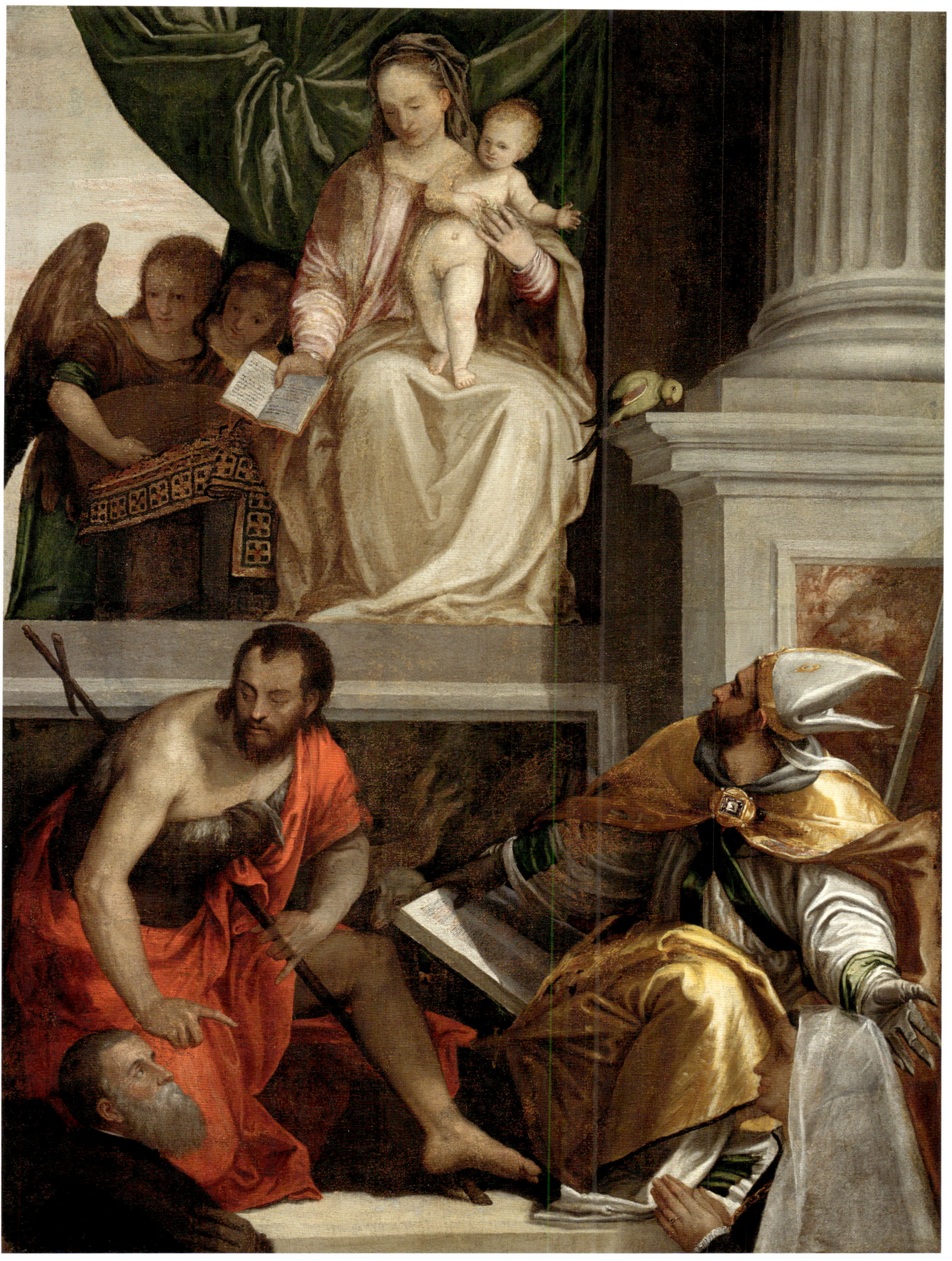

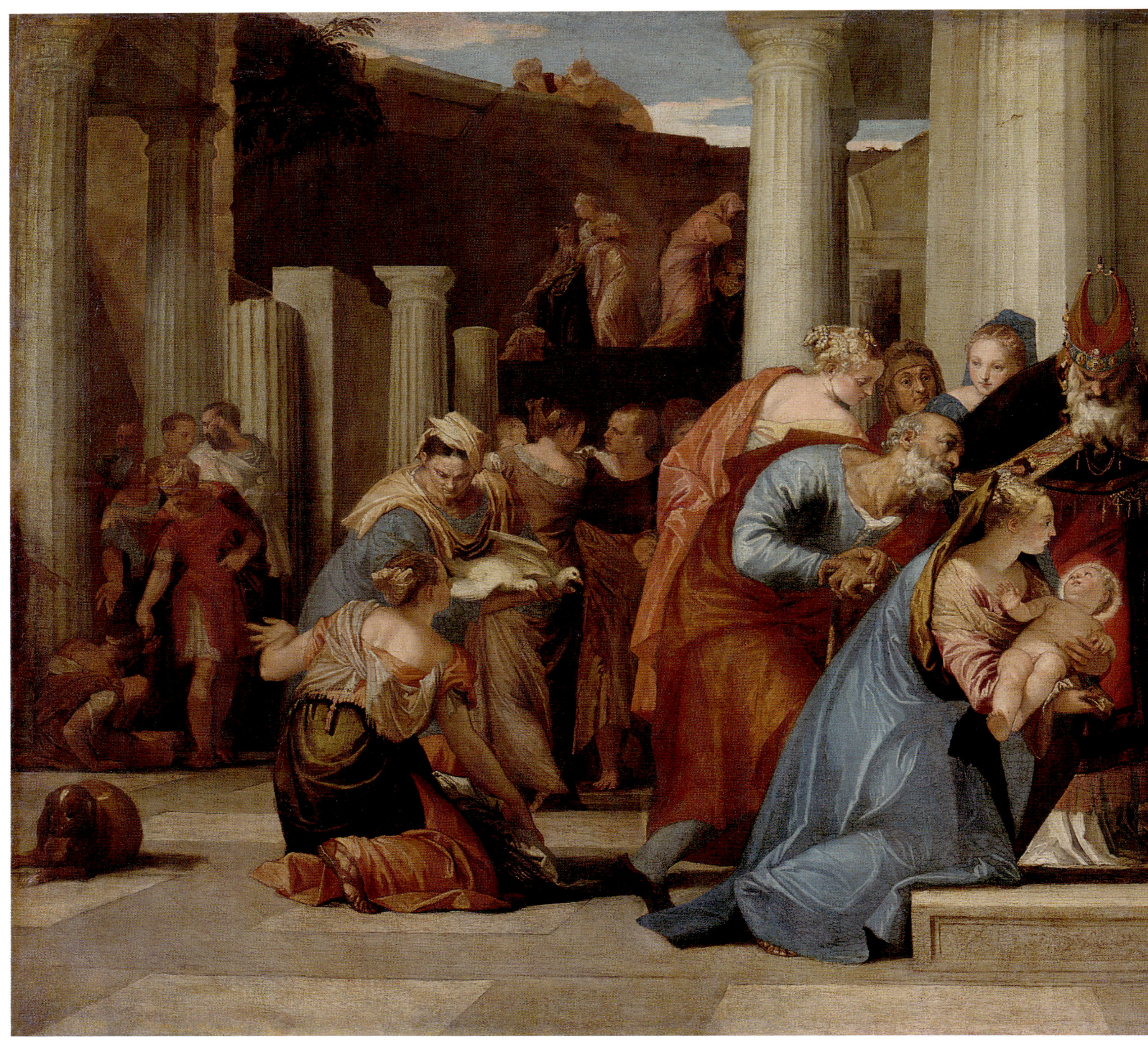

Presentation in the Temple, 1550-1553 (?), canvas, 186 × 417 cm. Dresden, Gemäldegalerie, inv. 223

The large canvas did not find concordance in its attribution: it was referred to Farinati and Montemezzano, as a work from the Veronese area in the middle of the century, with the figural and classicist situations typical of that pictorial contingency. It certainly did not benefit from having been cut off at the top: but it is an early work by Paolo, with some typical solutions and the dominant interest in architecture. There is a series of details which will become typical of Veronese: the profile of the second character to the left of the priest; the intertwining of the hands supporting the large vase, the solution of the putto's arms hugging the dog; the profile of the faun on the vase. Paolo Veronese is refining his repertoire.

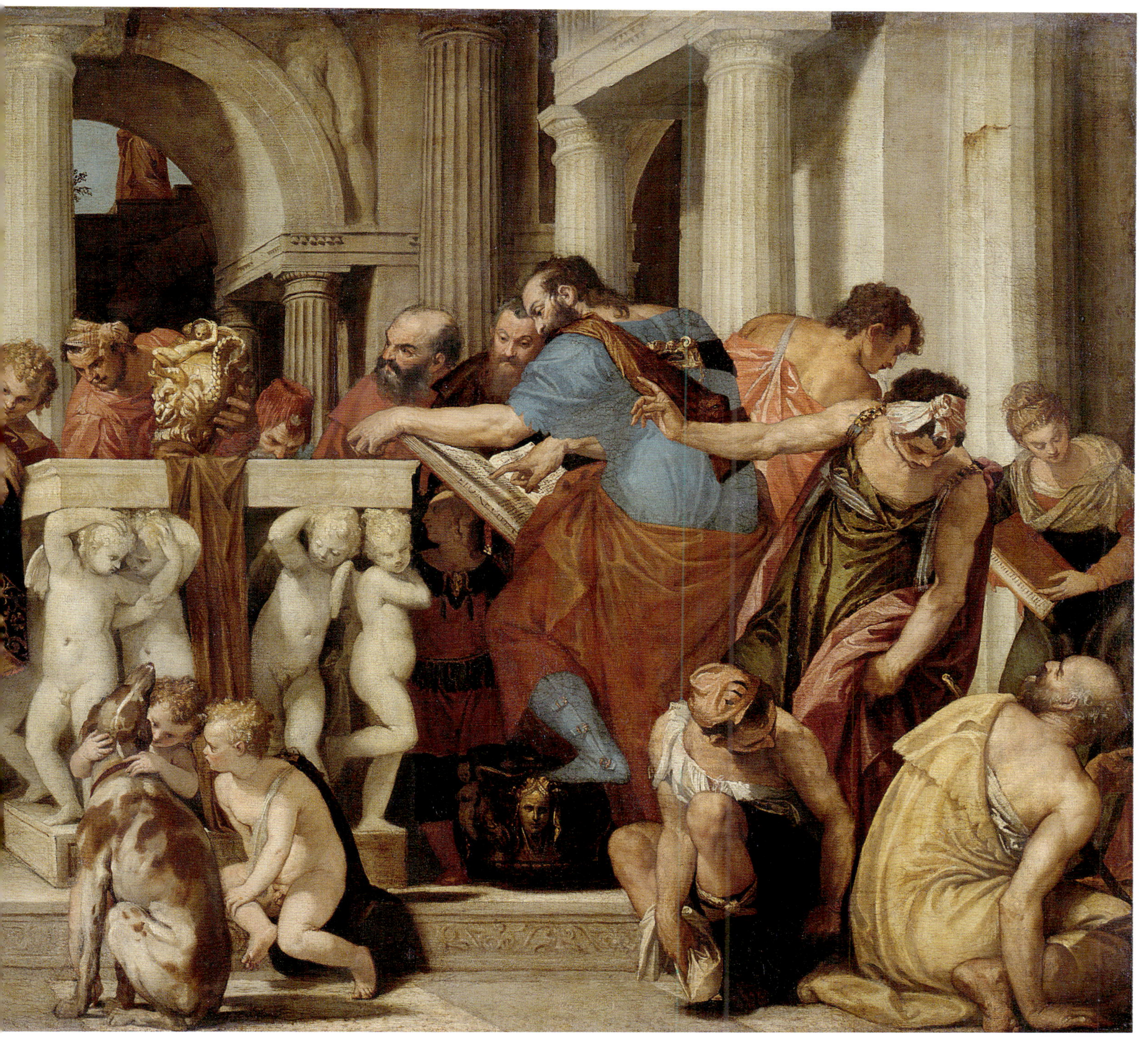

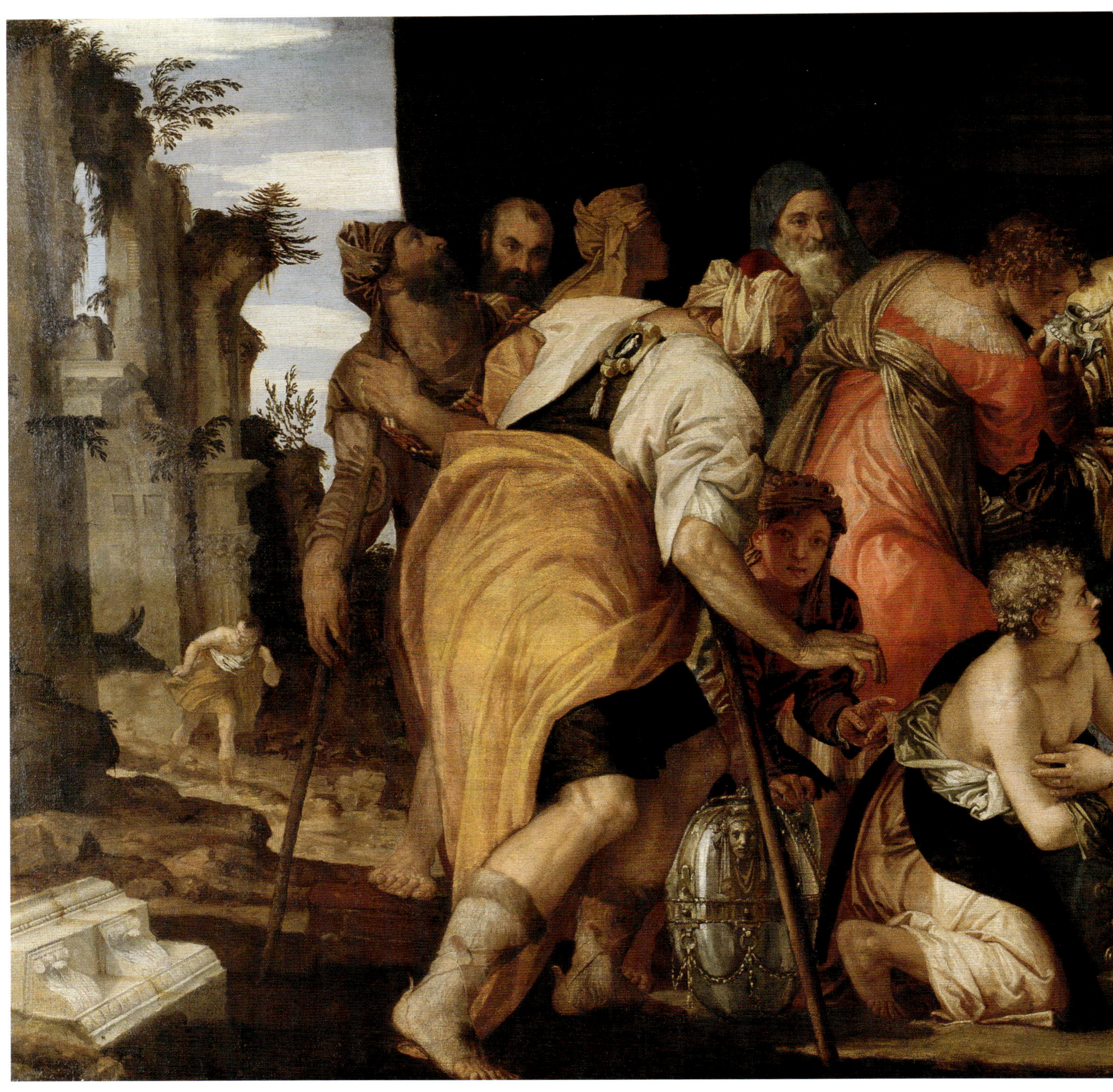

Consecration of David,
1552-1555 (?), canvas,
173 × 365 cm. Vienna,
Kunsthistorisches Museum, inv. 40

From the collections of the Duke of Buckingham, and auctioned in Antwerp in 1648, it will also be attributed to Farinati and Zelotti, then by modern critics almost unanimously given to Paolo Veronese. The two landscape glimpses present primary allegorical motifs: ancient ruins, modern basilicas. Antiquity reconstructed by the moderns. In the centre is the anointing of the boy, indication and confirmation of the rebirth of arts and faith.

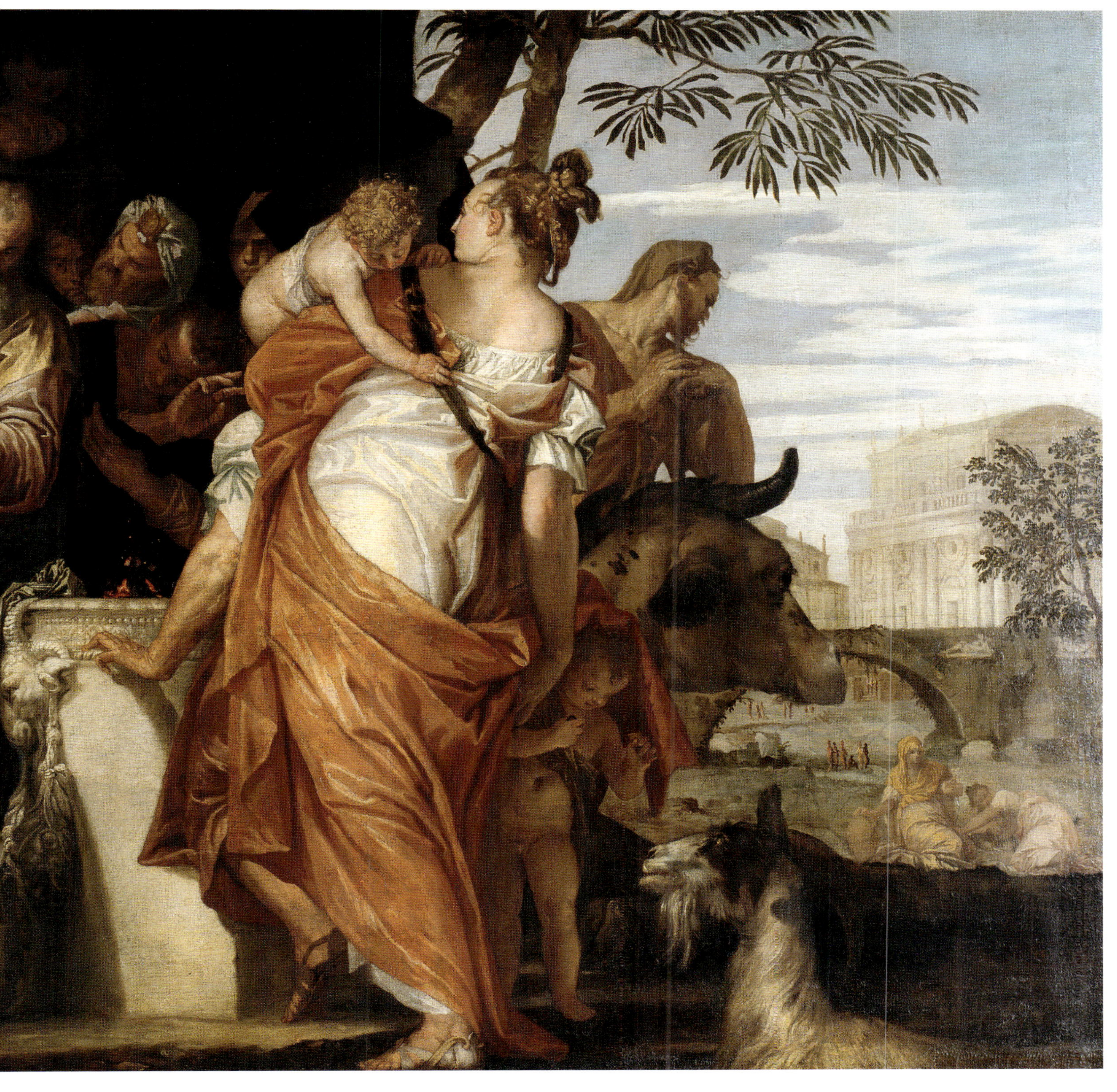

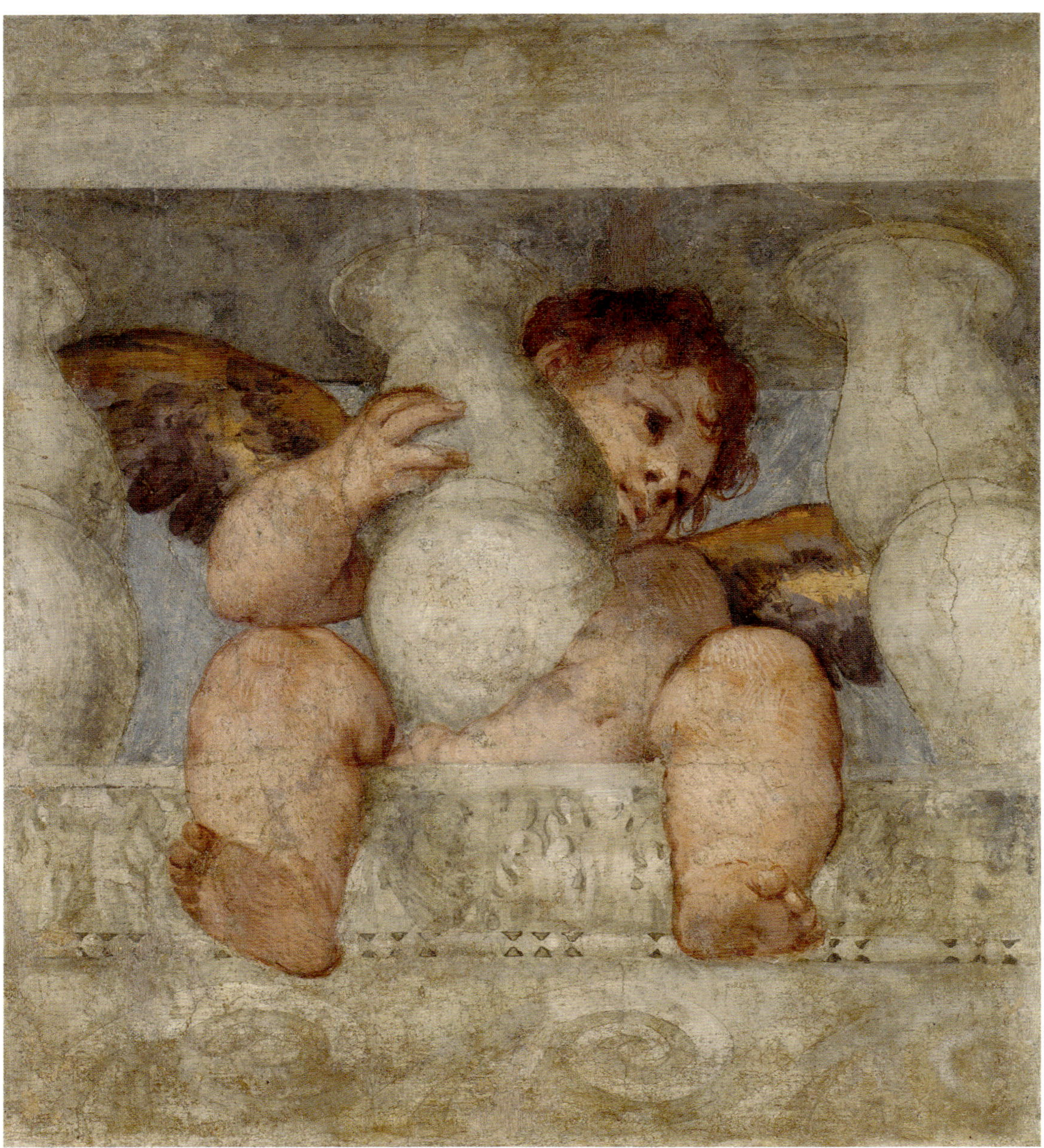

Winged Putto, fresco, 73 × 67 cm.
Vicenza, Museo Civico, inv. A 73

Another proof in that period is the *Lamentation over the Dead Christ* commissioned by the Hieronymites for the church of Santa Maria delle Grazie in Verona, the occasion for the acquaintance between Bernardo Torlioni and Paolo *spezapreda*. Here too the traits that would become his typical solutions are present: the group in the foreground from the side; the distant landscape background with its characteristic hazy skies; the foreshortened face of the Magdalene with Venetian hairstyle.

IN VILLA, ON THE BRENTA RIVIERA

Among these oil canvases, dated with uncertainty, there is a work that seems to have been done in a precise year, the commission due to the recommendation that would later open for Veronese the doors to great Venetian patrons. The very active Sanmicheli, the mentor who initiated him into the erudite and archaeological taste of the classicist tradition but also into the decorative experiences of Tuscan-Roman ancestry, must have provided him with the technical and theoretical tools of perspective, indicating how to decorate architecture and multiply it in illusionary direction. It is the decoration of the villa built by the architect from Verona for Alvise Soranzo, scion of a powerful Venetian family which numbered the fifty-first doge, and at the time administered large estates around Castelfranco Veneto. Like the Da Portos from Vicenza, the Pisanis and the Barbaros, all Paolo's future patrons, it was a "Roman-like" family, i.e. inclined to a less conflictual relationship between the Republic and the Papal See, not only in politics, but also in artistic orientations. Families who admired Michelangelo and Raphael, supported and directed the classicism of Sanmicheli and Palladio, appreciated the painting by Francesco Salviati, painter in the lagoon for Giovanni Grimani, and later admired Battista Franco, close to Sansovino.

Ridolfi saw and described the villa, completed in 1551 in Treville along the Brenta Riviera, judging it a jewel of country architecture with its classical loggia marked by mighty corbels and friezes, and the use of particularly soft rustic ashlar brought into dialogue with the natural landscape. The interior was decorated in the summer of 1551, the date reported on a fragment, by Paolo with his friend Giovan Battista Zelotti. As Vasari reminds us, both were "loved as children" by the architect. They worked in association with the twenty-year-old pupil of Caroto, Anselmo Canera, under the guidance and judgment of Sanmicheli, creating "many works, done with design, judgment and beautiful manner" as Vasari noted in the *Life* dedicated to the architect.

"At the Soranza – Ridolfi wrote – he painted columns, villages, the seasons and children with various fruits in their hands in the loggia of that Palagio. In the lunettes: Mars and Venus; Jupiter and Juno; Mercury and Pallas" and then much more; unfortunately what remains to us of that extensive and varied decoration is today completely fragmentary, minimal and incomplete. After decades of decline, the building suffered from looting and bivouacs by the French and Austrians. The abandoned villa was demolished in 1817: the nobleman Filippo Balbi, who had admired those decorations, carried out the tearing off of many dozens of frescoed parts with a new technique adapted by himself, favouring the figures. The chronicles indicate more than a hundred – 108, according to a list of the time –pieces saved and kept by Balbi, who personally donated some to the Cathedral of Castelfranco, then kept in its sacristy. The vast majority ended up in the rivulets of the antiques market, even in England, and are now lost; only about fifteen fortunately landed in different places, from the patriarchal seminary of Venice to the municipal art gallery of Vicenza. Some of these have been attributed to Paolo even if, after the removal, retouching and restoration of a nomadic life for two centuries, what remains is a faint testimony of the original inventions, however certifying the achieved ability as a fresco painter and that taste for great allegorical figures that will characterize all Veronese's production in the sixth decade.

The frescoes of Villa Soranzo follow a model that is now widespread in Veneto, declining classical inspiration – i.e. the indications relating to the decoration of the rooms taken from Vitruvius and Pliny – and proposing together architectural illusionism and unfounded landscapes, mythological episodes and allegorical figures. The experience of the Soranza, perhaps anticipated by more modest tests now lost, takes place in the representative environments where the young trio uses, with different abilities, the classical lexicon now widespread from Trento to Mantua, from Romanino to that Giulio Romano known by Veronese for the decorations of the apse of the Cathedral in Verona, executed by Francesco Torbido already in 1534 on cartoons by Giulio for a precise will of Bishop Giberti.

Among the few remaining fragments, *Justice* and *Temperance* and the large fragment with *Time* and *Fame* were unanimously given to Paolo. In the fragment of *Fame*, we admire the remarkable ability to propose the aerial movement of a *Fame* with large wings and clamorous yellow robe which turns orange in the shadows and collides and cools with the green band. As for *Time*, identified by the hourglass, the figure has retracted his wings and, stationary on the cloud, waits for human vanity to fly away. Then *Justice* is beautiful in the intent face, splendid in the worked, elegant fabric. She gracefully leans on her sword and carelessly holds the scales. *Temperance* and *Justice* are prosper-

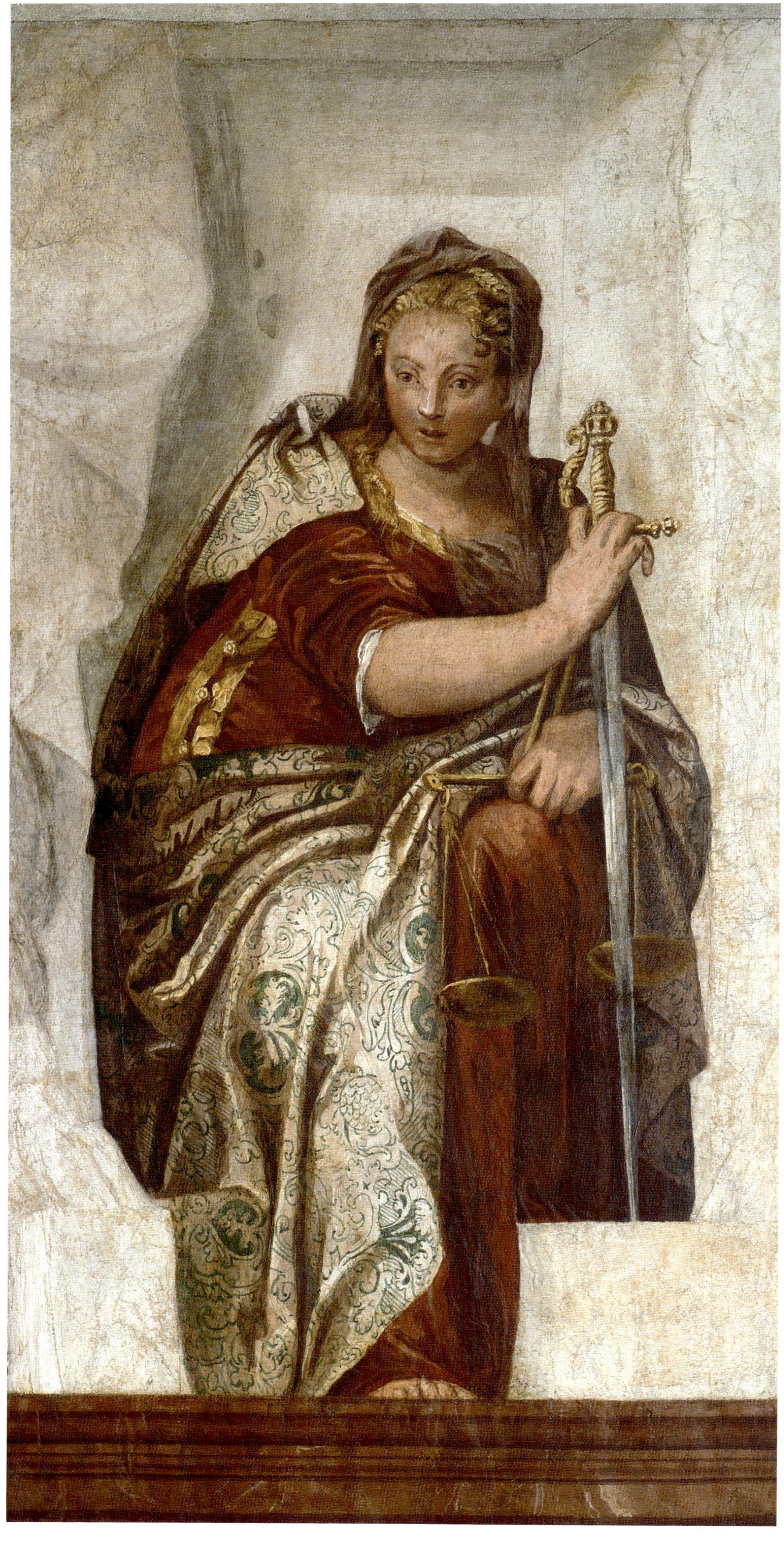

Justice and Temperance,
1551, frescoes mounted on canvas,
200 × 100 cm. Castelfranco Veneto,
cathedral (from Villa Soranzo)

The two frescoes of the Soranza propose the typical allegorical taste of the times, and expertly interpreted. Here is, for example, the young woman who observes, almost fearfully, a mirror with the Soranzo coat of arms: it is the image of the woman who must become aware of herself, mirroring herself into her ancestors. So Prudence or Temperance. The two allegorical figures were placed in false niches; the association with Fortress and Prudence would have completed the series of Cardinal Virtues, in all probability united in the decoration of the same space.

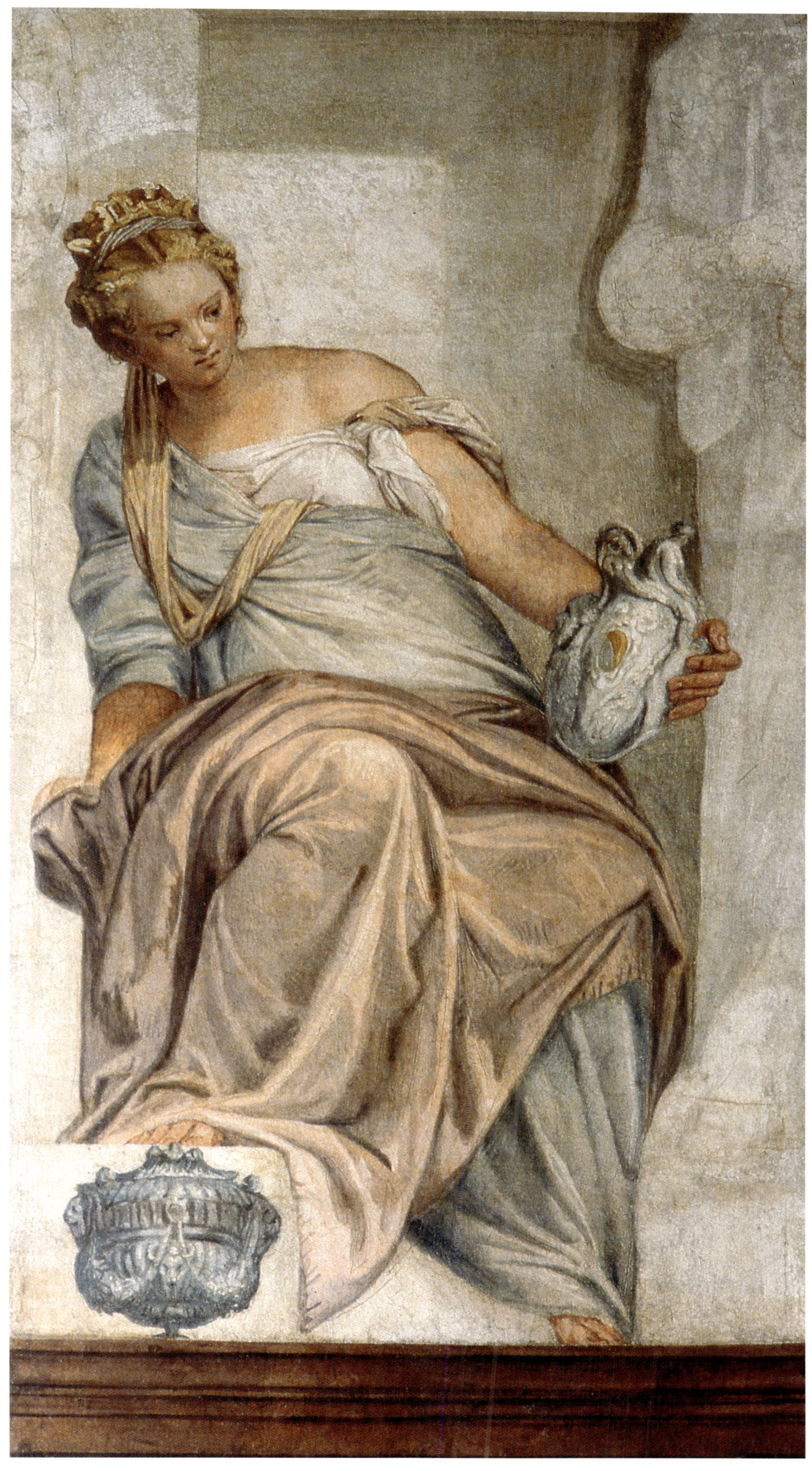

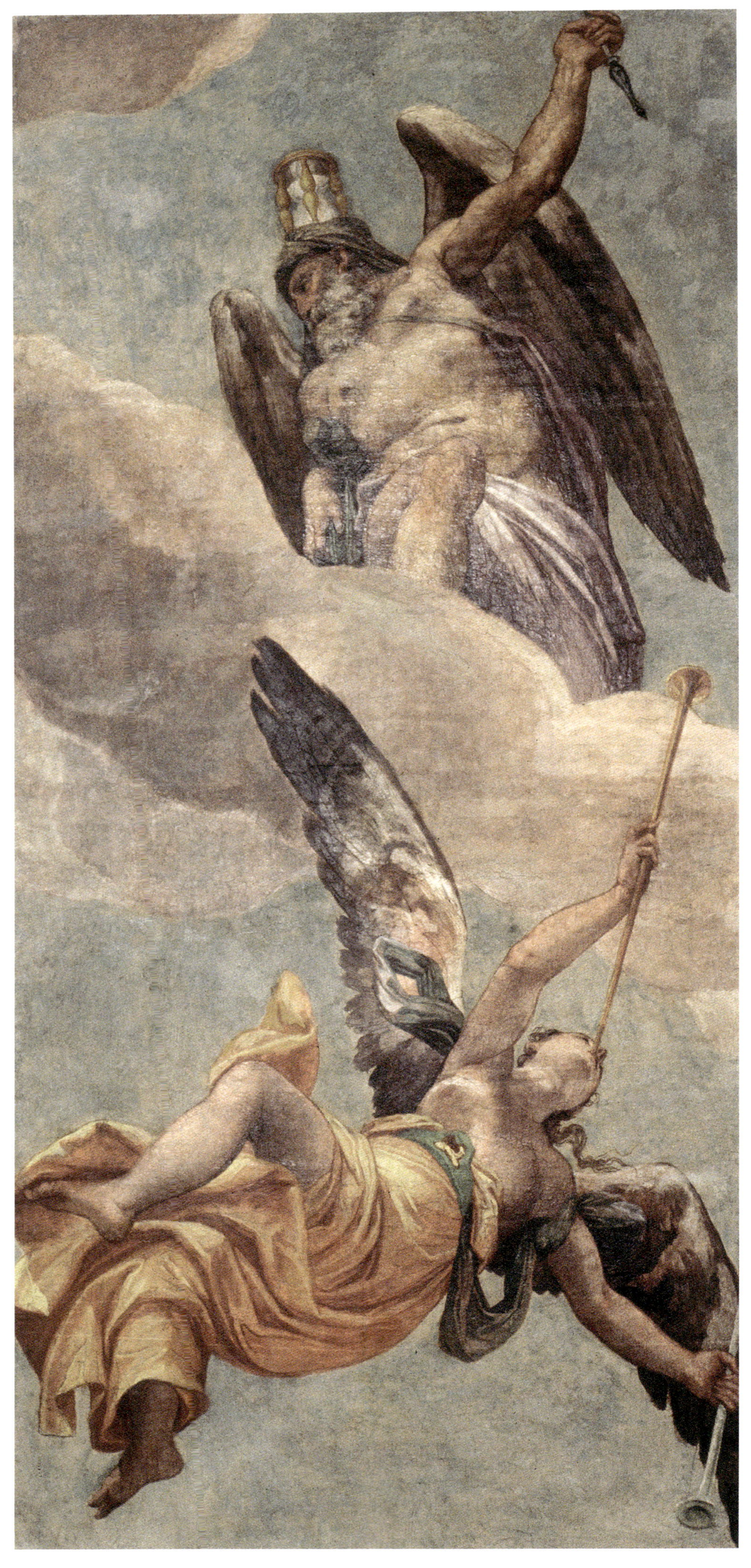

ous and seductive girls, they wear ancient virtues and, solid on plinths, they look out from niches admonishing us of their being necessary and warning presences. However, we note that both have a rather small head compared to the body: an indication that we will find in other early works, attributable to the careful study of Parmigianino's drawings and paintings. Then there is also, among the fragments of the Soranza, a delightful little *winged Putto*: he observes the world well embraced by the pot-bellied balustrade, wittily portrayed and proposed with luminous efficacy; immediately attributed to Paolo, capable of inventiveness and grace in taking up a common typology of figures.

Time and Fame, 1551, fresco mounted on canvas, 353 × 168 cm. Castelfranco Veneto, cathedral (from Villa Soranzo)

Decorations in the villa

These fragments allow us to document the painter's ability to try his hand at a large fresco decoration, his pictorial technique revealing to the fullest and best the confidence and speed of the artist, who, in a day's work, and without the possibility of significant repentance or corrections, must lay down confident brushstrokes on a few sketched lines to manage the necessary amount of colour. Work on the plaster that is still damp, just pulled, so as to guarantee the definitive setting of the colour. In terms of technique and genre characteristics, in the sixteenth century the fresco decoration in the rooms is different from painting: one is determined by the spatial and functional variety of the location, the other by the limit of the frame; the one is motionless, the other mobile. Decoration is seen as some sort of architecture, it is a comment on spatial measures, it expands or limits them, it is always determined by them; it circumscribes and opens the vaults, defines or goes beyond the walls, "breaks through" and supports. Compared to the architectural volumes and spaces, the decoration has different weights: sometimes little more than a filler, or a frame, other times autonomous in defining and suggesting. For some theorists, such as Sebastiano Serlio, decoration is an ancillary function: the prudent architect must govern it and must remain "master of all those who work in the building", in particular "of the painters whom he distrusts, since they are easier to be taken by inspiration" and "to show the vagueness of the colours and, not having anything else to do with it, they have disconnected and sometimes damaged any order, for not having considered placing the paintings in their places" as he states in his *Regole generali di architettura*, from 1537. If for Serlio precisely "the vagueness of the colours" could spoil the order and harmony of a building, for others, such as Sanmicheli, the internal decoration was an opportunity to underline the spatial and expressive choices; he probably agreed with the painters on the general lines of the quarterings, on the specific architectural design within which figures and landscapes, fruits, festoons, monochromes, and other decorative inventions would be placed.

The decorative setting of the villa in the Venetian countryside is in any case moved by the already fifteenth-century and Petrarchan ideology that sees the "rustic life" as intellectually industrious idleness; the decorations in the villa must suggest humanistic topics, themes of scientific naturalism, inspirations and examples of behaviour and moral warnings: all framed by rural motifs. We follow a sort of encyclopaedic glossary built through common headings: from Architecture and Astronomy, to Geometry, Justice, Mathematics, up to Temperance and Time. These are obviously ideological projections, since the reality is that of the manor house as managing and administrative centre of the agricultural activities of the fund, equipped in the *barchesse* with rooms for storing capital goods and transforming agricultural products.

THE PORTRAITS: FIDELITY AND INVENTION

The companion friendship of the Soranza, on excellent terms, will repeat itself in the decoration of Palazzo Canossa in Verona, also designed by Sanmicheli: the frescoes within a stucco decoration illustrated stories from the Old Testament, now lost. Precisely to the Canossas we could refer a first portrait considered by all to be autograph, the *Gentlewoman with Child and Dog* mentioned by Ridolfi and taken away from the Bevilacqua palace in 1797, prey to the Napoleonic troops. It is a portrait of suffused melancholy and great empathy: the young woman who looks at us without a trace of a smile is dressed in the simplest ways, the black dress over the fluffy white shirt seems to be a sign of widowhood. Her little child with curly hair clings to her, protected by her maternal hand. Also the child's face is almost sad, even though he looks affectionately at the faithful dog, whose moist and expressive eyes are turned to the female friend. What is the child holding? It would look like a bone, to be offered to the faithful animal: so, if we interpret it as a rebus, also typical of Lorenzo Lotto, dog+bone in Italian, i.e. can+osso, gives the name "Canossa", and in fact some historians have identified the lady as Isabella Guerrieri Gonzaga Canossa, widow by Galeazzo Canossa: the problem is that she was born around 1513, which certainly does not correspond to the person portrayed. She could be the daughter-in-law, Creusa Costanzo Canossa, who, however, married Girolamo, son of Isabella, only in 1560. Moreover, distant biographical events cannot add anything more to the moving portrait, already in Veronese style, and it is no coincidence that it has been shown over and over again in recent exhibitions.

Gentlewoman with Child and Dog, around 1553 (?), canvas, 115 × 95 cm.
Paris, Musée du Louvre, inv. 149

The portrait of the young mother has been variously dated (between 1548 and 1555), trying to attribute a name to the woman wearing simple clothes, apparently widowed. A precocious canvas certainly painted by Veronese, of remarkable empathy, particularly original in the group associating the child, the dog's muzzle, the clasped hands. The black robe is characterized by a refined treatment, an attention to the fabric that will become a constant in Paolo's art.

The beautiful dog next to the child, with caring eyes turned to the mother, can also be a symbol, as per tradition, of fidelity. But then, as we shall see, the dogs painted by Paolo only in his official works are many dozens – at least forty. Furthermore, he deals with every type of dog, hunting and lapdogs, pointing and watchdogs, companion pets. Most of them are sitting or lying down, many appear indifferent to miraculous facts; sometimes they bark, for example a very small one to defend Susanna from the old men, or they play roughly with a cat, or they prepare to escort their masters. Already Vasari admired Veronese's dogs simply because they were "alive and natural", and so should have done his contemporaries, who in painting wanted to see nature, and reality, simply improved, made more alive and therefore more appreciable; but then we must explain the fact that the lines of flight from the famous Veronese *Suppers* converge on a dog. If the painter proved to be a dog lover par excellence, he painted many other animals: first of all beautiful horses, free and saddled, runaway and tamed, and then cats, crouched and curled up, nervous and at rest, and monkeys, parrots, cattle... A love for animals to which symbolic and allegorical meanings can be attributed from time to time but, like fabrics, are above all an expression of the taste for the art of painting, in all its potential.

By now active and well known by the major patrician families, Paolo was called to work on a Palladio building site in Vicenza. Perhaps around 1552, in the Palazzo da Porto, in a phase not very distant from the experiences of the Soranza, he prepared two *Allegories* now in Rome in Pinacoteca Capitolina, *Peace* and *Good Government*, also interesting for having placed the allegorical figures not on the clouds but on very solid rock bases, which will be repeated shortly for another group of four canvases, also allegorical. The two inventions are beautiful: *Peace* with the torch wants to burn a mass of weapons, moreover metallic, with silvery luminosity; very delicate pinks ranging from antique to pastel, against a rock coloured by a variety of more or less burnt earths; the *Good Government*, sometimes interpreted instead as *Temperance*, holds a straight bar against the ruins of an ancient arch; the base in marble, the elevation in brick: the supports of an antiquity to be restored.

During his stay in Vicenza he must have had a prestigious request: to create the full-length portraits of the spouses *Iseppo da Porto* and *Livia da Porto Thiene*. The works, painted between 1551 and 1552, are now separate: Iseppo at the Florentine Uffizi and Livia at the Walters Art Museum in Baltimore.

The da Portos, among the most visible families in the city, pose with great naturalness, with the lively presence of their children, shy but curious. Almost life-size in two matching canvases, presumably located in the same room, perhaps separated by a window as suggested by the specular origin of the light. They are contained in a barely mentioned fake niche, dressed with refinement in family dignity, without formalities and trappings, but also without particular emotional

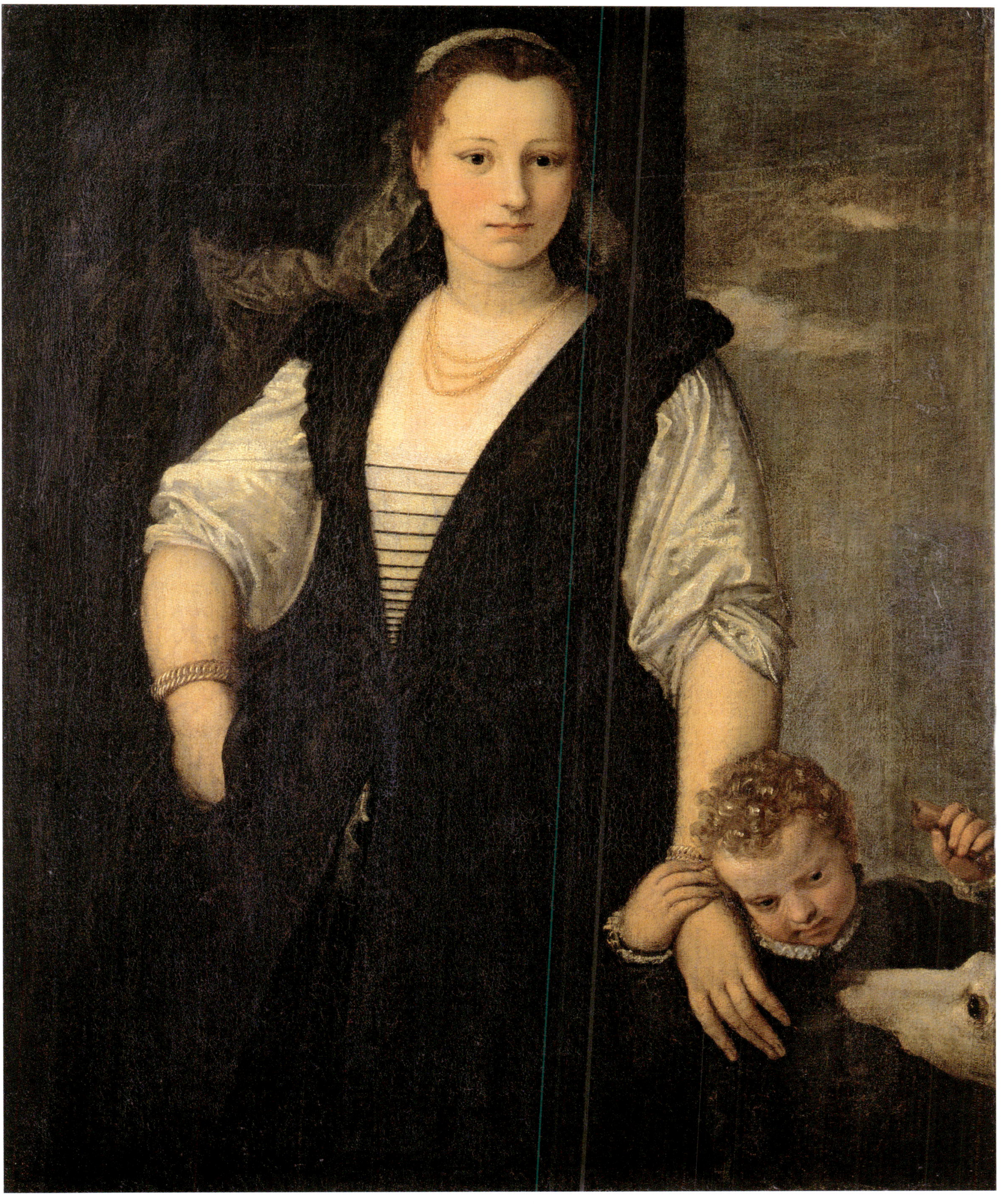

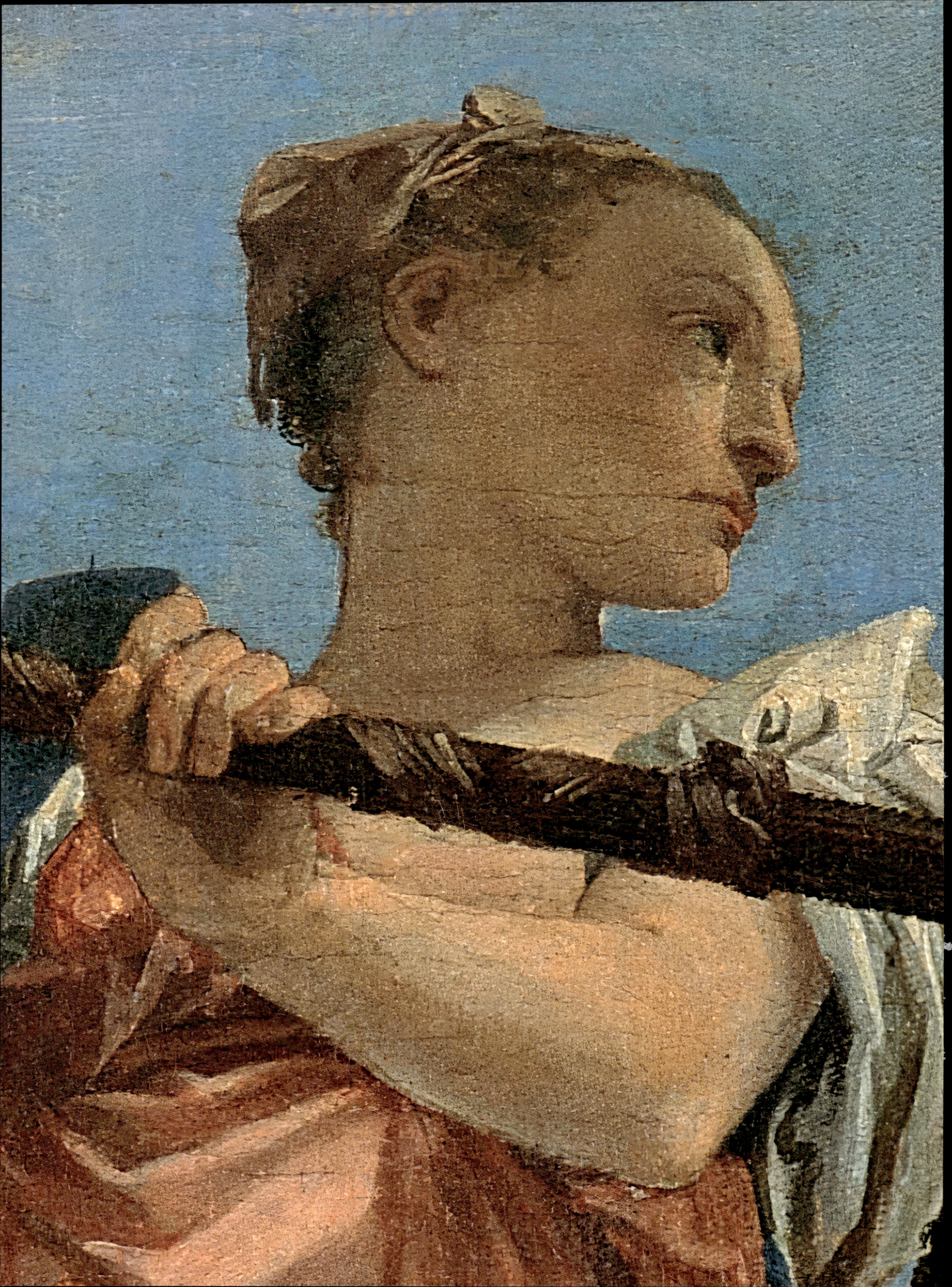

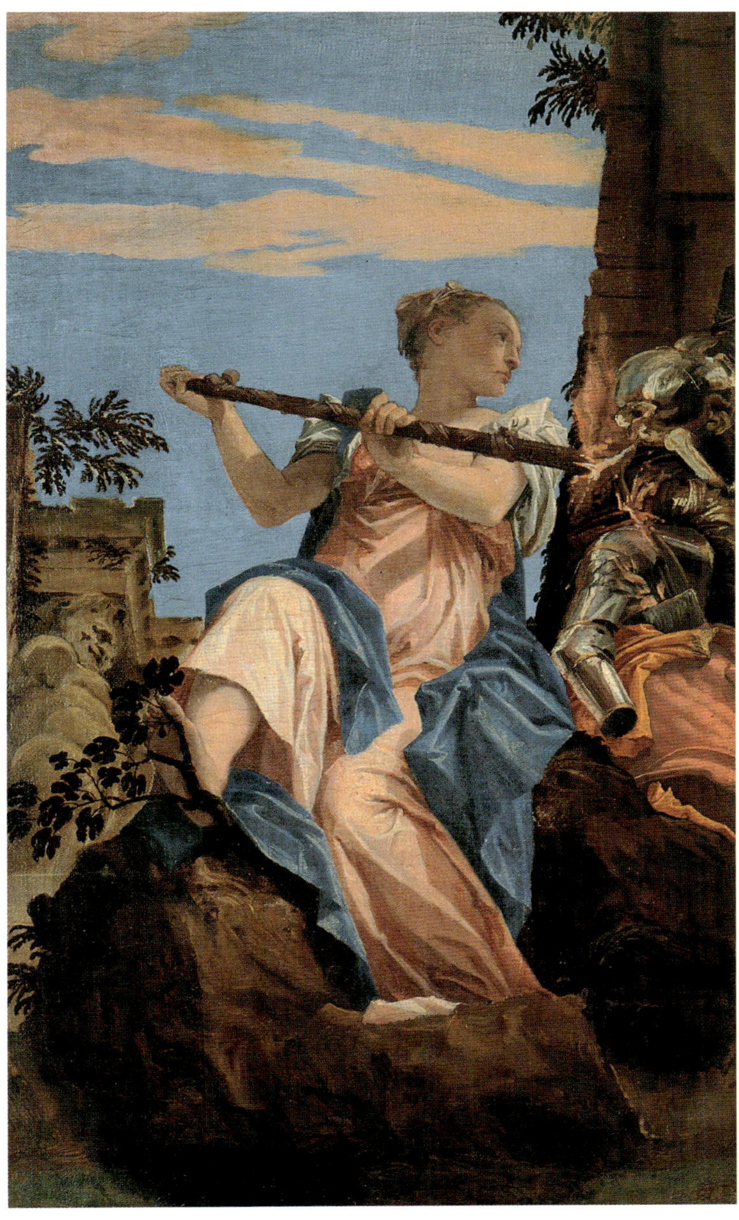

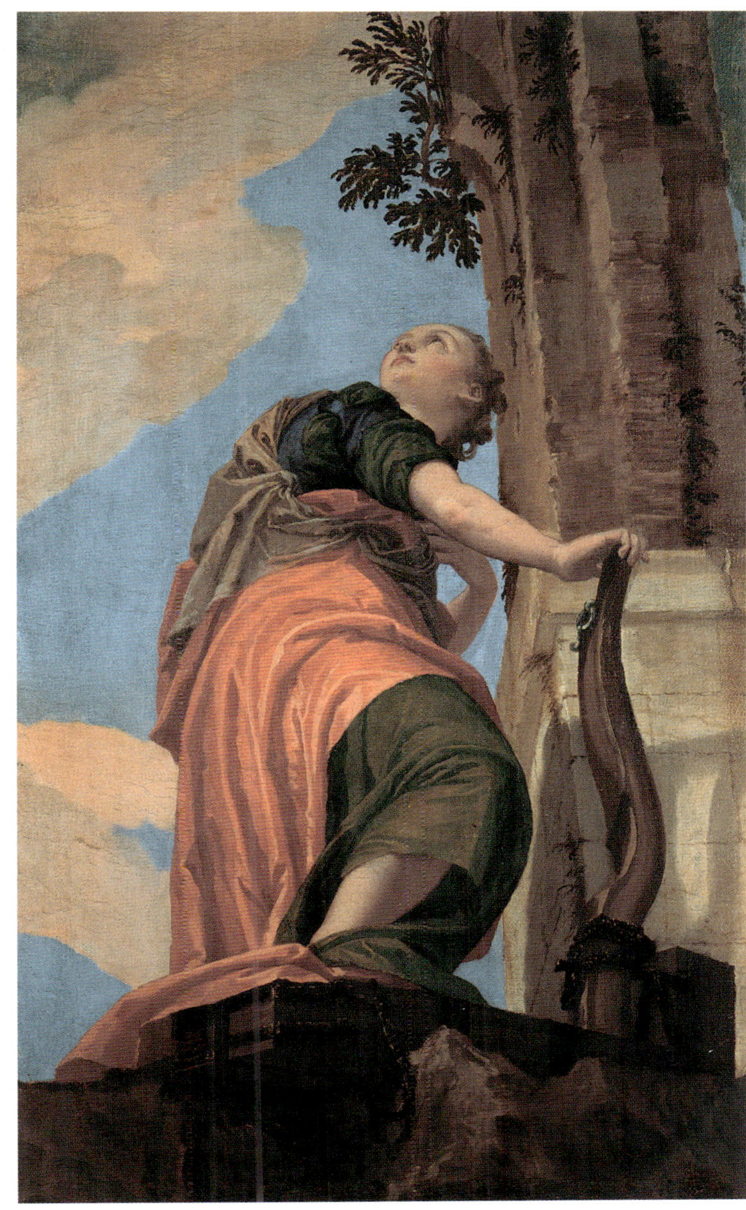

revelations. Iseppo da Porto, the master of the house, is portrayed with his son Leonida, to whom the same play of hands binds him as the melancholic young widow Canossa. The beautiful treatment of the dark coats, the careful work on the furs that border them, in particular the brightness of that of the child, show a level and originality that leaves no doubt about the portraitist's ability. Iseppo was a politically important character in Vicenza, with prestigious intellectual roles as well, an exponent of that circle that looked with great sympathy at the development of Calvinism, not without a Nicodemism which, moreover, did not save him from inquisitorial inquiries. He had married Livia Thiene in 1542, and they will have ten children. The painting should portray the eldest son, Leonida, born one year after the marriage, while alongside Livia there should be the first daughter, Deidamia, born in 1545; the children appear to be the right ages, confirming the dating of the work. The pretty Deidamia who looks at us curiously is caught in the same posture as the little girl who will spy on us from the illusion of a door in Maser.

Paolo will then often use the full-length format, uncommon in contemporary Venetian painting; his portraits will be mostly personal and private, to be placed in a home and not in public places, with institutional connotations. The portraiture of the Institutions of the State, doges and high officials of the government of the Republic, is aimed above all at Tintoretto's workshop,

Allegory of Peace, 1552 (?), canvas, 105 × 64 cm. Rome, Pinacoteca Capitolina, inv. PC 50

Allegory of Good Government, 1552 (?), canvas, 105 × 64 cm. Rome, Pinacoteca Capitolina, inv. PC 48

The foreshortened figures, on divergent lines, rest on solid rock bases, between the fragments of ancient ruins. The allegories in the tradition of Venetian humanism are constructed with effective skill, while the light pictorial application imitates the fresco. Placed in a patrician residence, predictably the Palazzo da Porto in Vicenza, they demonstrate the precocious inventiveness of the young painter, and also the presence, in the female profiles, of Parmigianino's lesson.

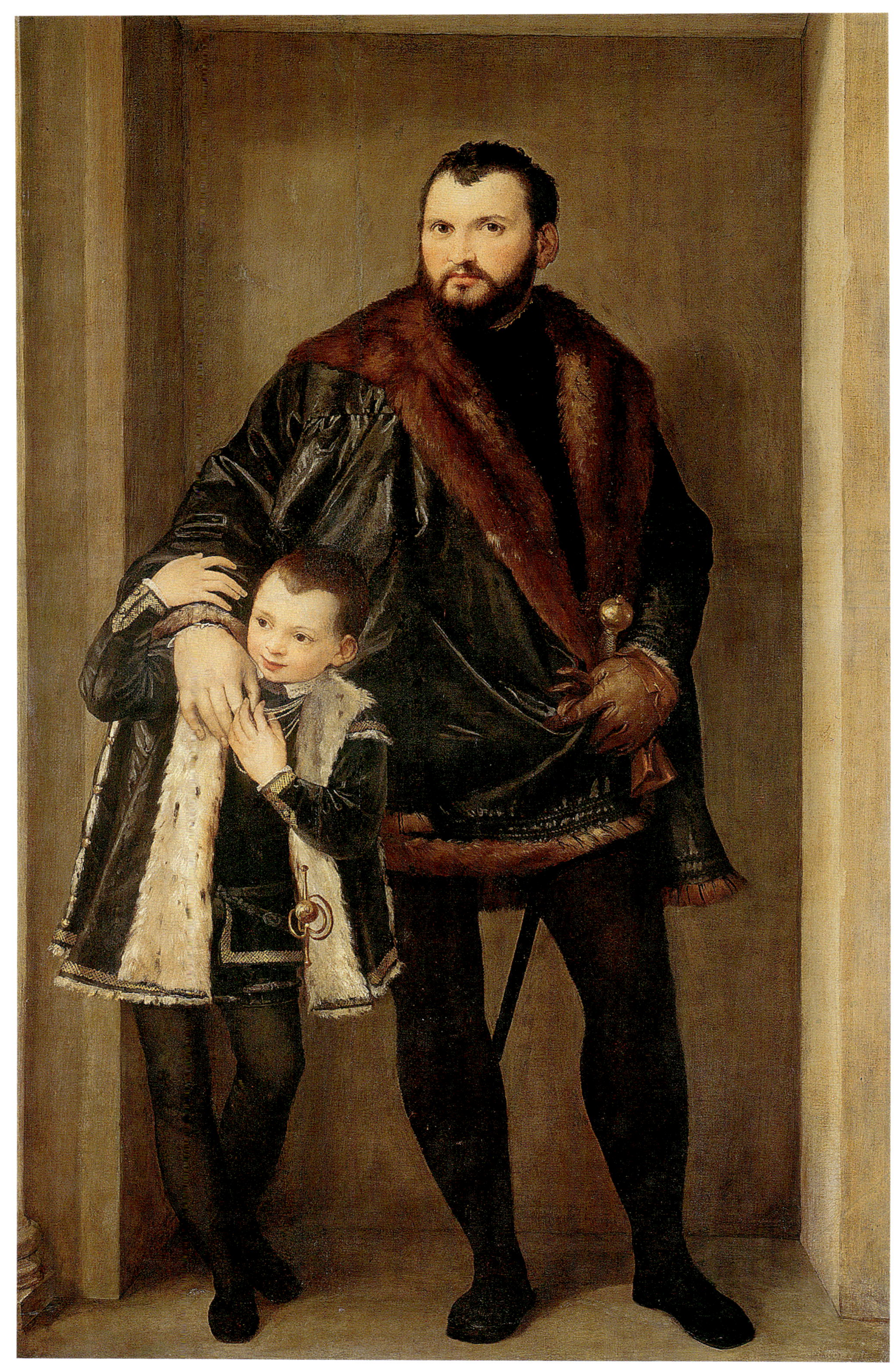

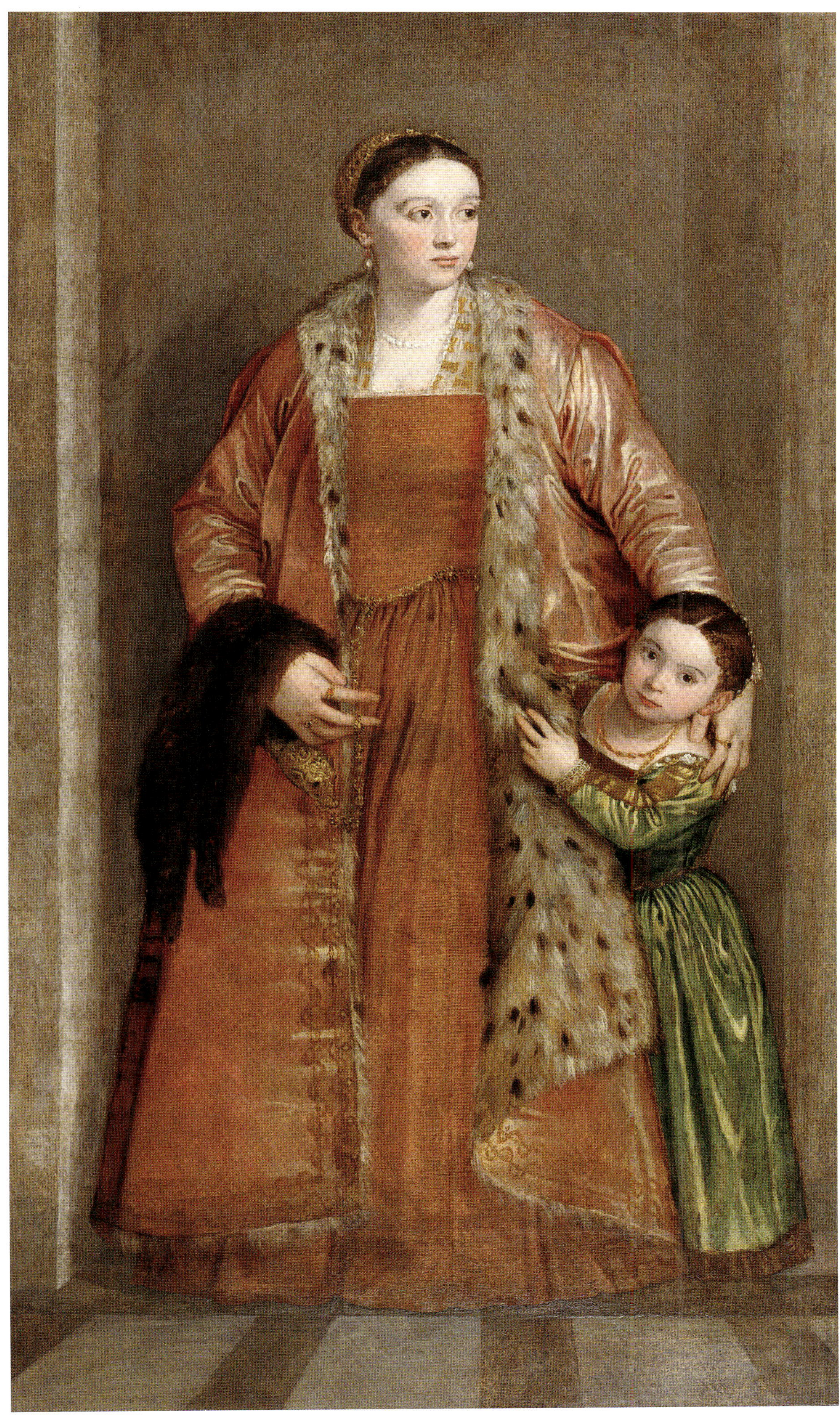

Iseppo da Porto with His Son Leonida, 1551-1552, canvas, 207 × 137 cm. Florence, Galleria degli Uffizi, Collezione Contini Bonacossi

Livia da Porto Thiene with Her Daughter Deidamia, 1551-1552, canvas, 207 × 137 cm. Baltimore, Walters Art Museum, inv. 37.541

The novelty of this famous pair of family canvases is twofold: the official nature of the full-length portrait is softened, made friendly and domestic with the protective and proud gesture of the parents, and the affectionate curiosity of the children. At the same time, the attention to the texture and material of the fabrics, the care in the description of the furs, the attention to the accessories, the gloves and the stole reveal the taste for observing the truth and the finesse in the definition of the backgrounds that will signal the Veronese to the Venetian public.

while Veronese responds to the requests of loyal and important patrons, emphasizing in particular their taste and elegance, expressed through dress and attitude. This is the prevailing message with respect to the emotional and psychological deepening, which instead had characterized the best portraiture of Lotto, Titian and Sebastiano del Piombo. Furthermore, in Veronese the physiognomic rendering will be less characterized in the female portrait, brought back to a basic model which he will repeat and vary dozens of times. In any case, his care in painting will limit the portraits to a few dozen, even including the controversial attributions.

For the young painter, other commissions quickly arrive. One, in particular, is very tempting: an altarpiece for the cathedral in Mantua. The person requesting it is Cardinal Ercole Gonzaga, who also hired Battista Del Moro, Paolo Farinati and Brusasorci, all from the "Veronese company", to decorate other three altars in a friendly competition. In the proposal made by Paolo there is the attention, perhaps even the enthusiasm for the solutions of Raphael's best pupil, that Giulio Romano who in Mantua had exhibited his inventiveness as a masterful decorator in the ceilings and rooms of Palazzo Te. To the highly esteemed Giulio Pippi, who recently passed away, the making of the canvas reveal the presence of Michelangelo, known through engravings, copies and drawings. The altarpiece offers one of the most popular devotional subjects, an occasion for infinite variations of expressive imagination, namely the *Temptations of Saint Anthony Abbot*. Here, however, rather than temptations we should speak of *Torments*, of *Tribulations* in the fierce struggle with the diabolical entities, in a gloomy and moreover sensual atmosphere that recalls Correggio. In the violent foreshortening of the overturned monk and in the gigantism of the diabolical being who wants to hit him with a horse's hoof, showing all the tension of a muscular system in vigorous evidence, the effect of classical statuary is felt, even if the reference is not necessary for the famous and variously known *Belvedere Torso*, for drawings and engravings: the widespread reproduction of the Roman plastic, so appreciated in Verona, is sufficient. The horse's hoof recalls the hippocentaur present in the life of the hermit narrated by Jacopo da Varagine; the Abbot Anthony had met the monster that merges horse and human appearance while going in search of the first hermit, Paul: an ambiguous encounter, a sign of the survival of the pagan deities, and hallucinations of solitude in the desert. Here Veronese shows his mimetic skills, or adherence to local tastes, and chooses tones that are unusual for him: dark, rusty, rare until late maturity. A ray of light softens the shoulders and chest of the seductive she-devil, who was unable to hide two horns and sharp, ferocious nails, ready to sink into the hand of the landed and shocked monk; or to bring the old hand to her youthful bosom. That disguised devil has a splendid hairstyle of golden blond hair, useful for giving light to the foreshortened face, and the pictorial skill will then be transferred to other female figures. The elements of the dress of the fierce sorceress are beautiful, in the shades of plum. Today we can observe the scene with eyes made shrewd by Freud, finding different meanings: for the cardinal and the painter, it was only the warning that the evil knew how to hide, blend, and tempt. It is an important canvas, also because the first document with a handwritten signature is linked to it, and with a certain date: on 11 March 1553, the painters from Verona, together, asked the prelate for payment for the altarpieces ordered the previous year, and now completed and not yet withdrawn. The request is signed by all: our Master signs with "Paullo spezapreda" at the bottom, as stated in the document kept in the Gonzaga Historical Archive in Mantua, EN, XLI, no. 2. The first and last time he uses the family identification name; in a few years he will choose the most noble, and maternal, Caliari.

The relationship with a patrician clientele, the colouristic qualities, the attention for central Italian pictorial facts necessarily lead him towards Venice. His first public presentation, in the most modern church, commissioned by Doge Gritti, is immediately prestigious. For the powerful Giustinian family he created the *Holy Family with Saints John, Catherine and Anthony Abbot*, an altarpiece for the altar of their chapel in the church of San Francesco della Vigna, still on site, a

Temptations of Saint Anthony Abbot, 1552-1553, canvas, 198.2 × 149.5 cm. Caen, Musée des Beaux-Arts, inv. 54

Outstanding juvenile masterpiece, immediately judged by Vasari as the best compared to the works of the young artists from Verona to whom Cardinal Ercole Gonzaga had commissioned the canvases, it manages to express a claustrophobic atmosphere of cavernous cave, a nightmare in which the only light is reflected on the marvellous flesh of the she-devil. A completely new palette for Paolo, with the varieties of the most vinous colours; the "inhuman" musculature of the diabolical being, shades dominated by shadows.

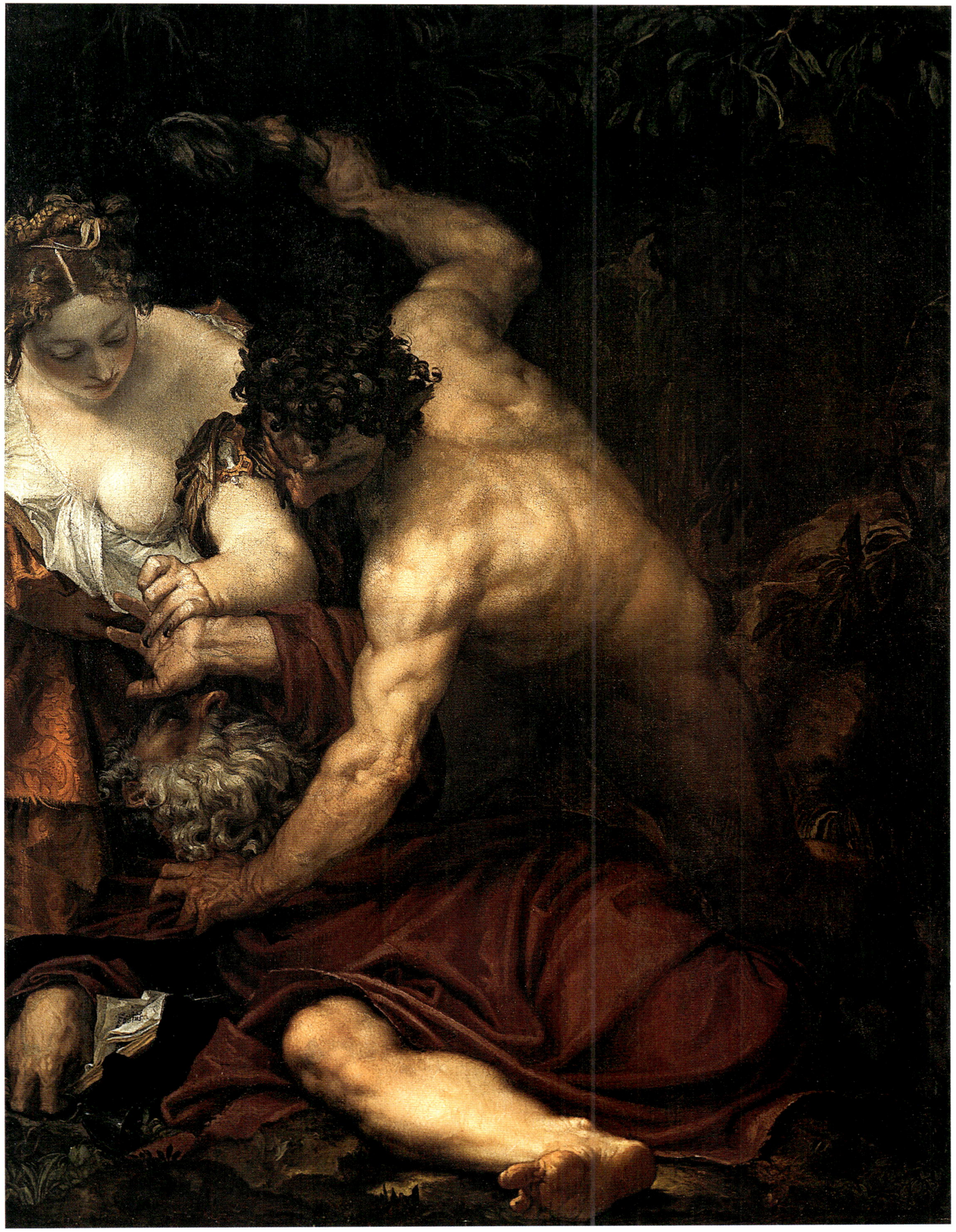

pictorial text that shows how the young man had already seen, understood and introjected the famous Titian solutions of *Pesaro Altarpiece*. It therefore represents a sort of transition between the explicit synthesis of the youthful formative period and the approach to the specific Venetian tradition, while always maintaining his identity firmly in the compositional and colour choice. The silk of Catherine's dress stands out and we also appreciate the beautiful design of her basket, which recalls how the Annunciation had caught Mary intent on domestic commitment and prayer; the basket rests on an architectural backdrop, very similar to that of the famous *Altarpiece of Saint John Chrysostom*, painted forty years earlier, at the time a highly innovative work of Sebastiano Luciani. Opposite to the signal of the announcement, we find the anticipation of the passion: the red of the blood and the white of the shroud, in the pillow on which the Child rests. Another sign is represented by the broken column on the ground on which Anthony's feet rest: it means the world that has now collapsed, overcome by the advent of the New Age of salvation. However, some uncertainties are shown on the canvas, remnants of youthful insecurities, such as the complicated and hesitant postures: it is not known where John could rest, even encumbered by the lamb, on an altar table or a very shallow step, while the abbot risks slipping on the rock of the column; and it is not clear whether Catherine goes on her knees or instead gets up with difficulty. Furthemore, the abbot's head is too small. But then we appreciate the strokes of light on the dress of the Alexandrian princess, boasting a rare splendour, and the sweetness of the faces, each one carefully characterized. Over the centuries, the altarpiece has lost much of its splendour, a comment that can be repeated for many other canvases by Paolo Veronese: not only because the colours, over time, alter, starting with the blues, but also because, in the past, all the original pigmented paint was taken away. Without forgetting that precisely because of the colour change many Veronese skies were repainted in the 19th century.

In any case, the work was appreciated by all: it is new, and it is an excellent viaticum. The Giustinian family is also linked to the "papalist" exponents, to the pro-Romanist circles of the Venetian patriciate, the best and most attentive patrons of Paolo, who entered through the main door in the circle of collectors and connoisseurs on whom the choices of public painting also depend. The church of San Francesco della Vigna had been commissioned by the great, and not forgotten, doge Andrea Gritti. Now is the time of a weaker and colourless doge, even sick, Francesco Donà, and the choices for the paintings in the Doge's Palace are taken by others: the Barbaros and the Grimanis. Through them, one can immediately get to the most prestigious public patrons.

Holy Family with Saints John, Catherine and Anthony Abbot, 1561-1562, canvas, 319 × 187 cm. Venice, church of San Francesco della Vigna, altarpiece of the Giustinian chapel

An important transitional work between the Veronese production, of which it maintains all the characteristics and some uncertainties, and the attention for the Venetian production, in particular the ever-present lesson of Titian.
It is also indicative of a work that should be the expression of accomplished colouristic skills and of the patron's tastes: the still life, the pillow, the fabrics, the feminine grace, the vagueness of childhood.

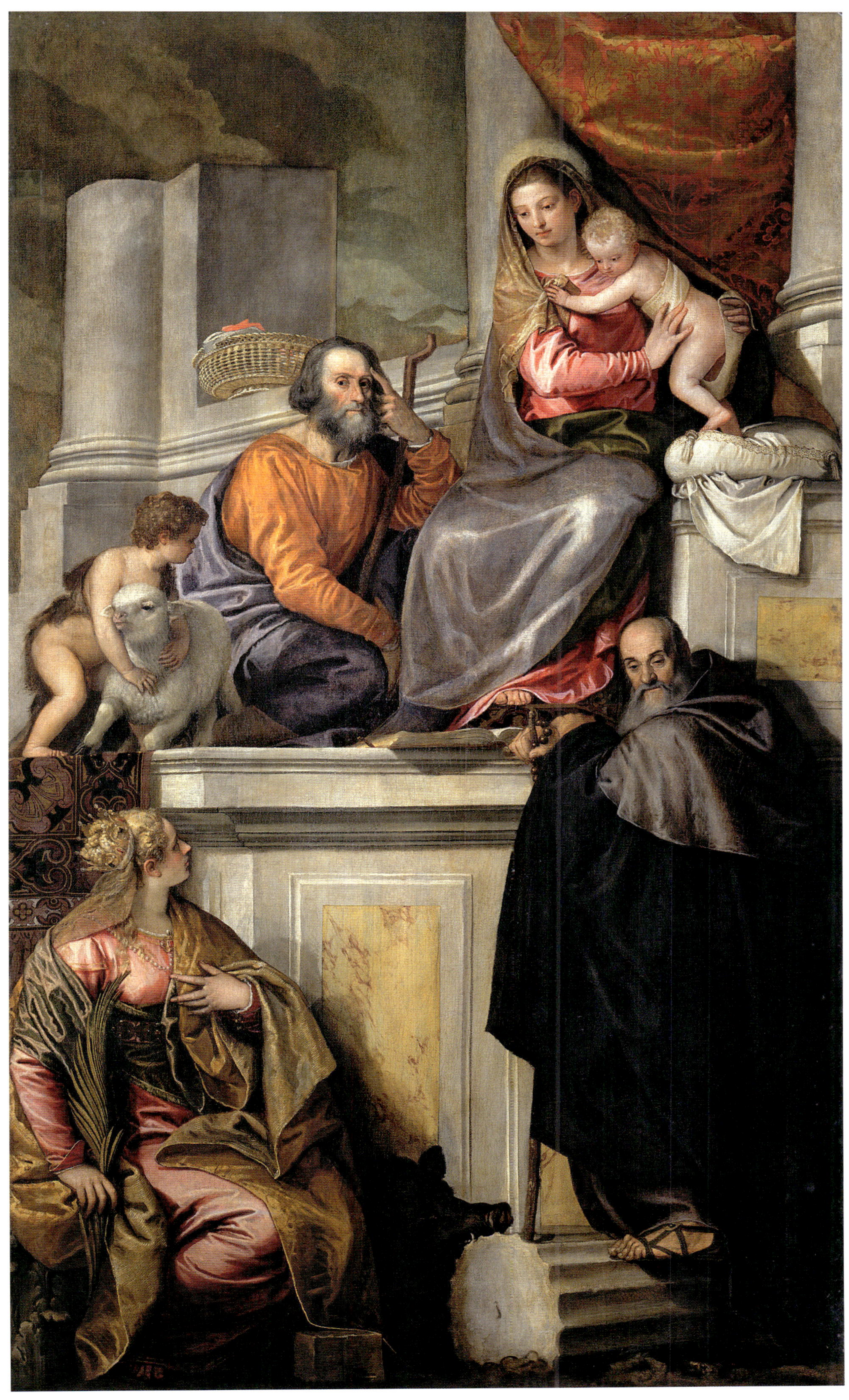

CHAPTER III
Summons with a Hug

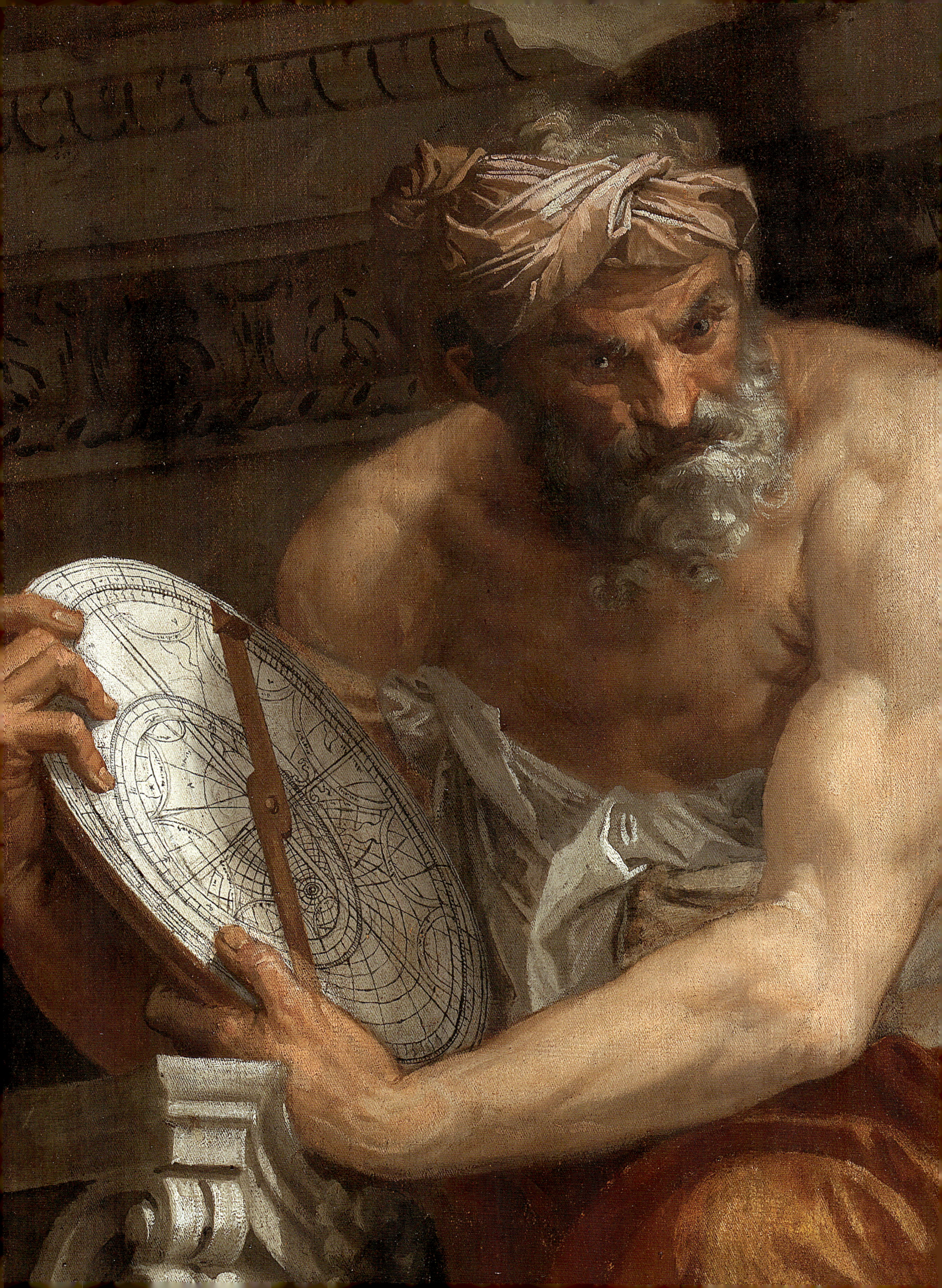

In the spring of 1553, two young Veronese painters, friends and mates, Paolo *spezapreda* and Giovanni Battista Zelotti, arrived, obviously by water, on the marble banks of Piazza San Marco. They had a proposal as high as it was prestigious: they were requested at Palazzo Ducale for the decoration of the ceiling of the Sala dei Dieci, the most powerful of the Venetian magistracies. Several characters guaranteed the invitation. However, according to Giorgio Vasari, the request for help from the painter in charge was essential, who, it is said, had not felt able to complete the imposing decoration on his own. It was an ecclesiastic with numerous prebends, Giovanni Battista Ponchino – known as "Bazzacco" or "Brazacco" or "Bozzato" – operating for a long time in Rome, and on very close terms with many of the most important Venetian families, all oriented towards improving relations with the Papal seat, in particular the houses of Grimani, Barbaro and Corner. In the second edition of his *Lives* (1568), Giorgio Vasari wrote:

> There was in Venice about this same time a painter called Brazzacco, a protégé of the house of Grimani, who had been many years in Rome; and he was commissioned by favour to paint the ceiling in the Great Hall of the Chiefs of the Council of Ten. But this master, knowing that he was not able to do it by himself and that he had need of assistance, took as companions Paolo Veronese and Battista Farinato, [...]. Now, although all three of them acquitted themselves well, Paolo Veronese succeeded better than the others.

In reality, Ponchino was a good artist, capable of satisfying the inclination for Michelangelo's art, then prevailing in the people responsible for the renovation of Palazzo Ducale: Daniele Barbaro and Vittore Grimani. And yet the clergyman had his troubles: denounced for heresy and sodomy to the Holy Office, he would also be censured by the suffragan bishop of Treviso, Giovan Francesco Verdura, for an altarpiece in the Cathedral of Castelfranco accused of "dishonesty" and "turpitudes". Perhaps also for this reason he was offered help to complete the enterprise, warrantors being Sanmicheli, Grimani, and Daniele Barbaro. Paolo, reliable by culture and character, capable of directing the associates, technically even sophisticated, appears capable of dealing with cultured patrons and complying with their requests. What more could one ask? Immediately to work; the undertaking for Palazzo Ducale will be crowned with success and esteem, he will become "the Veronese" par excellence, and will sign himself Caliari, a surname ennobling him.

The decoration concerns the new rooms intended for the Council of Ten, a magistracy with judicial and police functions, proceeding against the crimes of lese majesty, seditious people, counterfeiters. According to Francesco Sansovino, who wrote in 1561, the entire program of the three rooms - the *Sala delle Udienze*, the *Sala della Bussola* and the *Sala dei Tre Capi* – had been suggested by Daniele Barbaro, the future commissioner of the decoration in his villa in Maser, where Palladio follows the latest works; the humanist patriarch of Aquileia had known and appreciated the young Veronese painter for years, finding him close to his tastes and orientations. Barbaro had trained in the humanistic environment of Padua, he cultivat-

Allegory with an Astrolabe, 1553-1554 (?), canvas, 203.2 × 112.7 cm, detail. Los Angeles County Museum of Art, inv. M. 74.99.1, gift of Ahmanson Foundation

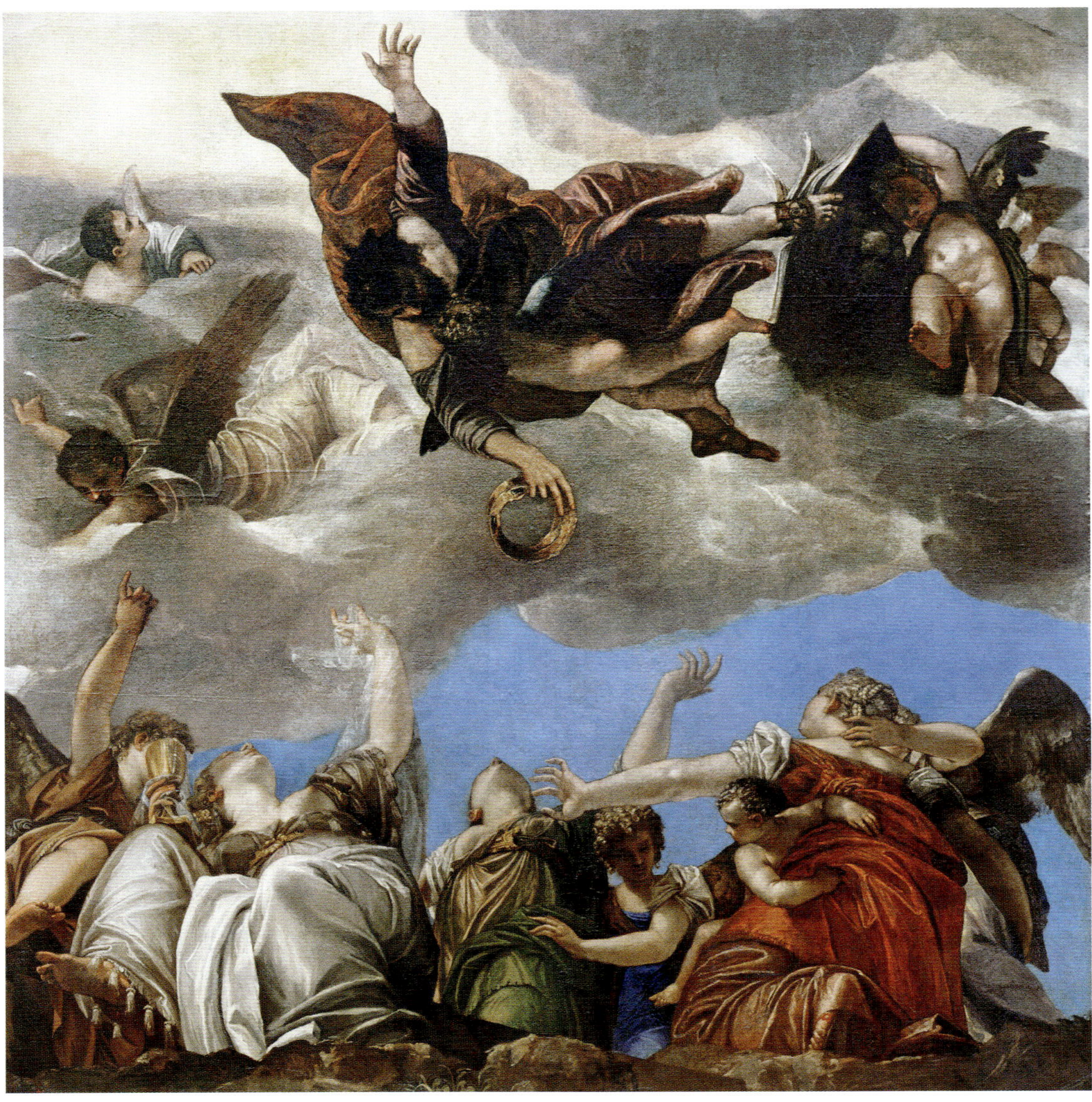

Saint Mark Crowning the Theological Virtues, 1553-1555, canvas, 330 × 317 cm. Paris, Musée du Louvre

Jupiter Hurling Thunderbolts at the Vices, 1553-1554, canvas, 560 × 330 cm. Paris, Musée du Louvre

By making these canvases for the halls of Palazzo Ducale, Veronese immediately presents himself with proofs of absolute skill, arousing immediate admiration from his colleagues and patrons. The technical knowledge in rendering the image from below is increased by the dynamics of the movements, by the freshness of the cold colours, while the enthusiasm of the Serenissima officials is aroused by the ability to merge religion with civic sense, Christian doctrine and tradition with the Venetian specificity, representing the virtues of government, and translating the moral values of public functions.

ed the family archaeological interests, had been interested in Roman formal novelties, in the decorative constructions of Raphael and in the ever new lessons of Michelangelo, and now he identified in Paolo the one who best translated his greatest passion into images: architecture, in the line of the classicism of the most appreciated Venetian architect, Andrea della Gondola, by now known as Palladio.

For the Sala delle Udienze Paolo prepared a large oval canvas – more than two centuries later it would be greatly appreciated by the Napoleonic men, who took it to the Louvre, so that now there is only the copy in its place in Venice – with *Jupiter Hurling Thunderbolts at the Vices*. The allegories are rather easy to read, which according to Francesco Sansovino were Sacrilege (not Heresy) with a roll of falsehood; Rebellion (with the rope around his neck); Sodomy (extremely easy: the two men are embracing); Falsification (taken with his hands in the bag of counterfeit coins). The authority of the judiciary and its repressive effectiveness is visually accentuated by the up/down effect and the crushing of the Vices, taken from Giulio Romano's *Fall of the Giants* in Palazzo Te in Mantua, with the intentional meaning of defeat for any attempt to offend the *auctoritas*.

Then it's the turn of *Youth and Old Age*, where the young woman is the good sister of the devil disguised as a seductress in Mantua, while the old man is taken exactly from the drawings, also made by Ponchino, of the statue of *Lorenzo de' Medici, Duke of Urbino*, a sculpture by

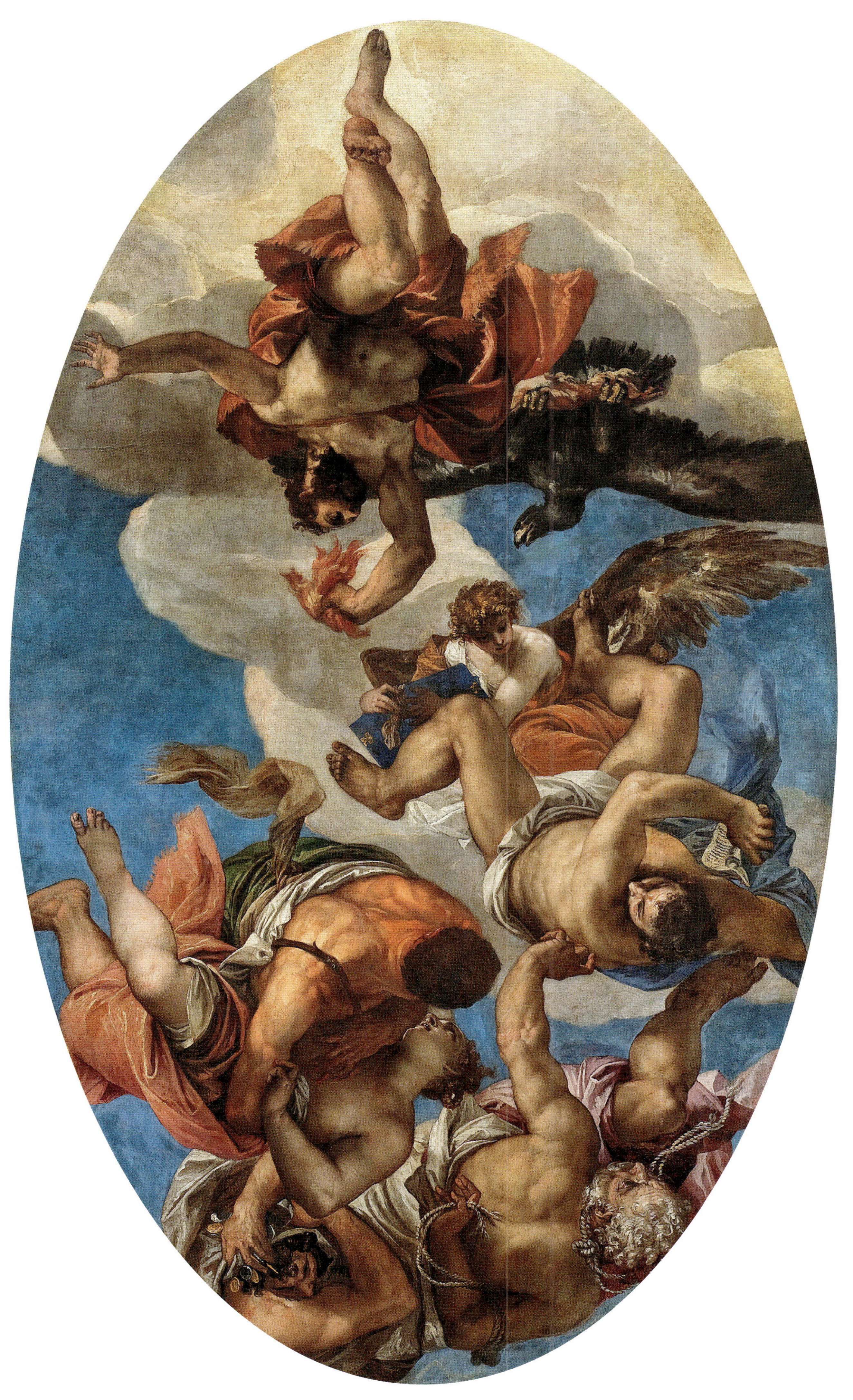

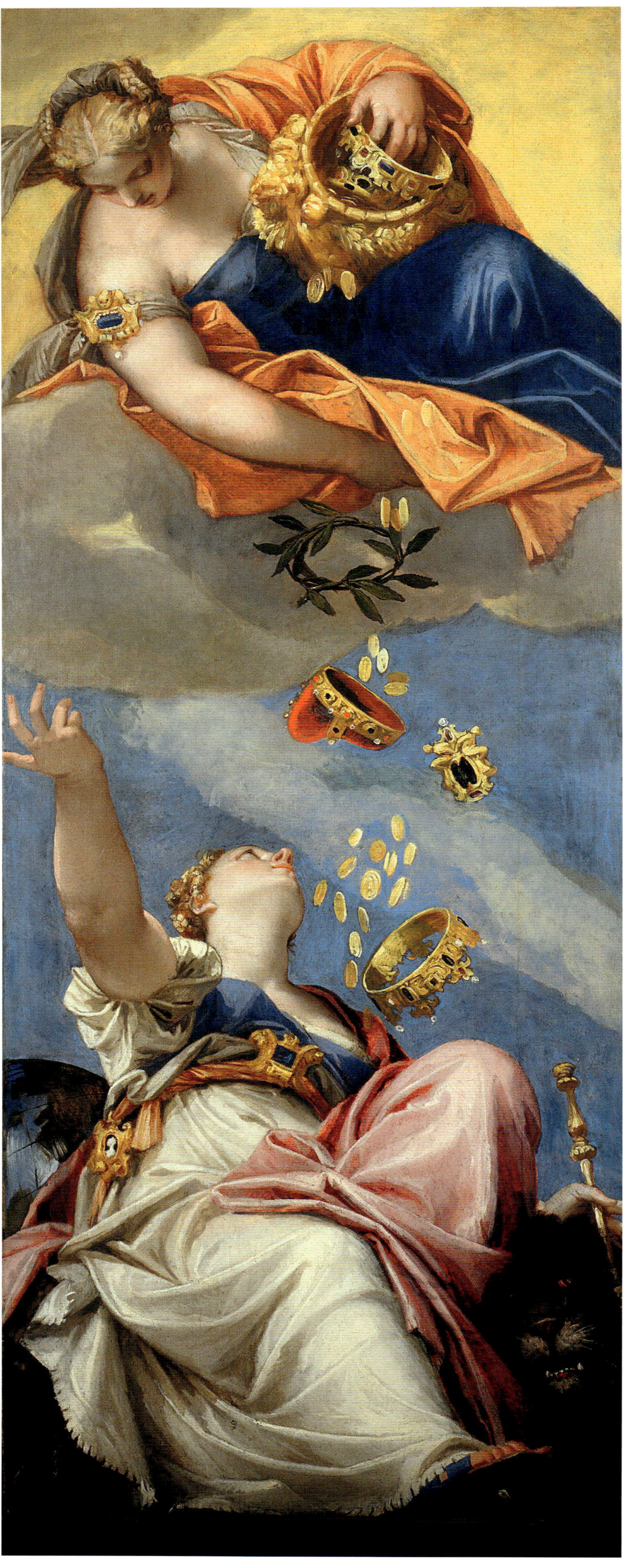

Juno Showering Gifts on Venice, 1554-1556, canvas, 365 × 147 cm. Venice, Palazzo Ducale

Youth and Old Age, 1553-1554, canvas, 286 × 150 cm. Venice, Palazzo Ducale

In these creations for Palazzo Ducale, Veronese offers – in his best colouristic draft – an evident homage to Michelangelo in the posture of Saturn, taking up *Lorenzo de' Medici* from the New Sacristy of San Lorenzo in Florence. The young woman is the *altera virgo* if compared to the female demon of the *Temptation* for the Cathedral of Mantua. The flood of jewels that Fortuna showers on Venice represents another element, of light and colour, which excited the contemporaries.

Following pages
Allegories

The four *Allegories* only recently recomposed, unknown for destination, commission and realization, are a point of arrival for the young painter in the first five years of the sixth decade: grandiose and statuesque, in the sign of the wisdom of the ancients and of the art of navigation, of geographical discoveries and the Arts – Painting, Sculpture, Architecture – are a perfect tribute to the culture of Venetian scientific humanism and new geographical knowledge. They show particular pictorial skill in the variation of lights, and in the drafting on canvas, which recalls the fresco technique for effectiveness and speed of the brushstroke.

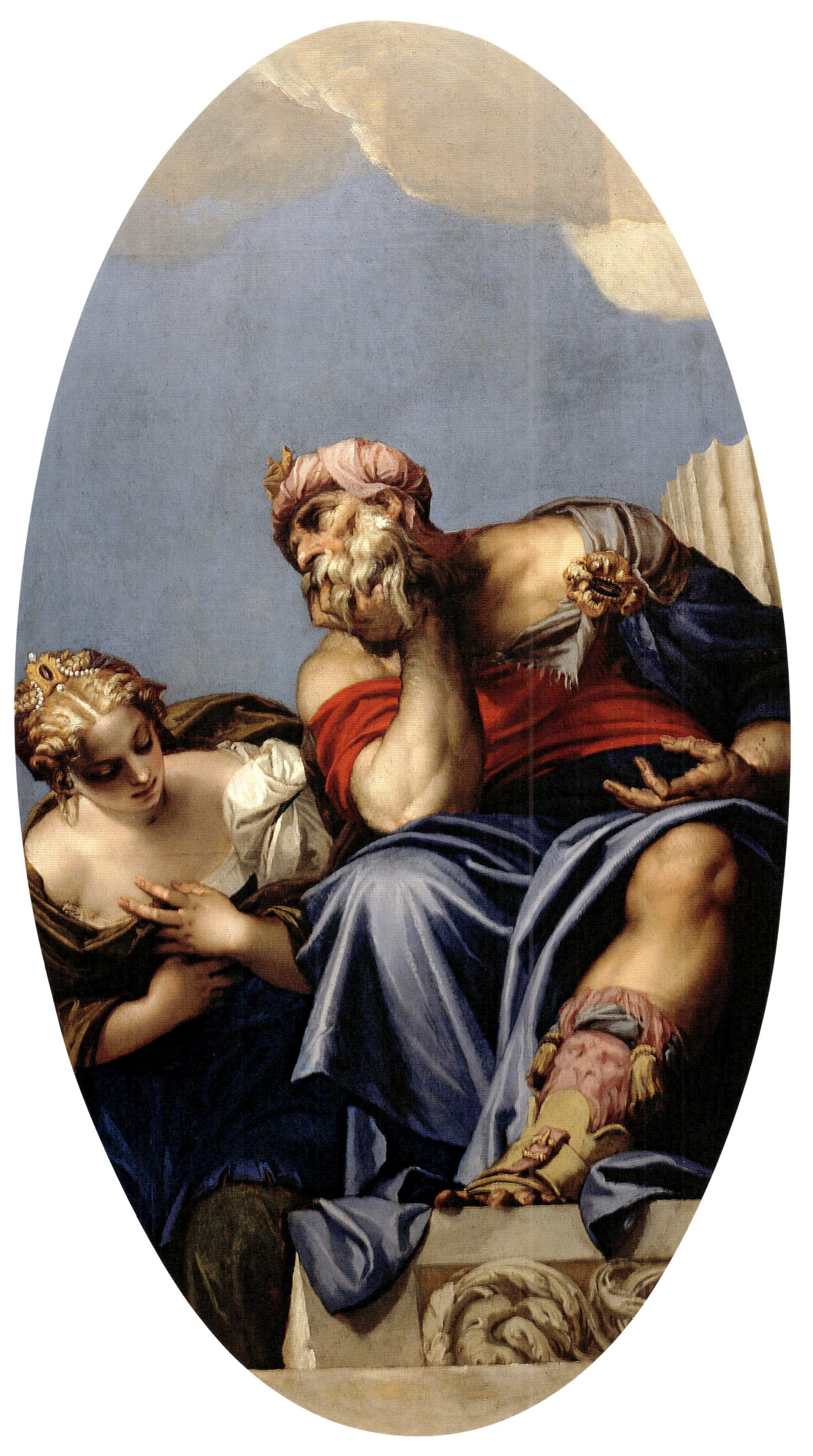

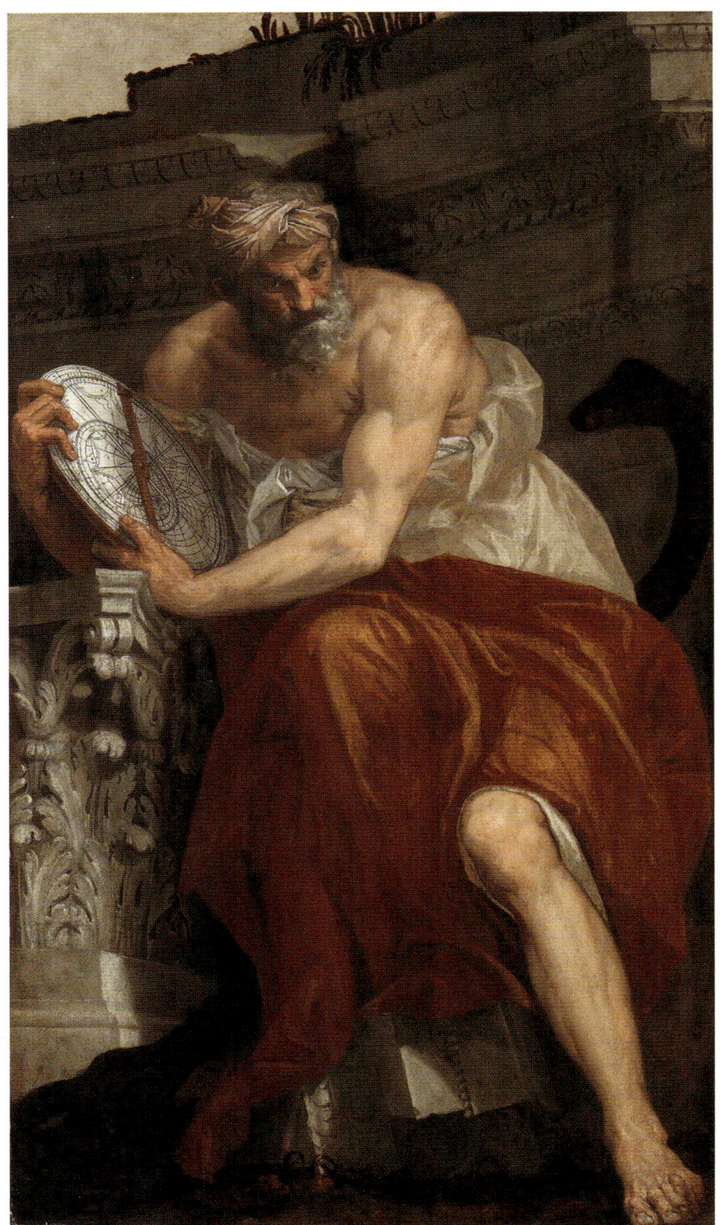

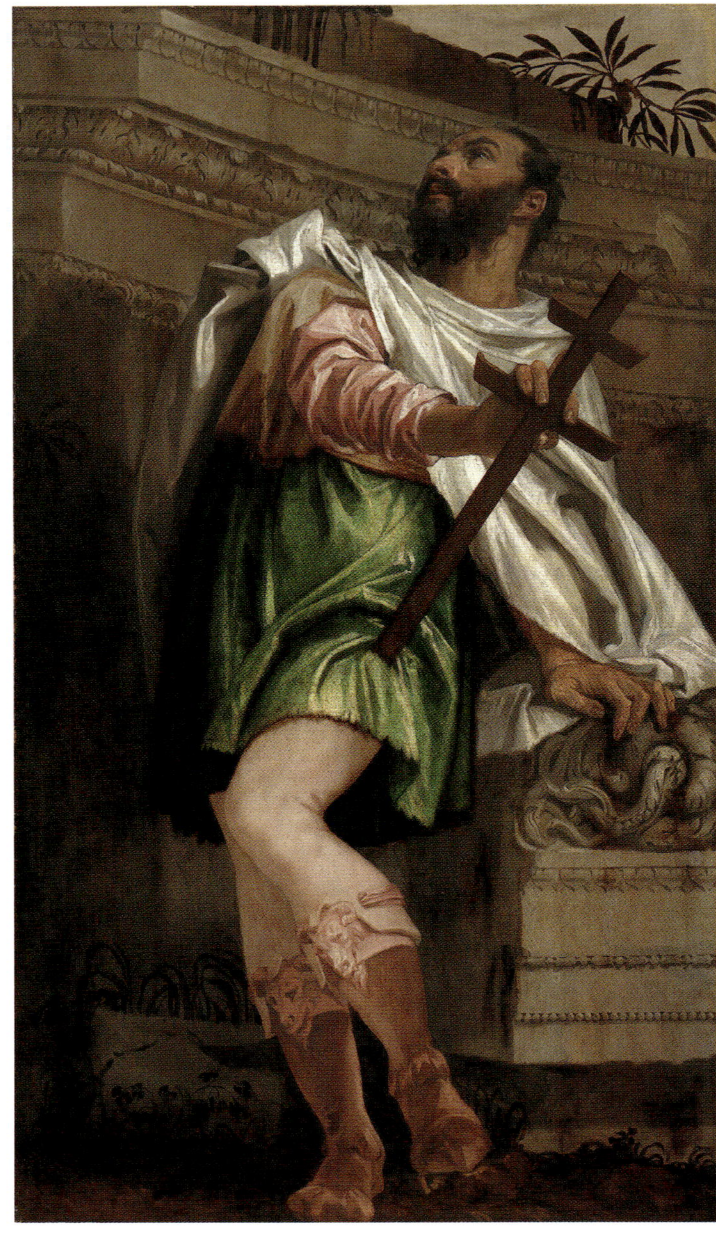

Allegory with an Astrolabe, 1553-1554 (?), canvas, 203.2 × 112.7 cm. Los Angeles County Museum of Art, inv. M. 74.99.1, gift of Ahmanson Foundation

Allegory with the Jacob's Staff, 1553-1554 (?), canvas, 204.3 × 116.8 cm. Los Angeles County Museum of Art, inv. M.74.99.2, gift of Ahmanson Foundation

Michelangelo in the New Sacristy of San Lorenzo. Then he created an image of pure encomiastic glory, though joyful and happy: the so-called *Juno Showering Gifts on Venice*, in which we do not find the attributes of the goddess, since it is rather a representation of Abundance who generously bestows crowns and ducal horn, jewels and mint coins, but also the laurel of the arts to a young and well-turned Venice, with the faithful Lion rubbing against her like a big cat. In the Sala della Bussola is the *Saint Mark Crowning the Virtues*, in which the Republic itself, personified by Mark, honours Faith, Hope and Charity.

On the ceiling of the Sala dei Tre Capi, whose centre is dominated by an octagon by Zelotti, Paolo painted again *The Triumph of Nemesis over Sin*, or *Virtue Triumphant over Vice* and the *Triumph of Virtue over Vice*; the Nemesis or Virtue is absolutely similar to the Vasti completed for the church of San Sebastiano, of which in this case she would be the first model. Notice the heavy chains with which the downed enemy will be immobilized: they are those of the Piombi.

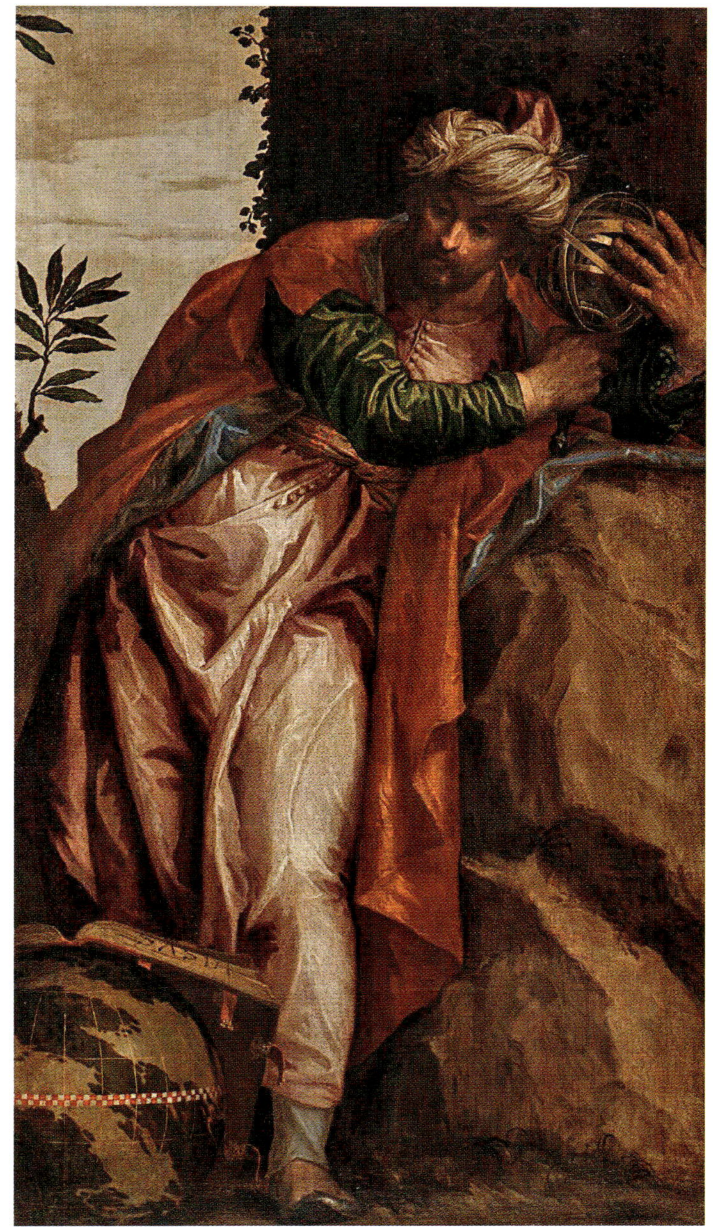

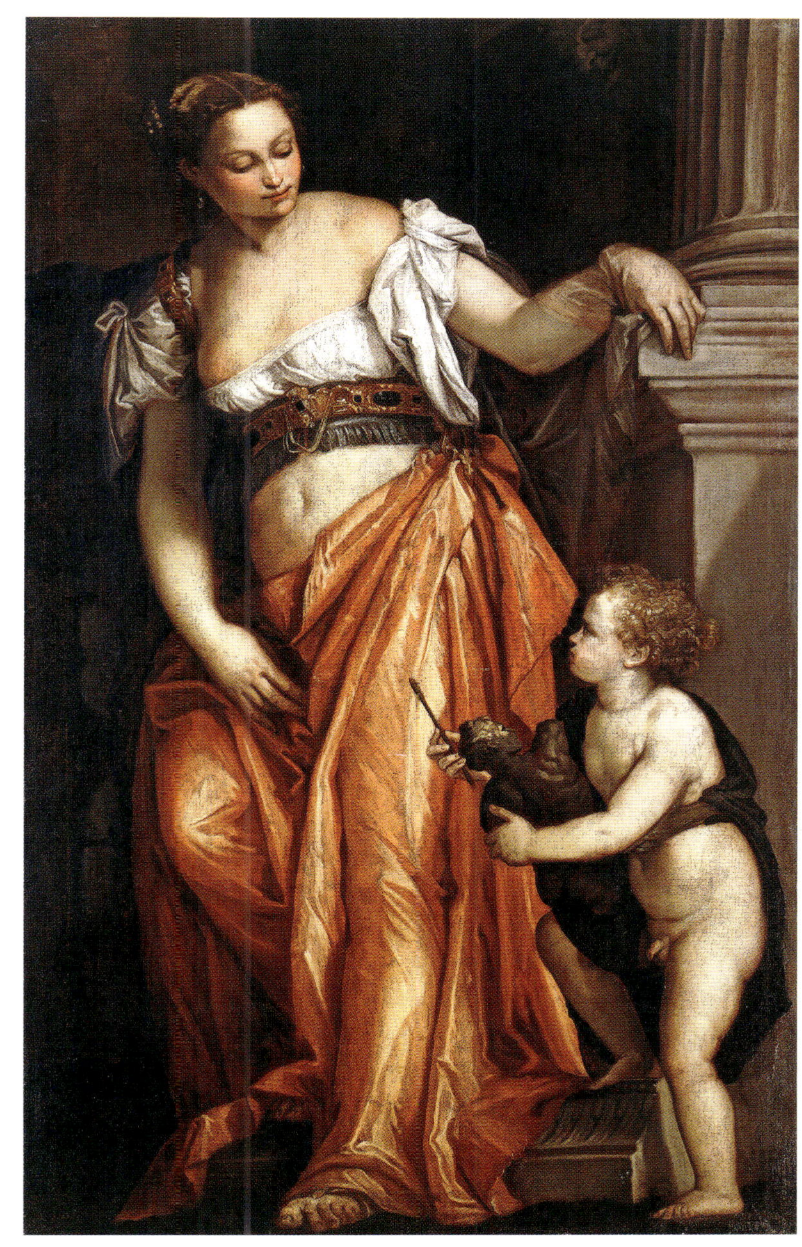

A WORKSHOP OF ALLEGORIES

Allegory with the Armillary Sphere,
1553-1554 (?),
canvas, 205 × 114.3 cm.
Regione Piemonte, Reggia
di Venaria, inv. 40297

Allegory of Sculpture,
1553-1554 (?),
canvas, 205.4 × 114 cm.
Regione Piemonte, Reggia
di Venaria, inv. 40296

Daniele Barbaro might have asked, or only suggested to Paolo another group of allegories that met the tastes of the humanist, translating knowledge and research into images. These are four canvases, flukeily brought nearer a few years ago, whose history is mysterious: certainly by his hand, they should not exceed 1554. Two are kept in Los Angeles - the *Allegory with the Jacob's Staff* and the *Allegory with an Astrolabe* – and two, rediscovered in 2015, the *Allegory with the Armillary Sphere* and the *Allegory of Sculpture* are on deposit at the Museo del Paesaggio in Verbania. Three canvases therefore interpret astronomical and geographical studies, at the centre of the interests not only of the patron but of any Venetian patrician, whose *cursus honorum* included a period of training in navigation on galleys. Therefore they knew the Jacob's staff perfectly – the instrument used to determine the height of the Sun and the North Star – as well as the astrolabe used to measure the height of the stars above the horizon. The armillary sphere is instead a model of the celestial sphere indicating also the equator line, which the painter underlines with a string of small red and white squares painted on the terrestrial globe. The three astronomical allegories are joined by a fourth of a completely different subject: it is Sculpture, isolated or perhaps connected to other images. The woman's gaze is turned to the putto who is holding a stick and a clay model of torso, which is being worked on; she looks like a reminiscence of Paolo as a child, the son of the *spezapreda* that Ridolfi described as being educated in modelling small clay figures, which will later become models to draw. The woman, the Sculpture that appreciates and inspires the childish labour, rests on an architectural structure with pedestal, plinth and column boasting Palladian features and from which a grinning grotesque emerges – a sudden and unexpected invention, whose meaning is difficult to grasp.

Dispersions and acknowledgements

The paintings now in Los Angeles appeared in English collections in the 19th century, arriving in the United States in 1911; presented again on the London market in 1973, they definitively reached the County Museum the following year, by gift. Much more mysterious are the vicissitudes of the other two canvases, which appeared in 1916 at Villa San Remigio in Pallanza, owned by a couple of cultured collectors, Silvio Della Valle di Casanova and Sophie Browne; the heir Ester Bonacossa donated the Villa to the Piedmont Region in 1977. It was only in 2013 that a young student, Cristina Moro, found them during her degree thesis work, immediately proposing them to her professors of reference, Giovanni Agosti and Jacopo Stoppa; the identification, thanks also to Vittoria Romani, was rapid, later confirmed by the restoration works, by the comparison with the American canvases and by the public exhibition. If the dating and patronage cannot be certain, it is nonetheless reasonable to consider them to precede Paolo Caliari's activity at Maser. It should also be noted that the face of the character with the Jacob's staff will later become that of Philip of the *Saints Philip and James the Lesser* in the National Gallery of Dublin, and that of the centurion in the canvas *Christ and the Centurion*, now at Prado. Works that belong to the sixties, in which we find the "typus" of the man at the end of maturity: bearded, with a receding hairline, with energetic features, the same large ears, wide nostrils and marked nose.

With the work in the Doge's Palace, and the ever more numerous requests within the city, Paolo had to settle down in Venice, without, however, separating his family relationships and the mainland clientele in any way. In the year 1554 he was already a tenant of the house and workshop of Vincenzo Zen: we know this because the Savi di Rialto should be notified of the year's income, and Zen's tithe was presented on 14 January 1554 *more veneto*, according to the custom for which the year begins with the anniversary of the mythical founding of the city. So for us it is already January 1555, referring in the declaration to the income of the previous year, as is still the case today. The house was in Corte Candela, which today is Campo dei Gesuiti, near the Santi Apostoli in Cannaregio. In the document Zen stated that "ser Paulo Veronese painter keeps everything for rent for thirty-two ducats". This choice of home is not fortuitous, since Zen is part of one of the great patrician families and of a circle of intellectuals which includes the architect Sebastiano Serlio and the publisher Francesco Marcolini, who will publish Daniele Barbaro's *Vitruvius* and made a fortune with Aretino's books. In 1556 he published the first edition, still without illustrations, of *Le imagini con la spositione de i Dei de gli antichi* by Vincenzo Cartari, then reissued in 1571. A book read and consulted by Paolo, who will draw from it feats and attributes of the ancient gods, even of the lesser known ones, as in the case of Eros and Anteros, characters who recur in many profane and sensual canvases.

The Venetian intellectual and patrician world is a dense interweaving of family relationships and friendships, to which the Veronese Paolo Caliari fits perfectly, immediately in relation

to the notables of the city, as previously in his Verona. Benedetto was always active alongside Paolo, so much so that from 1557 the Veronese registry offices no longer kept any news of the two painter brothers. Moreover, their father, Gabriele *spezapreda*, should have died by that date, so his widow Caterina would join their sons in Venice. The year is unspecified, certainly within 1562, since on 17 July Caterina is required to appear in court in Verona for a dispute relating to a house, and from Verona the magistrates turn to Venice, where she now has a permanent residence. In that same 1562 Paolo buys some land in a locality between Cittadella and Castelfranco Veneto, at the price of two hundred ducats: a certain Francesco Barbarella assists him as mediator, a name that will often appear in the documents relating to the purchases and management of the painter's land properties in the area of Castelfranco. Land properties, various rented fields, showing Paolo's interest in land investments, an interest that continued throughout his life, the result of a remarkable economic well-being, and of a constant and remunerated production for the city of Venice.
Paolo will be able to understand, grasp and represent all the tensions of the soul, tastes, requests of the city, he will exalt the myth in an allegorical form, the faith in the dimension of piety, he will illustrate it in the newspaper and in the sociality of the *Conviti*; in Palazzo Ducale he will show the myth of Venice, in the Hieronymites' church the heartfelt, painful and heroic faith, and then he will portray families and figures of a substantially cohesive patrician society, in large canvases exhibited in the *porteghi* of his patrons. Venice welcomes him with immediate pleasantness: it is a city with an attentive public who loves painting, not only patricians and clergy, and not only citizens. In every Venetian house there is an image painted, outside or inside, out of devotion, even only on coloured paper for the less well-off, since the prints are exhibited and sold by itinerant shopkeepers and vendors, even at fairs and in markets. The images are everywhere, on the decorated furniture, the chests, the headboards, while the taste is formed and orientated through the churches and the fresco decorations on the façades of the buildings. Venetian exteriors and interiors are a great book of figurative stories: sacred and profane, personal and collective, of deeds and fantasies.
The Venetian artistic production is based on family workshops able to satisfy every type of request, on the vast and stratified public, and on the absence of a court art subject to the tastes and wishes of the prince. All this had a result: Venetian painters are free to offer the public diversified works, always created independently; they also produced artworks in series, as in the case of images offered for private devotion, and made to order in the case of portraits, the "poems", allegorical, mythological, sensual inventions. In this way, a model of production and thematic freedom was established that was admired and envied in Spain and England, then applied in Flanders, in Antwerp; a model that allows the continuous variation of genres, themes and techniques.
While the Republic asks for large canvases with historical subjects, the ecclesiastics ask for large canvases with the facts of the New Testament; popular piety wants images of Mary and the saints; portraits and mythological scenes are reserved for patrician and intellectual classes, while citizens aspire to family groups proposed as a sign of prestige, or presented in the manifestation of their faith, portrayed while offering a sacred image to public devotion. For the most cultured and refined collectors there will be personal decorations, private "poems", allusive scenes, rare and conceptual allegories. Paolo Veronese will be able to design and create any type of images required by the patriciate, the Republic and the major religious orders; in his workshop he will have apprentices and workers, collaborators and pupils, and his brother as a faithful alter ego. In addition, Paolo Caliari knows how to dialogue on an equal footing with architects, offering patrons surprising camouflage results, opportunities for new decorative seasons, joy and wonder for guests and hosts.

THE NECKLACE AND THE HUG

Transfiguration, 1556,
signed, canvas, 555 × 260 cm.
Montagnana, cathedral

In proposing a habitual image and recurring in painting not only in Venice from the fifteenth century, Paolo Caliari underlines in more marked ways the distance between the manifestation of the divine, in its luminous stillness, and the drama in the world, in the astonished and landed postures of the apostles. It is a separation underlined by the cloud, which corresponds perfectly to the *transumanar* of the already incorporeal Christ.

The painter is very active and while working for the church of San Sebastiano he does not give up on offers. On 3 June 1555 he was in Montagnana; in Francesco Pisani's palace he signs the contract with the *fabbriceri* of the Duomo for "an altarpiece for the great altar in the Pieve di S. Maria di Montagnana." Patrons know the "quality of Mis. Paulo Caliaro Veronese living in Venetia" and asked him to create an "Altarpiece without frame by painting a *Transfiguration of Christ* with those figures that most adapt in terms of beauty and ornamentation with the mentioned altarpiece, and in that use very fine colours [...]". The remuneration for the work, of which executive freedom should be noticed – in any case always considered in the contracts of the time – will be compensated with "Gold shields, in pure gold, one hundred and thirty in three equal instalments", of which the first one will be paid immediately, as a deposit. Delivery by Christmas 1556. This document, now in the Archpriest's Archive of Montagnana, testifies to Paolo's use of the surname Caliari for the first time.
The Pisanis too, like the Giustinianis who commissioned the altarpiece in San Francesco della Vigna, were exponents of that "philo-Roman" orientation which combined a declared propensity for taste with a political position. Francesco di Giovanni Pisani (1509-1567) – the inscription on the summit frieze still stands out on that building today "FRANCISCVS PISANVS IO[ANNIS] F[ILIVS] F[ECIT]" – was a cultured and wealthy exponent of the Moretta dal Banco family branch, owner of thousands of fields, a large real estate inherited around the town. The palace had been inhabited for a very short time when Paolo was received with the deputies of the Community and the blacksmiths – later Francesco Pisani will host a small court of artists and men of letters – and obtained the ornaments of Alessandro Vittoria, author of elegant sculptures in hard stucco. Later Paolo will complete the splendid canvas with *Alexander the Great and the Family of Darius*, now in the National Gallery of Art in London, to be placed on the main wall of the large hall on the first floor of the Venetian palace. A canvas on the values of the patriciate with a refined allegorical complexity, as we will see.
The *Transfiguration* for Montagnana is also the first signed work: "Paulo/ Vero/ P." [Paolo Veronese painted], imposing and also original, with that Christ who becomes evanescent, as opposed to the apostles and fluttering coloured angels. The contrast between the hieratic nature of the Son and the expressions of amazement, astonished wonder and awe of those who witness the event, underline a by now complete skill and mastery of physiognomic design, as well as colour. Even if, it is obvious, Caliari adds little to the previous very high iconographic solutions of *Transfigurations*, from Lotto to Raphael. The plastic motifs of the Anthony Abbot from Mantua return in the foreshortened Peter, the fallen apostle.
By now fully Venetian, Paolo Veronese achieved a sort of official consecration with the decoration of the ceiling of Libreria Marciana, created by Sansovino: here he painted, in 1556, the roundels with *Honour, Arithmetic and Geometry, and Music*, three canvases each with a diameter of 230 centimetres. On 10 February 1557 the *Procuratori de Supra*, administrative judiciary, allocated 40 ducats "to pay for the paintings done in the library" to our "Paulo". The round of *Music* has some particular iconological aspects such as Love without wings, for which Vasari was able to affirm that he no longer flew, being linked to the musical arts, all engaged with stringed instruments, while Love accompanies him with a harpsichord. Instead, the satyr herm, the memory of the pan flute, refers to the wind instruments, which prevent singing. Music will be the most appreciated of the rounds given to the other six painters called to the decorative competition with Veronese,: Andrea Schiavone, Giuseppe Porta Salviati, Battista Franco, Giovanni de Mio, Giulio Licinio and Giambattista Zelotti. Vasari recounts that they had been chosen by the associates of the city's art dictators, namely Titian, Jacopo Sansovino and Pietro Aretino. They would have been the ones to propose the name of an artist who, most deserving,

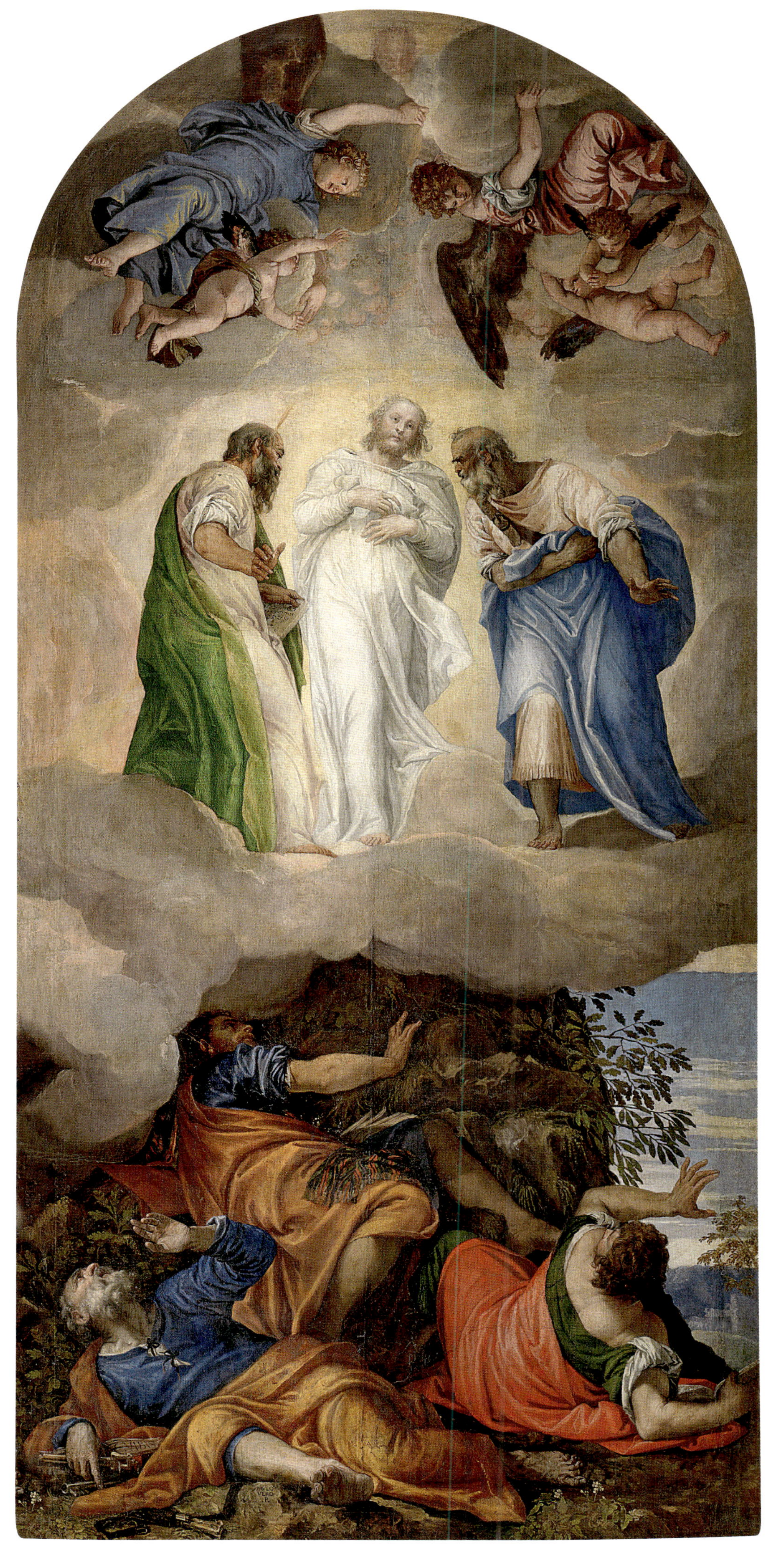

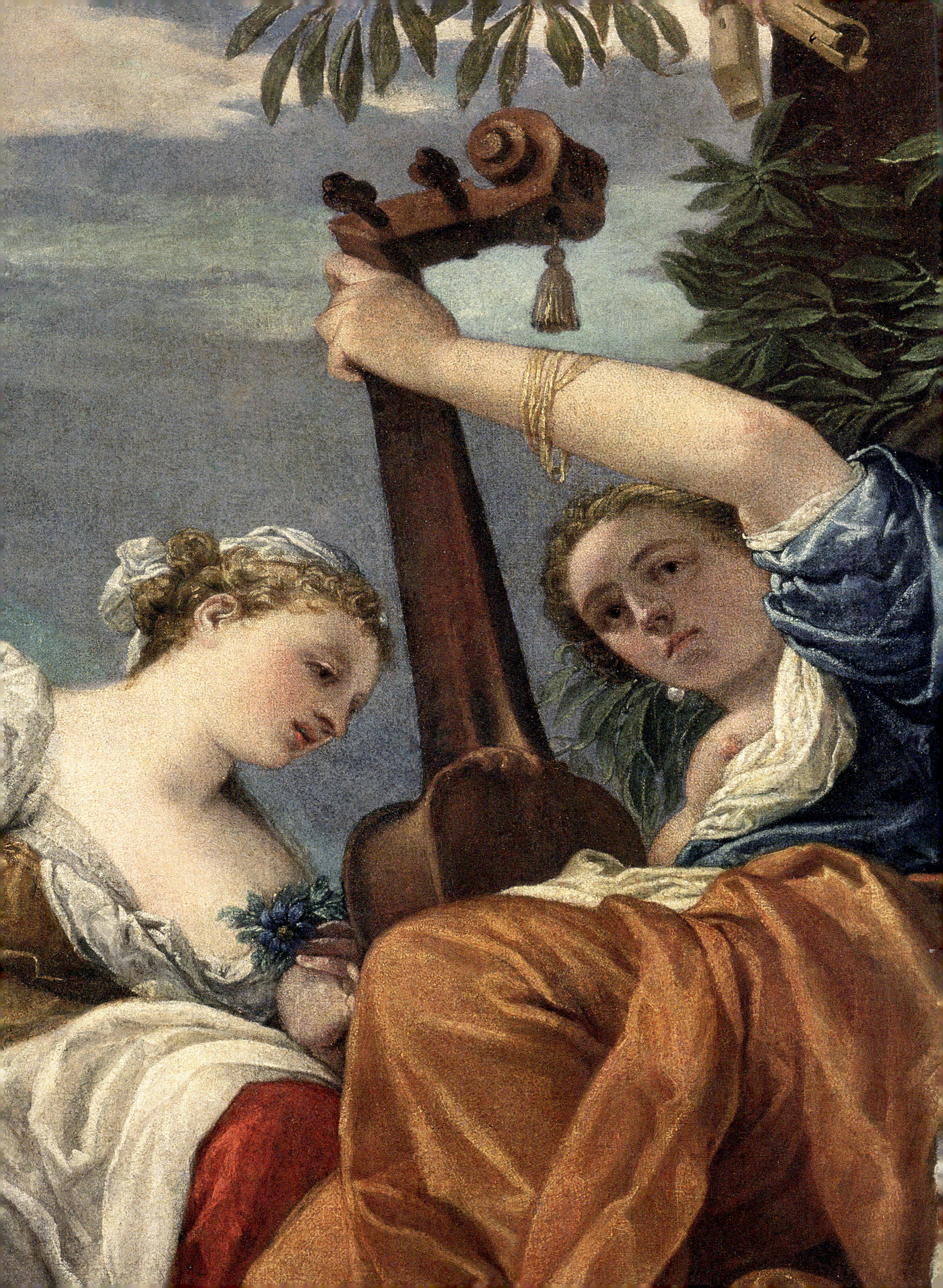

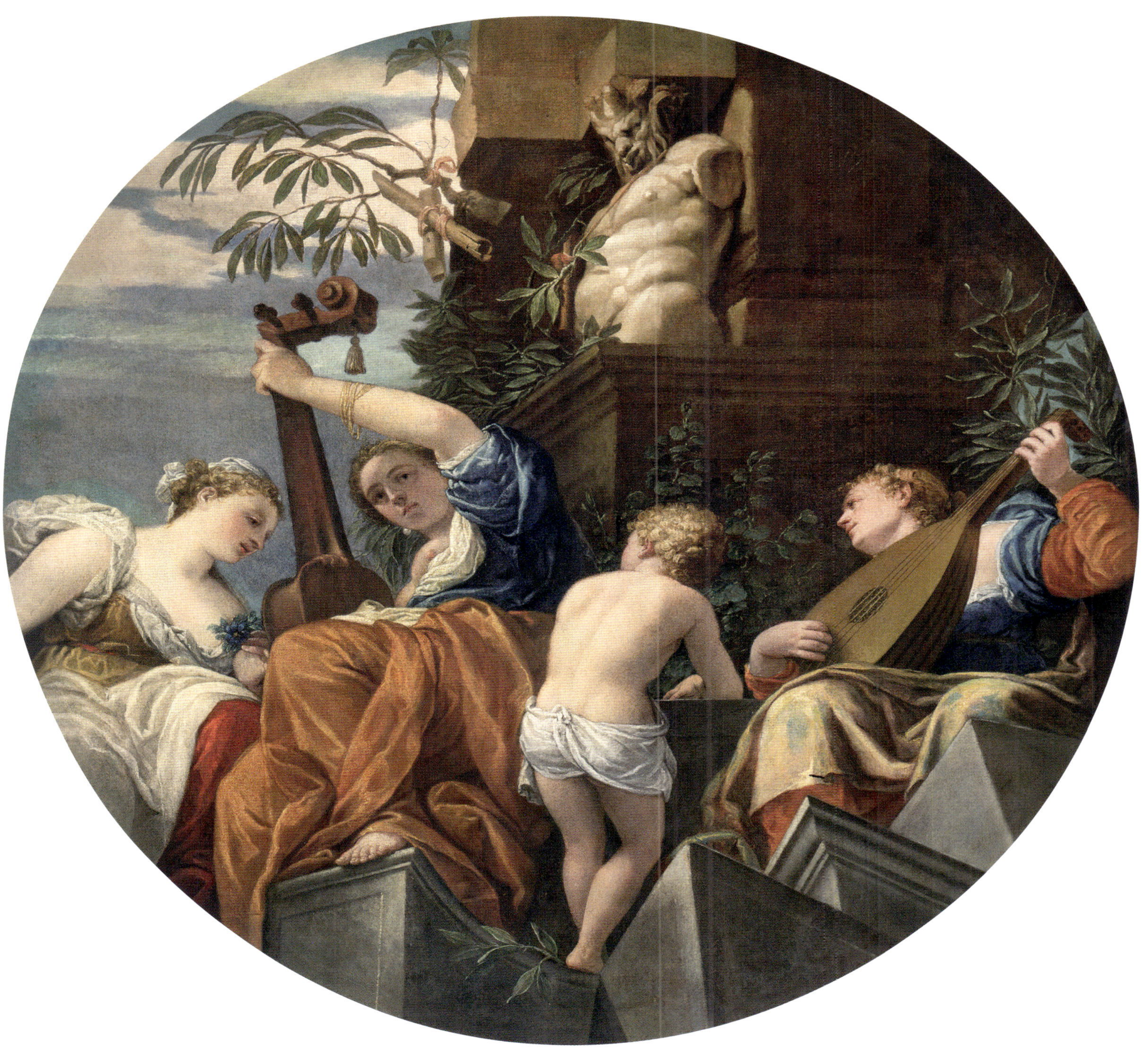

Allegory of Music, 1556,
canvas, Ø 230 cm.
Venice, Libreria Marciana

According to the narrative of the time, the tondo with the *Music* created for Libreria Marciana earned not only unanimous praise, but the prize of a gold necklace, still kept in 1648 by his nephew Giuseppe Caliari, precious testimony of his ancestor's glory. Vasari remembers the embrace of Titian, who recognized in Paolo the best of his generation and his worthy successor. The allegory is also praise, in the humanistic tradition, of Harmony, associated and exalted in Love, here without wings: since, according to Vasari, he must not fly away, depriving himself of Music. Noticeable the distinction between stringed and percussion instruments, accompanying the singing, and the wind instruments, around the satyr's herm: an expression of a more archaic and wild musicality.

would have obtained the gold necklace offered as a prize by the Prosecutors. The palm was given to Veronese, for colours and invention of *the Allegory of Music*: the painter had, with the necklace, the public embrace of Titian, a real legitimation, a sort of generational passage; with his approval he was recognized, at only twenty-eight, as the most talented of his generation.
Meanwhile the indefatigable Michele Sanmicheli finished a building in Murano, owned by the lawyer Camillo Trevisan. To decorate it he gathered a group of friends from Verona: with Paolo and Zelotti also Bernardino India and Battista del Moro. Of the vast decorative system there remains a hall of Olympus with Seven planetary deities, very difficult to read, evidence of the astrological as well as mythographic taste of Venetian humanistic culture.

IN SAN SEBASTIANO AGAIN

In 1558, between 31 March and 8 September, Paolo returned to San Sebastiano to paint the frescoes on the walls and the choir of the friars as well as the *Announcing Angel* and the *Virgin Announced* on the pendentives of the triumphal arch opening the presbytery. On the side walls of the nave he also created a simulated portico supported by twisted columns, with false niches occupied by the grandiose monochromes of Fathers of the Church and Sibyls. Subsequently on the walls of the choir of the friars he created the images of the cycle of the saint to whom the building is dedicated. He framed them in complex and articulated stage fronts, simulating columns so that they appear truly set on a stage. They are particularly animated visions: in the first, Sebastian, who miraculously survived being sentenced to death by being pierced by arrows, and was saved and cured by Irene, now publicly reproaches the emperor: it is the *Saint Sebastian before Diocletian*. But the despot, not at all converted, orders that the young tribune be beaten to death by ferocious hirelings: it is the *Martyrdom of Saint Sebastian*. If particular is the choice of setting up the scenes as a theatrical situation, equally blatant is the invention, under the scene of the rebuke, of the trompe l'oeil in which he pretends to be a monk who, from behind, enters a fake door, on whose doorstep lies another young monk. It is a prime example of the illusionistic games he will enjoy, and will delight us at Maser. Paolo will then carry out an even more daring invention by painting an *Archer* who shoots his arrow through the room of the church, hitting the *Sebastian Miles* tied to the column on the opposite wall, while the angel with the palm of martyrdom hurries over him. Particularly skilful is the positioning of the archer, assisted by two companions, who forcefully draws the bow, whose exact trajectory can be reconstructed from below. Sebastian tied up and naked, with a flowing loincloth, receives the palm from an angel who authentically seems to fall on his back with a slightly grotesque, but certainly very skilled effect.
The two compositions relating to martyrdom now show complete ingenuity in managing the crowd of figures around the protagonists. In the crowd we find cruelty, indifference, incomprehension towards the one who goes to death for his faith. There is a substantial ferocity in those beings who feel no mercy, and it seems to rediscover the horror of the crowds who enthusiastically witness the death sentences by the magistrates of the Republic, carried out among the columns of Piazza San Marco. But we also find the stories of the brutal indifference of the Turkish massacrers, of which bloody, terrible things were told.
Precisely some similarities in the expressiveness of the characters and the traits of a conquered technical maturity suggest that a large canvas now almost unanimously attributed to Paolo, *Christ among the Doctors*, today at Prado, is close to the frescoes of San Sebastiano. It illustrates the episode of Christ's childhood (Luke 2, 41-50) when the twelve-year-old Jesus was taken by his parents to Jerusalem to celebrate Easter. Mary and Joseph lost him in the crowd, to find him in the Temple discussing with the doctors. The superiority of the young man is represented at

Saint Sebastian before Diocletian, 1558, fresco, 350 × 480 cm. Venice, church of San Sebastiano

Martyrdom of Saint Sebastian, 1558, fresco, 350 × 480 cm. Venice, church of San Sebastiano

Of particular interest, in the two frescoes placed in *barco* of San Sebastiano, therefore visible only to the monks, is the complex monochrome painting framing them, attributable to the *scenae frontes* of Roman wall paintings. Not only does the Veronese take up those models, but he realizes the events narrated in overtly theatrical forms as for attitudes, motions and expressions, following the tradition of Sebastian's life.

Following pages
Three Archers and Sebastian Tied to the Column, 1558, fresco, both 270 × 130 cm. Venice, church of San Sebastiano

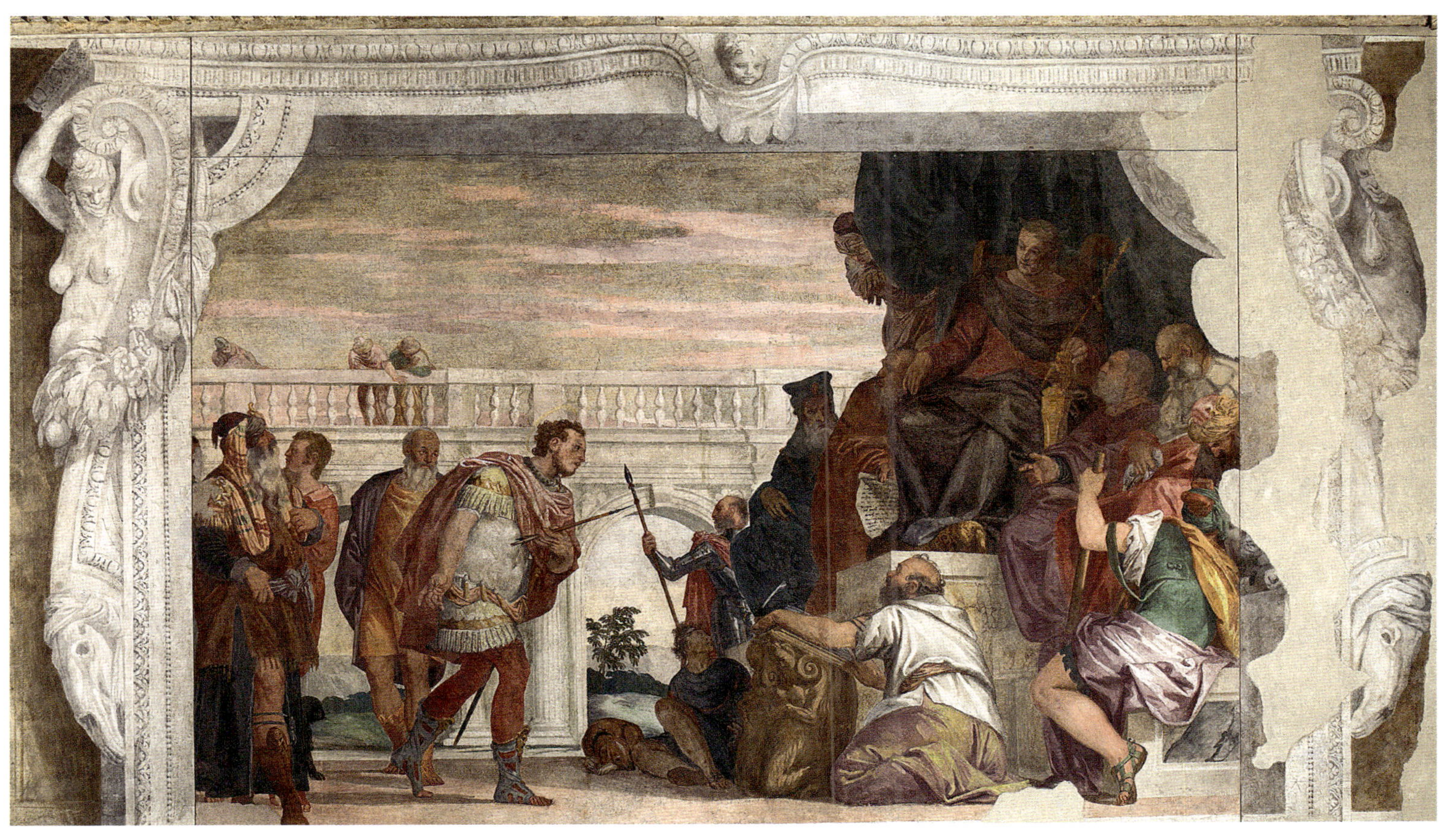

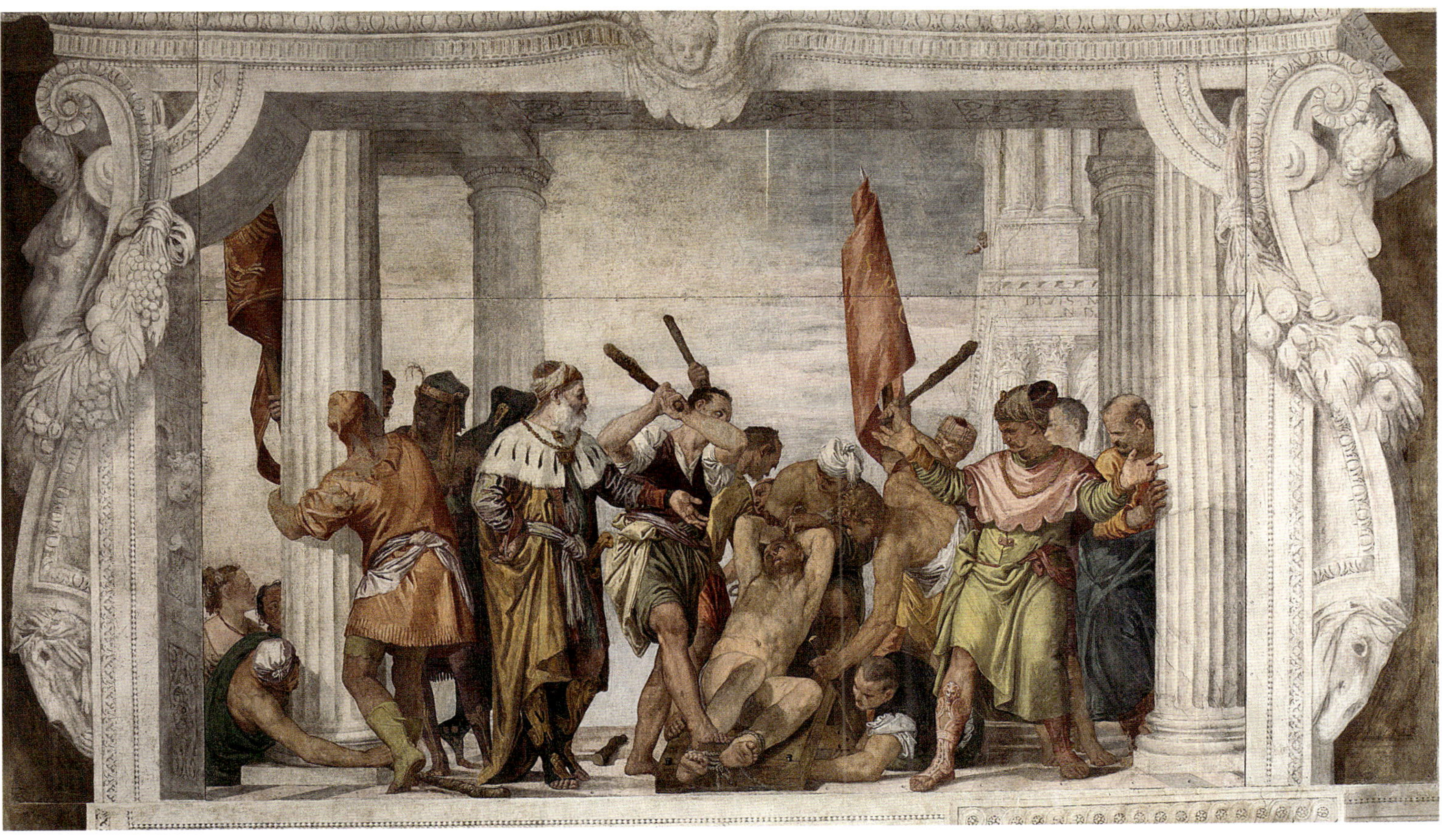

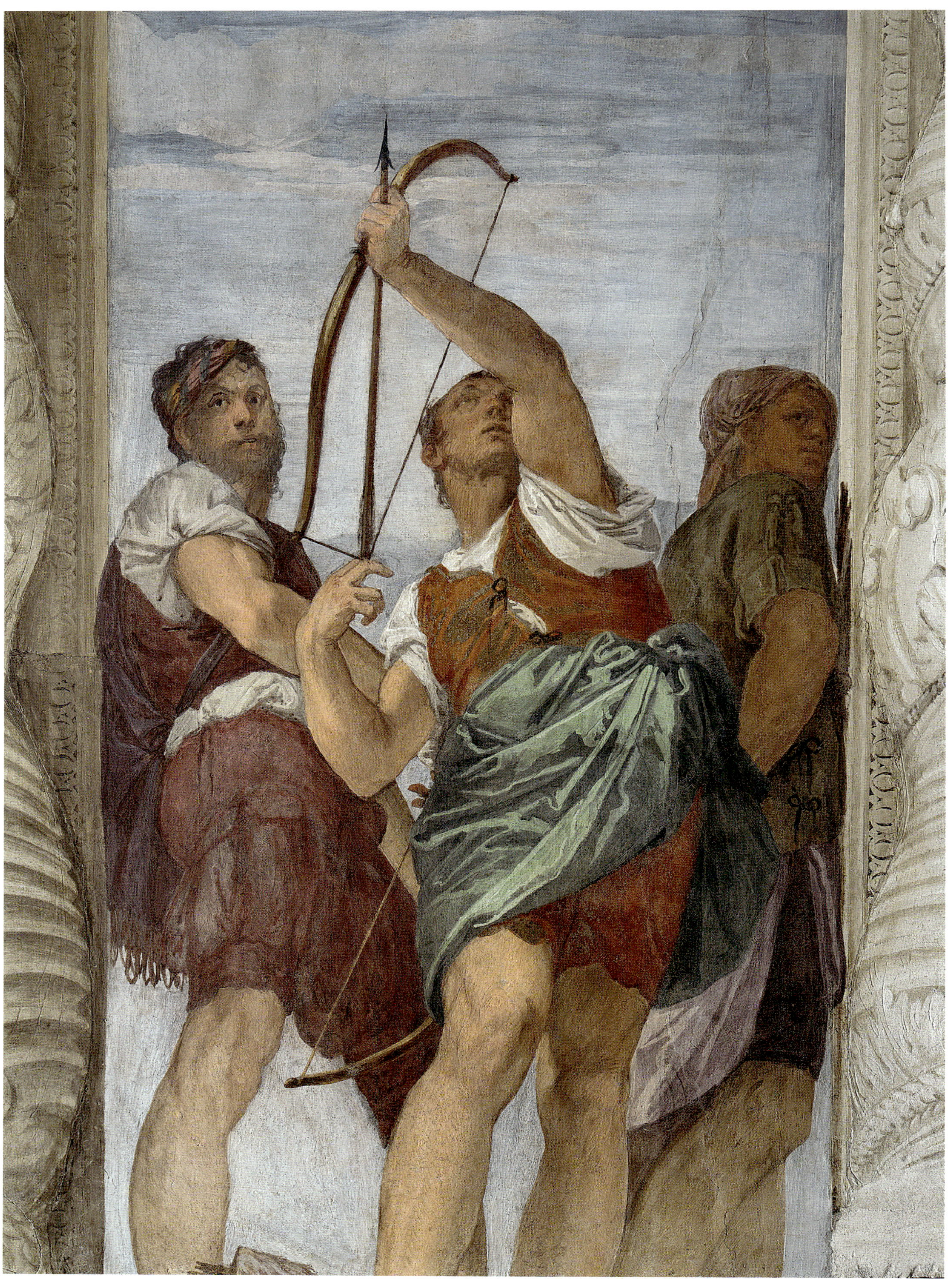

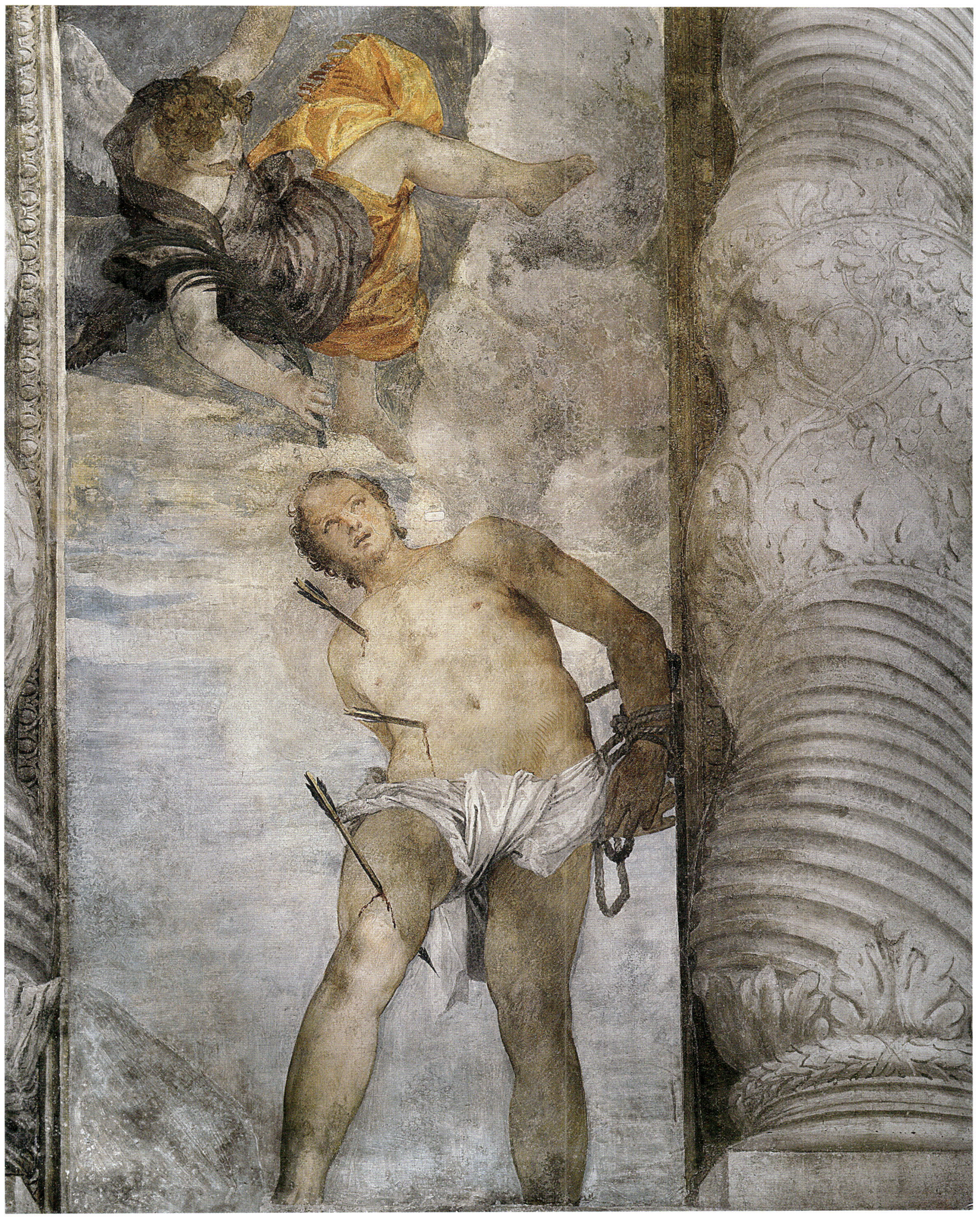

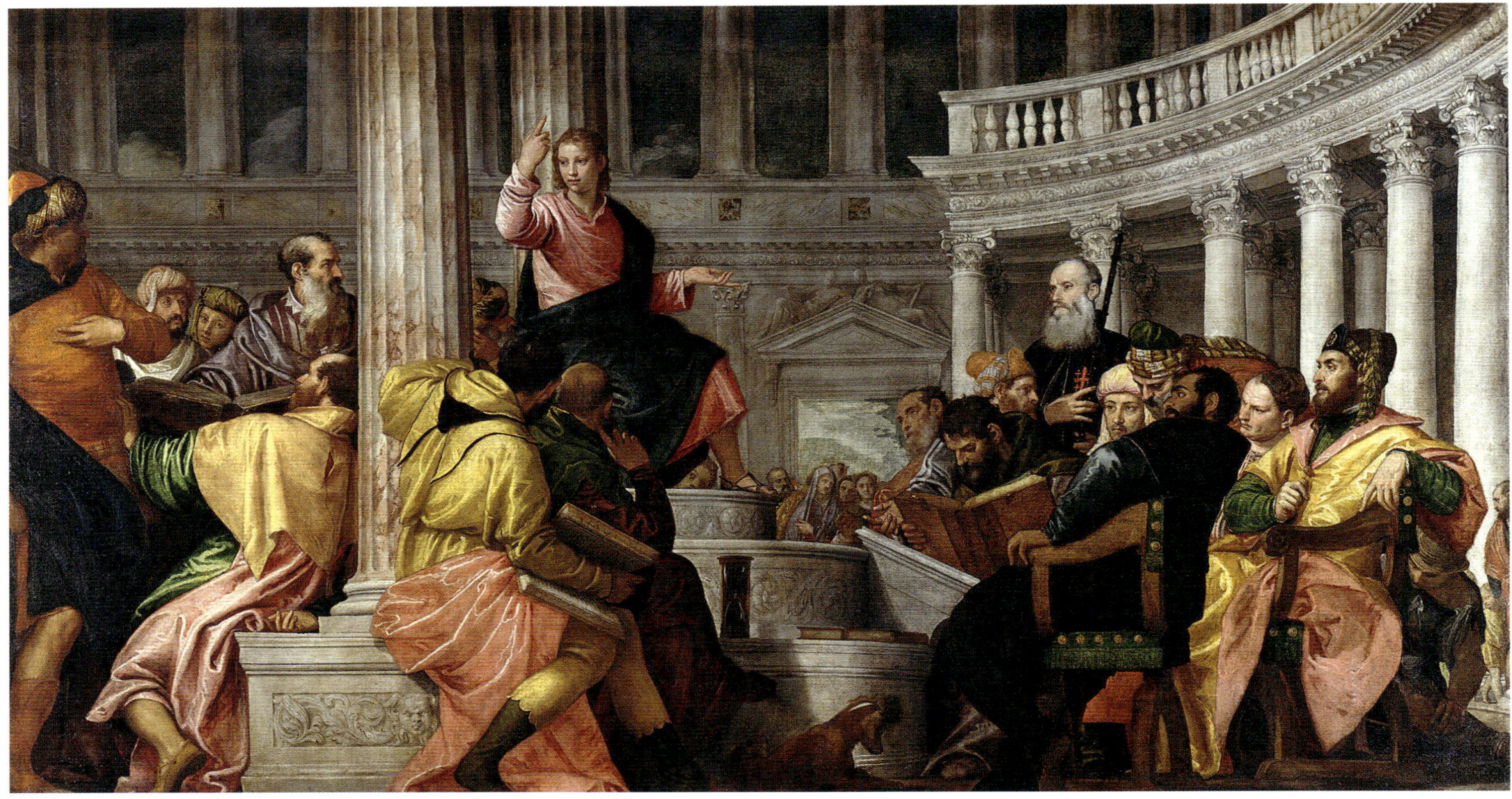

Christ among the Doctors, 1566-1567, canvas, 236 × 430 cm. Madrid, Museo del Prado, inv. 419

In the evident, methodical reference to the classical basilica architecture, as it was reproposed by Palladio, Paolo inserts a gallery of expressions, postures and gestures that we will find again in many of his narrative constructions. And, as on other occasions, he inserts and presents his patrons: here it is the unknown Knight of the Holy Sepulchre, with his staff, who soars over the bystanders, committed in listening to the Word of the divine young man.

the apex of the axis of the composition: expressive doctors of the Law look at him and glance at him, consulting their large books, while the divine child enumerates his arguments on his fingers. In an architecturally challenging space – a carefully studied reconstruction of a Roman basilica– the gathered lawyers show oriental headdresses, but above all the use of green in various shades stands out, in clothes and stockings. Only two characters, elderly and bearded, turn towards the Child in the attitude of the faithful: one, undoubtedly the man commissioning the artwork, wears the dress of a Knight of the Holy Sepulchre and holds a pilgrim's staff in his hand, and therefore the painting recalls his trip to the Holy Land, one of the most desired and coveted events for a faithful Venetian, as well as difficult and all in all adventurous. On a book consulted by the doctors of the law is painted "MCXLVIII" (1548), which initially led to place the work in the first juvenile catalogue, but the mastery is now wholly acquired and the architectural system, so carefully prepared, is derived from the engravings for the 1556 edition of Vitruvius. Of the canvas we only know that in 1648 it was in Casa Contarini in Padua, from 1686 it entered the Alcázar Palace in Madrid, perhaps purchased by Velázquez during his second trip to Italy (1649-1651).

Also in the summer of 1558 Paolo designed the organ case for San Sebastiano: it would be produced in autumn by the *marangon*, the cabinetmaker Domenico da Treviso, for a hundred ducats. Subsequently, on 3 September 1560, the engraver Francesco Fiorentino undertook to create the wooden cladding of the choir and the wall under the organ. The doors of the case, magnificently painted, will be delivered on 1 April 1560. With the doors closed, one can admire the *Presentation of Jesus in the Temple*; the architecture of the Temple in which the narration takes place is monumental and dominant, while the body of the Child supplies all the characters with light, and the old Simeon kneels, aware of the age of Grace open to humanity: the architecture, so magnificent, grandiose, well-kept and superb, testifies to its solidity and majesty.

When the music is played on the organ, the doors open and the scene of the *Probatic Pool* unfolds, where Paolo stages the story of John (1-17) in one of his most striking drawing tests: in

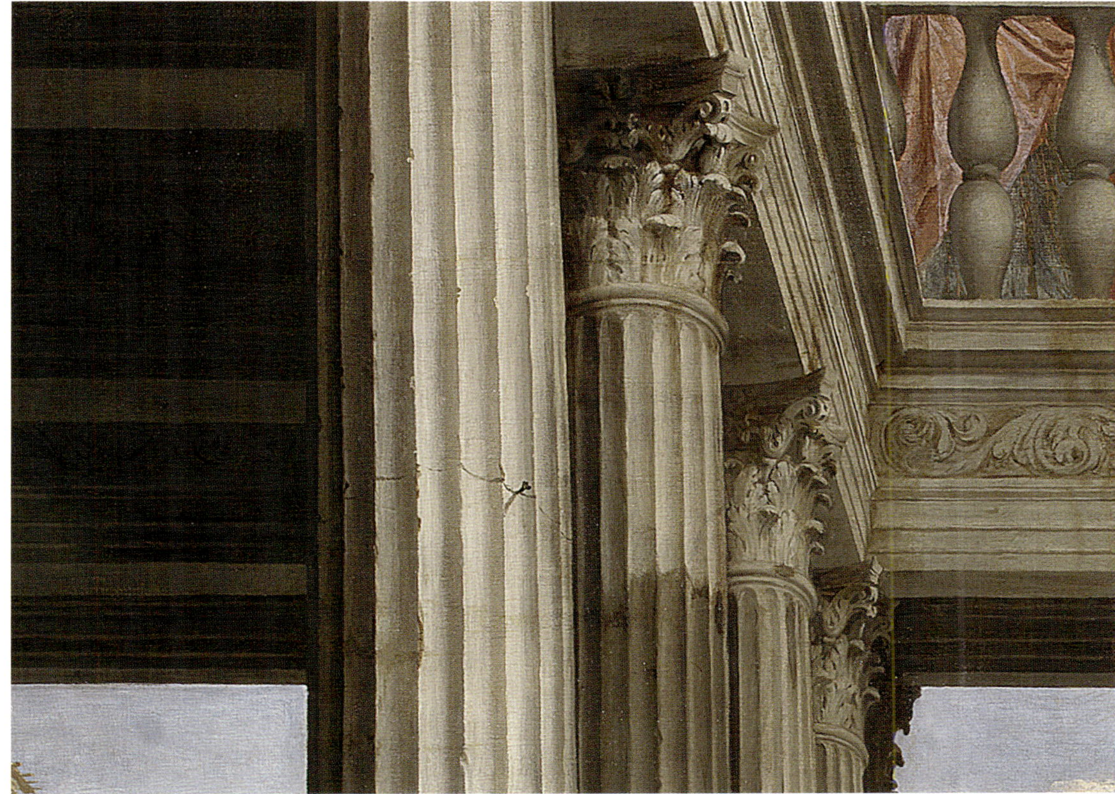

Supper in the House of Simon the Pharisee, approx. 1556, canvas, 315 × 451 cm, detail. Turin, Galleria Sabauda, inv. 580

In each of his works, Paolo Caliari proposed his own unique interpretation, a hidden detail, a hidden meaning: an allusive manifestation, sometimes in the keys of the comic, other times in the enigmatic taste of wit, so typical and present in his age. Here, for the last time, in a canvas conceived and created for the friars of a convent in his city, where his grandfather and his father had also worked, Paolo proposes on the column the trompe l'oeil of the driven nail, recognizable by the shadow; a nail that has caused a crack in the stone. This is how he recalls the name by which the family was known: the *Spezapreda*, stonebreakers or stonemasons in the local dialect.

the faithful transcription of the story, he proposed the foreshortening of the five porticoes with Corinthian columns, an elaborate trabeation in Sansovino style, a grandiose entrance with arch and reliefs. Here the angel falling upside down, hair in the wind, is impressively effective, while the figures of the sick have a realistic calibre given by the highly effective anatomical design. On the balcony of the organ there is also a *Nativity*, while two elegant chiaroscuro figures of Virtues complete the apparatus, with a *Saint Jerome* (on the left) and the *Blessed Pietro Gambacorta* (on the right). But those paintings on the lower part of the walls of the nave are not executed on the fresh plaster: Paolo used fat tempera to obtain effects of brightness, and so the image quickly decayed due to the salty humidity which corroded the plaster, and the four *Sibyls*, the eight *Apostles*, *David and Isaiah* would be much less legible in a few years.
The grandiose canvases for the organ case reveal how much Paolo Caliari, in 1560, perfectly mastered his technical means, the ones that Boschini, in 1674, would describe as follows:

> He mostly used to shade the cloths almost all of lacquer, not only the reds, but the yellows, the greens, and also the azures [...]. In highlighting them he used to take for the most part the yellowish, the orpiment, the red, and the minium; nor did he ever veil any cloth, be it of whatever colour one chooses: so that, if one sees a veiled cloth in a picture, believed to be by Paolo, one must consider it very carefully so as not to be deceived. And if the touch of the flesh does not have that vivacity so witty and lively, it will easily be something where he is tougher than Benedetto the brother, or Carletto the son, who also were followers of that vague manner.

In the meantime Paolo delivers an important canvas for the convent of Santi Nazaro e Celso in his native Verona, requested in 1556 (on 3 January he had signed a receipt for the down payment) but postponed due to the many commitments. It is the first *Supper in the House of Simon*. Made for the refectory, it was destined to play a proactive role in the succession of the famous Veronese *Banquets*, and it is also certainly, for Paolo, a sort of family affirmation, since just

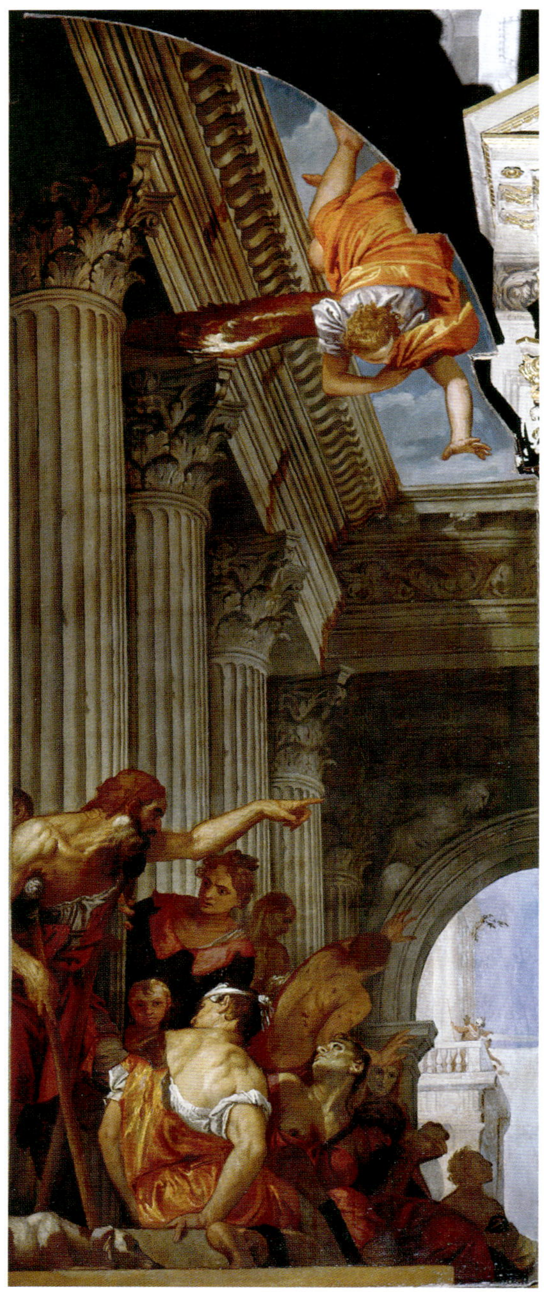

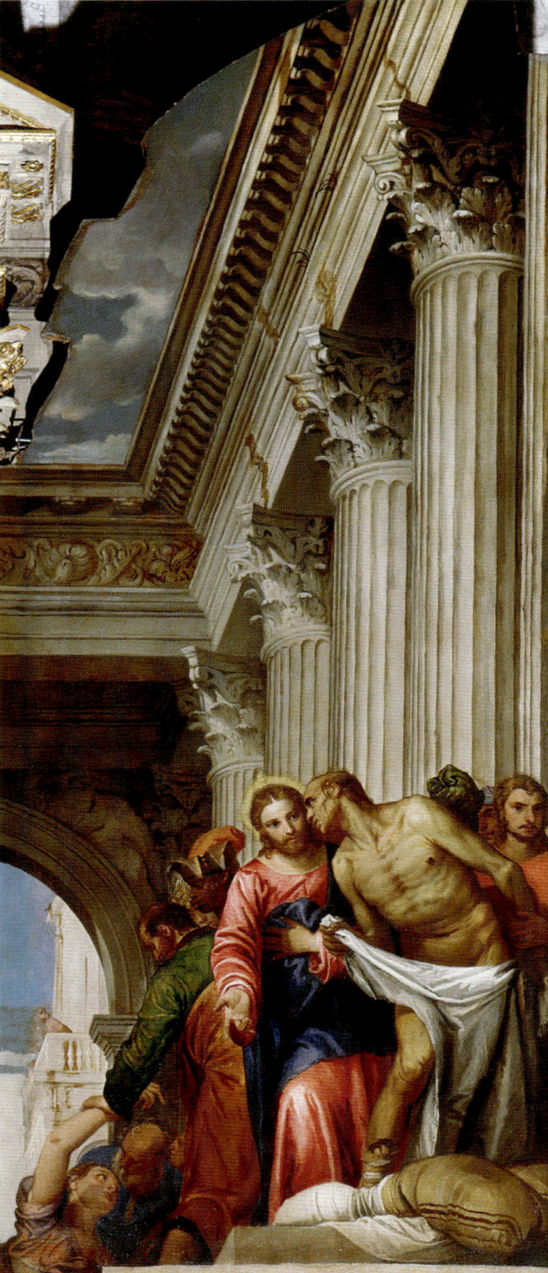

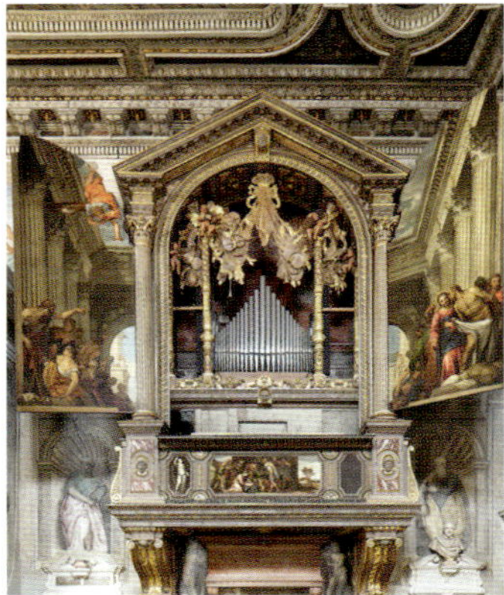

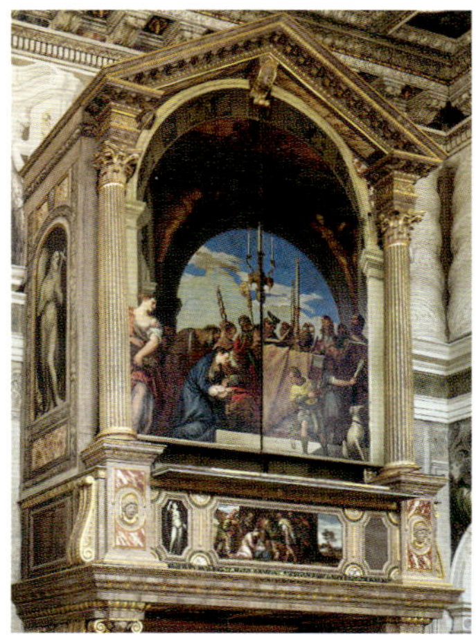

Probatic Pool or *the Miracle in Bethesda's Pool*, 1560, canvas, 490 × 190 cm. Venice, church of San Sebastiano, doors of the open organ

Presentation of Jesus in the Temple, 1560, canvas, 490 × 190 cm. Venice, church of San Sebastiano, doors of the closed organ

The centrality of architecture in Veronese's work is well represented in the general design of the organ case of San Sebastiano. From a monumental and properly structural point of view, the organ corresponds to the general design of Sansovino's Podacotaro funeral monument. The wooden structure designed by Veronese houses the four canvases, which in turn are supported by vaults and loggias and porticoes, rendered with the proportioned accuracy worthy of an architectural drawing manual. It is the original pictorial translation of the studies and drawings by Serlio and Palladio.

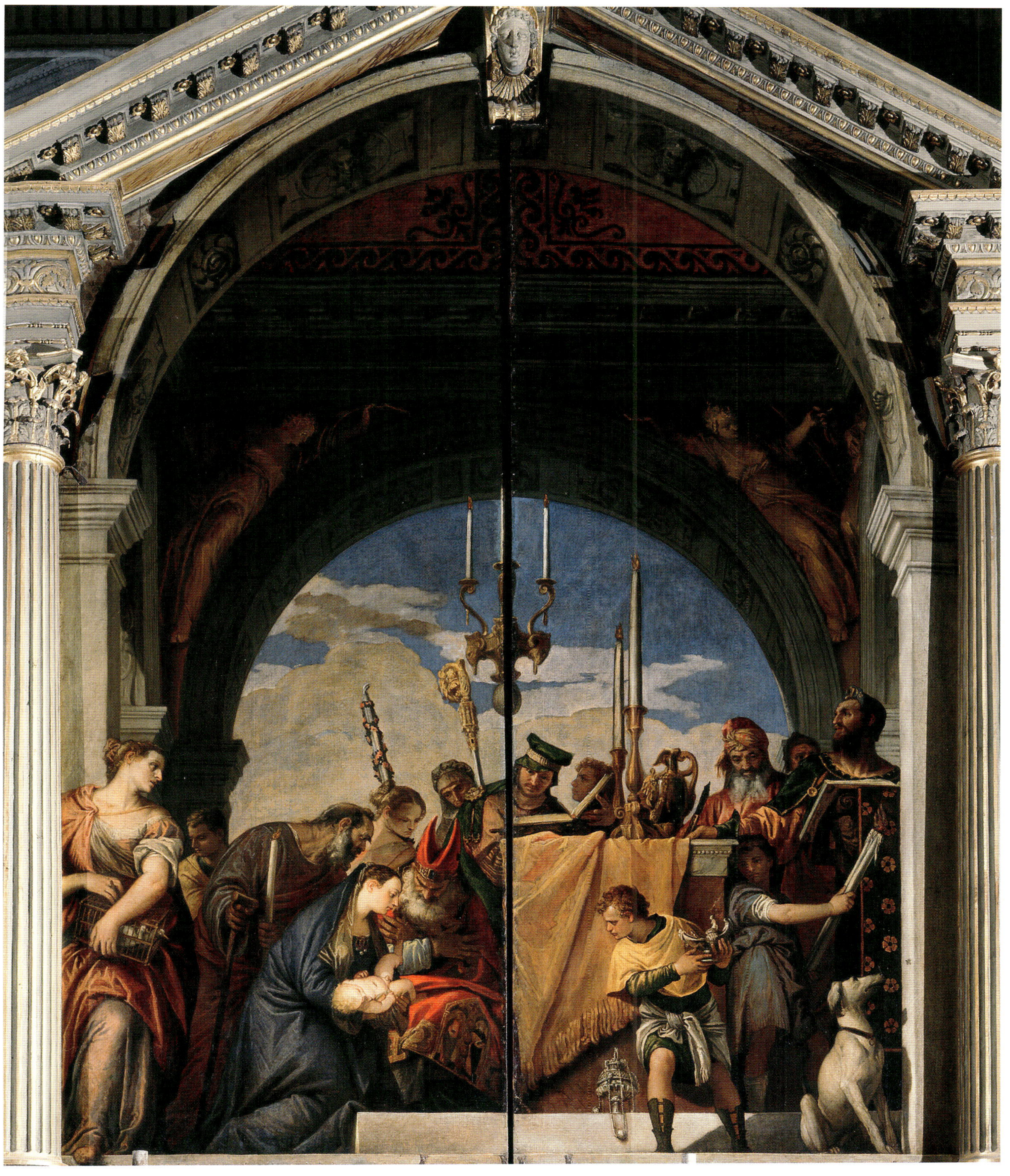

twenty years earlier his grandfather and father had created the floor of a chapel of the convent: that of San Biagio, by creating a design of perspective cubes in black basanite, Istrian white and red Verona marble. And it is no coincidence that right here, on the column in the foreground, Paolo paints a nail that seems to have created a fissure in the marble: it is the *spezapreda* nail. A proud signature in his hometown, in the places of his father and grandfather. It was an important commitment, because the reformed Benedictine order was a particularly important patron: Paolo would work at San Benedetto Po, at the abbey of Praglia, at Santa Giustina in Padua and above all in the very important, prestigious convent that occupied the whole island of San Giorgio Maggiore in Venice, right in front of Saint Mark stalls, at the entrance to the Giudecca canal, and facing the *Dogana da Mar*.

Madonna and Child, a Martyr Saint and Saint Peter, 1555-1560, canvas, 119 × 95 cm. Vicenza, Museo Civico, inv. A 77

Even the *Madonna and Child, a Martyr Saint and Saint Peter* – since 1826 in the Museo Civico of Vicenza by legacy of the Porto Godi family – should belong to a phase close to 1558. Here Paolo, in addition to exhibiting a Raphaelesque sweetness, is very remarkable for the representation of the typology of the elderly man in the bald Saint Peter, with a large beard, holding the keys of the Church with peremptory certainty, while the young Mother is all illuminated by the lily pink of her clothes, and strokes of brown lacquer provide thickness and depth to the whole group. The sweet saint on her right should be Saint Columba of Sens, identified both by the white dove and by the palm of martyrdom, and finally by the crown on her head: protector of fires and venerated in various Italian cities, her presence could be linked to the patronymic of the commissioner. It is a work of notable quality, especially in the supporting actors of the young Mother, very well defined.

And then there was another organ to decorate, this time for the church of San Geminiano; the necessary canvases were predictably put in place in 1560 since Francesco Sansovino already mentions them in 1561. Here too the architectural decoration is important: in an apsidal environment with a hemispherical dome, Paolo places two imposing figures of bishops: they are *Saint Geminianus and Saint Severus* while in niches he painted *Saint John the Baptist*, the contemplative life, and an armed saint, the active life of the Egyptian knight *Saint Menas*. The doors of the organ are now in the Galleria Estense in Modena.

The church of San Geminiano had been restructured in 1557 according to a project by Jacopo Sansovino. Once the work was completed, his father Benedetto Manzini had commissioned the monumental instrument. The figures painted by Paolo are truly impressive, created with fluid brushstrokes, with a light-colour exchange that produces luminescent effects. The copes are excellent, both decorated with Venetian fabrics of the greatest value; the portraits of elderly people are beautiful, especially the unknown bishop, perhaps Severus, the one who from Ravenna would have participated in a vision at the funeral of Geminianus in Modena. The choice is fully scenographic and reaches its peak in the knight Menas, confident of himself bordering on bravado, head held high and proud, gaze thoughtful, left foot beyond the limit of space with a perfect illusionistic effect. It is an episode of true pictorial joy, essentially acting on the expressive varieties of only two colours, red and bronze, which the haughty halberdier wears, capable of draping his cloak with extreme elegance. The flash of light on the sleeve of the white shirt tucked up on the muscular arm is of rare effectiveness, all warmed up by the strength of the colour. It could be said that the substantial adherence to a classicist line has allowed here the perfect fusion between the Roman legacies and the colouristic luminosity of the Venetians. But then, in the placement of the two saints in the apse coloured with grotesques, the tradition is also recovered in the "sacred conversation" of the Altarpiece of Saint Job by the unforgettable Giovanni Bellini.

When the church was demolished in 1807, the canvas with the holy Bishops entered the imperial Habsburg collections, from 1836 in Vienna, to then return to Italy in 1919, assigned to the Galleria Estense. The *Saint John the Baptist* was taken to the Imperial Villa of Stra, then to the

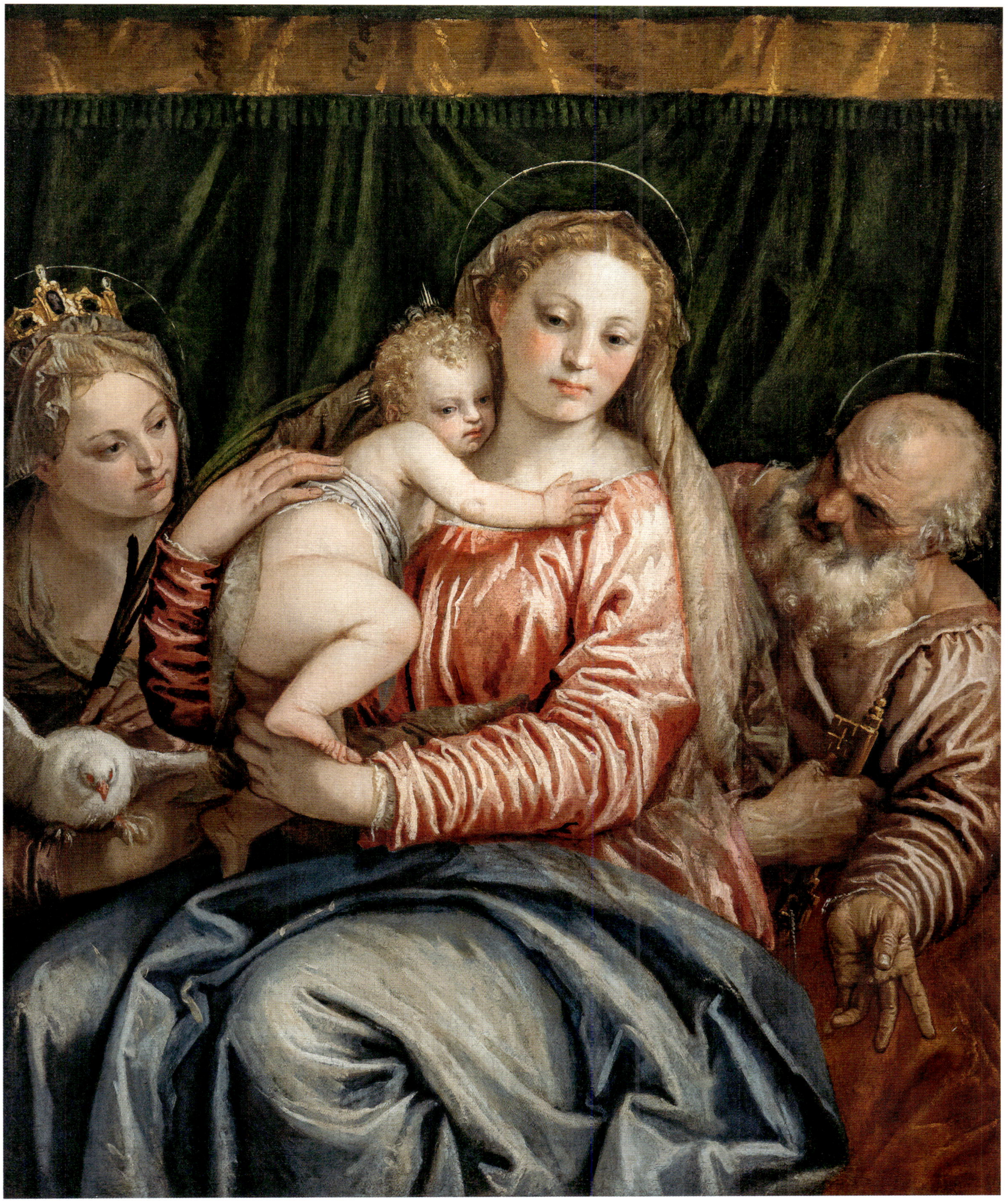

Royal Palace of Milan, to be reunited with its companions in Modena in 1924. The *Saint Menas* had instead remained in the warehouses of the Venice Academy, before being delivered at the Modena Academy of Fine Arts in 1811.

Is it possible that in these years, so crucial for the achievement and deployment of the narrative and expressive skills of the young painter, now in his thirties, Paolo found the time to go to Rome? This was Ridolfi's suggestion, saying that he would travel in the retinue of Girolamo Grimani, ambassador of obedience to the Pope. Grimani went to Rome three times, in 1555, 1560 and 1566; Paolo may have reached the city in 1560, when Michelangelo was alive and work was progressing on St. Peter's, still without a dome. A visit that would certainly have fortified him in two directions: the direct knowledge of the ancient world, formed from the earliest childhood with his father and the sure suggestions of Giovanni Caroto and Sanmicheli, and the direct appreciation of the works by Raphael and Michelangelo in the Vatican, known otherwise only through drawings and prints. However, we have no proof of this trip, or of a graphic memory: we know that it was necessary to be part of a retinue of a cardinal or an ambassador in order to be able to admire the ancient and modern works of art up close. It is unlikely that documents will emerge proving this stay, which was not decisive but certainly reinforcing for Caliari and his classicism. Through the multiple relationships with patrician families, whose exponents were in constant motion and brought descriptions, objects and a quantity of drawings from their travels, both Paolo and Benedetto were able to find suggestions and expressive solutions. In a letter from Benedetto to Giacomo Contarini, after Paolo's death, he expressly referred to the "faux paintings" or the trompe l'oeil of the frescoed "caves" or the imperial rooms that had recently been excavated. We do not know whether these, like the inventions of Perin del Vaga in Castel Sant'Angelo in 1545, were known directly or instead through notebooks of drawings and prints.

In 1561, the chapter of the friars decided to modify the windows of the presbytery in the church of San Sebastiano "come et quando ordinarà m. Paolo" ("how and when m. Paolo will order"). Meanwhile the painter is preparing to decorate the dome and the walls behind the altar with frescoes. Works practically lost, only the chiaroscuro images of *Saint Paul the Hermit* (left) and *Saint Onuphrius* (right), next to the altar, are saved, though reduced to a larval state.

In the summers of 1561 and 1562 Paolo Caliari returns to the mainland: it is the right season to paint. In Venice not only did the humidity and saltiness ruin the frescoes, but it was not possible to work on the plaster for most of the year due to the extreme cold. In the recent past there had already been years of exceptional rigor, such as the winter of 1547-1548, when Lake Garda was frozen; many still remembered having seen the entire frozen lagoon decades earlier: and in the previous century the thickness of the ice had been such that people went by ox-drawn carts from Mestre to Venice. And there will still be very harsh winters: those of 1568-1569, and of 1570-1571 with two meters of snow in Turin, and again the following year, with the port of Marseilles not navigable due to blocks of ice. Paolo and Benedetto and assistants must therefore have greatly appreciated the summers of Maser with the warm sun, the light auras, the exuberant nature, the ripe grapes. They must have been happy to decorate the villa of Daniele and Marcantonio Barbaro, the building designed and built with innovative architectural solutions by Andrea Palladio.

It will remain the most memorable civil enterprise in Veronese's exceptional pictorial career; even more exceptional is for us being able to fully enjoy its beauty even today, five centuries later.

Saint Geminianus and Saint Severus, 1560, canvas for organ doors, 341 × 240 cm. Modena, Galleria Estense, inv. 407

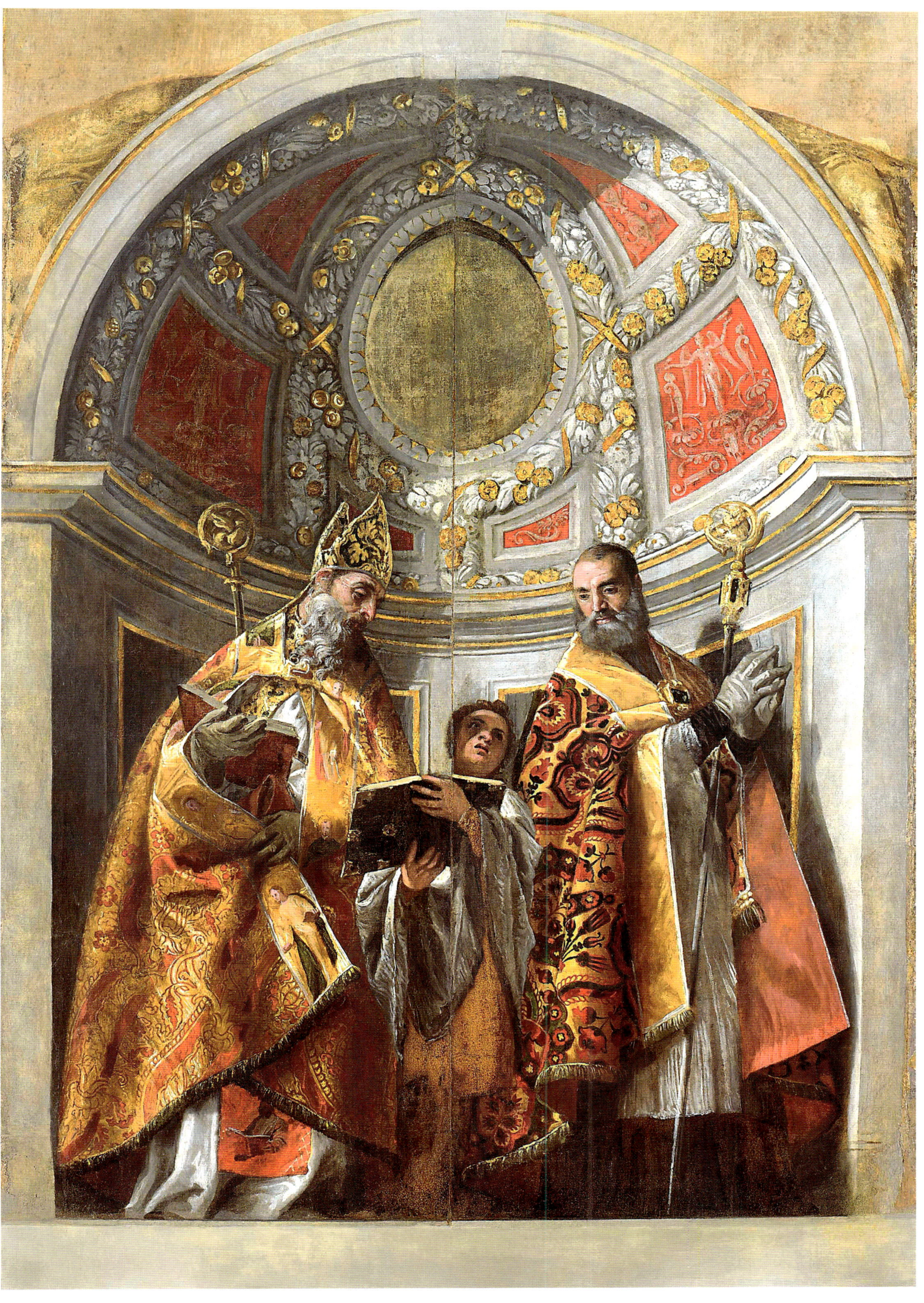

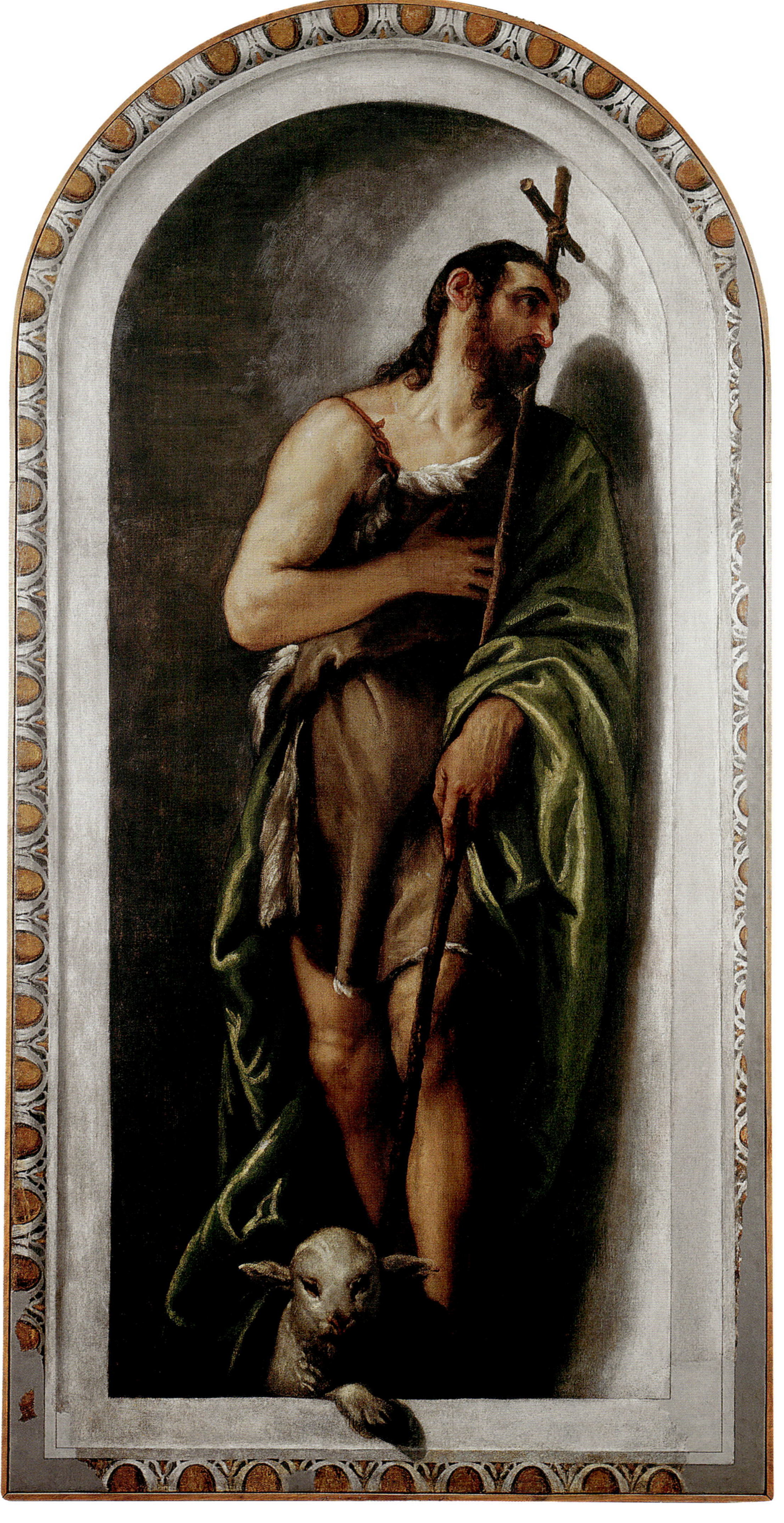

Saint John the Baptist, 1560,
canvas for organ doors,
247 × 122 cm. Modena,
Galleria Estense, inv. 408

Saint Menas, 1560,
canvas for organ doors,
247 × 122 cm. Modena,
Galleria Estense, inv. 409

One can only agree with Marco Boschini who indicated in the Saint Menas the "readiest, and most graceful figure, that the author made". The figure of the soldier, energetic and thoughtful, haughty and totally sure of himself, is accentuated by the contrast with the opposite, the humble, contemplative, resigned John the Baptist. Almost as if Paolo Caliari wanted to refer to human types, to the characters expressed by the theory of Temperaments: here the Sanguine and the Phlegmatic confront each other, with an energy and pictorial ability that was to be doubled in music, with open organ doors.

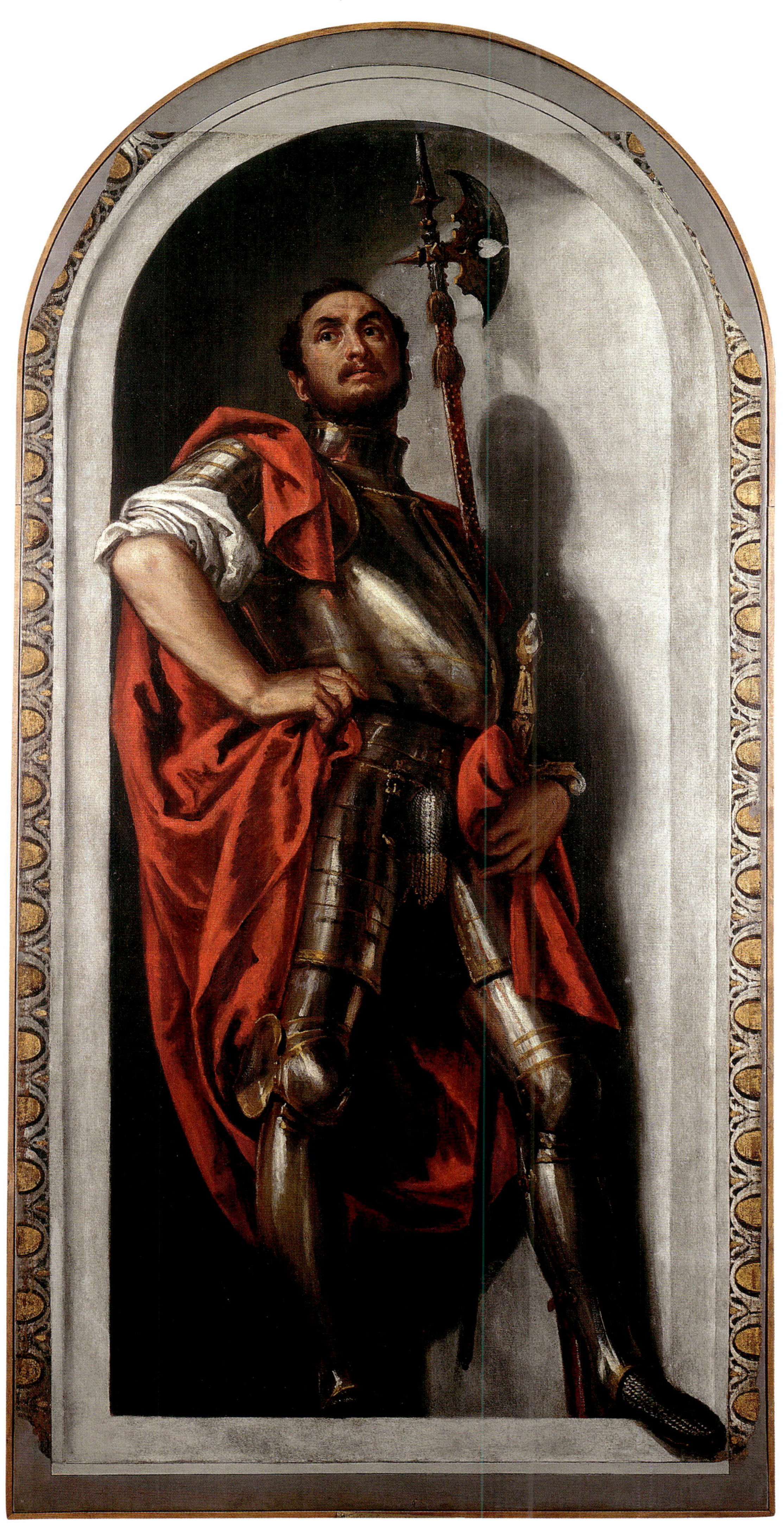

CHAPTER IV

Summers at Maser

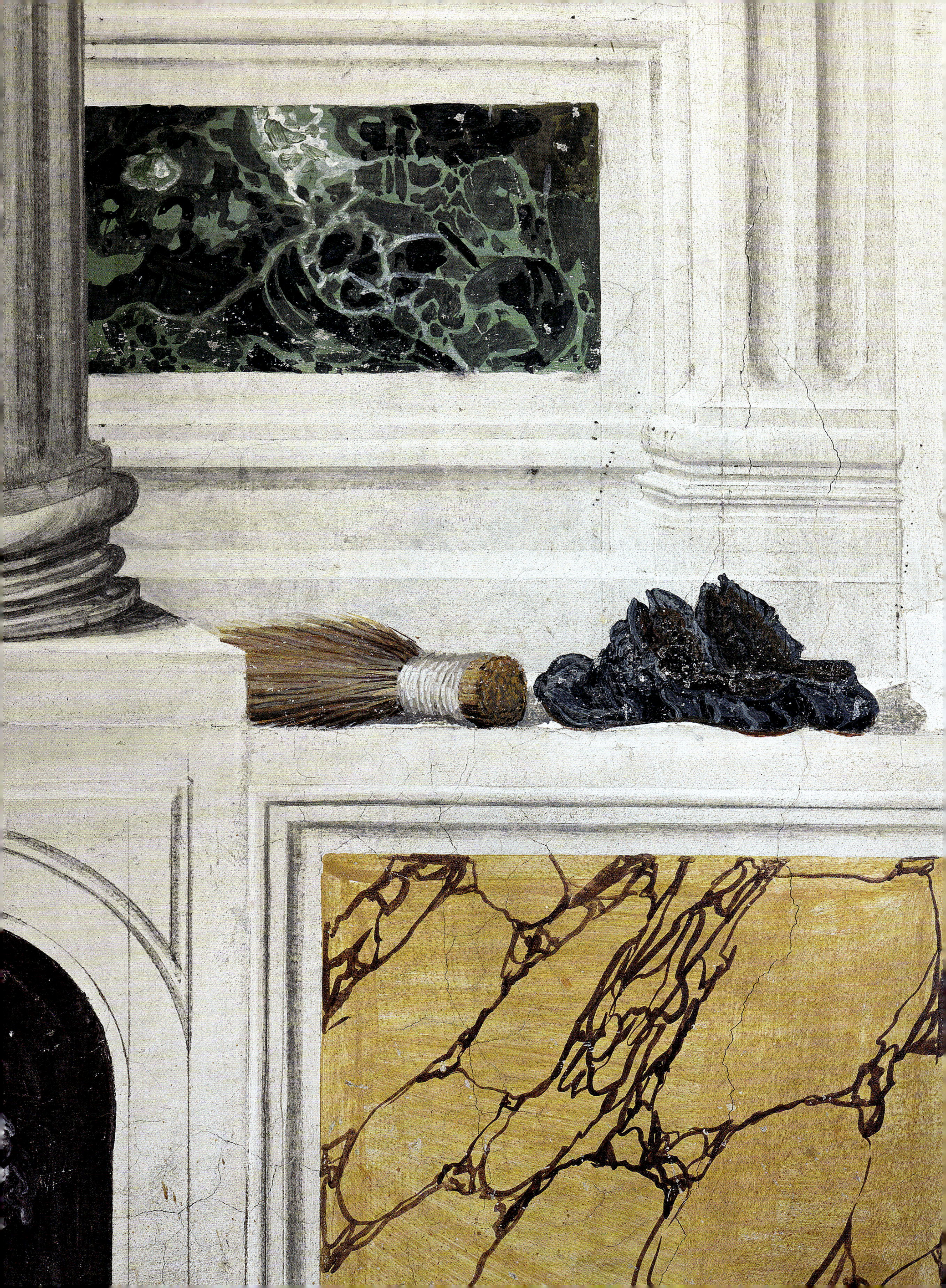

Who left them? Did they forget them, or did they just take them off? Why are they there? And how worn they are! Male or female? Work shoes or slippers? And why is there a toilet brush next to them? For five hundred years the shoes have been questioned, and obviously they don't answer. Veronese's shoes, obviously painted.

If in one of the frescoed rooms of Villa Barbaro in Maser, we do not look at the ceiling, where a great mythological play takes place, but on the walls that pretend to be elegant columns, we find a pair of slippers and a toilet brush. A trompe l'oeil by Paolo Caliari, a game and a small enigma, which however is seminal to understand how to read the whole, extraordinary decoration. Extraordinary for many reasons: it has been preserved despite neglect, changes of ownership, evolution of tastes, becoming dull, Austrian cannon fire, since Maser is not far from Asolo and Cornuda, it is on the right bank of the Piave, and the Austrian armies had fortified on the left bank, between October 1917 and November 1918. Movements of troops and artillery fire avoided the Villa: a narrow escape, a fate unfortunately not shared by all the marvellous residences of Venetian culture. Today Villa Barbaro is the only almost complete testimony of Veronese as a fresco painter of manor houses, from the Soranza onwards.

The series of frescoed rooms is new for the variety of scenes, meanings, inventive solutions, allegories and portraits, in the most grandiose private decorative system of the Italian sixteenth century. Where landscapes framed by columns, entablatures, tympanums, balustrades, windows, doors, architraves are followed by statues that pretend to be marble, fictitious bronze giants, glimpses of heaven crossed by winged geniuses and clouds on which they have settled, holding their emblems, figures of myth, allegories and similar elements, lively presences of the owner's family; and still pets and hunting dogs, lapdogs and hunting species, and musicians, and only painted doors from which pages and little girls look out, snooping. And much more.

Can we wear those shoes offered by the painter, placed on the threshold, to better read these illusions?

Their appearance should guide us: we just have to recover a verse by Petrarch, so well known that it became, at the time, an aphorism used to indicate the characters of a staging; to judge whether a work, or a verse, a poem, a prose, was "Matter of buskins and not of socci." It is the yardstick proposed in the *Trionfo d'Amore* (IV, 88) to separate the material of the noble, tragic theatre, where the actors wore buskins – elegant thick-soled sandals – from the thesis for which socci, the low and everyday shoes, slippers and poor clogs, were deliberately used by comedians.

In these rooms, the shoes painted by Veronese say so, the material is for "socci", there is no tragic height but human ambiguity: after all we are in the villa. And it will be comedy.

We will find the essential characters of the theatre that represents life and humanity, in its daily unfolding between drama and pantomime, ideal and desire, worrying and being moved, farce and joke. Movement, as we will go from room to room marvelling at each proposal, and singing, as instrumentalists welcome us with the most varied and joyful sounds, and other musicians will accompany us. There will also be an offer to Dionysus, present in the guise of Bacchus, in the room decorated with a large bower of grapes, offering the intoxicating drink

Toilet Brush and Slippers,
Room of the Conjugal Love,
1560-1561, fresco, 50 × 50 cm.
Maser, Villa Barbaro

The south wall is decorated with imitation marble plinths on which illusionistic columns rest. A sorghum toilet brush and a pair of work slippers have been painted in the intercolumn on the right, with quick strokes, superimposed on the architectural fresco. The cleaning carried out in 1958 demonstrated its authenticity: we presume it is therefore a typical expression of the Veronese taste for allusion and deception: not only an ironic trompe l'oeil, but a possible interpretation of the room and of the entire cycle, which proposes in each scene a high and cultured reading and a low and ironic reading, in the style of sixteenth-century comedy.

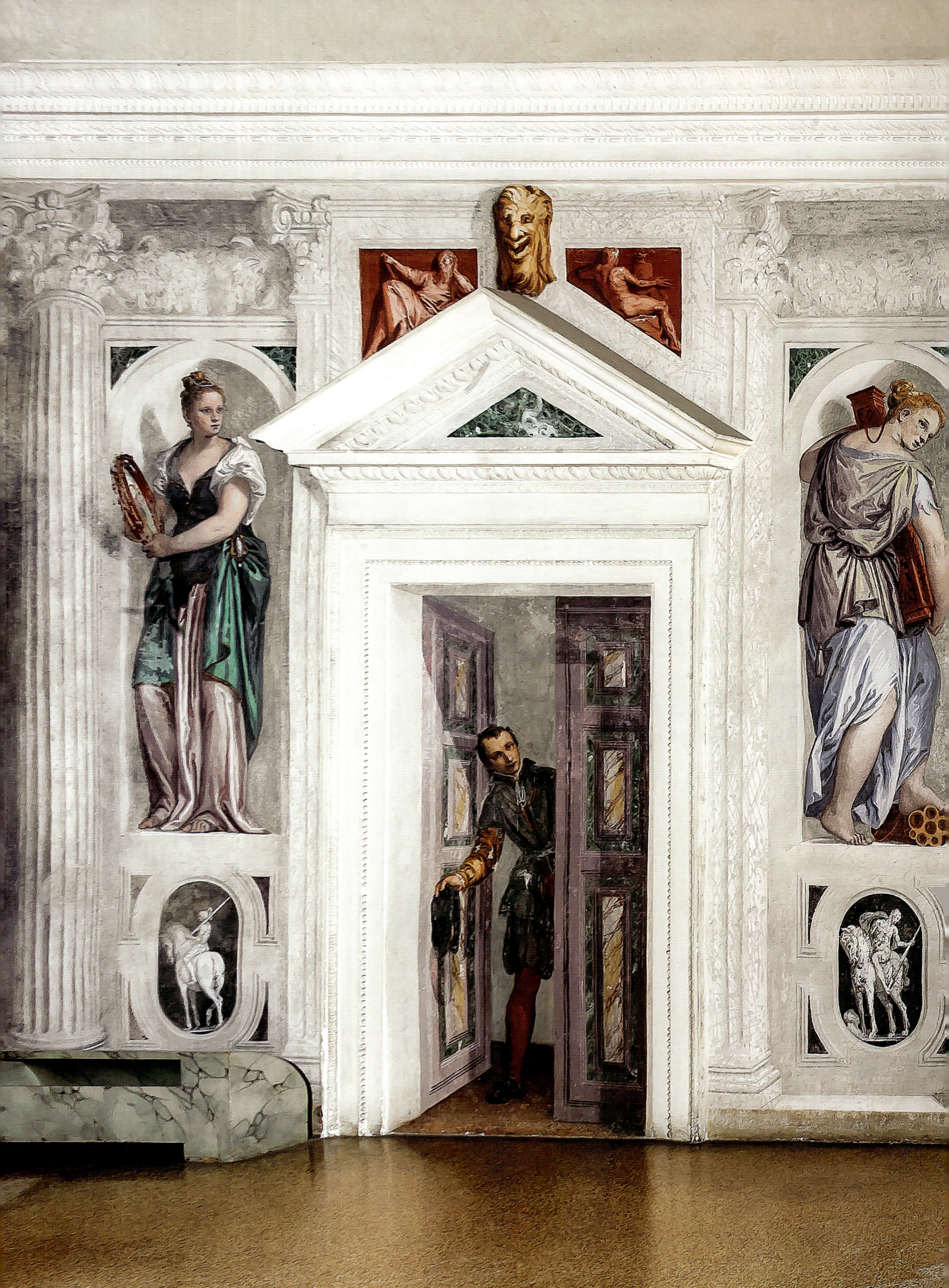

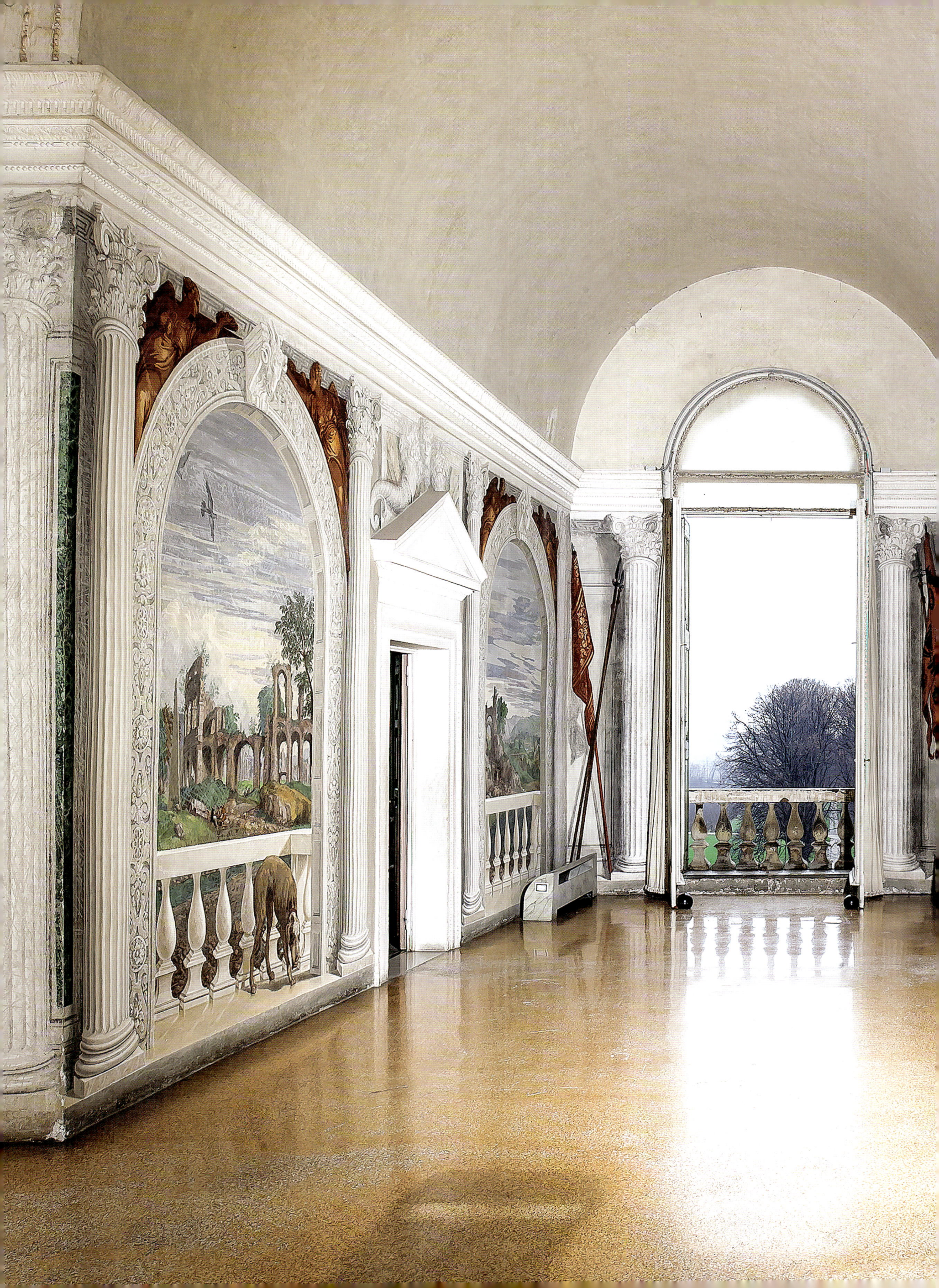

of which he is the master; and again the images are presented with the whole repertoire of misunderstandings, double meanings, various quarrels and possible jokes. Finally, like any comedy, it is ambiguous: it says and doesn't say, it lets itself be interpreted and hides; it alludes and does not resolve. It is exactly the typology of the comedies staged, with their own amusement and that of the spectators of the same social milieu, by the Compagnie delle Calze formed by young Venetian nobles.

It is necessary to go through the rooms without indulging too much in serious interpretations, which all in all are ill-suited to the place and time, to the painter and to the patrons, who appreciated and inhabited it, and to the lucky guests who were welcomed as "guests not guests", as stated by an inscription on the gable of the window at the entrance: "Nil tecti sub tecto/ hospes non hospes". Nothing secret under the roof, the guest is not a guest. Immediately on the façade, on the tympanum dominated by the imperial eagle of the Patriarchate of Aquileia with the coat of arms of the Barbaro, there is a scene that is not without ambiguity: two robust young men, symmetrical to each other, naked, from the back, riding monstrous animals kidnap, or at least seize with great force, naked maidens; at the extreme corners two cupids are having fun. Right from the entrance, the show is prepared, declined in variations of musical harmony: between human beings and anthropomorphic gods, sounds and images, landscape and dreams. But also between husband and wife.

The increased demand for decorations for private villas in the countryside was a phenomenon that characterized Venetian pictorial history for decades: none, however, had the quality and quantity of inventions as completed as the Villa Barbaro in Maser. Paolo Veronese will become the singer of the entire cultural horizon of the best Venetian intellectual patriciate, represented by the brothers Daniele and Marcantonio, linked by a common harmony of taste, educated in the cult of virtue and wisdom, with similar careers as very high republican officials, since Marcantonio was a magistrate and ambassador, decisive in negotiating the long peace with the Ottoman Empire, and Daniele was a scholar and "elected patriarch", moreover without taking sacred vows, as successor – but he never was – of the patriarch of Aquileia. As a matter of fact a magistrate of the Serenissima. Maser's project was asked to Andrea della Gondola, the master known as Palladio, because with him the architecture of the ancients truly lived again, in elegance and measure worthy of Pallas Minerva. Andrea directed its building until 1559, then the patrons wanted Veronese to decorate the representation and reception rooms, and the private studios; they certainly submitted to him a general idea and a program that the painter had to translate and interpret.

Daniele Barbaro, trained as a humanist, was also passionate about astronomy, a musicologist and above all a scholar of architecture and the science of perspective; his brother Marcantonio, a diplomat and merchant, was also passionate about the mechanical arts, a competent painter and amateur sculptor; the villa was supervised by his wife Giustiniana Giustinian as the great mistress of the house. Designed with authentic scenographic skill, functionality and classical rigour, there has been much discussion as to whether the illusionistic devices of the decoration dialogue or instead correct the Palladian architecture. The painter seems to multiply the spaces with deception: squares and breakthroughs towards landscapes of pure fantasy, memories of landscapes imagined or seen in other paintings and prints, in fact unreal even though it is a matter of a possible nature. Fantastic landscapes from ancient fairy tales, in the taste of classicism, inhabited by modern figurines.

Veronese will create fake doors and fake niches, large glimpses of luminous skies on plastered vaults, piling up balustrades, overdoors, illusory bas-reliefs, simulating bronze statues and polite little dogs; all in the spaces of eurythmic scanning. Palladio himself would have considered the decoration excessive and distorting, since he does not mention it in his presentation of Maser's project and drawing, in *I quattro libri dell'architettura*, which also lacks a reference to the plastic apparatuses of Alessandro Vittoria. But that emptiness can be explained by the publishing vi-

Previous pages
Cross Room, 1560-1561, fresco.
Maser, Villa Barbaro

The large room connects the different rooms. The walls are entirely frescoed with illusionistic architectural and marble effects. On the walls of the smaller wing, eight figures of women with musical instruments appear (interpreted as Muses). A Youth and a Maiden come out of false doors. Fantasy landscapes are on the walls of the main arm. Military garbs in the corners of the minor arm. Cameos with mythological figures on bases.

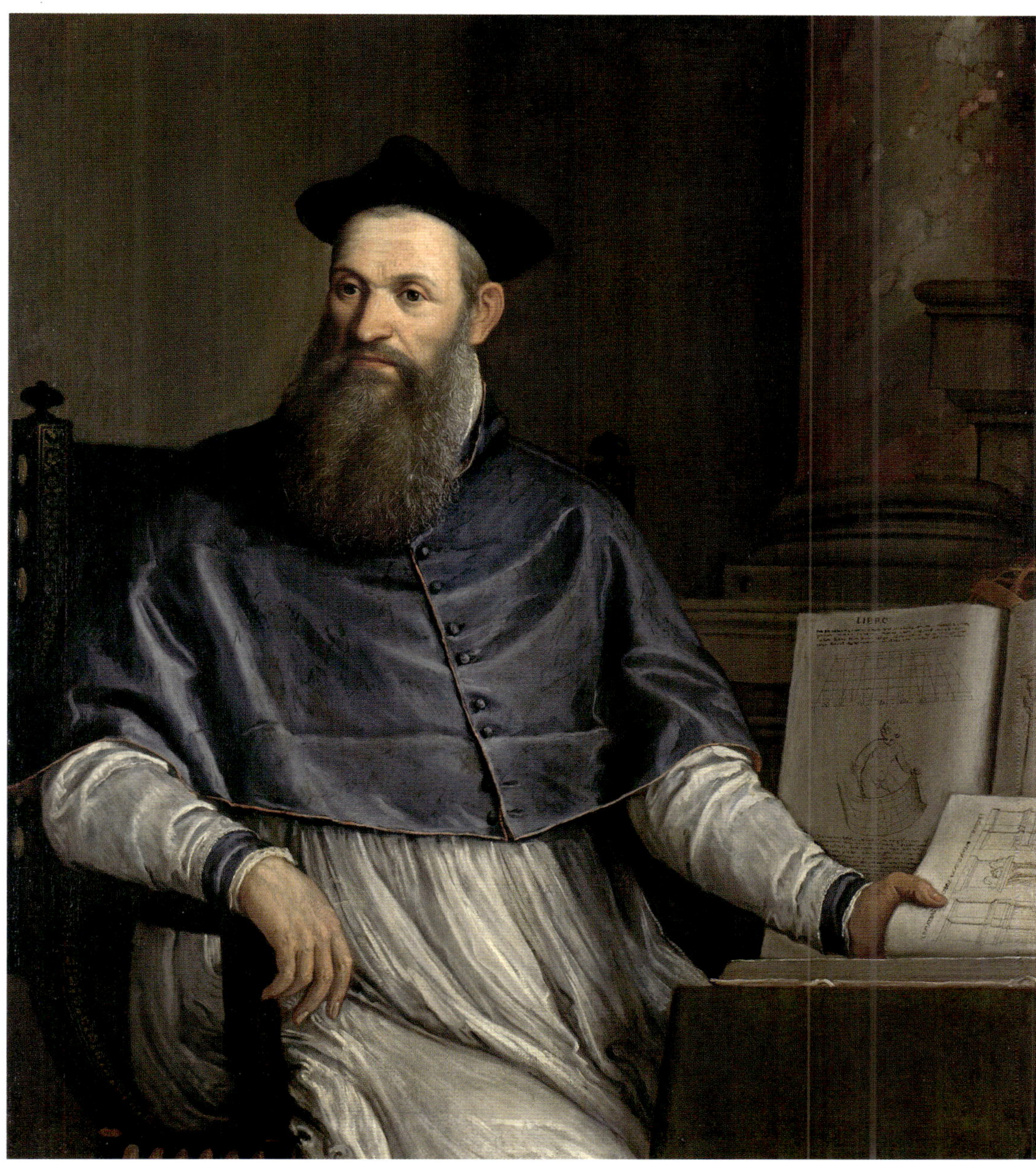

Portrait of Daniele Barbaro, 1557-1562, canvas, 121 × 105.5 cm. Amsterdam, Rijksmuseum, inv. 2529 B6

The portrait of Daniele Barbaro, the one who had promoted and supported Paolo's first activity in Venice, and then entrusted him, with his brother Marcantonio, with all the decoration of the Villa in Maser, is one of the highest proofs of Veronese as a portrait painter. The painter did not innovate from a compositional point of view, he exercised all his skill in the treatment of ecclesiastical robes, still proving to be a master in the articulation of shades of black and white, and then presented a portrait that not only corresponded to the physiognomy of the patrician but also portrays his interests in architecture and mechanics, his attitude as a scholar and humanist who restores antiquity, a serene explorer of the arts of building.

cissitudes of the book, while the intersections of mutual esteem between Palladio and Veronese are many and varied over the decades, even after that decorative cycle. In fact Veronese does not correct Palladio as he had not corrected Scarpagnino in San Sebastiano: he decorates in the taste of the time by superimposing narration on the neatness of the white spaces of architecture, above all he captures the light, he places himself in the spaces, sets backdrops, by their nature fictitious and temporary. But the architectural sign, the perfect spatial and human measure of Palladio remains in every environment; the internal decorations are built on an architectural design, the figures and images are inserted in the architectural order, like paintings or backgrounds, and the frame will establish their role: thus the landscapes that can be seen between the painted columns must evoke other spaces, rest the eye and build reminiscences. These were also the assumptions of the now lost decorations for the Paduan palaces of the humanists Alvise Cornaro and Marco Mantova Benavides.

Daniele Barbaro used a few adjectives to praise a "convenient" painting: vagueness, sweetness, quickness. The most suitable terms for Veronese, similar to the expressions that a painter and intellectual such as Federico Zuccari would use, the most international artist of his time, present in Venice between 1563 and 1565, working for the Grimanis of Santa Maria Formosa, and

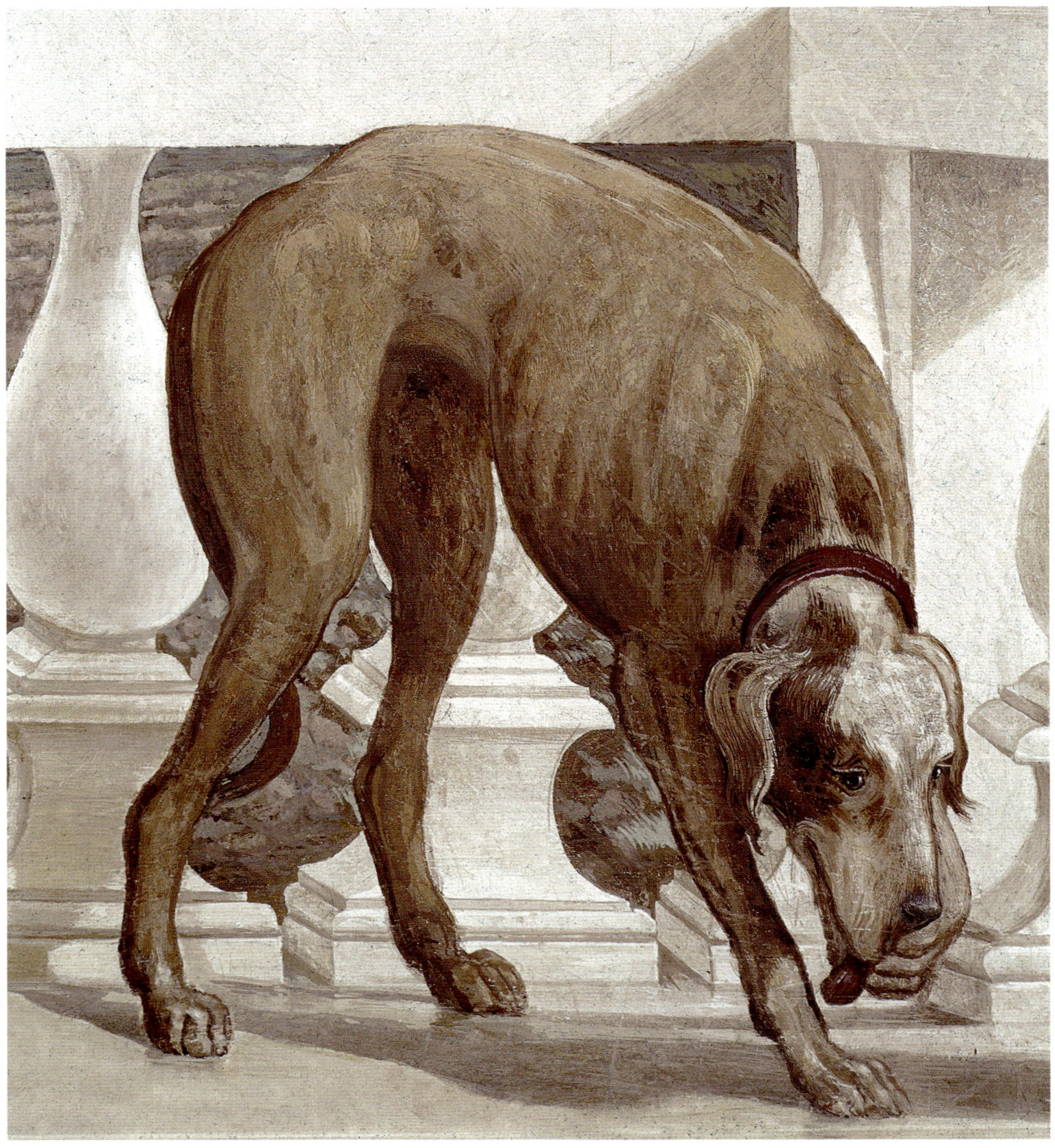

The Hunting Dog along the Balustrade, Cross Room, 1560-1561, fresco. Maser, Villa Barbaro

The appearance of the dog emphasizes even more the three-dimensional effect and the depth of the background with the landscape beyond the balustrade. The shadow play, which imitates a summer afternoon, is very careful. The dog that licks its paw, taken in an expressive moment, is extremely natural.

On pages 110-111
Room of the Conjugal Love, Ceiling, 1560-1561, fresco. Maser, Villa Barbaro

The scene on the ceiling of the east corner room has been interpreted differently. The characters are undoubtedly Hymenaeus, the patron god of marriage: he is sitting quietly and has left his sandals on the cloud; Juno leans on the (marriage) yoke, naked Venus invites silence with her finger to her lips, two spouses are followed by a character carrying the reins; Eros also appears. Is this the representation of marriage and the duties of the bride, or rather a Tribunal convened for a suspected treason?

accompanying Palladio on the Venetian shipyards. In his *Lamento della Pittura su l'onde venete*, he regretfully recalls: "But what shall I say about Paolo Veronese,/ Magnanimous, courteous, and excellent,/ Who gave an end to a thousand beautiful enterprises./ Of the most beautiful joys of the East/ This one placed a necklace around my neck, / And a large pendant of white pearls." He had personally known that painter of *zoie*, jewels, and had become his friend by frequenting his studio, as Ridolfi recalls: "While he found himself in Venice, this [Federico Zuccari] often visited his friend Paolo, and I procure some memory of his hands, and from old painters I have repeatedly heard people say that Zuccaro drew the two paintings in the Chapel of San Sebastiano".

Daniele Barbaro must have also proposed to Veronese the famous and almost proverbial anecdote narrated in the *Natural History* of Pliny the Elder, book XXXV, 65-66: the pictorial competition between two of the greatest painters of ancient Greece: Zeuxis and Parrhasius. Zeuxis unveiled his fresco: bunches of grapes of such realism as to deceive even the birds that try to peck them. Sure of victory, he invited Parrhasius to show his work to the judges, revealing it. But what he believed to be the sheet that covered the work was the work itself; so Zeuxis had to acknowledge his defeat. The deceived eye, the recreated illusion, to which we can add a precious note from Aristotle's *Poetics* (XXXV, 1461, b. 9): "In general one must bring back the impossible either in relation to poetry or

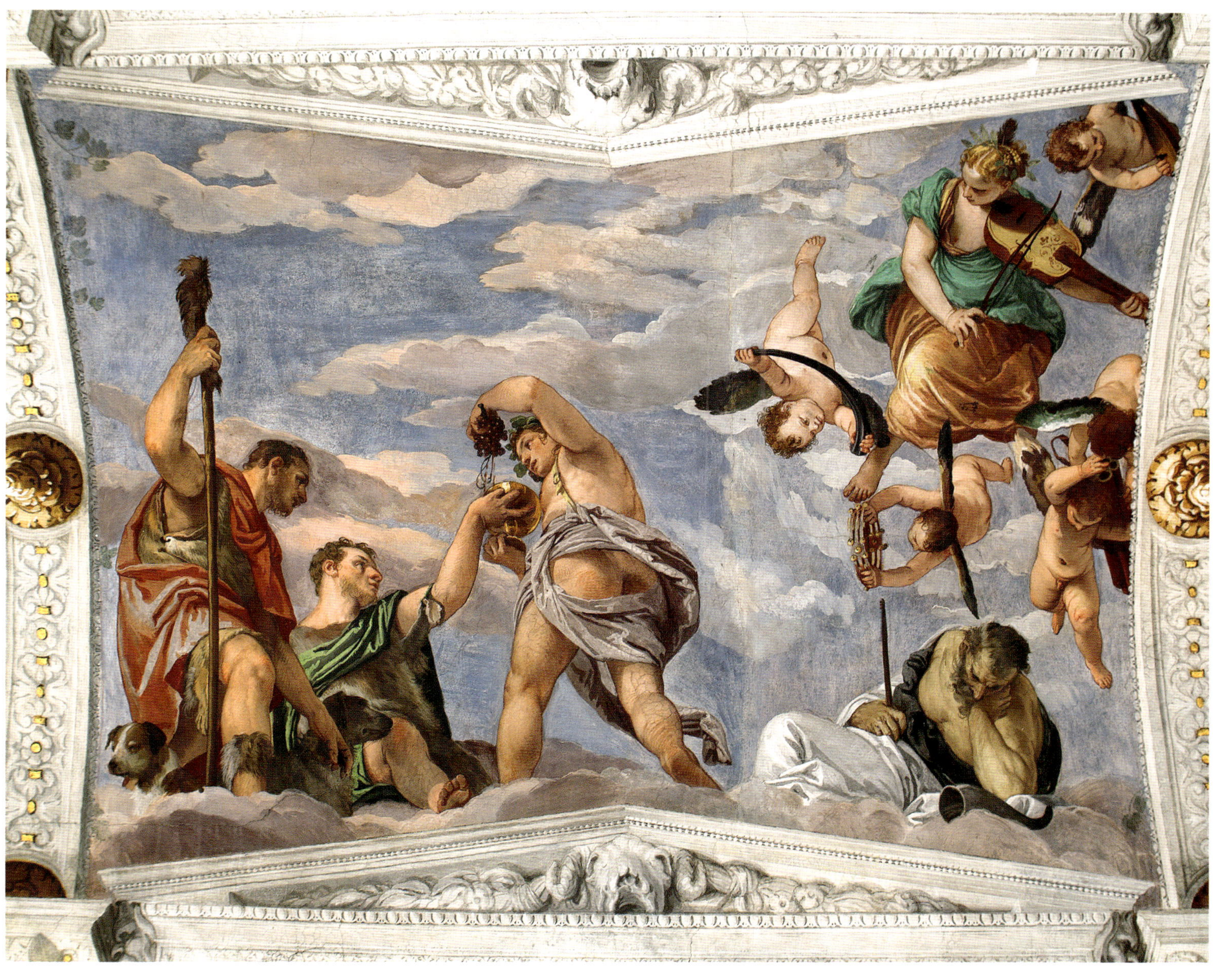

at best or to the common opinion. Since in relation to poetry the impossible credible (probable) is preferable to the incredible (improbable) but possible. And in relation to the best, the characters are such as Zeuxis painted them, because the work must be superior to the model", always remembering the common trait of tragedy and comedy, their "being imitations; but they differ from each other in three respects, namely by their imitation either in different materials or different things or in a different way and not in the same way" (1447 A). It is no coincidence that anthropomorphism corresponds to psychological naturalism: satyrs, tritons, winds, centaurs are represented as figures. In order to be understood by humans, they must partially assume their forms: the painted beings must be "fake", i.e. act. What the ancients liked and must be recreated, also adding the sophist Luciano's appreciation for overlapping colours and the use of shadows. But how to propose the dimension of imitation, of the deception of sight? How to read the image according to its rules? Pliny warns his readers that the image must be realistic in order to compete with reality, it must therefore contain the maximum of artifice, and at the same time bring about the admiring awareness that it is a deception. The image must be understood in its autonomy: and it can do so when the frame gives the possibility of seeing its fiction. Hence all the complex work of "quadraturism" in Maser: it must clarify how all that painted world is apparent. Mirror of reality and theatre, dream and staging.

Lares and Bacchus, the Sleep, Terpsichore, Ceiling of the Room of Bacchus, 1560-1561, fresco. Maser, Villa Barbaro

At the centre of the barrel vault ceiling, in the west corner room, we find a complex allegorical representation: the one offering the grape juice to the two mortals, in leather clothes, cloaks, accompanied by dogs, is Bacchus. The aerial figure playing the viola has been interpreted as Euterpe, muse of dance, but traditionally has other instruments, the tibiae or the flute. Perhaps does the man leaning on his hand represent sleep? On the door of the room is the motto "Et Genio et Laribus", hence the interpretative key, i.e. Bacchus paying homage to the ancestors. But the scene also seems to be the dignified disguise of the world of the countryside around the Villa: wine, dance, heavy sleep, shepherding. The patrician interpreters of the countryside.

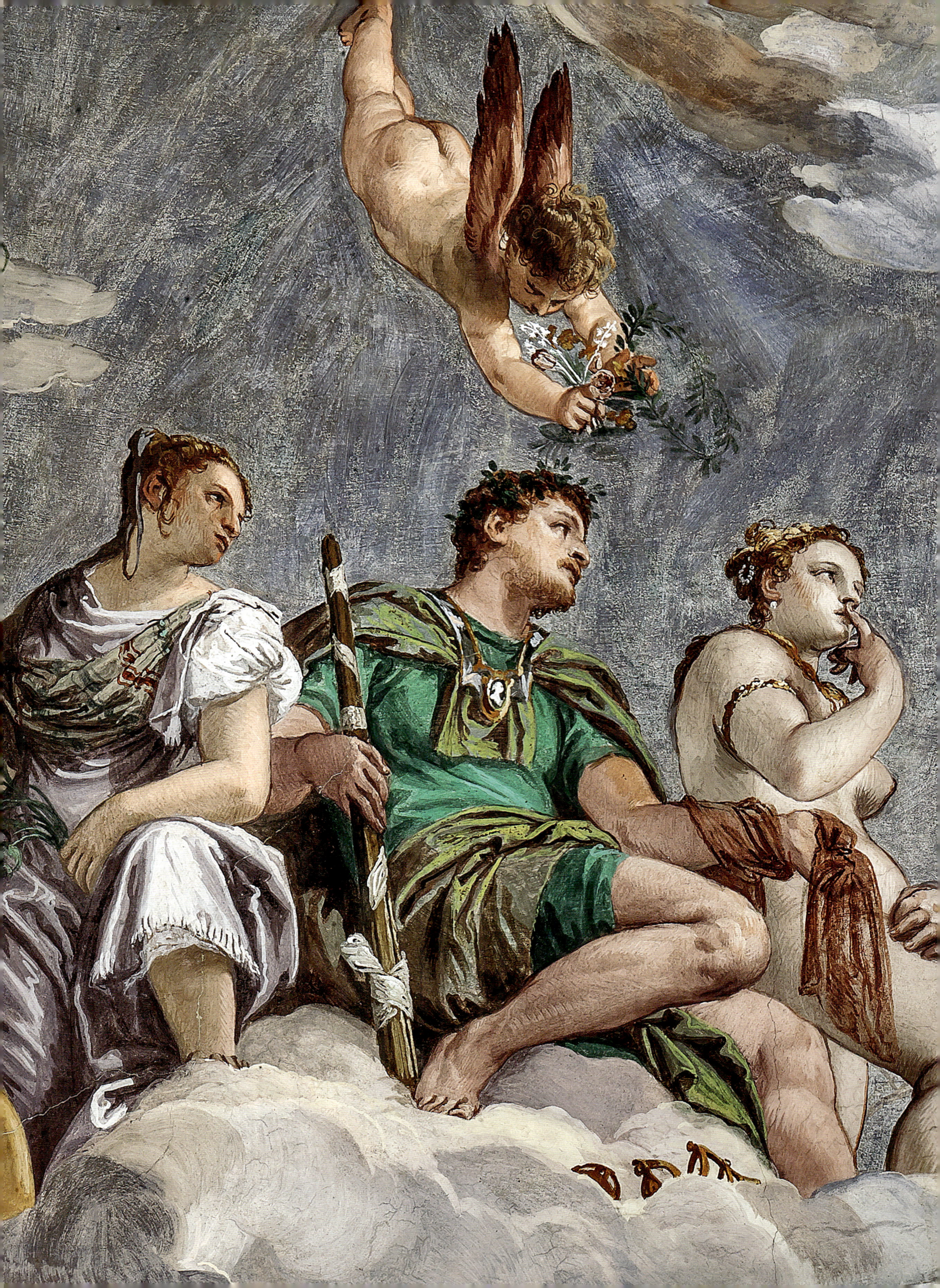

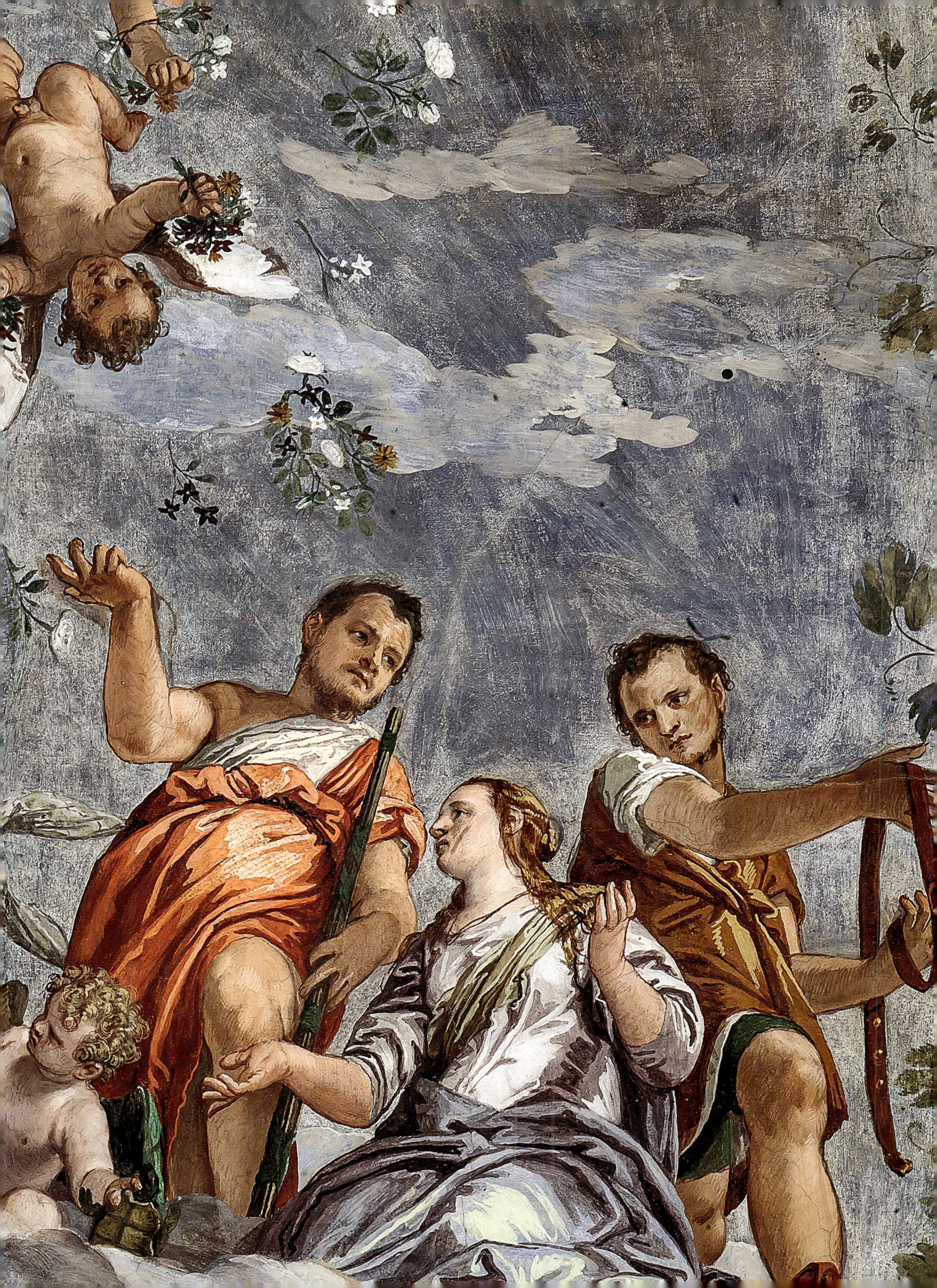

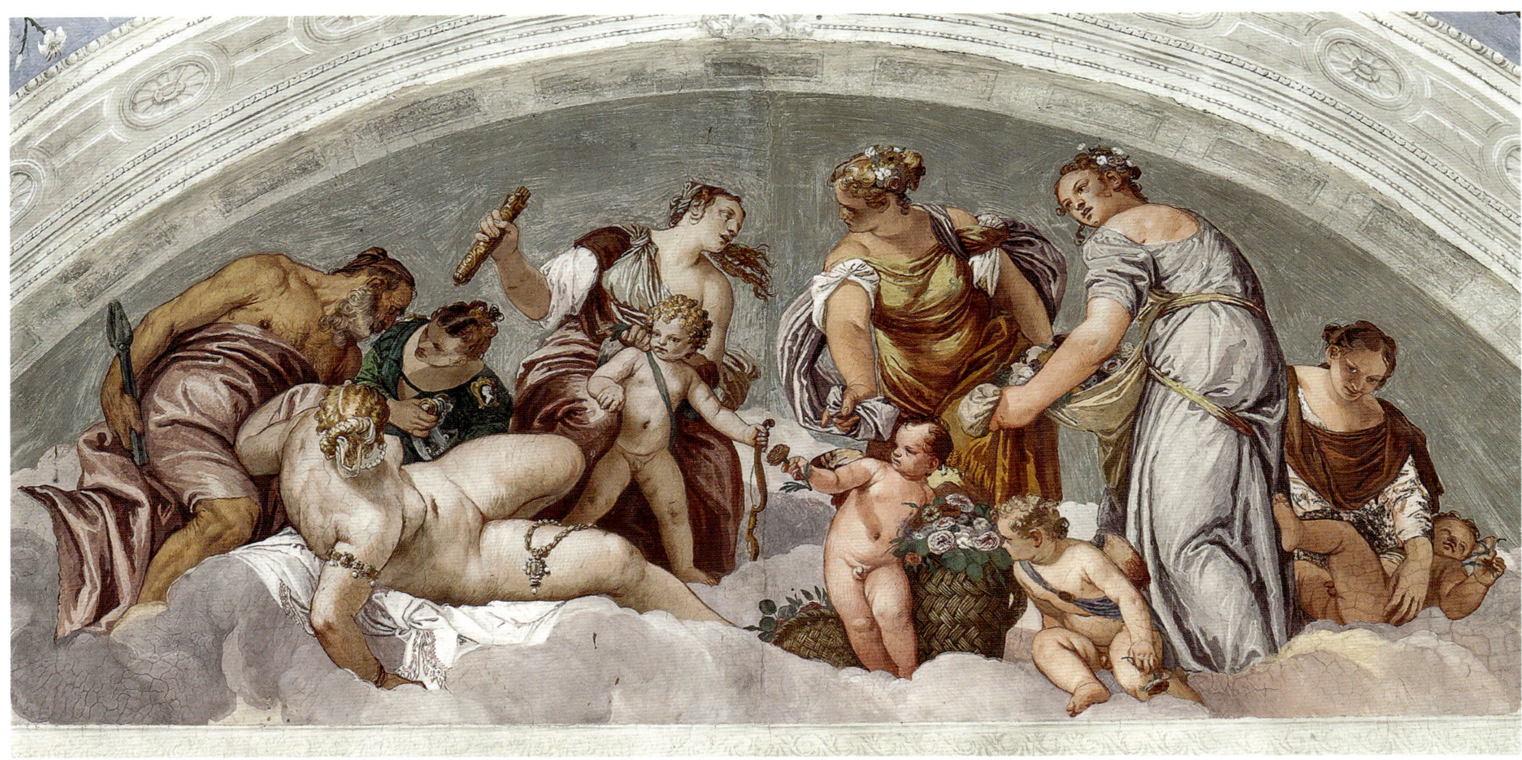

GODS AND HUMANS, THE PEOPLE OF ILLUSIONS

A short libretto is necessary to orient oneself in the show prepared by Veronese.
Over two summers, his fresco system created, with his helps, six rooms on the noble floor, which has a T-shaped plan. The central axis is given by the long hall, the Cross, which joins the façade with two rooms to the south, while the large square hall to the north overlooks the nymphaeum with rooms on two sides. The Sala a Crociera (Cross Room) presents a decoration with landscapes and, within painted niches, eight gigantic figures of musicians; on the walls there are also two fake doors from which a page and a girl look out, all within a fictitious architectural loggia, further decorated with simulated cameos.
The main room to the north is the Sala Quadrata (Square Room): the barrel vault is imagined as an architecture open to the sky, supported by spiral Corinthian columns. The simulation of a balustrade balcony rests on the cornice. On the ceiling, or rather in the light blue background, a seated female figure appears in a bright light, her arms outstretched: she flies on the back of a being who, from the details of the wings and clawed paw, we consider a dragon. Some gods crown her: Jupiter, Mars, Apollo, Venus, Mercury, Diana, Saturn; each with its own zodiac signs. At the corners, in four pentagons, the personifications of the elements: Water (Neptune), Air (Juno), Fire (Vulcan), Earth (Cybele); alternating in rectangular compartments in monochrome, allegories of Love, Fecundity, Abundance, Fortune. On the loggias, supported by twisted columns, a long balcony; a lady in an elegant dress, a child, an old woman with a small dog look out from the balustrade that delimits it. The lady has always been considered the landlady, Giustina Giustinian, with the youngest of her three children intent on watching a parrot, while the old nurse flanks her with her pet dog. On the opposite side two boys: one reads, the other with difficulty holds back a dog that barks at a petulant monkey; they are Francesco and Almorò Barbaro, eldest and second son of Giustina, or Giustiniana, and Marcantonio. That is not enough: on the two smaller walls, in the lunettes, other groups of figures: Venus, Vulcan, Proserpina and the Hours in one; Ceres, Hercules as a child, the Nymphs and Bacchus, in the other. Interpreted as the Seasons, Winter and Spring, Summer and Autumn. In the lower area of the walls, two

Olympus Room, Ceiling (opposite) and Lunette (above), 1560-1561, fresco. Maser, Villa Barbaro

The room presents the most varied and complex allegorical system. The barrel vault has been recreated as an architectural framework supported by twisted columns: beyond the framework the background, the sky of the gods and stars. All around a ledge, on which rests a fake balcony limited by a balustrade. From one side of the gallery, the viewer is watched by an elegant lady (traditionally identified with Giustiniana Giustinian, wife of Marcantonio Barbaro), an old woman, and a small child; on the opposite side a boy is reading, while another holds a dog (they are Francesco and Almorò Barbaro, teenagers). In the sky: Jupiter, Mars, Apollo, Venus, Mercury, Diana, Saturn around a woman leaning on a dragon. At the corners the four elements personified by Juno, Vulcan, Cybele and Neptune. In the rectangles: Love, Fertility, Abundance, Fortune. The two lunettes are also visible: Summer and Autumn interpreted by Ceres, the child Hercules; the Nymphs and Bacchus; winter and Spring (reproduced in the detail opposite) interpreted by Vulcan and Venus; Proserpine and the Hore.

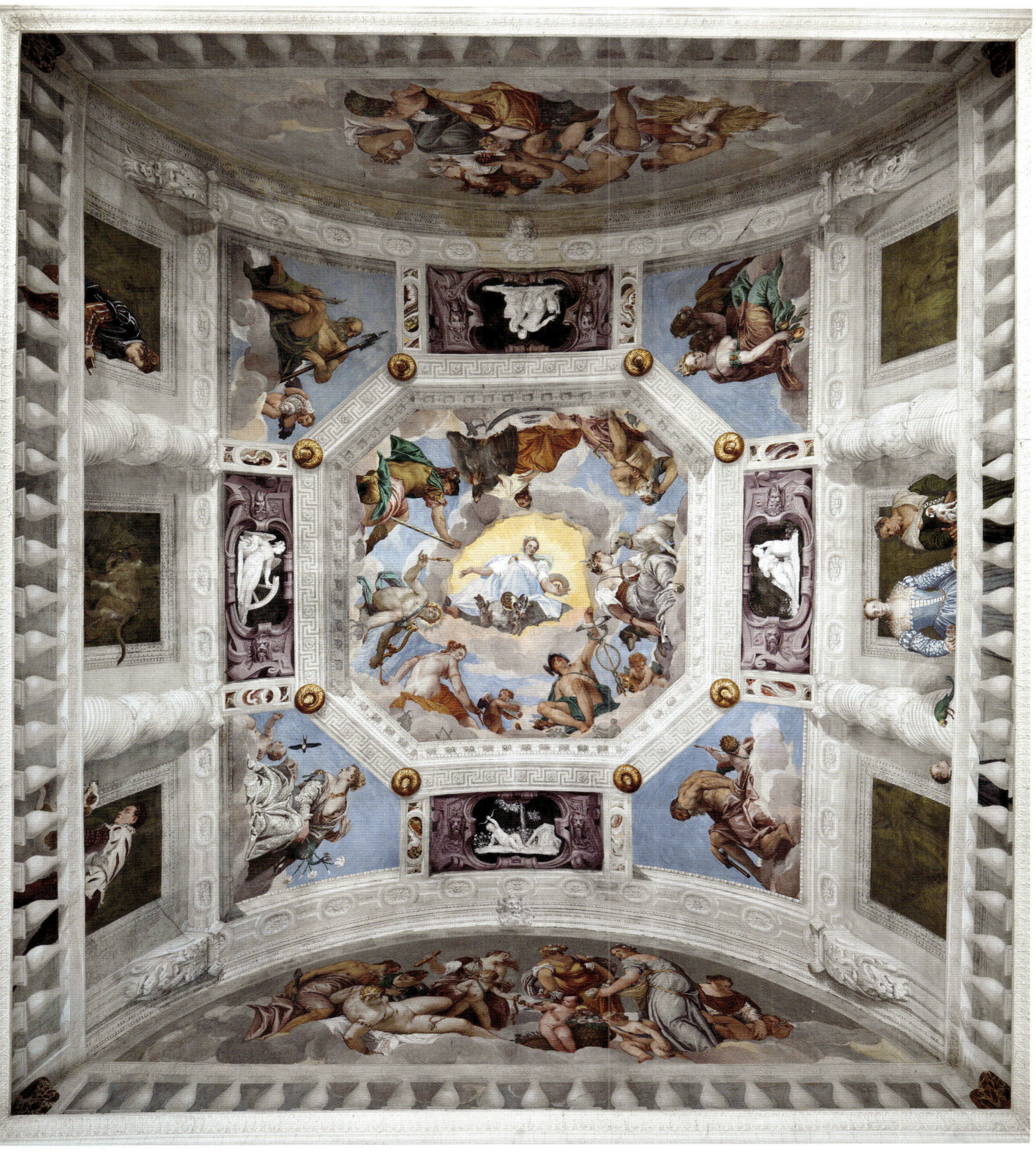

Francesco Barbaro Intent on Reading, Olympus Room, Ceiling, 1560-1561, fresco. Maser, Villa Barbaro

Francesco (1546-1616) was the eldest son of Giustiniana and Marcantonio; he will become Patriarch of Aquileia, followed by his death by his younger brother, Ermolao (Armolò in Venetian). He could be the young man intent on reading, not distracted by the barking of the dog and the noises of the countryside. Extremely elegant, in any case.

landscapes on each side delimited by Corinthian columns; on the doors that lead into the side rooms tympanums with monochromes, false sculptures; and towards the transept, separated by an arch, two figures, Peace and Discord appear to be in gilded bronze.

Two rooms are adjoining the square room. One is usually referred to as the Dog's Room, the other is the Lucerne Room. The room is called the room of the dog, because a pet specimen is sitting on the simulated base, and on the opposite side there is a crouched cat. On the walls columns, fake marbles, landscapes; in the arch of a lunette a *Holy Family with Young St John and St Catherine*. On the ceiling three allegorical figures: Abundance, Fortune and Envy; on the two sides of the cornice two pairs of figures: one seems to bring Time and History together, the other shows a naked woman, her hands on the crown of an old man dozing off. Here too the doors have tympanums decorated with fake statues: a human couple and a satyr couple.

The opposite Room of the Lucerne has a similar structure. On the ceiling is Faith who indicates Eternity (a snake biting its tail) to Charity who protects a poor man; on the cornices two couples: one appears to be Strength leaning on Prudence, with a mirror. In the lunette a Holy Family where the elderly Joseph offers a bowl with a spoon: it has always been the *Madonna della pappa* with features of accentuated tenderness. The image will be the one to address the last reverent thought in the evening and the first greeting in the morning – thus two bedrooms have been thought of.

On the opposite side, to the south, the other two rooms have a completely different iconographic perspective. The so-called Room of Bacchus offers fictional landscapes, statues, cameos, an imposing grape bower on one vault, while in the other a woman plays with a child on her lap (*Venus and Eros*) looking intently at a very young lyre player (*Apollo*). On the ceiling Bacchus offers a cup in which he squeezes the grape juice.

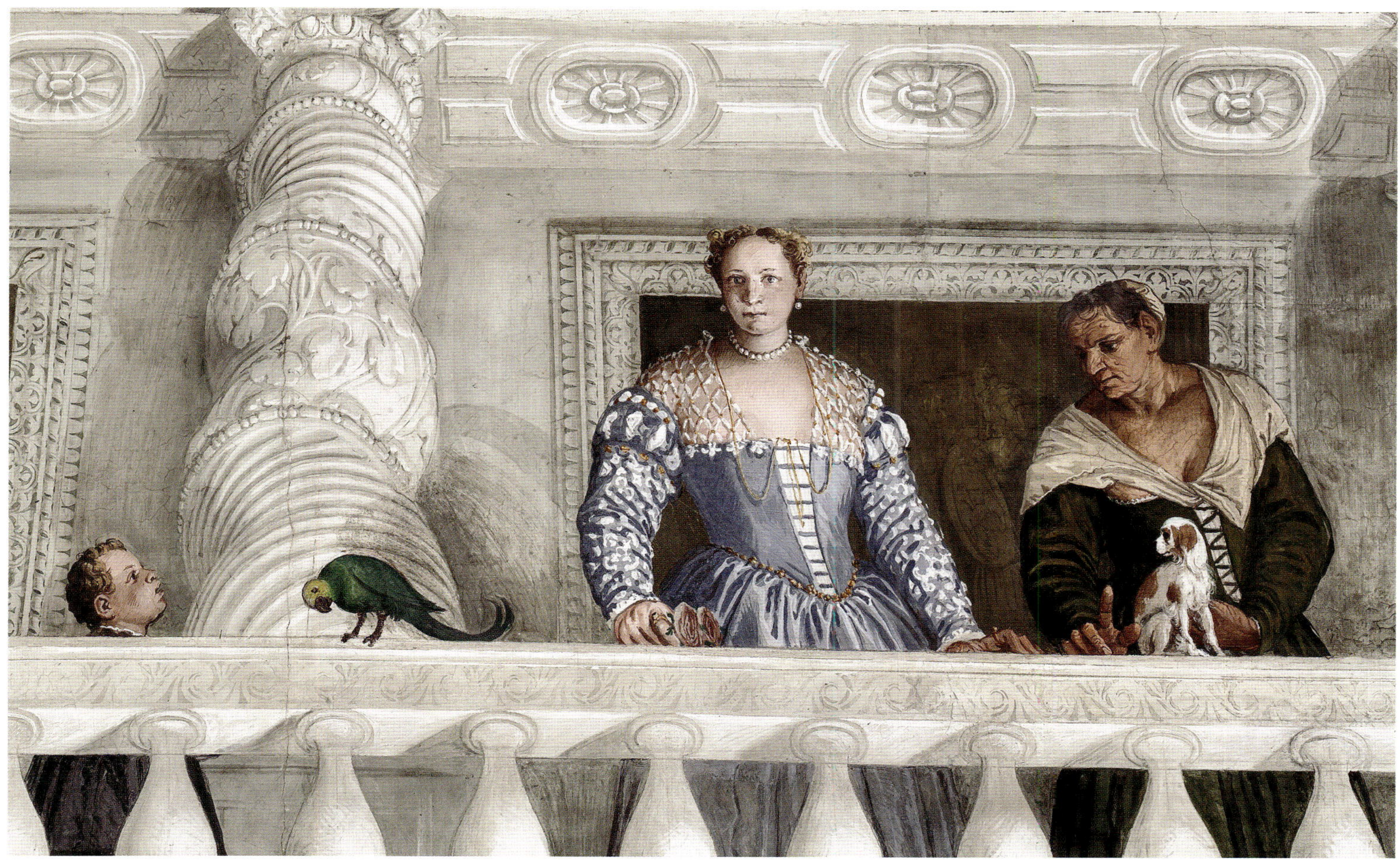

Giustiniana Giustinian with Nurse, Son and Parrot, Olympus Room, Ceiling, 1560-1561, fresco. Maser, Villa Barbaro

Giustiniana. The lady of the house who looks at us from the other – extraordinarily similar to the famous portrait of the "Bella Nani" by Veronese – wears a summer dress, with openwork lace, a row of large pearls and parure earrings. Summer roses are also interesting. The old nurse – a human type who follows conventions – indicates with her index finger her near future (up there, in the sky) while a lap dog does not worry about the petulant parrot, which intrigues the child with his upturned nose. A complete presentation of the real hosts, in the absence of fathers, brother-in-law and uncle.

The next room has been indicated as the Room of the Tribunal of Love: it will be necessary to decrypt the completely ambiguous image which is located in the centre of the ceiling and which gave the room its name. On the fireplace there should be the monochrome *Work* and *Peace*; and again, in addition to landscapes, two scenes: one presents two female players and a very young man with a bow; the other a woman and three cupids with silver vessels.
And then again, at the end of the two perspective escapes of the rooms, to the north a beater awaits us with a dog and hunting horn, to accompany us towards the bush. On the opposite side a lady with a fan, in the summer heat. Definitely incongruous to define them as a "self-portrait" and the "wife of Veronese": completely extraneous to tradition and inadmissible by the decorator, who if anything left his "signature" in the dog, the toilet brush and the slippers.

THE COMEDY OF HIGHLY CURIOUS THINGS

The six rooms have been interpreted overall as a cycle, proposed as a variation around Wisdom (at the centre of Olympus) which determines a cosmology in which human beings will find Harmony, Peace and those Virtues which, with help of Fortune, will see them accomplished. In 1939 Pallucchini limited himself to identifying the gods on the basis of their attributes, proposing the central figure of the ceiling of Olympus as Eternity. A profound connoisseur of Veronese, he judges Maser a "seminal moment", believing it was Daniele Barbaro "who suggested the allegories and symbols of the cycle of frescoes to Paolo. Perhaps today we are no longer able to know exactly the interpretation of some of those scenes: but from all of them emerges an elementary meaning of values, tending to exalt life and youth, through the symbols

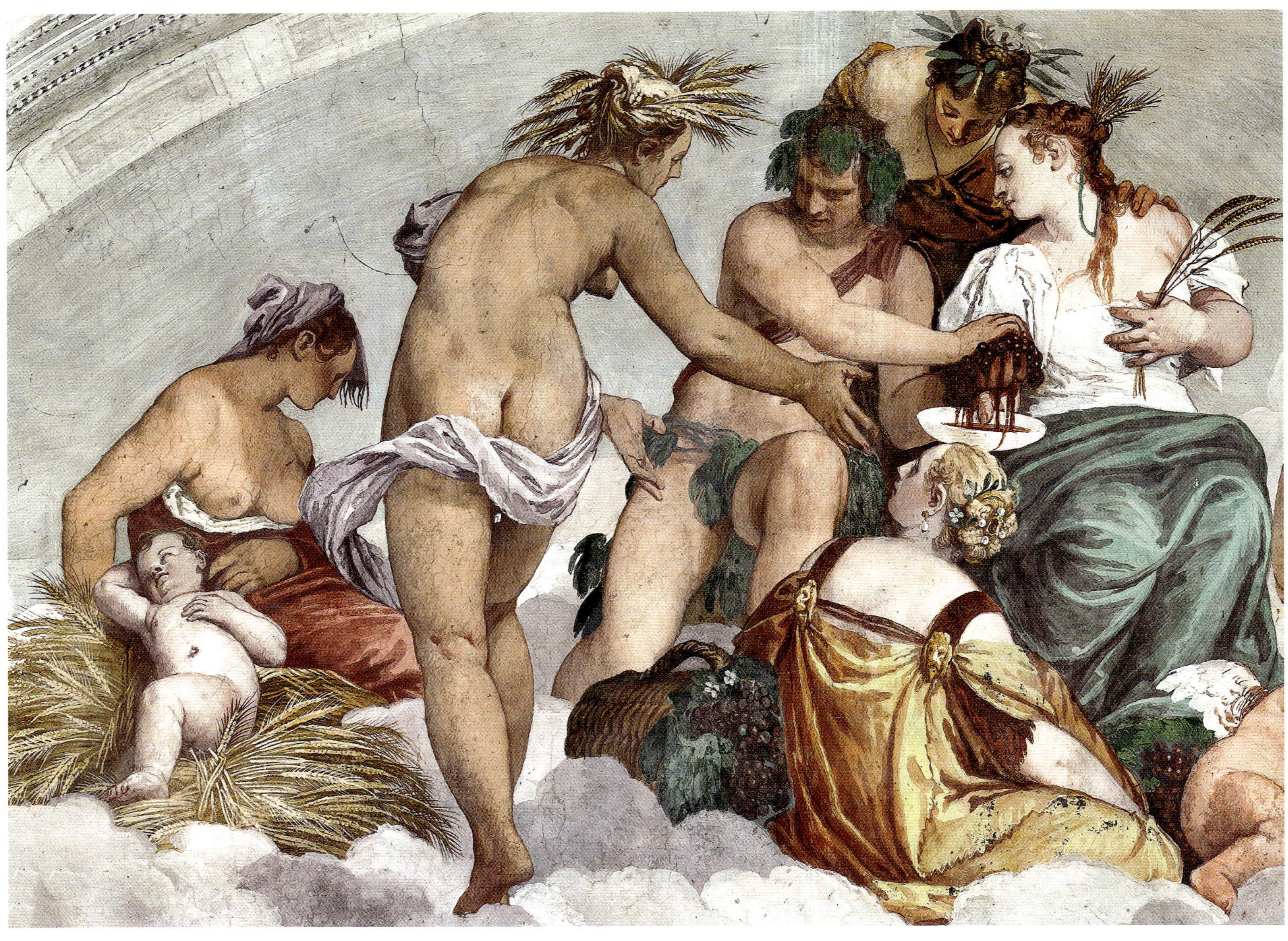

of classical mythology, which humanity will be able to understand, through the centuries, even beyond the allegorical veils."

Two decades after Alba Medea, in 1960, and Nicola Ivanoff, in 1961, proposed to consider Maser as a coordinated cycle: it represents Heavenly Harmony. The gods of myth interpret the planets, the foundation of astrological wisdom, while the dragon is a monster tamed by the Divine Wisdom. However, it should be remembered that in the Apocalypse of John, in chapter 12, after the first war in Paradise, there is the second earthly war of the Woman against the Dragon, always interpreted as Mary. And the reference to Mary, more in keeping with the culture of the Venetian humanist, would allow us to interpret the gods in the simplest way, i.e. the constellations, and therefore the cosmic order moved by divine love.

Otherwise, if the female figure is interpreted as Wisdom, it would be the defence against the reverses of Fortune, represented in one of the cameos with the broken wheel. In particular Nicola Ivanoff considers the scenes of family life an expression of the general theme of harmony, assuming a request from Marcantonio; to which Pallucchini, in 1563, replied that the rooms of Bacchus and the one known as the Tribunal of Love, where a naked Venus invites the kneeling bride to silence, show a completely pagan conception of life, exalting wine and love. Marini in the first catalogue that proposes *L'opera completa del Veronese* (Veronese's complete work), in 1968, accepts these various indications and so does Terisio Pignatti himself, author in 1976 of a more accurate and reasoned general catalogue, where he specifies "In essence, we face a con-

Summer and Autumn, Olympus Room, Ceiling, 1560-1561, fresco. Maser, Villa Barbaro

The translation of the cultured allegories by Paolo Veronese, in Maser, is always in the sign of comedy. Here it is well expressed in the tired reaper who has just nursed the big baby sleeping on the bundle of wheat, and they should be Juno and Hercules; while a conspicuously naked Ceres offers an abundance of gifts to autumn. The juice of Bacchus will gladden the three young ladies, evident scions of the Venetian patriciate, who pretend to be Nymphs.

Olympus, Olympus Room, Ceiling, 1560-1561, fresco. Maser, Villa Barbaro

At the base of the Olympian gods we find the signs of the Zodiac, the Elements and the forces that regulate existence: Love, Fertility, Abundance, Fortune. In the lunettes are the Seasons: it is a Cosmology that relates the human and the celestial.

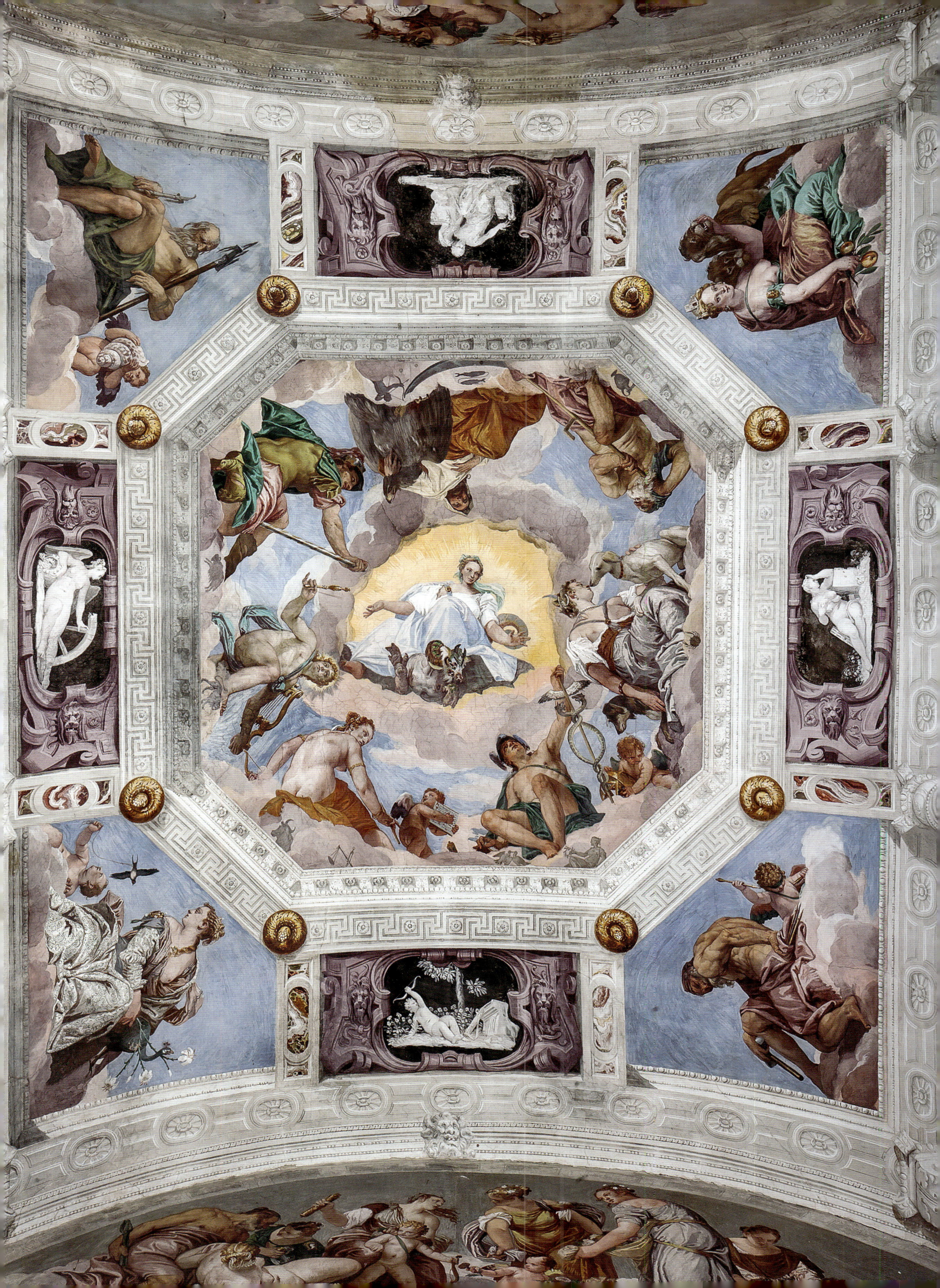

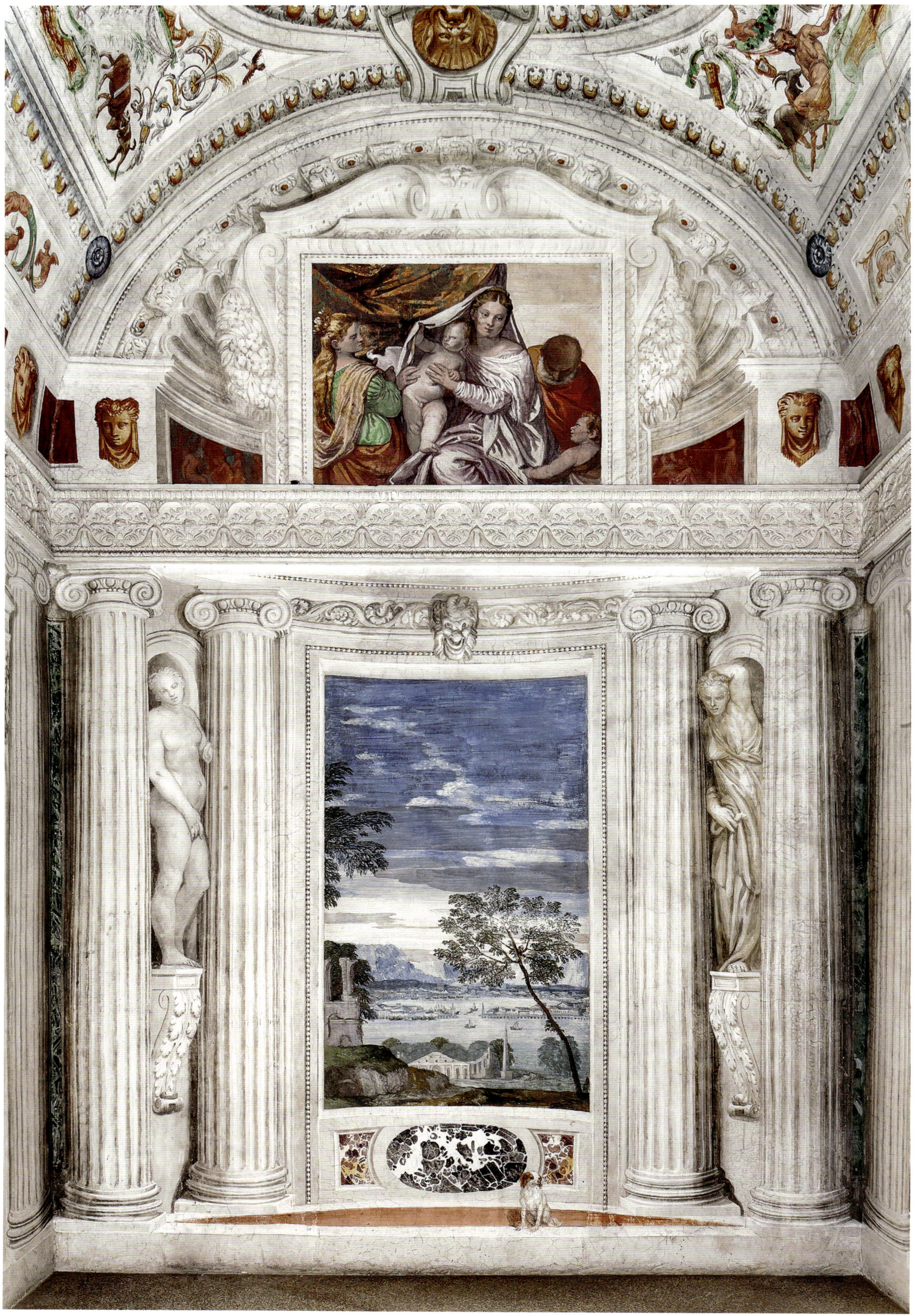

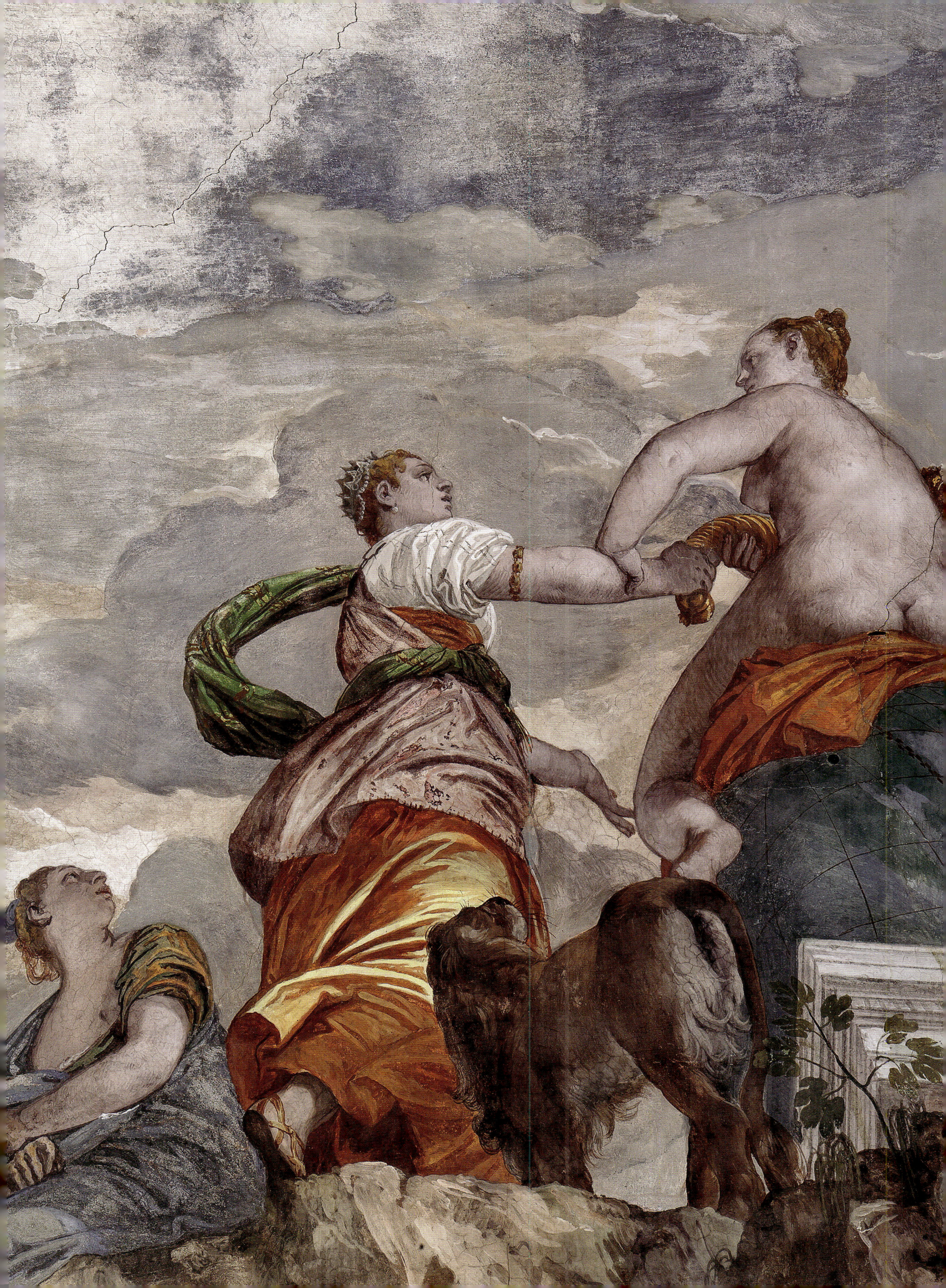

ception of the world that connects both to the personal philosophical beliefs of Daniele Barbaro, who was an astronomer and musician [...] and to his spiritual situation as patriarch of Aquileia", but then recognizes the exaltation of the pleasures of life, since the painter has "the intention to exalt the order and law represented by the patriarch of Aquileia within the universal harmony, with the abundance, fertility and happiness destined for Marcantonio"; he therefore concludes that the painter satisfies both patrons. Again in 1984 Pallucchini will confirm the idea of the centrality of Divine Wisdom and Harmony. A very careful scholar of Veronese, Luciana Crosato Larcher, in her *Considerazioni sul programma iconografico di Maser* recalled the work of an ancestor of the Barbaros, Francesco (1390-1454), author of a famous treatise, the *De re uxoria* printed several times also in the vernacular translation by Alberto Lollio, *Prudentissimi et gravi documenti circa la elettion della moglie* (Venice, Gabriel Giolito, 1548). Marriage for Barbaro – and it will remain so also for the following generations of the Venetian patriciate – is a legal bond, essential for the maintenance and generational succession of the family, which must be based on a harmony of personality and on the essential correspondence of social status. Thus it will be possible to form the progeny, educate the offspring, which is the primary and original task of the mother, guarantor of the progeny. This role of women in marriage for the ruling classes also derived from the strong concerns about dowry issues, which weighed more and more on family assets, and determined the kinship ties which, after the lockout of the Maggior Consiglio, were essential for the transmission of properties and prerogatives, also in relation to the cautious but necessary openings to relations with the more affluent citizens, through marriage strategies. Barbaro therefore indicates in the search and election of the "good wife" not necessarily the most beautiful or richest, but certainly the most morally gifted, an essential passage in the life of a gentleman. Hence a greater characterization of the female role than many other moralists, starting with Leon Battista Alberti. Among the various implications, confirmed by the mass of wills, the best guide for understanding female roles in aristocratic and non-aristocratic Venetian society is evidently that of a decisive and dominant role in domestic life. The woman is mistress of the house, she leads the servants, educates the children, the transmission of the nobility is matrilineal. Barbaro uses the ancient sources but at the same time mirrors the male dominance of the Aristotelian tradition. The success of the treatise by Francesco, Ermolao Barbaro's grandfather, published several times in Europe in the sixteenth century, could only be proudly confirmed by his great-grandchildren, the descendants Daniele and Marcantonio, and also illustrated in the system painted in their villa. In Paolo Veronese they will find a corresponding soul, since all his amorous allegories will be oriented towards the exaltation of conjugal love.

On the basis of this text, the scholar identifies the scene of the Room known as the Tribunal of Love identifying the god of the wedding, Hymeneus with the bride's veil, Venus pronuba who imposes silence, Juno in charge of the wedding with the marriage yoke, and then the Groom in the right age, the Bride who has every duty and therefore the success of the marriage; the last character, on the right, would be the "Master of the House" who holds the reins in his hands, in the act of offering them to the bride. In fact, she is the sovereign mistress of the house, the one who holds the reins to govern "the servants and the stuff" according to Francesco's words. The scene above the fireplace also refers to marriage, through three young women playing stringed instruments, while the monochromes represent Peace and Work. Other monochromes indicate the task of raising children, with the allusion to the revealed breast.

A Latin saying can be read on the fireplace in the Room of the Tribunal of Love: *ignem gladio ne fodias*, or literally "do not stir up the fire with the sword", a widespread motto, also present on the architrave of the fireplace in the Camera di San Paolo frescoed by Correggio in Parma. It was Erasmus of Rotterdam, in his well-known and appreciated *Adagia*, which he was enriching precisely in Venice for the edition with Aldus Manuzio, who provided a complete explanation of the motto. Do not strike fire with the sword, do not tease those who are already agitated with anger; do not provoke;

Previous pages

Holy Family with Young St John and St Catherine, Room of the Dog, 1560-1561, fresco. Maser, Villa Barbaro

It is the south wall; a splendid example of illusionism for having created a concave effect in the wall with an architectural structure and a landscape breakthrough, here an ancient port. At the base is an extremely real little dog, to be exact a Maltese, hence the name of the room.

Abundance, Fortune, Discord, Room of the Dog, Ceiling, 1560-1561, fresco. Maser, Villa Barbaro

Object of different interpretations: the one who possesses the cornucopia stops the hand of whoever requests it. So Fortune stops Ambition, which is in turn undermined by the woman who, on the back, already has the knife drawn: Betrayal. A metaphor of power.

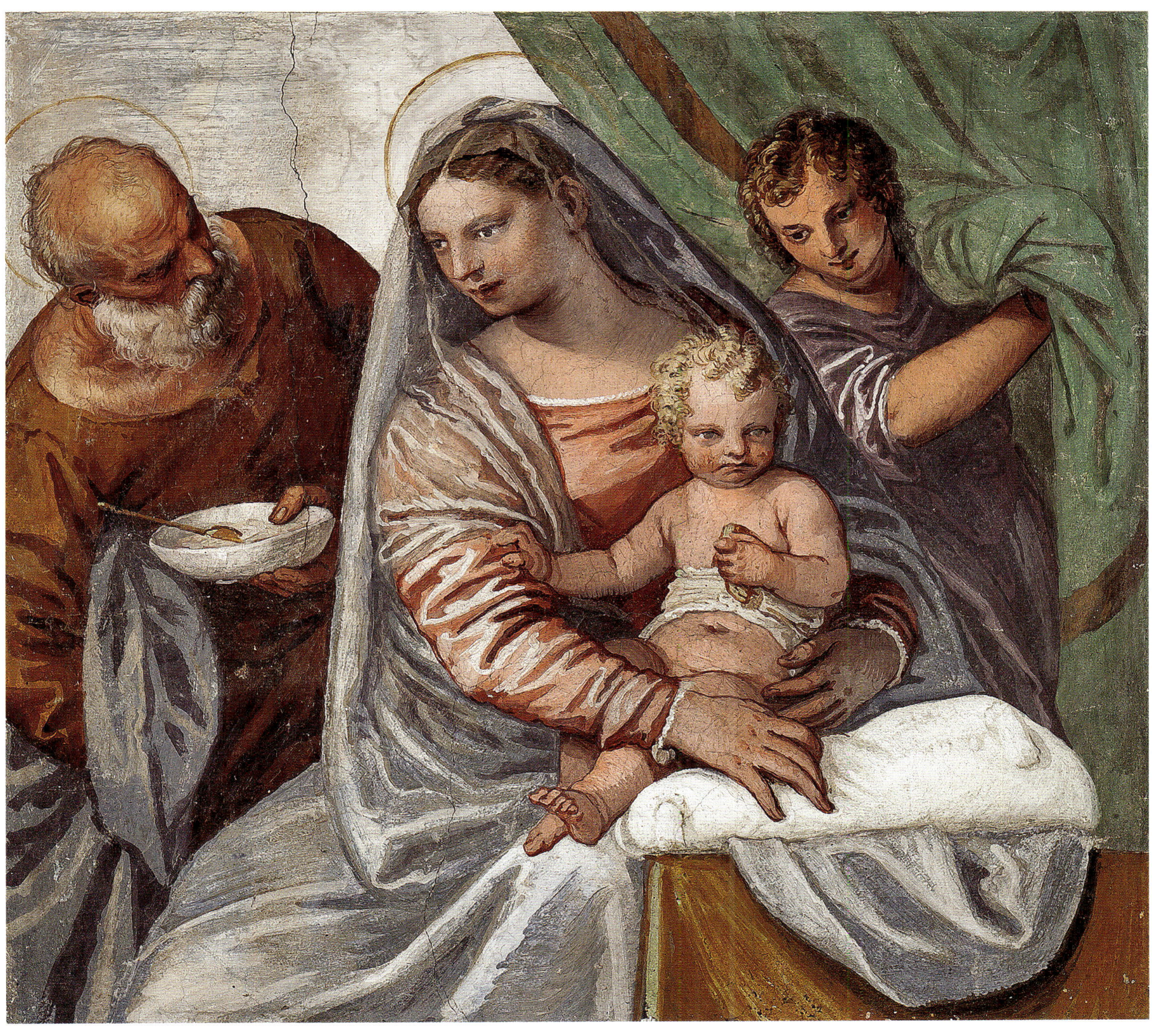

Madonna della Pappa, Room of the Lucerne, 1560-1561, fresco. Maser, Villa Barbaro

Two are the images sacred to Maser on the walls of Villa Barbaro, destined to study, concentration and rest rooms. In both cases they are familiar images: the most particular, almost private, very intimate, is this scene with Joseph who has prepared a meal for the Child. He hands it in the bowl with the small spoon, with a paternal domestic gesture.

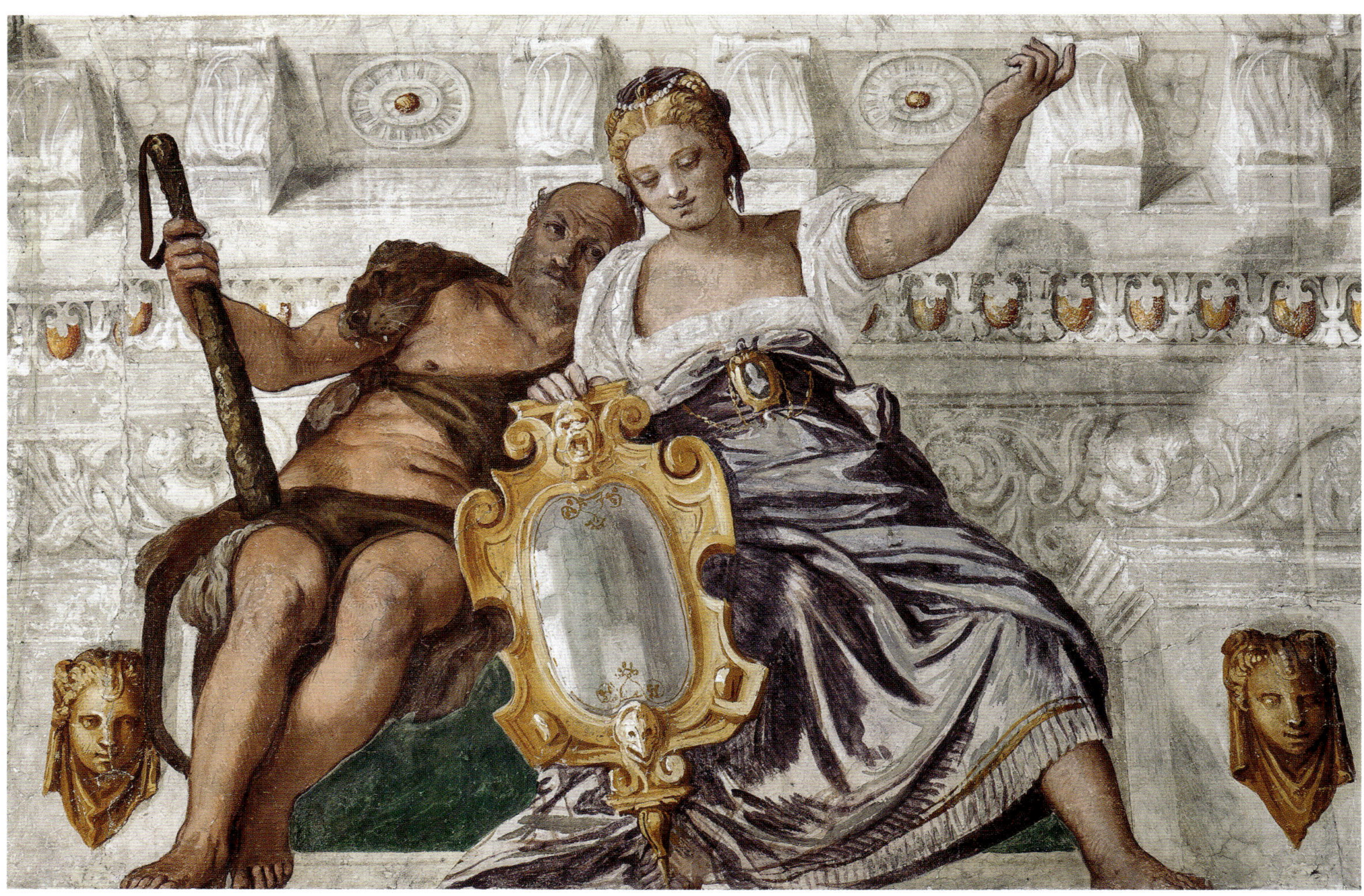

Strength Leans on Prudence,
Room of the Lucerne, 1560-1561,
fresco. Maser, Villa Barbaro

Prudence leans against a mirror, exposed towards us. The mirror shows what it really is, that is, the Truth. And it is precisely by leaning on the truth that attention and temperance will be achieved and will limit the brutal use of the Force, represented here by the mature man, in the shadows, holding a gnarled club. A somewhat aged Hercules.

and yet also: do not dampen passion with the cold sword. So: who is the ambiguous admonition addressed to, in that conjugal room? To the woman, of course, and she does it in the double meaning of not provoking anger by inciting her with her comments (she had been warned by the finger of Venus) and of accepting conjugal passion with pleasure, or at least not extinguishing it.

In fact, the Wedding scene seems interpretable in the light of *De re uxoria*: an "old-fashioned" scene in full humanist taste. And yet its meaning can be exactly reversed: the Groom presents to the wedding god a traitor Bride, to be judged; Venus suggests silence, Juno reminds her of the yoke, the master of ceremonies is ready to put the reins on her. It is characteristic of those Venetian generations to always play with meanings, allegories to be read in different keys, ambiguities as an intellectual game, hence the amazement in front of the double meaning as the ultimate outcome. In the Room of the Dog another small scene appears which refers to the love theme, once again in its duplicity. It is the challenge of Eros and Anteros, sons of Venus, who compete for the palm of victory between the impassionate love and the regulated love, but also between attraction and repulsion, the two polarities of the feeling of love. Eros for the Greeks, Cupid or Amore for the Romans, was originally indicated by Hesiod as a primordial, theogonic power of love; in the late period he becomes a divinity, always represented with his mother. Genealogies on his father multiplied and Pausanias already enumerated several; in the Roman world Cupid was the legitimate son of Venus and Vulcan, while Anteros was the son of Venus and Mars. Sometimes, Anteros is the expression of homosexual love in the Greek world; he is the avenger of unrequited love for Pausanias, he is also the expression of heavenly love. As Eros' adversary in the fight for the palm, he represents mutual love, and especially conjugal love for Themistius, and this was the favourite interpretation by

Italian humanists from Mario Equicola to Celio Calcagnini with iconographic results at the court of Ferrara, and later by Vincenzo Cartari in the *Immagini degli dèi* (Images of the Gods), a text known and used by Paolo Veronese. For Cartari, Anteros is the brother who allows Eros to grow when he is close to him; if he goes away Eros becomes a child again, which had worried Venus: "Therefore love grows when it is placed in a person who loves the same, and whoever is loved must love equally". Almost a paraphrase of Dante's "love, which exempts no one beloved from loving in return".

Paolo will depict Eros and Anteros over and over again, with insistence, also connected to the adulterous love of Venus and Mars. And it should also be noted that Anteros is indicated in several Renaissance poems as an expression of "Wrath and Indignation" or the "crude lord", the "true enemy" of courtly loves: it therefore appears "on the side" of Mars, the form of love as possession. Not forgotten by the "wrath" that moves Ariosto's Orlando, Anteros is therefore a very plural figure: in general, however, in the sixteenth century it is Reason that allows you to overcome Passions, the abnormal and absolute feelings that overwhelm the women of the myth, from Pasiphae to Medea, from Filli to Filomena. Finally, if Eros and Anteros contain opposites in themselves, every interpretation immediately produces the opposite: the palm of victory of one or the other will always be disputed.

The Room of the Dog presents another scene of double reading on the ceiling: Fortune, sitting on an unstable wheel, refuses Ambition who tries to grab the goods from the cornucopia, while below is Fraud, caught concealing a knife, as he prepares to rob goods from other areas. This instability of human fate is reaffirmed in the scene in which a large naked woman, with a rope beside her, "puts her hands" on the crown of an old sovereign with his sceptre. The old man has fallen asleep. By now he lacks strength and virtue: the young woman who deprives him of his attributes will be Destiny, Fate, ready to entrust to someone younger a power that is always and in any case transient. Ultimately, the campaign of Maser's frescoes produced a joyful, admirable flood of allegories, symbols, narratives, exposed for the pleasure of viewing and together with that of the cultured explanations by the hosts. They were given the opportunity to explain the enigmas represented, with cultured quotations and pleasant stories, discussing the ambiguity of the scenes with the cultured guest. Half a millennium away, we are left with the pleasure of the eyes, the wonder of deception, the subtle pleasure of the search for meanings, the praise for skill and the esteem for the intelligence of a century.

PORTRAITS OF LADIES AND GENTLEMEN

When Paolo Caliari descends from the scaffolding on which he created myths and allegories, in quick frescoes with amusing enigmas, and has to portray humanity on canvas, he produces legible masterpieces. Always, however, with a dose of mystery. As for two of the most admired, with the total absence of identification of the effigies.

One of the highest and best-known proofs of Paolo Caliari's portraiture is the so-called *Bella Nani* or the *Portrait of a Venetian Noblewoman*, now at Louvre. The appellation derives from the hypothesis that the painting belonged to the Venetian patrician family of the Nani, but the identity of the portrayed remains unknown. Stylistically, the portrait can be dated to the years of Maser's decoration: it is certainly the image of a married woman, an exponent of the Venetian patriciate in terms of hairstyles, dress and jewellery. One could recognize Giustiniana Giustinian, the lady looking out from Maser's balustrade, similar in physiognomy and attitude, remembering however that Veronese's female portraits tend to lack psychological analysis and individuality, approaching a model, a canon of female "virtuous" beauty in mid-century Venice. Here her virtue is all concentrated in the clear gaze, in the posture of the hand to the heart, in the dress, hairstyle and above all expressive serenity in the frank modesty, which show the condition of a happily married woman.

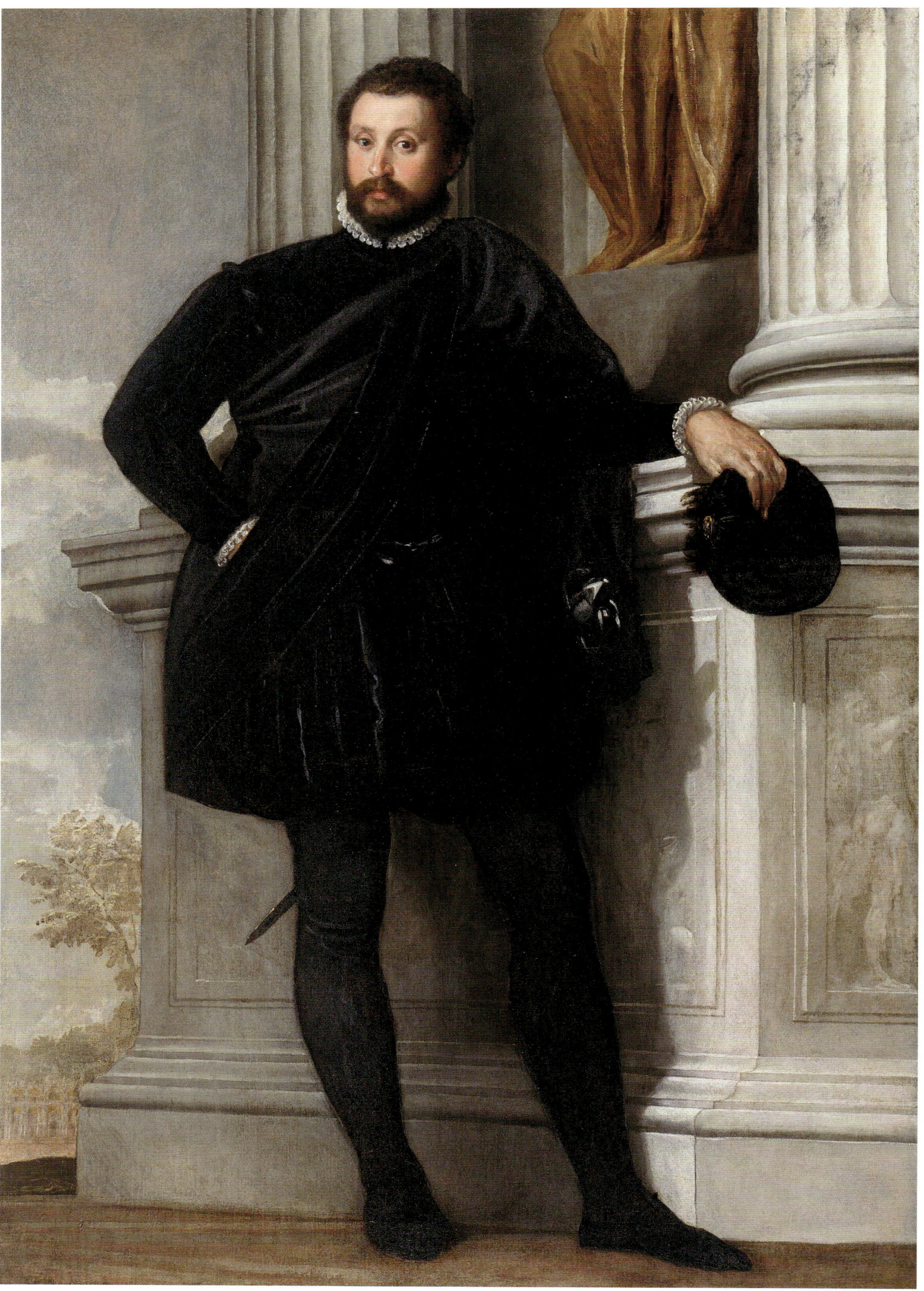

The dark background makes it possible to better bring out the fair complexion and blond hair, two essential attributes of feminine beauty, but then we will notice that also in this case, like that of Livia da Porto, the female body appears heavy under the clothes that hide it. This will also be the case in the family portraits and in the women present at the *Conviti*, in the allegories covered in drapery, such as Venice, and in the nudes of the Venuses. The aesthetic ideal has radically changed compared to the female models of the previous century, attracted by the long-limbed body of the Gothic age; it persists in a few Northern painters like Lucas Cranach. It is a radical change in the canon of female beauty: no longer narrow hips and small breasts, but wide hips and buxom breasts, but only in the nude; always in any case full flesh, chubby faces, sturdy legs.

Gentleman with Hat in Hand, approx. 1560-1562, canvas, 193 × 134.5 cm. Malibu, J. Paul Getty Museum, inv. A 71 P 17

Fashion

Women's and men's fashion in the mid-sixteenth century was necessarily conditioned by the type of fabrics and colours. Solid colour satin, *soprarizzo* velvet with different combinations and shades, the most varied brocades and brocatelles. Expensive and precious, black velvet remains the most suitable and preferred colour for men, since the taste for an austere masculine style predominates, distinguished by the *robone*, essentially a sumptuous overcoat. The young gentleman's wardrobe also includes a velvet dress, an overcoat also lined with fur for the harsh winters, a dark grey silk velvet jacket with a fur collar; and a necessary accessory: leather gloves. Over the years, fashion has made clothes more adherent, among other things, overcoming those cut, *stabbed* shapes, the slits along the sleeves and in the trousers that had dominated in the Thirties, while the shoulders are widening and the waist becomes narrower.

In common the two sexes share the shirt: in very fine linen batiste, also imported from Holland or France, thickly pleated, which in men emerges from the neckline of the doublet. The square necklines are also very wide, and often bring the gentleman's look closer to the feminine one: in his *Diaries*, Girolamo Priuli was scandalized that by now young people were wearing "high-priced shirts that looked like girls". The sleeves are no longer wide as at the turn of the century. On the other hand, trousers, which are short to be worn over tights, are increasingly swollen, especially for young people.

At the base of women's fashion, on the always very white shirt, a dress or tunic, over which the *camòra*, also called *zimarra*, is worn, wide and long open on the front, lined with fur for the winter. It is made of velvet, in the most sumptuous models in yellow-gold brocade, also in solid brick-red velvet. The dominant neckline is square. The *faldia*, a petticoat, was used to add volume and make the skirt stiffer. The shoulders are particularly developed, more square and supported by shoulder pads that can also become imposing, real rolls, and decorated with jewels, or even in silver. But the most evident character of Venetian fashion is given by very close-fitting bodices, which flatten the chest, with wide necklines, always rigidly squared. The bib placed under the jacket of various cuts - in England the *partlet* - has horizontal fastenings, often leaving the shirt uncovered, even slightly open. The skirt rises above the hips, also to highlight the very long necklaces and bejewelled belts. Boys and girls have similar clothing up to the age of seven, then boys are given the *cannoins*, puffy trousers, while girls have unique dresses with a long skirt.

The fundamental data of the second half of the sixteenth century is the end of the domination of Italian fashion and the emergence of specific fashions for England, Spain and France, which will influence, also and above all following the political events, the various Italian state regions. Venice is one of the few autonomous realities; exemplary will be, for example, the refusal of the most widespread accessory in the North, the gorget.

In the *Bella Nani*, the greatest attention is definitely paid to fabrics and, as per contemporary evidence, to jewels. Essential is the heavy gold necklace, traditionally with intertwined threads or links, long up to the belly which, as usual, ends with an imposing pendant. Equally usual for married women are pearls, as numerous as possible, and very large. The blue velvet dress, elegantly veiled by silk, is characterized by the belt formed by a twisted gold cord, interrupted at regular intervals by small roses with alternating rubies and sapphires, closed with a grotesque element, with gold scrolls and gems. That's not all: the dress is raised by two shoulder straps chiselled with pearls; on the wrists bracelets with segments in gold, rubies and sapphires, on the fingers three rings to underline the marital condition: a thin wedding ring is on the ring finger of the left hand, a ring with an emerald set on the middle finger, a ruby on the ring finger. The hand also directs to the very long, thin gold threads carelessly fixed to the neckline of the dress by clasps with sapphire gem. The pearls encircle the base of the *Bella*'s neck and then decorate the hair with hairpins and pins hidden in the laborious hairstyle, always loved by Veronese. Obviously her hair is that beautiful full blond to which every Venetian lady aspires, sunbathing on the roof terraces, with a suitable hat without a dome, wetting the hair with waters of perfumed essences; the curls frame her face.

Portrait of a Venetian Gentlewoman, (*La Bella Nani*), approx. 1558-1562, canvas, 119 × 103 cm. Paris, Musée du Louvre, inv. A.F. 2111

A few years later Veronese will propose a male portrait that represents the system of aesthetic and moral values of the gentleman. It is an exceptional full-length painting, an excellent work, also of refined psychological introspection: it is the *Gentleman with Hat in Hand* kept in the J. Paul Getty Museum in Malibu. The question of its dating is highly debated, ranging from 1560-1561 for Pignatti and Pedrocco, to more than a decade later for Rearick and others, including the museum, placing it between 1576 and 1578. For a painter like Veronese, who changes his stylistic choices significantly, dating is extremely difficult in the absence of documentary footholds. It is the case of this character: caught at the beginning of full maturity, very elegant in absolute simplicity, the sword at his side, leaning on a noble classicist architecture; in the distance a Basilica of San Marco located in the open countryside. The painter's working of a single colour is splendid, using all the shades of black: a single colour, but so slightly varied according to the fabric, that we can best admire the shoes and tights, the Spanish-style shorts, shredded and embroidered, the Venetian jacket and the satin cape.

The architectural apparatus is of reference: the figure leans lightly on a high marble plinth, on which two fluted columns rise on perfect attic bases. Between the columns a gilded bronze statue, predictably female. Very small, the profile of the basilica of San Marco, but located in the countryside, seems to be recognized on the seabed. An allusion? It could be: and even the cut of the eyes could refer to the refined diplomat Marcantonio Barbaro, Maser's other patron. What is certain is that the gaze and the expression show both distance and full self-control; the posture is that of the one who stops to allow the painter time to portray him, but he has other social and intellectual occupations. A gentleman, certainly: the "haughtiness of the painter", who with extreme skill represents all the possible nuances of velvet is, with evident psychological acumen, the "haughtiness of the gentleman", so distinct in the extreme elegance of simplicity.

If they were the Barbaro-Giustinian couple, they would still be in splendid harmony, like the Porto-Thiene; in any case we can and must admire them in their fullness of masterpieces with few equals in sixteenth-century Italian portraiture.

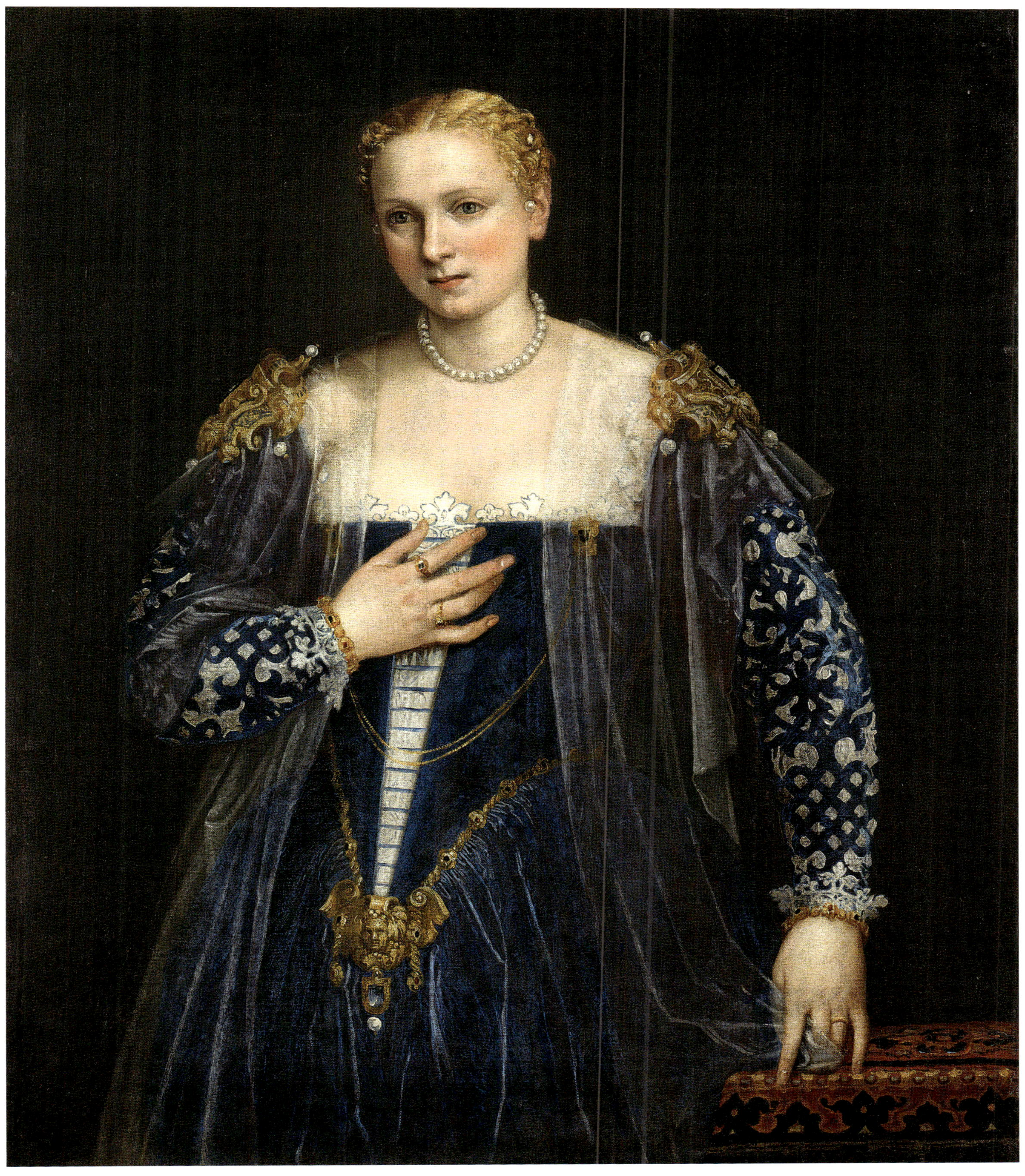

CHAPTER V

Venetian Winters

Established for home and workshop in Venice, Paolo and Benedetto often returned to Verona and to the mainland, while we have no documentary certainty of travels beyond the domains of the Serenissima. After the two – predictably - summers in Maser, Paolo agreed on a new important assignment: in January 1562 he accepted the contract for one of the most important decorations, the Sala del Maggior Consiglio in Palazzo Ducale. A commission obtained, in Ridolfi's opinion, thanks to the success of Maser's frescoes, with the task of painting a large canvas with a historical subject, an episode from the exploits of Frederick Barbarossa. Canvas with a short life: the devastating fire of 1577 reduced it to ashes.
Veronese is now perfectly integrated in Venice, even esteemed as a technician, with the assignment in 1563, in commission with Titian, Tintoretto, Schiavone, Sansovino and Iacopo da Pistoia, to judge the mosaics of the Zuccati in S. Marco, on which a controversy had developed regarding both the quality of the material and the timing of the work. The Venetian ruling class shared the opinions transmitted to us by Ridolfi:

> A few memorable sayings still refer to Paolo; that good judgment of painting could only be made by those who were well educated in the art; that this faculty was a gift from heaven, and that toil in it, without natural talent, was sowing in the waves; that the most worthy part of the painter was ingenuity and modesty, and that the images of Saints and Angels had to be painted by excellent painters, having to induce admiration and affection. He revered Titian as the father of the art, and greatly appreciated Tintoretto's lively wit. (Ridolfi 1648, pp. 78-79 – free traslation)

The active and professionally serious man that we have come to know through the few documents, the painter well aware of his own talent but also respectful of the great Masters, could only arouse envy and malice in a Venetian environment that has always nourished an inexhaustible source of gossip, often malicious and defamatory. Many foreigners who came to work in the city had noticed this, starting with Albrecht Dürer whose letters from Venice are significant and tasty testimonies of the jealousies accompanied by copying, plagiarism and imitations, constant in the Venetian arts milieu. Malevolent rumours began to intertwine about the Veronese, disguised as anecdotes; they will be transmitted for generations, authentic period fakes, such as the one that the Count de Caylus heard during his stay in the lagoon, almost two centuries later, in 1714. He informs us seriously – the guides have said and confirmed it! – how Veronese had spent years in the small monastery of the Hieronymites being in grave danger: he had painted the portrait of a Venetian nobleman, but then, having received the patron's complaints about a lack of resemblance in the painting, he offered to correct it. He returned it with the addition of a pair of horns, letting everyone know that now it lacked nothing to be truly similar. The furious and humiliated nobleman hired assassins to kill Paolo, who had to take refuge in the convent for years, so he had time to decorate it all. According to Caylus, the lie was true: one had to invent some little story about the very serious and punctual painter, who would not feed any anecdotal stories about himself. And on the other hand, how much anecdotes are loved by those who understand nothing about art!

Sermon of John the Baptist,
approx. 1562, canvas, 205 × 169 cm,
detail. Rome, Galleria Borghese,
inv. 137

THE MANIFESTATION OF THE SACRED

Baptism of Christ, 1561, canvas, 204 × 102 cm. Venice, church of the Redeemer, sacristy

Veronese's patrons were mainly religious orders, members of the patriciate and some rich and prestigious families in the city, but sometimes also less well-known merchants. Like the two characters portrayed in the right corner of the altarpiece for a chapel on the Giudecca. We are dealing with a Venetian shopkeeper, Bartolomeo Stravazino (Stravazin in his will dated 4 May 1565), portrayed in three-quarter view, humble and severe, ready to cast a withering glance at the less than devoted spectator, and his son Giovanni, who will only survive five years, ennobled with the small cross of pontifical knighthood. Giovanni devoutly "sees" the sacred scene: the model is that of the representation of the donors "in the abyss", i.e. not only in the corner, but in humility, in adoration but "external" to the sacred scene, according to a decidedly archaic scheme, evidently requested by the patrons, for life-like portraits.

This canvas with *The Baptism of Christ* was requested and created in 1561 to decorate an oratory, also characterizing it as a family shrine, in the small church of Santa Maria degli Angeli on the Giudecca. Part of the land occupied by the Capuchins, housed in a very poor convent, will be purchased, with other surrounding areas, by the Republic. On 4 September 1576 it was decided to build a rich church as a vow to defeat the plague that was decimating the city by laying the first stone on 3 May 1577 on the foundations along the great Giudecca canal: after the peak of the epidemic at the end of the summer, thanking for the miracle, the construction was entrusted to Palladio. The majestic building, clearly visible from San Marco and from the entrance to the Grand Canal, will be the famous church of the Redeemer. Over the centuries the memory of the event will remain with the annual votive procession to the sanctuary, and the dogal journey on a pontoon bridge to cross the canal is still the most loved and heartfelt of the many Venetian feasts.

The canvas with the *Baptism of Christ* was brought to the new building, placing it in the sacristy, a more hidden and less scenographic solution compared to the oratory for which it was painted. The perimeter addition transforms the altarpiece, originally arched, into a rectangular one, while successive energetic cleanings have impoverished the pictorial material; only a modern restoration has brought the damask of Giovanni's cloak back to its original colour, has made the colours more alive, closer to the original splendour. The bodies of Jesus and of the Baptist appear monumental against the background of the blue sky, where the clouds are harmless pink veils; John's position is higher up, according to the iconographic tradition, while the Baptized is in humility, his feet in the water, his head bowed, his arms folded in devotion. The face of Jesus is strongly foreshortened in an attitude of reverence, advancing one foot while bowing. The posture is moved and natural. The scene is attended, as in the tradition of so much Venetian painting, by two curly-haired, devoted and attentive angels, who combine the sexual identity of the male and female genders. We see the feet of a third angel. Winged cherubs, in Veronesian style "from bottom to top", escort the dove of the Spirit, bearer of an entirely transcendent, unnatural light, a true flash that makes the vegetation diaphanous: the instant of the Divine.

The Sacred manifests itself in Baptism as a prefiguration of the final Sacrifice: by accepting baptism in the Jordan as an act of purification, Jesus accepts his own human condition, the path of suffering and redemption that will take Him to Golgotha. The baptism introduces Christ into public life, it is the first theophanic manifestation, and the act is confirmed by the presence of the other persons of the Trinity, the voice of the Father and the descent of the Holy Spirit. Following Saint Paul, the descent of the Holy Spirit is the pledge of eternal salvation, and is the seal of brotherhood with Jesus Christ: "Do you not know that all of us who have been baptized into Christ Jesus were baptized into his death? We were buried therefore with him by baptism into death, in order that, just as Christ was raised from the dead by the glory of the Father, we too might walk in newness of life"(Romans 6:3-4). The high and sacred gesture of John the Baptist, the one who had prophesied "I indeed baptize you with water unto repentance, but He who is

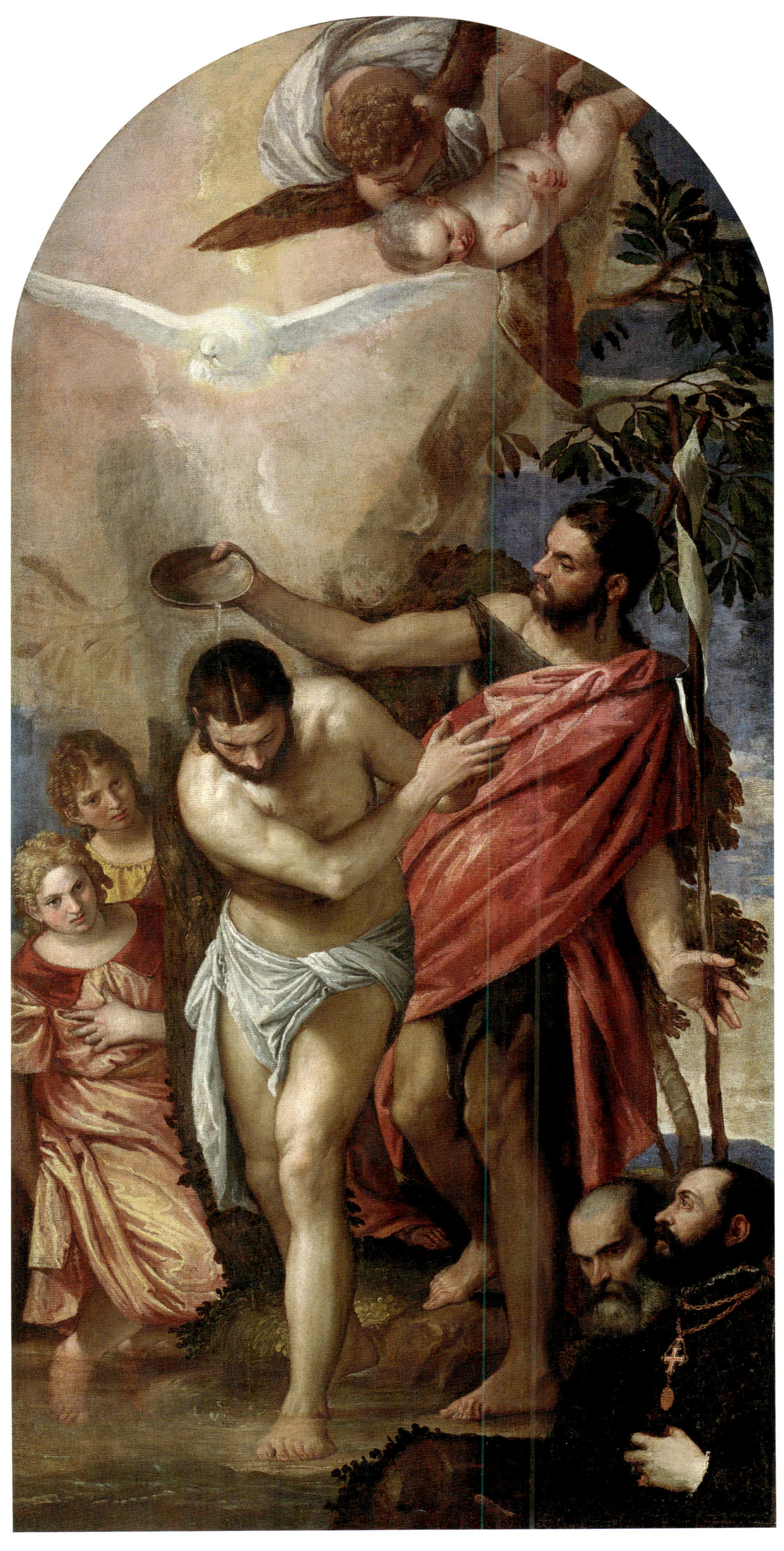

coming after me is mightier than I, whose sandals I am not worthy to carry. He will baptize you with the Holy Spirit and fire" (Mt 3, 11), underlines the lustral washing, purification and repentance, the spiritual rebirth and union with Christ.
Veronese has composed the scene with textual rectitude and visual concentration, enclosing the two bodies in an ideal rectangle. The dove with outstretched wings is grandiose, the two putti are acrobatic, the two angels are dignified observers, distant from the earthly reality of the donors "en abyme". On the compactly woven linen canvas support he limited the preparatory drawing, preparing a half tone ground with the subsequent application of light on dark tones. The decorative harmony and the serenity are given by the clear range of colours which, in the 1560s, opposed him to Tintoretto's "terribility", to those ghostly allusions which flicker in the mature Tintoretto. On the contrary, Paolo brings the taste for monumentality even in a canvas, like this one, of limited size, moved by the splendid reflections of the Venetian orange emanating from the angelic dress that illuminate the water of the Jordan and also shine on the golden bank. The chromatic orchestration of the robes – the red of John's mantle, the sky blue of the perizonium of the baptized person, the lead-tin yellow of the angel – is exemplary of Paolo's visuality.
The theme of Baptism will move the interest of the Master and his active workshop several times, in the search for different solutions; in particular John the Baptist is a recurring presence in Veronese's catalogue as a co-protagonist in the multiple Baptisms started with the canvases on the same subject today in Raleigh, North Carolina Museum of Art and in Braunschweig. He is also the protagonist of *The Preaching of John the Baptist* at the Galleria Borghese in Rome, where an ascetic addresses three "Orientals", represented through the three ages of life. Camel cloak, with a poor belt, the Baptist holds in his left hand the stick on which ECCE (obviously Agnus Dei) is written, and with his right indicates Christ the bearer of the good news to be preached to a group of waiting women. The woman with the child around her neck is a recurring appearance, from the *Anointing of David*.

EVERY GENRE AND SPECIES OF PAINTING

For an ecclesiastical and patrician clientele, Paolo creates in his workshop intense sacred scenes alternating with mythological scenes of open sensuality, marked by that evocation of antiquity and classical erudition that fascinates the intellectual world. And meanwhile he prepares great historical scenes for the elders, and panoplies of Venetian glory.
Thus, always premised on the questionable dating when documentary certainties are lacking, a canvas such as *Venus and Mercury Presenting Eros and Anteros to Jupiter*, today in the Uffizi. The painting contains all the elements of the most exquisite classicism: there are not only the characters of the myth, Venus in her perfect nudity, according to the canons of the time, Mercury with winged sandals and caduceus, and Jupiter recognizable by eagle and sceptre. There are the architectural references, with the high base supported by herms, and the Parian marble parapet. There is the vase and the cameo and the Arcadian atmosphere of the landscape, all the reconstruction of the classical world in the reading of the time. Curiously, we only see the legs of Jupiter, a choice of layout of great eccentricity and novelty, to which Veronese sometimes resolves with a compositional freedom that only the following century will be able to use.
Ridolfi remembered a series of canvases with the stories of Eros and Anteros in Giambattista Sanudo's house: a theme dear to the painter, for which Eros represents impulsive love, falling in love and passion, while his brother Anteros is the one who helps the growth of the little brother, that is, it makes love legitimate and lasting. The multiple versions of the Greek myth agree in narrating how Aphrodite, realizing that little Eros does not grow, asks Themis for the reason. The answer will be that love must be reciprocated in order to develop: Aphrodite will then gen-

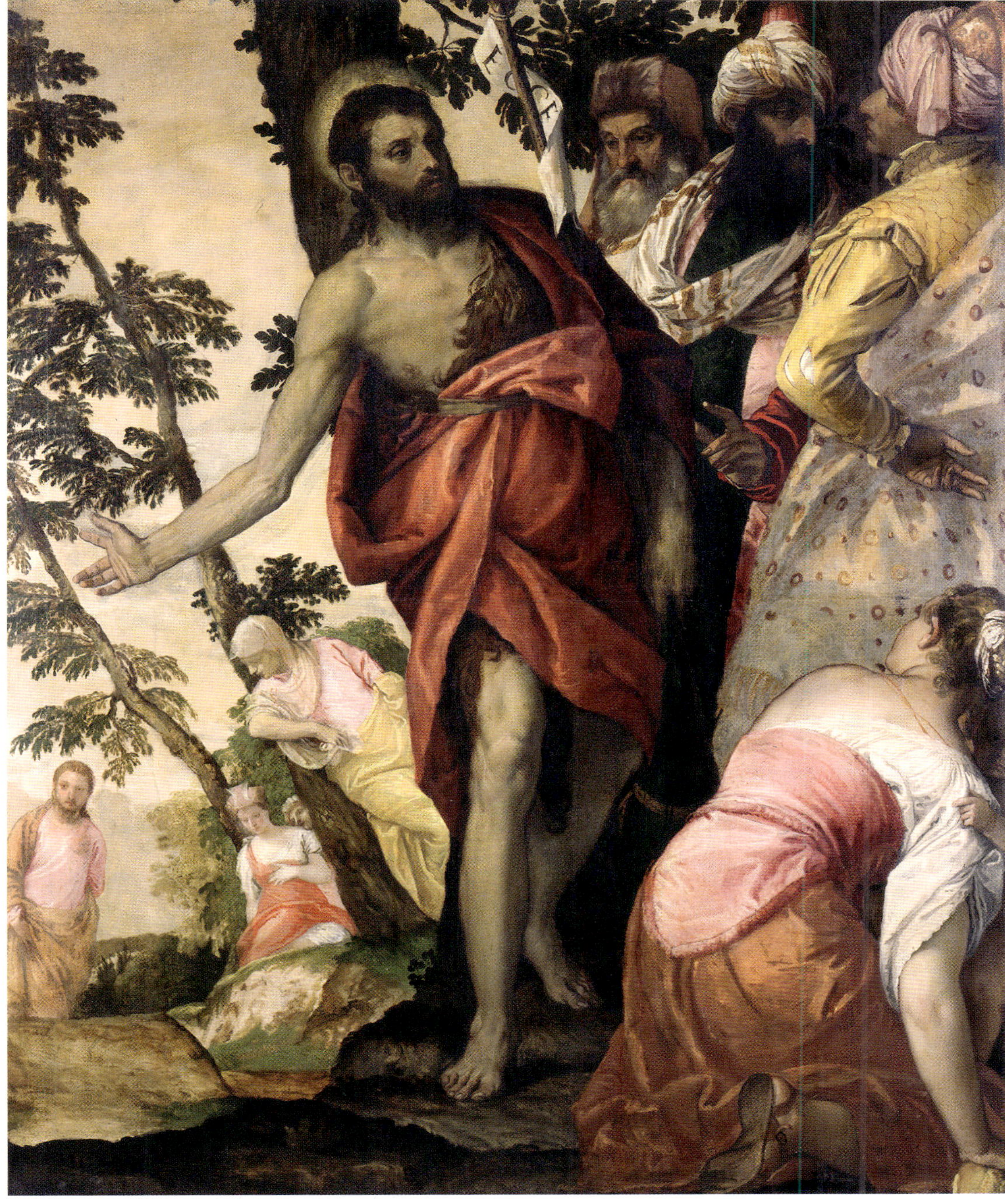

Sermon of John the Baptist, approx. 1562, canvas, 205 × 169 cm. Rome, Galleria Borghese, inv. 137

The canvas belonged to the Barbaro family. The chromatic system is remarkable, with the very light, almost nebulous tones towards the advancing Christ, and the brilliant, varied tones, moved by the strokes of light in the group on the right with the kneeling woman and the three oriental men, almost a tribute to Giorgione in the indication of the three ages of life.

erate with Ares another son, Anteros, often represented without wings, while Eros is winged, armed with a bow and numerous arrows in his quiver.

In the meantime, intense production for the monastic orders continues: already in March 1562 three altarpieces, for 98 scudi, are paid by the abbot of the Benedictine monastery of San Benedetto Po. The contract was signed on 27 December 1561, with the advance of 25 ducats. Made in a very short time, perhaps even one in a month, they will be seized after two centuries by the French, then sold and dispersed. They were compositions with few thickened characters and important colour solutions. The *Consecration of St Nicholas as Bishop of Myra* is now in the London National Gallery. Nicholas was bishop of the city on the southern coast of present-day Turkey in the 4th century; his relics arrived in Bari in 1087, stolen or bought, and the character is known today as San Nicola di Bari. Veronese's scene is inspired by the *Golden Legend*, which narrates how, on the eve of the election of the bishop, a voice announced that a young man called Nicholas had already been chosen by heaven: he would arrive first at the door of the

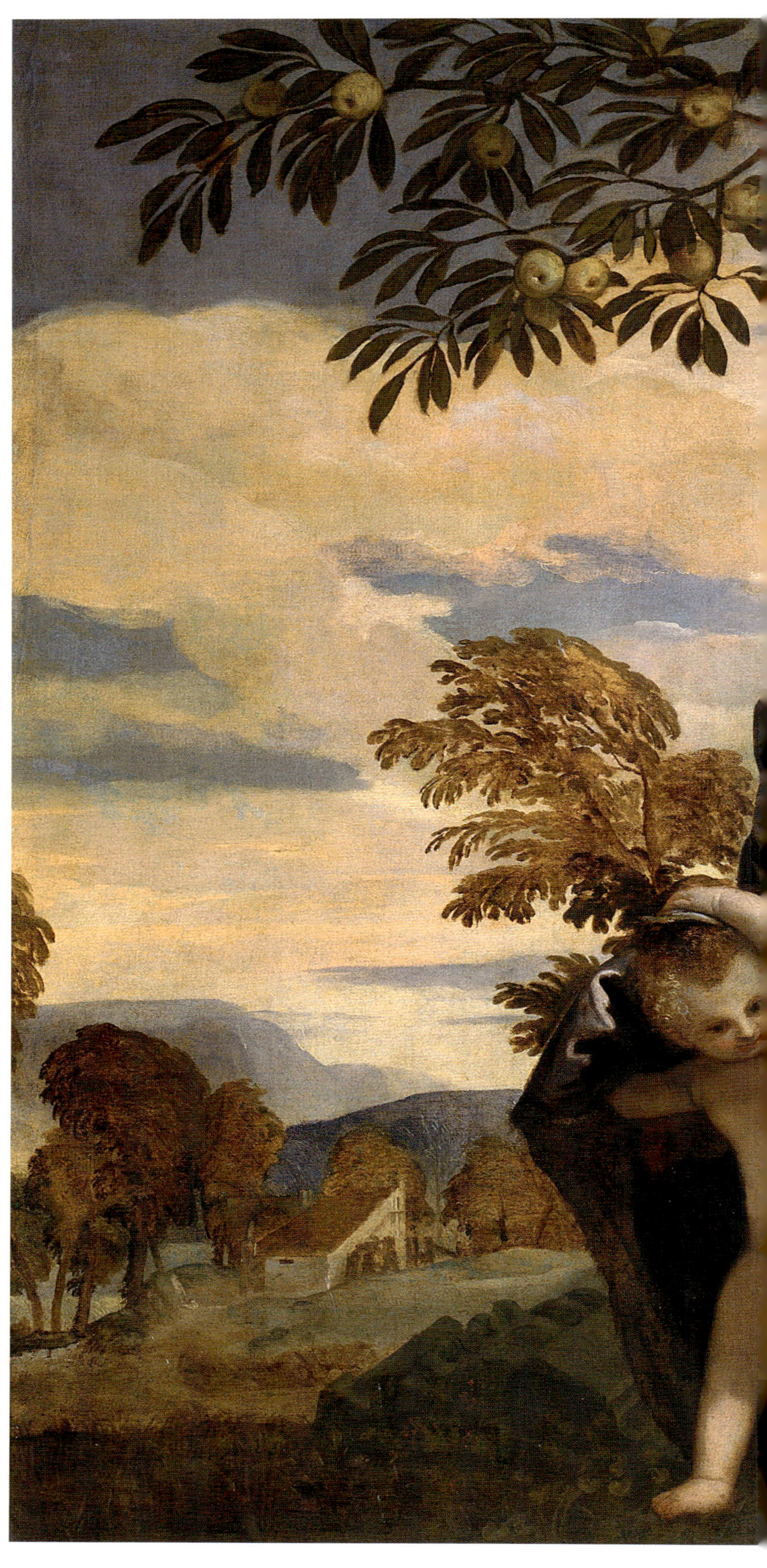

Venus and Mercury Presenting Eros and Anteros to Jupiter, 1562-1564 (?), canvas, 150 × 243 cm. Florence, Galleria degli Uffizi, Collezione Contini Bonacossi

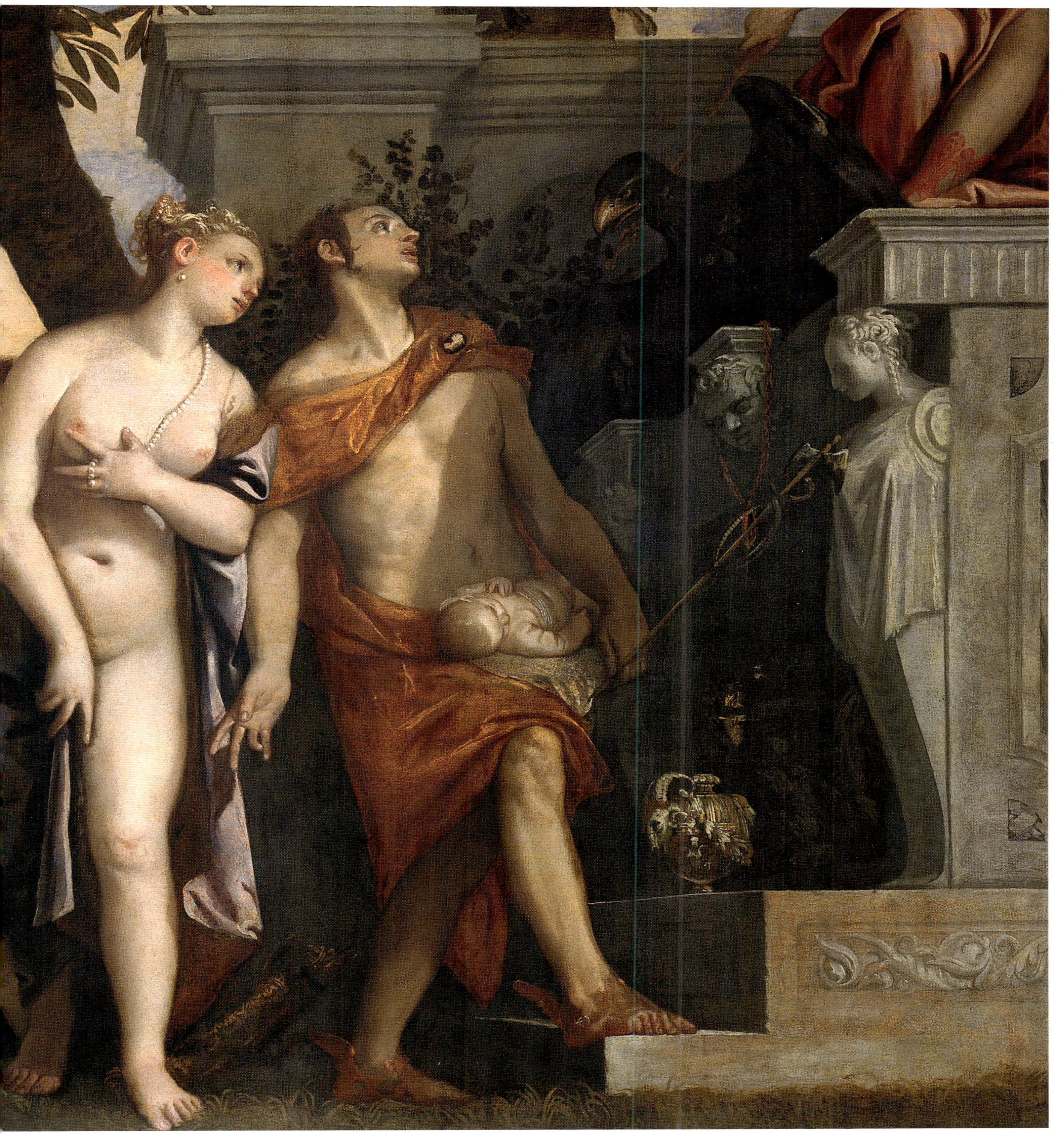

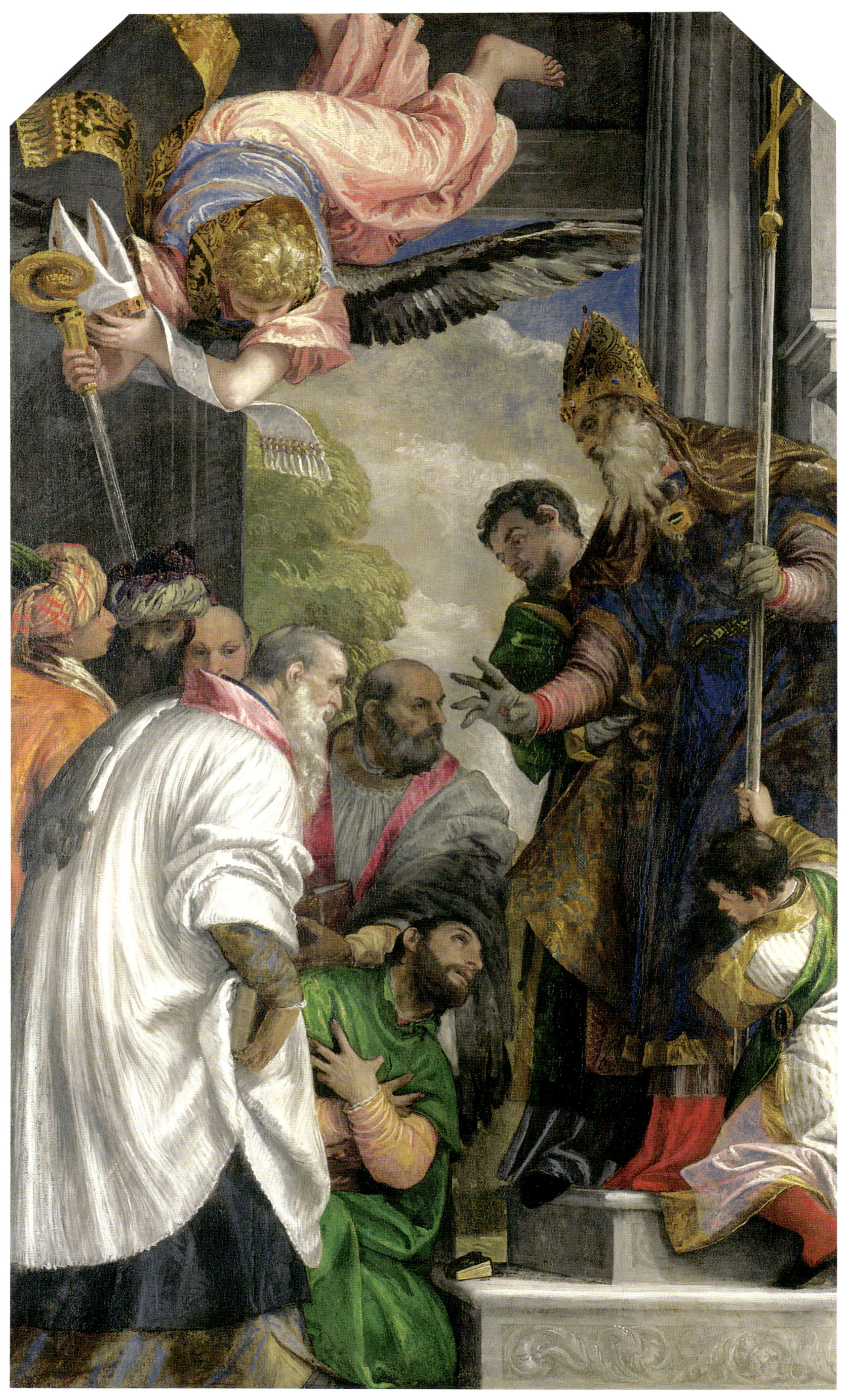

cathedral. The painter portrays him on his knees, in an emerald green robe, the main colour in the geometric centre, flanked by two older priests in white surplices, with a notable use of grey to highlight the folds. The angel carries the mitre, the stole and the crozier, attesting to the divine choice, while the turbans confirm the oriental setting. The altarpiece of Saint Nicholas was taken from the abbey church in the French capture of Mantua in 1797, then sold and purchased in 1811 by the governors of the "British Institution for Promoting the Fine Arts in the United Kingdom", becoming the first Veronese exhibited in a public institution in England. The other canvas with the *Madonna Appearing to Saint Jerome*, also purchased in England, was lost in a fire in 1836. The third, the *Apparition of the Madonna and Child to Saints Anthony Abbot and Paul* is now in Norfolk: after various auctions and at least five private collections, it was purchased by Walter Chrysler in 1954. In a suffused golden light, the Madonna and Child and a brief escort of angels appear to the two elderly, miserable hermits, roused from meditations. The abbot stands with difficulty on his stick, lifts the rosary with which he prayed; faced with the vision, Paul seems to fear for his heart, while the large book of scriptures on which he meditated slips from his knees. Bare feet, earthy bodies, unkempt beards, the signs of an ascetic life are marked with the browns of sackcloth; on the contrary there is the bright satin of the inhabitants of the celestial spheres: the silvery blue, a yellow of ripe lemons, a splendid emerald green that we still appreciate, after so many secular ordeals. The large and ancient abbey of San Benedetto Po was already at the end of its resources in the eighteenth century, and the abbot had had to sell the body of the Countess Matilde di Canossa to the Vatican to obtain the necessary subsidies to compensate for the disasters of the floods; with the arrival of the French, the church will lose its last treasures.

Again for the Benedictines, for the abbey of Santa Maria Assunta in Praglia, Paolo completes two canvases: an animated *Glory of Angels* that we see in the convent art gallery, with a wide use of blue for robes juxtaposed with pink, and *The Martyrdom of Saints Primus and Felician*, since 1886 in the Civic Museum of Padua. Spectacular for the solution of the dramatic beheading in the foreground, resolved in formal classicism in the wide sky between the column in the foreground, the distant glimpse and the flag raised to dominate the scene so full of characters.

The altarpiece for the sacristy of the Venetian church of San Zaccaria – *Holy Family with Saints Baptist as a child, Jerome, Francis, and Stella* – could be dated between 1563 and 1564; now it is in Venice Academy, also known as Bonaldo Altarpiece; it was taken to Paris and returned to Venice in 1815. The altarpiece had been offered for the sacristy by Francesco Bonaldo also in memory of his brother Girolamo and his son Giovanni who died, as written on the tombstone, at just twelve years, six months, seven days, ten hours: the calculation tells us how bitter the regret was. The family affair will be just as painful: Francesco Bonaldo will in fact be declared insane and locked up in his villa in Fiesso; his wife Stella will order a cycle for the family palace in San Stae, now dispersed in French collections.

Here, on the pedestal in the centre, with the mirror in red Verona marble – almost a signature – there is the little John caught placing his hand on the eponymous saint Francis, while on the opposite side is a tired and suffering Jerome, lowering his gaze; the figures refer to the remembered family members. Particular is the choice of the Madonna's large fringed mantle, the luxurious golden drape with plant motifs hanging in the niche: the fabric called *griccia*, the most precious Venetian material, refers to the activity of the family of the donor. The altarpiece is truly a beautiful synthesis of Veronese's journey from the time of his work for the Lazises: if the pyramidal construction is identical, now the expressive choices and portraiture quality are mature, even in the young woman, an exemplary Venetian beauty. The choice of colours is very skilful, starting with the light plum of the large coat; note also the complete skill in the rapid drafting on the canvas prepared with plaster and glue, without priming.

In the *Giustiniani Altarpiece* in San Francesco della Vigna (around 1551), as well as in the *Bonaldo Altarpiece* for the sacristy of San Zaccaria, Veronese compares himself with Titian in

Consecration of St Nicholas as Bishop of Myra, 1562, canvas, 282.5 × 170.8 cm. London, National Gallery of Art, inv. 26

Following pages

Apparition of the Madonna and Child to Saints Anthony Abbot and Paul, 1562, canvas, 285 × 170 cm. Norfolk, Chrysler Collection, inv. 71.527

Glory of Angels, 1562, canvas, 350 × 190 cm. Praglia, abbey of Santa Maria Assunta

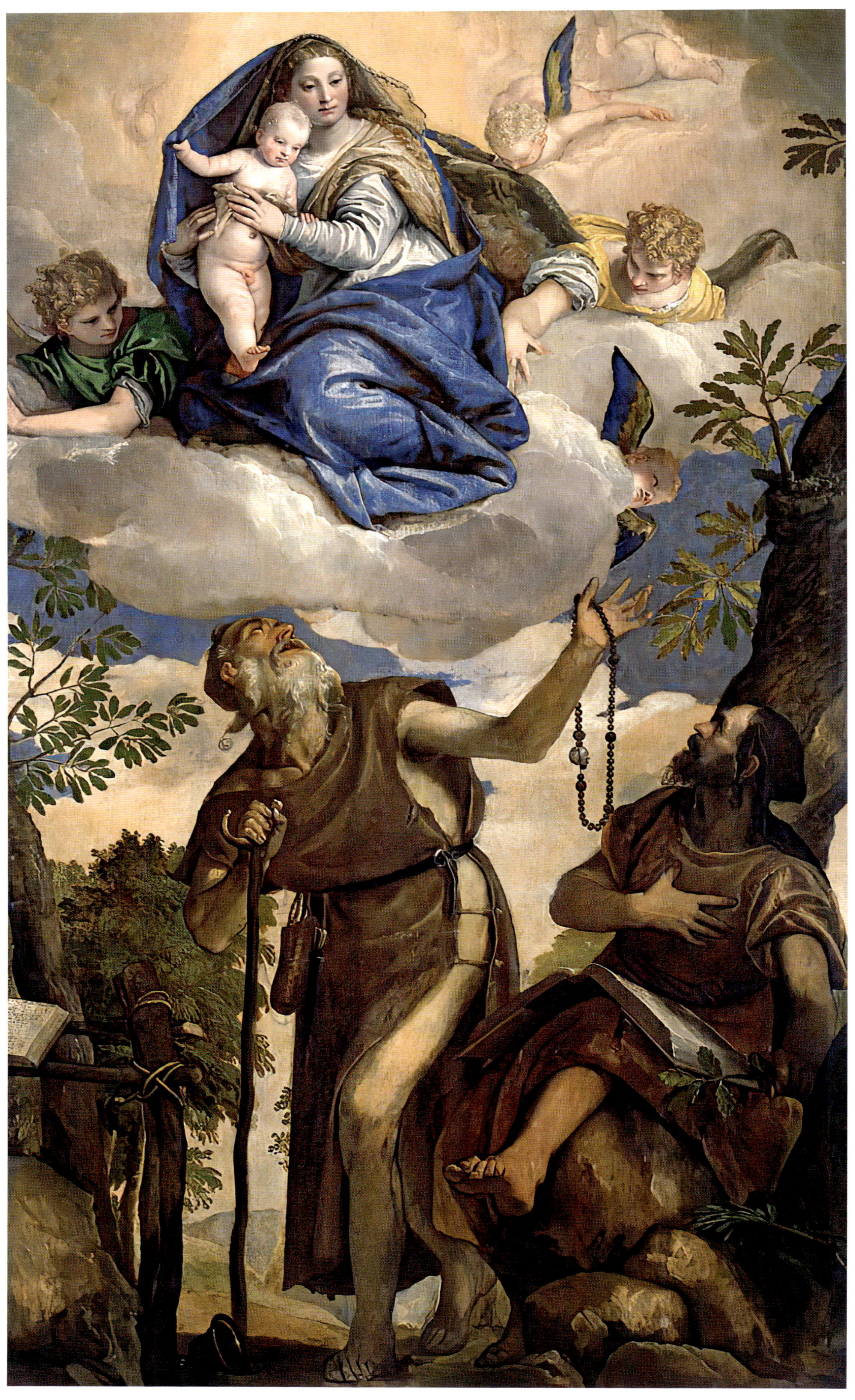

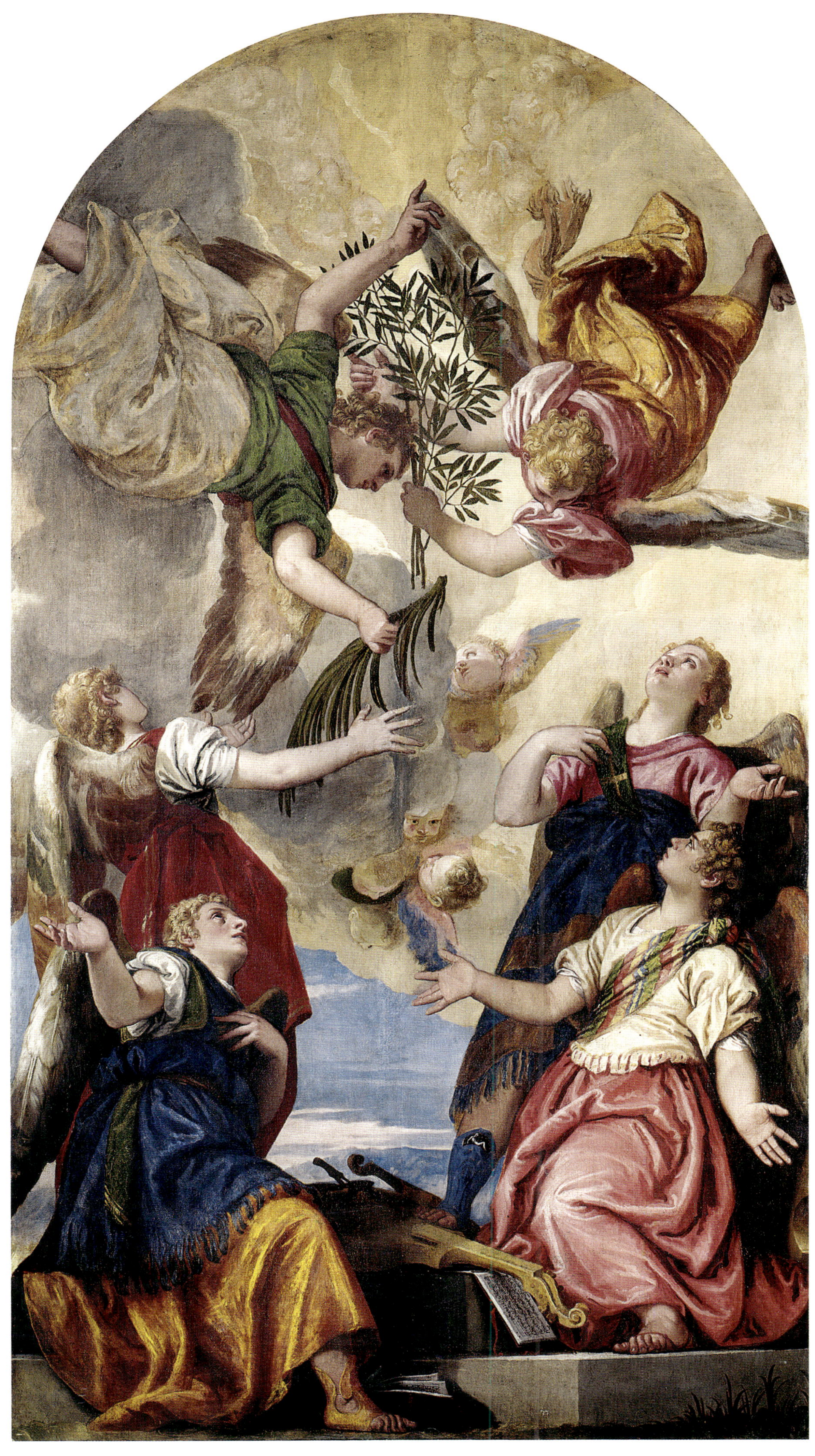

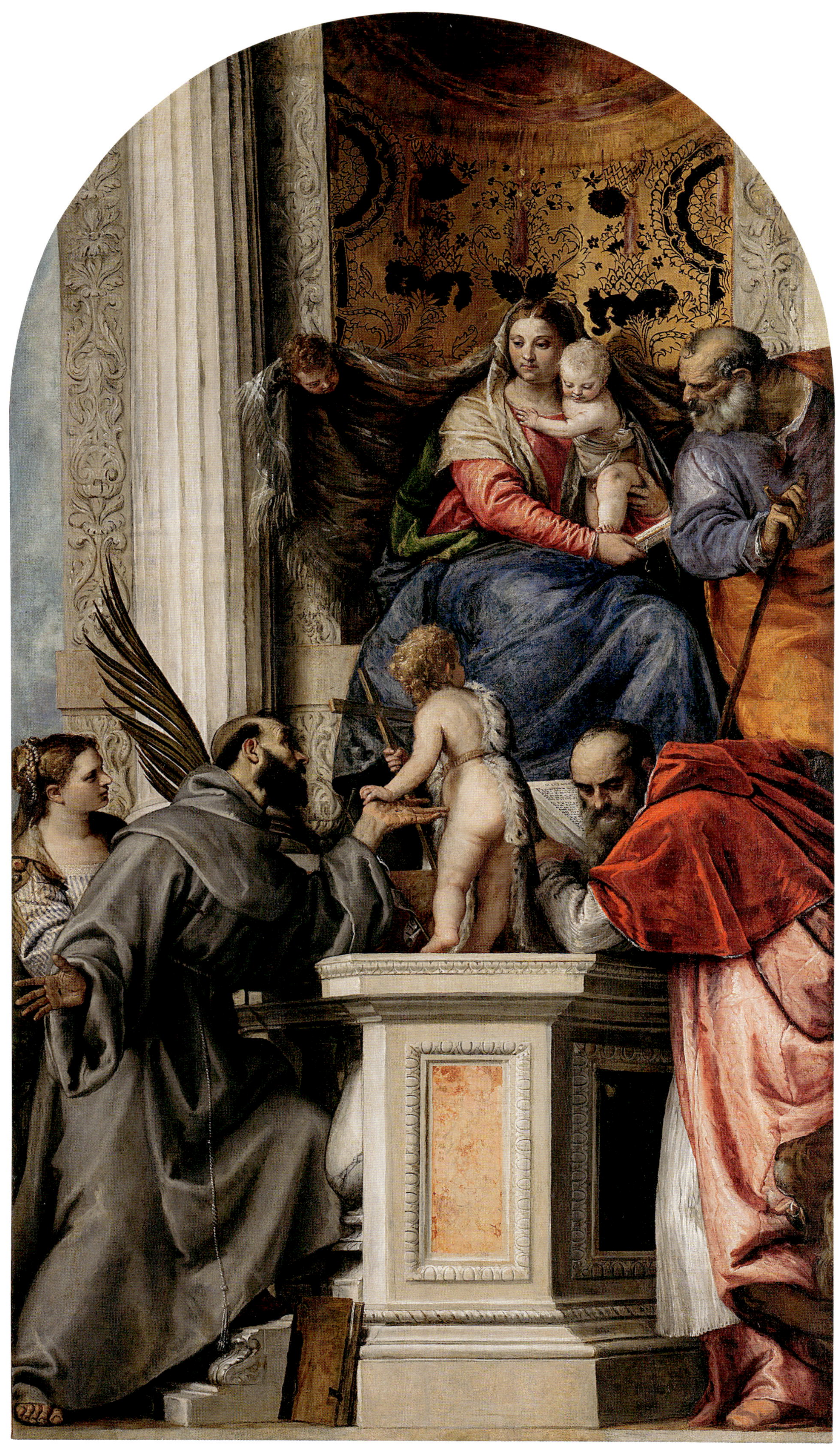

the choice of the diagonal foreshortening and in the general theatrical conception of the whole, but he chooses the almost front view of the characters to let the viewer participate in the sacred scene. This solution will be fortunate, becoming the ideal prototype of the "Madonna enthroned with saints", surpassing the model of "Sacred conversation" and obtaining narrative and dynamic effects with the theatricality of the postures and expressions. There is no longer the timeless fixity of Bellini's altarpieces, a gathering of saints to whom the faithful turn to ask for the intercession of the Madonna; now the scene is active: it is the saints themselves who show attitudes of prayers, emotional transport, asking the devotee for the same fervour.

With a large clientele and a well-established business, financial security and social recognition, Paolo thinks it is high time to get married: he is now thirty-eight years old. The bride has been known since the time of youthful acquaintances, she is the twenty-six-year-old Elena, one of the daughters of the painter Antonio Badile, his master, who has now been deceased for five years. The wedding is celebrated in the church of Santa Cecilia in Verona, and from Verona, is the ring bearer and witness, a long-time friend, the painter Paolo Farinati. Then the dowry deed is stipulated: with Farinati the other witness is Anselmo Canera, a pupil of Caroto who is also in a youth association with Paolo. With the arrival of the children and the presence of servants and journeymen, the need for space will grow. Paolo Caliari will not buy a house in the city but will rent, after the *mezado* of Vincenzo Zen, a building owned by Vincenzo Morosini for no less than sixty ducats a year and later a larger property in San Samuele, belonging to Jacopo Federici. Daily life, family and business are now and will always be permanently in Venice: he will return to the mainland for work but also to buy fields and a country house.

Around 1566, the year of his marriage to Elena Badile, the large and crowded canvas with the *Martyrdom of Saint George* must have been placed in S. Giorgio in Braida during a stay in Verona. In the place of honour in the presbytery of the important building, the altarpiece concludes the perspective of the ecclesiastical hall, which from the mid-fifteenth century belonged to the powerful congregation of San Giorgio in Alga, on the structures of a previous, ancient monastic building. The majestic dome on the short transept was designed by Sanmicheli, and finished by his disciple Bernardino Brugnoli. Eight chapels were decorated with altarpieces admired over the centuries, among others by Goethe, equally masterpieces of the Veronese: all, starting with Giovan Francesco Caroto, and then Paolo Farinati, witness to the wedding of Paolo and Elena; naturally Brusasorci, and Girolamo dai Libri, Pasquale Ottino, Francesco Montemezzano and Sigismondo de Stefani. In the apse the *Martyrdom* is immediately recognized as the best work also for the solution of proposing the martyrdom of the holy knight instead of the traditional challenge with the dragon. The canvas is above all enhanced by the grandiose architectural machine of the altar: four Corinthian columns support a sumptuous and dynamic tympanum, accompanying the apse in its curvilinear movement. This monumental frame, attributed to Bernardino Brugnoli, will have been, if not drawn, certainly agreed with Paolo due to the intrinsic quality of the relationship with the painting. In his *Osservazioni nella pittura* from 1580, a contemporary, Cristoforo Sorte, wrote that Veronese: "gave his marvellous decoration to the figures made in those clouds, thus in having made them figures of sweet colours, and divinely illuminated by supercelestial splendour, as also in having understood the perspective of the distance, both in the distant figures and in those who are in the plane and represent, as it is, the natural, are very well understood and done with perfect reasoning." The painted scene is very rich, divided between two levels: in the celestial one the Madonna is circumfused by the theological Virtues, the Faith with the chalice to whom Saint Paul addresses, the Charity with two infants, the Mother with the Child to whom Saint Peter looks with the keys; Hope asks to intercede for the holy martyr, in silent dialogue of glances with George who, below, is about to be martyred. A little angel glides carrying both the palm of martyrdom and the crown of glory with which he will reward the martyr, while the executioner prepares himself, leaning on his great sword. In vain, a bearded, livid pagan priest invites George

Holy Family with Saints Baptist as a Child, Jerome, Francis, and Stella (Bonaldo Altarpiece), 1563-1564 (?), canvas, 341.5 × 193 cm. Venice, Gallerie dell'Accademia, inv. 345

Painting it for the sacristy of the Venetian church of San Zaccaria, Paolo Veronese had to deal, even if not directly, with the altarpiece by Giovanni Bellini, already considered a seminal work. In fact, the study of light and the relationship with the apse, and even more the dialogue of colours, show the attention to the work of the Master. But then Veronese develops the theme with an absolutely familiar reference, through the eponymous saints, and a more personal and psychologically penetrating religiosity, always reaffirming his singular personality through the architectural elements and the work on fabrics.

to pay homage to a bronze idol. The whole scene is crowded by the actors of Paolo's now stable company: in the elaborate architectures, inhabited by classical sculptures, there are armigers, Orientals with their elaborate turbans, Moors and a distant crowd on the balustrades. Two horses seem to observe the scene with more pitiful looks than humans. Paolo Caliari has put his entire repertoire on the stage illuminated by the clear daylight. And all his colours shine brightly.
In the same period we find *The Adoration of the Shepherds*, for the chapel of the Silk Weavers in the church of Santa Maria dei Crociferi in Venice. Transported at the end of the 19th century to the current chapel of the Rosary in the church of Santi Giovanni e Paolo, it appears with the reckless perspective exercise of the upside down, and the portraiture exercise of the faces of the shepherds, a popular novelty in a painter for aristocrats; parallel is an *Annunciation*, equally reckless in architecture accentuated by large twisted columns, and an angel descending from the other on Mary who welcomes the news of her future motherhood with open arms, in total acceptance.
Within a numerous and varied production, including large altarpieces and mythological subjects, and always large canvases, while also satisfying a clientele that still asks for smaller devotional canvases, Paolo Caliari pays homage to his great patron, as well as "tutor" in Venice. He does so with the splendid *Portrait of Daniele Barbaro*, today at the Rijksmuseum in Amsterdam, proposing the highly esteemed patron with his work on Vitruvius in the edition prepared with the contribution of Andrea Palladio; there is also a leaflet dedicated to clocks, not a secondary technical, mechanical and scientific interest of the humanist scholar.

Martyrdom of Saint George, 1564, canvas, 426 × 305 cm. Verona, church of San Giorgio in Braida

BACK TO SAN SEBASTIANO

Paolo returned to San Sebastiano in 1565 for the installation of the altarpiece of the main altar, the *Madonna and Child in Glory with Angels Playing Music, Adored by Saints Roch, Sebastian, Peter, Francis, Catherine and Elizabeth*. They are the eponymous saints of the family members of Cataruzza Cornaro, sister-in-law of Alvise Soranzo who commissioned Treville and had acquired the right to be buried in the main chapel. The altar was built by Salvatore Tagliapietra to a design by Paolo, and financed by Elisabetta Soranzo.
This iconography of the "Madonna in glory with saints" will be even more successful than the "Madonna enthroned" in the space shared with saints and proposed in theatrical form with boxes, steps, thrones, canopies, colonnades. The "Glory", on the other hand, clearly separates the earthly and heavenly worlds, also indicating the ascent of Mary in body and soul, reaffirming a dictum of faith that much later would become dogma, and responding better to post-Tridentine mysticism.
For San Sebastiano Paolo Caliari will reserve two other grandiose canvases, masterpieces of his style as a painter of stories. To the left of the high altar we see *The Saints Mark and Marcellinus Led to Martyrdom*: two twins condemned for their faith accept death spurred on by Sebastian, in the armour of a centurion. The old mother despairs, dishevelled, her arms thrown to heaven, heartbroken, she would like to hold them back; the disconsolate father spreads his arms, the anguished wives show their little children, soon to be orphaned. Sebastian's gesture is imitated by a little monkey, a dog comes down the stairs, slow and worried: perhaps they warn that martyrdom will not be understood by the ignorant crowd, but only by the innocent.
The second canvas repeats the *Martyrdom of Saint Sebastian*, for the public of the faithful who cannot see the frescoes in the choir of the friars. Albanian signs and flags return, and a crowd gathering never seen before; some sort of *horror vacui* for which Paolo inserts into the painting every profile, every face, every possible turban and headdress, bare torsos and muscular arms, pages and beggars, Moors and abbots. An all-male crowd, the only female presence is a statue. It must have meant something.

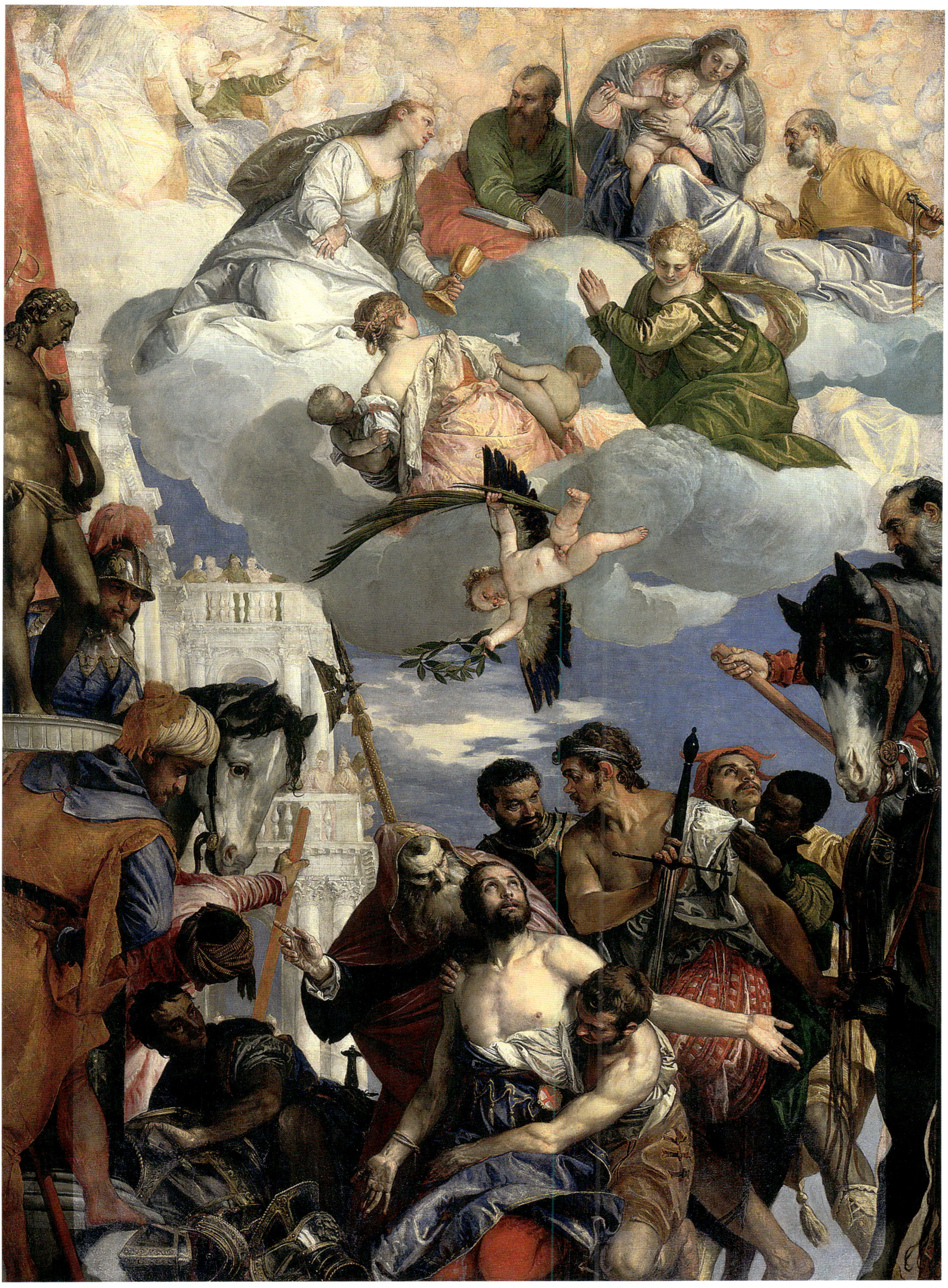

And again: on the terrible and gnarled stick with which the saint will be martyred, Paolo paints the word "Lazarum"; to understand its meaning, and its declination in the accusative, we need to refer to the initial verse of a well-known responsory, in ceremonies for the deceased: "*Qui Lazarum resuscitasti a monumento foetidum tu eis domine dona requiem*". The word on the cudgel turns from a prayer to a menacing and macabre warning in the hands of the executioner. Tremendous reference to the terribleness of the torture, warning of the fatal bludgeon, once again very "oriental".

The middle of the seventh decade corresponds to the fullness of Paolo Caliari's pictorial art, best expressed in a canvas always much admired by the lucky contemporaries who saw it, and then over the centuries by the guests of the Pisani family. Purchased after years of negotiations by the English royal museum for a sum so high at the time as to provoke a parliamentary question, considered Veronese's masterpiece by John Ruskin, the canvas has been one of the prestigious witnesses of Italian painting in the National Gallery in London since 1857. It is *The Family of Darius before Alexander*, painted for Francesco Pisani, perhaps shortly after 1565, for other historians around 1573 for the Pisani Moretta family in San Polo. It presents the Macedonian leader as a model of virtue, in the tradition of humanistic painting: after the defeat of the Persians, the mother, wife and daughters of Darius, fearing for their fate, went to the victor's tent at night, to implore his clemency. Alexander received them, flanked by his faithful friend and general, Hephaestion. Dario's mother prostrated in front of the latter, not recognizing Alexander: when she was told her mistake, she was even more afraid. But the magnanimous forgave her, indicating Hephaestion as the "other Alexander". Example of clemency and greatness of mind in fraternal friendship, according to Plutarch the nobility of Alexander was recognized by the defeated Persian king. The Greek biographer adds that the daughters of Darius married Alexander and Hephaestion. But the best-known source of the anecdote exposed by Veronese is the *Factorum et Dictorum Memorabilium* by Valerius Maximus, with numerous editions, translations and abridged versions printed in Venice. A sign of magnanimity and moral warning, the much admired scene was recreated by Tiepolo almost exactly at Villa Cordellina.

The event follows the flight of Darius III king of Persia after the defeat in the battle of Issus in 330 BC. Veronese presents the elderly Sisigambis in broad daylight on her knees in front of Alexander's friend, mistaken for the victor. Hephaestion, in armour, with an orange cloak, looks surprised and points to himself. Alexander comforts Sisigambis and with the gesture of his hands explains the right identity. Behind the elderly mother we see Dario's wife, Stateira, and the two young daughters dressed in the Venetian fashion of the Sixties, as can be seen from the shoulder pads. Hephaestion wears plate armour, typically Italian and contemporary, while Alexander's costume is a deep pink, the armour is painted on sculptural models, but the chain mail and sword are from the sixteenth century. The background is Palladian, a theatrical scenography accentuated by the low horizon: the whole scene is created in the taste of the mix between present and past typical of Veronese. The staging is theatrical: Sisigambis mentions Stateira, in turn presented by the man who accompanies them; her eldest daughter has her mother's crown on her arm; Dario's son is the child dressed in red who shelters next to his grandmother, in a large blue mantle lined with ermine, the dress of Venetian prosecutors. Crowded, rich and expressive as usual the group on the right, under the enormous head of a horse, the famous Bucephalus; various armed men, a dog and a page intent on curiously spying on the child in red, the vanquished heir. This page leans on a shield, apparently in leather, which shows a two-tailed siren, emblem of the temptation to which Alexander does not give in. A little monkey, symbol of unbridledness, inability to control itself, is well chained: Alexander therefore virtuously dominates instincts and temptations. Curious and particular are the "Egyptian" hairstyles of the slaves, where the dwarf fool takes refuge with the dogs: he will soon be a protagonist in the *Conviti*. The painting is above all a feast of colours; what Marco Boschini wrote is true:

Madonna and Child in Glory with Angels Playing Music, Adored by Saints Roch, Sebastian, Peter, Francis, Catherine and Elizabeth, 1562, canvas, 420 × 230 cm. Venice, church of San Sebastiano, altarpiece of the main altar

Following pages
The Saints Mark and Marcellinus Led to Martyrdom, 1565, canvas, 355 × 540 cm. Venice, church of San Sebastiano

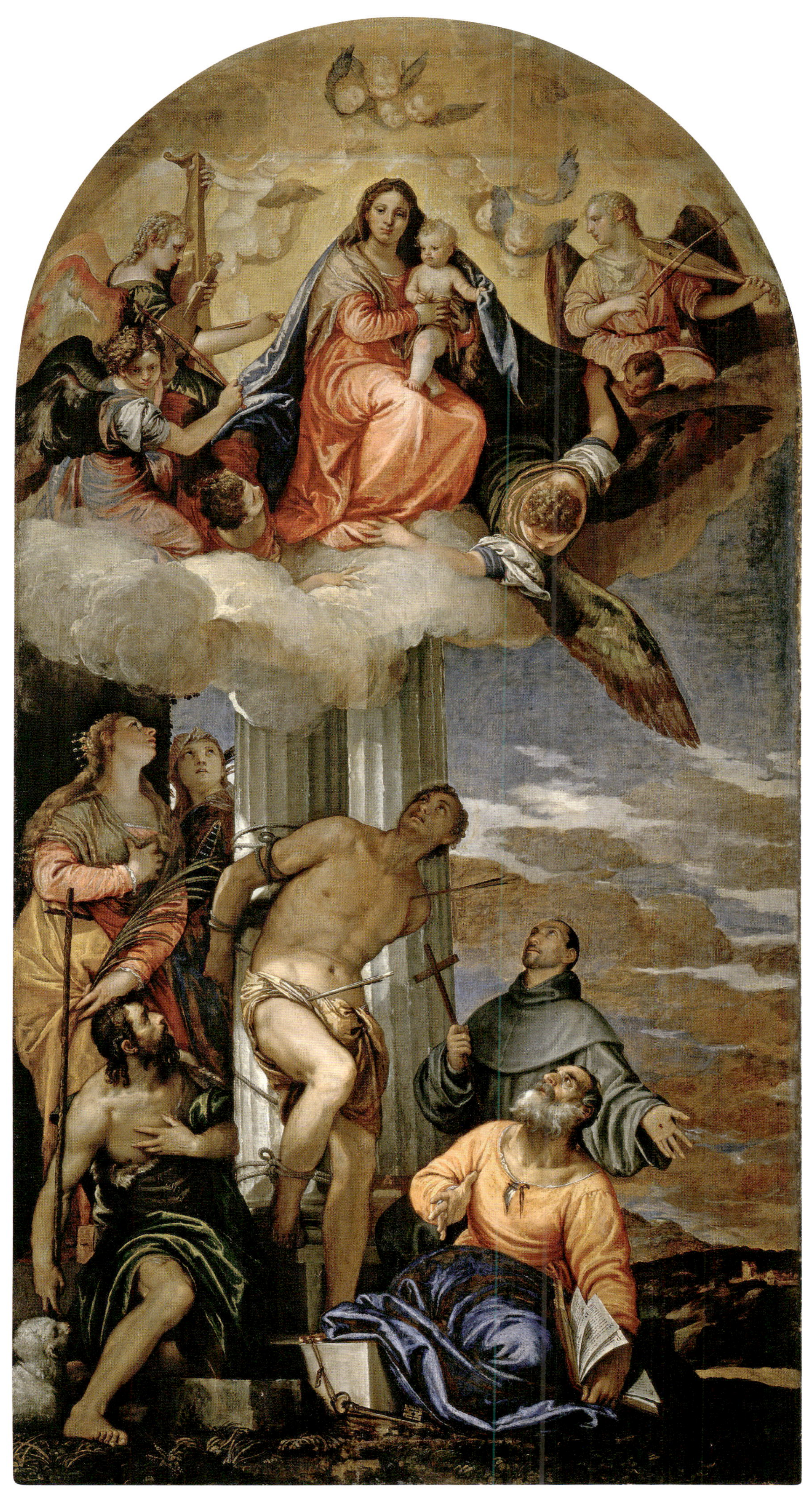

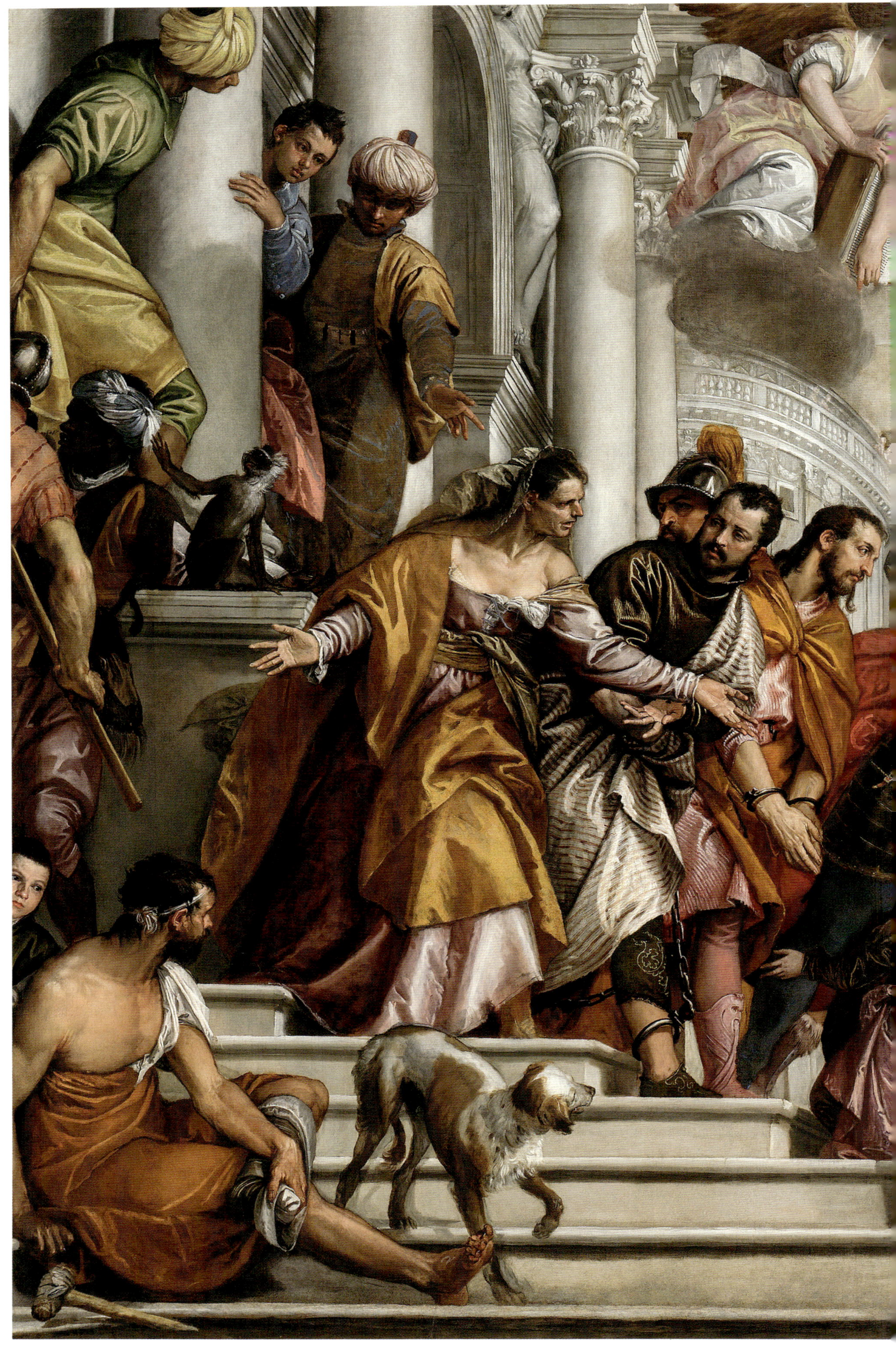

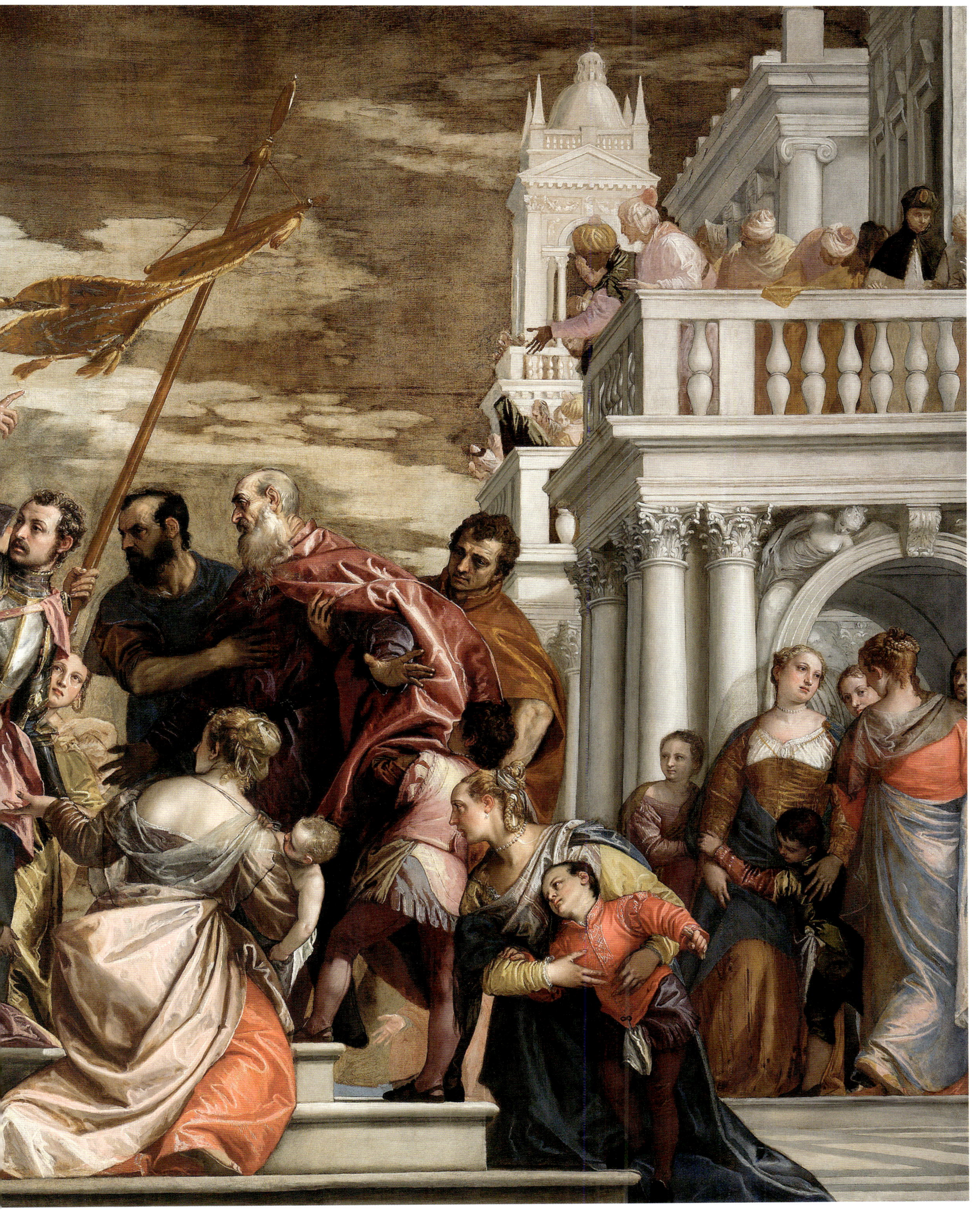

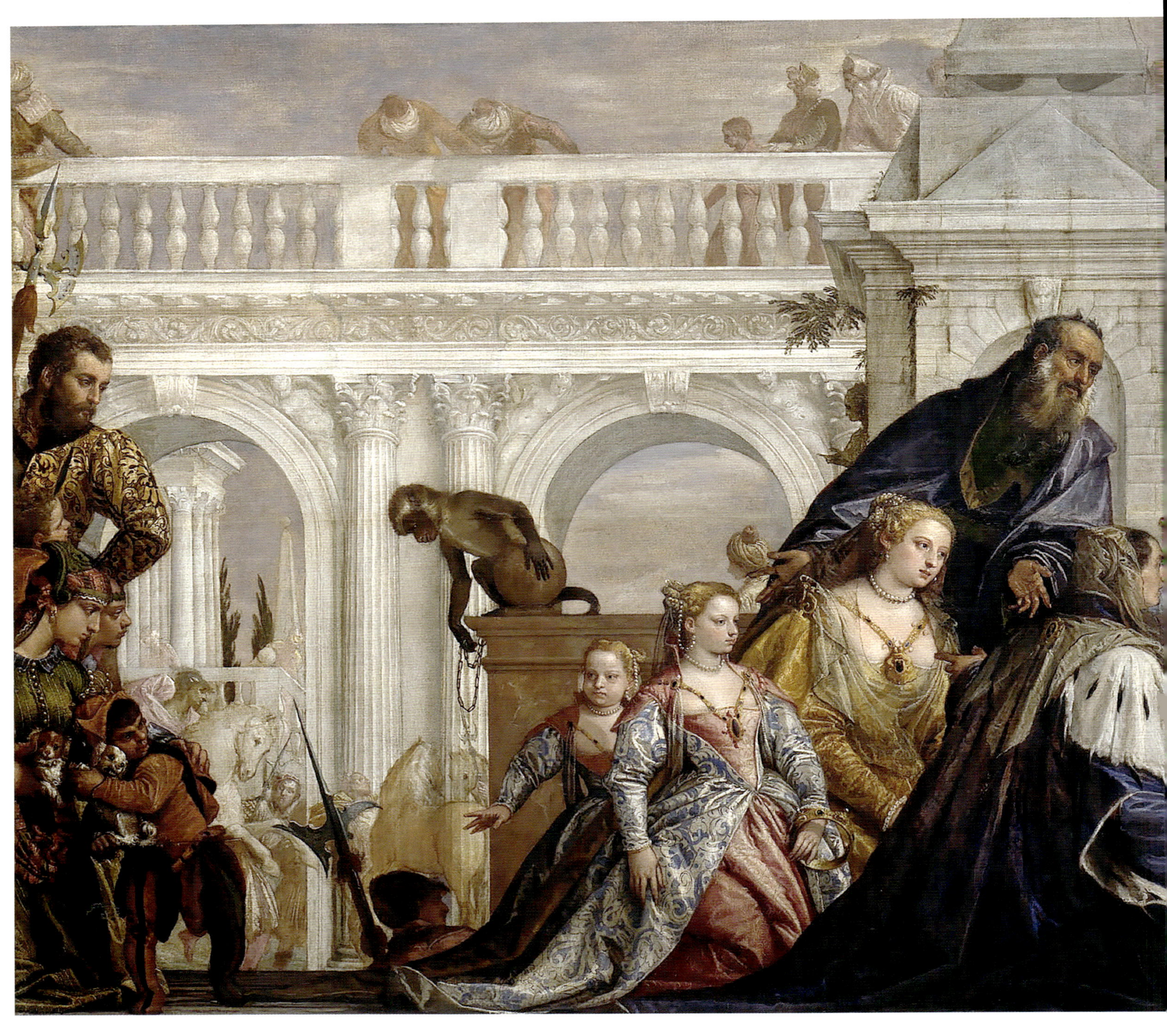

The Family of Darius before Alexander, between 1565 and 1573, canvas, 236 × 475 cm. London, National Gallery of Art, inv. 294

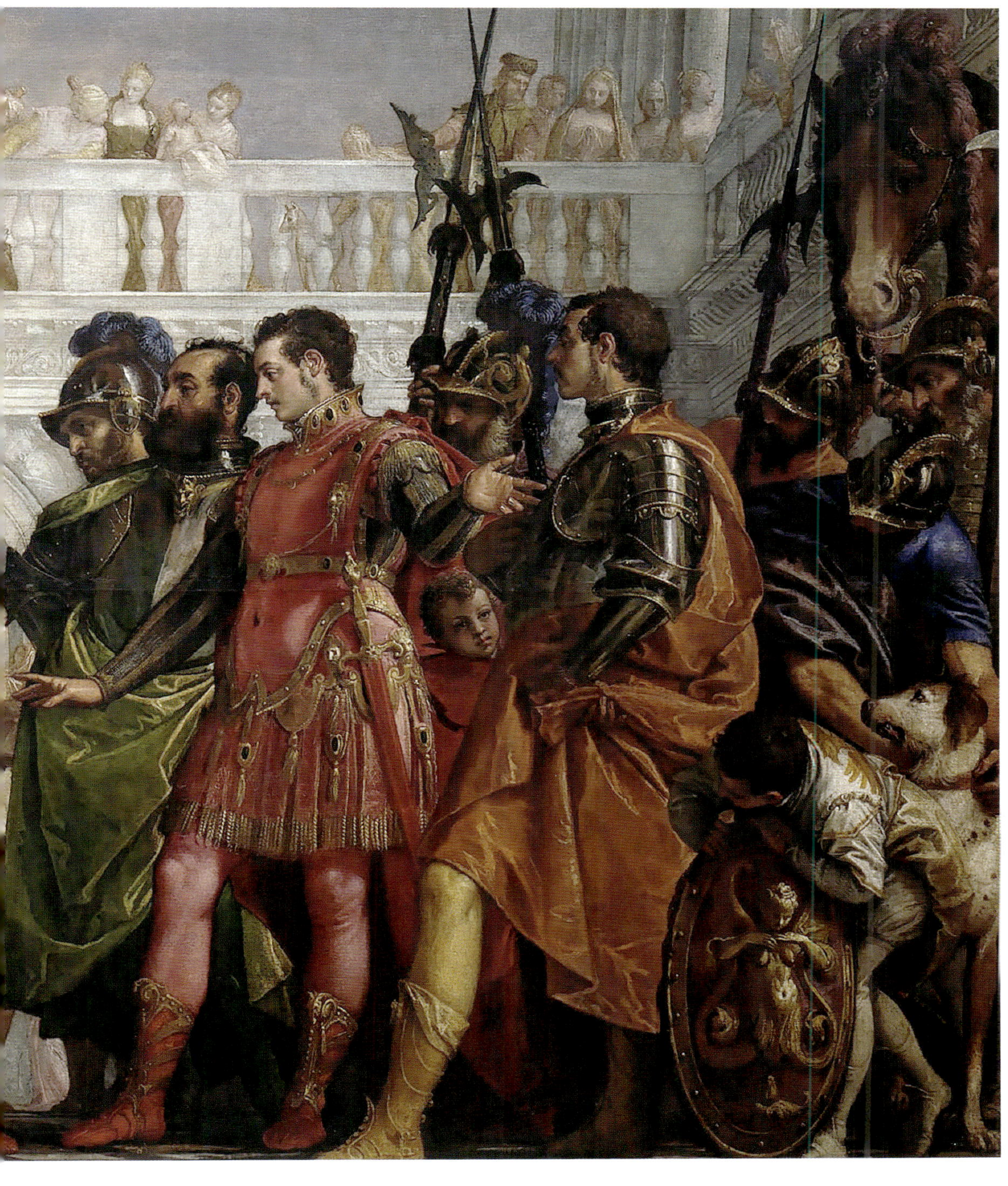

The Vision of Saint Helena, 1570, canvas, 198 × 116 cm.
London, National Gallery of Art, inv. 1041

"We could say that to obtain these effects the painter mixed gold, pearls and rubies and more than fine emeralds and sapphires and the purest and most perfect diamonds". The jewels represent the brilliant luminosity of Veronese's painting, the diffused light that reflects and shines on objects obtained from juxtaposed and not merged colours, the sum of luminous qualities given by the proximity of complementary colours that generate white light, clear luminosity.
But Paolo Caliari will also be able to vary on a few shades: beautiful and exceptional for its sobriety is *The Vision of Saint Helena* from the National Gallery, datable to 1570 and taken from an engraving by Marcantonio Raimondi. It was carried out with a taste of monochrome, working only on shades of pink, with great skill and rigor. The premonitory dream of Constantine's mother, the vision of the cross then searched for and found in Jerusalem is still a varied subject: *The Dream of Saint Helena* in the Vatican Pinacoteca is a real catalogue of fabrics, moreover of rare skill. For Veronese, the dream, as in the medieval tradition, is a vision in which the transcendent can manifest itself, here represented by the angel bearing the cross.

Fabrics in Veronese's Art

It was the Church that encouraged the use of the most sumptuous fabrics in liturgical practices, with allegorical decorations on backgrounds woven with gold and silver threads. The velvety drapes will be particularly praised and requested for example by Carlo Borromeo, they are those "sumptuous gold-embroidered drapes of Venice" that Shakespeare will recall in the *Taming of the Shrew*. Curly velvet, determined by the stitches that emerge from the weave, alternates with cut velvet, with thick and satin pile, in particular *soprarizzo* velvet obtained by combining the cut to define the design, and curly velvet for the profiles. The *soprarizzo* will enjoy maximum success and seems to be the most illustrated by Veronese. Other fabrics also appear in his canvases: damask, where silk creates the glossy / opaque effect; *lampas*, which uses silk with gold and silver wefts; the textured and figured velvet, featuring eye-catching colour combinations and typical oriental designs, with jagged leaves and palmettes. The counter-cut has an intense crimson red colour decorated with concentric rosettes alternating vertically with heraldic crowns supported by the union of two twisted branches: it is the fabric chosen by the highest institutions.

Paolo's work is absolutely refined in mixing hues and obtaining a rare palette, where complementary pairs such as indigo / orange yellow; orange-red / cyan; green / magenta, and then purple pink and yellow-green, and a whole other series of shades, are proposed in unprecedented combinations. In particular, the variations around orange and blue allow luminous flashes, plays of shadows generated by the silks of garments. Also for this ability Veronese will enthuse Delacroix and Ruskin and the impressionists, although very distant from him for mythographic and religious sensibility.
Thus Eugène Delacroix wrote in his *Diary*:

> There is a man who manages to clarify without violent contrasts, who paints en plein air, which we have always been told is impossible: this man is Paolo Caliari. In my opinion, he is perhaps the only one who has been able to grasp all the secrets of nature. Without having to exactly imitate his manner, one can pass through many streets on which he has placed indicating torches. I owe everything to Paolo Veronese.

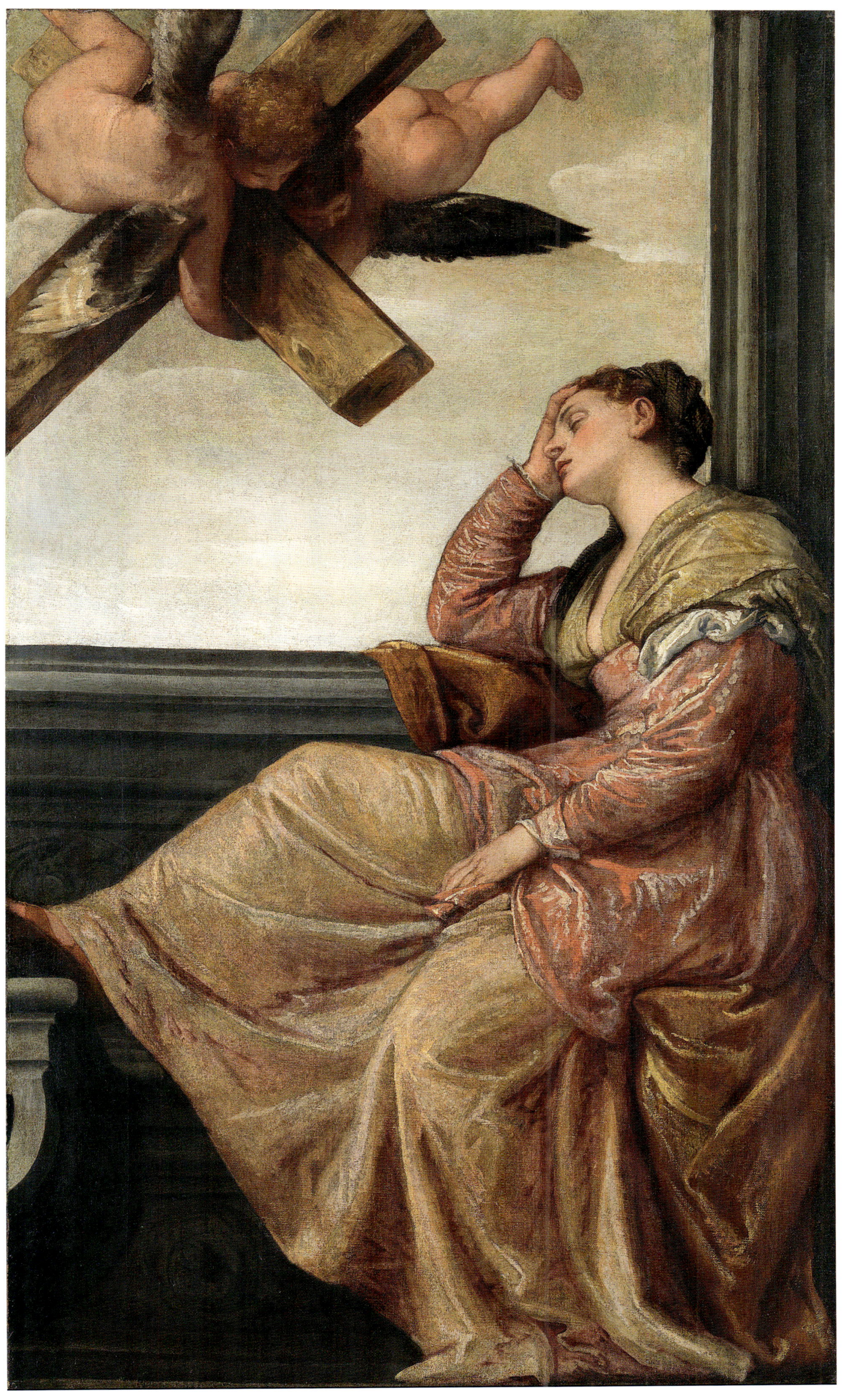

CHAPTER VI
Weddings and Suppers at the Theatre

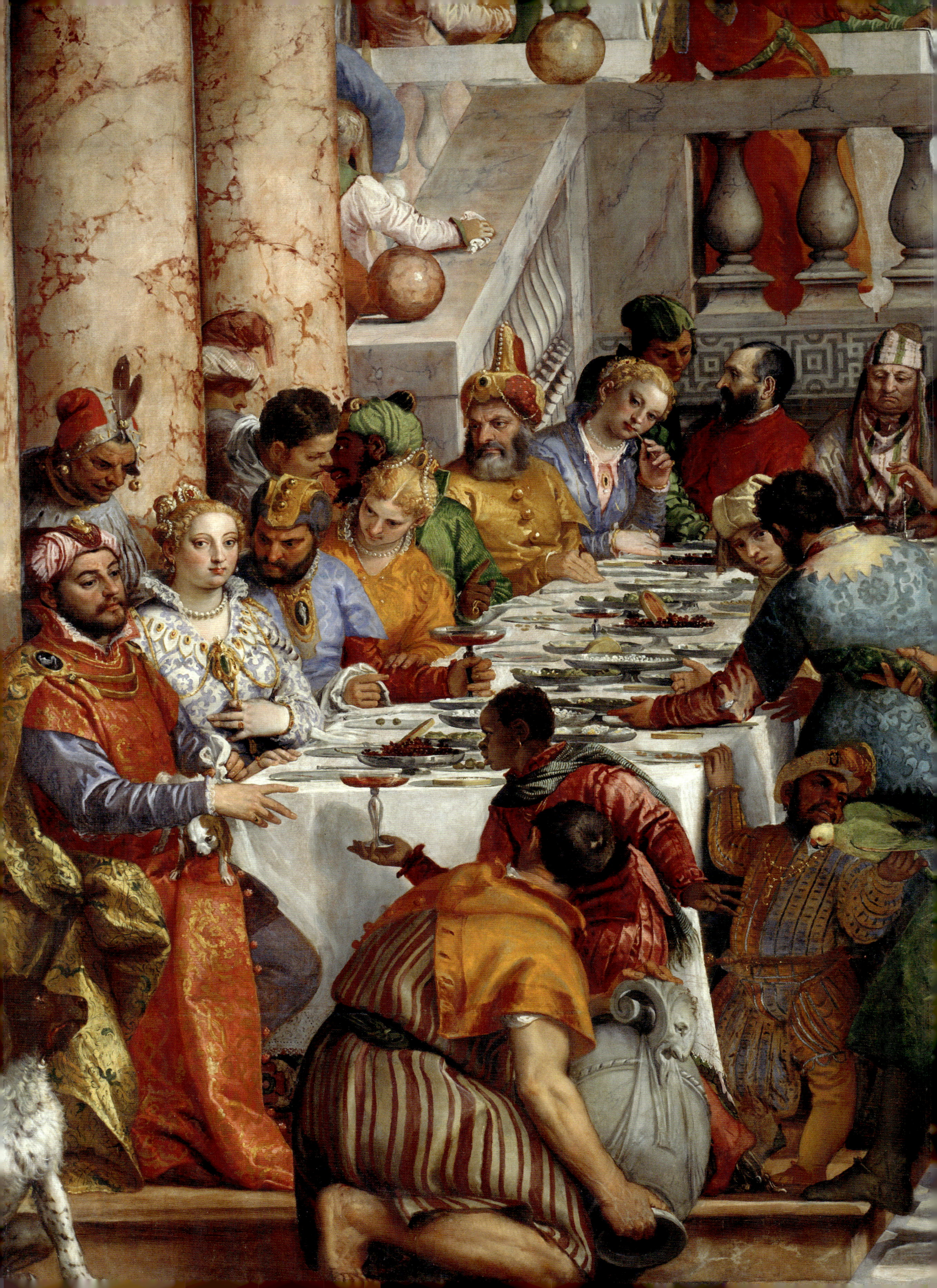

The greatest fame of Paolo Veronese remains entrusted to the modern public to a series of grandiose canvases, with similar subjects: they are the so-called *Cene*, i.e. banquets inspired by evangelical episodes, representations of sumptuous symposiums, expressions of Venetian society in the mid-sixteenth century. These canvases, unique for their architectural construction and immense vastness, have made the painter immediately identifiable and remain in the tourist memory, if only because the Louvre welcomes, presented in the very popular hall that houses the *Mona Lisa*, the most impressive painting, *The Wedding Feast at Cana*, one of the grandest canvases in the history of painting: 9 meters and 90 centimeters by 6 meters and 66 in height, more than Tintoretto's *Paradise* for the Sala del Maggior Consiglio, even more than the *Coronation of Napoleon* by David, or *Guernica* by Picasso. The sixty-six square meters painted by Veronese are inhabited by a number of characters: one hundred and thirty-two "figures" in an architecturally defined space. Characters presented frontally, fixed in a movement, an expression that requires a progressive, linear reading, attentive to every nuance, to the rhythm of gestures and postures; the entire scene will then be captured as a sum of snapshots.
"What avenues have been opened in it to decorate the place with architecture, and how many of these he has used to increase spectators at the party! What affections he portrayed in each of the principal actors, and so perfect for that time!" Thus Luigi Lanzi in his *Storia pittorica della Italia* printed in 1795; in the spatial dimension created by the geometric rigour and the perspective artifice, there is the possibility of grasping the sacred, or rather its manifestation "here and now", which must be sought, perceived and recognized, not being immediately flashy and central.
This was what the priors and abbots were looking for: they wanted a scene from Paolo for the refectories of convents – a backdrop set populated according to the painter's taste, to make us understand the manifestation of Christ in real life, within the story of a chaotic and mundane, confused present, from which the monk draws himself out. During the meal consumed in silence, with the mere presence of the Word spoken by a reader, the friar will be able to understand, in his soul, the presence of the sacred stopped on the large canvas that represents the world. It is a daring, intellectually sophisticated challenge, an example of sixteenth-century religiosity.
But in organizing those scenes marked by worldly luxury it was also necessary to consider the other function of the convent refectories, starting with the most famous, precisely the one for which *The Wedding Feast at Cana* was intended, the building of the Benedictines of San Giorgio Maggiore. The refectory space, already designed by Palladio as a large theatre which is accessed by a double entrance with steps – i.e. the door decorated on the sides by large basins – was not intended only for the meals of the friars, it was open to occasions of reception and prestigious visitors, it was the public and hospitable part of the monasteries. Like the Rolli palaces of Genoa, so too the Venetian convents had to receive and host illustrious visitors and delegations from the Republic, high ecclesiastics or figures with roles of particular importance, and their entourage, always numerous. At San Giorgio, for example, Cosimo dei Medici had been hosted during his years of exile, receiving a splendid collection of manuscript books as thanks.

The Wedding Feast at Cana, 1562-1563, canvas, 666 × 990 cm, detail and, on the following pages, whole. Paris, Musée du Louvre, inv. 1192

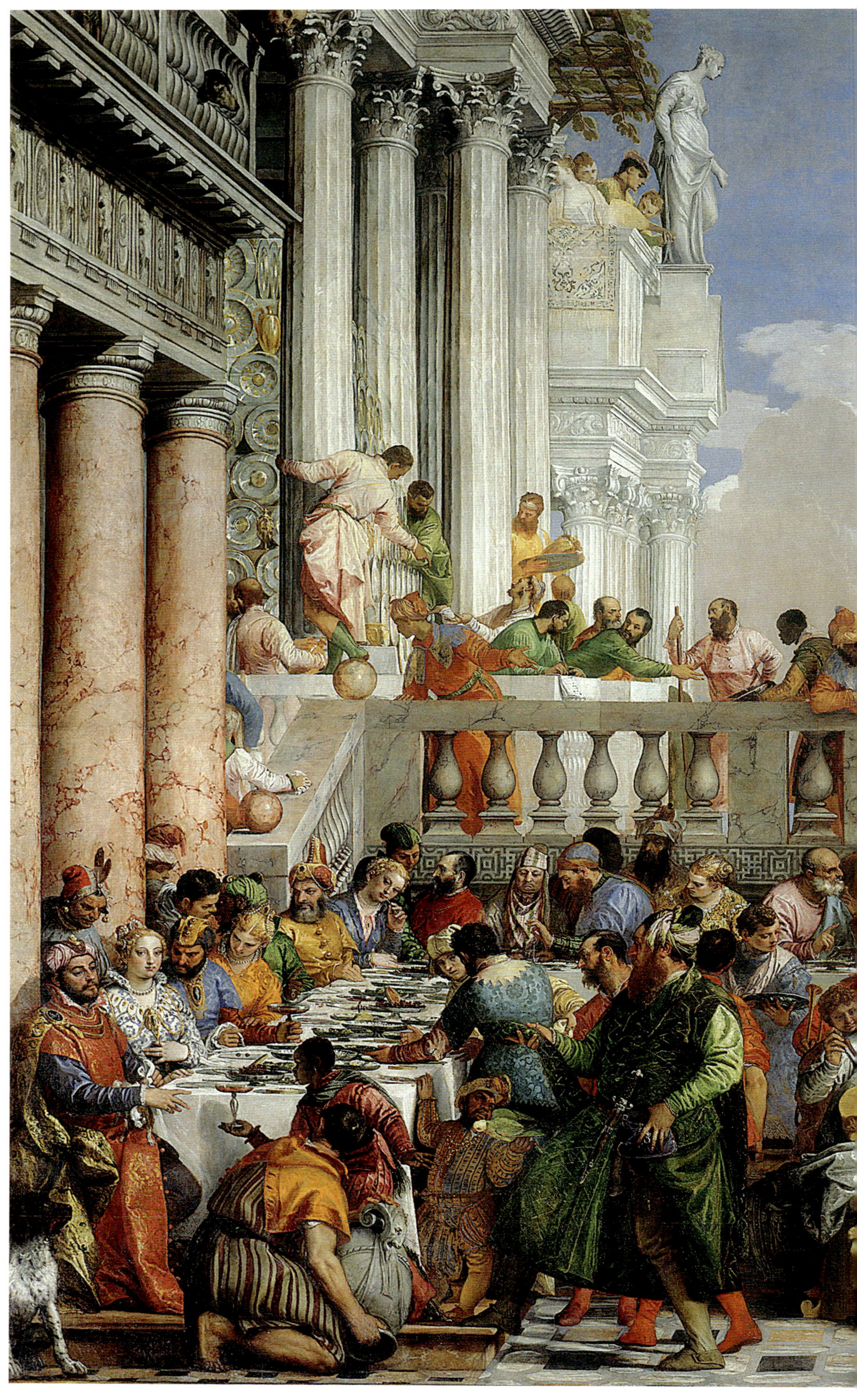

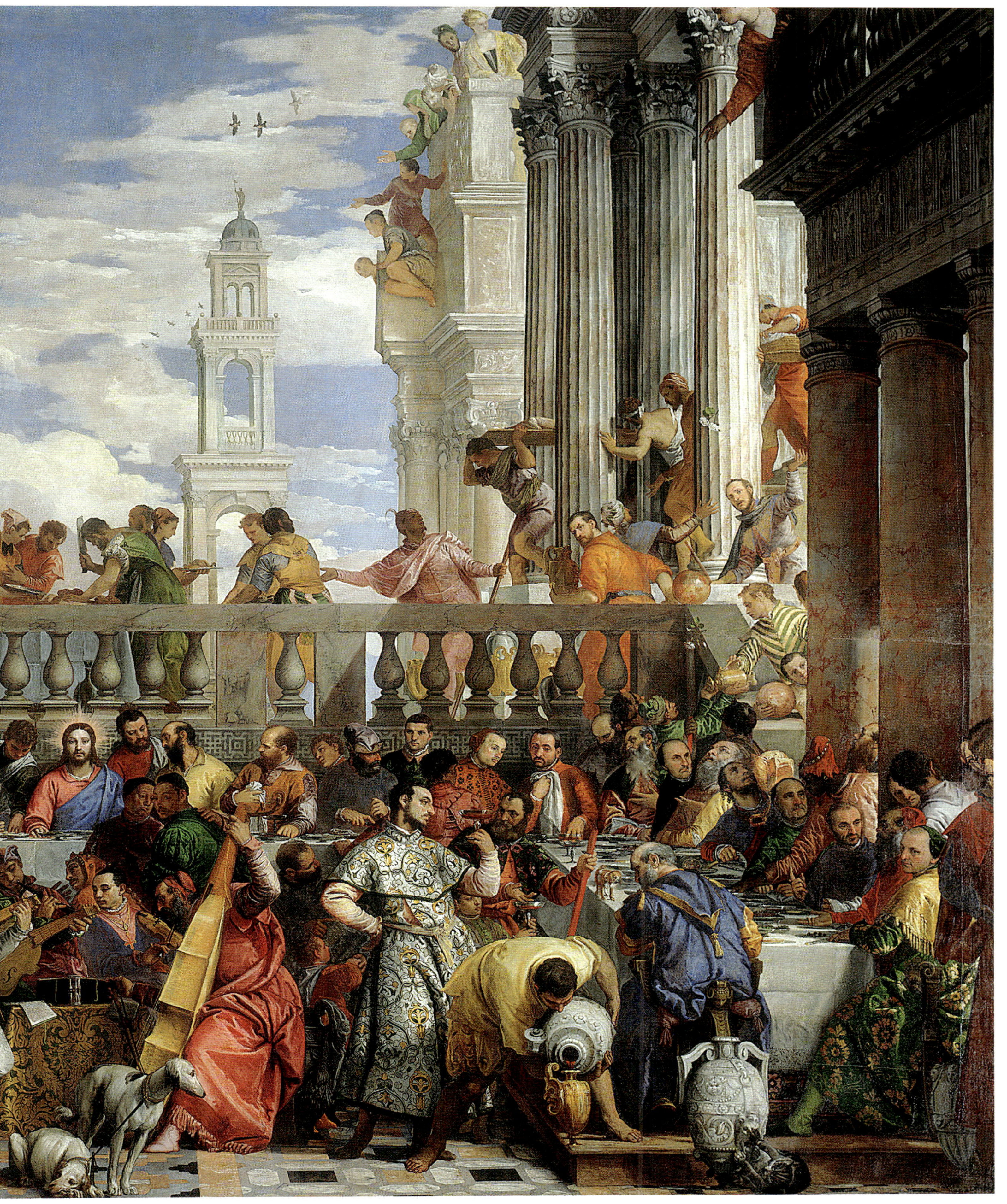

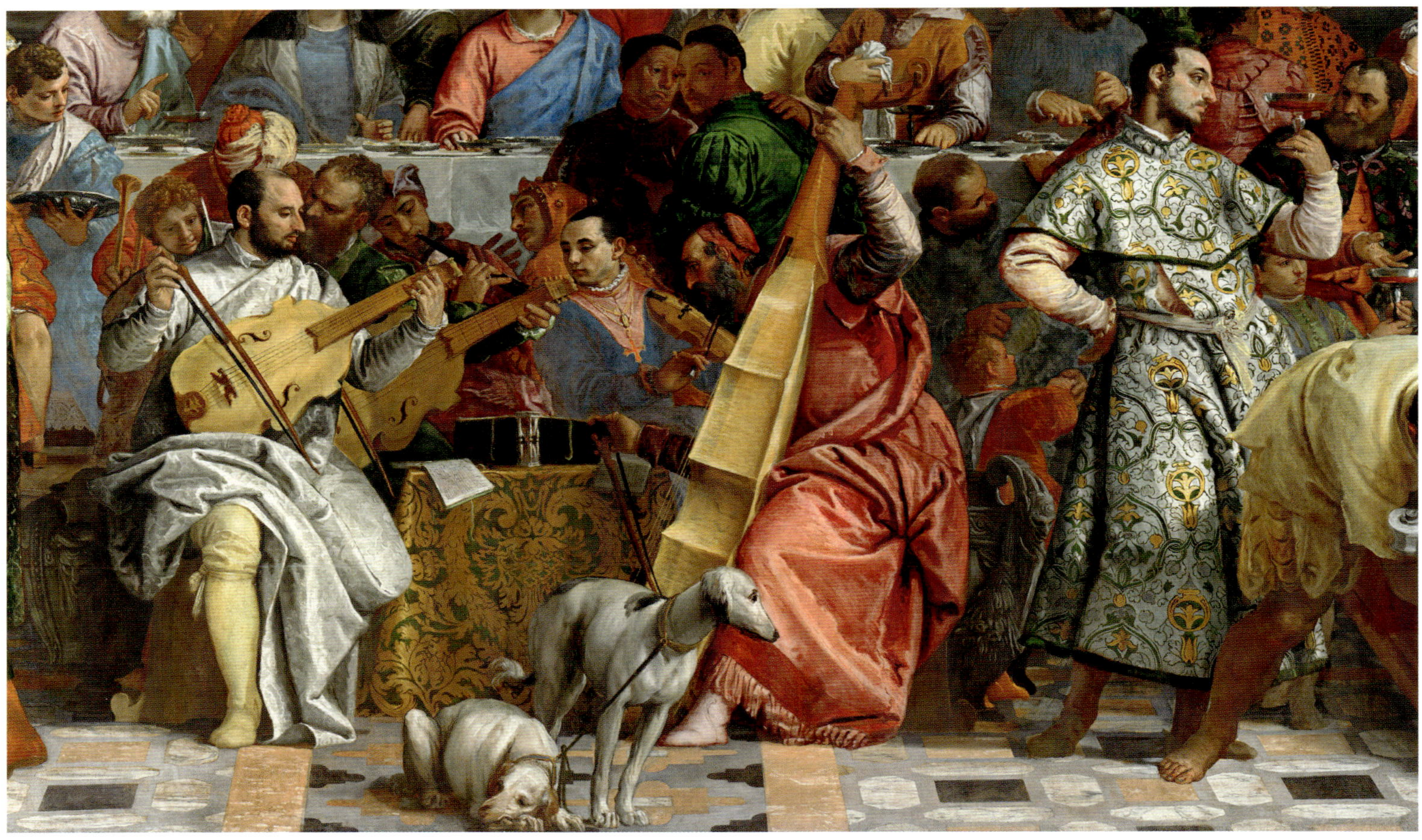

The Wedding Feast at Cana, 1562-1563, canvas, 666 × 990 cm, detail. Paris, Musée du Louvre, inv. 1192

The Banquet: Food, as Well as Sideboard and Table Services

For Venice, the banquet was a codified and ritualized social occasion, an expression of power, a manifestation of prestige, a pretext for talking, listening to music, entertaining business relationships; also an opportunity to admire the taste of the landlord, the art of the carver and the sideboard services. An expression of the civilization of the Venetian table, the banquets offered by the Republic were particularly splendid, organized by the Doge and Dogaressa for dignitaries, ambassadors, guests, but also representatives of brotherhoods and professional bodies. This exhibition of community agreement also offered to hundreds of people took place five times a year: on the days of Saint Mark, the Ascension, Saints Vitus and Modestus, of Saint Jerome and of Saint Stephen.

The banquet is a social occasion: conversations, exchanges of information, political choices. It will have a considerable duration and will not be dedicated only to food. Among the various "services", or courses, there will be moments of pause, in which the diners can get up, talk, attend some common moments, at least three: poetry readings; listening to music played and sung; presentation and commentary of works of art.

The long tables (on planks arranged on trestles) will be covered with three tablecloths: a first one on which the last service will be presented, destined to remain on the table; a second one, narrower, and a third on which the table is immediately laid. On it are placed: trophies of flowers, fruit and herbs, some porcelain (the "Bassano") for acid sauces, some silver, crystals with drinks; then a large plate that will remain until the end, a smaller plate changed at each service; a fork, sometimes a knife and a spoon. One, maximum two glasses. When the guests arrive, the "first sideboard service" must already be on the table.

During the banquet, the "sideboard services" and the "kitchen services" alternate. The first are the cold dishes: vegetables, fruit, cured meats, desserts; some hot preparations such as fried foods are brought to the table on common trays, from which the diners serve themselves using their fingers, or small forks with two prongs; on other trays are cups for broths, glasses with tiny preparations of soups, and other liquid preparations. At the end of the "sideboard service" the common dishes and the saucer on which the diner has placed and consumed what he chose are collected. The "cooking services" are instead the single courses served directly by the cook in the kitchen.

The organization includes a "carver", director and room manager. He presides over everything, presents the cooked courses, eventually brings the large dishes from the sideboard to the table, fulfils the requests of the diners. The "carver" is responsible for preparing the sideboard dishes: he slices cold cuts and hams, divides cakes and cheeses, any non-single aspic, peels the fruit and distributes the portions. All in mouthfuls: you don't have to use a knife; there will be only one spoon on the table. The team is completed by a "cupbearer" who is responsible for preparing the "vases" or carafes of wine and various drinks, which the diner serves himself. The "cook" remains in the kitchen, but can assist the carver or replace him in the presentation of the dish, which he will illustrate with some annotations that entice the diners.

The banquets, an expression of the antiquarian and ceremonial culture of the Venetian patriciate, also reflected the health guidelines proposed by medicine and became a real fashion. The success of a character like Tommaso Rangoni was decisive, very rich – the only one who appears in a statue, by Sansovino, on the pediment of a church, San Giuliano, with trilingual epigraphs in his praise – inventor of the diets that promised to make people live in health up to one hundred and twenty years. The vast literature on dietetics, one of the four parts of medicine for Galen, is combined with a renewed passion for rustic plots, orchards and gardens: from which herbs, fruits and vegetables are harvested that make up, together with spices, an endless vegetarian and healthy gastronomy. Vinegar, mead, mustards, brines, jams, verjuices – prepared with unripe grapes – sugared almonds, cider are indicated from time to time in the diet by different doctors. And reading the cookery texts shows how careful the carvers were in organizing banquets that satisfied the palate without excessively offending the stomach, with the bitter-sweet, aromatic-milky, sweet-and-sour associations that sixteenth-century palates liked. The passion for spices and herbs, sweet and savoury jams is dominating; poultry meat is preferred – pigeon, guinea fowl, pullet, lapwing – to the others, with the exception of the ubiquitous veal; freshwater fish, such as sturgeon and pike, are the favourite. That particular, all-Italian preference for cured meats and entrails, brains in particular, and liver, and for sauces, pickles, marinades, was beginning then. Fresh dairy products dominate, obviously seasonal fruits, or candied and sugared almonds, and then the passion for the different types of pepper, ginger, juniper, cinnamon, saffron and turmeric, cloves and nutmeg is manifested; for garlic sauces, vinegars, and mustards. For all types of honey and aromatic and bittering honeydews; without forgetting sugar: brown, bitter and aromatic.

Among the foods that could never be missing eels, the different types of caviar, bottarga, smoked herring; dates and dried fruit. Various jellies with which to prepare all sorts of what we call aspic. Vegetables are always present: hops, asparagus, artichokes, fresh broad beans, peas, snow peas; and the flowers: mallow, nasturtium, borage, rosemary, violet, purslane; salads: wild chicory (dandelion), rapunzel (*Campanula rapunculus*), and fragrant herbs to enrich them: lemongrass, curly mint, basil, tarragon, fennel, sorrel; all kinds of lettuce, gherkins, fennel. And then legumes: chickpeas, lentils and grass peas. Fruits: pears, melons, watermelons, almonds, walnuts. Fruit, vegetables and legumes strictly follow the seasonal trend.

The progressive transformation of Venetian commerce and craftsmanship in the direction of the production and export of luxury goods finds in banquets an exemplary opportunity to show, through an articulated codification, exclusivity: fabrics, glass, goldsmithing. Veronese offers in his *Conviti* tableware of excellent workmanship and fine Murano glasses, silverware and even a minor product, however admired and exported: the lace used to decorate and embellish the tablecloths. Even the tablecloth was a sign of wealth: a series of fine fabrics were placed on the tables also because, in the absence of napkins, the guest was allowed to wipe his hands on the tablecloth; arranged one on top of the other, they were changed following the succession of services; in the *Feast in the House of Levi* Veronese will also paint, under the tablecloths, the table

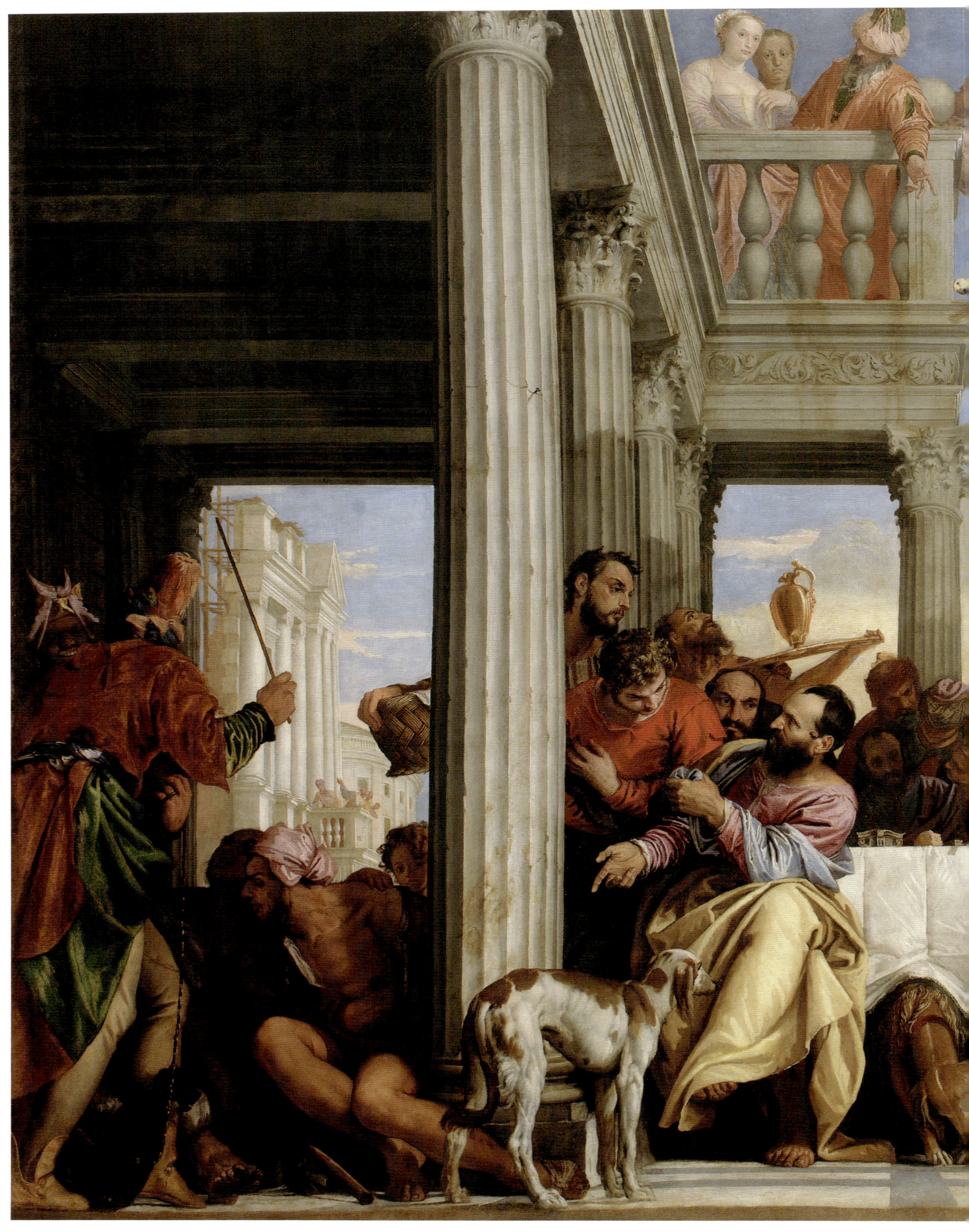

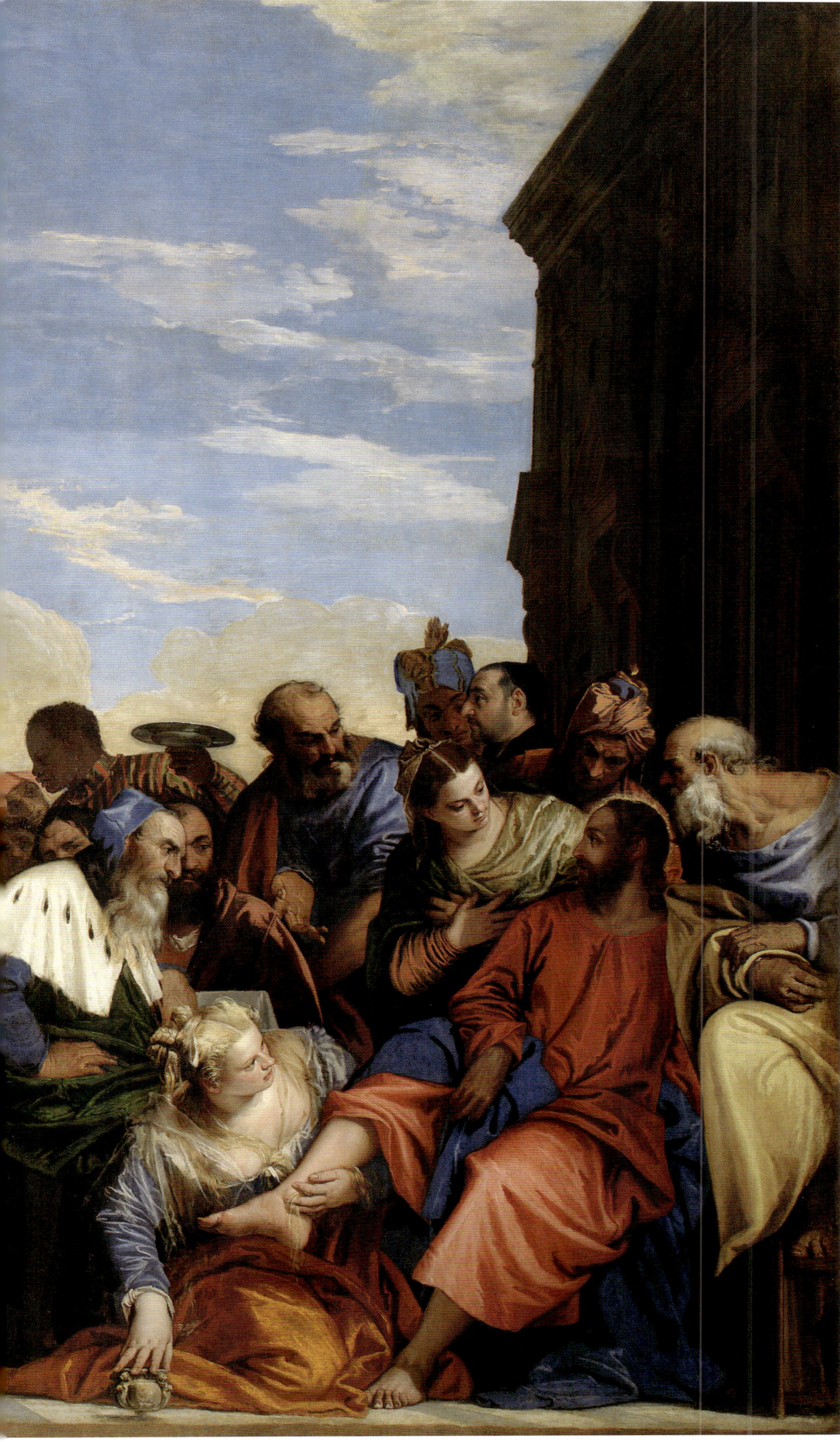

Supper in the House of Simon the Pharisee, approx. 1556, canvas, 315 × 451 cm. Turin, Galleria Sabauda, inv. 580

carpet, typically Venetian. Therefore, in observing the "staging" of the banquets we must first of all understand their social value in order to better appreciate the pictorial data, considered by contemporaries as an excellent public proof of Veronese's art, one of his inimitable peculiarities.

GUESTS AND SPECTATORS

Between 1555 and 1556, the series of *Conviti* opens with the first *Supper in the House of Simon the Pharisee*, commissioned by the Benedictine monks of San Nazaro and Celso for the refectory of their convent in Verona. In the church building, on the altars, are already works by all Veronese friends, from Antonio Badile, Orlando Flacco, Battista del Moro and Domenico Brusasorci; the vault of the presbytery and the apse basin will be frescoed by Paolo Farinati, who will also be present with the canvases on the sides of the choir.
By signing himself with an allusive sign, which can only be appreciated in Verona, namely a nail driven high up in the column, a nail that causes a more visible, extensive crack, Paolo reveals himself as Paolo *spezapreda*, the talented, hopeful young of a few years earlier. Now famous and appreciated, he organizes a very interesting frontal scene, to be admired in its entirety and reviewed step by step. It will be sold by the few surviving monks, reduced to poverty after the plague of 1630, reaching the Spinolas in Genoa, then the Durazzos and finally the Savoys; today it is a precious jewel of the Galleria Sabauda in Turin.
The reference "in the house of Simon" is to the episode narrated in the Gospel of Luke (7:36-50):

> When one of the Pharisees invited Jesus to have supper with him, he went to the Pharisee's house and reclined at the table. A woman in that town who lived a sinful life learned that Jesus was eating at the Pharisee's house, so she came there with an alabaster jar of perfume. As she stood behind him at his feet, weeping, she began to wet his feet with her tears. Then she wiped them with her hair, kissed them and poured perfume on them.When the Pharisee who had invited him saw this, he said to himself, 'If this man were a prophet, he would know who is touching him and what kind of woman she is – that she is a sinner.' Jesus answered him, 'Simon, I have something to tell you.' 'Tell me, teacher,' he said.

And Jesus will tell the parable of the two debtors, thus making us understand the meaning and significance of the forgiveness of sins: the woman who has sinned a lot now shows a lot of love, and she will be forgiven.
But in the Gospels there are different versions of the anointing episode: for John the scene takes place in Bethany during a supper, after the resurrection of Lazarus, six days before Easter. Lazarus sits among the diners, Martha serves at the table, Mary, the other sister, carries a vase containing an oil with pure spikenard balm, expensive and precious extracted from a plant of Persian origin; she anoints Jesus' feet with it, then dries them with her hair. Judas is indignant at the waste, remembering that the perfume was worth three hundred denarii, with which the poor could have been helped.
And this is precisely the version chosen by Veronese, *The Supper at Bethany*: in fact we see Jesus addressing Martha, Judas protests holding a pocket-shaped edge of his cloak in his hand, but then a figure confirms the hypothesis: in the centre of the scene a character is in a conspicuous shadow, he looks in front of himself, observed with curiosity by three men, very close, one in particular seems to want to check his features and his breathing. The character is then clearly indicated by a man who, from the balustrade, points him out to two dumbfounded ladies: it is therefore precisely him, Lazarus, in the centre, who has been resurrected. In fact John 12: "Meanwhile a large crowd of Jews found out that Jesus was there and came, not only because of him but also to see Lazarus, whom he had raised from the dead. So the

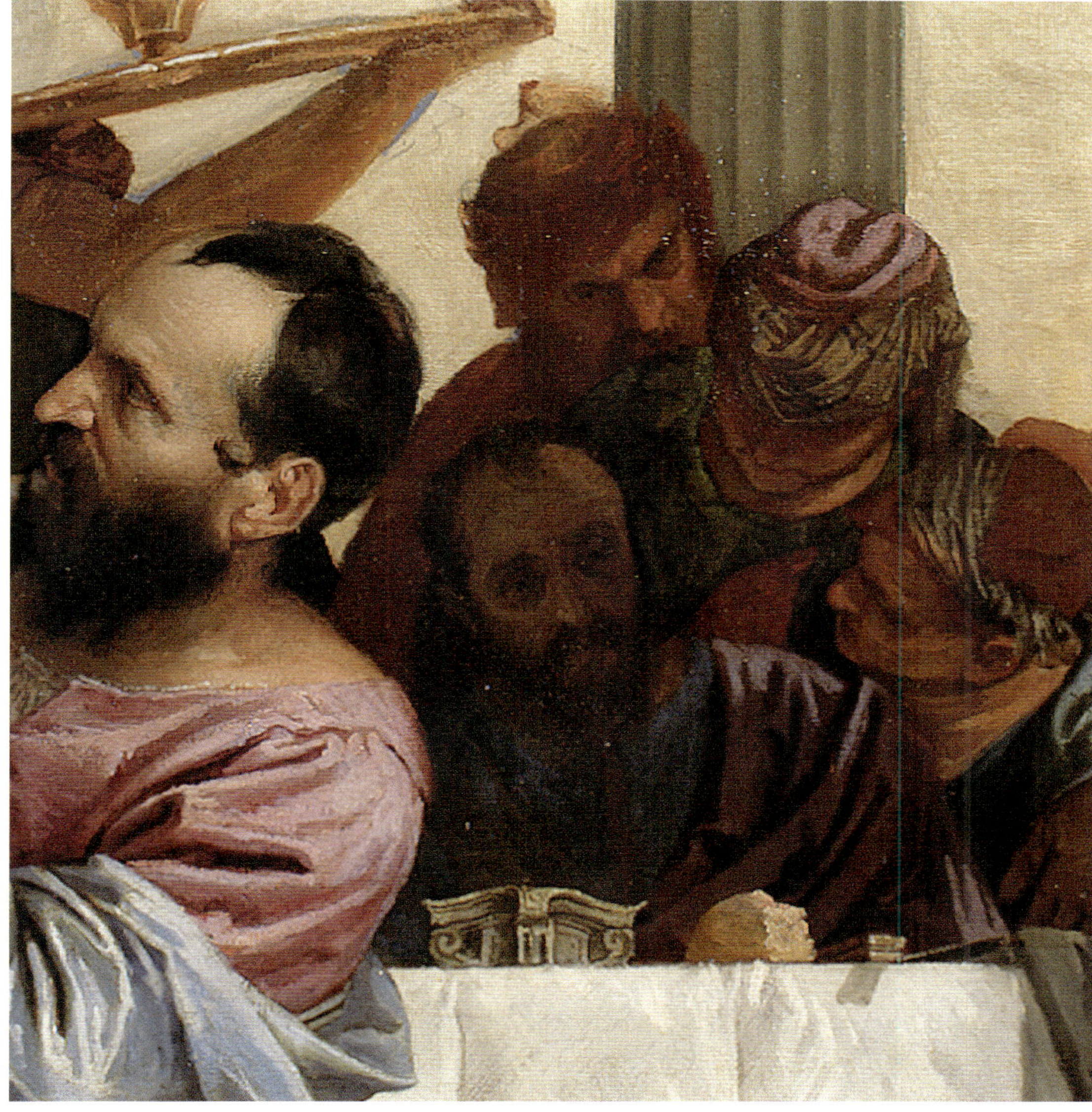

Supper in the House of Simon the Pharisee, approx. 1556, canvas, 315 × 451 cm, detail. Turin, Galleria Sabauda, inv. 580

chief priests made plans to kill Lazarus as well, because many Jews were leaving because of him and believed in Jesus."

In the shadow of the Palladian loggia, to the left, are some beggars and beautiful dogs. The beggars refer to the practice of charity, to the exercise of virtue, the two animals could refer to that fidelity, to the deep friendship that bound Jesus to Lazarus and his sisters. Leaving apart, of course, Paolo's absolute predilection for dogs.

Even in the evangelical stories of Mark and Matthew, which are similar to each other, the scene of the banquet with a woman who shows her love for Jesus takes place in Bethany, but with a Simon "the leper", two days before Easter. An unnamed woman carries an alabaster vase containing perfumed oil – Mark also specifies that it was spikenard oil – with which she impregnates Jesus' head, arousing criticism in those present for the obvious waste : hence the rebuke of Christ, who feels it is a compassionate gesture, a warning of his imminent death.

On the evangelical episode in the different versions, the comments, the allegorical and theological interpretations are innumerable. Historical approaches underline figures and admonitions, isolate and explain the figure of the prostitute who uses perfumed oils for patrons, ask the meaning of the "leper", in itself a pariah who certainly could not have been invited to the table, and therefore should be understood as a person cured of leprosy. In any case, the scene, which is of great literary effectiveness, conveys the forgiveness of sin and the manifestation of female

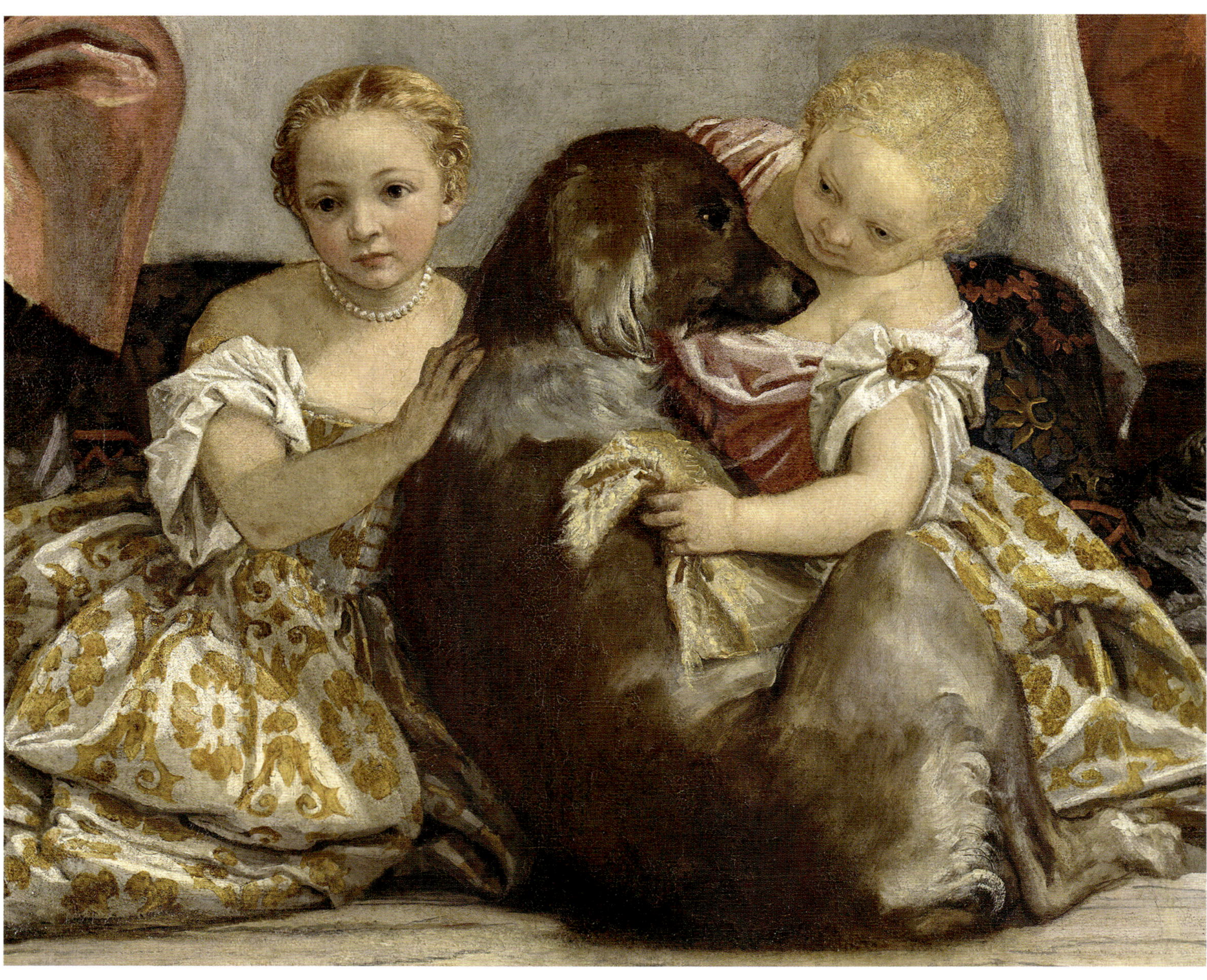

Supper at Emmaus, approx. 1560, canvas, 242 × 416 cm, detail. Paris, Musée du Louvre, inv. 1196

respect and devotion. The woman who honours Jesus is often referred to as Mary Magdalene, sometimes identified with Mary of Bethany, sister of Lazarus and Martha, or with the sinner of the supper in the house of Simon the Pharisee, to then become the Mary of Magdala that John points out like one of the women, the other is Mary of Cleopas, present at the crucifixion and at the visit to the empty tomb, after the Resurrection. In any case Paolo Veronese stages the touching act, and the reproach of Jesus towards those who do not understand the meaning of virtuous homage. Also for this reason the setting can be placed in an ahistorical present.

The *Supper with the Pharisee*, which should be renamed the *Supper of Bethany*, is followed by a singular but significant *Supper at Emmaus* for a private commission. Probably executed around 1559-1560 and destined for some *portego* of a prestigious family, it will arrive in France in the collection of Cardinal Richelieu. It is a surprising canvas, exemplary of Paolo's figurative tastes, of his thickening of figures in a loose and also ironic narration. The episode in Luke 24, 14-35 presents an event following the death of Jesus crucified on Golgotha: two disciples, after learning that the sepulchre in which the Master's body had been placed is empty, head towards Emmaus, the place of a hot spring about ten kilometres from Jerusalem. On the road they meet a traveller, who listens to their sad considerations; the two, amazed at his ignorance, recount the dramatic events of the last few days, considered by the traveller as the fulfilment of the prophecies in the Holy Scriptures. The two, one of whom is referred to as Cleofa, invite him to stay with them for supper "because it's getting dark". "He sat down to eat with them, took the bread, and said the blessing; then he broke the bread and gave it to them. Then their eyes were opened and they recognized him, but he disappeared from their sight."

Veronese paints exactly the moment of the blessing of the broken bread, the instant of recognition, while a plate with food arrives at the table. Outside the loggia, in the distance, the meeting between the two and the pilgrim. But a crowd of people witnesses this scene, just like on an attended stage: no less than fifteen, actually sixteen counting a profile of a young Moor in the background; and what an audience! There is a child who affectionately holds a small spaniel in his arms, a pair of delightful twins who caress a very sweet beagle; three bearded adults, a very Venetian lady with the last born in her arms; little boys and girls. There are also very ambiguous characters: a rather gruff innkeeper pays no attention to Christ at all; another in service, dignified and bearded, with a nice cloak, shows instead sudden attention, turning around, while his hands advance towards another table; next to it an elegant child looks at Christ with pure eyes. Only the three men show a certain gravity in understanding the scene, while the lady observes us indifferently, holding the last born; some boys and girls are bored enough, they haven't found a place to play. Which family? What relationships between men, what Venetian lineage asked to be present on the sacred scene? Are there hidden allusions in the different attitudes? Could the exception of the classic drapery of some dresses refer to people who died at the time of the family portrait? Nothing is known, and the spectator is amazed at this contiguity between the reconstructed sacred text and the observation of a very daily group, a civilized and wealthy family, who posed in their best clothes, and who show themselves with dignity but also a little shamelessly, in his private family chronicle. Meanwhile, on the left, far beyond the threshold of the important loggia, the Pilgrim accompanies the two wayfarers towards Emmaus. What he leaves behind is not only the distant, thickened Jerusalem, but a nearer ruin: it is a classical world that now belongs to the past, already fallen in the face of the new faith. The architecture in the background scene can also allude to the disciples' inability to see Christ, as if that past, so exalted by humanists, represented an obstacle. There will be other triumphal arches, vestiges of an outdated past, in Veronese's canvases, other fragments of ruins: from time to time they will represent the end of the Mosaic law, the decline of the pagan world, but also the transience of man's works faced with the eternity of the divine word.

On 6 June 1562 Paolo agrees with the procurator and the cellarer of the convent of San Giorgio Maggiore in Venice "to make one of our paintings in the new refectory of the same width and length of the façade, making it completely full, making the history of the supper of the miracle performed by Christ in Cana, Galilee, making that quantity of figures that he will be able to comfortably enter and that is required for such an intention." The large refectory had been renovated in 1560 by Andrea Palladio; at the end of the masonry work it had been furnished with benches and reredos; the canvas was to be placed on the short wall opposite the entrance, above the seat reserved for the abbot. The monastery will buy canvas and frame, the painter will receive 324 ducats, the work will have to be done on site, in the refectory, the monks will provide the painter and assistants with meals, or "the mouth expenses that will be eaten in *Refec.rio*". Therefore Veronese will work under the daily gaze of the monks, probably also listening to observations and suggestions, to be accepted or not. Paolo takes care to point out in the contract that all the expenses necessary for the work are borne by the convent: everything is specified in the document in the State Archives of Venice, San Giorgio Maggiore, processo n. 10; the execution is foreseen for the "festa de la Madona de sep. 1563", thus on 8 September. The payment of the gigantic canvas will be done on 6 October 1563, with mutual satisfaction.

In this *Wedding Feast at Cana*, now in the Louvre, after two and a half centuries of adventurous transfers, the scenographic ability, the inventive variety, the extreme realism and the colourful

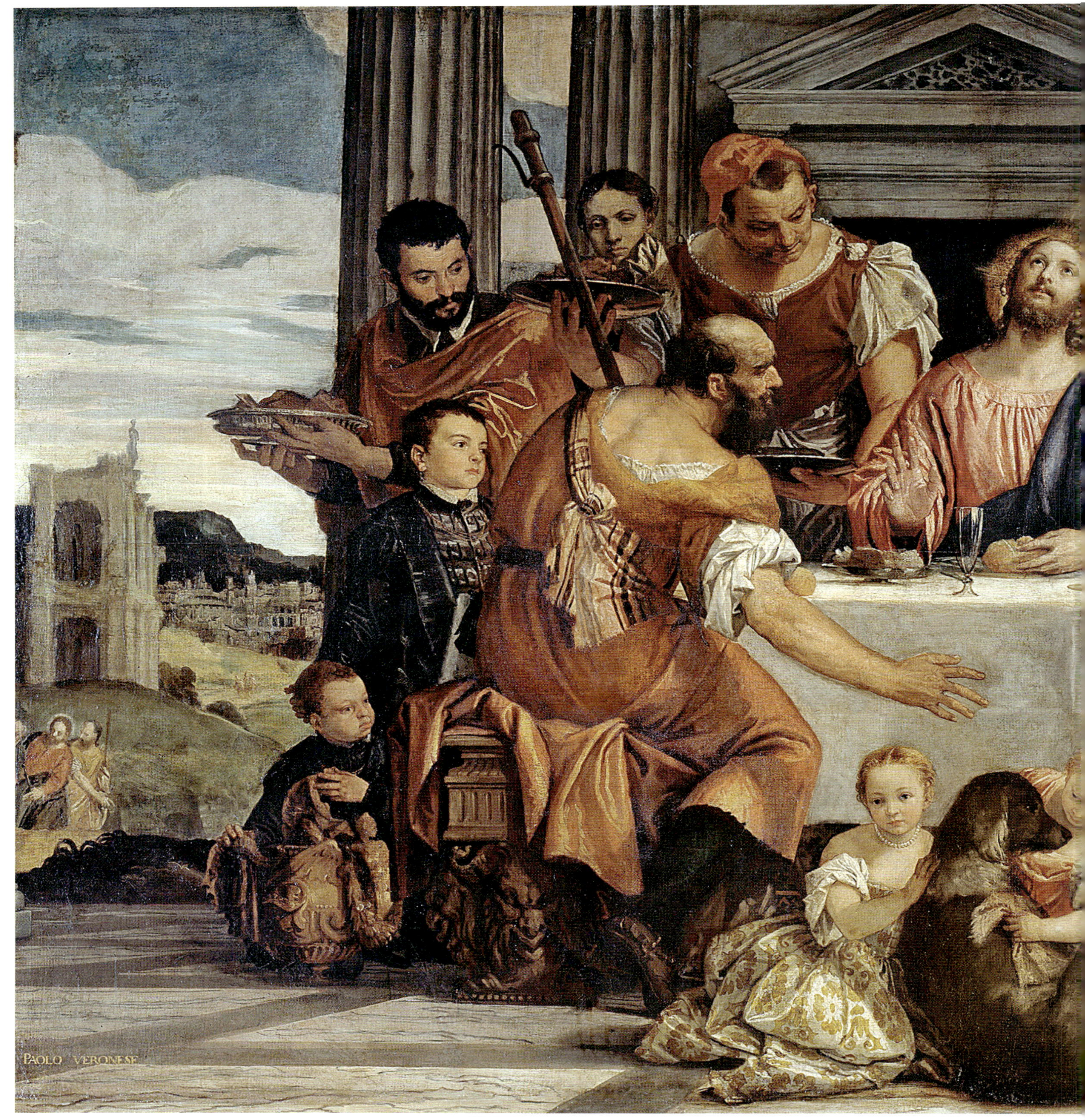
PAOLO VERONESE

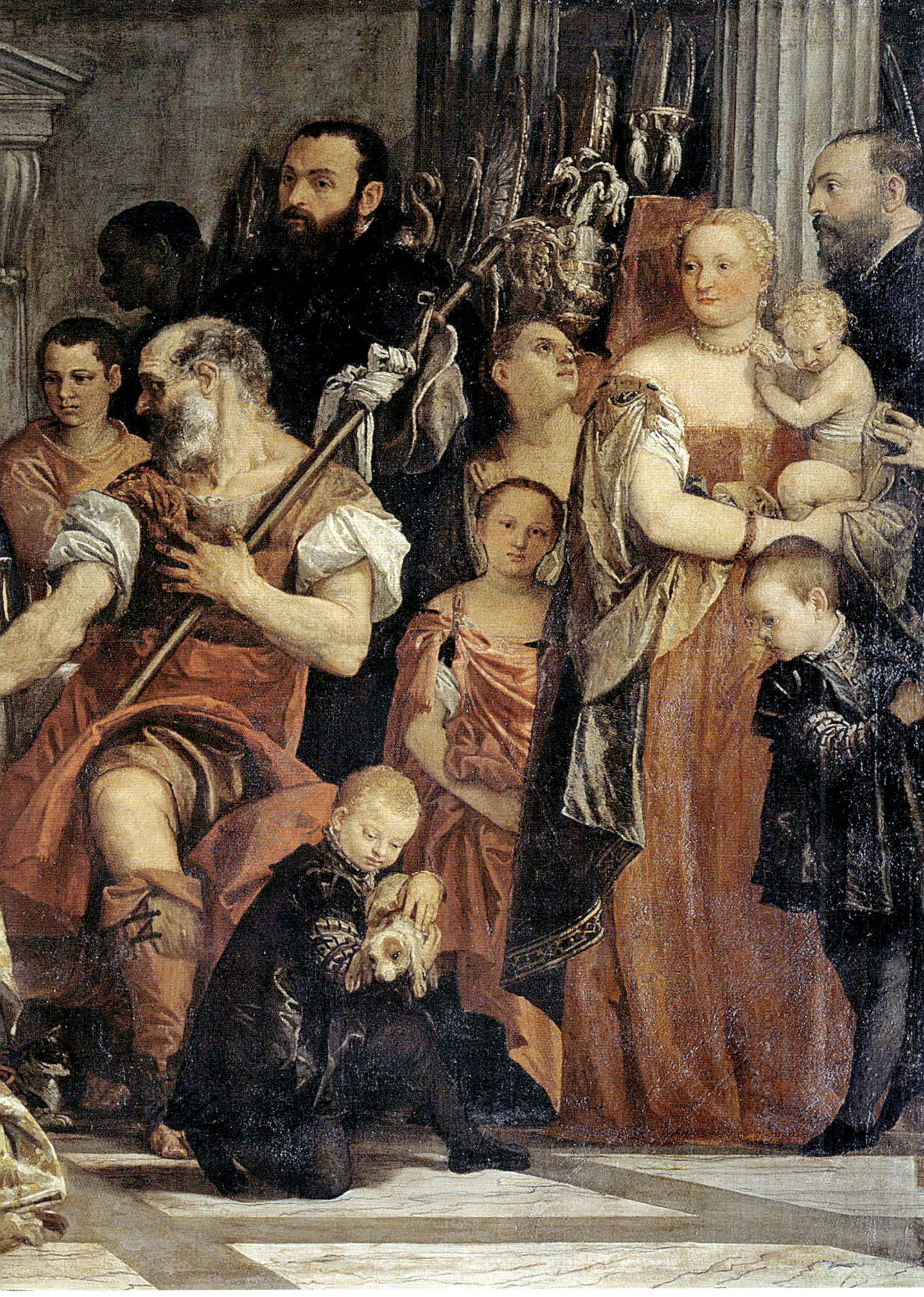

Supper at Emmaus, approx. 1560, canvas, 242 × 416 cm. Paris, Musée du Louvre, inv. 1196

impact reach their maximum effects on the spectator. Because there are those absolutely "Veronesian" colours – malachite green, salmon pink, amaranth and carmine, and then gold and silver, the variations from raw yellow to deep orpiment, the turquoise: all with incandescent effects. And yet we can no longer go back to the reconstruction of its original appearance: centuries and men have changed the painting. It has been cut down to the sides; the whites have become transparent, the background has in any case yellowed, various colours such as the red lacquer have darkened, the copper resin has acquired amber tones; all colours are generally more opaque. Folded in two and rolled up by the French after the requisition in 1797, straightened and stretched, repainted, stuccoed, and partially repainted with the means and ideas of the early nineteenth century, after half a century it had to be "restored" again in the Musée Napoléon, now Musée Royal du Louvre. The work completed in 1854 was judged very bad by various connoisseurs, who saw the original harmony destroyed. The official defence of the Louvre did not appease the controversy: the sky had been completely repainted, the seneschal's dress had turned red, in particular, as confirmed by recent non-invasive analysis techniques, the two faces that today baffle us had been repainted moreover, precisely those of Christ and Mary. A seventeenth-century copy, visible today at the entrance to the Refectory on the island of San Giorgio Maggiore, shows a much more expressive Jesus, different from the current idealized and frankly romantic face, and moreover with his gaze fixed on space; of the original painting there is only a very thin veil on the clearly visible texture of the canvas. Mary's face appears even more reconstructed, it is "dazed", it has a grey-pink colour instead of ochre, her skin tones are different from the tones of the other characters, close or distant. Veronese has never painted such a dull Mary. The wedding will arrive in these conditions until the radical restoration work, carried out for many months by several dozen restorers, concluded in 1992.

The evangelical episode of the Wedding at Cana (John, 2, 1-12), the first miracle attributed to Christ, is set in an architectural construction that continues the environment in an illusionistic way, allowing a distribution of the figures in harmony and an articulation of passing lights, giving only very clear shadows. Around Jesus everything is a festive animation of poses and gestures, of expressions and moods. The Eucharistic sense is given by the board with the slaughtered lamb on the balustrade above, while Mary alongside appears as *sponsa Christi*, alluding to the Church. But then, for the number and quality of the guests, clothes and pottery, the banquet is all Venetian, official and grandiose like the one imagined by Pietro Aretino in his *Quattro libri de la humanita di Cristo* from 1539. Boschini in 1660 limited himself to exalting the pictorial values by defining Paolo in the *Carta del navegar pitoresco* as "the treasurer of art and colours", a "true Apolo inlauranà" for whom "This is not painting, it is magic / Which enchants the people who see it / A truly divine virtue / which personifies the soul and conquers the hearts!". After that, a full two hundred years later, known physiognomies were sought in various figures of guests: it was Zanetti in 1771 who wanted to recognize Alfonso d'Avalos and Vittoria Colonna in the spouses on the left, Francesco I and his wife in the characters next to them, Acmer II king of the Turks and, in the corner, also a portrait of Charles V. In reality only one is certainly a portrait: in the eighth place of the table on the right Veronese added a face, probably of a prelate, executed on paper then applied to the canvas. It could be the abbot of San Giorgio, Andrea Prampuro da Asolo, elected to this office in 1564, after the delivery of the painting. Which would mean a nice gesture of vanity equivalent to a possible portrait of his predecessor, Girolamo Scrocchetto, the third diner from the right in a blue suit.

What is certain is that immediately after its implementation, the canvas became one of the marvels of the city and of painting, on a par with Raphael's *School of Athens* or Leonardo's *Last Supper*, so much so that Giacomo Barri in his *Viaggio pittoresco* from 1671 was able to write that "whoever comes to Venetia and leaves without seeing it can say that he has not seen anything". Copied by legions of artists, often commissioned by foreign princes and intendants, in 1705 the monks gathered in chapter decided to limit its reproduction. Then its quiet existence was interrupted. An adventure as dizzying as it is reckless begins.

On 14 May 1797, French troops landed unopposed in Venice. The Serenissima ends in the most inglorious way, betrayed by the Great Council. Two days later, in Milan, Napoleon imposes the tributes to be paid on the Venetian envoys: there will also be works of art, as well as two symbols: the horses of Saint Mark and the winged lion, for many centuries with San Todaro on the highest columns, protectors of the city. The painters Barthélemy and Tinet, and the chemist Berthollet, are delegated to seize the canvases: they will confront Pietro Edwards, curator of the works of art in the lagoon; he manages to save several Tintoretto's paintings, but he will have to give up the Veronese's works, which are particularly admired and coveted.

The Voyages of the Wedding Feast

The commissioners begin operations to transfer the large canvas to the now occupied convent, using at least crude soldiers. The large canvas is unnailed from the wooden frame, laid on the ground, folded in two, then slowly wrapped around a large cylinder, interspersed with sheets of paper at each rotation. It takes almost three weeks to finish the job. On 8 August, in Palazzo Grimani, the large roll is placed in a custom-made case; on 26 September it is embarked on a barge to take it beyond the mouths of the port. It is hoisted with difficulty on a 32-gun frigate, *La Sensible*. This starts sailing in the open sea; first the Adriatic, then the Ionian, the route to France. The arrival in Toulon takes place four months later, on 22 January. Change of vessel in the port: the crate is placed on the railing of the *Créole*, a small tonnage barge, which passes Marseilles, then goes up the mouth of the Rhône, arriving in Arles three weeks later. She begins the ascent of the Rhône up to Lyon, then sails on the Saône, and again enters the Central canal which connects to the Loire, then goes up to Nevers. It is summer, the river is low, ao they have to change barges, often digging a little channel in the river. Other channels: Briare, then Loing; at the end she reaches the Seine.

On 26 Messidor of the year Sixth, or 16 July 1798, the barge anchors in Paris. Waiting for a few days, the Directory wants to worthily celebrate the anniversary of the beheading of Robespierre, the bloody defeat of the Jacobins, on 9 Thermidor. The carts with the crates of Venetian prey move an imposing procession towards the new Musée de la République, created to "liberate" the works of art that were hidden from the people, in the convents and palaces of power. Here, finally, the boxes are open: luckily there are no mice's nests, but the situation is certainly not optimal, the pictorial layer is thin, clouded, dry and cracked: it has fallen off in several places. Yet the *telero* is proudly exhibited on a temporary frame, on 8 November; but then, and immediately, they must intervene. Cleaning, working with hot mastic, giving it a new canvas lining. An operation that makes the painting even more fragile. Years of work, interrupted by partial exhibitions. The last draft of the paint is officially reached on 2 April 1813. The year of Leipzig, then the end of Napoleon, and the end of Napoleon Museum.

The Emperor of Austria wants *The Wedding Feast at Cana* back, and he wants it immediately, to et back to Venice, which is by now his. Now it is the French Vivant Denon who opposes with every argument: the painting is too fragile, another journey will be deadly, the re-frame makes it impossible to rewind it on a roller; the journey is too long, there are no ships. Also on offer is a counterpart: a canvas by Charles Lebrun representing the Pharisee's Banquet with the Magdalene at Christ's feet. To verify the humiliation it can still be seen today at the Academy, after a long deposit at Palazzo Pisani. The authentic mortification is immediately deplored: Antonio Canova clearly said that it was an offense to the honour of the country, letting the Emperor know. But then Lebrun's canvas, dated 1650 and ugly, had to be accepted, while the Veronese became a source of inspiration and study admired by entire generations of artists, from Delacroix to Cézanne. In the middle of the century, in 1851 and then for years to come, other interventions, cleaning, partial varnishing, colour fixing, re-linening, repainting. The restoration denounced as outrage and contempt: Delacroix would write that "poor Veronese was killed by that unfortunate Villot", Frédéric Villot, conservator of the paintings in the Louvre. But the hardships did not end: on 3 September 1870, in the midst of the Franco-Prussian

war, the conservator received the order to send the most precious canvases at ì Brest Arsenal. New disassembly, necessarily rushed.
The canvas will return after a year: and further washing and repainting operations will have to be carried out. Isolated and solitary in the Salon Carré during the war of 1914-1918, the *Wedding Feasts* resumed their wanderings from 28 August 1939, on the roads of France in search of the salons of isolated castles that could accommodate it. Anxious searches: difficulty in handling it, accidents in transport, then humidity and continuous changes in temperature: Chambord, Louvigny, the abbey of Loc-Dieu, Montauban. In secret, traveling along secondary roads, the Italians must not notice it, since they could perhaps take the opportunity to take it back. Then in November 1942 it returned to the Louvre, under full German control.
After the war it was renewed, moved, a new wooden structure was created, and while the coveted restoration was being completed, an accident occurred: on 3 June 1992, the scaffolding collapsed and the canvas ripped, visibly: four large fractures. Today they are invisible. At least they.

To still be able to admire *The Wedding Feast at Cana* is almost miraculous, after all these ordeals, so quickly summarized. It is the result of the radical restoration operation carried out between 1989 and 1992, a work of great complexity that has moved dozens, indeed hundreds of scholars and technicians, restoring good legibility and removing the red paint, apograph though ancient, from the seneschal who now appears dressed in green, on the left of the painting.
Although exemplary, the intervention cannot restore the impression of those who saw the painting by Paolo Caliari for the refectory of San Giorgio Maggiore, as soon as the scaffolding had been taken down, in the month of September of the year 1563. However, today we are first of all impressed by that movement of characters which sucks in the view, does not let the eye stop, accompanies us in a movement which no other painting can generate. We follow the characters, one by one, there are one hundred and twenty-six of them, including seven women, we see them come to life in the moment fixed by the brush. It is the entire Venetian society, from top to bottom, from the patricians to the rich city bourgeoisie; the clerics and scholars; traders, craftsmen. And then thirty-three servants with different functions; six jesters, a dwarf, two children and the musicians. And dogs, a cat and a parrot.
To cheer up the banquet there is also a group of players: tradition has it that the elderly Titian is identified with his usual cap, and a young Tintoretto behind the player who should be the self-portrait of the painter, however identical to the little cupbearer further on, appraising the wine in the beautiful glass. So Paolo and Benedetto, very similar to each other. The so-called Titian gives time on the bass to the two younger ones who play the violas. Each one touches different strings with the bow, but their accord is harmonious, and it is that of a trio that recognizes the different roles and at the same time reproduces a music that is heard in full consonance; it is the harmony that Andrea Gabrieli created at the time. If it were truly a tribute to the other two greats of Venetian painting – to which Bassano would also like to be added, becoming a quartet – it would illustrate a fact, the contemporary coexistence of three very different artists, all worthy of the greatest esteem on the part of the lagoon public. Not hatred, envy and entirely invented polemics: since due to the variety of patrons in Venice, from private individuals, religious orders, magistracies, public works, decorative proposals from architects, in short, due to all the variations of tastes and genres, there is space for every painter, especially if of quality and also of high price. Titian, Tintoretto, Veronese and Bassano don't need to compete with each other for patrons: each has requests, each has orders from admirers. However, even if a certain resemblance between the elderly musician and Titian is true, and if indeed the violone player and the cupbearer appear to be brothers, there is no resemblance between

the players identified as Tintoretto and Bassano; then it would be truly unusual for the prior to accept a blatant staging by living painters.

A highly admired and prestigious work, the pride of the administrators of San Giorgio, always in demand by visitors who could not be denied admiring the work, harassed by the painters who wanted to copy, reproduce in more human sizes or in details, the seminal work, the large canvas represented the best confirmation of the power of the monastery that occupied the entire island of San Giorgio Maggiore.

UNEXPECTED DINERS

The *Wedding* for San Giorgio should be followed by the *Supper in the House of Simon*, 1567-1570, for the Hieronymite convent in Venice, always requested by Prior Torlioni. Since 1817 it has been exhibited in Milan, at the Pinacoteca di Brera. It presents significant innovations such as the movement to the extreme left of the main theme, the offering of the Magdalene kneeling at Jesus' feet, and then, exactly in the centre of the scene, the fight between two dogs and a cat. It is difficult to investigate its ultimate meaning, if there was one, beyond a possible reference to the conflicting history of the convent.

A little later (1570-1572) is the *Supper in the House of Simon* for the refectory of the convent of Santa Maria dei Servi, the Servites of Venice, donated in 1664 by the Republic to Louis XIV and now in deposit in Versailles. The canvas was already damaged by humidity when the monks chose to sell it to the Republic: it was restored in France and exhibited in a salon that wanted to recreate the original milieu, recalling the architecture of the painting.

Between these two, in memory of Veronese's interrogation in front of the Inquisitor in 1573, a lost Supper would have been created for the Maddalene convent in Padua. Furthermore, the series for the Cuccina family includes the *The Wedding Feast at Cana* (1571-1572), now in Dresden, Gemäldegalerie Alte Meister, and the *Supper of Saint Gregory the Great*, completed in April 1572 for the refectory of the convent of the Servites at the Sanctuary of the Madonna di Monte Berico, in Vicenza, a destination for Marian worship since 1435. It is still on site, after a dramatic recovery: the canvas was torn into thirty-two pieces by soldiers of the Austro-Hungarian Empire after the battle of Monte Berico on 10 June 1848; it was Franz Joseph himself who compensated for the havoc.

The architectural structure elaborates the Corinthian colonnade of the *Supper in the House of Simon* in the Servi di Maria, adding an arch in the center to further frame the scene towards which the spectator's attention must focus, where the pilgrim Jesus and Pope Gregory the Great, the "Servus Servorum" in pontifical dress, are seated in front of a low balustrade, with the broad celestial background behind them. Thus they are strangers to the world, and only the prior of the convent, Damiano Grana in his black suit, witnesses and understands the miracle, while behind him an entire family group, the mother with a child in her arms and two elderly people receive a charitable act, testimony of the good works of the Servites. The fact is that while the prior understands and follows the apparition of Christ with attention and participation, the cardinal who is also in front of him does not look at the plate containing the Lamb – the body of Christ which reveals to the Pope the identity of the pilgrim – neither seems to understand the event; the other cardinal does even worse: he holds an eyeglass to scrutinize the poor who sit at the table, the twelve invited by Pope Gregory to remember the Last Supper. Here too, as in each of the *Suppers*, the concern for caritas is present, in the figures of the poor to whom bread is brought.

Both in the *Supper of Saint Gregory the Great* and later in the *Feast in the House of Levi*, the multiple fire porticoes derive from the experience of Palladio, with the *serliane* of the arches

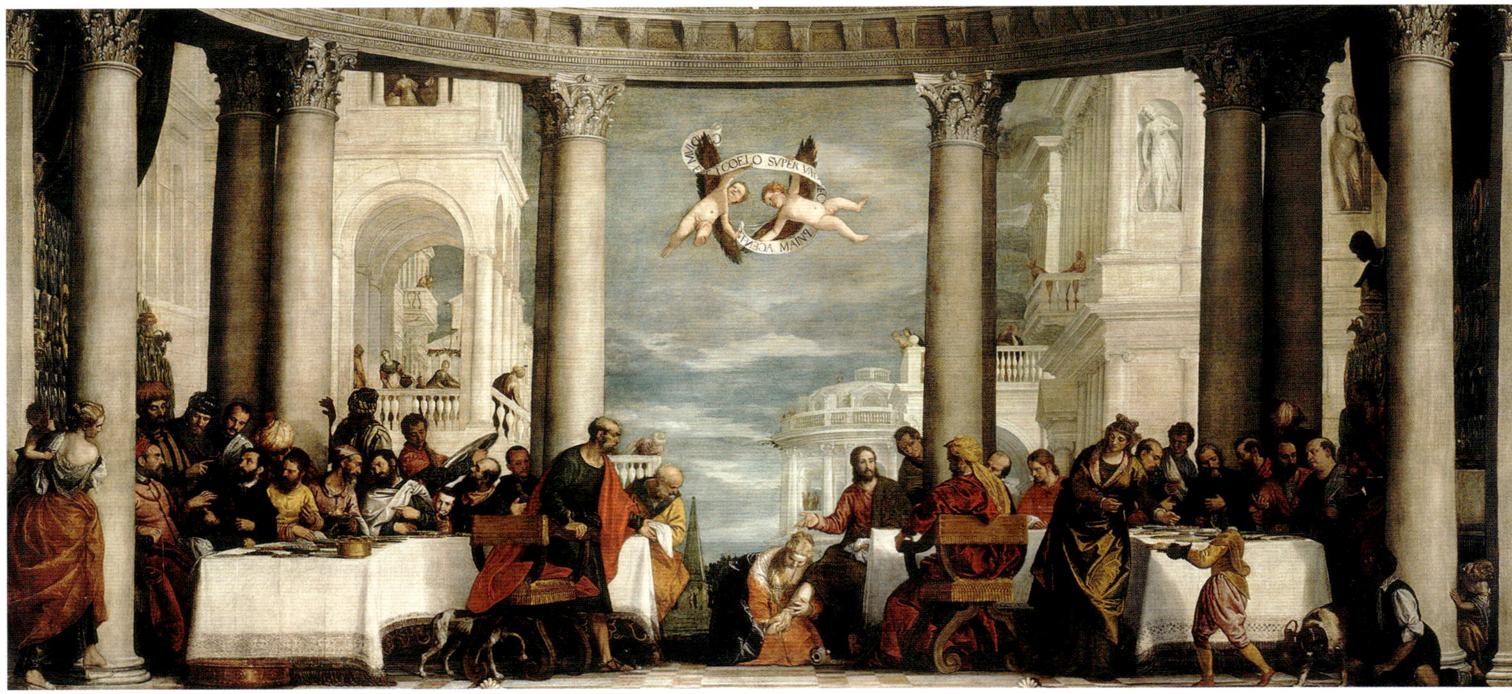

and their supports inspired by the Basilica in Vicenza. The two canvases, executed in succession, also share the "dead staircase", or the double lateral staircase.

Supper in the House of Simon, 1570-1572, canvas, 454 × 274 cm. Versailles, inv. M.V.8181 (Louvre, inv. 143)

Supper in the House of Simon, 1567-1570, canvas, 275 × 710 cm, detail. Milan, Pinacoteca di Brera, inv. 140

The Veronese production of banquets ends with the *Last Supper* from the church of Santa Sofia in Venice, prepared for the *banco* of the Scuola del Sacramento, and currently exhibited at the Pinacoteca di Brera, in Milan: the last trial, in 1585, with an evangelical banquet, conforming to the Tridentine dictates. The table is placed in perspective, according to Tintoretto's typical scheme, the various apostles appear, identifiable, beside some further characters: the innkeeper, two servants, one of which is black, a cripple, a girl offering bread, and an inevitable dog. The scene refers to the Eucharist, and that bread can also reach the crippled, human suffering. Then there is also a very domestic cat, which observes a pair of sandals, lost amidst the confusion in front of Christ's message: someone among you will betray me.

As can be seen, apart from two privately commissioned works, it is the Benedictine, Hieronymites, Servite and Dominican orders that ask for these *teleri* for their refectories: the *Suppers* are an opportunity to reflect, while nourishing the body, on the meaning of the food of the Word – in the silence of the meal there was the reading of a text, sacred or of religious interest – comforted by the food of sight: that is the Icon, the sacred Scene.

The success and requests of the *Cene* is an entirely Venetian phenomenon between the seventh and eighth decades of the sixteenth century, with two different protagonists: Tintoretto and Veronese. Tintoretto paints at the request of the schools of the Sacramento, the minor, popular schools, and represents scenes of great emotional intensity, rich in religious references and marked by the everyday and popular world. On the contrary, Veronese represents the great official *Conviti*, the religious references appear almost marginal, and inserts the theatrical show in grandiose architectural contexts. The pictorial exceptionality of his *Conviti* has always been acknowledged, and one of the most balanced and exact judgments is the one formulated in 1855 by the Swiss art critic Jacob Burckhardt:

> Paolo's most famous paintings are his banquets, which exist in all sizes, from the smallest to the largest. They represent the necessary maturation of painting in real life, free from the last constraints of historical representation, which requires only a barely justifiable pretext to glorify with an irrepressible joy all the

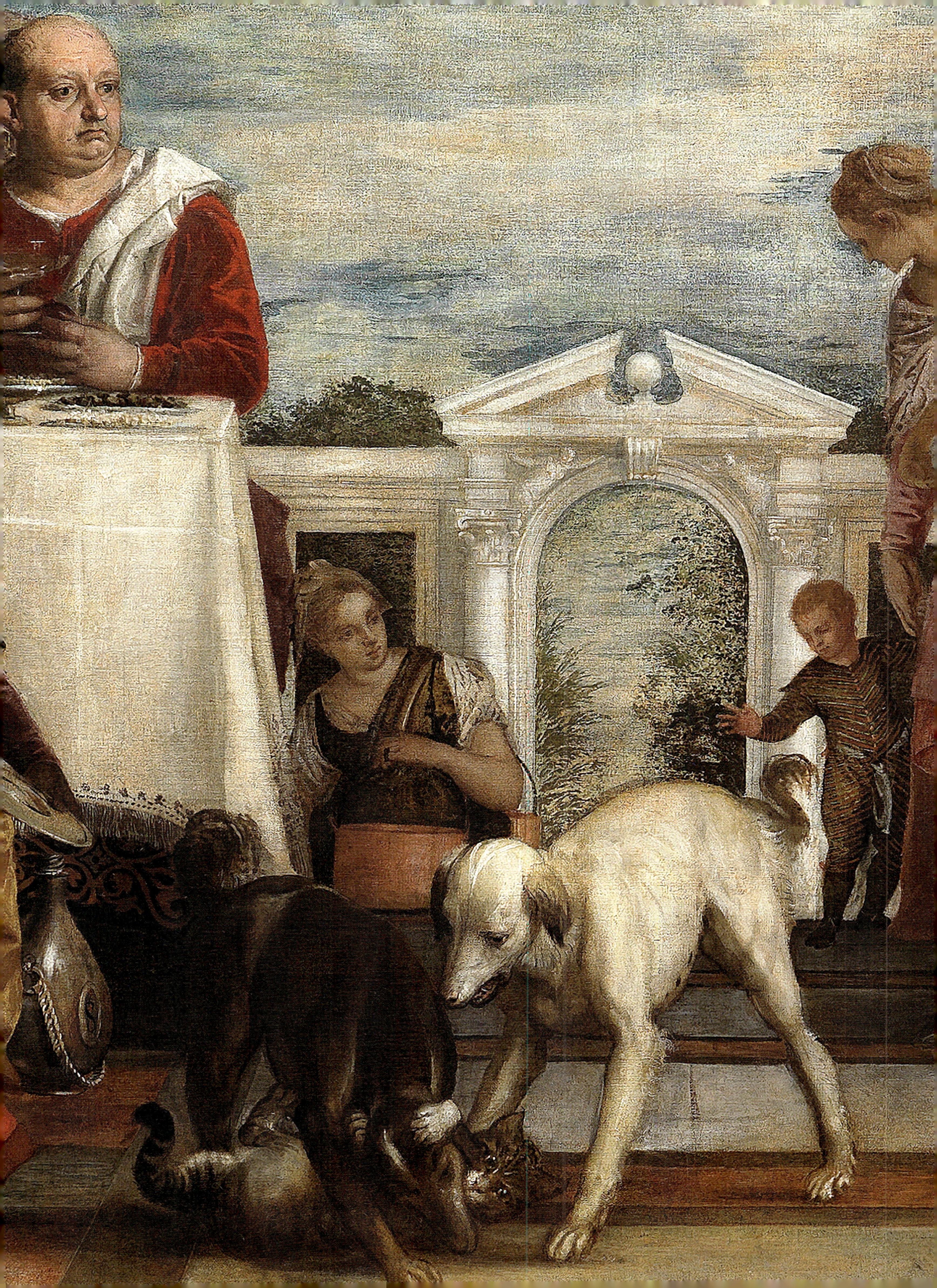

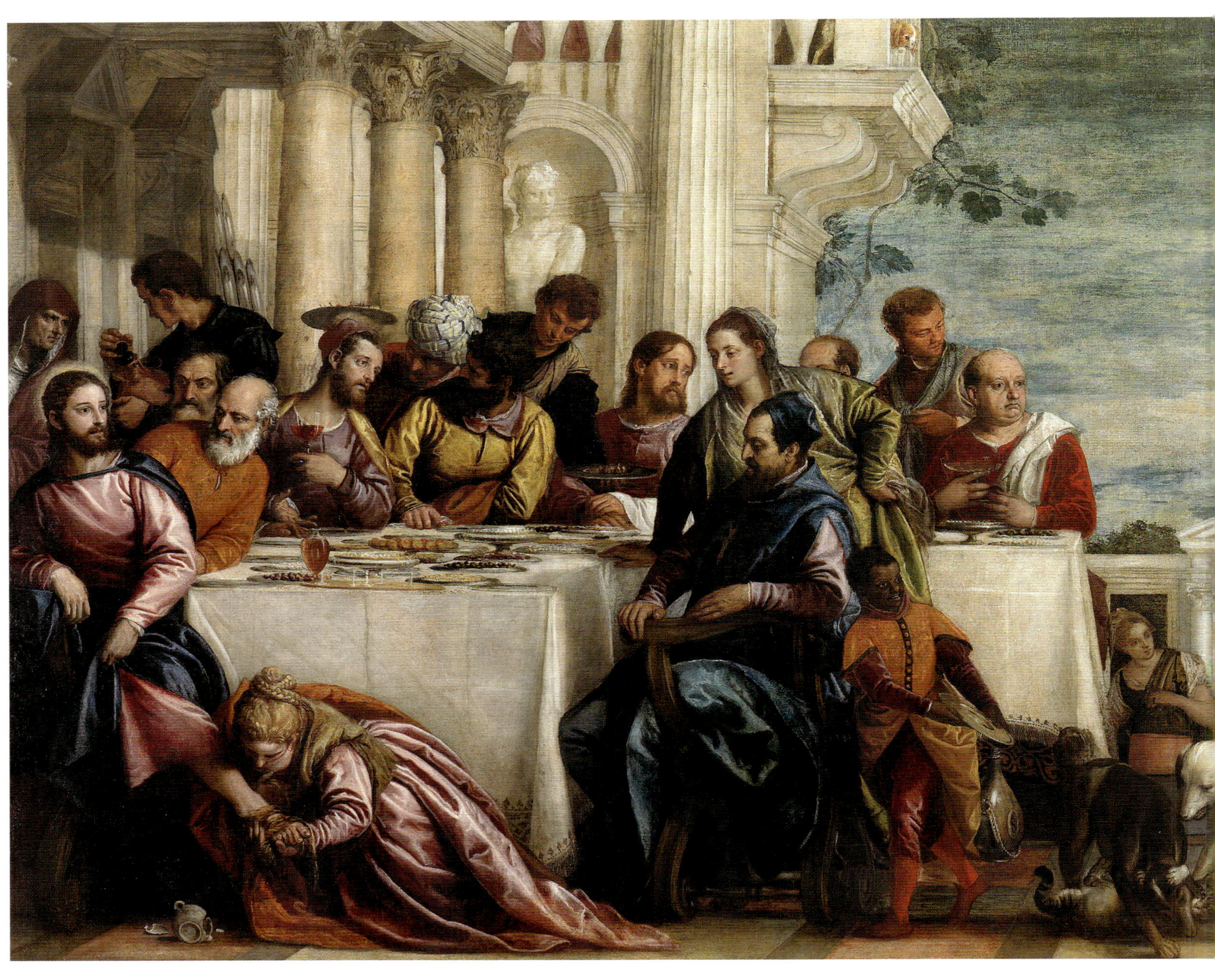

Supper in the House of Simon,
1567-1570, canvas,
275 × 710 cm, whole and, on the following pages, detail. Milan, Pinacoteca di Brera, inv. 140

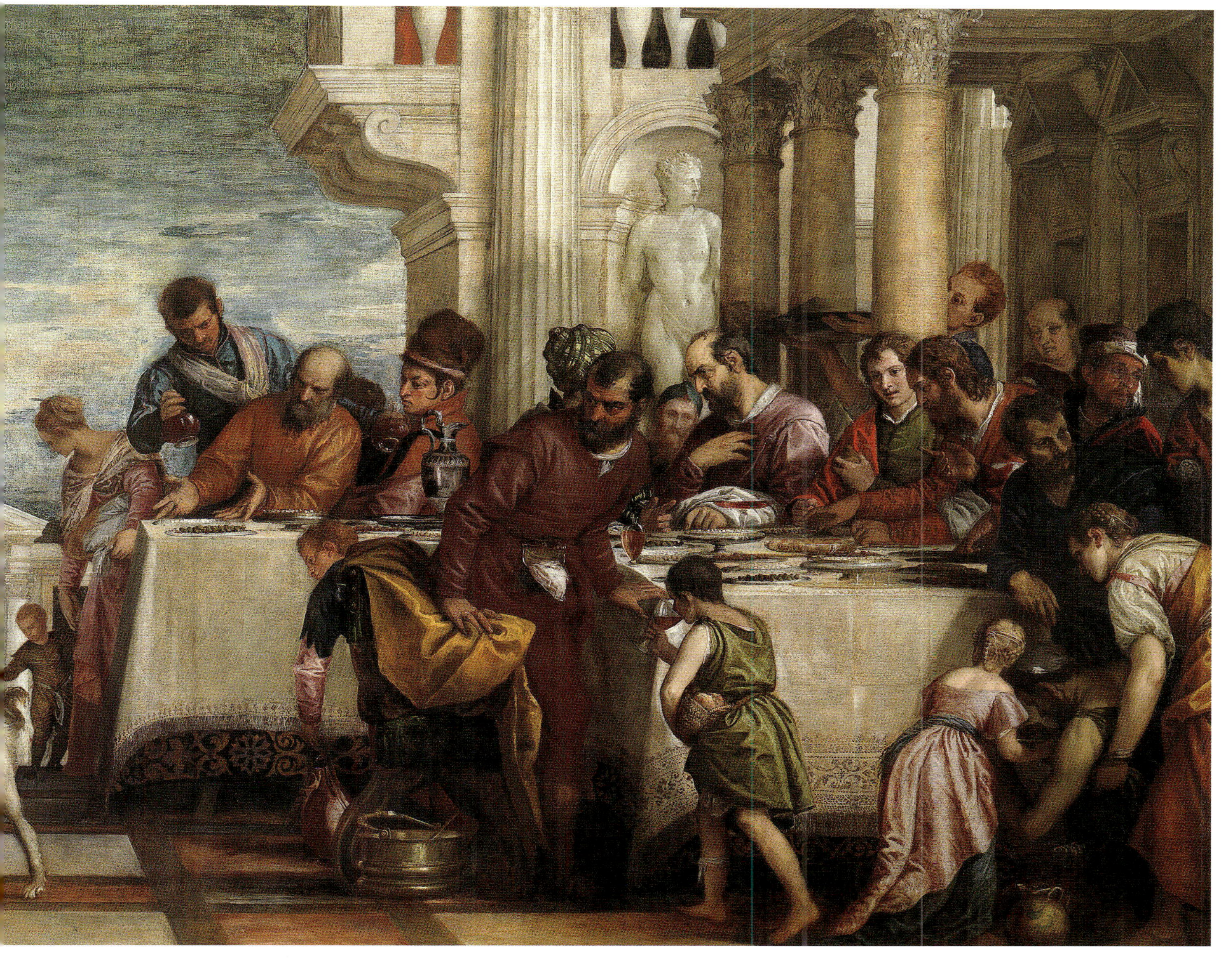

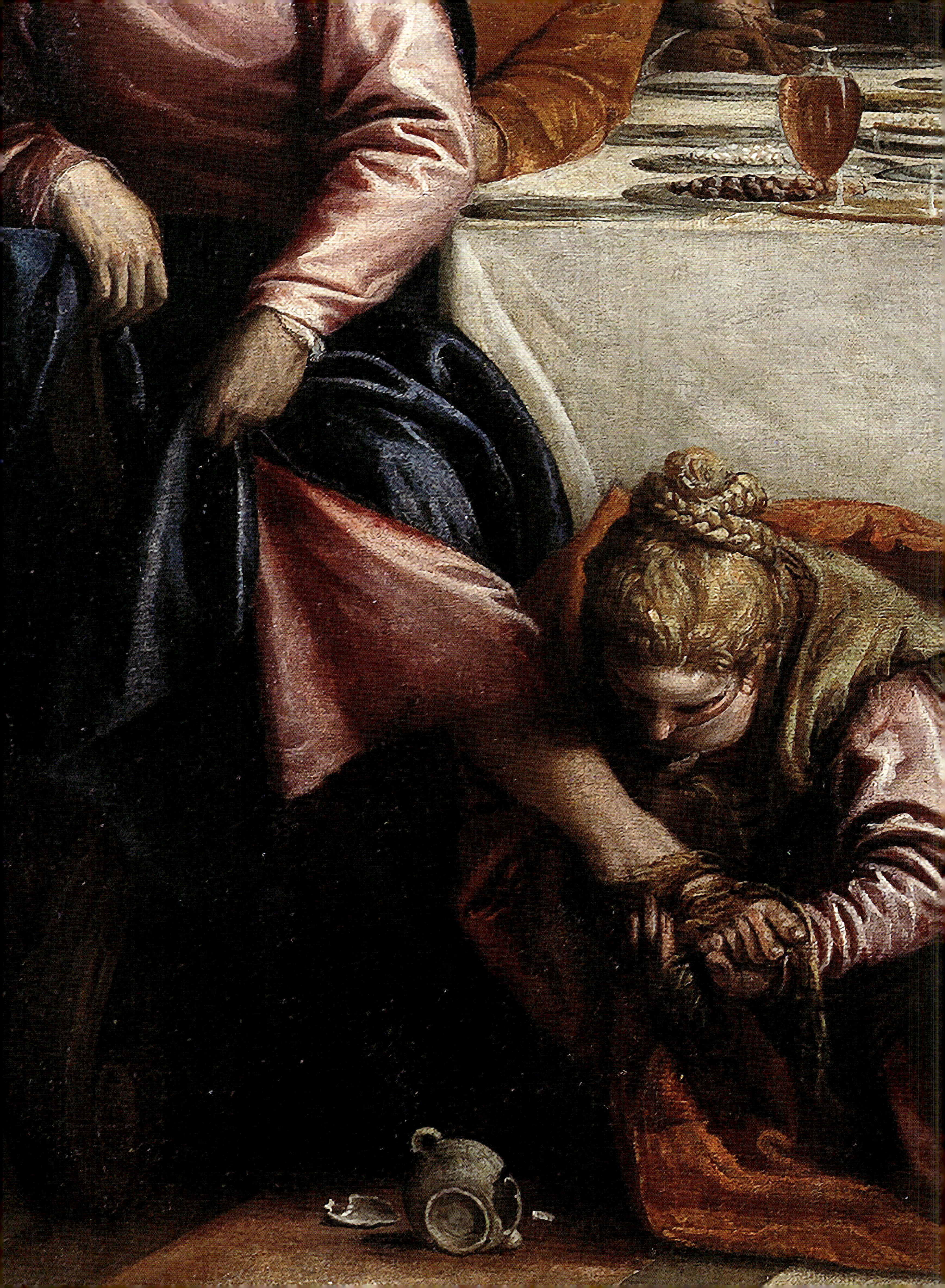

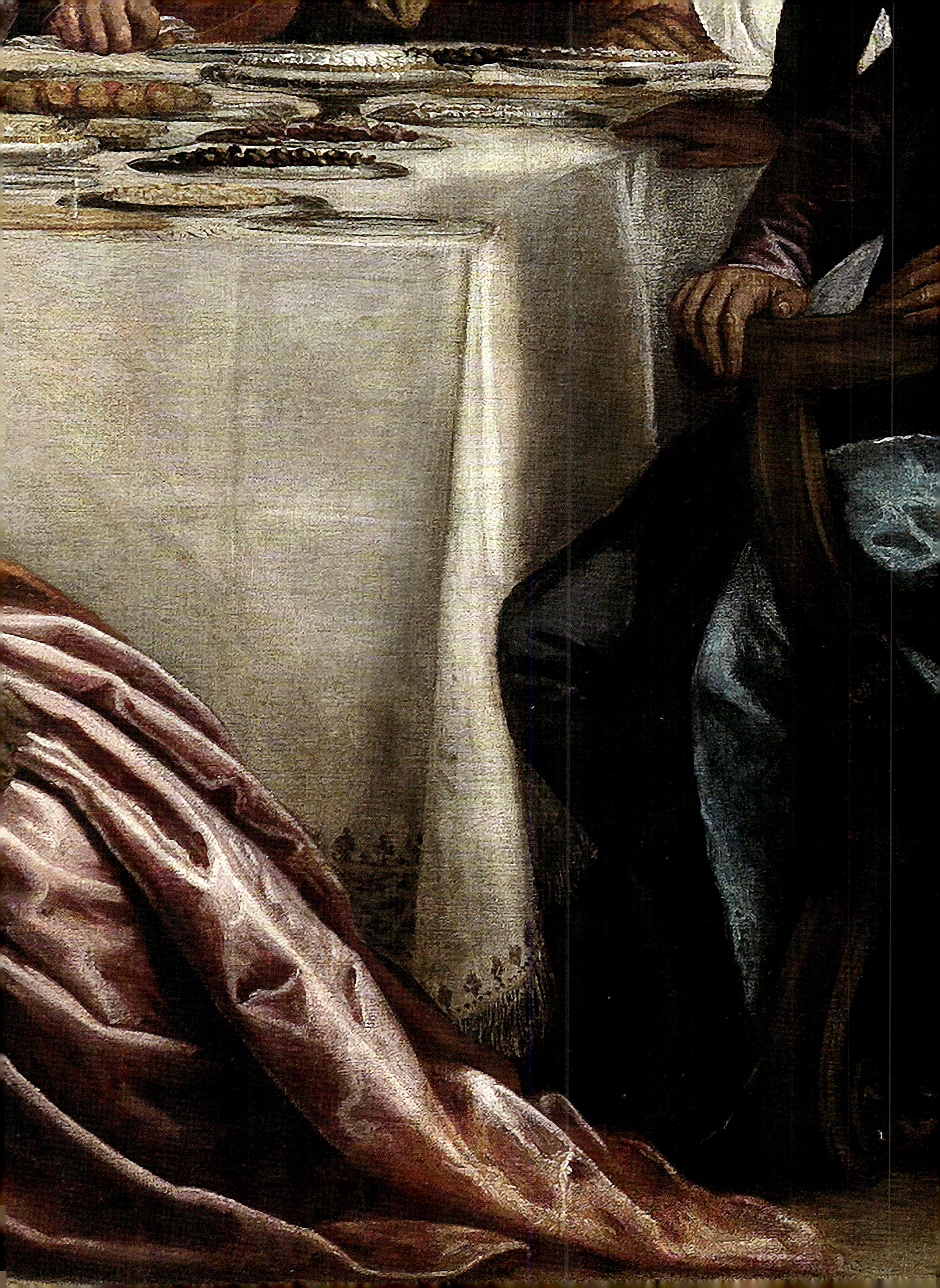

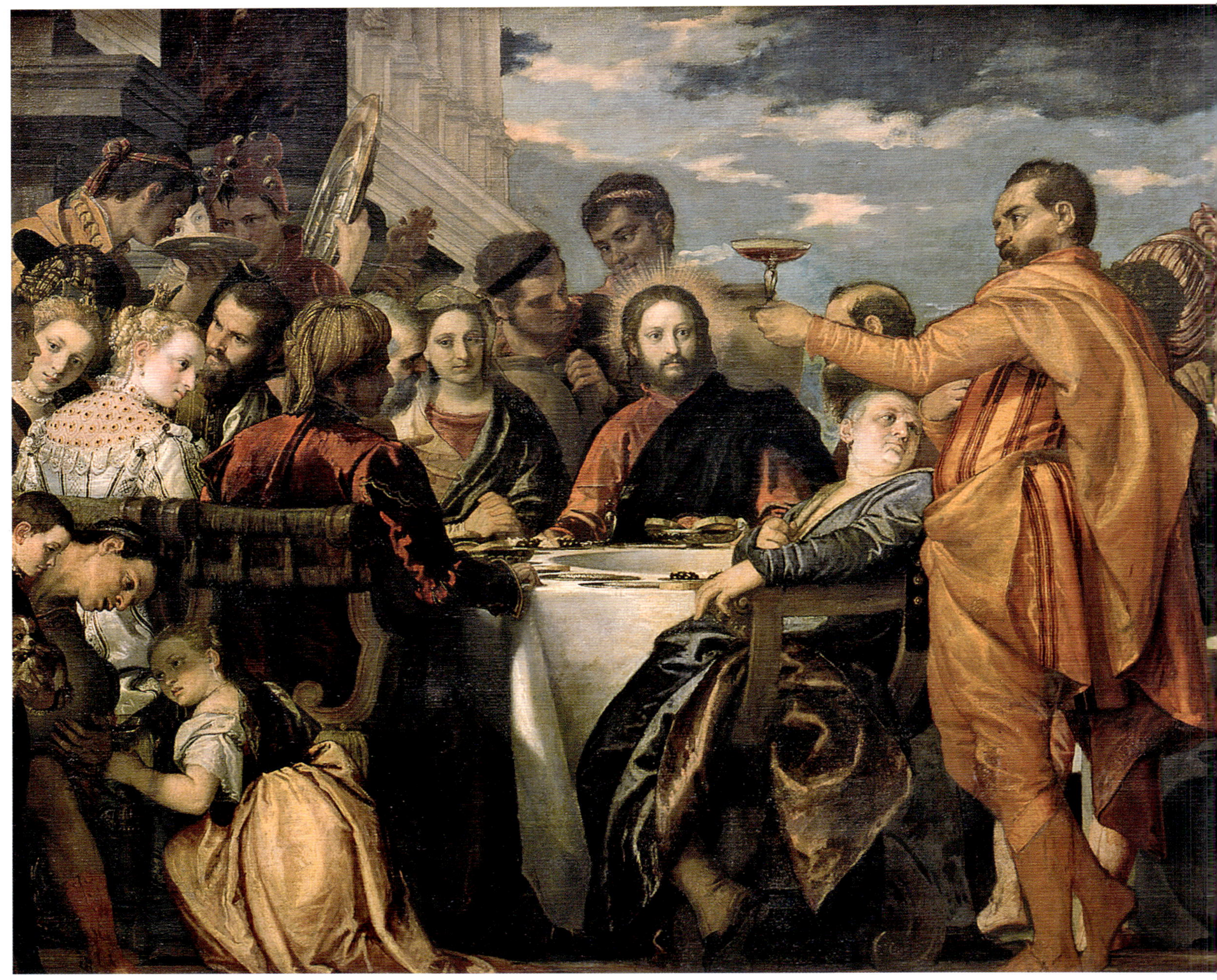

magnificence of this world and particularly of its generation, beautiful and free, in full enjoyment of the view. [...] Veronese always found some biblical banquet that lent him the sure basis for the invention and whose ceremonious content he could counterbalance by animating details. Architecturally and prospectively marvellous places constitute the scene on which guests are arranged and episodes take place, which are moved with great richness of elements, but without jumble. The best and greatest of these paintings (Louvre) are perhaps – as far as the so-called pictorial setting is concerned – the most beautiful paintings in the world; the perfect harmony of a chromatic scale is imposed in them and it is not reflected in other paintings; but the scale of all these lives gathered in one bundle that includes them all is basically an even greater miracle.

The Wedding Feast at Cana, 1571-1572, canvas, 207 × 457 cm. Dresden, Gemäldegalerie Alte Meister, inv. 226

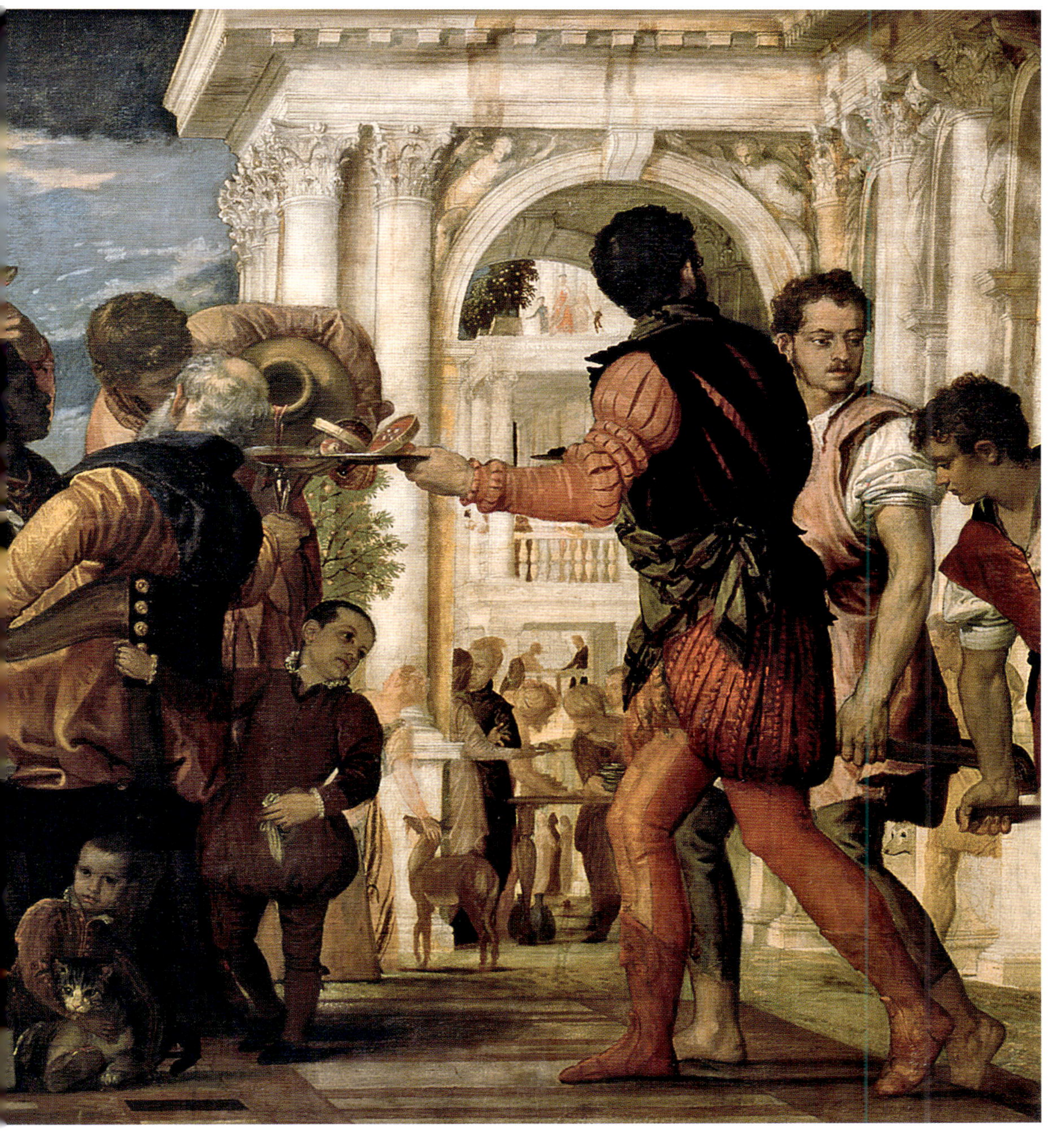

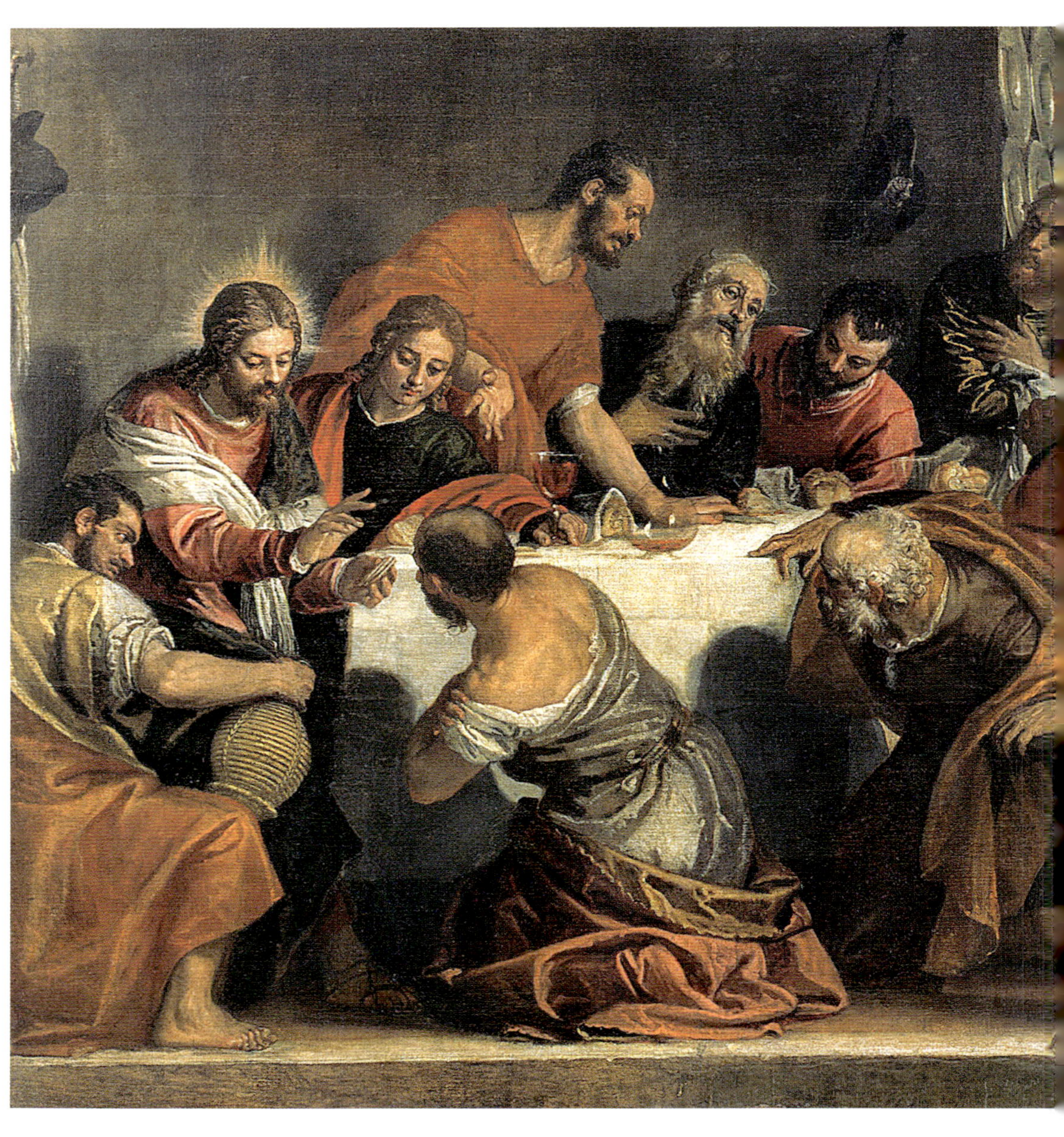

The Last Supper, 1585,
canvas, 220 × 523 cm.
Milan, Pinacoteca di Brera,
inv. 141

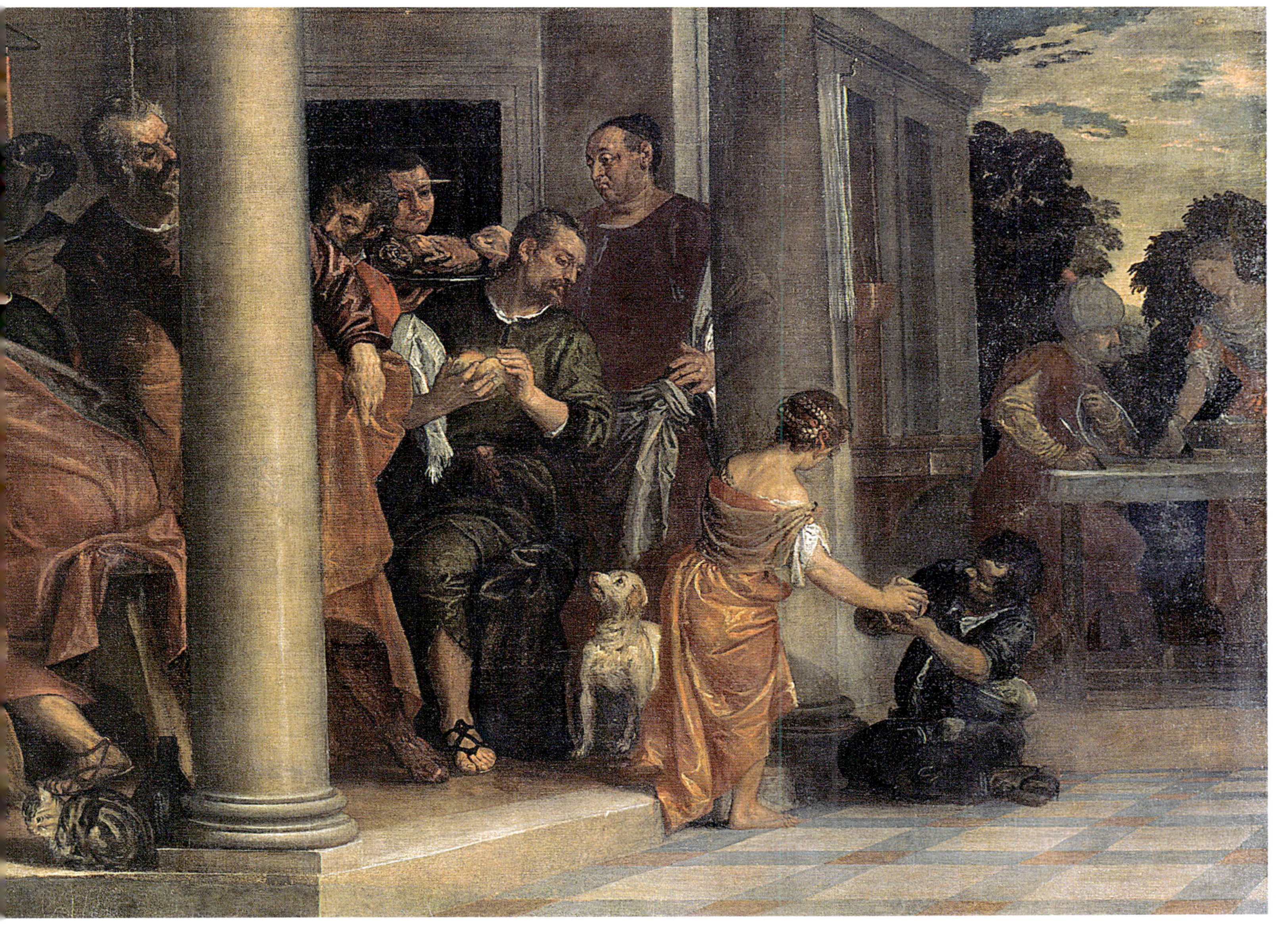

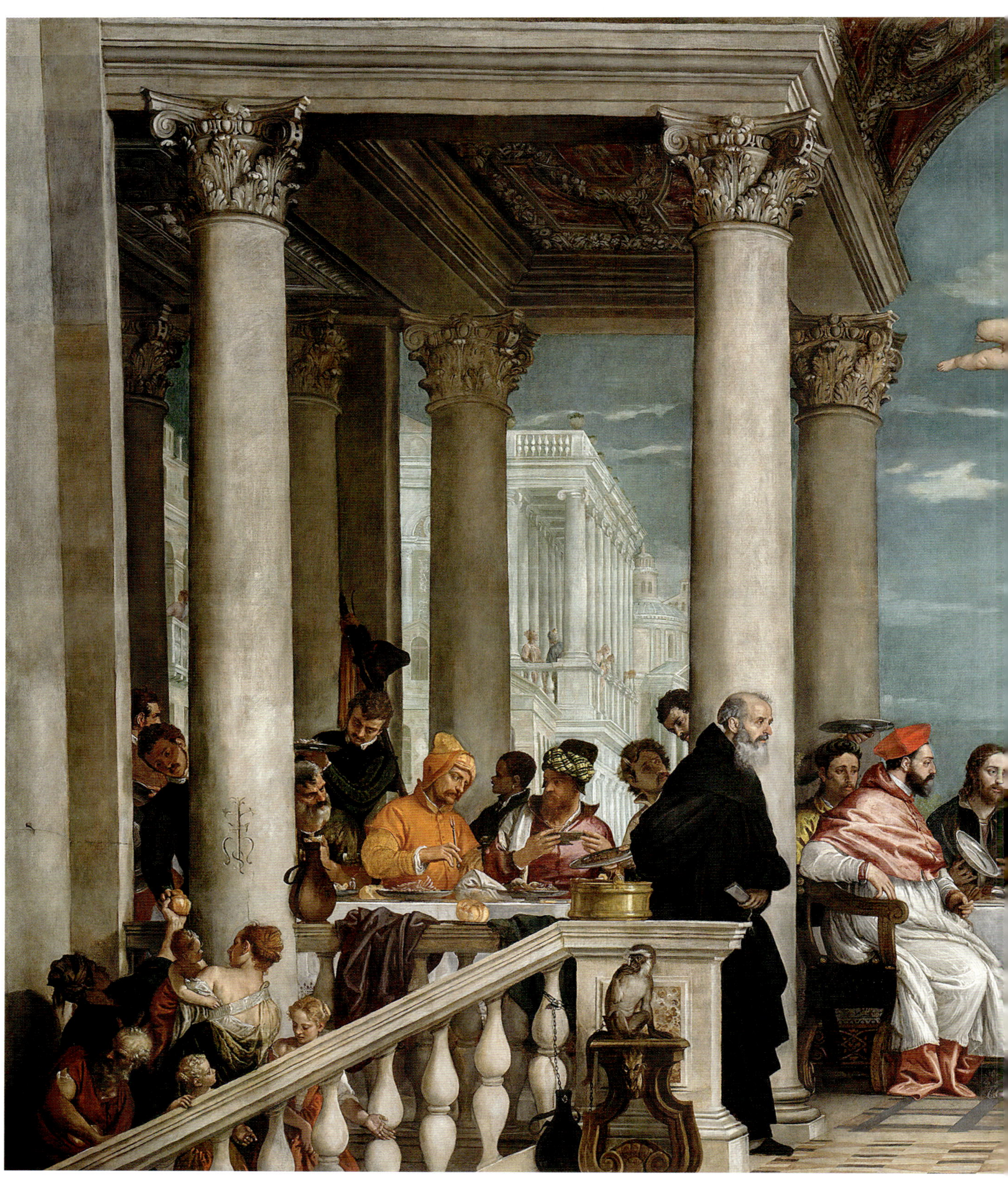

Supper of Saint Gregory the Great, 1572, canvas, 477 × 862 cm. Vicenza, sanctuary of the Madonna di Monte Berico

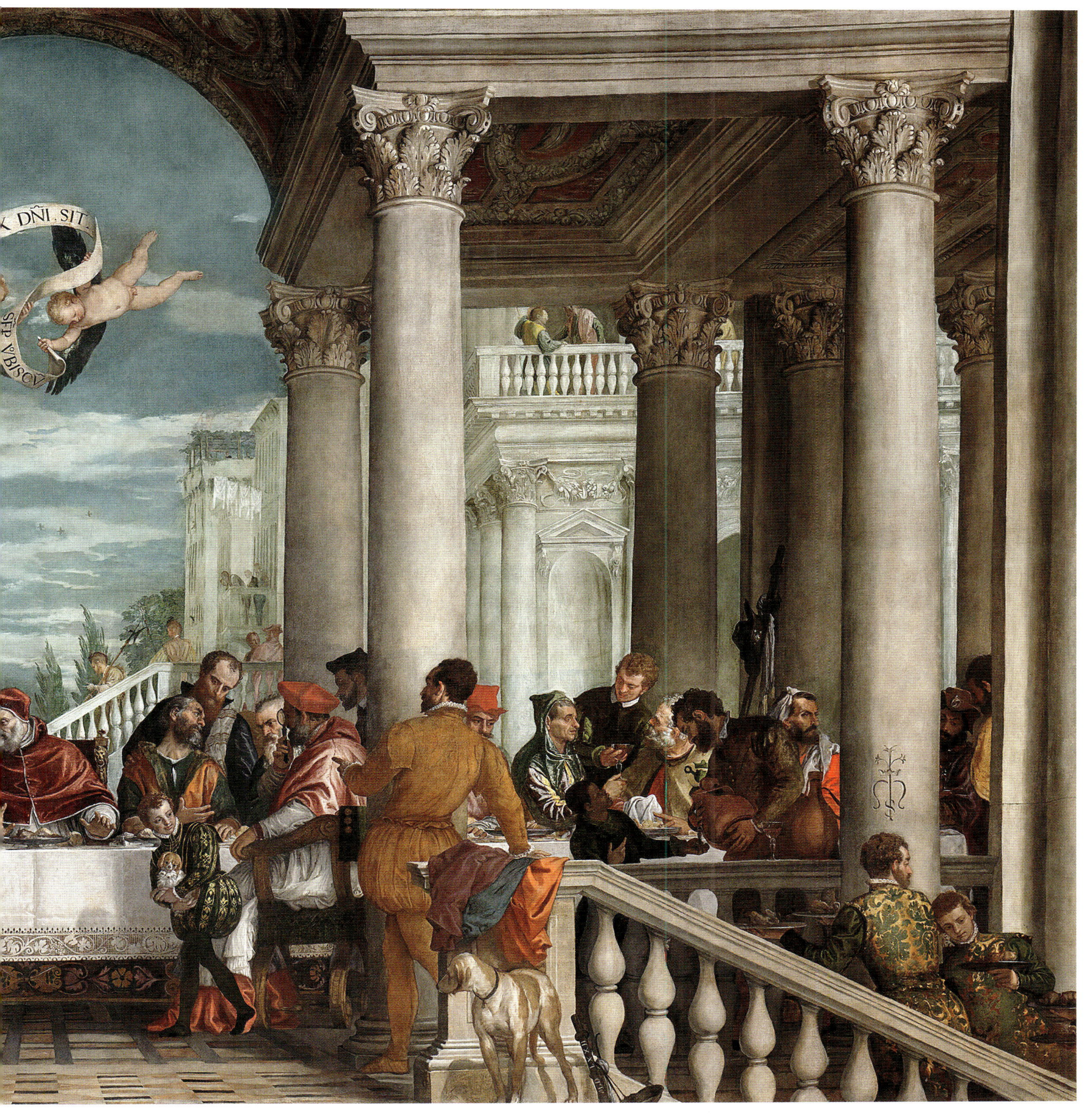
DÑI SIT
SĒP V̄BISCV

CHAPTER VII
Supper with the Inquisitor

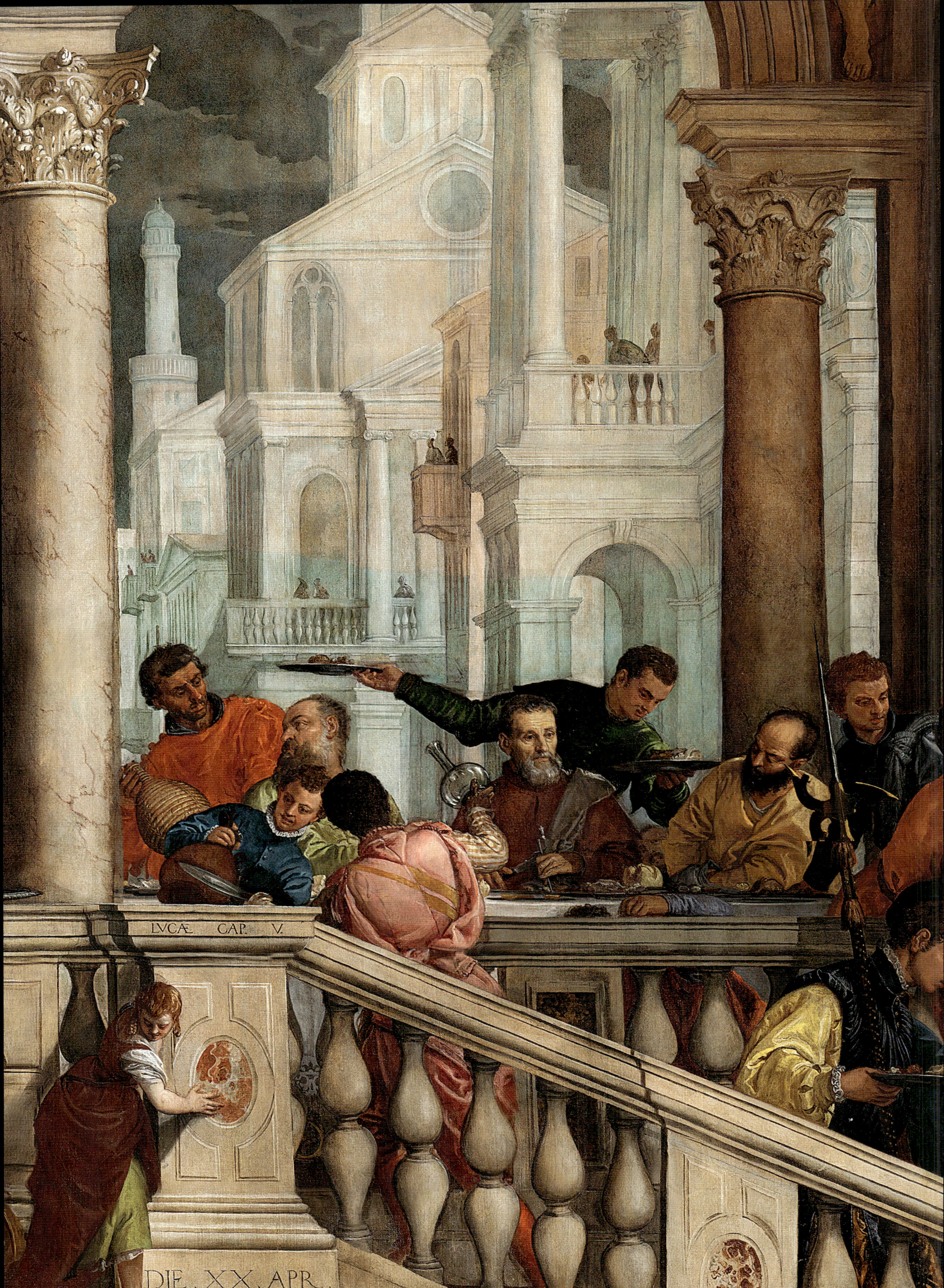
LVCÆ CAP. V.
DIE . XX . APR.

On 20 April 1573, the large refectory of the Dominican convent of Santi Giovanni e Paolo in Venice received, on the back wall, an enormous canvas, another *Convito* by the famous Paolo Veronese. This work is expressly named in clear letters: above the date inscribed on the piers that delimit the balustrades of the stairs on the left there is a quotation "FECIT D[OMINO] CO[N]VI[VIUM] MAGNU[M] LEVI" or "Levi made a great banquet for the Lord", on the right the evangelical reference LUCA CHAP. V. Written, however, in smaller body than the dates entered below.

The *Feast in the House of Levi* is exhibited at the Gallerie dell'Accademia in Venice, impressive in its gigantic dimensions: 555 × 1280 cm. At first glance, and it was even more so at the back of the large refectory, it amazes with its formidable architecture, three gigantic bays of a loggia made up of double *serliane*, which can be accessed by two "dead stairs". In addition, monumental winged victories are inserted in the spandrels, whose grandiose virtuosity is accentuated by the effect of "going out" from their space. It is not about quadraturism, it is the expression of an idea of painting capable of giving unity to space, using architecture and sculpture. In the erudite debate on the supremacy of one over the other, which Venice liked so much, the pictorial proposal of Veronese, as in Maser, in San Sebastiano, in Palazzo Ducale, offers the synthesis of the different languages.

The masterful perspective solution proposes the viewer a variety of points of view: a theatrical solution like the one built in the Teatro Olimpico in Vicenza by Vincenzo Scamozzi, with scenic alleys in divergent axes. So no longer a single central vanishing point: by truncating the elusive orthogonals he encourages the eye to follow the shorter ones, so the entire exposure on the surface of the canvas is not grasped at first glance, the eye must observe every portion of the loggia to appreciate its extent and perspective.

Once again Paolo Veronese is a supreme painter of architecture, a quality not always recognized in the past, when many art historians attributed these works to Benedetto and his workshop. Instead they are the "figure" of Paolo's production, always constantly attentive, as documented by the organ of San Sebastiano or the Martyrdom of San Giorgio in Braida, to the architectural and stone "frame" of his pictorial inventions. In this *Cena* he also realizes his most accurate, imaginative, multiple and inventive idea of the city, with fantastic constructions, Towers of Babel, loggias and compositions of every order in a metaphysical space in which the best Italian pictorial tradition can be found, from Fra Giovanni from Fiesole, the daring Angelico with early Christian Rome reinvented in the Niccolina Chapel, up to Bramante and Peruzzi, Raphael, Michelangelo and Giulio Romano.

According to the narrations of the first sources, starting from Ridolfi, the Supper was ordered and paid for by the friar Andrea de' Buoni, with his alms and a little patrimony, and the painter would have accepted the minimum payment for love of the place and of the art, generously wanting to make up for the loss of a *Last Supper* by Titian, which disappeared in the arson of the refectory, caused by the soldiers who were staying there, on 14 February 1571. The hypothesis of the friar who pays from his own pocket is an opportunity to present the painter in the guise of a devout and meek believer: in this case we don't have a contract, but there is no reason to justify the anecdote; perhaps it is possible that a friar contributed significantly to

Feast in the House of Levi, 1573, canvas, 555 × 1280 cm, detail and, on the following pages, whole and other details. Venice, Gallerie dell'Accademia, inv. 374

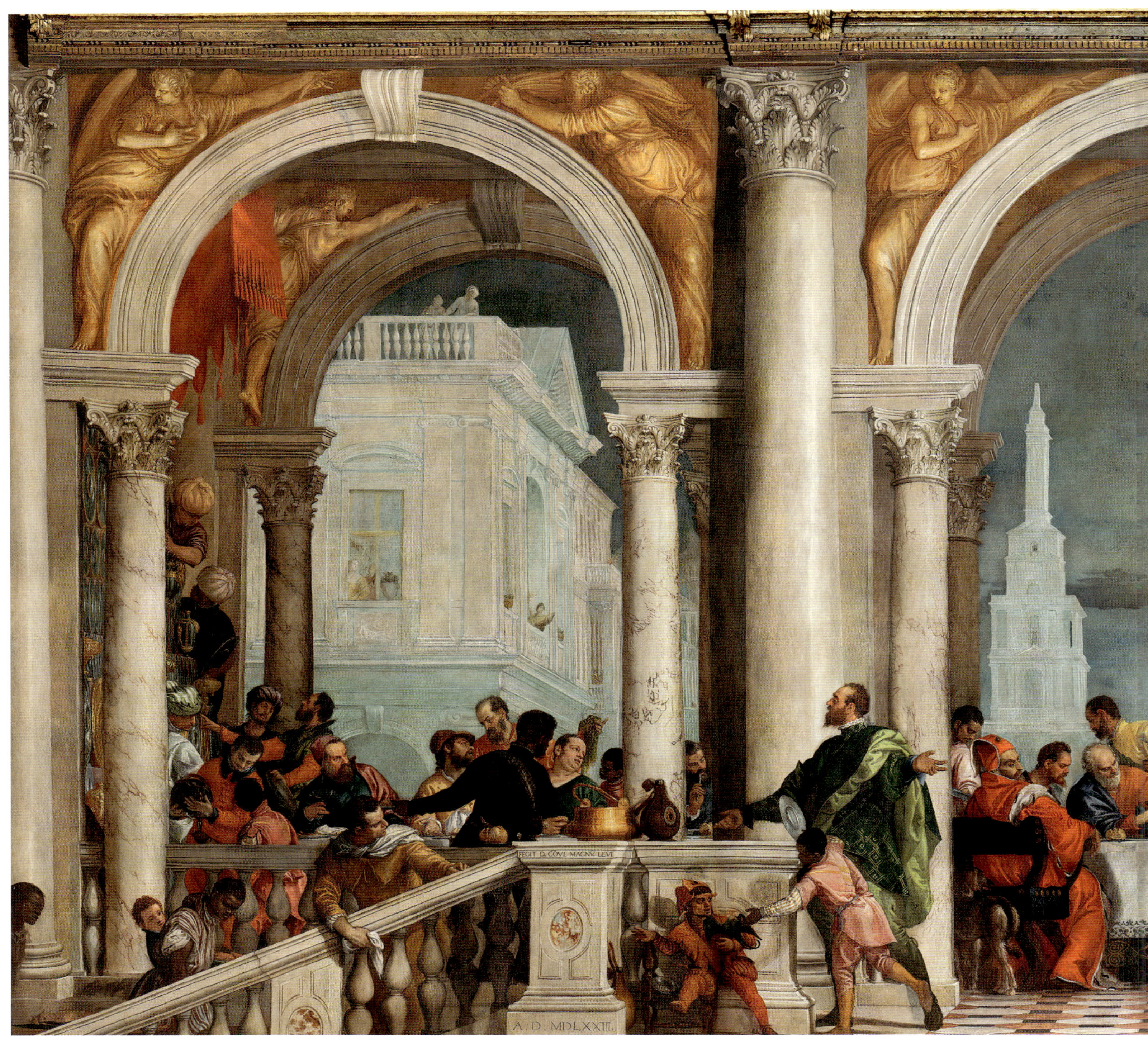
FECIT D. COVI. MAGNV. LEVI
A. D. MDLXXIII.

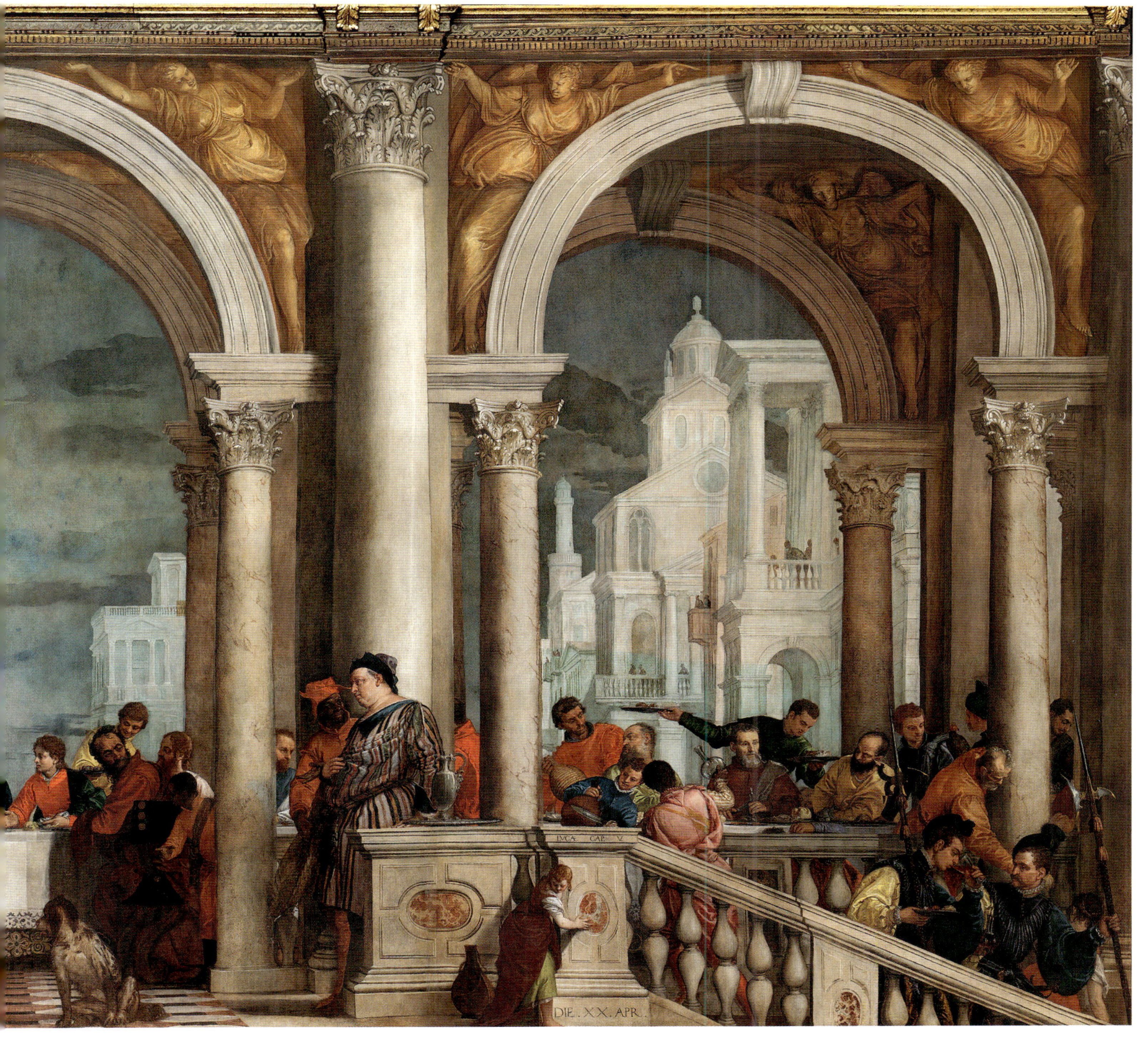
LVCA CAP. V
DIE. XX. APR.

remunerating the artist, but the amount requested would have been similar to that obtained from San Giorgio Maggiore.
Writing for the fourth centenary of his birth in the *Nuova Antologia* from 1928, Adolfo Venturi, as an authentic art critic, neatly reviews the sumptuous palette, the first and main reason for enjoying the work; the writing is exemplary for the analysis criteria:

> The usual pictorial whims, which Veronese favours and repeats with subtle variations, enliven the scene, continually attracting the amused eye: the Moretto, stretched out towards the dwarf, with the purplish shadow bubble of his face amidst the splendour of a pink silk and a plate of pure silver, inclined to mirror the light as in the Supper at Cana; the face of a page boy between figures in red and yellow, illuminated by a few touches of those two colours; the reflections of the blue and yellow of the garments on the halberds of two soldiers; the very mobile interweaving of ribbons over a green dress; the cat with the phosphoric nose; the multi-coloured striped tunic of a fat figure to the right; and, everywhere, bottles and glasses, tilted by the servants to make the glitter of the rays converge on the glass, and flasks with gilded straws, gold and silver utensils. The colours in Levi's Cena are a succession of clear, fresh, spring-like notes: canary yellows, faded pinks, lilacs, ruby reds. The reds shout celebration throughout the picture, interrupted on the front by the dark green mantle of a declamatory gentleman and the blue-gold, white-gold striped tunic of a fat character. And the bright pink tunic of a moretto in the foreground, the pink of dawn that dyes the clouds on the tender sky and from the clouds reverberates on the air-coloured buildings, blue and pink, reverberate, here and there from the loggia, the last delicate echo of that festive concert of reds.

The Problematic Convito

The Dominicans of the Basilica of Santi Giovanni e Paolo who had requested the work, since Titian was unable to renew what had been burned both due to his advanced age and his very slow processing times, were strictly dependent on the choices of the Venetian state, right from the building of the enormous church. The prestigious doge tombs built by the Lombardos were raised in the ancient and grandiose building, and the military glory of the Serenissima was celebrated in the funeral monuments dedicated to the commanders of the fleets. Here the rituals were officiated for the patricians who, at a high price, obtained the possibility of being remembered with marble cenotaphs. Here above all, at the time, the best orators of the Order were welcomed and preached, and here the learned theologians of the University of Padua expounded theses and arguments. State councillors, intellectuals, exponents of high-ranking families made up the management team of a rich and prestigious convent in which many friars maintained the family properties, had their own income, enjoyed absolute freedom of movement, had study rooms and private libraries. All this not only for at least flexible rules, but also for the specific will of the Priors. Inside the convent there were clear hierarchies, friars who took care of daily life, of the regular rites, others only of studies, others of financial administration; still others, for essentially family reasons, exercised a real political and cultural orientation role.
All these autonomies that had characterized the city convents, open to various welfare and charitable initiatives, to relations with the city administration, to study and teaching, to itinerant preaching, were frowned upon and hindered by the "Observants". These friars, in collaboration with the Holy See, pressed for a return to a more rigid observance of rules, behaviours and doctrine. To the "Conventuals" they opposed an observance which concerned both the essential purpose of the order, preaching and study, and the rigid rules of life in common, liturgical observance and respect for the vows of chastity, obedience and poverty.
The convent of Venice had been the furthest from the discipline, it was the fortress of the "Conventuals", friars accused of being "naughty", rebellious and riotous, too free in their movements according to the pontifical see itself. From 1531, the Vicaria of San Domenico was to supervise the return to the origins and to a reform of life, under the authority of a delegate, obviously observant, appointed by the General of the Order; but bringing the Conventuals back to obedience generated continuous tensions, especially between the Venetian fraternity linked to the Serenissima and to the identity of San Zanipo-

lo, and the Observants sent from outside to study theology; between the prior and the vicar obviously, but also within the same convent, between the different roles that corresponded to class origins and level of studies. Often very harsh, or threatening, clashes in which the secular power also had to intervene diplomatically, but sometimes militarily. Suffice it, within a rich documentation exchanged with Rome, to report these expressions of the nuncio Girolamo Verallo, written on 15 March 1537 to Ambrogio Ricalcati andregarding the convent of Santi Giovanni e Paolo: "if they live so dissolutely, also keeping bad women, and worse still, publicly, which is the greatest infamy in the world, without any respect and without any fear of God and shame of the world, if they fight among themselves and want to gouge out their eyes, which is a great thing (...) if they sleep all day, then making a thousand riots at night to kill each other, so that it can be held much safer walking in a wood than there; and so little obedience, indeed none, to their priors and prelates, that is a great reproach." The document (reported in *Nunziature di Venezia*, vol. II edited by Franco Gaeta, Rome, Istituto Storico Italiano, 1960, n. 49, p. 105), shows the truly scandalous situation of the most important Dominican convent in Venice, confirmed by the number of "apostate" friars, i.e. released from their obligations and reduced to the lay state: this is the majority of the deceased in the convent, in the sixties and seventies.

When Paolo Veronese was called, the situation had certainly improved due to the action of Vincenzo Giustiniani, but there were still many occasions for tension: in particular, the friars of San Zanipolo contested the accusation of not being "good priests", an accusation which they overturned on the clergy curial, denounced of hypocritical pharisaism. At the same time the convent remained under the strict protection of the Doge, following the evolution of the conflicts between Rome and the Serenissima. And that significant link between the convent and the Doge will be well illustrated by a canvas painted by Francesco Guardi in 1782 which portrays the refectory, still adorned on the back wall by Veronese's canvas, on the occasion of Pope Pius VI's farewell from the Doge. The painter shows the choral participation of dozens and dozens of guests from each other's entourage, a procession of prelates and politicians in the refectory where state elders and prestigious guests usually welcome.

The clash between the Observants, headed by the prior Eliseo Capys in office from 1571 to 1573, and the conventuals present in Sanzanipolo is therefore related to the judgment on the good prelate: and the *Feast in the House of Levi* seems to refer precisely to the criticism of scribes and Pharisees by Jesus. In fact, this particular convent situation had not been considered by historians and art critics until an unexpected discovery. In the issue dated 1 July 1867 of the prestigious *Gazette des beaux arts*, on page 378, there is a short article entitled "Paul Véronèse appellé au Tribunal du Saint Office à Venise, 1573". The author is Armand Baschet, a well-known and appreciated scholar, who spent five years in Venice studying the state archive of the Serenissima in depth, writing important studies on the relations between the Republic and France. The article begins by acknowledging: "I do not believe that any biography of Paolo Caliari known as Veronese has signalled that this honest man had anything to do with the Holy Office. Instead, here is a document that shows it", and he goes on to confess that he had no suspicion going through the documents relating to that court; if anything, he thought he'd find some paperwork against people like Pietro Aretino, certainly not against a mirrored painter like Veronese. Baschet adds that the tribunal of the Inquisition in Venice is very different from the Spanish or Roman ones, has a much more limited power, and combines three ecclesiastics – the nuncio, the patriarch and an inquisitor Dominican friar – with three laymen, the Savii all'Eresia, indicated by the Republic, in office like all magistrates for only one year. It is therefore a court less bound by the dictates of the Church than the name and fear suggest. Given the premise, the scholar translates the document, or the constitution, an ancient legal term to indicate the interrogation. It must be said immediately that this paper is unique, other documentary pieces are missing, i.e. the denunciation, the interrogations of other witnesses, the minutes of any other sessions: nothing except the summons, the minutes of the interrogation of Paolo Caliari, until then completely unknown, neither hinted at nor suspected by biographers and sources.

After 1867 art historians will have to take this into account, and they will do so in different ways: some deduce a real risk, observing that Paolo will no longer paint banquets in his particular style; for others it is the heroic testimony of the artist's freedom, in a kind of Galilean trial against art; others will highlight the relative bonhomie of an Inquisition which limited itself to a warning asking for changes at the expense of the painter, which by the way were not carried out. Since the essence of the criticism, rather than the accusation, is having placed on the scene of the painting unbecoming, unsuitable and offensive characters and situations in a sacred situation. But this is because it would be a Last Supper, therefore a scene covered in sacredness even if the image is placed in an unconsecrated space. The risk would be that of offering arguments to the ultramontane heresies.

The document is important because it records, albeit in the form of a report, the direct opinions of Paolo Caliari; presumably written during the exam, it shows the usual summary dryness, but also cancellations, abbreviations, elimination of questions, absence of arguments and details; moreover, the manuscript does not say who is asking the questions, while from the answers it seems that Paolo is addressing several people. The interrogation must therefore be contextualised, compared with the previous and subsequent ones, understood through the procedures of the time. As Gino Fogolari did very well in the past (in *Il processo dell'Inquisizione a Paolo Veronese*, in "Archivio Veneto", XVII, 1935, pp. 352-386) and Philipp P. Fehl (*Veronese and the Inquisition. A Study of the Subject Matter of the So-called 'Feast in the House of Levi'*, in "Gazette des Beaux-Arts", LVIII, 1961, pp. 325-354) with the best analytical result, extremely illuminating, finally offered by Maria Elena Massimi, first in a doctoral thesis of 2004, then in the book *La cena in casa Levi di Paolo Veronese. Il processo riaperto*, published by Marsilio in 2012. We follow the manuscript text with the erasures.

THE INTERROGATION

So on Saturday 18 July 1573 Paolo Caliari was summoned before the Inquisition court: the place is not indicated, but it should be the church of San Teodoro next to the Doge's Chapel, i.e. the Basilica of San Marco; here from 1541 to 1615 the archive of the Tribunal was kept, under the responsibility of the chancellor of the nuncio.

As mentioned, we do not have the names of the judges, which should be reconstructed by deduction, on the basis of the documentary sequence; the Dominican inquisitor is Aurelio Schellino, from Brescia, while the three lay Sages in charge were Giacomo Foscarini, Alvise Zorzi and Niccolò Venier. We must add that the doge in charge, Alvise Mocenigo, had clear anti-papal political sentiments. If present, the incumbent patriarch must have been Giovanni Trevisan, at the time seventy years old, but it is more probable that he was replaced by a delegate; the third clergyman was plausibly Giovanni Battista Castagna, bishop of Rossano, appointed nuncio to Venice on 15 June; he will then be recorded in history for the shortest pontificate, with the name of Urban VII: only twelve days.

Then the interrogation begins:

> a Dominus Paulus Callarius Veronensis pictor habitator in parochia Sancti Samuelis [is asked about his identity – confirmed – and job]: Respondit Io depingo et fazzo delle figure. [A precise answer, exactly corresponding to one of the kind of activities of the men enrolled in the Art. And to the question whether he knew of the summons:] Respondit per quello, che mi fu detto dalli Reverendi Padri, cioè il Prior de San Zuane polo, del qual non so il nome, il qual mi disse, che l'era Stato qui, et che Vostre Signorie Illustrissi-

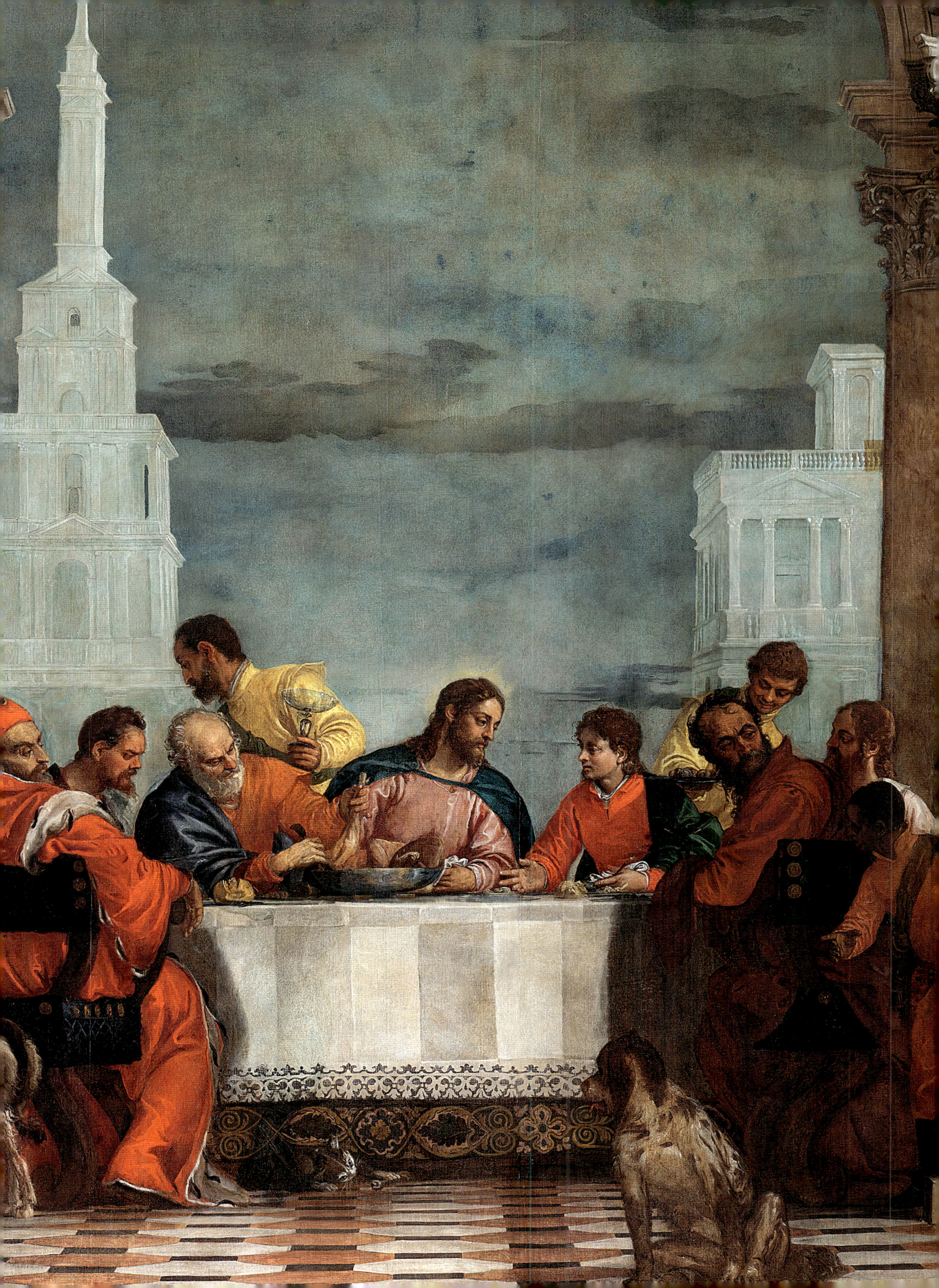

> me gli haveva dato commission che 'l dovesse far far la Maddalena in luogo de un Can. Et mi ghe risposi, che volentiera haveria quello et altro per honor mio et del quadro. ~~Ei dictum~~ Ma che non sentiva che tal figura della Maddalena podesse zazer che la stesse bene. ~~Ei dictum~~ per molte ragioni, le quali dirò sempre, che mi sia dato occasion che le possa dir.

I reproduce the text exactly, including the deletions, which identify implied and unregistered questions (*Ei dictum*). The first answer is already disconcerting: don't you know the prior's name? Yet it was Adriano Abriani, who had communicated to him the results of the meeting with the Inquisitor, and the request to paint the Magdalene (instead of the dog!), or to make the scene clearly a "Supper in the house of Simon". And Veronese had refused; he is asked to be right, precisely the *Ei dictum* was cancelled, the sentence appears as the only answer, and the question is missing; in any case Veronese simply says: she didn't look good in the painting. But why? the painter would have explained it, perhaps, later. The interrogation continues by subtly asking which painting he was referring to: *Questo è un quadro della Cena ultima, che fece Giesu Christo ~~al~~ con li suoi apostoli ~~Ei dictum~~ In casa di Simeon*. The Last Supper then, but where? he would have been asked: and the answer is surprising: the Last Supper would have taken place in Simon's house. The most singular aspect is that no one disputes this undue relationship between the Upper Room, or the room of a "hotel" in Jerusalem where Jesus meets with the disciples, washes their feet, warns of the imminent betrayal and indicates in the bread and wine the manifestation of his memory, and Simon's house, where the episode of the Magdalene had taken place.

The inquisitor, or someone on his behalf, asks where the painting is – *In refettorio delli frati de San Zuane polo* – inquires about the measure and also asks *havete depento Ministri*? That is Apostles. The questioned replies: *E'l patron dell'albergo Simon, oltra questo ho fatto sotto questa figura uno scalco, il qual hò finto chel sia venuto per suo diporto à veder, come vanno le cose della tola*. This detail, the presence of the "patron" who wants to control the canvas (the *tola*), would seem to refer to a different source than the *Gospels* and the *Letter to the Corinthians*. It could once again be *I Quattro Libri de la Humanità di Christo*, the Marcolini edition from 1538 which contains a reference to the "owner of the inn" where Jesus and the apostles dine; he knew Jesus and reserved a private room for them, and therefore he brings the food and can "enter the scene". At the Inquisitor's request, how many and which "Last Suppers" were painted by Caliari, the painter recalls those of Verona and that of San Giorgio: at this point someone among those present: *Li fu detto questa non è cena, ne si domanda della Cena del signor. Respondit Ne ho fatto una nel refettorio di Servi di Venetia, et una nel Reffettorio di San sabastian qui in Venetia. Et ne hò fatto una in Padoa ai Padri della Maddalena*. In fact, the observations do not concern the wedding at Cana or the supper at Simeon's, but only the Last Supper, and the interrogation points to the most inconvenient, dangerous and suspicious situations:

> che significa la pittura di colui che li esce il sangue del naso? Respondit L'hò fatto per un servo, che per qualche accidente li possa esser venuto ~~al~~ il sangue del naso Ei dictum Che significa quelli armati alla Thodesca vestiti con una lambarse per una mano? Respondit E'l fa bisogno, che dica qui vinti parole. Et dictum che'l dica. Respondit Nui pittori ~~havemo la~~ si pigliamo licentia, che si pigliano i poetti et i matti, et ho fatto quelli dui Alabardieri uno che beve, et l'altro che magna appresso una scala morta i quali sono messi la, che possino far qualche officio parendomi conveniente, che 'l patron della Casa che era grande e richo secondo che mi è stato detto dovesse haver servitori. Ei dictum Quel vestito da Buffon con il papagalo in pugno à che effetto l'havete depento in quel Telaro? Respondit Per ornamento, come si fa.

Paolo's answer, the license of painters is that of poets and fool, is not original but, in general form, it is the popularization of the famous thesis of Horace, in the *Letter to the Pisoni*, known as *Ars Poetica* in verses 9-10 "Pictoribus atque poetis quidlibet audendi semper fuit aequa potes-

tas." The *dictum Horatii* (painters and poets have always been granted the right freedom to dare in everything) was well known to painters and lovers of the arts, ecclesiastics as well as men of letters. Paolo defends himself by affirming the principle and autonomy: I painted what I liked to paint, for ornament, as one does. As for the invention of the "dead stair" or the double lateral stairway that defines two levels, also used for the Monte Berico canvas, he proposed it to further underline the distance and the difference between the banquet hall and the social space . On this scene he sets the scurrilities of which he will be accused: they take place beyond, outside, with respect to the sacred area, defined by the portico.
However, one cannot deny the imprudence of the questioned person in confirming that the nosebleed is really nosebleed, which happened by who knows what accident; equivalent to the statement that the dog was better off than the Magdalene, and that the halberdiers were suited to the rich guest.
Another rather serious question: what is Peter doing with his hands on his plate? *Respondit s'l squarta l'agnelo per darlo all'altro capo della Tola*, the apostle then cuts the lamb into pieces to give it to the other apostles arranged along the table; and who is sitting to receive the dish? *l'è uno, che ha un piron, che si cura i denti*. That is, he uses the small fork with two prongs, an elegant Venetian innovation to bring pieces of food to his mouth, a new habit, given that hands and spoons were usually used at the table. But what are the others doing, besides the Apostles? Who requested them?

> Credo che si trovassero Christo con li suoi apostoli; ma se nel ~~spa~~ quadro li avanza spacio io l'adorno di figure ~~si come mi vien commesso et~~ secondo le invenzioni. Ei dictum se da alcuna persona vi è stato commesso che voi dipengeste in quel quadro Thodeschi et buffoni et simil cose. Respondit Signor no: Ma la commission fu di ornar il quadro secondo mi parese, il quale è grande et capace di molte figure si come à me pareva. Ei dictum se li ornamenti che lui pittore ~~so~~ è solito fare dintorno le pitture o quadri ~~a torno le~~ solito di fare convenienti et proportionati alla materia et figure ~~princip~~ principali o veramente a ~~caso~~ beneplacito secondo che li viene in fantasia senza alcuna discrittione et giudizio. Respondit Io fazzo le pitture con quella consideration che è conveniente, che'l mio intelletto può capire. Interrogatus se li par conveniente, che alla cena ultima del signore si convenga depingere buffoni imbriachi Thodeschi ~~arma~~, nani, et simili scurrilità. Respondit Signor no.

No one has suggested his characters to the painter: here it seems that we are trying to obtain a possible accusation against the Dominicans of the convent; but the painter claims them as his own and, to top it off, confirms that in fact buffoons and Germans shouldn't be in a sacred Supper! So?

> Interrogatus Perché dunque l'havete dipinto, l'ho fatto perché presuppono che questi sieno fuori ~~dove~~ del luoco dove si fa la cena, Interrogatus Non sapete voi, che il Alemagna et altri lochi infetti di heresia sogliano con le pitture diverse et piene di scurrilità, et simili inventioni diligare, vittuperar, et far scherno delle cose della Santa Chiesa Catholica per insegnar mala dottrina alle genti Idiote et ignoranti. Respondit Signor sì che l'è male: ma perché tornerò anchora quel che ho ditto, che ho obbligo di seguir quel che hanno fatto li miei maggior.

Therefore: the "scurrilous" characters are outside the sacred space; there are heretics who can think badly, but after all I paint like the Masters before me: and he proposes Michelangelo as an example who painted nudes in the Pontifical chapel. The inquisitor's answer is obvious: that is the Last Judgment, where no dressed beings are presumed, and in any case there are no antics. Veronese's referring to Michelangelo is dangerous: everyone knows that the latter's Judgment in the Sistine Chapel had been the subject of fierce discussions, controversies and criticisms

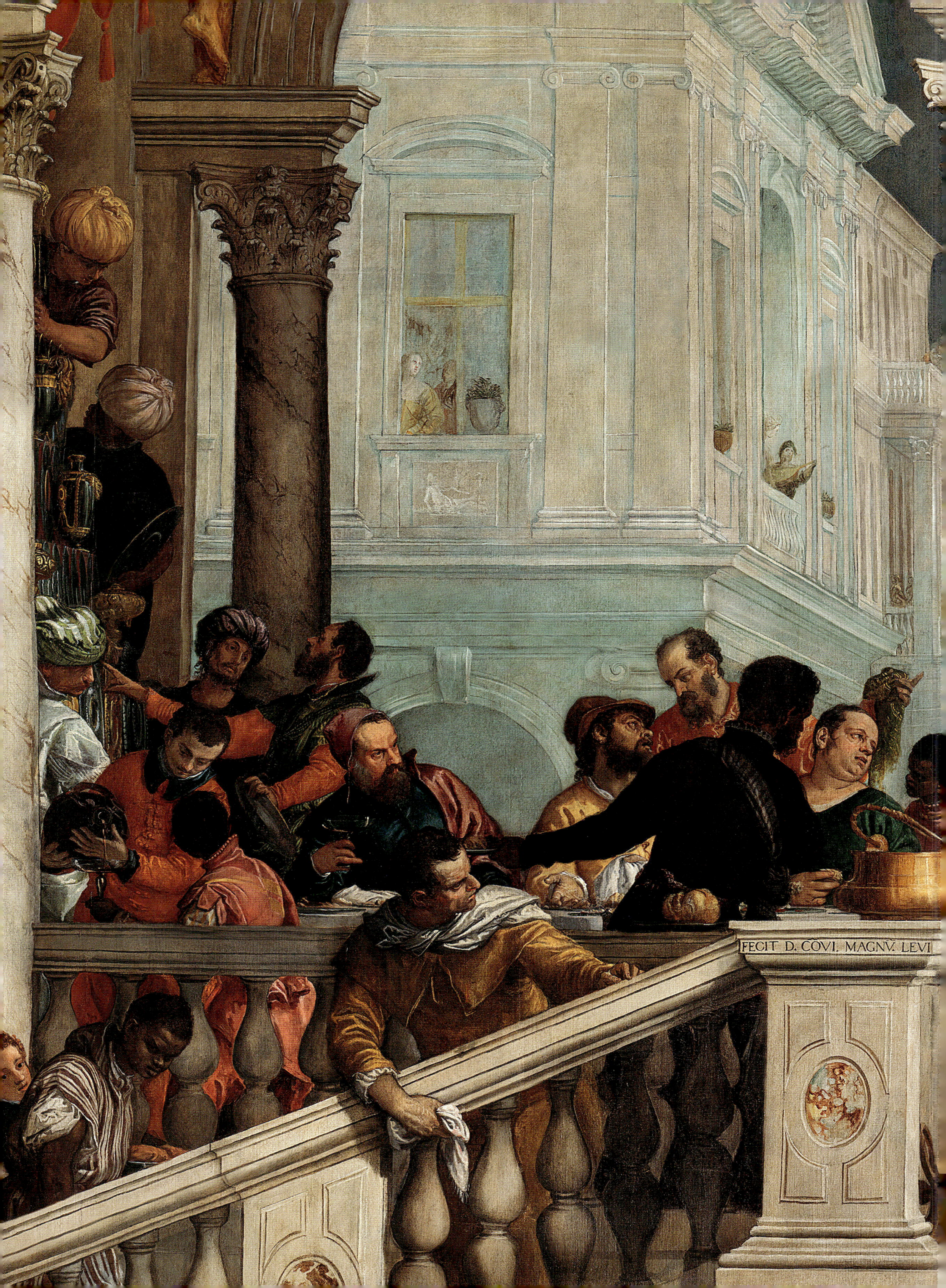
FECIT D. CŌVI. MAGNV̄. LEVI

and that a few years earlier, in 1565, Daniele da Volterra had been called to cover the genitals, acquiring for himself the nickname of "braghettone". Then comparing a refectory to the papal chapel is undue also from the point of view of the typology of images. But in short, does Paolo Caliari want to defend his so dangerous picture? *Respondit Signor Illustrissimo no che non lo voglio defender; ma pensava di far bene. Et che non hò considerato tante cose, Pensando di non far desordene nisuno tanto più, che quelle figure di Buffoni sono fuor del luogo dove è il nostro Signore.* At this point the interrogated resumes the same line of defense, i.e. that he hadn't thought about the consequences of his choices, and the interrogation ends. Quibus habitis it is decreed that Paolo is obliged to *corigendum et emendandum* the painting within three months and at his expense. If it is not done, there will be a penalty. *Et ita decreverunt omni meliori modo.*
At the end of the reading, the impression is that the inquisitors wanted to understand and know if there was a message in those choices of figures and situations, unsuitable for the representation of the Last Supper, and who was the prompter. Veronese assumed full responsibility for it, claiming his own freedom, underlining the difference between the sacred space and the narrative one; he was elusive and often tautological, refusing interventions on his work, even with an impudent attitude.
As known, in the end no modification was made to the canvas which, however, received (or had it already received? Since there is no evidence of an intervention subsequent to the Inquisition's request) that reference to the Gospel of Luke. Let's read the text again: Luke 5.

> 27 After this, Jesus went out and saw a tax collector by the name of Levi sitting at his tax booth. "Follow
> me," Jesus said to him, 28 and Levi got up, left everything and followed him. 29 Then Levi held a great
> banquet for Jesus at his house, and a large crowd of tax collectors and others were eating with them.
> 30 But the Pharisees and the teachers of the law who belonged to their sect complained to his disciples,
> "Why do you eat and drink with tax collectors and sinners?" 31 Jesus answered them, "It is not the
> healthy who need a doctor, but the sick. 32 I have not come to call the righteous, but sinners to repen-
> tance." 33 They said to him, "John's disciples often fast and pray, and so do the disciples of the Pharisees,
> but yours go on eating and drinking." 34 Jesus answered, "Can you make the friends of the bridegroom
> fast while he is with them? 35 But the time will come when the bridegroom will be taken from them; in
> those days they will fast.

So the *Feast in the House of Levi* reveals a harsh criticism of the hypocrisy of the Pharisees (i.e. the Observants), justifying the disciples, who eat, drink and are in the world with tax collectors and sinners (i.e. the Conventuals). So the *Feast* could be a polemical manifesto in defence of the Conventuals. The interrogation raises many questions, and no answer: how come the Inquisition questions about that canvas, first summoning the prior, then the painter? Who reported the scandal? Is it believable that Veronese painted all the animated action just to "fill" it, following only his own creative judgement? Without tips and comparisons?
Let's try to go back to the commentator closest to Veronese, Ridolfi, to understand how the enterprise was understood seventy years after its completion. Our source has no doubts: it is the supper in the house of Levi, later known as Matthew; and for this there are many and varied actors; no orthodoxy problem:

> The table is simulated under a spacious loggia, partitioned into three large arches, outside which one can admire the beautiful structures of palaces which make for a delightful view. In the middle rests the Saviour, opposite Levi dressed in a purple robe, and with him sit many publicans, and others mingled with the Apostles, in whom he composed very rare heads in singular effects, and portrayed Friar Andrew in a corner with a towel over his shoulder, from whose effigy one would draw as a good advantage what was spent in the work; and among the things of admiration is the figure of the innkeeper leaning

> on a pedestal, who besides dividing the quality of the character individually, is of such fresh flesh that he seems alive. Near him is an Ethiopian servant with Moorish dress and basket in hand: he is laughing and moves whoever looks at him to laughter. Finally, the whole work is handled with great skill, as much as can be done in this genre (...).

Therefore, let us carefully watch the unfolding of the play set in the gigantic architecture, against an urban background of fabulous complexity, perhaps also the bearer of different meanings, starting with that sort of tower of Babel in the centre. Each character is fixed in an expressive instant, there is no "civil conversation with music" as in the *The Wedding Feast at Cana*, with postures and gestures of the "etiquette" of the time. Here we are faced with characters and situations in motion, in a web of relationships that are difficult to dissolve.

Jesus appears very calm, while the young John is talking and, with words on his lips, enumerates three arguments, indicating with his gesture the action of Peter, to the right of Jesus. He is about to cut a leg of lamb; the bread is intact in front of him. Behind is a servant, carrying a glass goblet, a wine glass, perfectly clear. The evangelical reference this time goes to Matthew 23-26:

> Jesus said: "Woe to you, teachers of the law and Pharisees, you hypocrites! You give a tenth of your spices – mint, dill and cumin. But you have neglected the more important matters of the law – justice, mercy and faithfulness. You should have practiced the latter, without neglecting the former. You blind guides! You strain out a gnat but swallow a camel. Woe to you, teachers of the law and Pharisees, you hypocrites! You clean the outside of the cup and dish, but inside they are full of greed and self-indulgence. Blind Pharisee! First clean the inside of the cup and dish, and then the outside also will be clean.

Jesus was controversial with the Pharisees, and no less so with the chief priests and the elders, those who have the task of ruling, guiding, instructing the people belonging to the Lord, to whom he addressed a parable in Matthew 20.1-16. The owner of a vineyard is absent: responsibility for the work has been entrusted to the vinedressers. When the time comes for the harvest, the master sends servants to collect the fruits that are due to him: but the tenants mistreat them and drive them away; "Last he sent his own son to them, saying: 'They will have respect for my son!'" And instead, just seeing him, "the peasants said to each other: 'This is the heir. Come on, let's kill him and we will have his inheritance!'" The parable is clear: God is the master of the vineyard, that is of the people of Israel, the tenants – the priests and the elders – felt they were masters, they drive out all the prophets, they want the death of the Son of God.

Perhaps it is because of these reproaches that the tall figure in red, whose coat is lined with ermine – the prerogative of prosecutors – and whose peculiar hat is adorned with a pin, turns annoyed. It cannot be Levi or the apostle Matthew, it is no coincidence that the *Heredes Pauli*, when they redo a *Feast in the House of Levi*, in San Giacomo della Giudecca, will set up a very different relationship between the guest and Jesus.

Another character with bushy eyebrows turns equally annoyed to our right, while behind him a young cupbearer smiles in amusement, carrying a plate from a sideboard. What prompted the annoyed reaction? And why does the carver "à la Vitellio", reproducing a famous Roman face from the Grimani collection, look almost annoyed at the situation, while the young Moor makes a comment, laughing? It seems that no one has appreciated or understood both Peter's action, the carver's job, and what perhaps Jesus has already said, or what John is asking, or saying, or repeating.

At the table everyone expresses an expectation full of uncertainty: under the arch on our left the characters are either surprised (at the far end the bearded man with a skullcap) or question themselves without giving an answer (the man with the felt hat frowning at the interlocutor) or appear amazed and perplexed (the fat man) or hesitant, or indifferent (the one picking his

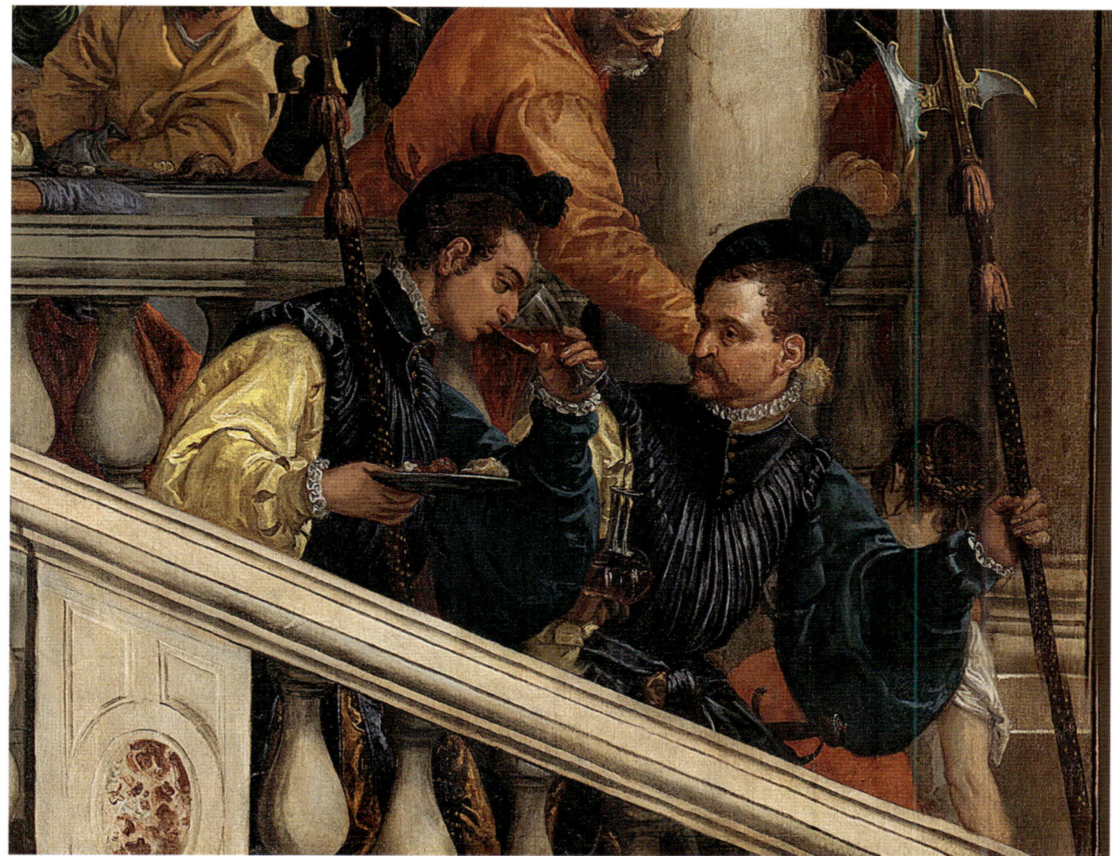

teeth between the columns). On the right the same: some observe without intervening, only one with a napkin over his shoulder looks towards the public in the refectory, eating with cutlery (the patron?); the last one on the right, in yellow, puts his hand in a bag of money (Judas?).

The other characters, the pages, the servants, the halberdiers, the buffoon dwarf, all appear extremely agitated. Out of breath and defaulting: the jester has retreated to drink from the flask and feed the parrot, instead of entertaining the guests; the dog does not bark at the cat playing with a bone; the servant takes care of the epistaxis and does not help the young carrying the heavy sled of meat; the halberdiers drink and leave the scene. The plates are missing, the master of ceremonies stirs and solicits with truly theatrical gestures; the carver stands apart, disgusted by it all and without action. Are they all in the service of tax collectors, acting like the Pharisees in hypocritical and false ways?

To the many questions proposed by this canvas, the possible answers are different, not all clear or definitive, not resolved, indeed tangled by the interrogation report. Overall, the evidence remains of a controversy between Conventuals and Observants, one accusing the other of hypocrisy, and they are scandalized by a behaviour judged inappropriate, worldly and "naughty". Fascinating and complex pictorial text, almost enigmatic. It is perhaps better to return to the readings of Ridolfi and Adolfo Venturi; perhaps, the ultimate meaning of this *Convito* remains the personal heritage of Paolo Caliari alone.

CHAPTER VIII

Lepanto and beyond

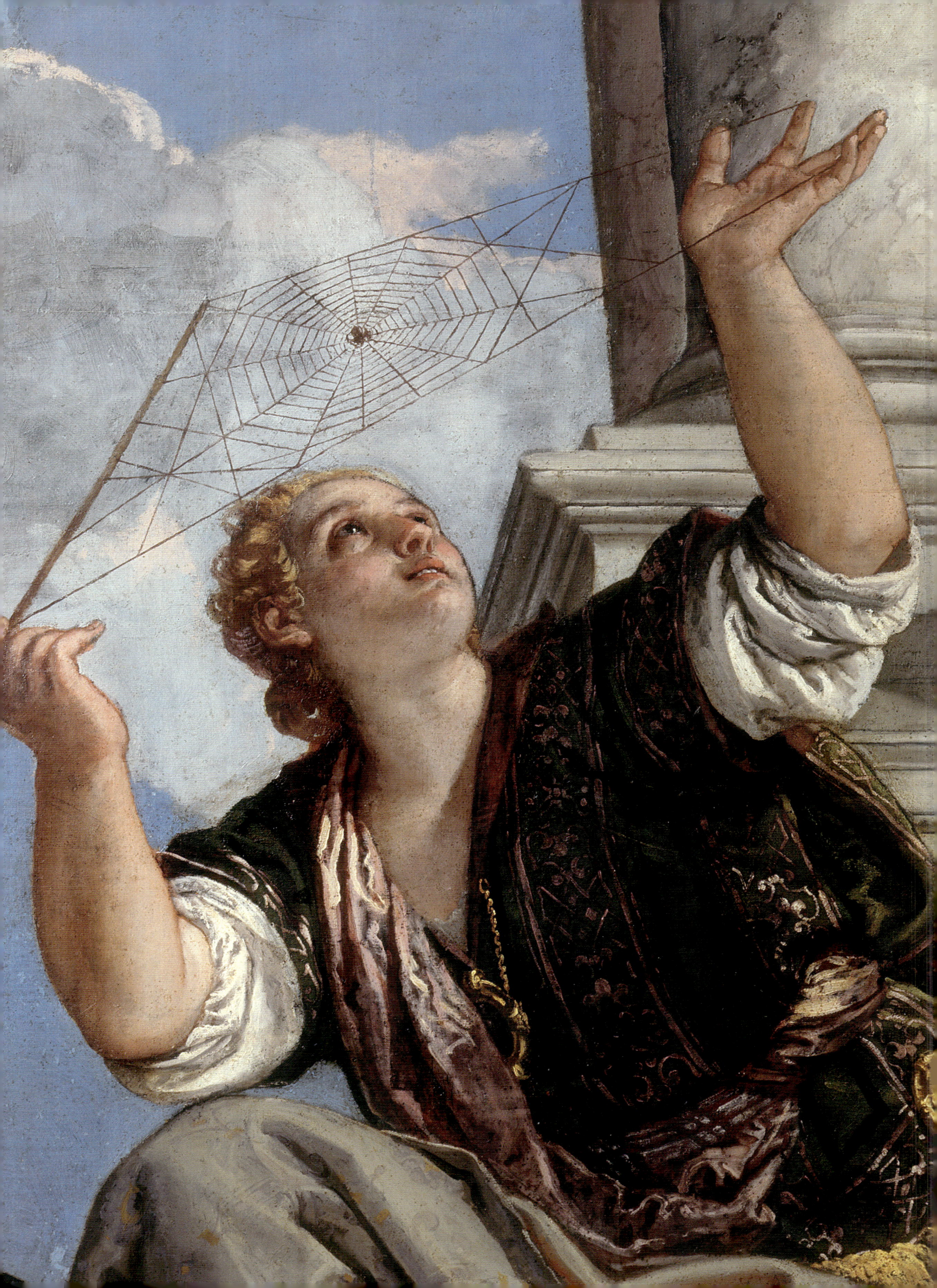

The battle of Lepanto against the historic enemy, the Ottoman Empire which had now taken possession of Cyprus, was a victory felt by the Venetians as redemption and revenge, and perhaps also the end of a centuries-old conflict; a peace seemed possible, indeed finally "Peace". The news of the success reached the lagoon a good eight days later, on 17 October, and it was an anticipated Carnival. Like other enthusiasms, the rejoicing lasted the time of the intoxication; after the chants and the Te Deums, the glory of the combatants and the count of the damages, it was understood with increasingly bitter disappointment that the questions remained open, Cyprus was definitively lost, and negotiations had to be carried out, obviously without glory and without clamour.
The separate peace with *Signor Turcho* and the confirmation of the definitive loss of Cyprus, which was very badly received by the allies of Venice, Spain and the Papacy in the lead, again suspicious, was experienced with regret and some sighs of relief in the lagoon. A brief calm will follow, until the next, unexpected but always feared scourge.
By creating the *Allegory of the Battle of Lepanto* for the Scuola della Madonna del Rosario in the church of San Pietro Martire in Murano, today in the Gallerie dell'Accademia, Paolo Veronese summarizes the encomiastic reading of the battle. The calendar placed the heroic day under the patronage of Saint Justina of Padua, an ancient martyr; to her the painter adds the patron saints of the allied nations, Peter for the papacy and James for Spain; but it is Mark who presents the Virgin with a figure completely veiled in white: Boschini explains the mysterious lady as the "Virgin of the Adria", or the Gulf of Venice, the domain of the Serenissima.
In the bipartite structure between celestial scene and naval battle there is the whole tradition of ex-votos; Veronese gives us the impression of a close, ferocious clash in the wooded forest of the masts of the opposing ships and the like; only the banners distinguish the vessels, on the left the Venetian flagship hoists the winged lion, gilded on a red background. On the usual preparation of plaster and glue, Veronese uses his palette: white lead, azurite, very fine cinnabar with an idea of red lacquer; then traces of carbon black, red ochre. The mixtures are picked up by the tip of the brush, managed in minute touches, immediately gleaming.
Another work by Paolo linked to Lepanto is the *Agostino Barbarigo* at the Museum of Art in Cleveland. The Provveditore Generale of the Venetian fleet is portrayed posthumously, in emotionally felt effigy: he shows, like a new Saint Sebastian, the arrow that killed him in the sea of Lepanto. The link between Paolo and Barbarigo was also personal. The patrician had been the godfather at the christening of his eldest son Gabriele, just three years earlier, on 7 September 1568. For the Paduan basilica dedicated to the saint of the auspicious day, in 1575 he painted the *Martyrdom of Saint Justina*, with the documented and autonomous help of Benedetto, probable author of the ever more evanescent group of angels and the crowd of seraphim. The glory of the triumphant Christ dominates the martyrdom of the virgin; from the presbytery the scene sends a message of patronage to the city. To the saint Veronese had dedicated a youthful *Martyrdom of Saint Justina,* now in the Civic Museum of Padua; it had been considered contemporary, but the majority of historians anticipate it by almost twenty years for the arrangement of the characters around the emperor, similar to the tondi of the Marciana, and for the scene on the right, with the woman with bare

The Dialectic, 1576-1577, canvas, 150 × 220 cm. Venice, Palazzo Ducale, Sala del Collegio, ceiling

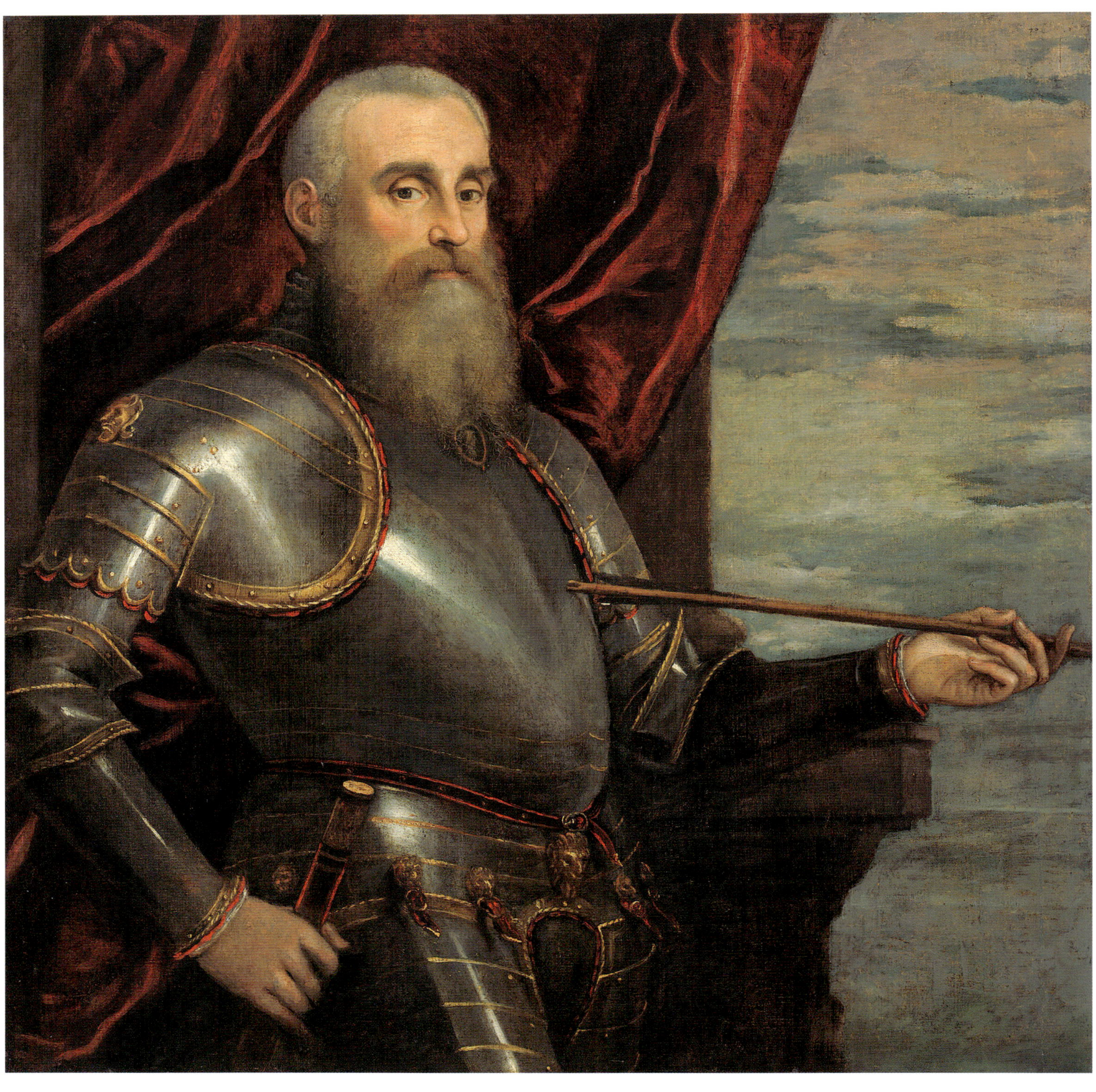

Portrait of Agostino Barbarigo, 1572, canvas, 102.2 × 104.2 cm. Cleveland, Museum of Art, gift of Mrs L.E. Holden, Mr and Mrs Guerdon S. Holden, and L.E. Holden Fund 1928.16

Allegory of the Battle of Lepanto, approx. 1572, canvas, 169 × 137 cm. Venice, Gallerie dell'Accademia, inv. 136

For the church of San Pietro Martire on Murano, Paolo Caliari proposes a canvas in which we recognize his typical allegorical choices in the upper part, while the lower part is carried out in the tradition of the ex voto, with a military and naval subject, common at the time on the walls of churches. It is a novelty, almost unique in Paolo's production, careful here to restore the sense of a close, violent and chaotic clash, without documentary concerns.

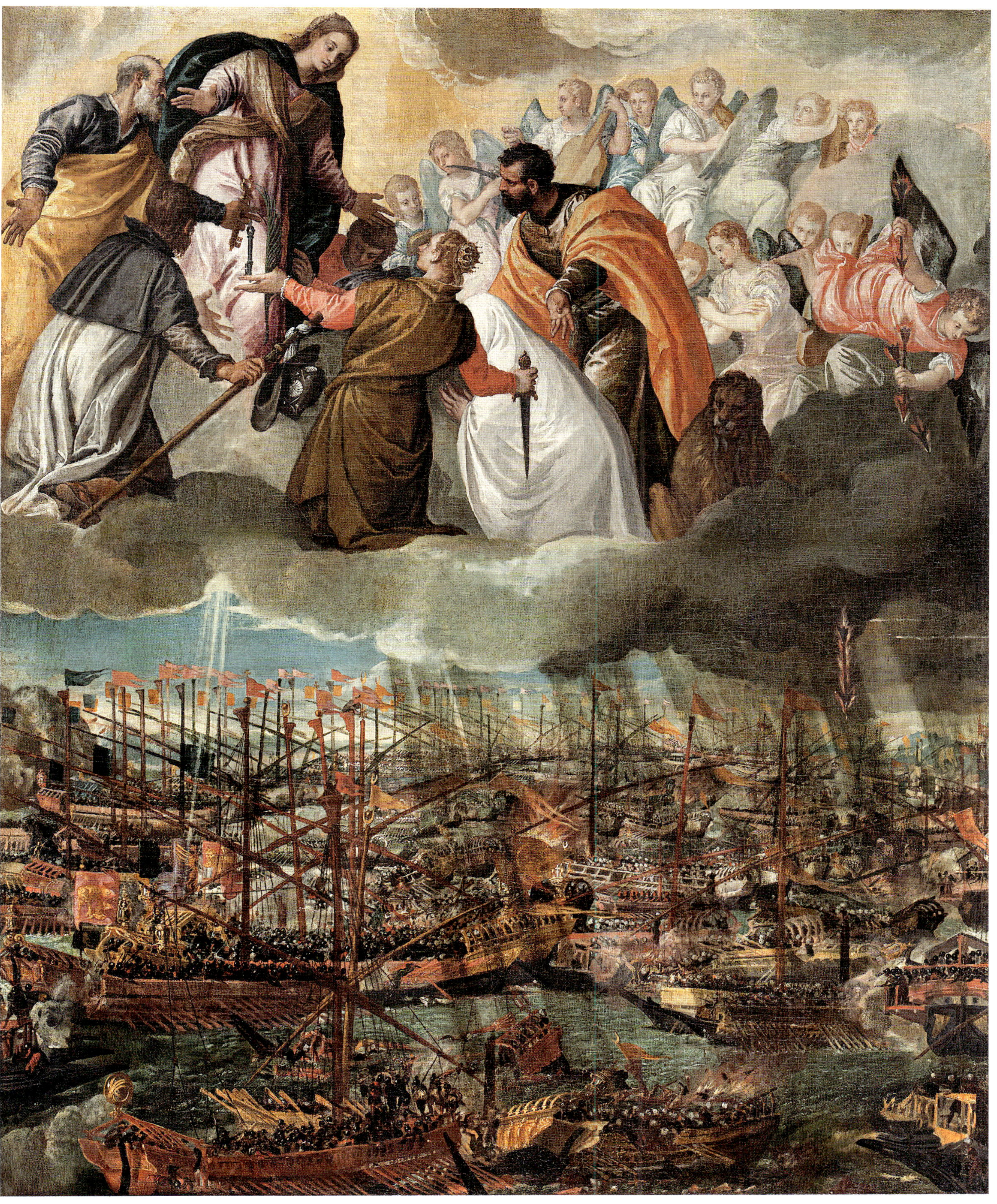

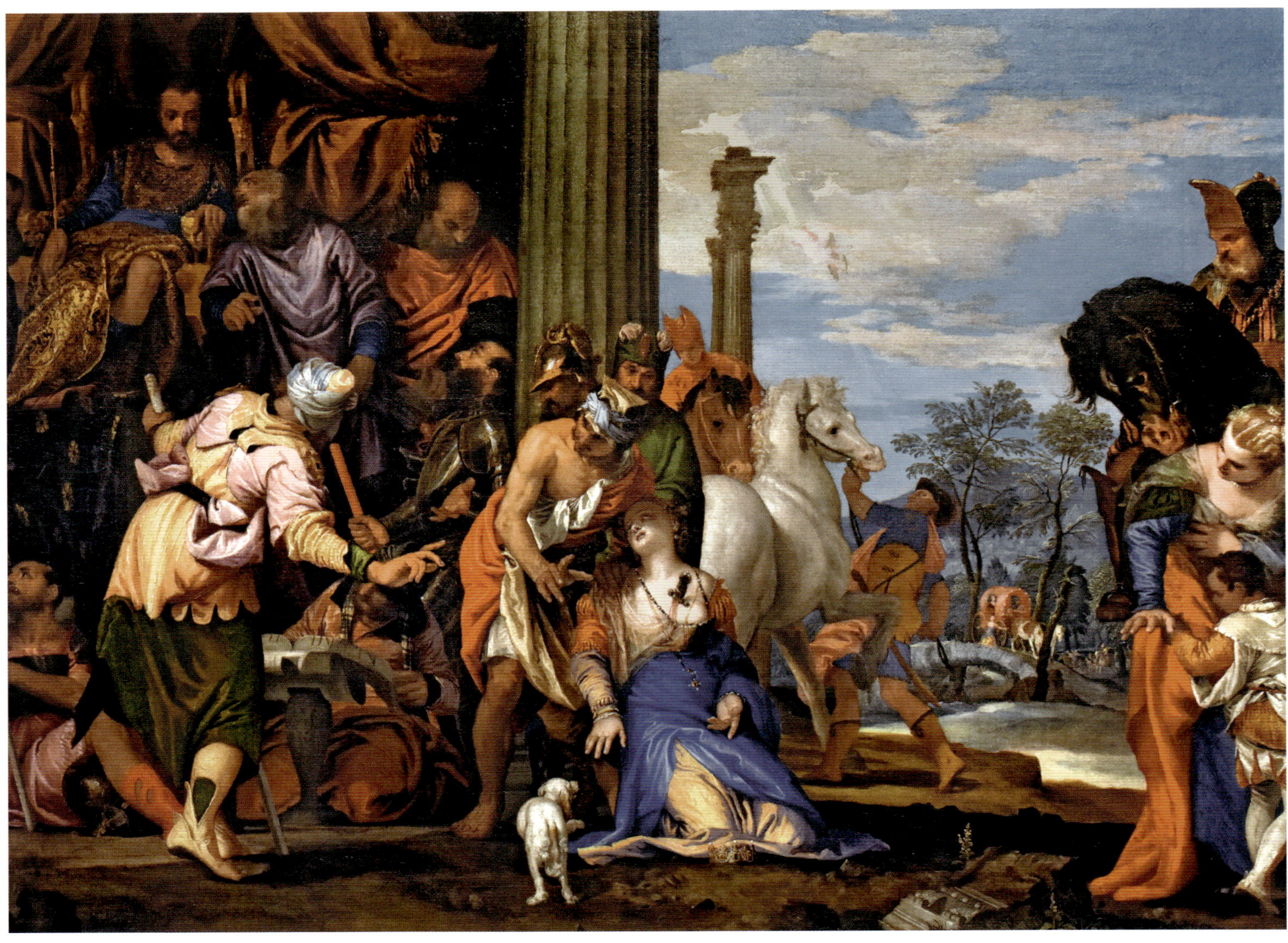

Martyrdom of Saint Justina, 1576, canvas, 525 × 240 cm. Padua, Basilica di Santa Giustina

shoulders, the white horse that trembles, hardly restrained, the landscape background. Youthful traits such as the silvery flashes on the soldier's armour, the bewildered little dog who assists, the theatrical gestures of the many characters who would like to intervene, indicate, solicit, verbalize: meanwhile the dagger is stuck and the saint can bleed out peacefully; a messenger of eternal happiness comes from the rosy sky. The group of magistrates is in the shadows, on the opposite side of them a woman – very Venetian in her traits – consoles the dark-haired page, frightened of her, who takes refuge on her lap so as not to see the violence. Touching scene that refers to the need to convert infidels and educate slaves. The effect obtained by the *Martyrdom of Saint Justina*, today in the Uffizi, is lower: in a reduced version two characters, the patrons, perhaps father and son, witness the martyrdom with an attitude of meditation or compunction, certainly without particular emotion.

SUBJECTS AND VARIATIONS

By 1572 Paolo Veronese, with his whole workshop, completed a grandiose private order: four large canvases for the decoration of the Coccina family hall, in their palace on the Grand Canal. It is known today as Palazzo Papadopoli, headquarters of the Aman hotel, internationally famous for its ephemeral and sumptuous social occasions.

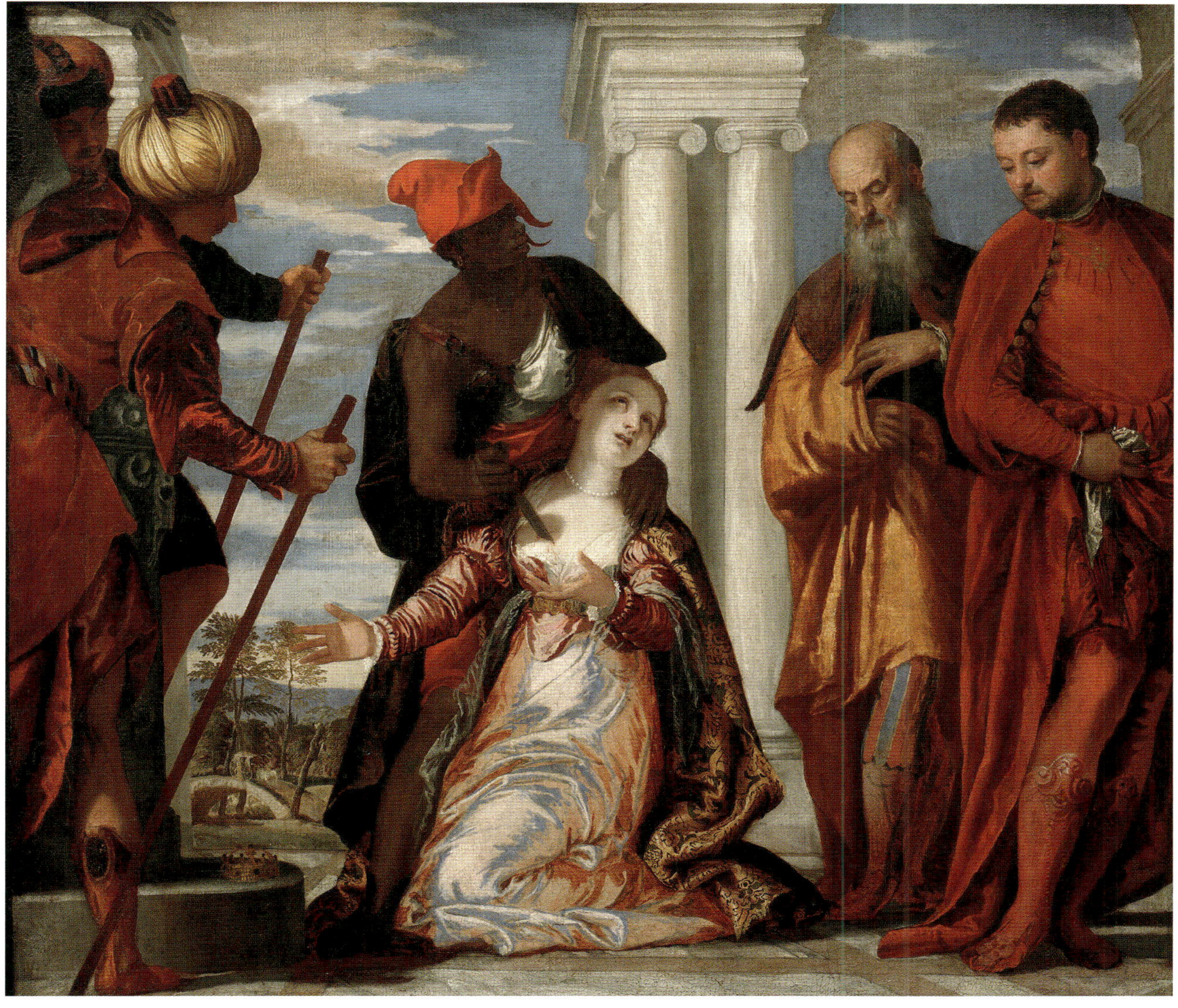

Martyrdom of Saint Justina, approx. 1570-1575, canvas, 103 × 113 cm. Florence, Gallerie degli Uffizi

These Còccina -- but are also referred to as Cuccina, or even in local documents Cuzina, Cozina, then Cocina and Coccino in more recent ones – were jewellers and drapers, originally from Bergamo and enrolled in Venetian citizenship. Initially they lived in a modest residence in the parish of San Felice, trading in Rialto under the portico of the drapery. After developing a manufacturing activity, the brothers Girolamo and Giovanni Coccina created a considerable fortune, invested in funds on the mainland and annuities which allowed a standard of living worthy of patrician families. Thus they had the prestigious building designed by the Bergamo fellow Giangiacomo dei Grigi and built in the parish of Sant'Aponal; the façade in Istrian stone presents a scenographic synthesis: central serlianas following Sanmicheli, lateral tympanums inspired by Palladio, cartouches of the attic à la Sansovino.

By the end of the works, in 1568, the brothers Girolamo and Giovanni had already been buried in San Francesco della Vigna, and it was the heir Alvise di Girolamo who indicated the family palace that appears in the background on the right of the large canvas *Presentation of the Coccina Family to the Virgin*, which together with the *Wedding Feast at Cana*, the *Adoration of the Magi* and the *Ascent to Calvary* complete the impressive decorative project of the wealthy citizens. On the canvas we find the patron saints of the founder brothers, Saint Jerome and Saint John the Baptist; the head of the family is kneeling beside his bride, Zuanna; brother Zuanantonio is behind the column while the other brother, Antonio, shakes the hand of Faith and is supported by Charity. Alvise's seven children follow: Giovanni, Francesco, Girolamo, Andrea,

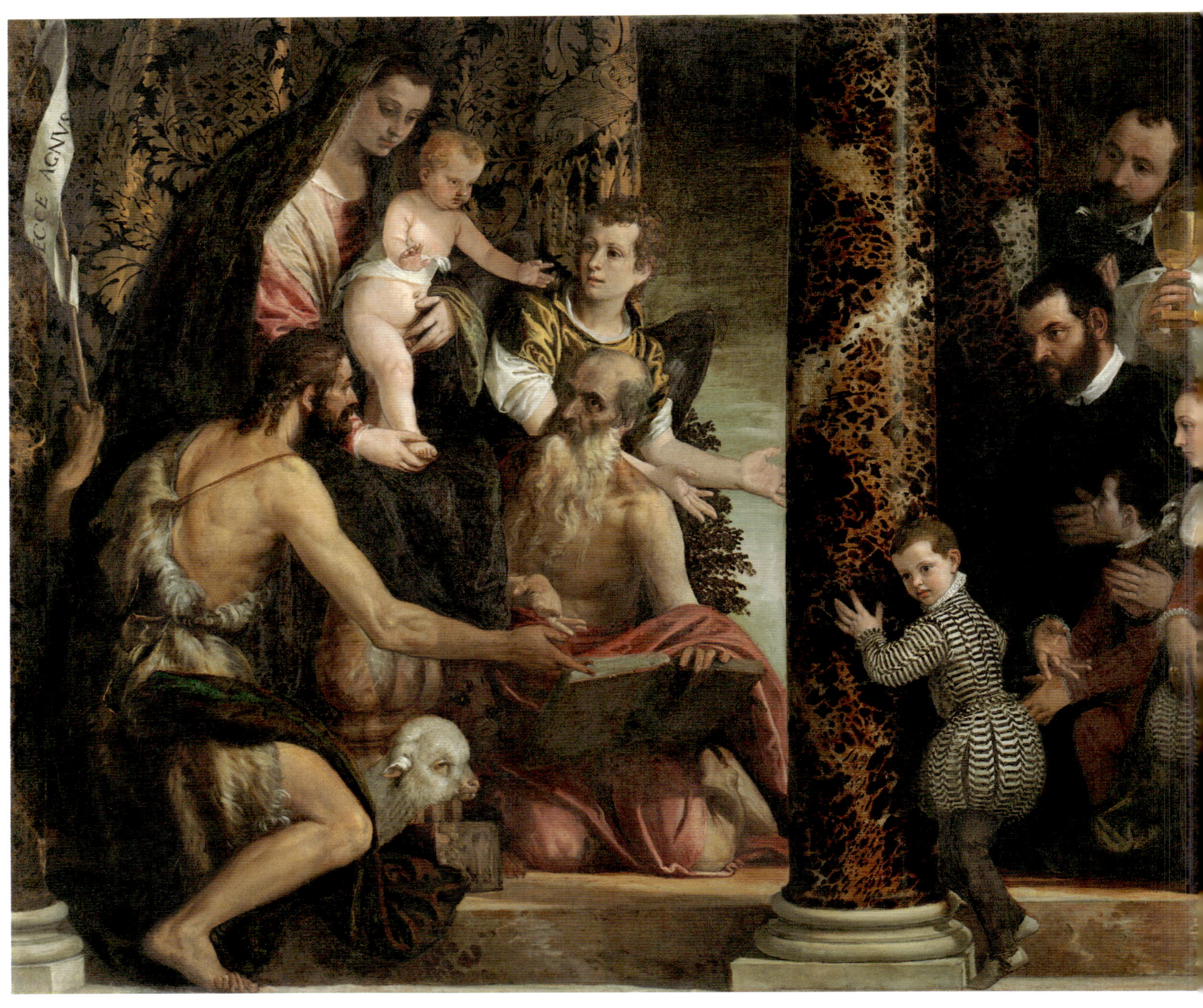

Presentation of the Cuccina Family to the Holy Virgin, 1571-1572, canvas, 167 × 414 cm, whole and detail on the following pages. Dresden, Gemäldegalerie Alte Meister, inv. 224

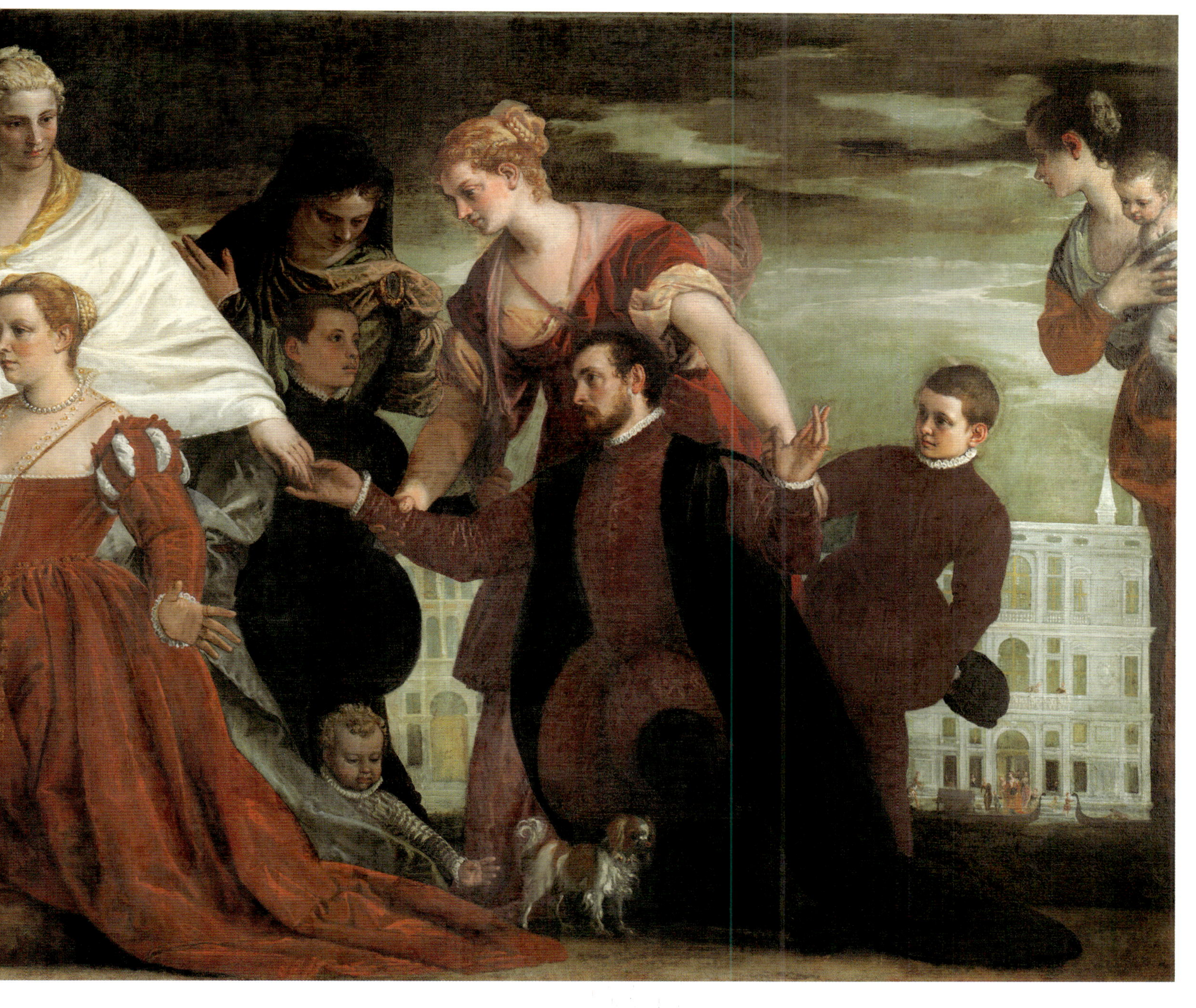

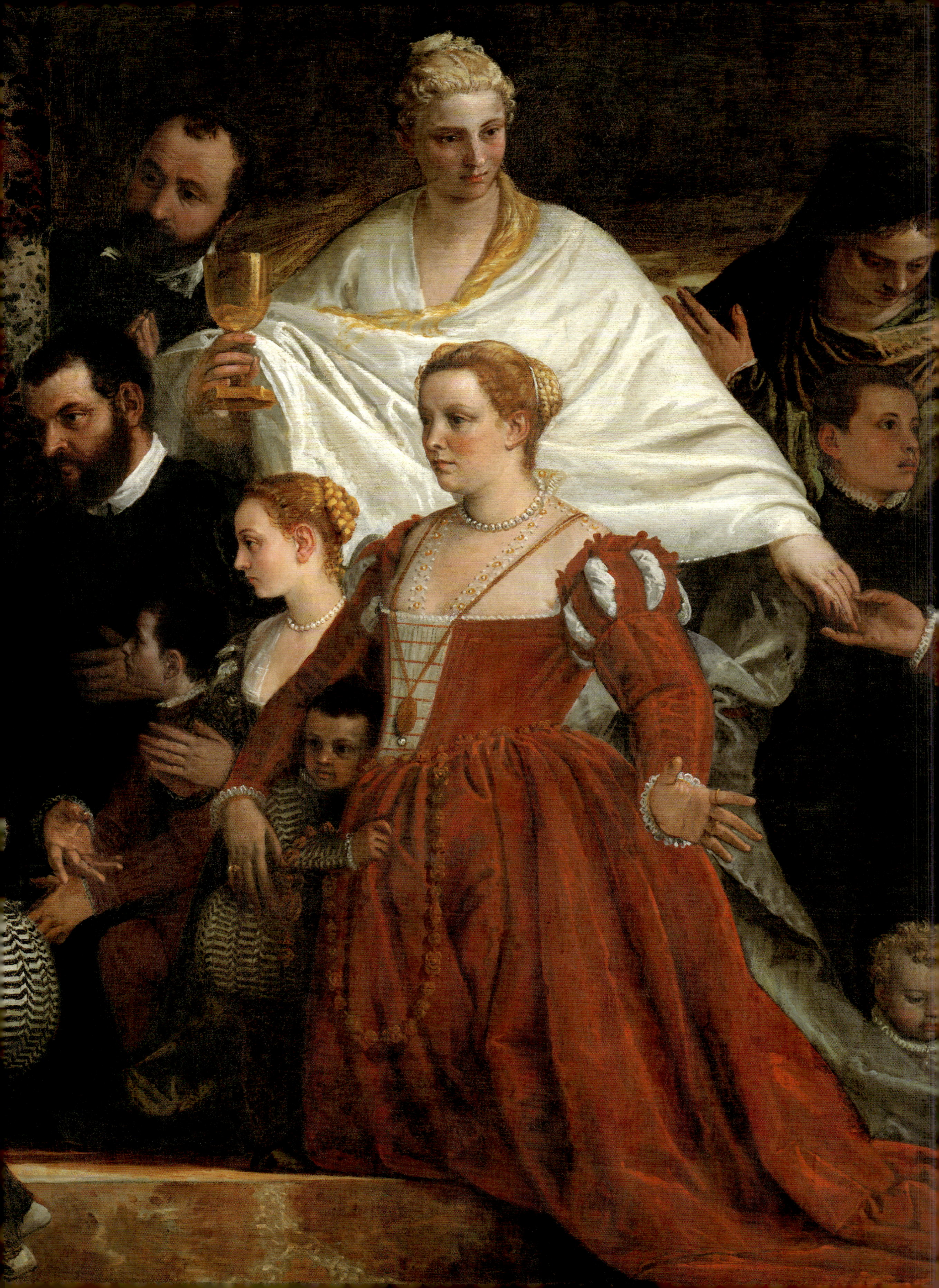

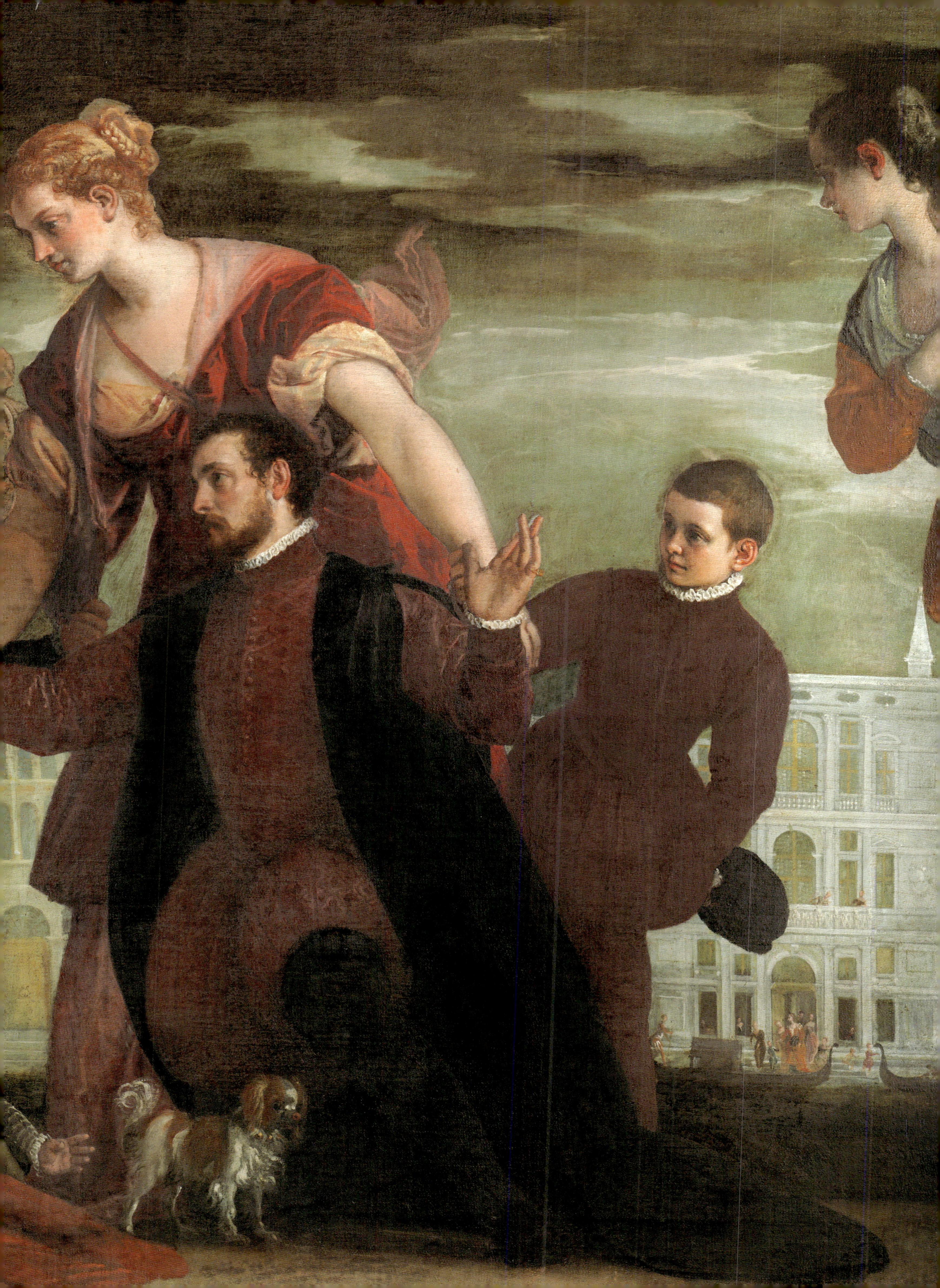

Domenico, Marcantonio and Gianbattista in the nurse's arms. The little child is destined for an ecclesiastical career, since he will be monsignor, dean of the Rota in Rome, a leading figure in the Roman curia. As of 1631, we know from a letter sent to Cardinal Francesco Barberini, who absolutely wanted to buy some works by Veronese, that the canvases were all still in the family palace, valued at extremely high prices.
The family also wanted to appear in the other scenes: in the *Calvary* we recognize the portrait of Antonio, and the sons reappear in the *Wedding Feast at Cana*. Paolo Caliari had excellent relations with all of them: we have documentary confirmation of this when the only daughter of Elena and Paolo was baptized: *1572 adì 15 novembre. Vittoria et Ottavia fia de messer Paulo Caliari pittor veronese stantia in calle de ca' Mocenigo in le case de messer Jacopo Federici, fu battezzata adì sopradicto. Fu compare messer Alvise Cocina fo di messer Zuanne. Il Piovan* (Venice, church of San Samuele, Archivio parrocchiale, Battesimi, reg. 1). It is also through these links that the esteem and social recognition of the Caliari in Venice is confirmed. In a sequence of masterpieces for merchants and citizens, in that eighth decade of the sixteenth century, we also find *The Adoration of the Magi* in Santa Corona in Vicenza, exhibited in 1574, of which the Vicentine Guido Piovene wrote very well, recalling the effect of that canvas on him as a teenager:

The Adoration of the Magi, 1574, canvas, 320 × 234 cm. Vicenza, Basilica di Santa Corona

The subject enjoyed a significant fortune in Paolo's catalogue and later in the workshop, with variations and inventions. The Vicenza canvas is not only a pictorial masterpiece, a splendid theatrical staging with characterized characters, creating an effect of depth of the seabed with a strongly lowered horizon. It provides a powerful and dominant allegorical interpretation through the building behind the Holy Family: the column against which the Mother stands out underlines her role, while the classic portico, full of Palladian echoes, appears supported by the wooden skeleton, symbol of the new Christian age, but also of the possible recovery of the ancient.

> The picture of Santa Corona, neglected at the time by the critics, produced in me perhaps the first effect, today we would say of drugs (the only effect, in my opinion, that one must ask of art), which the Veronese offers to those who look closely. That already nocturnal sky and clouds in the background, nocturnal but very clear, illuminated by a special light-shadow or light-darkness, different but no less light than daytime, that sumptuous gathering of iridescent satins and velvets, in invented foreshortenings and perspectives, for which we need to refresh the adjective wonderful, they composed the vision of something never seen, which however did not contrast with the truth, and had the virtue of drawing us inside itself without giving us the slightest sensation of changing our lives. (Marini 1968, p. 7 – free translation)

The altarpiece placed in the chapel of Sacra Spina had been requested by a cloth merchant, Marcantonio Cogollo. For the third time in a span of a few years, Veronese returns to the theme, after the *telero* for the Coccinas and the one, just the year before, for the Venetian church of San Silvestro, now in London. Here the absolutely innovative idea is the solution given to the hut, a wooden skeleton, a sort of scaffolding to complete a Palladian portico. The theme of the renewed and rebuilt classicism after the advent of Christianity is accentuated by the first of the Magi dressed in the superb dogal cloak, woven in gold. The supreme Venetian authority prostrates himself before the sacred, as in tradition, making the event topical; on the canvas typical features of Paolo: the beautiful horse's head, the poles with flags, the procession that comes from the distant horizon; also the invention of a donkey and an ox that stick out their muzzles completely intrigued. The severe and intent character, bearded, behind the Moorish king is in all probability Marcantonio Cogollo. Here too, however, the protagonist is neither the subject, nor the patron, as Filippo Pedrocco wrote:

> Colour thus confirms itself as the true protagonist of the Veronese world: a colour different from Titian's tonalism or from Tintoretto's and Bassano's luminism, but which discovers the increase in luminosity derived from the juxtaposition of complementary colours, i.e. those which fused together make up white, the brightest hue; a colour that creates a myriad of faceted planes of light on the surfaces, with an unreal effect of extraordinary intensity. The local hues thus take on the luminous reflections of those nearby; black is abolished and the shadows themselves are coloured, in such a way that the luminosity of the painted scene becomes greater than the real one: an effect which gives rise to that eminently decorative spirit which finds triumphant application in the frescoes of the villas in Veneto countryside. (Pedrocco 2010, p. 114 – free translation)

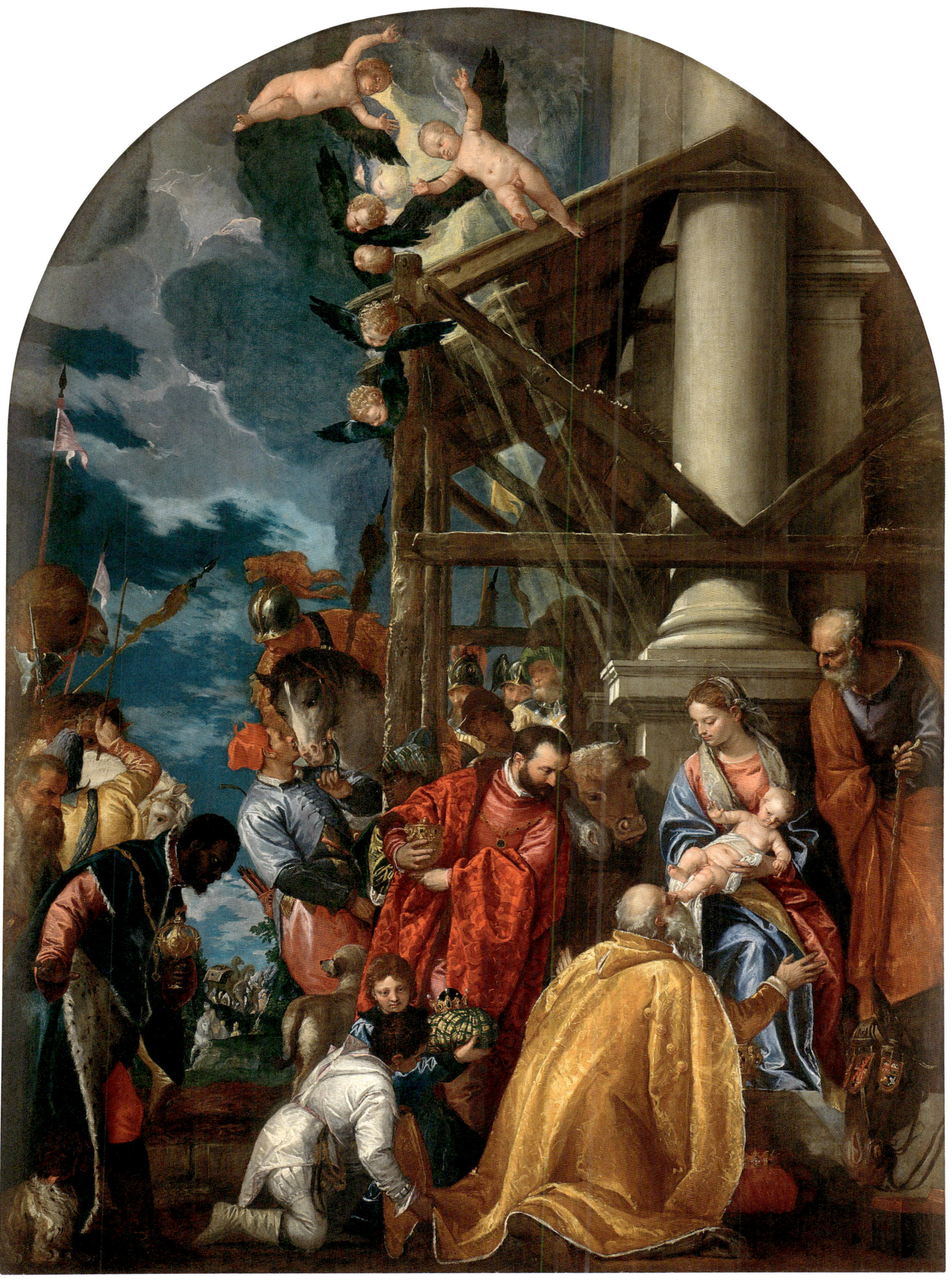

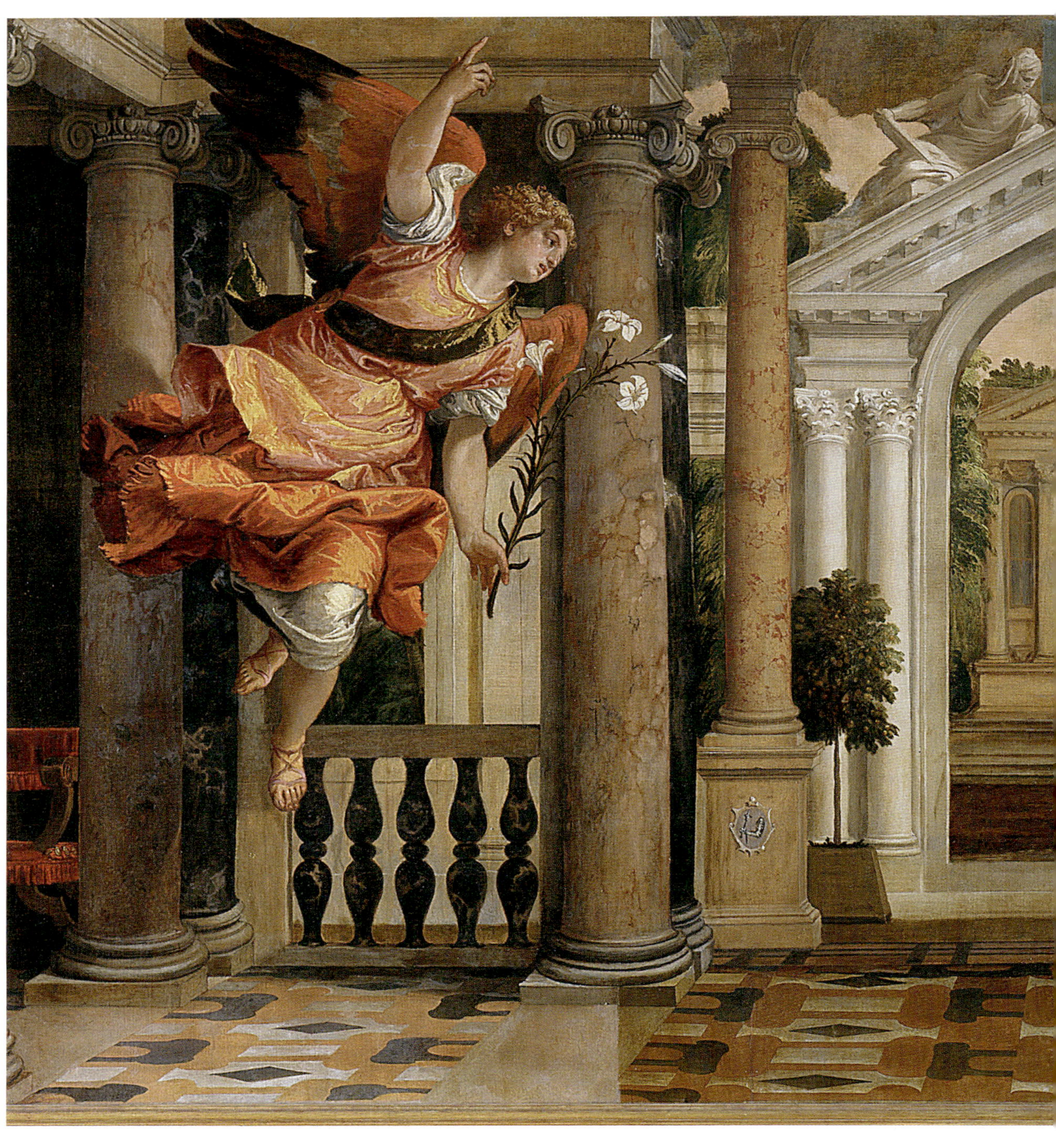

Annunciation, 1578,
canvas, 240 × 303 cm. Venice,
Gallerie dell'Accademia, inv. 315

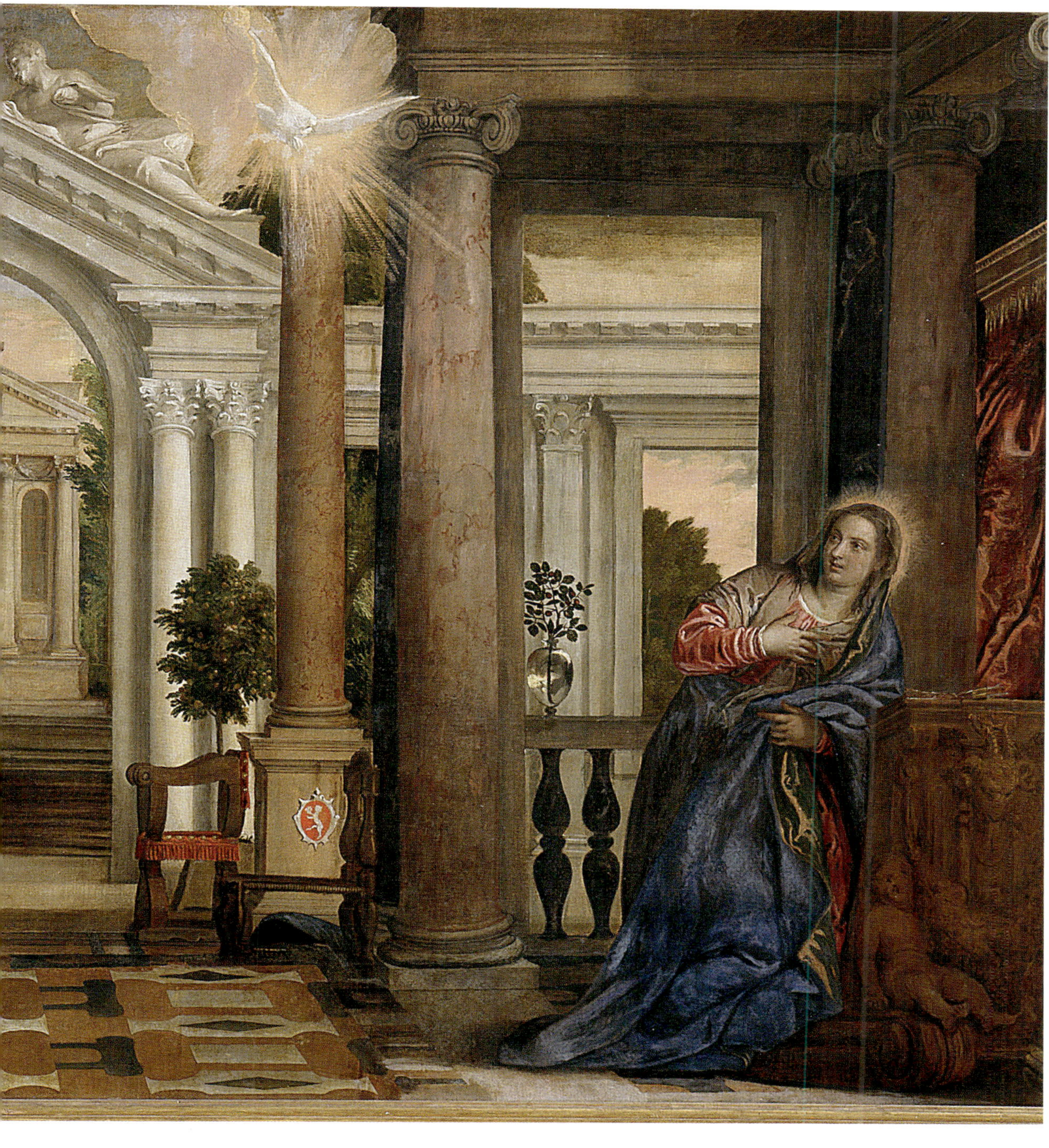

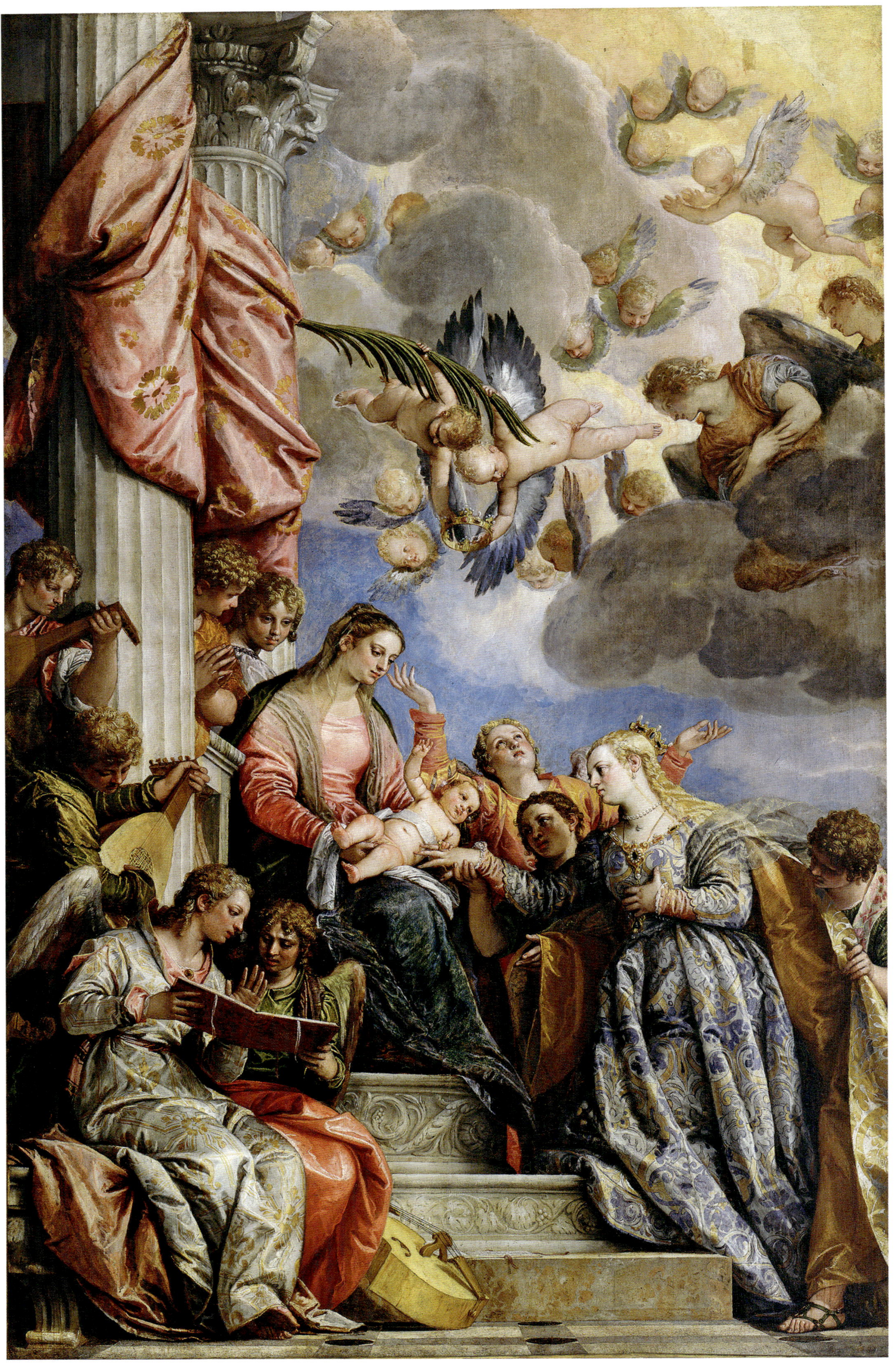

At the same time, for another patrician patron, Paolo created the altarpiece with *Saints Jerome, Lawrence and Prosper* in S. Giacomo dell'Orio, following the death of Girolamo Malipiero, at the request of his widow Laura Barbarigo; in the sacristy of the same church the Caliari workshop was present in the oval ceiling with the *Faith*, four tondi with the *Doctors of the Church* and an *Adoration of the Shepherds*, perhaps a juvenile work.

Relatively limited are the subjects required for altarpieces, such as the *Annunciations* and *Resurrections*. For them Paolo Veronese seeks new solutions, varied compared to other painters: an example is the imposing *Annunciation* for the Scuola dei Mercanti at the Madonna dell'Orto in Venice, datable to 1578, now in the Gallerie dell'Accademia. The emblem of the Confraternity, a hand blessing the cross, is at the head of the arch in the center of the painting. In the dominant care for the architectural design, the Virgin is almost secondary, amazed by the arrival of the Angel, moreover moved and dynamic. Already Pietro Edwards in 1811, at the time of attributing it to the Academy, defined it as "a composition that could be called theatrical, rich in architecture, statues, sumptuous drapery and the most flourishing colour that can be said." The façade of the small temple refers to the Palladian solution of San Francesco della Vigna. According to Daniel Arasse, who worked a lot on the subject of the Annunciations, at least seventeen are to be referred to Paolo Veronese and his workshop, including the *Annunciation* in the Thyssen collection, while the one at the Escorial, signed and dated 1583, has been largely attributed to Benedetto. From the very first Annunciations, like the one today in the Uffizi, the architectural datum is dominant, two thirds of the canvas are occupied by architecture, by the fluted columns of a vast portico with the central escape towards a triumphal arch: space is the protagonist, and is the key to understanding: it indicates the place of the Incarnation, or rather the Basilica, the Church in which the Eucharistic mystery is renewed.

Another example of successful subjects, and repeatedly taken up again, is *The Mystical Marriage of Saint Catherine*; a masterpiece, formerly in the church of Santa Caterina dei Sacchi and now in the Gallerie dell'Accademia. It is dated around 1575, mentioned by Sansovino as early as 1581. It is an authentic cascade of colours: greens, greys, unprecedented pinks, the blues, oranges and reds in dazzling nuances. It is perhaps the work that has best preserved the original colours, for which Giannantonio Moschini was still able to write in his guidebook in 1815: "Respected by time, it is one of the few works which allow us to recognize how happy that great man's brush was". Veronese's painting reaches its exemplary peak in the luministic effects, or rather in obtaining that fabrics, and also jewels and metals, give the effect of shining. This ability to work the "lume", obviously highly appreciated at the time, is obtained by combining the appropriate whites, yellows, ochres in "pure touches" obtaining the "luster", the same that we can best appreciate in the angel's satin dress in the foreground: a silvery satin that communicates the same sensation of a living fabric, worn in full light. For the high altar of the church, annexed to an Augustinian female convent, Veronese prepared the grandiose altarpiece, with a superb ascending structure, characterized by the exclusive female presence: the only male, in his sexual evidence, is the Child; the angelic variation is very rich, also oriented towards the feminine. The scene is a Venetian patrician wedding: the bride dressed up and adorned with jewels, a small crown on her head, receives the wedding ring from the Child. For the profusion of fabrics, timbre elegance, expressive organization, the altarpiece was the most suitable for the convent of nuns where the young Venetian patrician women were educated for marriage. The theme of the "mystical marriage of Saint Catherine", also requested for a name day, allows to dress the beautiful and cultured princess with the utmost elegance, in the legend martyred with a cogwheel; Paolo had chosen it since the 1550s, with the beautiful *Holy Family with Saint Catherine*, which also features an elderly Anna and two angels playing and singing in a frame of Ionic columns.

The few emergencies that we remember in a production that is always exceptional in terms of quality and quantity must find an explanation in organizational terms. Veronese, Hans Dieter

The Mystical Marriage of Saint Catherine, approx. 1575, canvas, 337 × 241 cm. Venice, Gallerie dell'Accademia, inv. 1170

The chromatic score of the entire scene is particularly brilliant in the celestial movements and in the marble solidity of the imposing architecture. For the church of the Augustinian female convent dedicated to Saint Catherine, Veronese prepared an all-female scene, with the saint – Mary's twin sister – in the clothes, hairstyles and postures of the Venetian bride. Furthermore, the setting of the fabrics is all Venetian, as is the musical accompaniment, in the best tradition of the time. The canvas is thus presented as an absolutely exemplary example of Paolo Caliari's sacred production of the seventies.

Huber confirms, produced more in the century than any other painter; forty years of continuous, qualitatively homogeneous and constantly successful activity. This was also the result of the organizational talent with which he created and directed his own workshop, active from the early sixties, of which we are certain thanks to the story of the heirs. Many young apprentices were trained in the workshop and various masters worked there, always with the presence of his brother Benedetto, a true alter ego, able to lead construction sites and independently carry out a series of tasks, as well as being a guide for the assistants. He then had from his sons Gabriele and above all Carlo an essential contribution to the great cycles of the ninth decade.

Family Workshops

At the time, the majority of Venetian master painters were helped by some worker or apprentice, collaborations were limited to decorative construction sites; in the fifteenth century there were two great family painting workshops, the Vivarinis in Murano and the Bellinis in Venice; much more numerous, for obvious production reasons, were the stonecutters' workshops which employed dozens of people, starting with the famous Lombardo dynasty. In the sixteenth century the workshops of the Vecellio, Robusti, Caliari, Da Ponte and Palma families became places of prestigious training, creating a tradition renewed until the eighteenth century with Tiepolo and Guardi. Organized as a family business, the workshops guaranteed a continuous production, a stable qualitative yield, managed a congruous and continuous portfolio of orders with a constant income, capitalizing over time models, cartoons, finished copies, plaster casts, and more furniture, objects, sculptures, costumes and clothes, as well as a quantity of working tools. And above all drawings: today at least two hundred autographs of Paolo Veronese remain in the most diverse typologies: studies, very rapid sketches, sketches finished in chiaroscuro, completed ideas and projects. A precious material for attributing and reconstructing the genesis of a work. Moreover, what has come down to us is only the smallest part of a very rich production, the true capital of the workshop which allowed for copies and variations, different associations, repetitions of details.
The labour standards guaranteed by the statutes and rules of the Arte dei Depentori were controlled by a special judiciary, the Giustizia Vecchia, founded in 1173 and made up of three magistrates, active in dispute cases through commissions of experts. Without authorization from the Guild, it was not possible to work in Venice: so Albrecht Dürer wrote to his friend Pirckheimer in 1506, explaining that he was rather annoyed at having to pay four florins to practice his trade. When you were born in the workshop, or were children or grandchildren of the Master, the practices became very fast: Carlo Caliari signed an altarpiece when he was just sixteen.
The organization of the work was based on the effective division between masters, apprentices and journeymen: the Master was responsible for the *inventio*, the creation of original compositions oriented to the patrons' will. Paolo Caliari had the appreciated ability to vary the same theme with originality, renewing the composition: this is the case of the many *Baptisms*, of the different declinations of the *Mystical Marriage of Saint Catherine*; of *Martyrs* and *Madonnas Enthroned* or *in Glory*. In the single composition some figures, architectures, ornaments are assimilated and varied by the closest collaborators, also producers of copies or replicas on which the Master intervenes with final, guarantee touches. In the case of the *Heredes Pauli* it will be verified how the workshop knows how to take up and reassemble with originality typical models of the deceased Master: architectures, postures, types of portraits.
Ridolfi accurately describes the practices of Vecellio's workshop, which produced far fewer works than Veronese, since Titian intervened several times on the canvas, with resumptions at intervals of weeks or months, before finally dismissing it; on the contrary, Tintoretto's workshop was known for its extreme executive speed and great working capacity, as well as for the qualitative uniformity achieved, and it is no coincidence that in the will of 1594 Iacomo Tintoretto established: "I want my son Dominico to finish the works of mine that remain imperfect, by his hand, using that manner and diligence that he has always used on many of my works". This family centrality and dynastic fostering will also characterize the Caliari workshop.

In his forty years of work, Paolo was therefore able to count on collaborators, help and substitutes. While some masters, the circle of friends with whom he had collaborated in his youth on decorative construction sites, always continued by looking at the production of the most talented contemporary, such as Zelotti, Paolo Farinati and Giovanni Antonio Fasolo, other masters were trained in the workshop. Like Dario Varotari (1539-1596) who was supposed to work with him in the 1560s, and then autonomously created cycles of frescoes for the Praglia Abbey, in Villa Emo in Montecchio, and various interventions in Padua. Varotari would marry Samaritana Ponchino, daughter of Giovan Battista, from whom he had Alessandro in 1588, destined to greater fame as "il Padovanino", while his daughter Chiara was an excellent painter, also remembered for having created a much praised art school in Venice. To Dario Varotari could have succeeded as assistant Antonio Vassilacchi (1555-1629), known as Aliense, "the foreigner", for having spent part of his childhood in Greece. Started off on an honourable career, Vassilacchi was a contemporary of Francesco Montemezzano (1555-after 1602) from Verona, from a family that had specialized in construction for generations, pupil and active collaborator of Benedetto Caliari. Their nephew, Luigi Benfatto, known as Alvise Del Friso (1544-1609), also returned frequently to the workshop. He was already trained as an adolescent by his uncle and then, according to anecdotal traditions, became his imitator, skilled in understanding his ideas, anticipating him.

Much younger, substantially the same age as his firstborn Gabriele (1568-1631) and Carlo (known as Carletto) Caliari (1570-1596), were Claudio Ridolfi (1570-1644) and Pace (Pase) Pace (1574?-1617). Ridolfi, trained in the workshop, would then go to work in Corinaldo in the Marches, while Pase Pace would testify to Benedetto's last wishes and in May 1598 he would be Gabriele's best man. Therefore an intimate painter of the family, a pupil in the last years of Paolo's life, then probable assistant of the *Heredes Pauli* to conclude with his own catalogue, from a monumental *Madonna* for the Church of the Carmini to a *Footwashing* in the church of Santa Croce in Venice, and subsequently canvases in Brescia and Bergamo areas.

It is not easy to identify the presence of all these masters in the works attributed to or connected to Paolo's workshop. It is difficult to isolate the single contribution, to distinguish their hand even though we know it through personal works. In fact, those who worked with Paolo were not oriented towards autonomy but towards collaboration, mimesis, if not minute imitation following the model of Benedetto, always the less gifted alter ego of his brother. Paolo intervened on the final drafting of a canvas – which Rubens will also do – with chromatic elevations, for example in the garments and in the flesh tones, while he was less present in the architectural quadratures, in the marbling, or in the "fake bronzes" and in the monochromes, in the cameos.

A possible assessement of the typology of the workshop production can be found in the two large canvases now in the Galleria Sabauda in Turin: *Moses Saved from the Waters* and *The Gifts of the Queen of Sheba to Solomon*, requested by Carlo Emanuele I of Savoy in his early twenties. The young Savoy ruler was completely enthusiastic about Venetian painting, he loved Titian – and moreover bought works by a completely different hand like Vecellio – and asked Veronese for several canvases, which would be much appreciated at court. In these compositions we recognize typical figures of Paolo, taken from drawings or cartoons, perhaps even some compositional ideas, but these works lack any brightness, colours, and the grace of the autographed works. They are canvases made by several hands, in particular by Benedetto, and it would seem above all his nephew Alvise to have played a significant role. In *Moses* the narrative solution is then very curious: the princess with maids and pages stands on the top of a sort of short channel, on which the basket floats, while she entrusts the baby to the mother who shows her breast ready to feed him. Mother and son are presented to the princess by a young man dressed in the Spanish fashion of the time at the court of Turin, with a marked starched ruff. Even the carriage in the background responds to the shapes of the time.

In *The Gifts of the Queen of Sheba* we find women's clothes, postures, but also vases, little dogs, camel heads, all typical of Paolo, while Benedetto should be given the execution of architectures, statues and busts. Here too there is a particular idea, with a substantially clumsy solution: Solomon is enthroned at the top, in the corner and in deep shadow, with the features of a little boy. The impression of accumulation of solutions created in the past is even more evident. The reason? Either Paolo was very tired

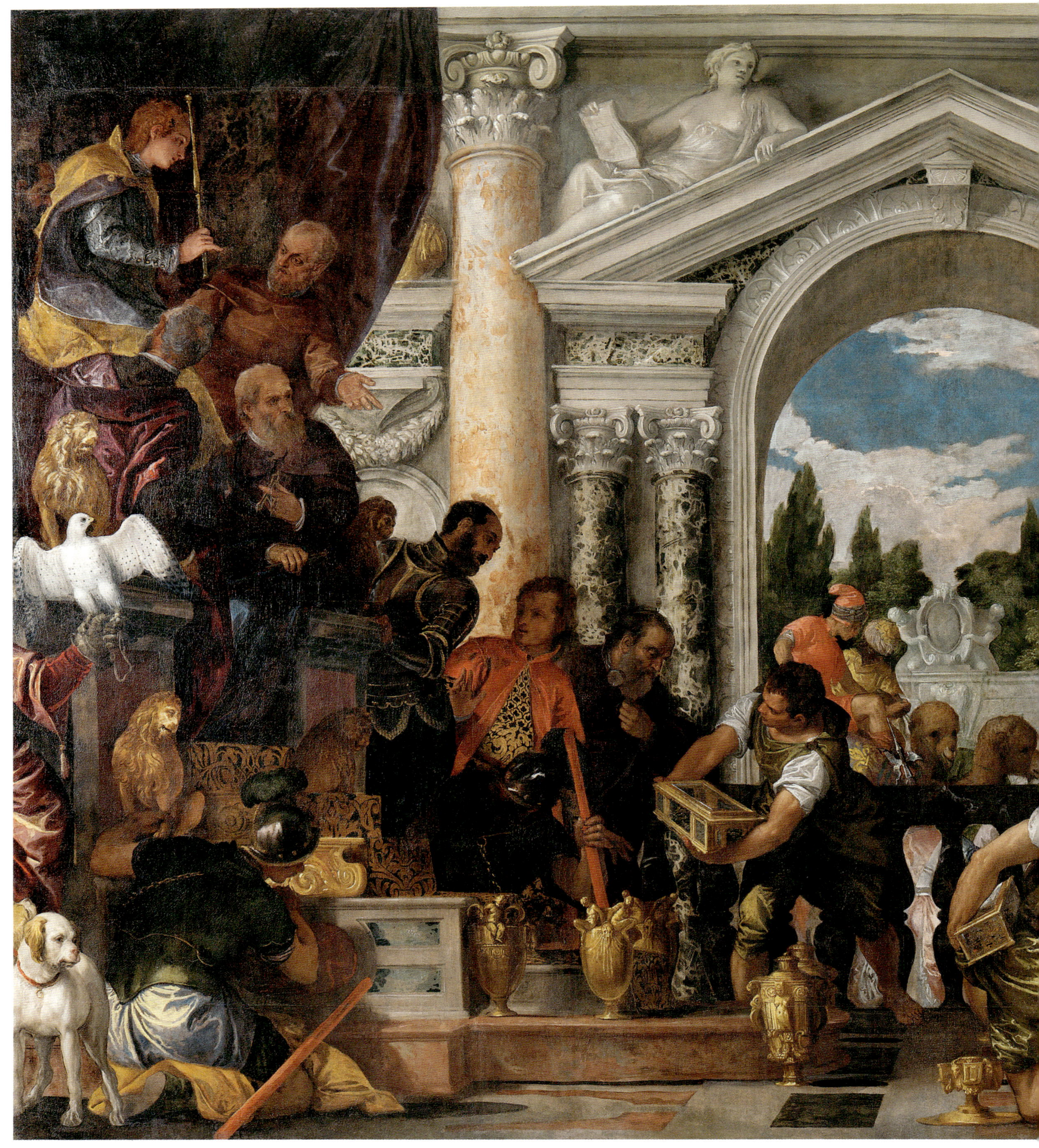

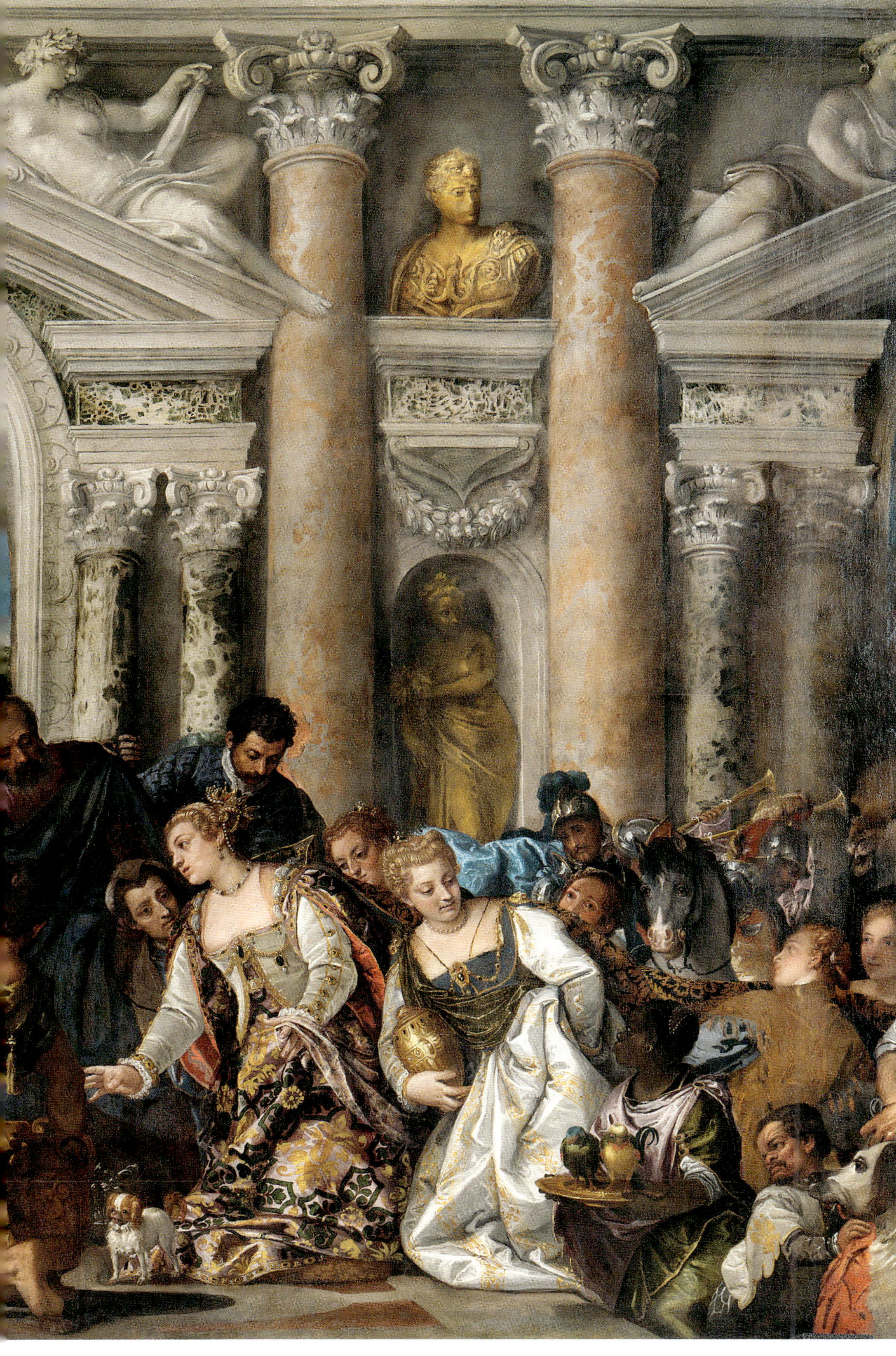

The Gifts of the Queen of Sheba to Solomon, after 1582, canvas, 344 × 545 cm. Turin, Galleria Sabauda, inv. 464

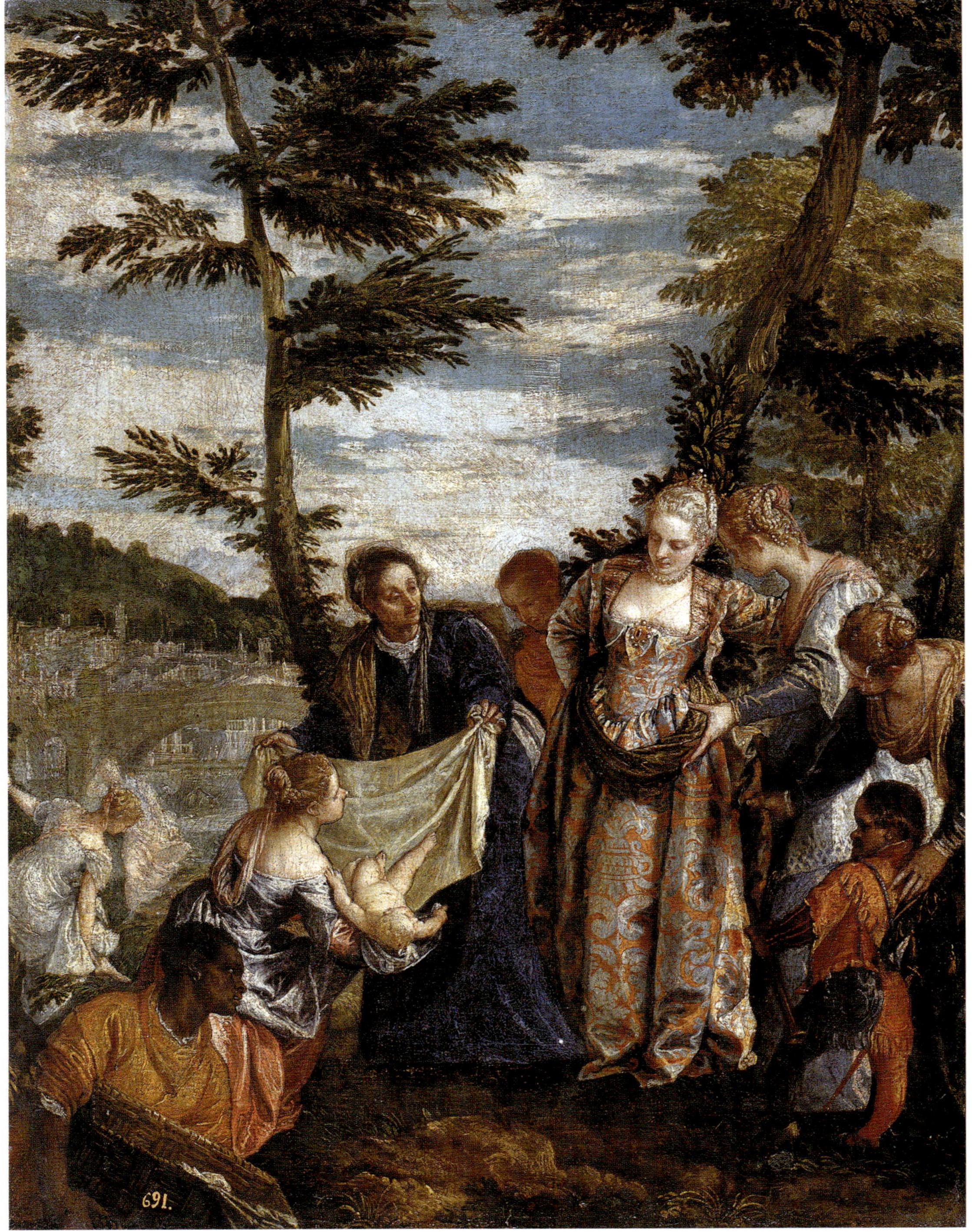

Moses Saved from the Waters, 1581 (?), canvas, 50 × 43 cm. Madrid, Museo del Prado, inv. 502

Supreme demonstration of Paolo's ability in the small format, compendium of finesse and summation of the possible variations of the scene, it is one of the best, if not the most significant, of a very varied subject even in the workshop, in large formats. Every detail shows that joy of painting that both enthusiasts and students - even virtual - recognized in him, starting with Tiepolo, who would always return to the motif of leaning trees to direct light and perspective.

and distracted and let the work for a court that little interested him be done by others, or he thought of approaching the "modern" tastes of the patron, on the outskirts of Italy, which promptly happened. If the workshop produces a lot, when the work is destined for Venice, the Master takes up the brushes again, as in the *Resurrection* for the church of San Francesco della Vigna, the fourth chapel on the right side, purchased by Sebastiano Malipiero and then taken over by the Badoers. It was one of Veronese's most discussed canvases until recent times, when the authorship, at least substantial, appeared to be shared, placing the work around 1580. Conception and composition by the Master, uncertainties about Christ and backdrop. It remains an example of the "Venetian colouring" in which the single brushstroke determines the pictorial structure by building legibility through the lighter colours, bearers of the structuring light.

In the golden sunrise little angels appear. Jesus' head is surrounded by a ray of light, a glorious Christ with traces of wounds on one foot, not on his hands and side. A few fragments outline a barren and rocky landscape, where the sepulchre is just hinted at, on the ground, bare and formed by common slabs. The soldiers who guarded him have been annihilated: the soldier in the centre, wrapped in a coral red cloth, looks bewildered and frightened into the sarcophagus. On the left side, a soldier on the ground looks up, shocked by the event; at his side the companion with the intense yellow armour opposes the shield, he has left the bow behind, the arrows abandoned near the tomb. He fell down in surprise. Another sentry with helmet and sword almost trips in trying to defend himself, his water bottle falls, a companion brandishes his spear against Christ, an absurd but understandable defence. Their decomposed postures show dismay in the face of the shocking event and trace the pyramidal compositional structure, ended by Christ with his own crusader banner, his arms wide: the upward motion is a sinuous momentum.
In the refined chromatism, all the Venetian colours are present: azurite, indigo, cochineal lacquer, orpiment, realgar. The harmonic construction of the greens is beautiful, dazzling in the mantle on which the great divine light shines, obscured by the group of trees and in the thick foliage. The windy morning is transfigured by the light of the Risen One, which clears things up, makes the leaves translucent, pale in the radial emanation. The dynamic engagement of the canvas is evident if compared to the other two paintings attributed to Veronese and boasting the same subject: one, better known, is in the Hermitage, while the other, perhaps created for private devotion, is in the Gemäldegalerie in Dresden, where Christ, ascending with open arms, wrapped in a red mantle, is contrasted by the various landed soldiers who protect their eyes with their hands and clothes, while another, with a green, silvery mantle, try the defense with the shield. In the background, an angel shows the empty sepulcher to the two Marys, veiled and amazed.

SCOURGES AND APOTHEOSIS

Even if the illusions inspired by Lepanto had died down, there is always one last feast to impress the royal visitors to Venice: in the hot July of 1974, Henry III of Valois, called to the throne of France, was welcomed on the Lido by a gigantic triumphal arch designed by Palladio, with canvases from the workshops of Tintoretto and Veronese, who had been working day and night; there Henry would be able to relax with the most celebrated courtesans.
Recreation did not last long: on 25 June 1575 a family from the Trentino valleys arrived in Venice, a guest of fellow villagers. A few days later, everyone gets sick. Fever, pain, then oedema, the symptoms that doctors know well; the Lazzaretto reopens, in short the new plague spreads in the district, even if immediately isolated. But the disease escapes, reappears here and there, does not end, regains strength after short breaks. The luckiest can cross the lagoon to take refuge in some corner of the mainland, for those who remain the danger is fatal: in the end the population will be reduced by a third, at least fifty thousand individuals will die. Between progressions and pauses, restarts and crises, from July '75 to July '77, the plague opens spectral voids in all neighbourhoods, decimating the poor and fragile population who cannot escape. In fact, the vast majority. Even the patricians and citizens who did not want to leave die; among the many Titian, alone and abandoned in the empty house of Biri Grande. The greatest painter is buried in the Frari, without the glorious ceremonies due to the most famous and prestigious of European painters. His loss will then be felt as the final seal to the great season of Venetian painting.
The entire Caliari family survived, probably taking refuge in the lands acquired over the years. In addition to Gabriele and Carlo, with Paolo and Elena and Benedetto are little Vittoria and Orazio Bortolo, born on 3 September 1571. The last child, Camillo, will be born after thirteen years of marriage, dying after less than a month, in September 1579.

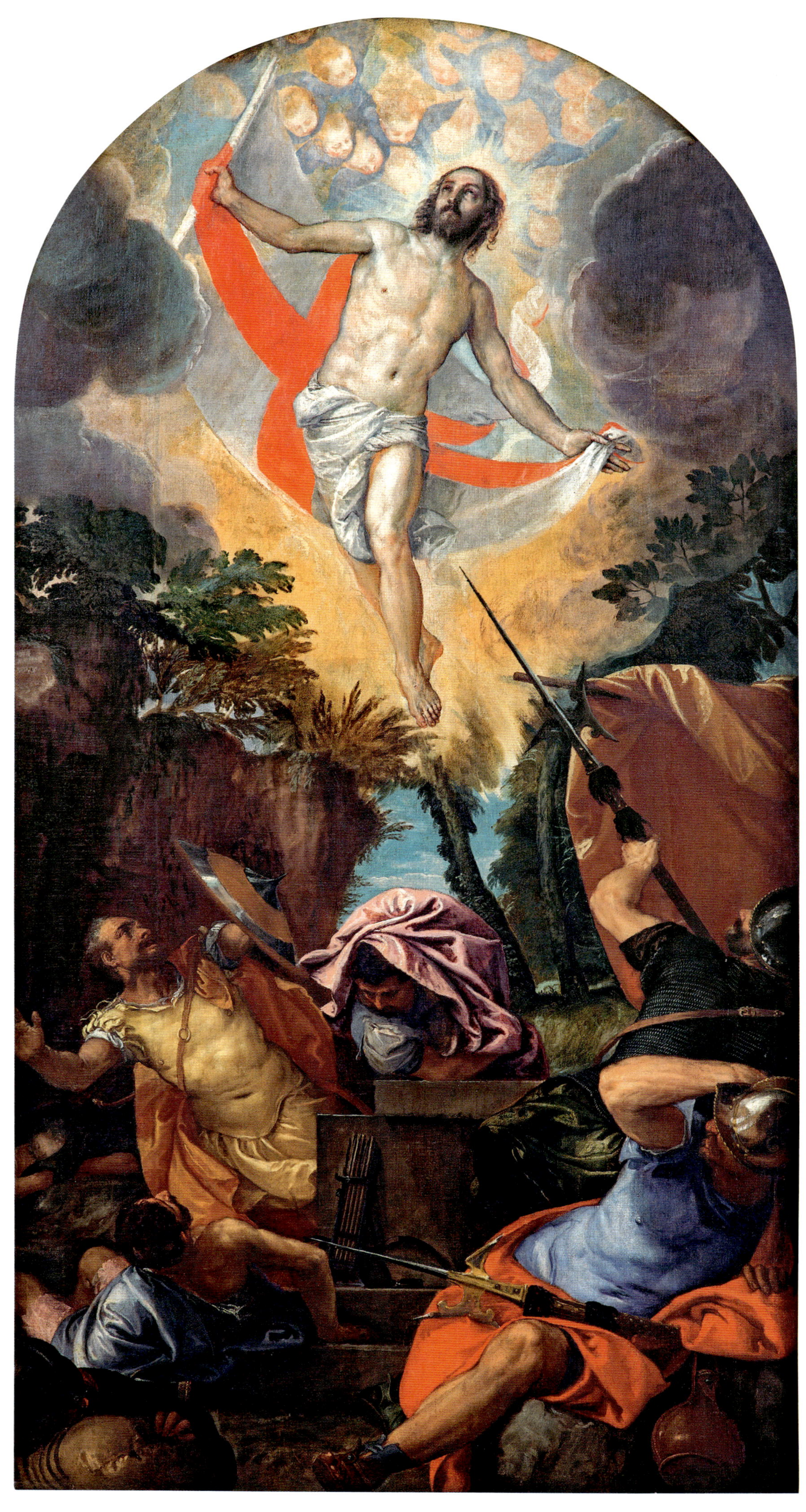

Paolo, Ridolfi tells us, was "careful in spending so that he had the possibility to acquire many farms and accumulate riches and furnishings". Veronese invested fees and huge profits from his workshop on the mainland by purchasing, among other things, twenty-five fields in Treviso area, with a villa "that he keeps for his own use"; he leased the estates obtaining bushels of wheat and half of the wine produced. He also financed mortgage loans on the conventual property of the Benedictines, who turned to him for liquidity needs. Among others, a loan of no less than five hundred and fifty ducats is documented, which yields interest for forty-five ducats a year. Another example is the agreement signed on 17 November 1586 with the prior of the convent of the Carità, for a census, a sort of loan with guarantee of land near Ravenna, from which he derives another financial income. His children will enjoy the proceeds, and will still make a loan to the same convent on 30 July 1590, after their father's death. Among the intense economic relations of the decade we also find the offer of two hundred ducats to the convent of San Sebastiano, where Paolo wants to be buried: it is a *mansionaria* or a legacy for a weekly mass.

Resurrection, approx. 1580, canvas, 325 × 160 cm.
Venice, church of San Francesco della Vigna

A furious fire on 11 May 1574 destroyed various rooms of the Doge's Palace: the reconstruction was entrusted to Antonio da Ponte, with the advice of Palladio. Veronese was called to decorate the ceiling of the Sala del Collegio, he worked on it from 1575 to 1578 during the reign of Sebastiano Venier. For that cycle, probably conceived by Marcantonio Barbaro, he created three central compartments, one oval with *Faith* and two rectangular: *Venice with Justice and Peace* and *Mars and Neptune*, and as many as eight T or L-shaped panels. A series of allegories which have been referred to as: *Reward*, *Purity*, *Meekness*, *Loyalty*, *Prosperity*, *Vigilance*, *Dialectic or Industry*, *Moderation* plus six chiaroscuro with allegorical figures on the ceiling. On the wall, above the courthouse, he also painted the grandiose canvas with *Sebastiano Venier Kneeling in the Act of Giving Thanks for the Victory of Lepanto*. Located above the doge's seat, it represents the *Capitano generale da Mar* introduced to the Redeemer by Saint Mark and Saint Justina. Venice is the matron who offers the dogal horn, while on the left it is Faith herself who offers the Eucharistic chalice – thus faith and political authority collaborate on the same level – while the fallen in the battle, in the background, are epitomised in the figure of Agostino Barbarigo, operational commander of the *left horn* of the fleet.

One of these allegories has been alternatively referred to as the Dialectic or instead Industry, alluding to the methodical and perfect work of the spider. More stimulating to understand it as "The Dialectic", since the figure supports, arms raised, a geometric plot without admiring it as the gaze is beyond, towards infinite space. The dialectical tension goes beyond the imitation of nature; philosophy, like art, becomes a free reworking of reality, looks to the other world, to allegory and illusion.

These canvases by Veronese in glory of Venice show a world far from reality, "admirable inventions", figures of the world of ideas in the "wonderful palaces". They speak a cultured and rhetorical language: *ut pictura poesis*, like poetry so painting that arouses admiration and wonder, amazement and questions.

For the hall of the Magistrato delle Biade he proposed *Venice Receives the Homage of Hercules and Ceres*, a canvas cut into a four-leaf clover from the original format, due to subsequent damages. A matronly Venice decked out with her best fabrics is honored by a curiously bald Hercules and a conspicuously naked Ceres, in a skilful perspective game, while the putti carry bundles of wheat, remembered by Ridolfi: "bundles of corn, as a sign of the abundance of grains, of which the Venetian state is rich". Veronese is very realistic in reproducing the bundles with the precision of someone who has seen them tied up by peasants while they are harvesting their lands.

Precisely from the year 1578 we have a group of letters, now divided between the British Library, the Pierpont Morgan Library in New York and the Getty Research Institute, showing the attention with which Paolo Caliari follows his land ownership, while always an attentive and

Venice with Justice and Peace, 1575-1578, canvas, 250 × 180 cm. Venice, Palazzo Ducale, Sala del Collegio

prudent investor. These are letters to Marcantonio Gandino, a nobleman from Treviso, attorney, consultant and mediator for Caliari. Another prosecutor will later be Francesco Soranzo; from the correspondence we learn that Paolo also bought land near Mestre for the sum of seven thousand ducats; he often travelled visiting his possessions, for purchases and negotiations, he also used the journeys to accompany portraits, always between Padua, Treviso, Castelfranco. From other hints we discover how branched the clientele was, how close the relationship was with the Venetian patriciate, not only Venetians, and also how attentive the painter followed the events of the convents, the policies of the various priors. For his part, he is sharp-eyed and wary: presenting his *Redecima* to the Dieci Savi sopra le Decime, or the denunciation of real estate, on 9 August 1582 (it is in the State Archives of Venice, X Savi delle Decime, Redecima 1581 Castello, b. 157 bis, n. 456, estimo 1582), he protested that he had miserable tenants who paid with barrels of wine, a bushel of wheat, a pig, two hens, and fifty eggs. A misery!

After another devastating fire at the Doge's Palace on 20 December 1577, which destroyed Guariento's *Paradise*, a supreme example of the most gilded and resplendent Gothic, an expression of the ideology of the myth of Venice and its government, Paolo Caliari created one of the largest panels in the ceiling of the Sala del Maggior Consiglio. It is the utmost manifesto of the glorification of Venice, a synthesis of the image of the Serenissima for Veronese: young and beautiful, virtuous and noble; she is Venus, she is the Queen of the Gulf, she is Justice. She is the Virgin Mary. Commissioned in 1579 and delivered by 1582, *The Triumph of Venice*, grandiose and spectacular, will exert a profound influence on subsequent Baroque decorative painting: it is an immense oval canvas that celebrates the Sovereign, loved and honoured by the people who pay homage to her. Seated on a cloud, Venice appears in front of a monumental triumphal arch supported by grandiose cochlide columns. She is crowned by Victory, while Fame, the tallest figure, with the top hat, announces glory. A flood of allegories follows, a display of Paolo's rhetorical skills: on the cloud we find Honour with the laurel; Peace with the olive tree; Security with the caduceus; Happiness is naked, like Abundance with the cornucopia full of harvests; on the right there is also Liberty with the cap of the Roman freedmen. On the balcony is the crowd of citizens and tributaries: men and women, ecclesiastics and aristocrats, Christians and Orientals, in different generations. And below, at the base where the winged, golden Lion of San Marco dominates, there is the confusion of horses, knights, a prison and the anonymous crowd of craftsmen and workers.

According to many critics it represents the work that closes the cycle of sumptuous and worldly painting by Paolo Veronese, decorative painting with happy colours. But the artist still has a lot to say and teach. In that year Agostino Carracci visits him, to make the engravings of six subjects of the Master, and becomes a friend as well as an admirer. He will be joined by his brother Annibale, who was also immediately devoted to Veronese, as Giorgio Vasari annotates in his *Lives*: "*Questo Paulino i[l] quale ho io conosc[iuto] et visto le bell'ope[re] sue era degno c[he] si scrivesse delle [s]ue lodi un gran vol[ume] essendo che le s[ue] pitture dimostra[no] egli non fu seco[ndo] ad alcun altro p[ittore], e questo ignoran[te] se a passa con qua[ttro] righe. E ciò perc[hé] egli non fu fior[enti]no*" (Perini 1990, p. 159). Thus the Bolognese reacts, scandalized by the few lines, calling the Tuscan Vasari "ignorant", denouncing that partisanship of which everyone, however, had noticed, and which will remain in the reconstruction of Italian art, where Tuscany with its "renaissance" and "mannerism" has set itself as the centre and measure of painting. In this regard it is worth remembering Roberto Longhi in the famous *Viatico per cinque secoli di pittura veneziana*:

> "Mannerism!" The same convenient mental scheme that was used by the German *monatti* of art history to throw Tintoretto's "serpentine" body into the cart, has also been tried to knock on Veronese's door. But Veronese was out... The fact is that mannerism appeared to Veronese as a natural custom of the time, as a modern world that needed to be represented, but dissolving it in a fabulous "universal harmony" again calm and resolute as in Titian, in Ariosto and, now, in his friend Palladio. (Longhi 1946, p. 27 – free translation)

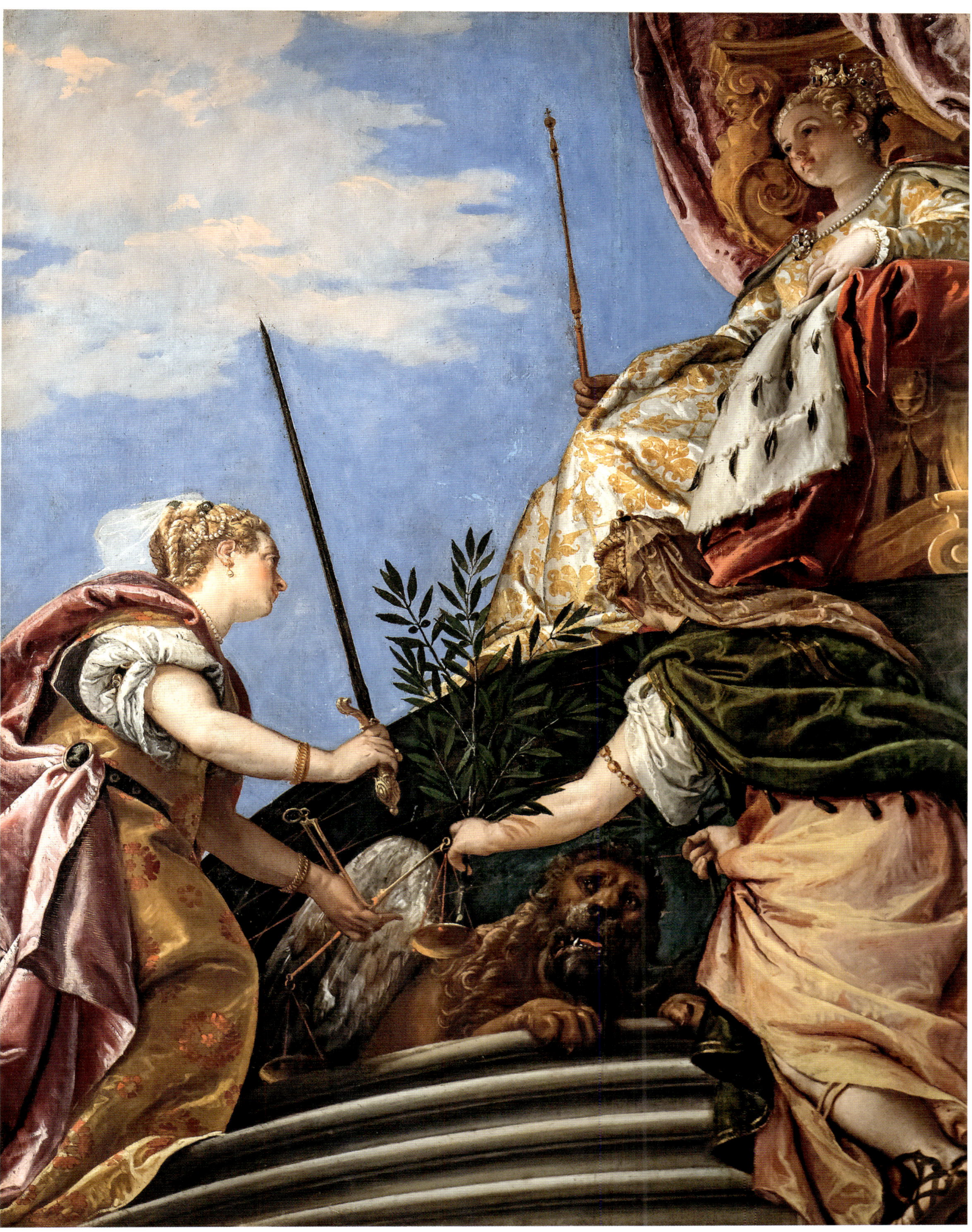

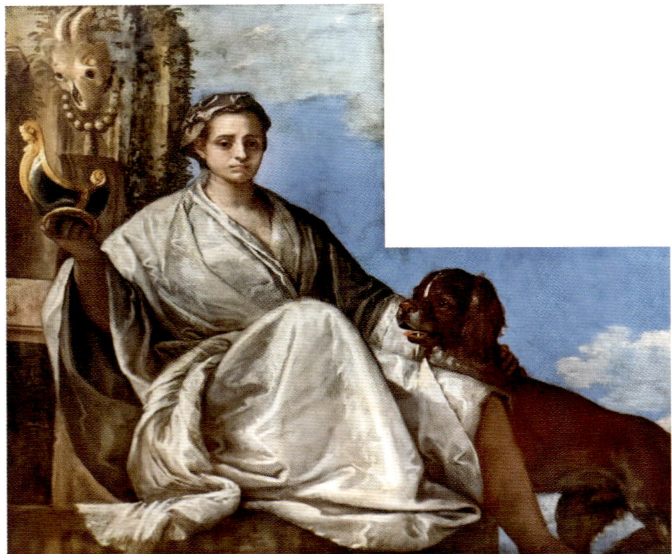

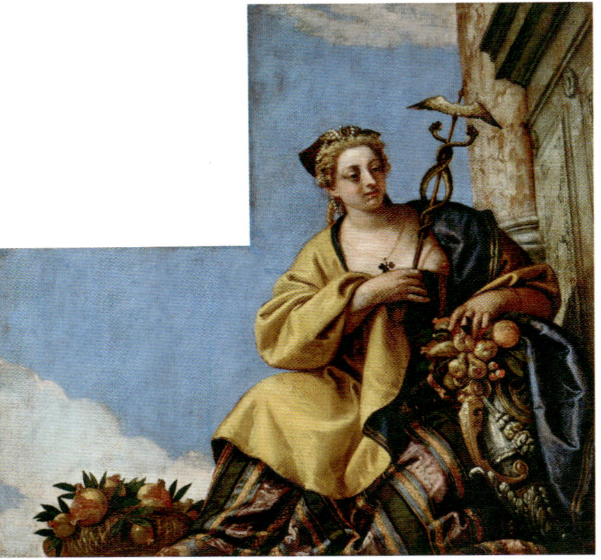

Loyalty, Prosperity, Vigilance, Moderation, 1575-1578, canvases. Venice, Palazzo Ducale, Sala del Collegio

For the room, in addition to the Triumph, Paolo also created two minor canvases, *The Capture of Smyrna* and the *Defense of Scutari*. He was unable to paint that Paradise which had also been commissioned from him, with Francesco Bassano, and of which a sketch remains. He did not have the time and, after his death, the commitment went to Tintoretto.

THE SENSES OF THE MYTH

Author of famous and celebrated *Suppers*, requested for imposing altarpieces, greatly admired by the most cultured aristocrats, painter of history and glory, Paolo Caliari also produces, and always with an absolute mix of contemporaneity, canvases dedicated to mythological themes drawn from classical literature, with obvious sensual if not erotic allusions.

The best example is the *Rape of Europa*, today in the Anticollegio hall at the Doge's Palace in Venice, painted for Jacopo Contarini's palace in San Samuele; it will be donated to the Serenissima at the end of the eighteenth century by the last heir of the glorious family; a highly appreciated canvas, which barely escaped the Napoleonic predators. Contarini, unmarried and childless, was one of the most cultured intellectual patricians and collectors, rich in interests and skills, a friend of Palladio and then of Galileo; he asked Paolo to illustrate the fable of the *Metamorphoses*, already proposed by many, and by Titian in particular. Veronese's iconographic choice focuses on a pronubus and nuptial climate: there is no fear in Europe, which already gives in to love by showing her breasts uncovered while she adapts to her mount, there is no fear even when the bull reveals its intentions calmly heading towards the sea, and she seems to want to push away the caring and fearful maids: she greets them without regrets when at sea the bull heads towards Crete, where Jupiter will love her. It is a nuptial climate in the colours, in the crowns of flowers, in the gestures of the cupids, and then there is that detail, the tongue of the bull that delicately licks Europa's foot, which always aroused a particular thrill in the enthusiastic admirers of Veronese's invention, lovingly taken up by Giambattista Tiepolo, even in the wooded setting, traced by bent trunks and broad fronds.

A setting that returns with other interesting and new solutions for another icon, the small but precious *Moses Saved from the Waters*, created in the early Eighties; replicated in at least seven other versions, always admired, still an occasion for a tribute and a second thought by Giambattista Tiepolo. It is a true compendium for further tests, including workshop ones, in

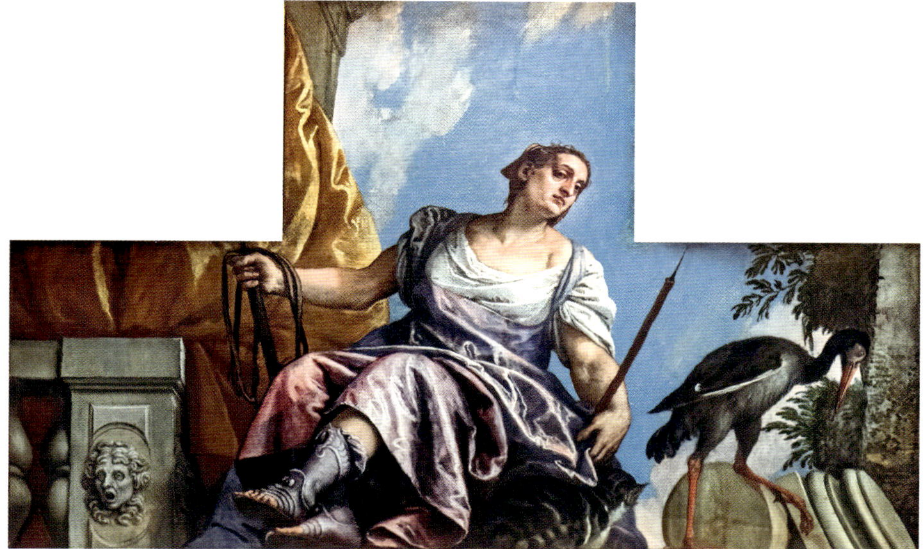

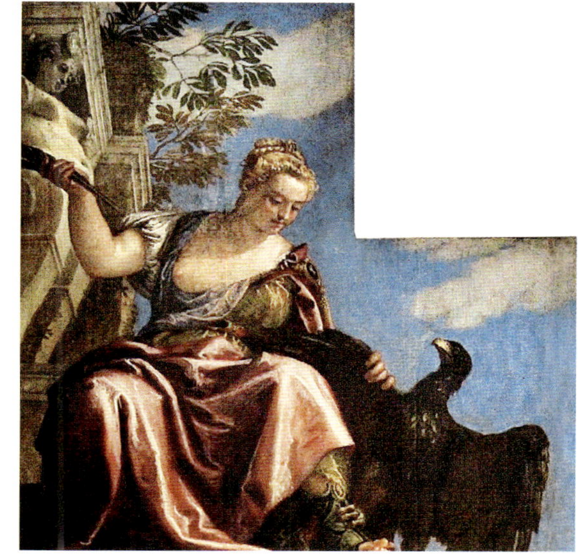

the measure of the airy atmosphere with backgrounds of a complex city and a majestic bridge, separated from the episode in the foreground by two sinuous trees to form a large inverted triangle: this is how we orient ourselves on the protagonist, the elegant princess who observes with a slight gentle smile the exposed child, presented by four maids; three more appear in the background, plus a Moorish servant and a dwarf. At the center of this court the princess wears a splendid brocade dress, she leans on the nearby caring maid, her right hand is behind her back, as if to support her. It is the very naturalistic posture of a pregnant woman, the sash on her belly confirms it. The invention is by Veronese, it does not belong to the biblical story in which the Pharaoh's daughter went to bathe when the child was found abandoned in the basket, since the sovereign had given the order to kill all the male children of the Jews, by now too numerous. Her daughter will disobey, paying the child's mother a "salary" to nurse him; when he is weaned she will adopt him, naming him Mosheh, the "Saved from the waters". As usual, Veronese rereads the episode in its contemporaneity: the adoption of abandoned babies was a frequent practice amongst wealthy Venetian families, and here its generosity is underlined, since the adoptive mother was already pregnant; perhaps the canvas referred to some family history.

Very interesting are the moralizing and nuptial solutions in a series always considered as an example of Veronese as a sensual if not erotic painter. Indicated with the generic title of *Allegories of Love*, it is uncertain as to its destination and request, although a long-standing tradition hypothesizes it was painted for the Emperor Rudolf II, an avid and ravenous collector, who also created a spectacular Wunderkammer. These are four square canvases, the pride of the National Gallery in London, indicated as *Infidelity*, *Contempt*, *Respect*, *Happy Union*. Intended for the view from below, for composition and diagonal cuts, each one has its own light; while they could hardly be placed on a single ceiling, it is interesting to think of them in pairs, for two bedrooms: thus they have an evident and transparent moral meaning, opposing Infidelity to Happy Union, Contempt to Respect. However, interpretative doubts remain, even in an apparently transparent scene such as the so-called *Happy Union*, where we see two spouses holding the same branch, while Anteros protects them and accompanies them, with a dog – symbol of fidelity. But who is the naked and busty woman who crowns the wedding? She is seated on a jar, or sphere, good fortune with a cornucopia beside her, thus an allegory of Fortune; she has a belt that holds nothing, but it is a sign of commitment. So best wishes for the licit union. On the contrary, the woman in Infidelity is held on one side by a worried man about to get up, on the other hand she hands a mysterious note to a rather arrogant young man.

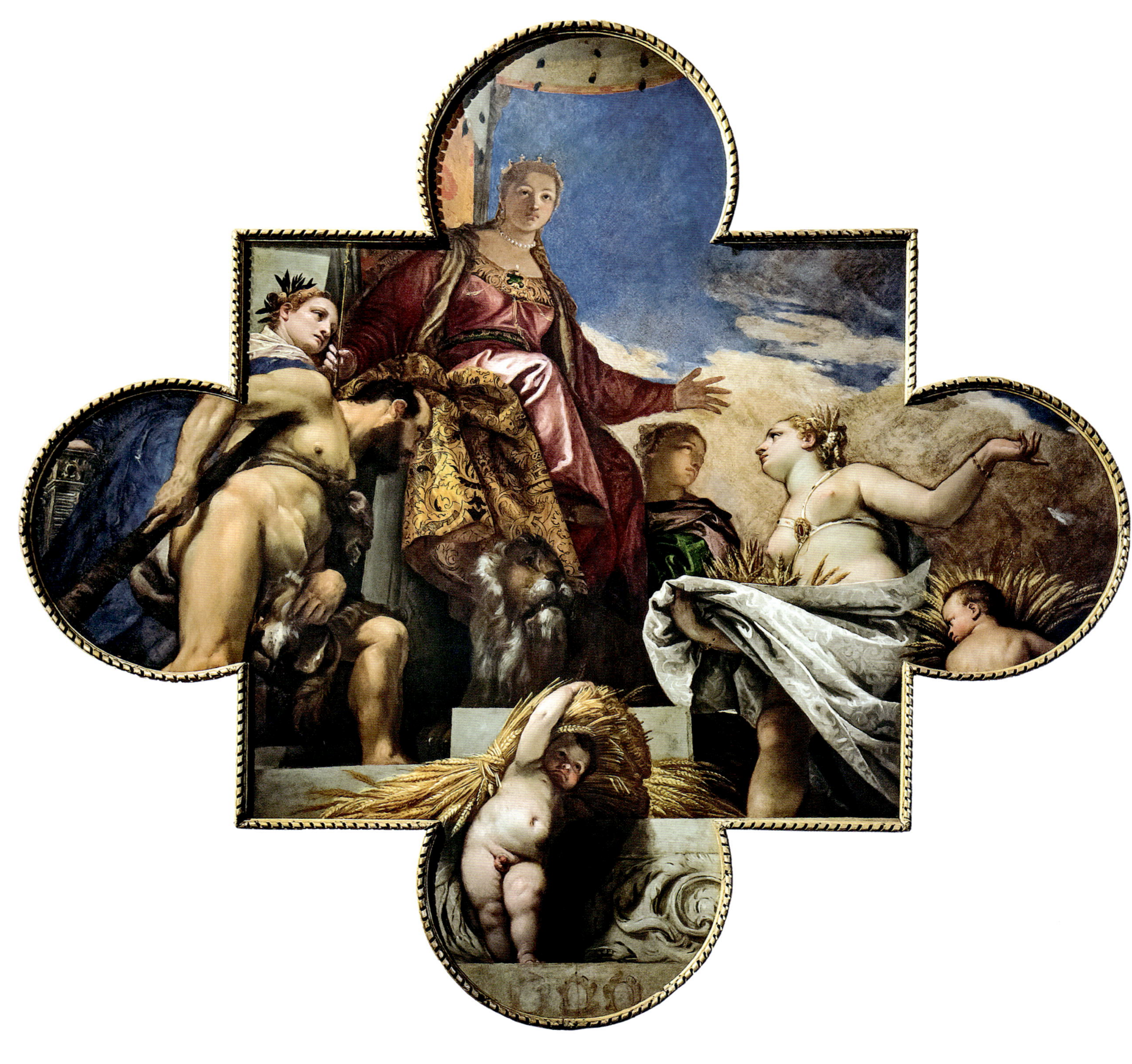

Venice Receives the Homage of Hercules and Ceres, 1575, canvas, 308 × 327 cm. Venice, Galleria dell'Accademia, inv. 45, formerly: Palazzo Ducale, Sala del Magistrato delle Biade

The Triumph of Venice, approx. 1582, canvas, 904 × 580 cm. Venice, Palazzo Ducale, Sala del Maggior Consiglio

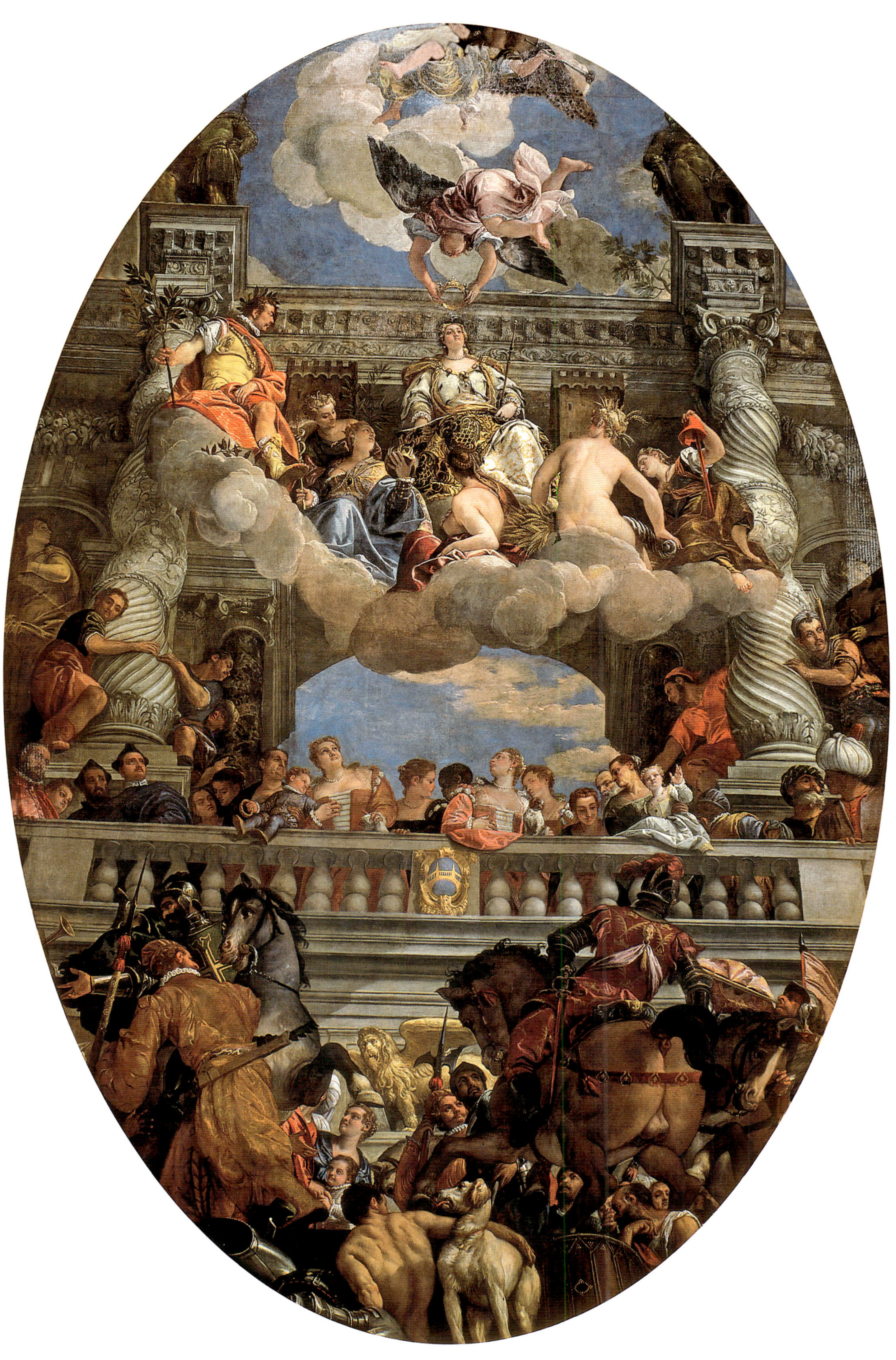

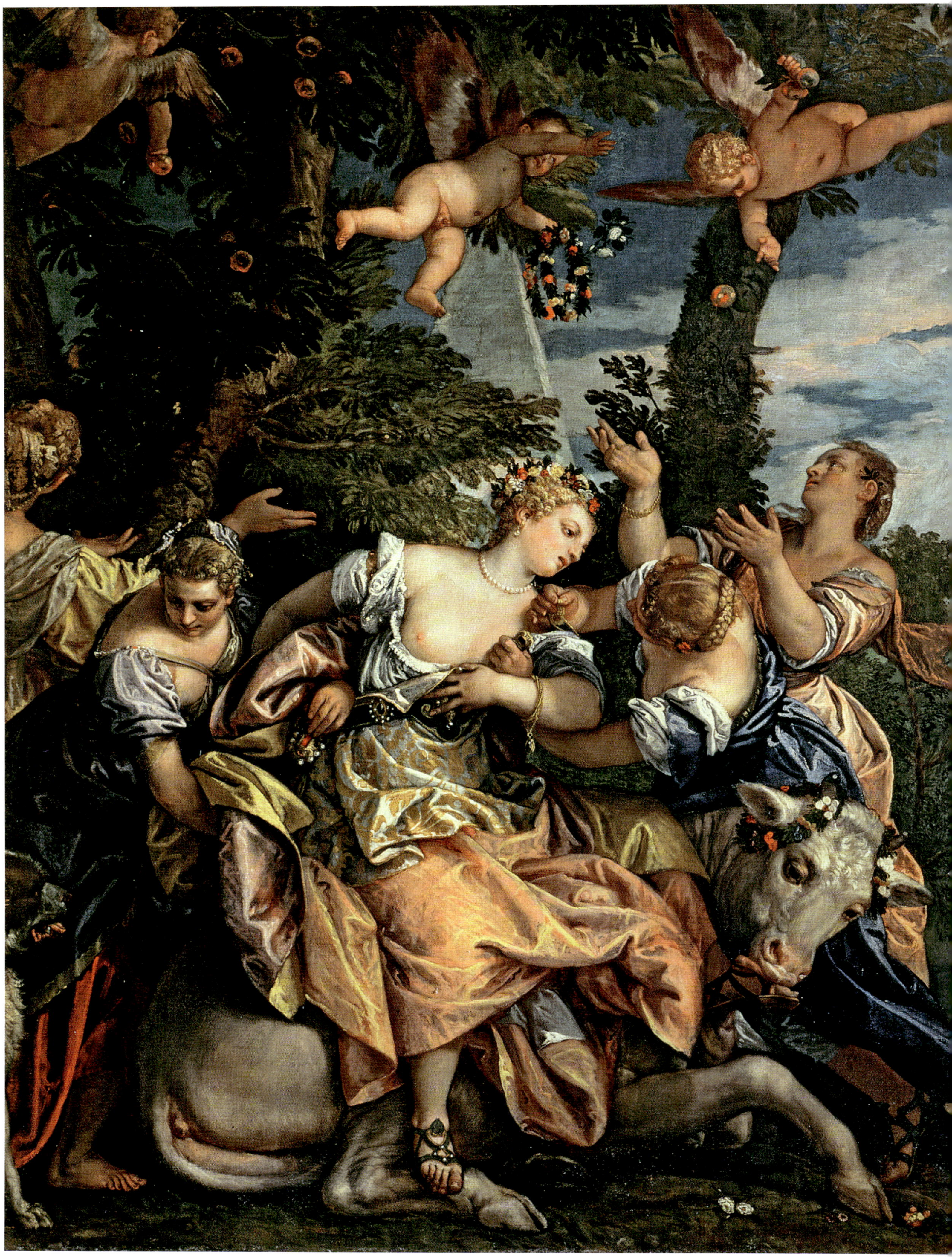

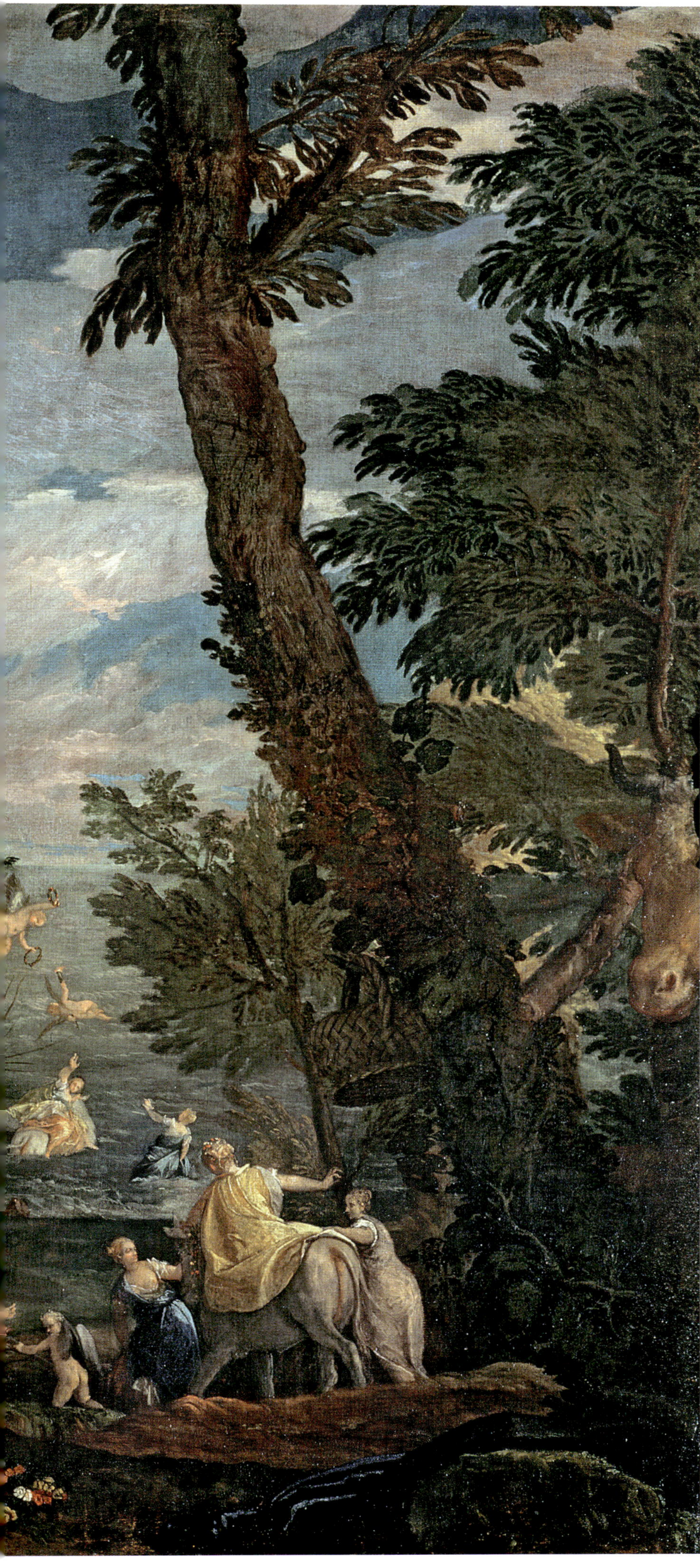

Rape of Europa, approx. 1578, canvas, 235 × 296 cm. Venice, Palazzo Ducale, Sala dell'Anticollegio

The canvas, part of Jacopo Contarini's collection, was judged among the most beautiful by contemporaries and even more so in the eighteenth century with the replica by Tiepolo. Narration of seduction and loving passion, devoid of any tragedy, indeed entirely interwoven with matrimonial tones.

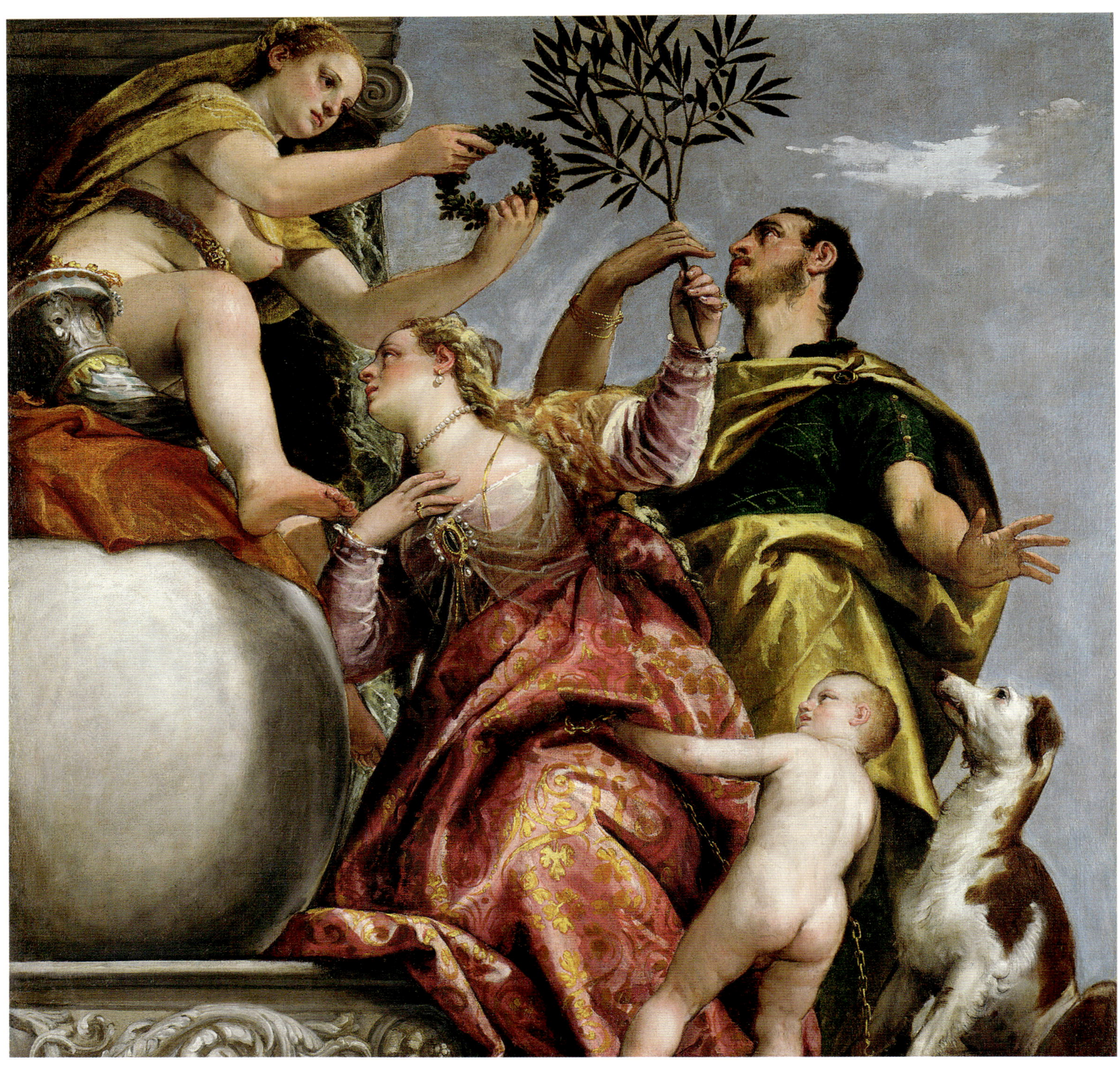

Allegories of Love: Happy Union,
approx. 1570, canvas,
187.4 × 186.7 cm. London,
National Gallery of Art, inv. 1326

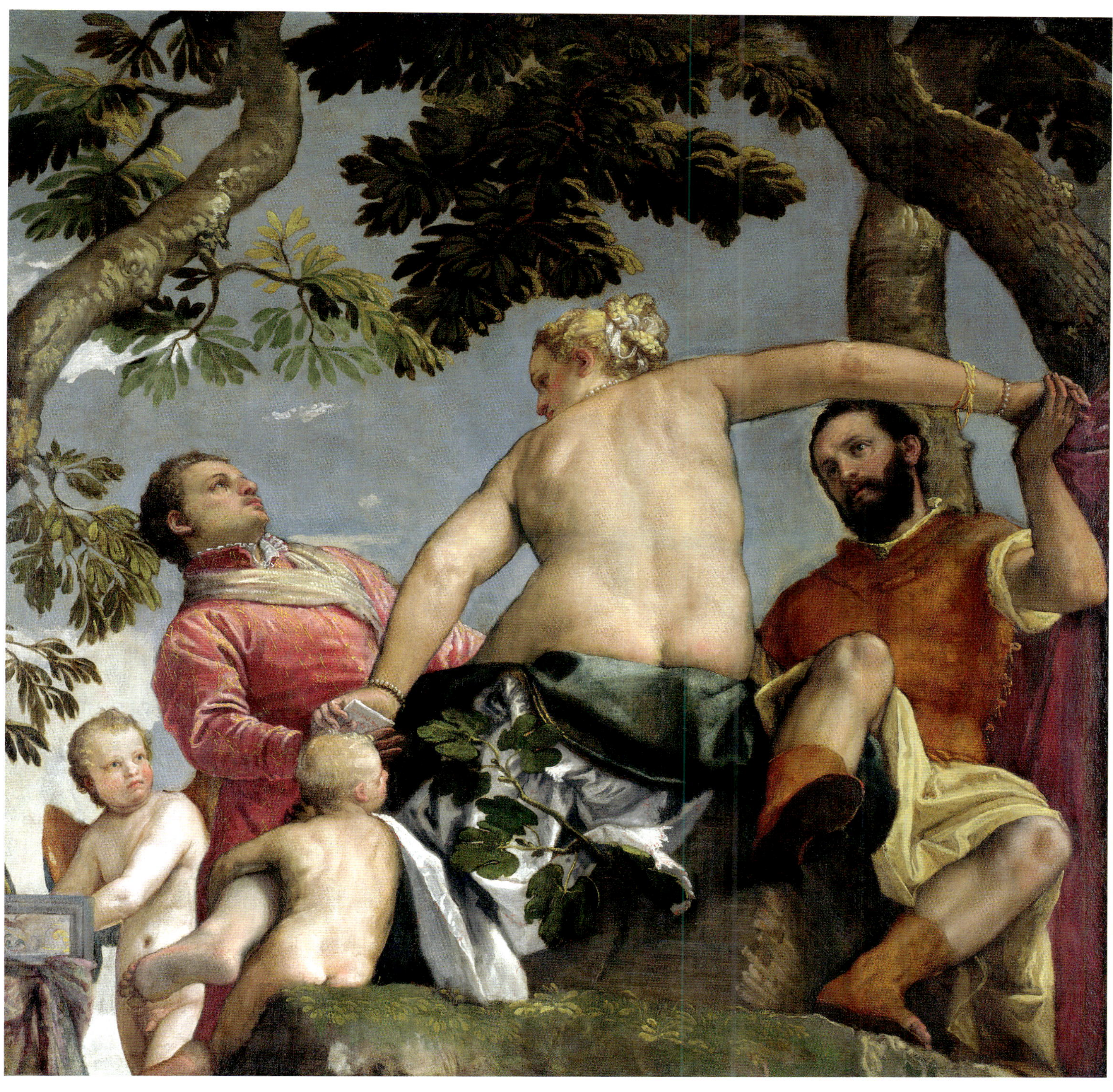

Allegories of Love: Infidelity,
approx. 1570, canvas,
190 × 190 cm. London,
National Gallery of Art, inv. 1324

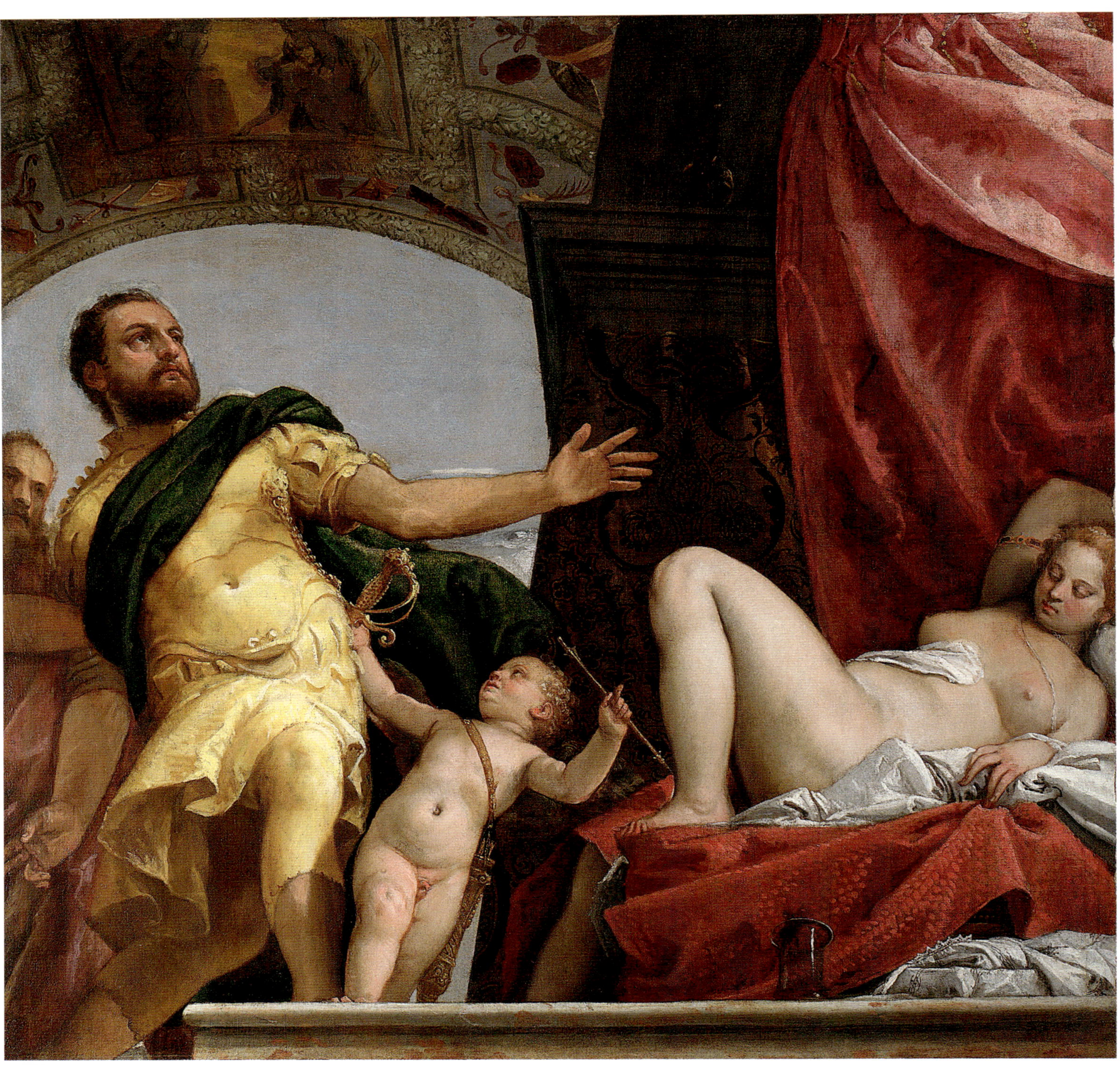

Allegories of Love: Respect,
approx. 1570, canvas,
186 × 194.3 cm. London,
National Gallery of Art, inv. 1325

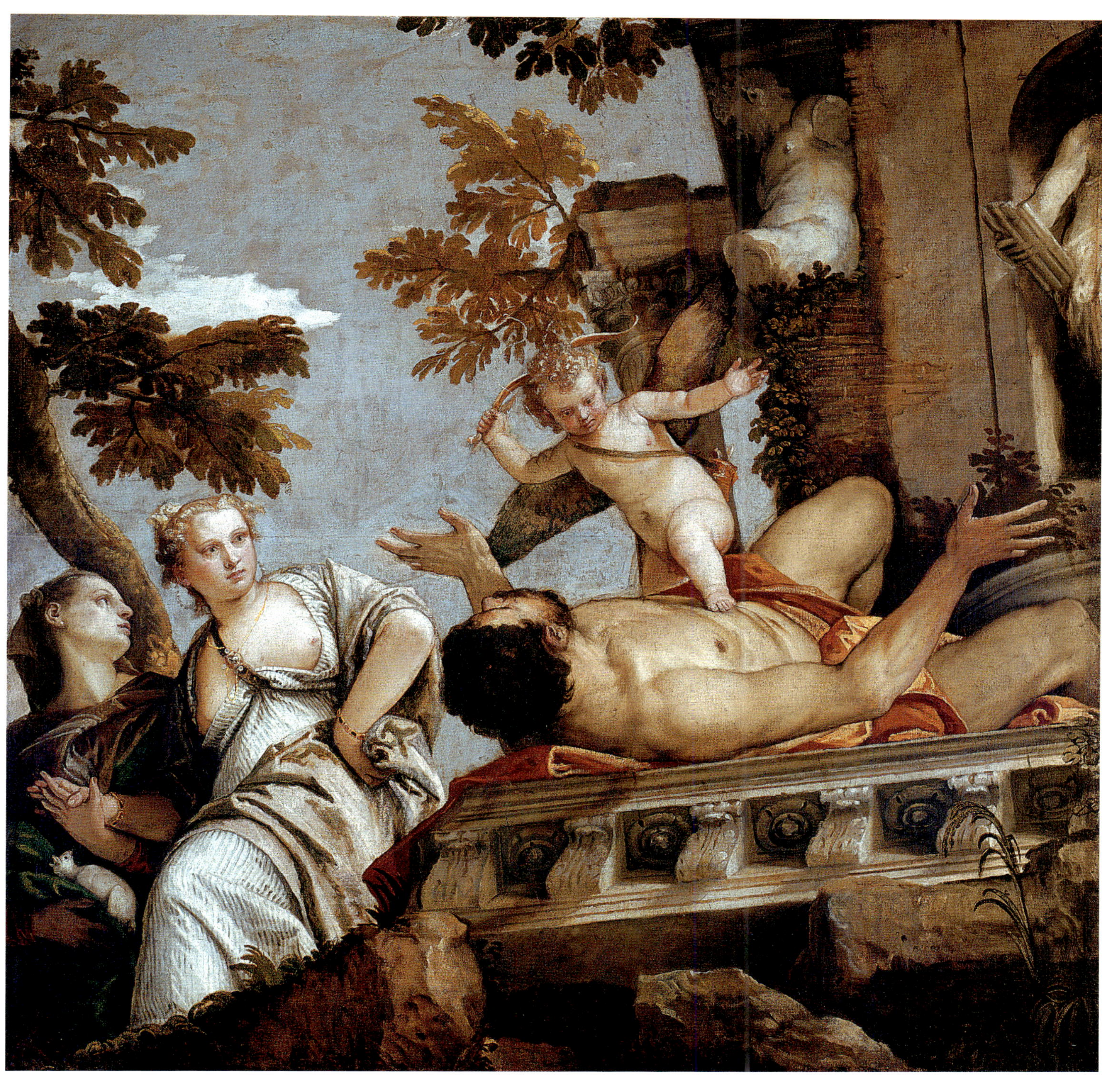

Allegories of Love: Contempt,
approx. 1570, canvas,
186.6 × 188.5 cm. London,
National Gallery of Art, inv. 1318

Here Anteros tries to hold back the unfaithful, now naked, ready to offer her graces; another putto plays a virginal, perhaps a seductive melody.
The scene called *Respect* shows Eros, armed with an arrow, who would like to lead a restrained knight to love, a virtuous man in a beautiful armour, armed with a sword, and you will notice the upright hilt held by the cupid, with phallic evidence. Eros leads him towards a woman abandoned on blankets, naked and immodest. The virtuoso does not look at her, also because she is held back by a man in the shadows, who vigorously grabs her arm. The dart has not been shot, the virtuous should resist the temptation. On the contrary, in *Contempt*, Eros, whose bow has an untied string, whips a knocked-down man, deceived by passion, observed with contempt by a woman, in an old-fashioned tunic, perhaps Chastity, who tries to take away another woman, very unveiled. Perhaps a wife and a lover, betrayed by him who has been drawn into illicit love? In any case Veronese has built moral lessons where only Anteros is saved, lasting and faithful love.
The same morality lesson can be found in the exceptionally small but beautiful canvas in the Galleria Sabauda in Turin, which shows *Mars and Venus with Love and a Horse*. Here Mars and Venus are undoubtedly preparing to weave an intimate dialogue, which we understand not only for the nudity of both, but also for the obvious footwork. And yet the moment is suspended. The beautiful head of a horse has suddenly appeared out of nowhere, the long bridle is entrusted to little Eros who holds it by the bit. The horse has always represented the uncontrollable erotic impulse, and here we see it tamed: is therefore a warning to Mars, the warning to moderate one's ardour in the act of love? Or maybe something else? Obviously, for the painter and patron or buyer, poetry consists precisely in the ambiguity of the allegorical formulas. For the lover of painting, the small canvas will be in all respects – lights, choice of colour sharpness, drapery, beautiful animal head, the detail of the blue blanket in the corner of the bed – a brilliant business card of the best Caliari.
In completely different sizes and with abundance and greater complexity of reading, it returns to the theme with *Venus and Mars Bound by Love* exhibited at the Metropolitan Museum in New York. Here we find all the elements of the classical iconography: Venus naked and suckling, Mars perfectly dressed in armour and cloak; Eros and Anteros and the horse. And in addition a herm, a petrified satyr to hold up a ruined wall. The landscape is woodland. What do cupids do? One arrests the caparisoned horse brandishing the sword of Mars, the other instead undertakes to tie the legs of the lovers with a ribbon. Armed, equipped with a cloak, the god is seated, Venus is naked, her dress carelessly thrown on the wall: only the cloak of Mars, who doesn't even look at her, partially protects her nakedness. The left hand of the goddess touches the man's shoulder, the right is at the suckling breast. A jet of water comes out of the stone fountain, to the side. What meanings did the painter give to the *lactatio Veneris*? The analyses have shown that every detail is original, wanted by Paolo. So it forces us to read its meaning, there must be a solution to this sort of rebus which places side by side a plurality of signs, each endowed with an allegorical sense, but whose overall construction is elusive.
Another canvas with explicit erotic allusions is *Mercury, Herse and Aglaurus* at the Fitzwilliam in Cambridge. It is signed "Paulus Caliar / Veronensis faci". The myth is found in Ovid's Metamorphoses (II 708-832). Aglaurus is the daughter of the king of Athens: she notices the presence of Mercury who wants to enter a room where her sister Herse is. Mercury confides in her his desire to meet Herse, and Aglaurus, full of envy, tries to bar the door to the god. As punishment for her, the god turns her into stone. Another variation on the loves of Venus and Mars is *Mars Stripping Venus with Cupid and Dog*, where the dog plays with a beautiful cupid, while a shadowed Mars rears a majestic crest.
Another dimension of Venus is the lover who wants to keep with herself the young, beautiful hunter Adonis. This story is one of the most complex and varied myths. Adonis was born from an incest propitiated by a mother who pushes her daughter to lie down with her husband, who

is also the daughter's father. The young man born of that love will be handsome and charming, much desired also by Persephone, the goddess of the underworld. This unleashes the hatred of Apollo and the mortal jealousy of Mars: he will die wounded by a boar. Veronese repeated several times the scene of the loves between Venus and Adonis: in particular the goddess is lovingly protective in *Venus and the Sleeping Adonis* at the Prado. She is holding a rectangular fan, fashionable at the time, while Eros keeps a hound at bay ready to hunt, and the other dog sleeps like the master, in a position of total abandonment.

A reflection by Bernard Berenson is also valid for these scenes: "... When I contemplate Veronese's paintings, I feel such a complete and perfect satisfaction that I feel it engulfs my whole being, my senses, my feelings, my intellect. If it is true that Paolo paints with less subtlety than Velázquez or Vermeer, he nevertheless creates, through his figurations, a House of Life, all the more than the other two, and therefore, all in all, I love him at least as much as I love any other painter who has ever painted..." (B. Berenson, *Introduction,* in *Palladio Veronese e Vittoria a Maser*, Milan 1960, p. 9 – free translation).

Following pages

Mars and Venus with Love and a Horse, approx. 1570, canvas, 47 × 47 cm. Turin, Galleria Sabauda, inv. 683

In its reduced dimensions, the canvas is of exceptional care and quality: the body of Mars, in the tense musculature, in the energy of the torsion recalls the style of Giulio Romano engraved by Marcantonio Raimondi, but then the scene of erotic value is as if suspended in the dreamlike atmosphere given by the appearance of the horse held by Cupid.

Venus and Mars Bound by Love, 1579 (?), canvas, 201 × 161 cm. New York, Metropolitan Museum, inv. 10.189

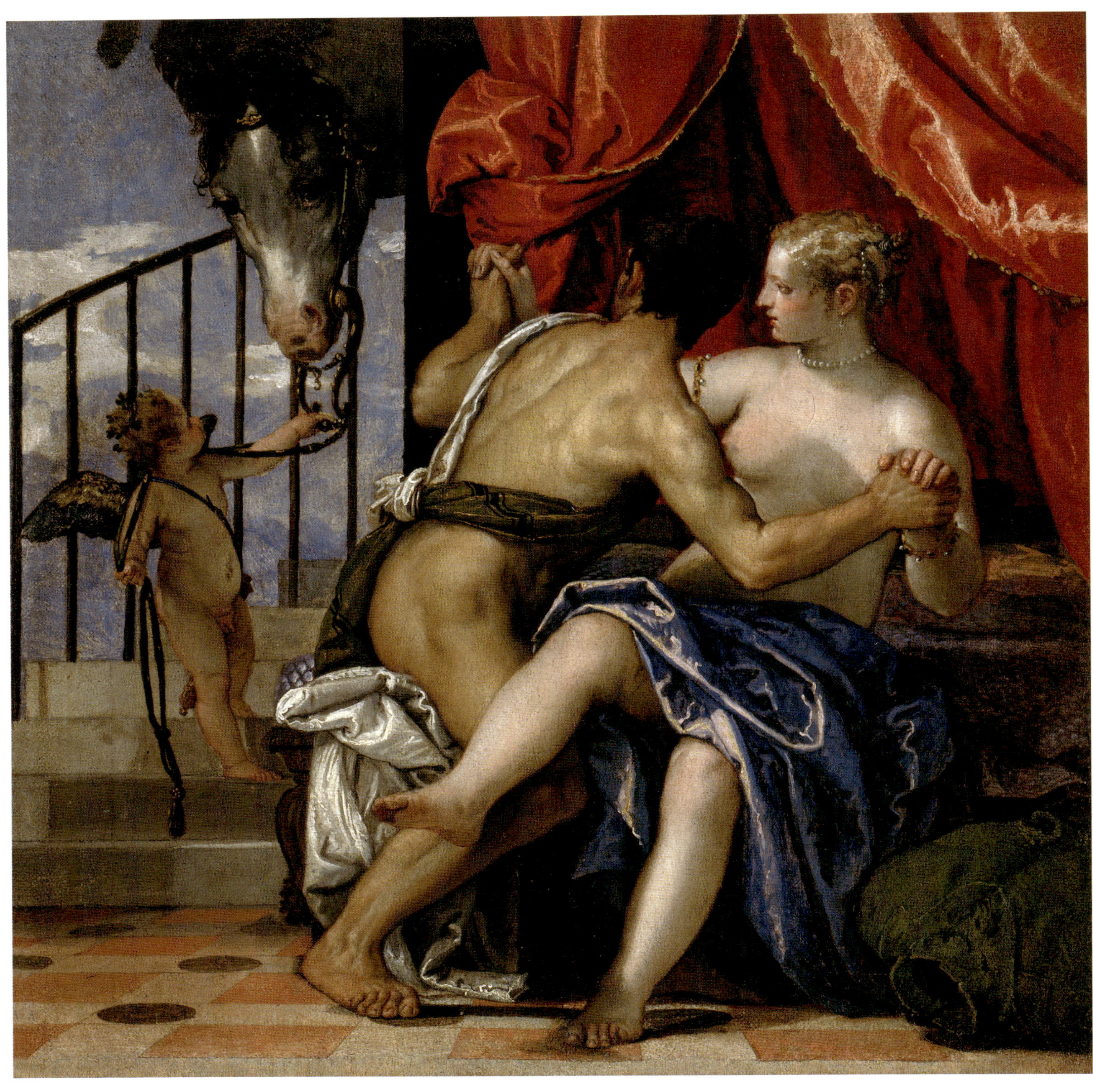

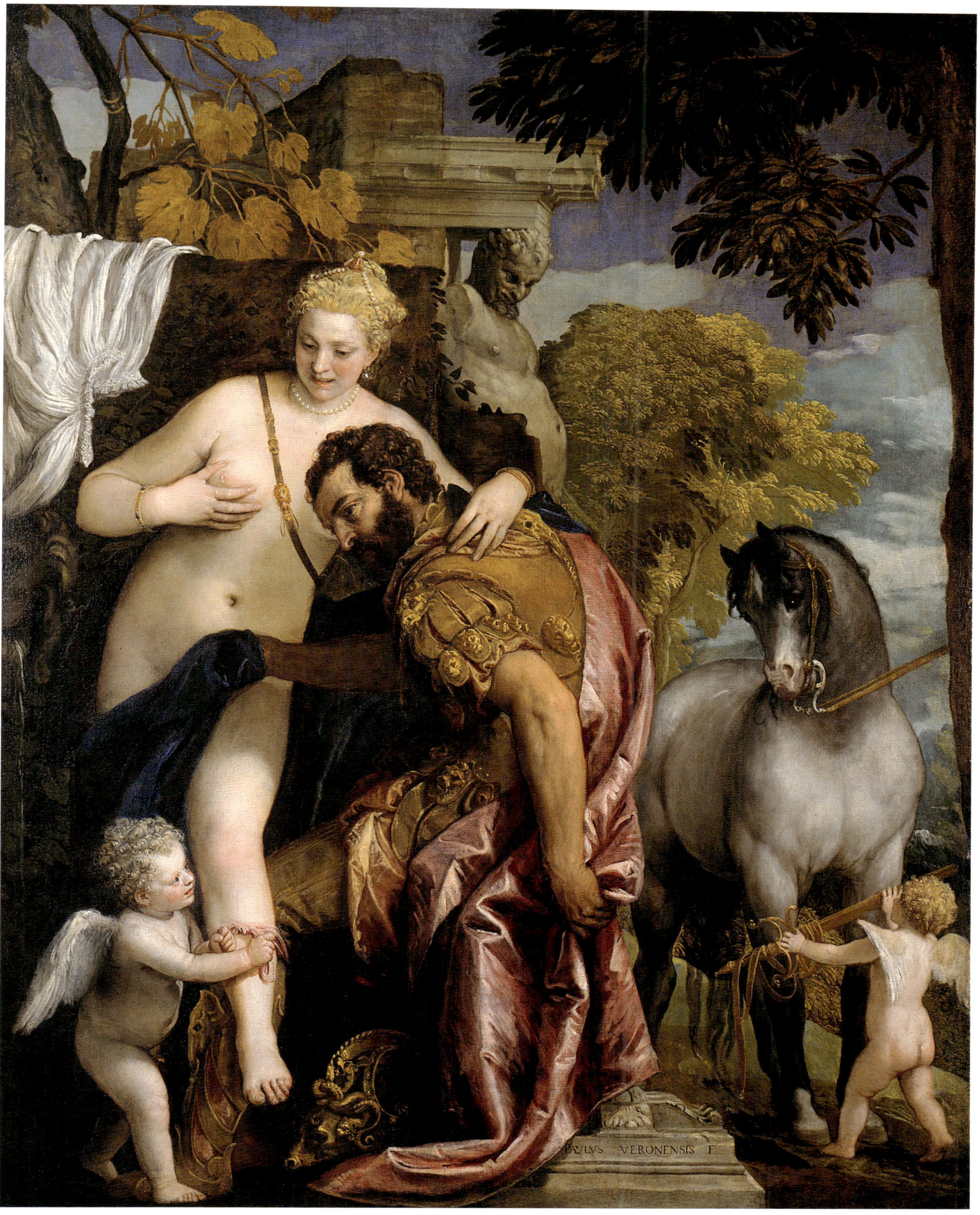
PAVLVS VERONENSIS F

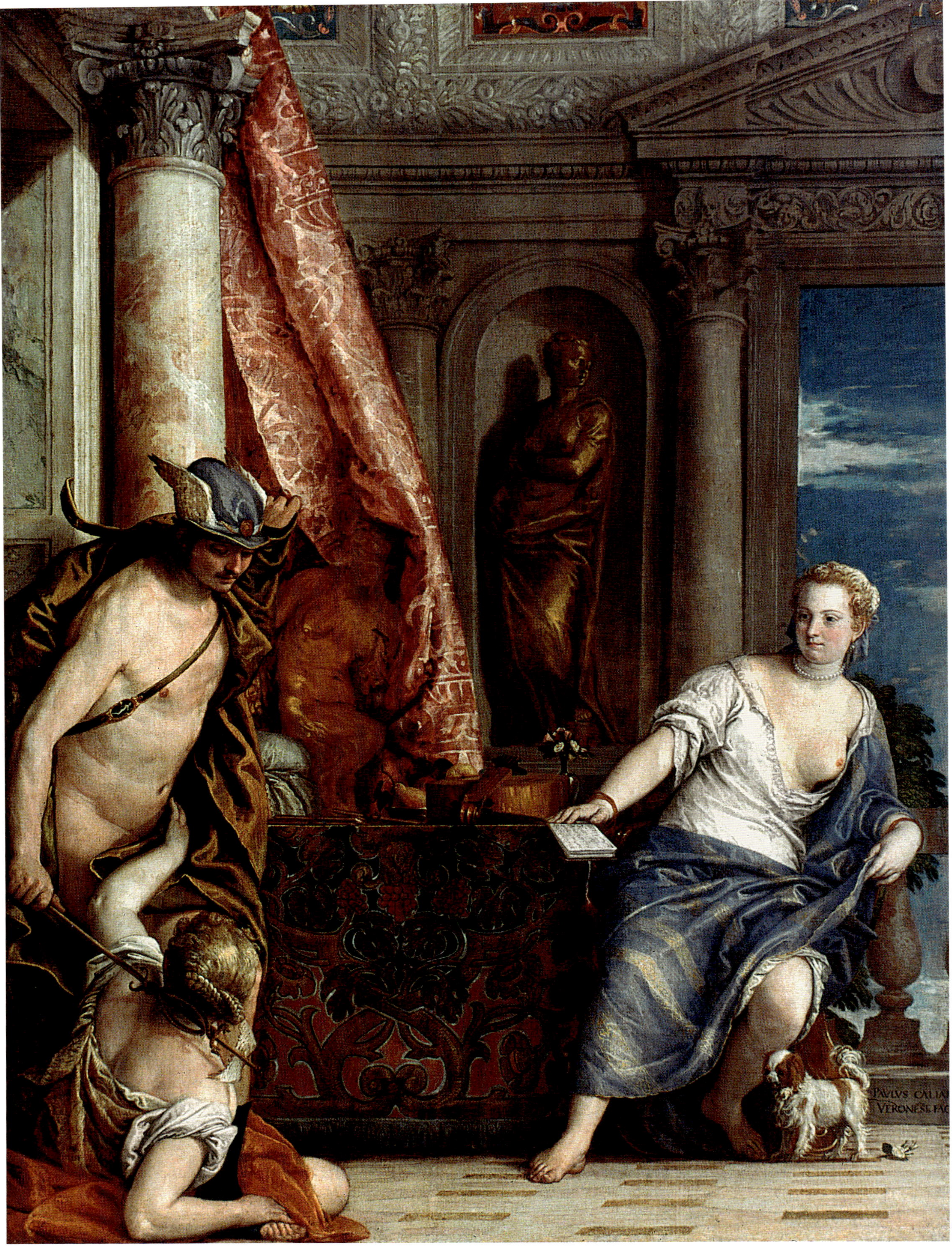
PAVLVS CALIA
VERONESE. FAC

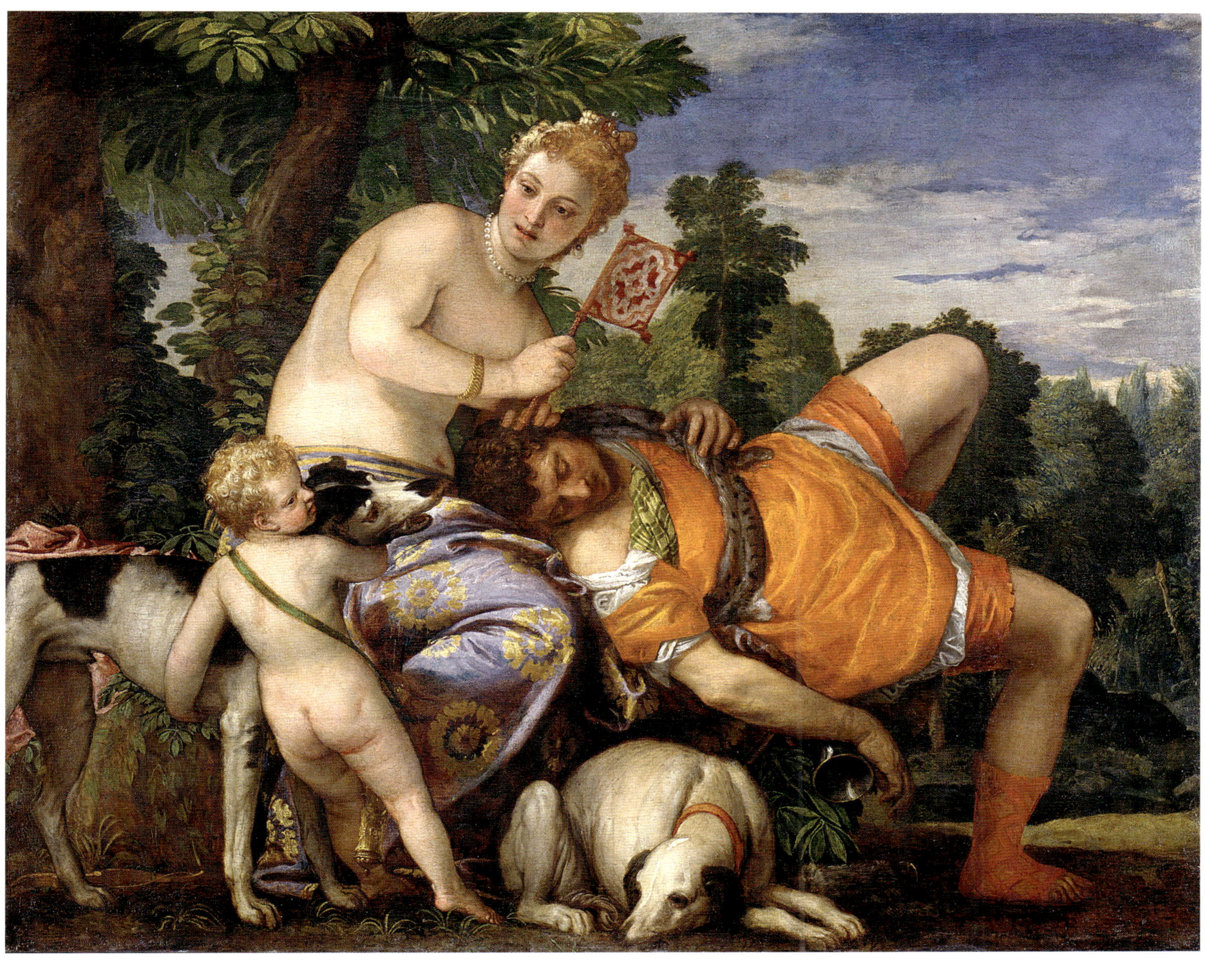

Mercury, Herse and Aglaurus, 1579 (?), canvas, 232 × 173 cm. Cambridge, Fitzwilliam Museum

Venus and the Sleeping Adonis, 1581 (?), canvas, 212 × 190 cm. Madrid, Museo del Prado, inv. 482

CHAPTER IX

"A lume spento" / "With Tapers Quenched"

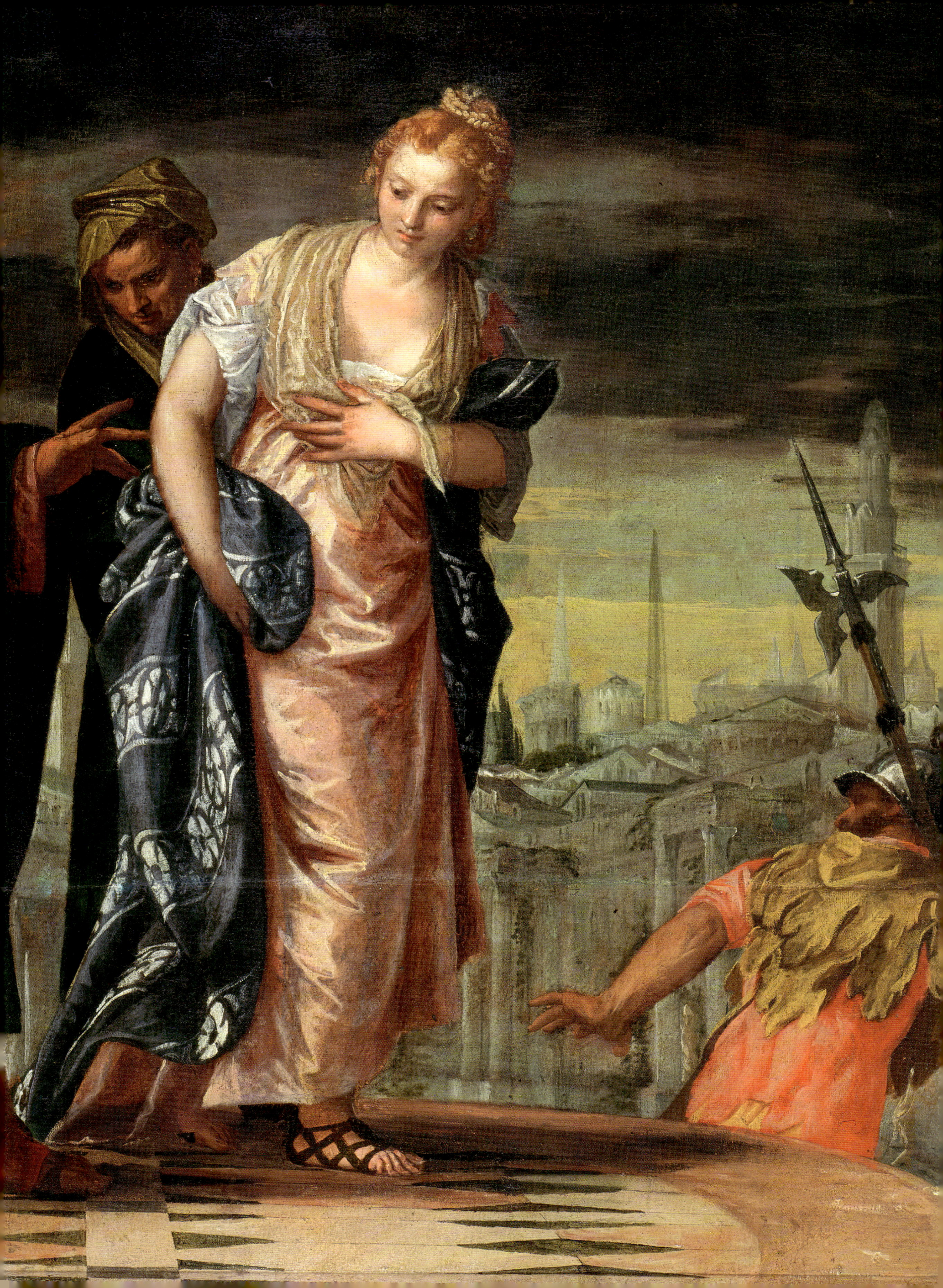

In the years following the plague which had terrible effects from Veneto to Sicily, other military and economic episodes testify to the decline of the Adriatic power; the Republic holds, confirming the sacredness of the institutions, maintaining efficient judiciaries and all the manifestations of Justice with which the withering away of Power is contained. Paolo Paruta discusses *Della perfettione della vita politica* (1579) considering, well before the declarations of the American colonists, that the purpose of politics is happiness, and happiness is peace, it is the guarantee of tranquility and institutional balance, it is the acceptance and maintenance of a balance based on harmony, that of the Republic. However, Paruta does not hide a biting melancholy for a glorious age, already gone; the gaze remains turned to the past, the memory recovers an experience that will not return: the Serenissima triumphant on the seas.

A whole world is tired of itself. The Renaissance is far away, researching tensions and experimental leaps have no more strength. The drive that had designed the new Rome has run out, had believed in endless cultural hegemonies and prestige. The return to order, dictated by the Church, was affirmed, the merchants falling back on secure incomes, on unadventurous investments in lands. Diplomacy cautiously observes the growing strength of national monarchies, Spanish rule and its feet of clay, the continuous convulsions of France, the disaster of Flanders, with which cultural and economic ties were primary and essential in the past. Relations with the entire Nordic world, now definitively separated by faith and culture, are loose. The rigid control of consciences and ideas is also astonishment in the face of the energies of renewal that the Catholic Church finds within itself, promoted by new orders, engaged in every intellectual and artistic expression, in the promotion of new constructions and inexhaustible, increasingly splendid ornaments of churches, in the revision and updating of the pastoral attitude; even so the Venetian diversity, the use of religion as the ideological cement of the state crumble. The identity of a civilization that had felt, in many moments, autonomous and different, is slowly being lost.

Now artistic commissioning collaborates more than before in social regulation, in the construction of consensus, in the transmission of behavior models. At the end of a season that represents the apex of the Venetian pictorial form, with the last Titian, the expressive fullness of Tintoretto's realism, the luministic mastery of Veronese, the cultural climate is changing. The conclusion of the Council of Trent penetrates and determines the forms of piety and the Catholic rite in different ways, while threatening clouds warn the arrival of the storm on the legendary Venetian freedoms, starting with the publishing activity which was, for a century, the most varied , enterprising, rich and productive of Europe.

There is a bitter restlessness in the most fragile, most impoverished city, deprived of so many inhabitants, so the joyful and glorious painting, the happy and bright colours, the specificity of Veronese's art, tend to fade away, to transform. Even Paolo Caliari, always energetic director of a very active workshop, perceives a different cultural climate compared to the world before Lepanto. In the eighties he sets the scenes in less luminous atmospheres, in more shady interiors, he tries nocturnal scenes, illustrates a more aching religiosity, paints many painful variations of

Duke of Buckingham Series: Christ and the Adulteress,
1580-1588, canvas,
143 × 288 cm, detail. Vienna,
Kunsthistorisches Museum
Inv.-Nr. GG 3676

Crucifixions. The adherence to the indications of the Council of Trent is more heartfelt, and his sacred painting has a greater gradient of conviction and edifying will, offering the example of the martyr saints for meditation. His scenes are increasingly crowded, as if to communicate a need for presence, and his profane and sensual world always offers a moralistic message.

Even for the beloved church of San Sebastiano the tone changes. For the Hieronymites Paolo painted various works now lost: the church banner to be carried in procession, a hermit Saint Jerome in the passageway to access the sacristy, some frescoes in the cloister. There will be more in his last decade of activity: on the altar of the chapel formerly belonging to the Grimani family, the third on the left, there will be the small *Madonna and Child, Saint Catherine and Friar Michele Spaventi*; the friar arrived in Venice in 1578, the palette is still very fine, but undoubtedly less creative, more dull. The *Crucifixion* on the third altar on the right, in the Garzoni chapel, on the other hand, already has those withered colors, the melancholy tone that belongs to the later production. The fainting of the Mother, who looks at the Son on the cross, fosters an intense bond, as for expressions and colours of clothes, and rustle of fabrics, between three women, while a suffering John is isolated, foreshortened to the right.

FAITH ILLUSTRATED

The images of Christ multiply, with variations around iconographic motifs less frequented by Paolo in the past. Intimism dominates, as well as more nocturnal settings, a more heartfelt and participatory religiosity. The canvas with the *Dead Christ Supported by Angels and Saints Jacob, Mark and Jerome*, exhibited in the Strazzaroli chapel, in the very popular church of San Giuliano on the way to the Mercerie, is already an exercise on the lights of a last sunset and on the weight, the tiredness, the suffering of the body. The work, very particular, was mentioned by Borghini and always seen on site, still praised by Anton Maria Zanetti at the end of the eighteenth century, but already considered almost illegible due to the consequence of the smoke of the countless candles offered over the centuries, and neglected by connoisseurs until modern restorations. Veronese composes a double scene: below, three saints in a pyramidal scheme, in the physical and natural space, above, separated by a blue-green sky, a tragic, evocative Pietà. The face of the dead Christ, still clawed by the crown of thorns, is in the shadows: he is contrasted by an angelic face in full light, the expression altered by a very human affliction. Of another angel there is almost only a profile lowered into the shadows. It is Jacob, the pilgrim apostle, the wayfarer with the shell to collect water with which to quench his thirst on the infinite journey. He sees the scene in his mind. He is leaning on his cane, over a step. The Pietà is also the image conceived by those who have to write it, communicate it in the sacred texts, by the evangelist Mark, in a green robe and orange cloak, with his right hand touching a lion – this too with a humanly afflicted expression – and by Jerome, kneeling, hand to chest. This silent conversation takes place in the triangular composition, a sacred conversation of high intensity in the space marked by the buildings of History. But now all the architectural elements, the steps, the plinth, the cornice are neglected, the grass and plants grow between the cracks, the stone is corroded by time. Jacob, the pilgrim par excellence, comes from an abandoned world, communicates the meaning of that Pietà, of sacrifice, to those who will bear witness to it. A reading fully in line with the Tridentine interpretations.

Even more intense and heartfelt, but not dramatic, just tired and painful, is the depiction of the *Pietà (Dead Christ, the Madonna and an Angel)*. An exceptionally simplified composition, reduced to three characters, evidently aimed at devotion, perhaps created for a Dominican of the convent of Santi Giovanni e Paolo in Venice. Agostino Carracci engraved it with a burin, with faithful attention. It already entered the English royal collections in the early seventeenth century, and then passed through different properties, until its purchase in 1772 by Catherine II of Russia. The work

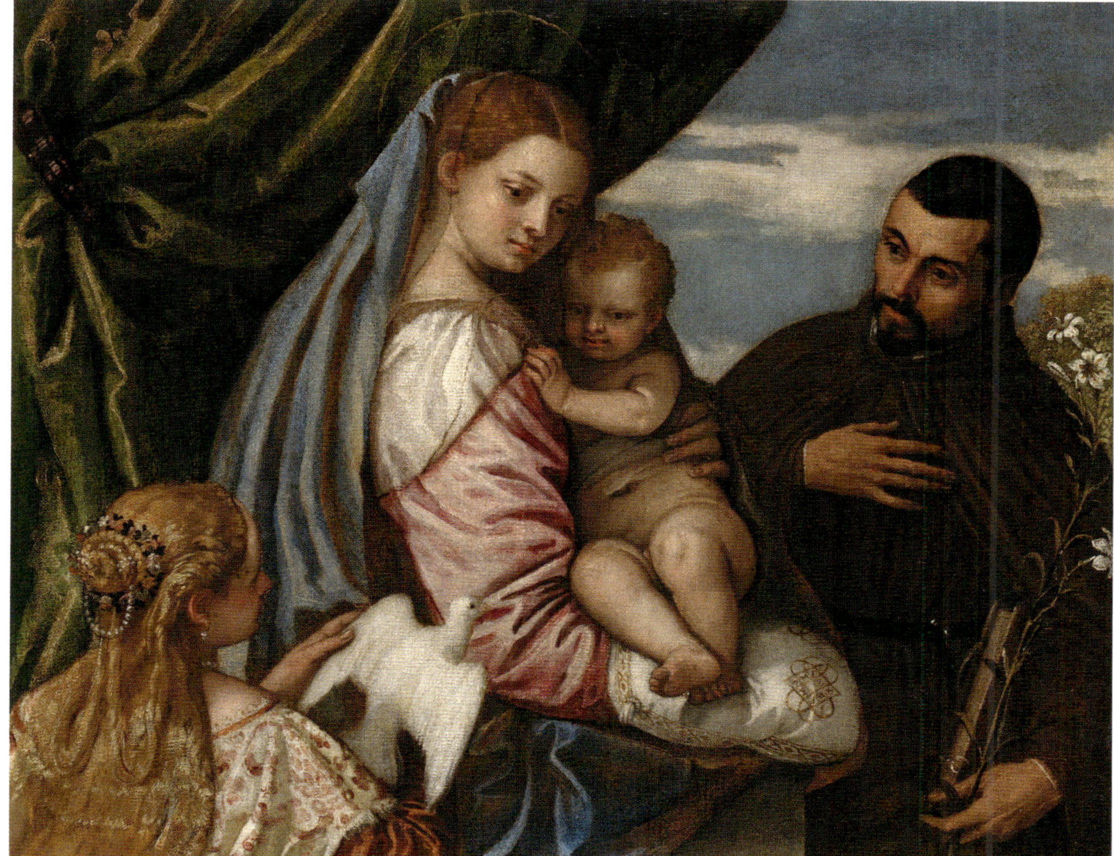

Madonna and Child, Saint Catherine and Friar Michele Spaventi, after 1580, canvas, 56 × 67 cm. Venice, church of San Sebastiano

has always been appreciated for the intense relationship between the three faces, that of a bloodless Christ, in the serenity of liberating death after extreme suffering, that of a young Mother, moved by all her affection, that of an angel who shows us with the effect of chromatic evidence, his vital fingers intertwined with the exhausted hand, wounded by the nail. Three different conditions and emotions pass through the faces, illuminated by a very delicate light; but then each figure has a decided monumentality, a weight evident above all in Christ. The contrast between the rosy red of the angelic garment and the earthy tones of the dead man, bled out on the white of the shroud, is in the register of the best Veronese.

Around the images of the crucifixion and piety Paolo creates works of great intensity, each with a precise identity, in a research without tiredness and without repetitions. Two examples that are significantly different from each other, yet created after a short time, are the *Crucifixions* of the Venetian church of San Lazzaro dei Mendicanti, and that of the Louvre. The first presents a deliberately simple, almost medieval layout. The painter conveys all the solitude of the event, that blood shed by the Crucifix with a saving function; painting, through the mediation of colour and reduced light, is capable of interpreting the anxieties of the historical present and of contrition in front of the divine sacrifice.

The canvas is different, particularly in the choice of reduced sizes in an unprecedented square format, prepared for private devotion, a beautiful and problematic *Calvary*: the three crosses appear tall and isolated, against the dark cloudless sky which actually occupies four-fifths of the painting. Far away is Jerusalem, the Mother has fainted in John's arms. But then her glance is drawn to the mysterious protagonist, a female figure entirely wrapped in a conspicuously yellow-orange cloak, her face completely hidden, only the gesture of her hands clasped to her chest testifies to contrition, anguished consternation in the face of pain. The figure turns to Mary, with suffering and pity. For the viewer the task to identify himself in this scene, and identify her.

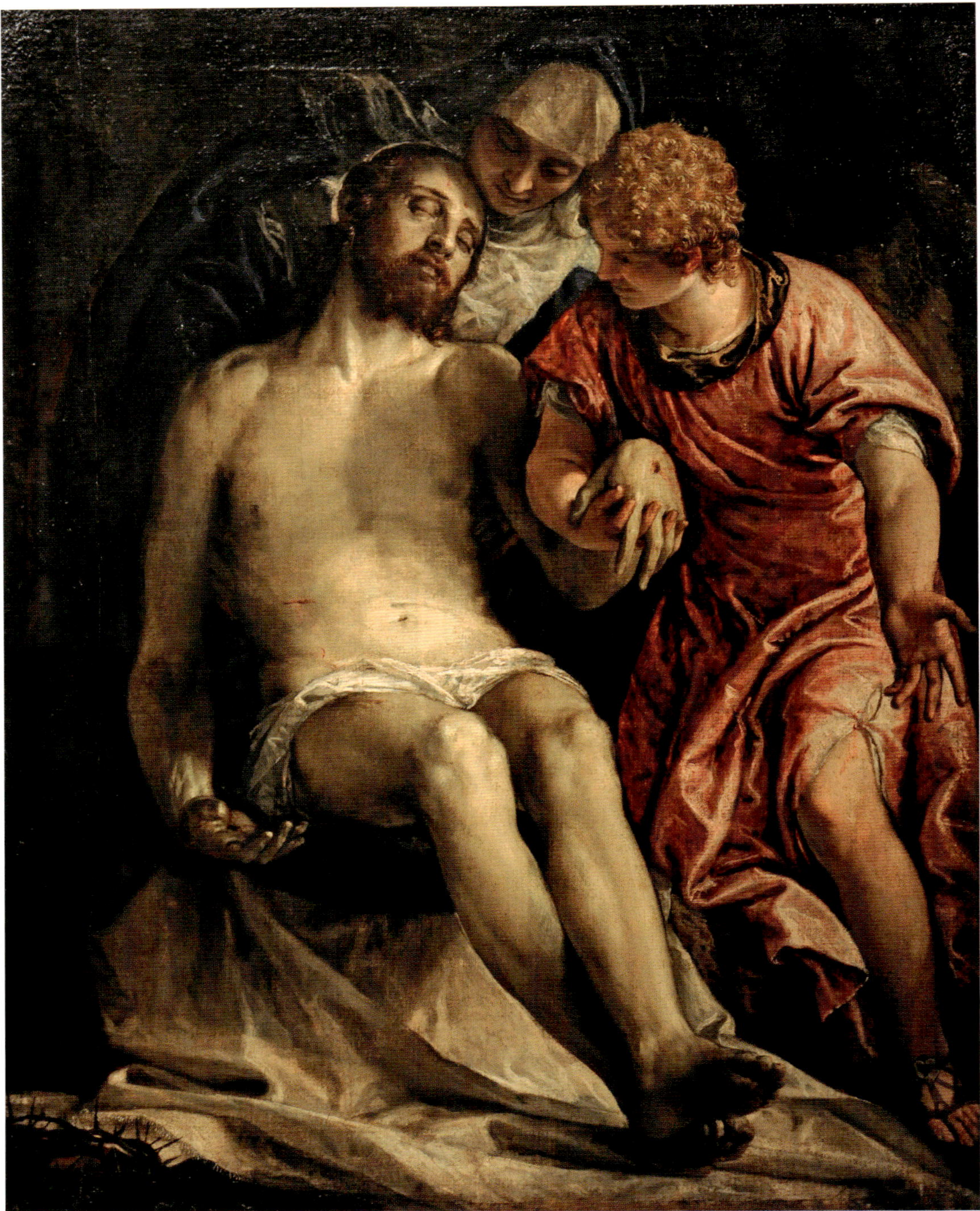

Dead Christ, the Madonna and an Angel, 1580-1581, canvas, 147 × 111.5 cm. Saint Petersburg, Hermitage

Indeed, even on a stylistic level, the works that Paolo created in the ninth decade mark an evident, albeit limited, change, with a lesser definition of the drawing, a brushstroke closer to the tonal painting of the Venetian tradition. The painter has just passed his half a century, he is in full force: the change should not be attributed to age but precisely to the new cultural atmosphere, to the dialogue and expectations of the patrons, and above all to the reasons for painting, to the attention and sensitivity with which he observes the new experiences that are maturing in Italian painting, and the intellectual ferment of the various Academies.
This is the case of the *Coronation of the Virgin* created for the Venetian church of Ognissanti and today at the Accademia, paid for on 23 October 1583 by the female convent annexed to the church. It is a very crowded canvas, in which all the figures generated by Paolo's inventions seem to add up. At the top is the coronation scene, with two angels who are placing a ducal mantle

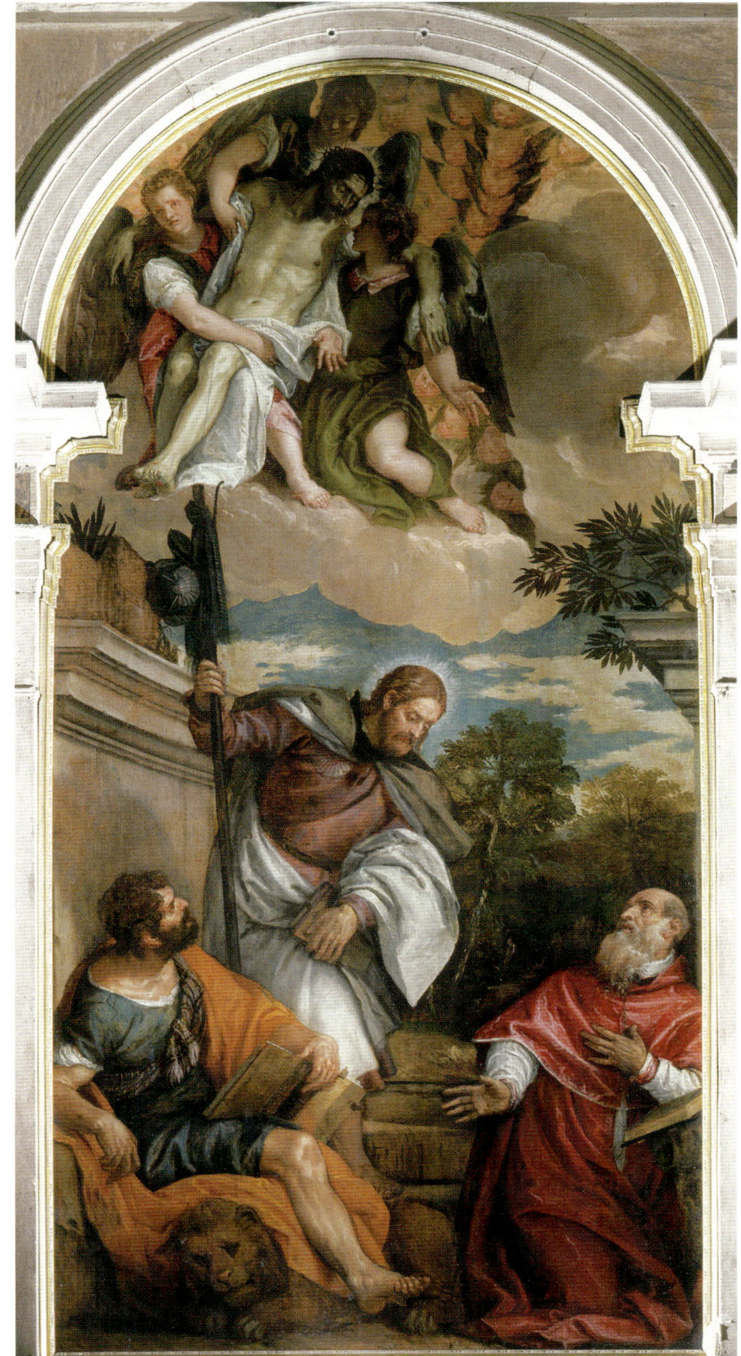

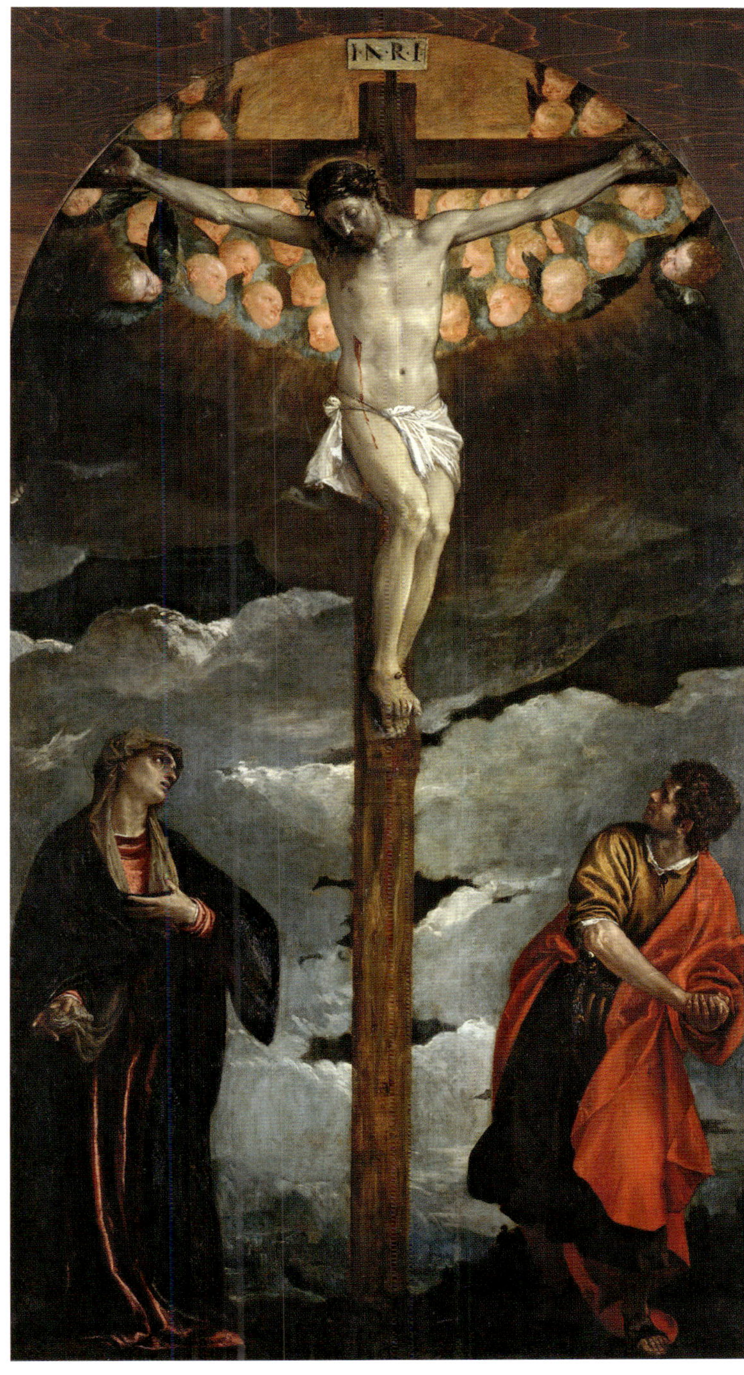

on Mary, dressed in light blue brocade. She has just been crowned by the Father, and her Son hands her the sceptre. A crowd of cherub heads escort the dove into the clearest light. In the lower part, about fifty apostles, evangelists, martyrs, saints, fathers of the Church, a crowd sitting or standing on mattresses of clouds. Particularly perceptible is the image of a Benedictine nun, who could represent Saint Scholastica, who indicates the scene in dialogue with a martyr, perhaps Lucy. A portrait or at least a tribute to the abbess Lucia Michiel, the patron, maybe. Precisely the different faces in which we recognize someone already glimpsed in the *Conviti* and in the sacred scenes, or the entire Veronese company, as well as a certain didactic and scrupulous choice of attributes, had led to consider this canvas as a great workshop work, supervised by Paolo but conducted by hands that conformed to cartoons and drawings, to ways of colouring that had been imitated for years. In the work on the lights, on the more distant, almost evanes-

Dead Christ Supported by Angels and Saints Jacob, Mark and Jerome, 1581-1582, canvas, 365 × 181 cm. Venice, church of San Giuliano

Christ Crucified between the Madonna and Saint John, approx. 1580, canvas, 305 × 165 cm. Venice, church of San Lazzaro dei Mendicanti

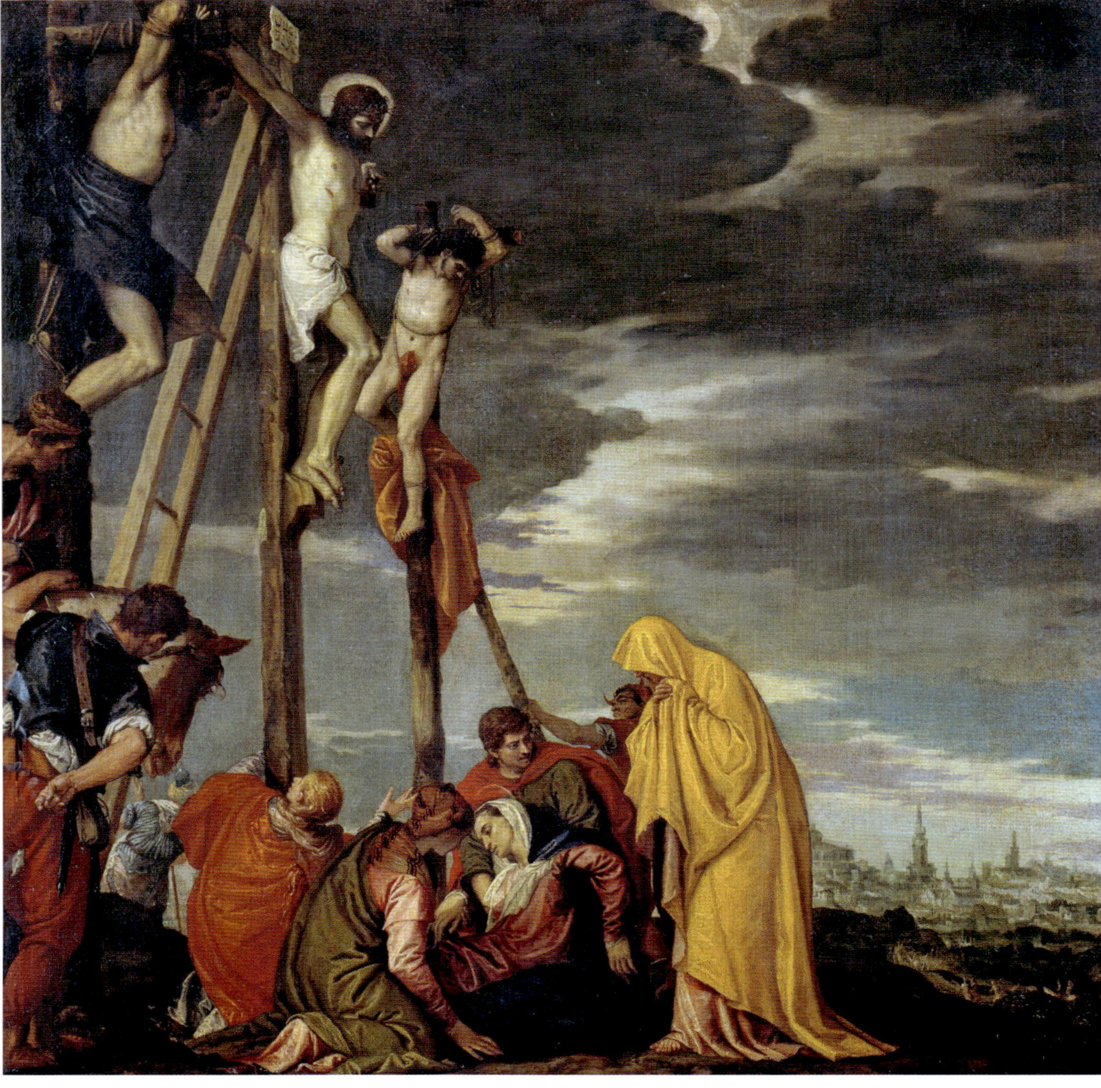

The Calvary, 1580,
canvas, 102 × 102 cm. Paris,
Musée du Louvre, inv. 1195

The canvas was probably intended for private devotion: it is certainly one of the best, most intimate and painful expressions of Paolo's religiosity. Very skilful in the light illuminating the Crucifix, in the distant Jerusalem on the very low horizon, and then in the mysterious figure in yellow, in whom the pious believers can identify themselves.

cent figures and on some faces in full shadow, the theatrical game so typical of the Maestro was recognized. And yet we have a drawing, certainly by Paolo, where the names of various saints are also indicated; it should be, as in other cases, a reminder, but it directs us towards autography also in detail and not only in the overall design. The work, underestimated, not mentioned (Pallucchini), attributed to others (A. Venturi), was for Boschini "the table with all the saints, one can well say the Portrait of Paradise, made by the singular brush of Paolo Veronese" and Zanetti reported it as "excellent in the composition, and the parts are beautiful". It will be the very presence of the Oxford drawing that first convinced Cocke and then Rearick both of the autography and of the quality. In front of it the distance of Veronese's journey is measured in forty years: a slow and progressive becoming, a change of taste that "feels" his time, a reinvention that is already an anticipation and intuition of the following age, the results of which will converge in the great season of the Roman Baroque.
Indeed, back in 1988 Sandro Sponza confessed the first impression of "cumbersome cumbersomeness, confused jumble" which obviously depends on the twentieth-century taste, refractory to so much seventeenth-centuryism. If one is not attracted by the invention of postures and iconographic attributes, if one does not have the taste for appreciating an expression that refers to a virtue, a gesture that qualifies, a measure of holiness such as a dense dialogue, an engaging commentary on the Holy Scriptures between Jerome and Paul, immediately at the entrance to that whirlwind of Paradise, near which even Lawrence leans out to converse with someone

holding the palm of martyrdom while not leaving his griddle: in short, if one does not appreciate the cumulative invention, one denies Veronese the invention of the scene. While the ability to pass from the serious and deep colour tones in the lower part, close to the viewer, to the diaphanous and dissolving peaks that accentuate the sudden appearance, on the solid cloud, of the cloaked Virgin is still all Paolo's. It is always the Virgin/Venice in glory. It is the mature Caliari, on the threshold of an old age that fate will prevent him from going through.

TWO MISSING CYCLES

Crucial, in evaluating the final Veronese phase, was the fact that we could no longer appreciate, together and locally, the wide-ranging undertakings that would have given us back, such as San Sebastiano and Maser, the creative complexity and the state of Paolo Caliari's pictorial art in his sixth decade of life, the fourth decade of his profession. These are two fundamental cycles, one created for the Venetian church of San Nicolò della Lattuga, the other known as the Duke of Buckingham Series, sometimes hypothesized for the monastery of the Converts on Giudecca. These two homogeneous groups were dismembered after a few years, sold passing through different collections, and today the individual canvases are scattered among various museums, which makes it difficult to compare and reconstruct the relationships between the scenes.

The small convent of San Nicolò, known as "della Lattuga", better known as San Nicoletto, was governed by a particular constitution, welcoming well-deserving and elderly Franciscan friars. The building, although close to the largest Franciscan convent in Venice, the Frari, did not depend on the order, but on the Procuratori di San Marco: and this was clear right from the foundation wanted by Nicolò Lion, procurator, miraculously healed from a serious illness thanks to the lettuce (lattuga in Italian) grown in the convent garden. The community, about ten friars, enjoyed considerable intellectual and economic autonomy and freedom, was endowed with a very rich library and organized readings and lessons on Sacred Scripture, Logic and Philosophy: for public benefit, as clearly indicated: "for public benefit to transform that place into the form of a college, where the auditors have to practice in disputations, lectures and other acts usual to be done in good Academies" (Venice, State Archive, San Nicolò, b. 2, c. 18r-v). The guardian of the convent in the seventies, Andrea Michiel from Bergamo, skilful and enterprising, undertook a restoration and preparation of the church, which ended with the consecration, on 17 September 1582, of a building completely decorated with the grandiose cycle of canvases by Paolo Veronese and all the family members: Benedetto had created a Christ before Pilate, Alvise del Friso the Way to Calvary, Carletto, the young and very gifted Carlo Caliari, had been entrusted with the Resurrection, the Deposition, the Last Supper and two more canvases. There will also be the presence of Gabriele Caliari: we owe Zanetti the confirmation and identification of all of Paolo's relatives, each with independent evidence in the Christological sequence of a Via Crucis in line with the dictates of the Council of Trent.

The church was suppressed in 1806, and the precious series of paintings ended up dispersed: the inspector of public paintings Pietro Edwards sent some of them to the Academy, others were left in deposits. Edwards, who since 1777 was active in organizing interventions on public paintings on behalf of the Senate, also as academic professor, secretary of the College of painters and director of the public restoration laboratory located in the refectory of Santi Giovanni e Paolo, was instrumental to try to maintain the Venetian artistic heritage during the years of the French storm. He then obtained in the Kingdom of Italy the appointment as "preserver of all paintings and other art objects", delegate for the selection of works of art in the suppressed buildings, and "preserver of the gallery of the Academy of fine arts in Venice and of the Farsetti

Gallery". Actions of defense but also of dismemberment: works sent to Brera, others exhibited, some stored, several sold, with enormous consequences for the artistic heritage. Among those saved from French greed is the altarpiece originally on the high altar of the church of San Antonio in Torcello, with *Saint Anthony Abbot between Saint Cornelius and Saint Cyprian*. Now at Brera, it was brilliantly restored and enlivened by a graceful and witty page boy in total green, fashionable puffed trousers over tights, who holds the great tome on which Pope St. Cornelius reads. Overall it is one of the brightest tests for fabrics.

The cycle of San Nicoletto connected altarpieces, canvases for the ceiling, for the presbytery and the side chapels: in the end, about eighty canvases produced not only by family members, but also by all the different participants in the workshop, even in different eras: beyond to aids, pupils and collaborators, there was the Venetian circle that referred to Paolo's work, such as Jacopo Palma il Giovane, Marco Vecellio and Paolo Fiammingo, for which Rodolfo Pallucchini could conclude: "Compared to the last Veronese activity, this complex decoration corresponded to what had been the decoration of the church of San Sebastiano in his youth, but the whole school was also present in San Nicolò".

Among the canvases in San Nicoletto, the *Baptism and Temptations of Christ* stands out for its innovative solution, visible today in Brera. The contemporary representation of the two events is rare and theologically interesting, in the logic of *Imitatio Christi* where, in opposition to Lutheranism, the need is imposed both for purification and temptation, or rather for the fight against sin, fulfilled through Reconciliation, Confession, act of humiliation like that of Christ who is baptized and accepts the diabolical temptation. In the same way the believer will be able to imitate Christ by entrusting himself to the intercession of the Church. All those who saw the original arrangement of the canvas in San Nicoletto – Ridolfi, Sansovino, Boschini and Zanetti – noticed that above the canvas of the *Baptism and Temptations* there was another scene that united two moments: the *Last Supper* and the *Footwashing* painted by Benedetto Caliari, where the washing of the feet, humiliation, is associated with the purification in the Eucharist, what the faithful reaches through confession and contrition. The theological message contained in Paolo's canvas is strengthened and clarified.

In the very rich decoration of San Nicoletto eleven canvases were attributed to Paolo: on the ceiling the *Adoration of the Magi*, the four *Evangelists*, *St. Nicholas Confirmed Bishop of Myra* and the *Stigmata of Saint Francis*, now on the ceiling of the chapel of the Rosary in the church of Santi Giovanni e Paolo. Having suffered serious damage over time, the format had to be reduced and changed in the 19th century, so today the *St. Nicholas* is a tondo without the side lobes, of which we know through copies. The final effect of the ceiling was undoubtedly grandiose, with the multiplication of crowded figures, while the luminosity thickens, the architectural scene loses its classicism. It seems to see a work by Pietro da Cortona, the Roman painter who will best represent the "neo-Veronesian" passion of the third and fourth decade of the seventeenth century, when Paolo is admired and sought after more than Titian, and his canvases acquire dizzy evaluations.

Also "many small figures" characterize the *Crucifixion* today in the Gallerie dell'Accademia, marked by the accentuated pyramidal composition on the left, while a larger story descends from a gloomy Jerusalem, silhouetted against an increasingly cloudy sky. A dangerous ride unites Golgotha and the city, while a group of seated women seems almost extraneous to the sacred event, the soldiers play dice for their clothes, on the right the dead come out of tombs uncovered by the earthquake. This is really the feeling after the Great Plague, in a Venice that hasn't forgotten the voids and the dead, the end of so many activities and the tiredness of the survivors. From a pictorial point of view, Paolo Caliari is still and always the Master: those landscapes of his towards Jerusalem will be taken up and traced by so much painting of the artists following Tenebrism, and absolutely by 16th-century art.

Saint Anthony Abbot between Saint Cornelius and Saint Cyprian, approx. 1570, canvas, 270 × 180 cm. Milan, Pinacoteca di Brera, inv. 150

Following pages
Baptism and Temptations of Christ (Cycle of San Nicolò della Lattuga), approx. 1582, canvas, 248 × 450 cm. Milan, Pinacoteca di Brera, inv. 151

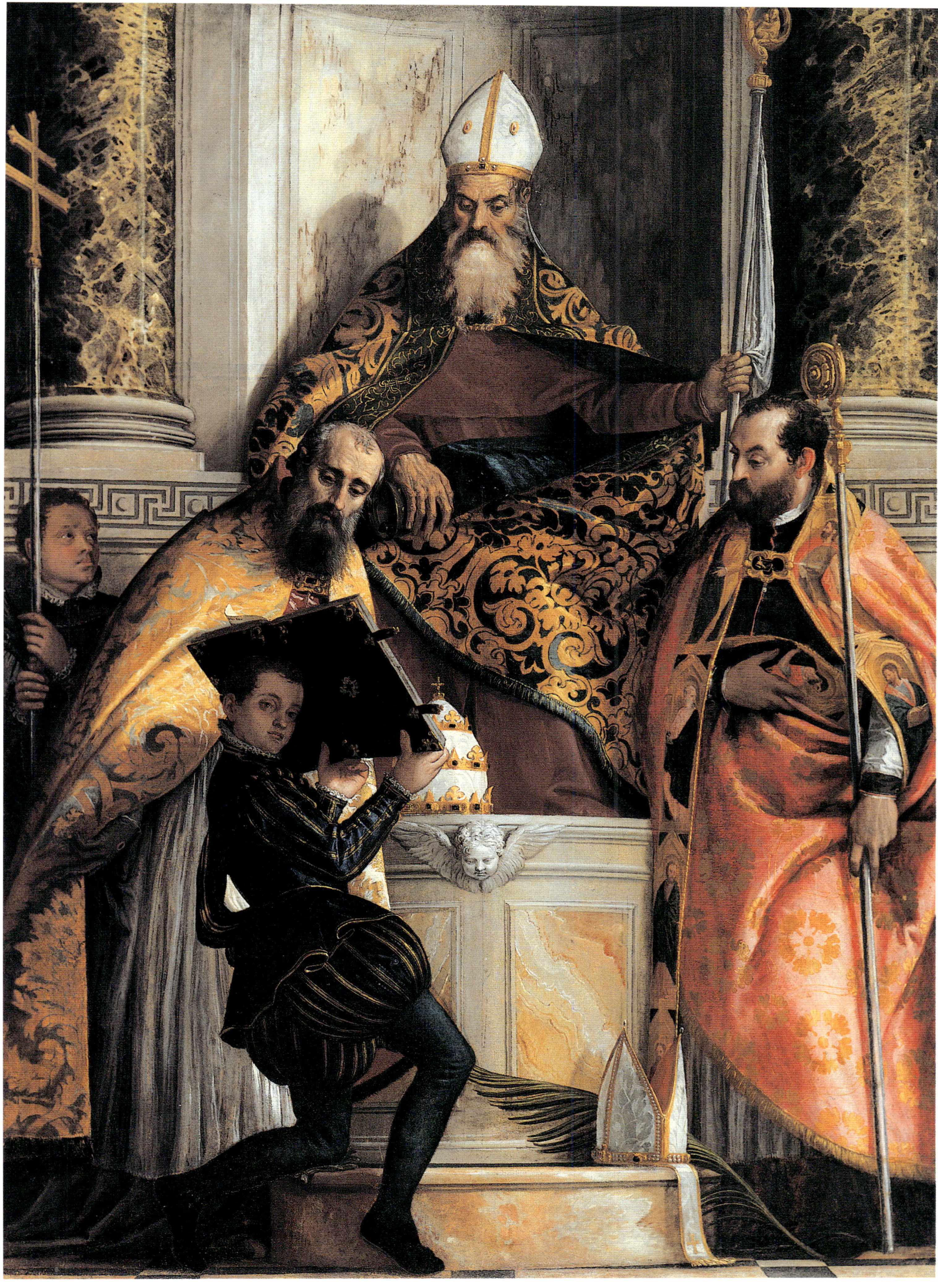

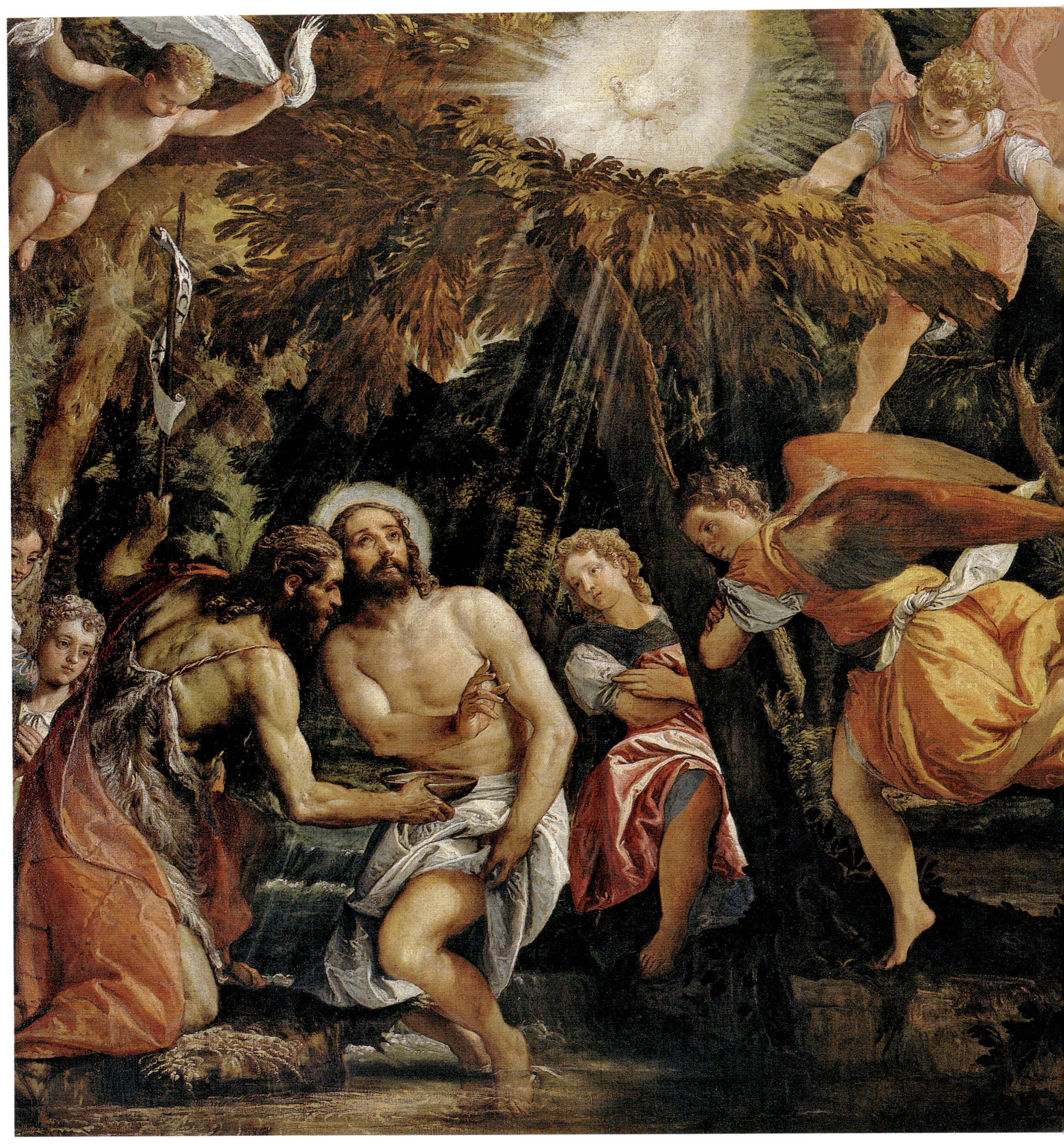

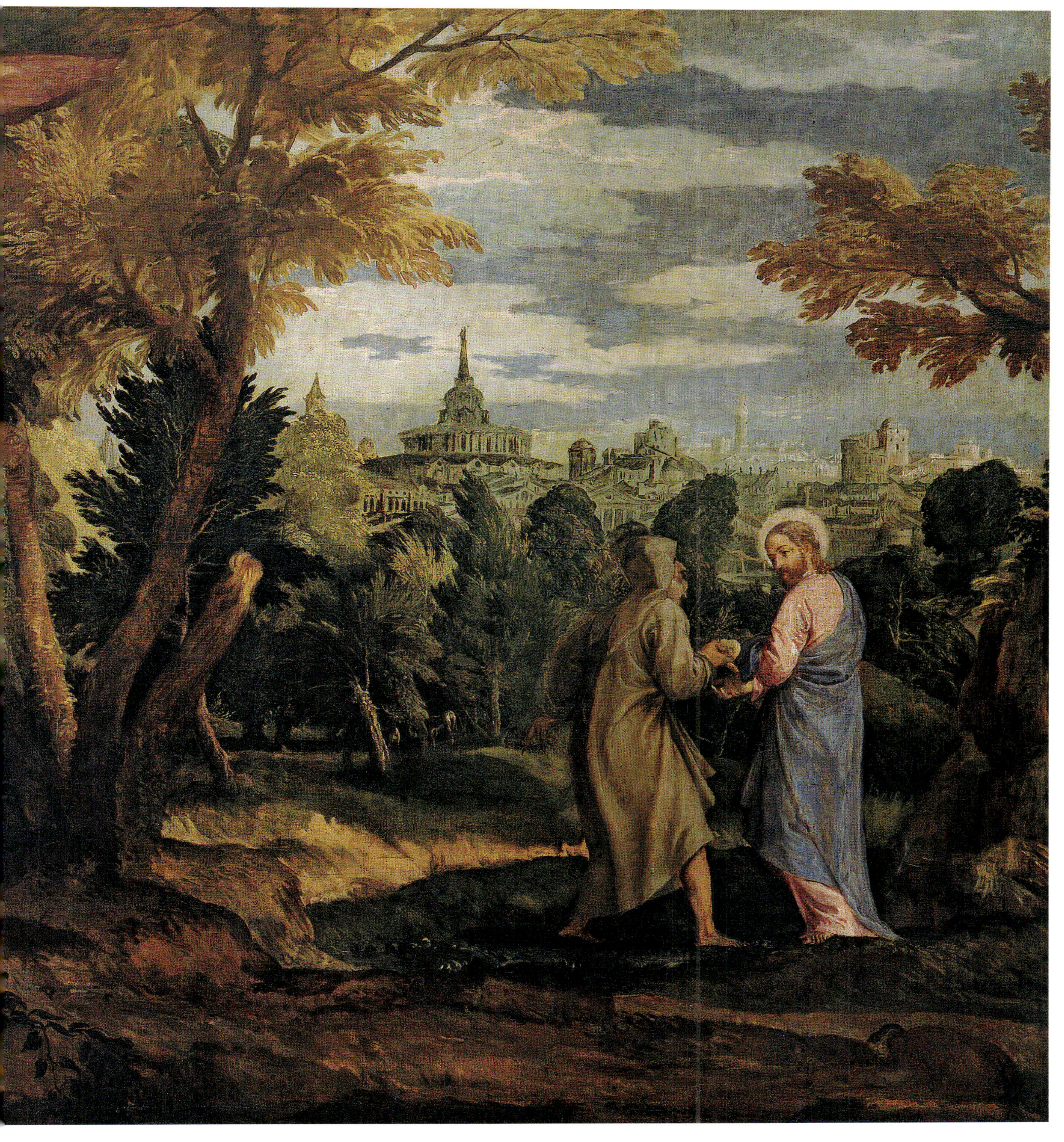

The so-called *Duke of Buckingham Series* is a cycle of stories from the Old and New Testaments; a group of canvases purchased in Venice by Charles de Croy, then passed to the collection of the English duke, returned for sale in 1648, purchased by the Archduke Leopold William, and finally reaching the Habsburg collections in Vienna and Prague. The subjects are: *Christ and the Adulteress*, *Susanna and the Old Men*, *Christ and the Centurion*, *Esther and Ahasuerus*, *Christ and the Samaritan Woman*, *Hagar and Ishmael*, *Lot and his Daughters*: today in Vienna; *Footwashing* and *Adoration of the Shepherds* in Prague, *Rebecca at the Well* in Washington. They measure around 140 by 280 centimetres. They were probably exposed at the top on the wall, having in common the lowered point of view. Mostly they illustrate events connected to female figures, and therefore it was thought they were originally destined to female convents, or churches in hospitals, asylums or jails, for "women of sin converted to God" or former prostitutes. Some Venetian institutions dedicated to them were famous, such as the Converts monastery which became later a women's prison; others had been created just before the last decades of the sixteenth century. But each search yielded only hypothetical results.
The cycle of canvases, although very interesting, is the result of the work in Caliari's workshop, always considering Paolo's creative role; some scenes, such as that of Agar in a landscape in dark green tones, refer to a decidedly Tintoretto-like taste, much closer to Benedetto's sensibility than to that of Paolo. The same is true for Rebecca, while in Esther's fainting we find the usual buffoon dwarf, as per drawings and cartoons. These works await exhaustive studies.

LOOKING FOR SHADOWS

The time for originality was waning: warm and dark tones appear already in the *Apparition of the Madonna to Saint Luke*, on the main altar of the Venetian church bearing the same name. Francesco Sansovino presents it succinctly: "The Saint sitting above the Ox in the posture of writing the Gospel, looking at the Virgin who appears to him from heaven". The evangelist patron of painters has next to himself the tablet on which he portrayed Mary and the work tools, according to the hagiographic tradition. A face already seen, while the young man holding the bishop's crozier, behind the saint, is curious and an evident reference to a patron.
In those shades of shadow, Veronese succeeds in a masterpiece, around 1583: *Christ in the Garden Supported by an Angel*, to be admired in Brera, where it arrived in 1808; an extraordinary nocturne created for the church of Santa Maria Maggiore. The effect of the narrative misalignment, shifting the entire emotional event to the left, allows a large part of the canvas to linger in the atmosphere of the night. Only the light of the Spirit emerges as a blade, makes the angel bodily, a mystical manifestation. It was again Pietro Aretino who imagined Christ fainting in the arms of the angel at the awareness of the Passion: the *Humanity of Christ* was still a source of inspiration. The group of sleepers exhausted by fatigue, the glimmer of dawn behind the typical trees with bent trunks, the cloaks piled up on the far right are just as many proofs of skill, with very little use of colour. The *Assumption of the Virgin*, formerly in the church of Santa Maria Maggiore and today in the Accademia, is to be placed in the ninth decade: it re-proposes inexhaustible inventions, with two apostles leaning on the balustrade and others, who have walked up the stairs, astonished at the Assumption in swirls of robe and cloak. The characterization of the faces and the shadows descending from the clouds is typical of the late Veronese, while the repeated little angelic heads and the usual architectural preparations saw the work of aids.
Curiously, contrary to the conciliar recommendations, supported in particular by Cardinal Borromeo, the portraits of the offerers multiplied in Veronese's sacred painting. This is the case of the *Adoration of the Shepherds* in the version of San Giuseppe di Castello, with the

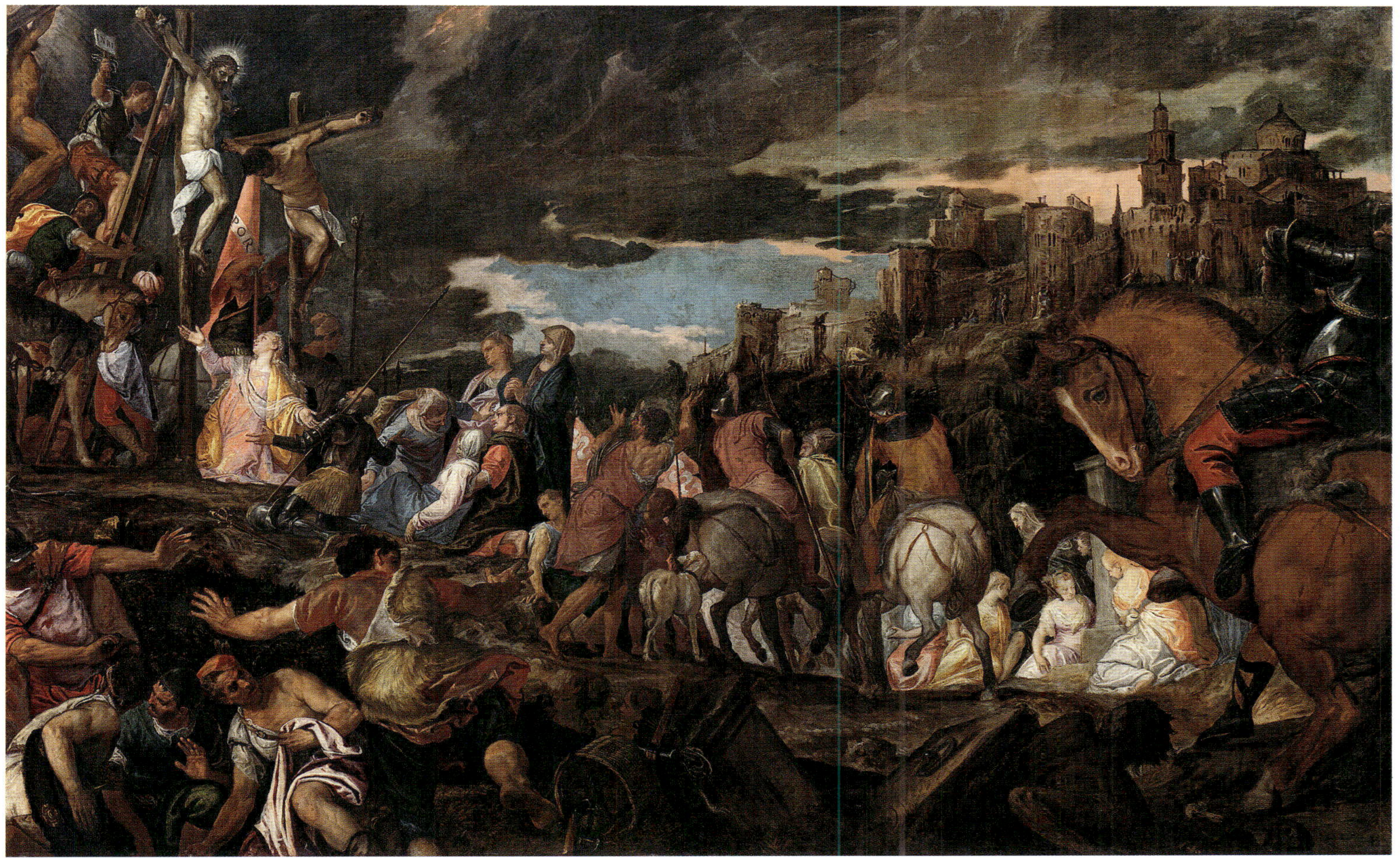

Crucifixion (Cycle of San Nicolò della Lattuga), approx. 1582, canvas, 287 × 447 cm. Venice, Gallerie dell'Accademia, inv. 317

beautiful portrait of Cardinal Girolamo Grimani in the guise of the eponymous saint, with a lion crouched at his feet. In the animals and in the common people, one can verify how much the presence of the Bassanos, with whom Carletto was trained, grew in the workshop, and how dull that brightness of the young Veronese is now.

A final creation, from 1587, is the *Conversion of Saint Pantaleon* for the church of San Pantalon, commissioned by Bartolomeo Borghi, titular parish priest; hagiographic diligence and new use of shadows make it exemplary. Although paid for with only thirty ducats, Paolo committed himself as usual, studying the idea in rapid sketches – one is kept at the Louvre – with the gesture of a doctor addressing the sky. According to legend, Pantaleon, much revered in the Byzantine church, had been educated as a Christian by his mother and trained in the medical profession, practiced with such skill as to bring him to the imperial court of Maximian: we are in the third century. However, it was the miraculous healing of a boy bitten by a snake thanks to the invocation of divine intervention that brought Pantaleon back to faith, conversion and subsequent martyrdom. At the centre of the scene is the doctor who no longer needs the tools kept in the case offered by the page: heavenly help is the blade of light on the face of the boy on the ground, in the arms of the parish priest, resurrected or healed. An angel brings Pantaleon the palm of martyrdom, the notice of the forthcoming sacrifice. In the dark corner on the right the deadly serpent tears itself apart. The saint wears doctors' robes, a red mantle lined with ermine, signalling his very high role as court physician, but the mutilated bust in plain sight is an allusion to an ineffective medical art, the false culture of the gentiles. The priest in white surplice and stole reaffirms the office of charity even in that poor and squalid environment: since at the end of the miserable narrow street a wooden latrine appears protruding over the little street, something truly unusual in Veronese's oeuvre. A realism to which Tintoretto had accustomed us, not Paolo. Meanwhile,

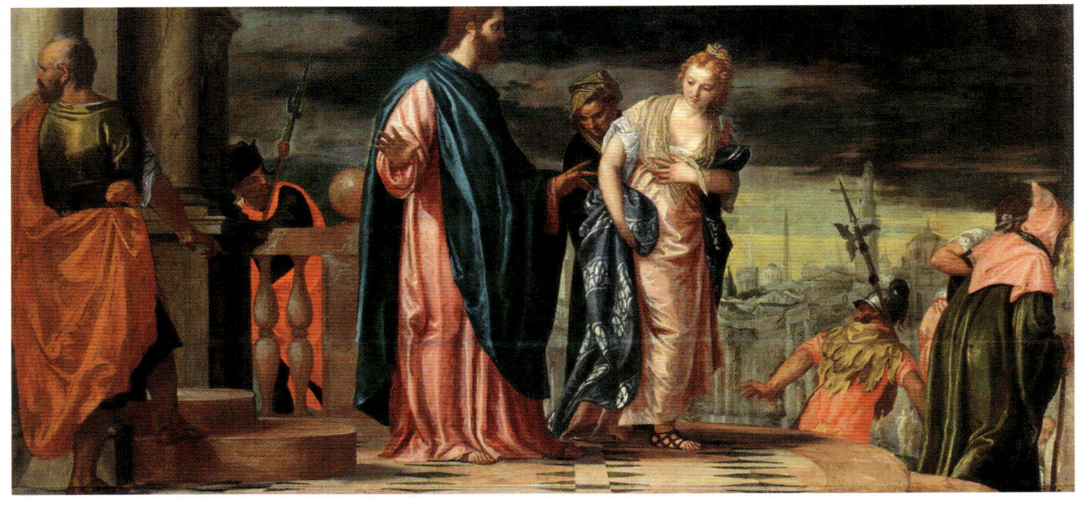

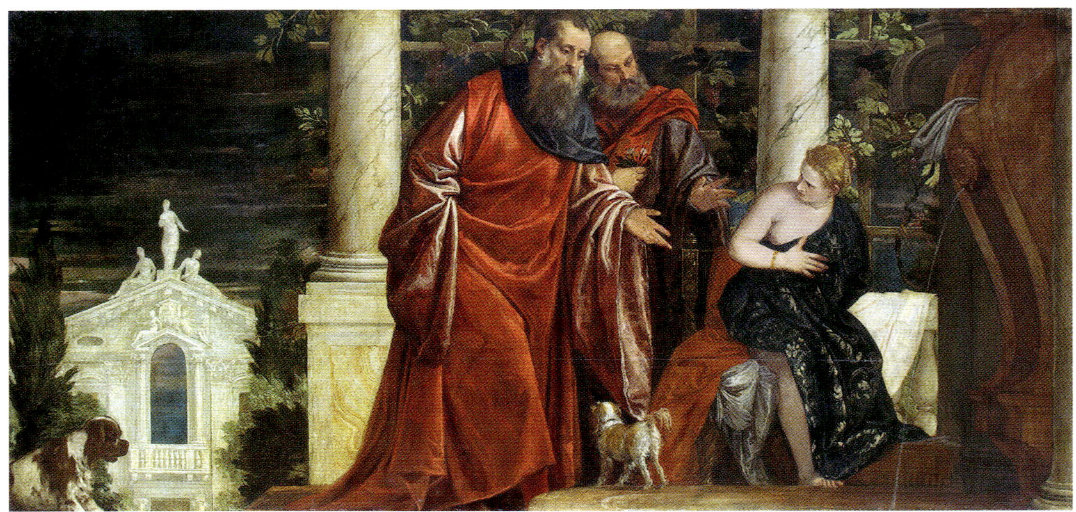

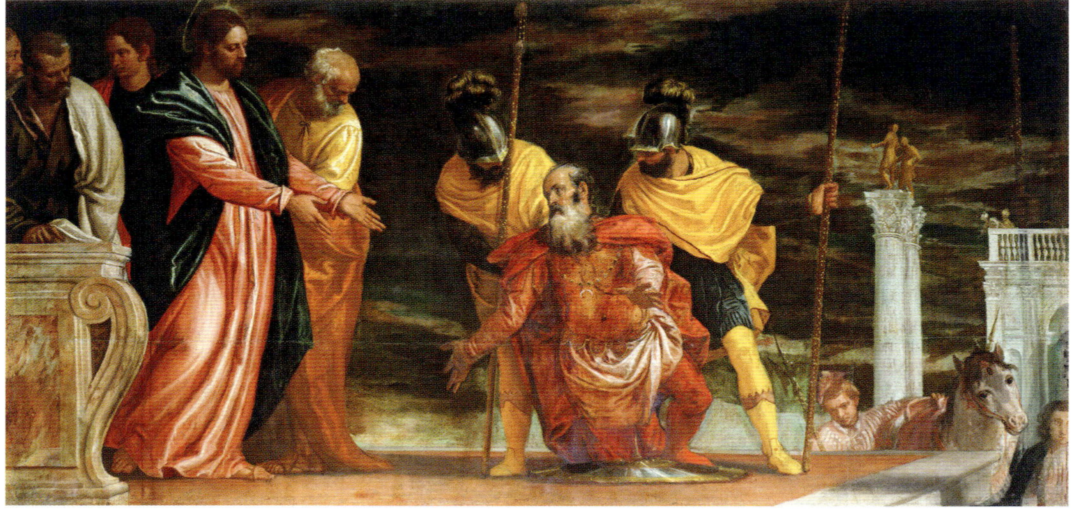

Duke of Buckingham Series.
Vienna, Kunsthistorisches Museum

Christ and the Adulteress,
1580-1588, canvas, 143 × 288 cm, inv. 3676

Susanna and the Old Men,
1580-1588, canvas, 140 × 280 cm, inv. 15

Christ and the Centurion,
1580-1588, canvas, 140 × 280 cm, inv. 3675

Esther and Ahasuerus,
1580-1588, canvas, 141 × 289 cm, inv. 3677

Christ and the Samaritan Woman, 1580-1588, canvas, 143 × 289 cm, inv. 19

Hagar and Ishmael, 1580-1588, canvas, 140 × 282 cm, inv 3673

Lot and his Daughters,
1580-1588, canvas, 138 × 262 cm, inv. 3672

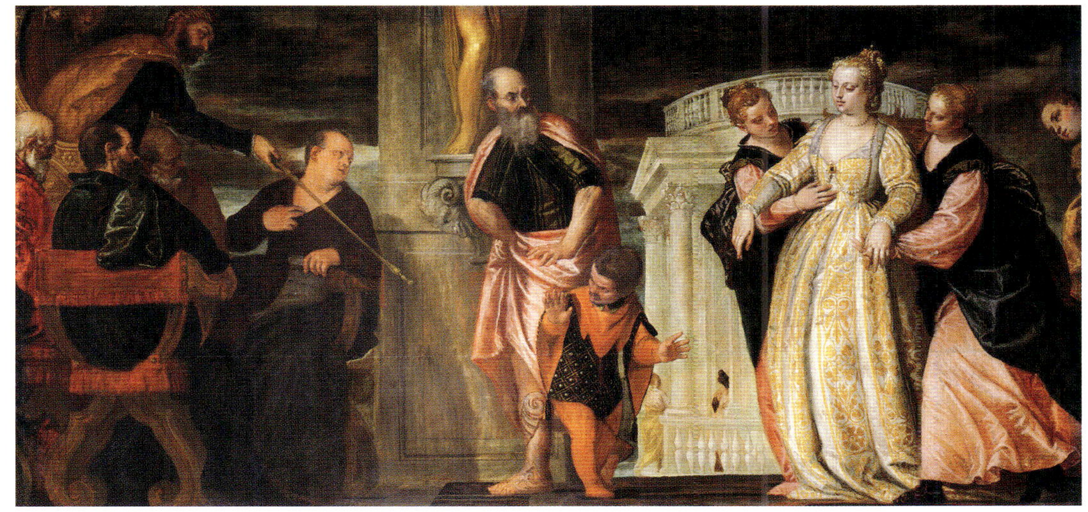
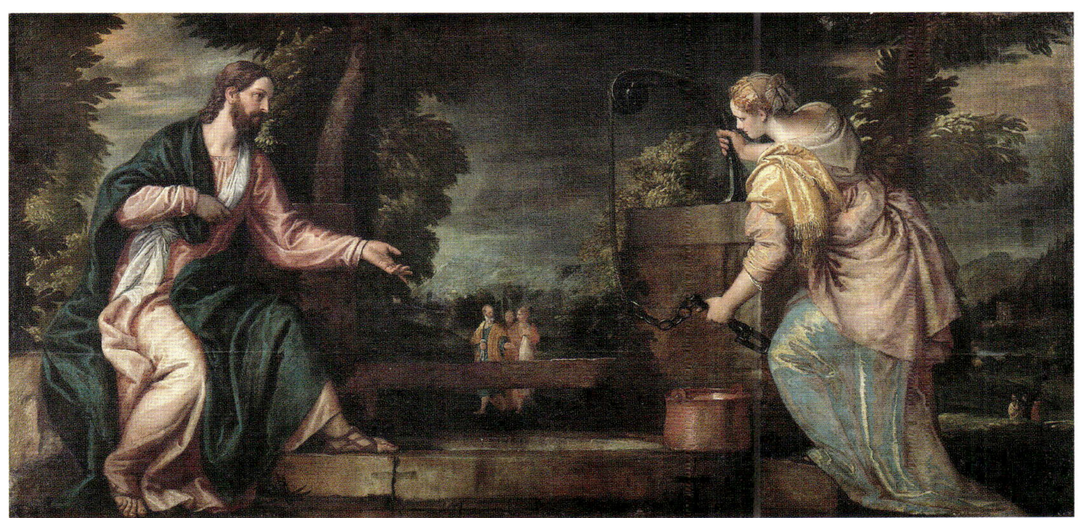
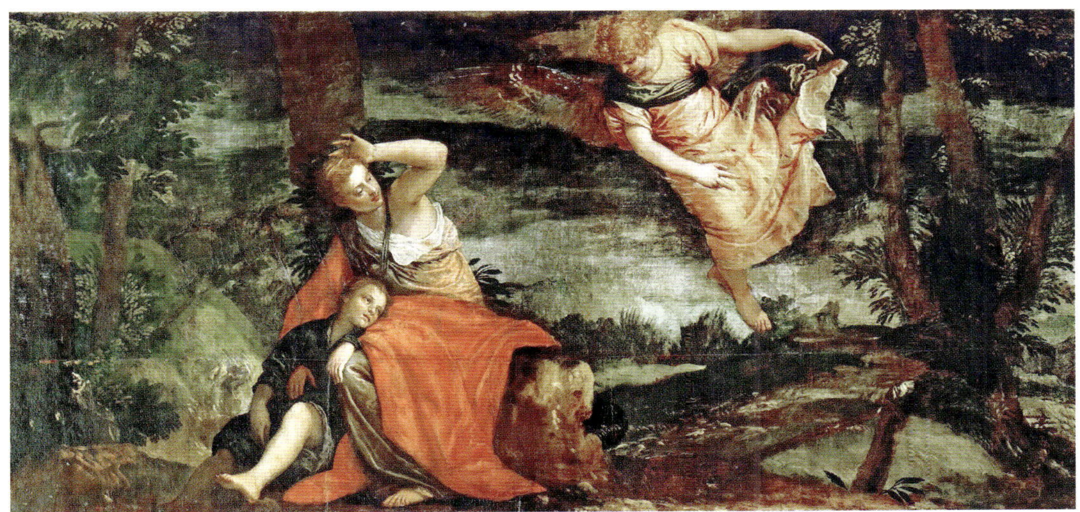
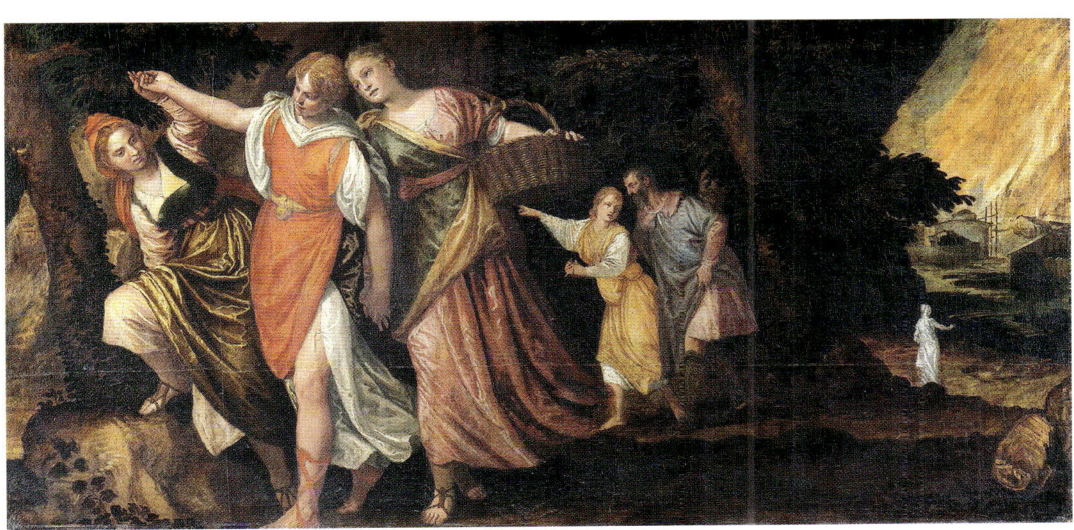

the limited chromatic scale determines a sort of melancholy, the nebulous evening atmosphere is impregnated with the tired sadness of the doctor who no longer trusts his art.
The case of the church of San Pantalon is actually unique in the lagoon: if the parish priests had a personal role in the commission and typology of the works of art adorning their church, the *Miracle of Saint Pantaleon with the Parish Priest Bartolomeo Borghi in the Guise of Hermolaus*, as the altarpiece should be titled, shows the prelate not only as an active participant on stage, but even transfigured in the body of Saint Hermolaus, the presbyter who would have convinced Pantaleon to ask for divine help rather than relying on art. It is an exaltation of the ecclesiastical patron not permitted by the Tridentine will, forgotten here. While in the slightly earlier altarpiece, *Saints John the Evangelist, Peter and Paul* (c. 1581) for the altar of the patriarch Giovanni Trevisan in San Pietro di Castello, the patron, the highest religious office, was only alluded to by his own eponym.

Returning once again from a visit to his possessions at San'Angelo di Treviso, in April 1588, Paolo Caliari fell ill. His fever and weakness would suggest calling a doctor, who in all probability would have observed that all the signs showed a perturbation of the phlegm, the mood that from the head, in the transition from cold to heat, would have descended to upset the balance of the blood as well. A catarrh that weighs on the breath invades the lungs. The course will not be benign, on the contrary, the patient will be more and more in pain; breathing difficulties and chest pains will increase. It is what will be named pneumonia centuries later.
On 19 April 1588 Paolo Caliari died in his home in San Samuele. The register on which the death is recorded uses these exact words: *morto de febre e de punta* (died for fever and phlegm). The unexpected disappearance of the 60-year-old, always active and hardworking, is not just a family trauma. It represents an irreparable loss for the more cultured part of the city: the painter who interpreted its culture and vision of the world had disappeared, capable of translating the narrative of glory and configuring the myth of the city. He who had resolved the dispute over the arts with the supremacy of colour, decorating palaces and churches. The regret, rather than diminishing, will increase over the years, always waiting for a "reviving Veronese". It will appear only a century and a half after the death of Paolo Caliari, and it will be the last, highest expression of Venetian painting: Giambattista Tiepolo. All the work started, the relationships, the goods and the commitments were not to be lost: and they were not. Benedetto, Gabriele and Carlo maintained the relationship with the patrons, completing the works started and accepting others; they continued to live with Elena, administering her assets, also relying on the attorney Monsignor Francesco Soranzo, a constant presence. Guided by Benedetto, the sons kept the workshop in full swing, also reserving private orders, as had been the case for some time. But when the work resulted from a common commitment, the signature clearly indicated the collective work with the words *Heredes Pauli Caliari Veronensis*. Thus, neither by copying nor imitating, but not even in full originality, they guaranteed the continuity of an idea, of a style, of now famous compositional solutions. They used drawings, perhaps cartoons, in any case well-known reference prototypes, and perhaps even semi-finished parts. They started from known elements, even the most appreciated by the public patron, to vary the composition, in a new imitative creation.

Duke of Buckingham Series: Esther and Ahasuerus, 1580-1588, canvas, 141 × 289 cm, detail. Vienna, Kunsthistorisches Museum, inv. 3677

Returning to the *Book of Esther* from which Paolo's Venetian story began, the painter chooses the episode in which the bride falls unconscious in front of the sovereign, to whom he must report the betrayal of Amman. The scene is absolutely consistent with the stylistic solutions that had ensured the fame of the *Suppers*: idealized female faces, sumptuous hairstyles, dresses in classic cuts, the different Venetian fabrics, architectural backgrounds. The whole series of canvases, where biblical episodes with heroines prevail, collects the pictorial motifs and solutions that made Paolo Caliari the most appreciated painter of his time.

Heredes Pauli Caliari Veronensis

The *Conversion of Saint Paul* from 1589, in the Basilica of Santa Giustina, Padua, is one of the paintings signed *Heredes Pauli Caliari Veronensis*. Among the most important paintings of this family association there are also the *Adoration of the Shepherds* at the Gallerie dell'Accademia in Venice and the *Feast in the House of Levi* in San Giacomo alla Giudecca, now in Palazzo Barbieri in Verona, a work that has recently been restored and reveals much of the activity of the heirs. It was the point of arrival and the strength acme of a series of canvases for the church of San Giacomo alla Giudecca, belonging to

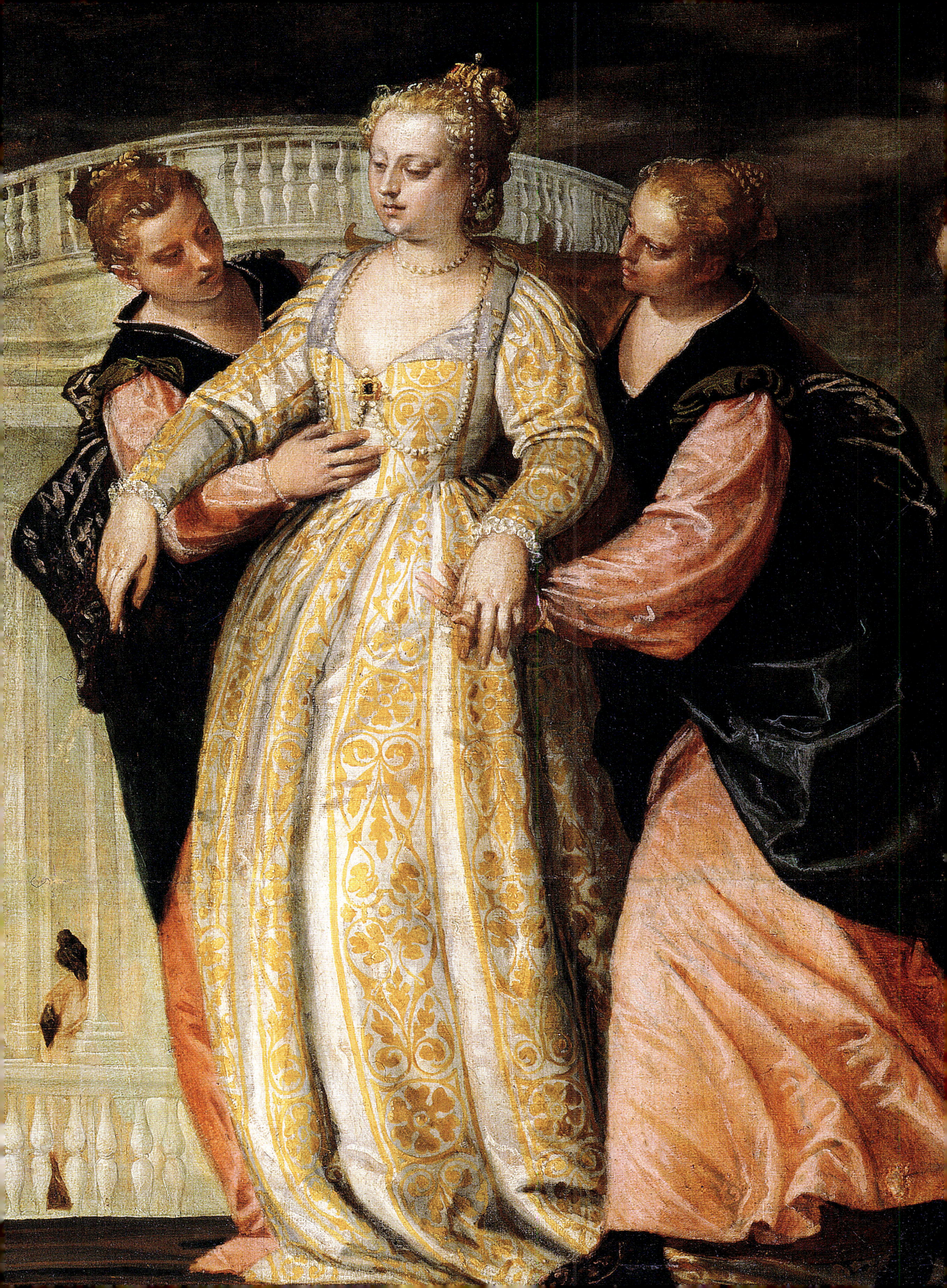

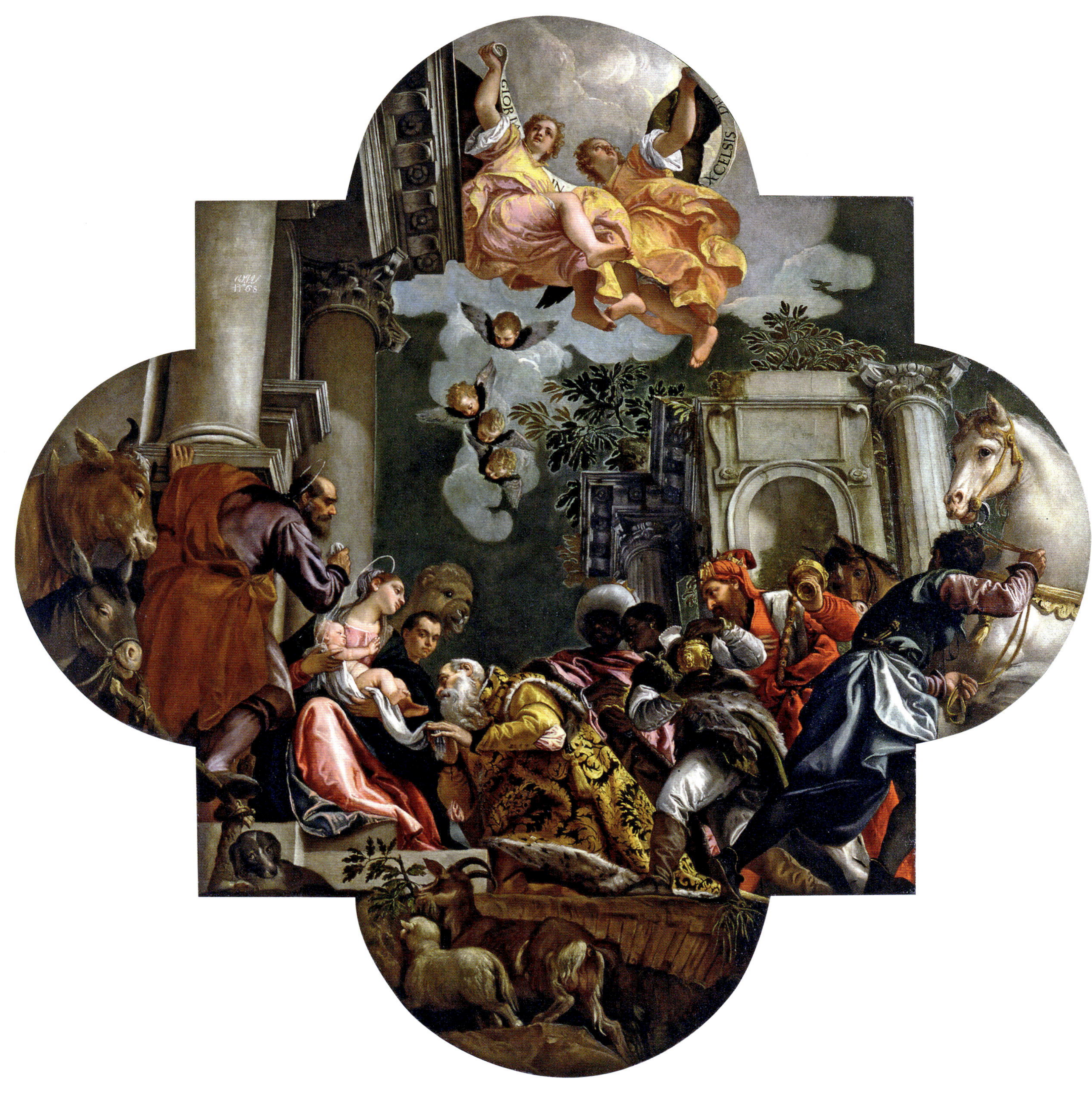
GLOR
XCELSIS

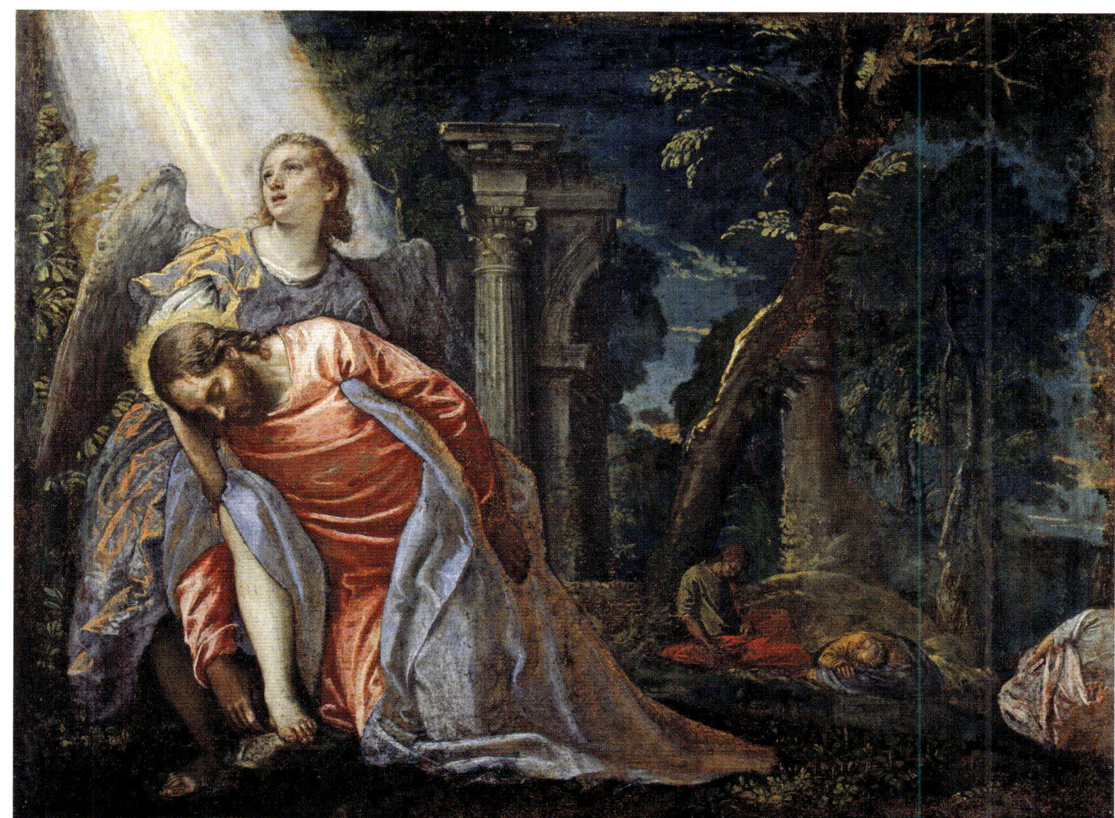

The Adoration of the Magi, 1581-1582, polylobed canvas, 420 × 420 cm, Venice, church of San Giovanni e Paolo, Cappella del Rosario, from Venice, church of San Nicolò della Lattuga

Christ in the Garden Supported by an Angel, canvas, 108 × 180 cm, Milan, Pinacoteca di Brera, inv. 241

the Servi di Maria. Three ceiling paintings and a frieze had also been prepared for the Serviti refectory: everything will be paid in installments by March 1591. The architecture here is also absolutely impressive: a grandiose loggia where the columns support a balustrade enclosed by three arches which open directly onto the urban space, characterized by a religious building with an octagonal dome, multi-storey patrician palaces, lively views. The scene is divided into two groups, also in this case very crowded and somewhat messy; in the middle two little boys are playing. Christ is leaning with his arm on the table, listening to the remark of his guest, the rich debt collector who has invited him, and to the criticism to which the doctor in ermine will submit him, in a rhetorical and bold attitude, reproaching him for not having proceeded, with his companions, to the ritual ablutions before the meal. Christ listens: the reprimand against the Pharisees is left to the imagination of the spectator. It is a significant canvas for understanding how much Benedetto and the Caliari sons had learned from Paolo, but also in which direction their style was moving. Demonstration, in any case, of the autonomy and culture of Benedetto, perfectly capable of proposing and interpreting allegories and requests, as demonstrated by his letters (Venice, Biblioteca Marciana, Mss. lat., cl. XIV, cod. CLXV [= 4254], f. 76).

For eight years the workshop continued to produce and was highly requested: the laborious enterprise was interrupted by another unexpected event. On 28 December 1596, still in San Samuele, Carlo died at the age of just twenty-six – the talented Carletto, a painter who had been active for a decade, and already much in demand and appreciated of his own (the obituary is in the State Archives of Venice, Provveditori alla sanità, Necrologi, b. 826).

Two years later, the figure of reference, Benedetto, disappeared. It would be the end of the enterprise: Gabriele got married and closed the workshop, devoting himself to other commercial activities, managing the significant inheritance and administering the substantial income of Elena Badile Caliari.

Benedetto had left several wills: the first in 1591, leaving both nephews heirs of everything, goods and shop. He bound two thousand ducats for the dowry of his niece Vittoria, Paolo's only daugh-

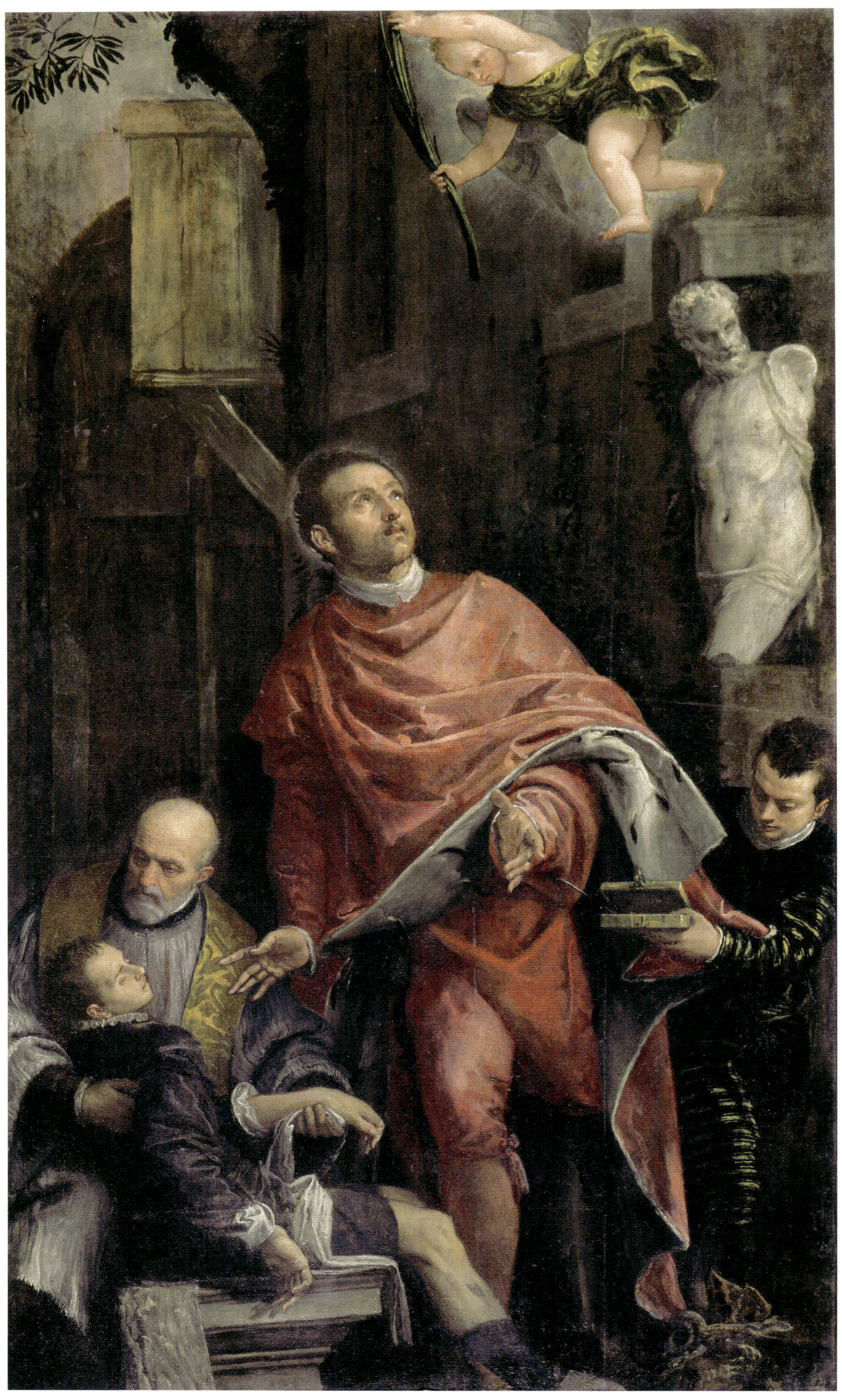

ter, and recommended himself to Gabriele and Carlo: "And because I know one needs the other, however I pray, indeed I oblige as much as I can, to stay all united together with charity and love, without dividing if possible, except by death, helping each another, and this under pain of losing five hundred ducats of the portion that belongs to them from the inheritance that I leave them (...)". A second will follows that first one, drawn up and concluded after the deed of dowry of Vittoria Ottavia Caliari, who married Domenico di Michele Dotto, a citizen of Castelfranco.
In this last writing dated 1 March 1598, moving and interesting, he who had lived his entire life in the shadow of his brother, partly also in his service, and without a family of his own, recalls as follows:

> Let it be known that I, Benedetto, son of Messer Gabriel Caliari, and the quondam Messer Paullo, most excellent painter, brother, who from the early years, separated from our other brothers (...) and thus united here in Venice, loving me as a father, and as the one who had been favoured from God and had a better lot than me, and I truly loved him as son and brother, for the benefits that I should receive from time to time. We spent around 40 years of life, then it pleased God to take him away from the world, and I allow myself to be able to dispose for the satisfaction of our souls what is permitted by law, having always been united with him, even though I can say that I have nothing to my credit, because he was the one who earned (...). (Caliari, 1888, p.183 – free translation)

For forty years he had been in fraternal association with Paolo, a type of society quite common in Venice. Now he left everything to his nephew Gabriele and his sister-in-law Elena, who he appointed as executors. A few days later, on 27 May, Benedetto died.
With Gabriele's final choice, the family enterprise ended: certainly not the memory, the active inheritance, the fortune of the works of Paolo Caliari, the Veronese. A fortune that has overcome the obstacles and quicksand of modernity. An intellectual of rare perspicacity such as Roberto Calasso wrote:

> Alpers and Baxandall are right when they write that, for Tiepolo, 'Veronese was painting'. Because Veronese is painting, for anyone. It is the remote, luxuriant and golden background from which images overflow, without the weight of meaning. It is the pure relaxation of the figures on the surface, like so many unrolled carpets. (R. Calasso, *Il rosa Tiepolo*, Milano 2006, p. 66 – free translation)

With another language, and the same passion, Marco Boschini exalted him:

> The great Paolo Veronese must be called the treasurer of painting; since all the jewels of its precious treasury have been imparted to him by it, with the faculty of being able to distribute them at his free will: in such a way that one sees the whole world jewelled by his brush. The supreme deities allowed him to be able to insert their Portraits into his works; and for this reason every figure of Paolo has something of God in it. Architecture has put in his hands the most well understood and the most proportionate shapes, of which anyone can make use in the most decent buildings. Invention has made him its arbiter in placing and arranging the Concerts of the Historie, decorating them with the very serious forms and expressions of Characters so pompously dressed that they can serve as models and suggestions to Princes, about how majestic they must appear in the presence of the World. In short, the Graces all had the ambition to always assist him, so that he can be called the delight of the world, since in him there is everything that the art of painting seeks, and the universal taste as well. (Boschini 1674, f. LXXIVr – free translation)

More cannot be said.

Conversion of Saint Pantaleon (Miracle of Saint Pantaleon with the Parish Priest Bartolomeo Borghi in the Guise of Hermolaus), 1587, canvas, 277 × 160 cm. Venice, church of San Pantalon

Following page
The Beater with Two Dogs, last room to the east, doorway, 1560-1561, fresco. Maser, Villa Barbaro

Painted in the doorway, visible in perspective from the Olympus Room, the autographed fresco has been interpreted as a *Self-Portrait* or as a *Gentleman Returning from Hunting*. A self-portrait in someone else's house was not so sensational in the pictorial practice of the time, nor does the character return from hunting. Instead the young man with jacket and knee breeches holds a skewer, and carries a beautiful hunting horn by his side, with which he will incite the dogs and give signals to the hunters; the long spit will be used to flush out the boar. The faithful dog waits for the order and the start. Thus he is the Beater. It is the last, joyful, very natural and festive greeting from Paolo Caliari to his admirers, and hunters of meanings.

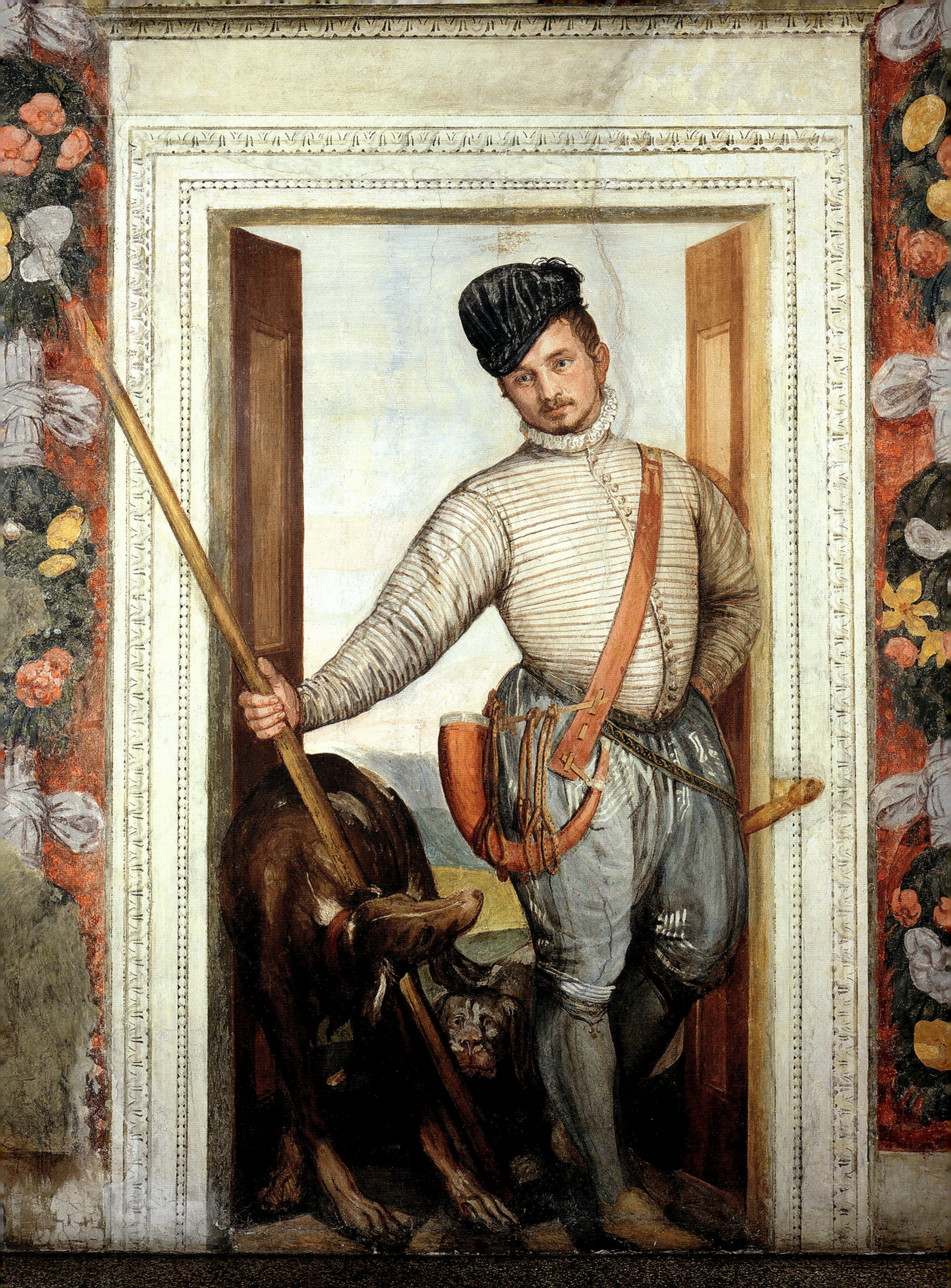

Bibliographical Note

The main ancient sources are:

Francesco Sansovino, *Delle cose notabili che sono in Venetia. Libri due*, Venice 1561.

Giorgio Vasari, *Le Vite de' più eccellenti pittori scultori e architetti*, Florence 1568.

Francesco Sansovino, *Venetia città nobilissima e singolare*, Venice 1581.

Raffaello Borghini, *Il riposo*, Florence 1584.

Carlo Ridolfi, *Vita di Paolo Caliari Veronese celebre pittore*, Venice 1646.

Carlo Ridolfi, *Le meraviglie dell'Arte ovvero le vite degli illustri pittori Veneti e dello stato,* Venice, 1648.

Marco Boschini, *La carta del navigar pittoresco*, Venice 1660.

Marco Boschini, *Le ricche minere della pittura veneziana*, Venice 1674.

Pietro Caliari, *Paolo Veronese. Sua vita e sue opere*, Rome 1888.

The book contains the following cross-references:

Rodolfo Pallucchini, *Mostra di Paolo Veronese. Catalogo delle opere*, Libreria Serenissima, Venice 1939.

Roberto Longhi, *Viatico per cinque secoli di pittura veneziana*, Sansoni, Florence 1946.

Remigio Marini, *L'opera completa del Veronese. Presentazione di Guido Piovene*, Rizzoli, Milan 1968.

Terisio Pignatti, *Veronese*, 2 voll., Alfieri, Venice 1976.

Rodolfo Pallucchini, *Veronese*, Mondadori, Milan 1984.

Francesco Valcanover, "Il colore ritrovato", in *Paolo Veronese. Restauri (Quaderni della Soprintendenza ai beni artistici e storici di Venezia*, 15), pp. 9-14, Venice 1988.

Massimo Gemin (ed. by), *Nuovi studi su Paolo Veronese*, Arsenale, Venice 1990.

Giovanna Perini (ed. by), *Gli scritti dei Carracci. Ludovico, Annibale, Agostino, Antonio, Giovanni Antonio*, Nuova Alfa Editoriale, Bologna 1990.

Terisio Pignatti, Filippo Pedrocco, *Veronese. Catalogo completo*, Cantini, Florence 1991.

Musée du Louvre, *Les Noces de Cana de Véronèse. Une oeuvre et sa restauration*, Editions de la Réunion des musées nationaux, Paris 1992.

Hans Dieter Huber, *Paolo Veronese Kunst als soziales System*, Fink, München 2005.

Museo Correr, *Veronese. Miti, ritratti, allegorie*, Skira, Milan 2005.

Lucia Nadin, *Migrazioni e integrazione. Il caso degli albanesi a Venezia (1479-1552)*, Bulzoni, Rome 2008.

Filippo Pedrocco, *La pittura della Serenissima. Venezia e i suoi pittori*, Electa, Milan 2010.

Giulio Manieri Elia (ed. by), *Veronese le storie di Ester rivelate*, Marsilio, Venice 2011.

Maria Elena Massimi, *La cena in casa Levi di Paolo Veronese. Il processo riaperto*, Marsilio, Venice 2012.

Alessandra Zamperini, *Paolo Veronese*, Arsenale Editrice, San Giovanni Lupatoto 2013.

Paola Marini, Bernard Aikema (ed. by), *Paolo Veronese. L'illusione della realtà*, Electa, Milan 2014.

Xavier F. Salomon, *Veronese*, National Gallery, London 2014.

Vittoria Romani (ed. by), *Quattro Veronese venuti da lontano. Le 'Allegorie' ritrovate*, Officina Libraria, Milan 2014.

Monica Molteni, Ettore Napione (ed. by), *Il 'Convito in casa di Levi' di San Giacomo alla Giudecca*, Zel, Treviso 2015.

Archival Sources

Mantua, Archivio Storico Gonzaga, EN., XLI, n. 2.

Montagnana, Archivio Arcipretale.

Venice, Archivio di Stato, Mani morte, Convento di San Sebastiano, b. 93, processo 7.

Venice, Archivio di Stato, Mani morte, Convento di San Sebastiano, b. 6, processo 69 (mansionarie).

Venice, Archivio di Stato, Provveditori alla sanità, Necrologi, b. 826.

Venice, Archivio di Stato, San Giorgio Maggiore, processo 10.

Venice, Archivio di Stato, San Nicolò, b. 2.

Venice, Archivio di Stato, X Savi delle Decime, Redecima 1581 Castello, b. 157 bis, n. 456, estimo 1582.

Venice, chiesa di San Samuele, Archivio parrocchiale, Battesimi, reg. 1.

Verona, Archivio di Stato, SS. Nazaro e Celso, reg. 11.

Verona, Archivio di Stato, Anagrafi della Contrada Santa Cecilia, reg. 149.

Verona, Archivio di Stato, Anagrafi della Contrada San Paolo, reg. 889.

Furthermore:

Nunziature di Venezia, vol. II *(9 gennaio 1536 - 9 giugno 1542)*, edited by F. Gaeta, Rome 1960.

The record of the inquisitorial interrogation was transcribed first by Gino Fogolari, in "Il processo dell'Inquisizione a Paolo Veronese", in *Archivio Veneto*, XVII, 1935, pp. 352-386, and then by Philipp P. Fehl, "Veronese and the Inquisition. A study of the subject matter of the so-called *Feast in the House of Levi*", in *Gazette des Beaux-Arts*, LVIII, 1961, pp. 325-354. The exact transcription in Maria Elena Massimi, *La cena in casa Levi di Paolo Veronese. Il processo riaperto*, Marsilio, Venice 2012.

Photo Credits

© 2014 RMN-Grand Palais (Musée du Louvre) / Franck Raux / Dist. Foto Scala, Florence
© 2019 RMN-Grand Palais (Musée du Louvre) / Adrien Didierjean
© 2023 RMN-Grand Palais / Dist. Photo Scala, Florence
© Archivio Fotografico – Fondazione Musei Civici di Venezia, Venice
© Cameraphoto / Scala, Florence
© Christie's Images / Bridgeman Images
© Dario Grimaldi / Bridgeman Images
© Erich Lessing / K&K Archive/ Mondadori Portfolio
© Francesco Turio Bohm. All rights reserved 2023 / Bridgeman Images
© Gemäldegalerie Alte Meister, Staatliche Kunstsammlungen Dresden. Photo: Elke Estel / Hans-Peter Klut
© Gemäldegalerie Alte Meister, Staatliche Kunstsammlungen Dresden, Photo: H. Boswank
© Kunsthistorisches Museum Wien, Gemäldegalerie
© Luisa Ricciarini / Bridgeman Images
© Mark Edward Smith / Bridgeman Images
© Metropolitan Museum / Art Resource / Scala, Florence
© Musée du Louvre / RMN Grand Palais / Dist. Foto Scala, Florence
© Musei Reali di Torino / Bridgeman Images
© Museo del Prado, Madrid
© Peter Willi / Bridgeman Images
© Photo Josse / Bridgeman Images
© Photo Scala, Florence
© Pinacoteca di Brera, Milan / Bridgeman Images
© Scala / Cameraphoto
© Scala / MBACT
© Scala, Florence / BPK
© The Devonshire Collections, Chatsworth. Reproduced by permission of Chatsworth Settlement Trustees / Bridgeman Images
© Versailles / RMN Grand Palais // Dist. Foto Scala, Florence
© Vincenzo Pirozzi / Bridgeman Images
Akg-images / Mondadori Portfolio
Album / Alamy Foto Stock
Album / Mondadori Portfolio
Artefact / Alamy Foto Stock
Bridgeman Images
Cameraphoto / Scala, Florence
Cameraphoto / Scala, Firenze ; © Archivio Fotografico – Fondazione Musei Civici di Venezia, Venice
Colin Dutton; Courtesy of Save Venice; Diocesi Patriarcato di Venezia, Venice
Courtesy Los Angeles County Museum of Art
Courtesy National Gallery of Art, Washington
DeAgostini Picture Library / Scala, Florence
Foto Art Media / Heritage Images / Scala, Florence
Foto Scala, Florence
Foto Scala, Florence ; © Archivio Fotografico – Fondazione Musei Civici di Venezia, Venice
Foto Scala, Florence - with permission of the Ministry of Cultural Heritage and Activities and Tourism
Galleria degli Uffizi (formerly Collezione Contini Bonacossi), Florence, Italy – Foto Scala, Florence – with permission of the Ministry of Cultural Heritage and Activities and Tourism
Ghigo Roli / Bridgeman Images
Ian Dagnall Computing / Alamy Foto Stock
Jozef Sedmak / Alamy Foto Stock
Magite Historic / Alamy Foto Stock
Matteo De Fina / Courtesy of Save Venice; Diocesi Patriarcato di Venezia, Venice
Mondadori Porfolio / Electa / Marco Covi
Mondadori Portfolio / Electa / Cesare Somaini
Mondadori Portfolio / Electa / Sergio Anelli
Peter Horree / Alamy Foto Stock
Prisma Archivio / Alamy Foto Stock
Rita Guglielmi / Alamy Foto Stock
Soprintendenza archeologia belle arti e paesaggio per le province di Verona, Rovigo e Vicenza
With permission of the Ministry of Cultural Heritage, Gallerie degli Uffizi, Florence
With permission of the Ministry of Cultural Heritage, Gallerie dell'Accademia, Venice
The National Gallery / Scala, Florence
Verona, Musei Civici, Archivio fotografico (photo Umberto Tomba); (BAMSphoto)

Silvana Editoriale S.p.A.
via dei Lavoratori, 78
20092 Cinisello Balsamo, Milano
tel. 02 453 951 01
fax 02 453 951 51
www.silvanaeditoriale.it

Reproductions, printing and binding in Italy
Printed by Tipostampa, Moncalieri (Turin)
in October 2023

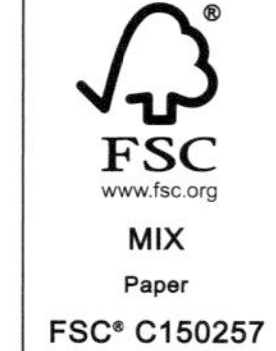